# Cruising Guide
TO
# MAINE - VOLUME II
## ROCKPORT TO EASTPORT
## Second Edition

**by Don Johnson**

**Edited by Julius M. Wilensky**
**all photos, sketch charts, and diagrams by the author**
**unless otherwise indicated**


published 1995 by **Wescott Cove Publishing Company**
P.O. Box 130, Stamford, CT 06904



1st Edition — 1987
2nd Printing — 1994
3rd Printing — 1995
2nd Edition — 1995

Library of Congress Catalog Card No. 94-60165
ISBN No. 0-918752-18-3
San No. 210-5810

# TABLE OF CONTENTS

Town Dock, Head Harbour, Campobello Island, Chapter 17

# EDITOR'S PREFACE

Westcott Cove has had exactly the enthusiastic response that we hoped for to Don Johnson's "Cruising Guide to Maine—Volume I, Kittery to Rockland." Reviews have been excellent and readers' calls and letters, and dealers' feedback have all been great. Both Volumes have been updated, Volume I Second Edition in 1994, and here's Volume II Second Edition.

This book starts at Rockport just above Rockland on the west shore of Penobscot Bay and Don takes you into every harbor and anchorage all the way to Eastport. Our title would indicate that our coverage stops there, "Rockport to Eastport." It doesn't. Don covers Campobello Island in New Brunswick, the U.S. shores of Passamaquoddy Bay and a little of Canada and up the St. Croix River. This river forms the boundary between U.S.A. and Canada (Maine and New Brunswick). We deliberately left the title at Eastport, because most sailors know where that is. Comparatively few have heard of Calais or the St. Croix River. Eastport is frequently mentioned in weather reports, and generally thought of as the easternmost town in the USA. Actually this honor belongs to nearby Lubec, but Maine sailors don't quibble about it so we won't either!

Many cruising sailors consider the area around Penobscot Bay, Mount Desert Island, Blue Hill Bay and Frenchman's Bay to be the quintessence of Maine cruising. Certainly it rates high. Few sailors cruise east of there, but Don makes it easy for the more adventurous who have time. Like Volume I, this book has a complete set of harbor charts, and enough regional charts, with all points of interest located on the charts. Don not only helps you find your way safely into harbors, but tells you what's ashore and exactly where it is. As in Volume I, there is extensive material on tidal currents, ecology, and history. He deserves your thanks and ours for his extensive research, and time consuming exploration. We think you'll like Volume II.

*Photo courtesy Yachting Magazine*

Editor Julius M. Wilensky

One of Maine's drawbacks is the frequency of fog. Don gives you a series of waypoints on the big folded charts inside the front and rear covers. These have latitudes and longitudes, so they are useful for GPS or Loran C.

Again, we give the reader a full set of harbor charts with all points of interest, afloat and ashore, located on the charts, and we also provide regional and general charts on useful scales. Though we have included a full set of revised charts in this edition, these are not to be used for navigation. Don's text tells you how to make a passage, how to enter a harbor, where to anchor, moor, or dock your boat, and where to find supplies, ice, fuel, showers, laundry, groceries, marine supply stores, repairs to hull, engine, sails, etc. It also describes sightseeing ashore, cultural attractions, transportation, museums, art galleries, restaurants, recreational opportunities, historical sites, and other points of interest, and shows exact locations of these on the charts. Don also gives you some of the history and ecology of the area so you can better appreciate what you're looking at. You can get some of this from competitive guides, but Wescott Cove still prides itself on publishing a more complete description in an easy-to-use format, and this is the only guide with a complete set of charts. It is Otabound, designed to lie flat anywhere you open it. It is meant to be used aboard, not left on your coffee table.

Although this book contains a full set of charts on useful scales, these charts are not intended for navigation. They are intended to supplement the National Ocean Survey charts with additional information, not to replace them.

Don Johnson presently lives near Eastport in a house he built himself, with the aid of his brilliant, well mannered teenage son, Ewan. Don formerly lived near Camden, and has cruised the Maine Coast for many years. A man of many talents, Don has been a commercial artist, and was a shipbuilder in Maine. He built his 27 ft. schooner "Nakomis" himself and sailed it to the Azores, Ireland and the Caribbean. He's an excellent navigator, knows what cruising sailors are looking for, and we think you'll find his advice on passages and harbor entries most helpful.

Don was born in Minnesota and educated at the University of Minnesota and the University of Illinois. Though self-sufficient and independent, Don is a friendly, intelligent gentleman with a sense of humor. The two volume cruising guide to Maine has been a massive undertaking. We've enjoyed working with Don Johnson, and are proud to again present his work to you.

Julius M. Wilensky
Stamford, CT
July, 1995

# INTRODUCTION

To most sailors, mention of the coast of Maine brings forth an image of rocky, windswept shores and a "land of the pointed fir." To others, it brings to mind high tides with their swift and erratic currents and a shore mostly shrouded in fog. This keeps many people from cruising Maine. It is true that if your keel accidently greets the bottom, it would not be as forgiving as sailing in an area like Chesapeake Bay. It is also true that there is occasional fog. But with careful planning and prudent sailing, certainly requirements for sailing in any area, there should be nothing to frighten you away. The most important element for optimum enjoyment is knowing in advance what to expect and to be prepared for it. This makes for relaxed and pleasurable cruising. The main function of the *Cruising Guide to Maine* is to accomplish this. It will describe how to enter and leave a harbor safely, where the best channel is, and important characteristics, e.g., landmarks, unmarked obstructions and errant currents, etc. It will tell you what to expect in the harbor in the way of anchorage or moorings and dock space at marinas or yacht clubs. It describes what services are found ashore—groceries, laundry and restaurants. Special features of the area that would be of interest are described—museums, historic houses, nature walks. These will all be numbered when first referred to in the text and keyed to their exact location on the reproduced chart segments. Finally, a brief history of the area is given.

I have lived in Maine for many years now, and believe there is no finer area for the cruising sailor. It is an extensive coast with about 3,000 miles of shoreline, containing innumerable islands, bays, sounds and rivers. To do justice to this long coastline, the Cruising Guide has been divided into two volumes. The first volume covers the area from the New Hampshire border to Rockland in Penobscot Bay. This second volume starts at Rockport and continues to Calais on the St. Croix River.

Although this coast is familiar to me, last summer I sailed to Rockport and visited every harbor described in this volume to gather first-hand information.

If you know of a remote desirable cove or anchorage that we've overlooked, please let us hear from you. You can contact me through Wescott Cove Publishing Company, address on the title page.

To give the reader a frame of reference, my boat "Nakomis" is a 27-foot schooner, designed by William Atkin in 1924. Her design is based on the Chesapeake Skipjacks, and has a full length keel and a 4 foot draft. Her auxillary power is a single cylinder, air-cooled diesel engine, which under optimum conditions will push her at 4 knots. Towing a dinghy reduces it to 3½ knots. This summer, my crew consisted of my 14 year old son, Ewan, and Willy, an English Bull terrier.

So if a boat that doesn't point well to the wind, does not maneuver quickly due to her long keel, and has an engine with minimal power, can negotiate the tides and currents of this coast, I am sure that almost any other boat out there can do it too.

Come and enjoy our downeast sailing. It's "finestkind!"

Don Johnson
North Perry, Maine

Photo by Julius M. Wilensky

Author Don Johnson

# LIST OF CHARTS, SKETCHES, MAPS, AND DIAGRAMS IN THIS BOOK

Following this list is another list of all the NOS publications and where to buy them, including many of the charts listed below. You will note that many chart excerpts in this book have suffixes, i.e., 13316A, B, C, etc. Don't try to buy these charts. The NOS charts that these excerpts were drawn from, have no suffixes. We used these suffixes to make it easier for you to refer from the text the proper chart excerpt in this book. As mentioned elsewhere in this book, these charts are not to be used for navigation. They are designed to supplement the NOS charts, not to supplant them.

| | | | |
|---|---|---|---|
| 168 | Bunker Harbor | Sketch Chart | |
| 169 | Harbors East of Schoodic Head | 13324 | 1:40,000 |
| 170 | Corea Harbor | Sketch Chart | |
| 173 | Petit Manan | 13324A | 1:40,000 |
| 175 | Narragaugus Bay | 13324B | 1:40,000 |
| | | Reduced approx. 10½% | |
| 177 | Pleasant Bay and Eastern Harbor, Cape Split | 13324C | 1:40,000 |
| 179 | Eastern Bay and Moosabec Reach | 13325 | 1:80,000 |
| | | Reduced approx. 9% | |
| 181 | Eastern Bay and Moosabec Reach | Sketch Chart | |
| 182,183 | Eastern Bay and Moosabec Reach | 13326 | 1:40,000 |
| | | Reduced approx. 9% | |
| 188 | Roque Is. | 13326B | 1:40,000 |
| 189 | Roque Harbor | Sketch Chart | |
| 190 | Machais Bay to Cutler | 13325A | 1:80,000 |
| 191 | Harbors in Machais Bay | 13326C | 1:40,000 |
| 195 | Little River, Cutler | 13327 | 1:40,000 |
| 197 | Haycock Harbor | Sketch Chart | |
| 199 | Harbors Between Little River, Cutler and Lubec | 13327A | 1:40,000 |
| 200,201 | Lubec, Campobello Is. Eastport, Western Passage | 13328 | 1:40,000 |
| | | Reduced approx. 5% | |
| 206 | Eastport | 13328 Inset | 1:15,000 |
| 209 | Cobscook Bay | 13328 | 1:40,000 |
| | | Reduced approx. 8% | |
| 210 | Gleason Cove | 13328B | 1:40,000 |
| 212 | St. Croix River, Calais and St. Stephen | 13328 Inset | 1:40,000 |
| 213 | St. Croix River | 13328C | 1:40,000 |
| Inside Rear Cover | Folded General Chart, Petit Manan Is. to St. Croix River | | 1:80,000<br>1:40,000 |
| | | Reduced approx. 11% | |

## LIST OF CHARTS, PUBLICATIONS, SOURCES

### National Oceanic and Atmospheric Administration, National Ocean Service charts and other publications covering the area described in this book, including current prices and where to buy them.

We cannot urge you strongly enough to cruise this magnificent coast with a full set of up-to-date NOS charts. The charts in this book are designed to help you enjoy your cruise and to ease finding your way afloat and ashore, but they are not to be used for navigation. They are intended to supplement the NOS charts, not supplant them.

| Publication | Price |
|---|---|
| U.S. Nautical Chart Catalog No. 1 | Free |
| U.S. Coast Pilot No. 1—Eastport to Cape Cod (new edition published every year) | $20.00 |
| Tide Tables, East Coast North and South America | $10.00 |
| Tidal Current tables, Atlantic Coast of North America | $10.00 |
| Marine Weather Services Chart—Eastport, ME to Montauk Point, NY. MSC-1 | $1.25 |
| U.S. Coast Guard Light List, Vol. I, Atlantic Coast from St. Croix River, ME to Ocean City, MD (Published annually) | $31.25 |

**NOS Charts**

| Chart No. | Description | Scale | Price |
|---|---|---|---|
| 13260 | Sailing Chart Bay of Fundy to Cape Cod | 1:378,838 | $14.00 |
| | Includes Loran C and Omega lines of position | | |
| 13306 | Sailing Chart West Quoddy Head to New York | 1:675,000 | $14.00 |
| | You don't need 13306 unless you're starting from south of Cape Cod | | |
| 13278 | Portsmouth to Cape Ann | 1:80,000 | $14.00 |
| | Hampton Harbor | 1:30,000 | |
| 13286 | Cape Elizabeth to Portsmouth | 1:80,000 | $14.00 |
| | Cape Porpoise Harbor | 1:10,000 | |
| | Wells Harbor | 1:20,000 | |
| | Kennebunk River | 1:10,000 | |
| | Perkins Cove | 1:10,000 | |
| 13288 | Monhegan Island to Cape Elizabeth | 1:80,000 | $14.00 |
| The last three charts listed above are needed only if you start from south and west of Penobscot Bay. | | | |
| 13302 | Penobscot Bay and Approaches | 1:80,000 | $14.00 |
| 13312 | Frenchman & Blue Hill Bays & Approaches | 1:80,000 | $14.00 |
| 13325 | Quoddy Narrows to Petit Manan Island | 1:80,000 | $14.00 |
| All of the 1:80,000 scale charts listed above have Loran C Lines of Position | | | |
| 13303 | Approaches to Penobscot Bay | 1:40,000 | $14.00 |
| 13305 | Penobscot Bay | 1:40,000 | $14.00 |
| 13307 | Camden, Rockport, and Rockland Harbors | 1:20,000 | $14.00 |
| 13308 | Fox Islands Thorofare | 1:15,000 | $14.00 |
| 13309 | Penobscot River | 1:40,000 | $14.00 |
| 13313 | Approaches to Blue Hill Bay | 1:40,000 | $14.00 |
| 13315 | Deer I. Thoro. and Casco Passage | 1:20,000 | $14.00 |

| | | | |
|---|---|---|---|
| 13316 | Blue Hill Bay | 1:40,000 | $14.00 |
| | Blue Hill Harbor | 1:20,000 | |
| 13318 | Frenchman Bay and Mount Desert Island | 1:40,000 | $14.00 |
| 13321 | Southwest Harbor and Approaches | 1:10,000 | $14.00 |
| 13322 | Winter Harbor | 1:10,000 | $14.00 |
| 13323 | Bar Harbor | 1:10,000 | $14.00 |
| 13324 | Tibbett Narrows to Schoodic Island | 1:40,000 | $14.00 |
| 13326 | Machias Bay to Tibbett Narrows | 1:40,000 | $14.00 |
| 13327 | West Quoddy Head to Cross Island | 1:40,000 | $14.00 |
| 13328 | Calais to West Quoddy Head | 1:40,000 | $14.00 |
| | Eastport Harbor | 1:5,000 | |

Coast Guard Light Lists should be ordered from:
Superintendent of Documents
U.S. Government Printing Office
Washington, DC 20402

All other publications and charts listed above can be ordered prepaid (payable to NOS, Dept. of Commerce) by mail from: Distribution Branch (N/CG33), National Ocean Service, Riverdale, MD 20737-1199. Orders must be accompanied by a check or money order. Telephone orders can be placed by calling (301) 436-6990. Visa and Mastercard are accepted for phone orders.

For Canadian Charts and Publications, write to:
Canadian Hydrographic Service
Dept. of Fisheries and Oceans
Institute of Ocean Sciences
P.O. Box 8080, 1675 Russell Road
Ottawa, Ontario, Canada KHG 3H6
'Phone (613) 998-4931

## Authorized Nautical Chart Agents in the area covered by this book are:

| | |
|---|---|
| **Bar Harbor** | Harbor Place Ships Store, 1 West Street, 04609, 207-288-3346 |
| **Bass Harbor** | Bass Harbor Marine, Granville Road, 04653, 207-244-5066 |
| **Belfast** | Canterbury Tales, 52 Main St., 04915, 207-338-1171 |
| **Blue Hill** | Mc Vays Hardware Inc., 408 Main St., 04614, 207-374-5645 |
| | North Light Books, Main St., 04614, 207-374-5422 |
| **Brooklin** | Brooklin General Store, Rt 175, 04616, 207-359-8817 |
| **Brunswick** | Great Island Boat Yard, Great Island, 04011, 207-729-1639 |
| | New Meadows Marina, 5541 Bath Road, 04011, 207-449-6277 |
| **Bucks Harbor** | Pettegrow Boat Yard, Starboard Cove, 04618, 207-255-8740 |
| **Camden** | Owl & Turtle Bookshop, 8 Bay View, 04843, 207-236-4769 |
| | Wayfarer Marine Corp., Sea St., 04843, 207-236-4378 |
| **Castine** | Four Flags, Main St., 04421, 207-326-8526 |
| **Cutler** | Village Market, Rt 191, 04626, 207-259-3922 |
| **E Blue Hill** | Harbor Marine Supply Co., Main St., 04629, 207-374-5820 |
| **Eastport** | Moose Island Marine Inc., 108 Water Street, 04631, 207-853-6058 |
| | S L Wadsworth & Son Inc., 42 Water Street, 04631, 207-853-4343 |
| **Ellsworth** | Branch Pond Marine, 269, High St., 04605, 207-667-2268 |
| | Sterling Marine Supply, 162 High Street, 04605, 207-667-2600 |
| **Jonesport** | Churchs True Value, Main St., 04649, 207-497-5441 |
| | T A King & Son, Main Street, 04649, 207-497-2274 |
| **Machais** | Coffins True Value Hardware, US Rt 1, 04655, 207-255-8387 |
| | Eastern Maine Books, 65-67 Main St., 04654 207-255-4908 |
| **Northeast Hbr** | F T Brown Co, Main St., 04662, 207-276-3329 |
| **Rockland** | Huston-Tuttle, 365 Main St., 04841, 207-594-5441 |
| | Rockland Boat Inc, 23 Sea St. Pl, 207-594-8181 |
| | Williams Co, Shore Village Book Shoppe, 308 Main St, 04841, 207-594-2336 |
| **Rockport** | Maine Sport, Rt 1, 04856, 207-236-8779 |
| **Searsport** | Hamilton Marine Inc, Rt 1, 04974, 207-548-6302 |
| **Southwest Hbr** | Hinckley Ship Store, Shore Rd, 04769, 207-244-7100 |
| | Manset Yacht Service, Shore Rd, 04769, 207-244-4040 |
| **Stonington** | Atlantic Avenue Hardware, Atlantic Ave, 04681, 207-367-2369 |
| | Billings Diesel & Marine Service, Moose Island Rd, 04681, 207-367-2328 |
| | Dockside Books & Gifts, W. Main St, 04681, 207-367-2652 |
| **Vinalhaven** | Calderwoods Wharf Inc, 12 Main St, 04863. 207-863-4831 |
| | Vinals News Stand, Main St, 04863, 207-863-4826 |

## HOW THIS BOOK IS ORGANIZED

This book starts with two chapters describing weather conditions, tidal currents and general notes and recommendations ranging from anchoring to fishing. Following these are 16 more chapters, each describing one or more islands, harbors, and anchorages in great detail.

Harbors are described in sequence as though you were starting at Rockport on the west shore of Penobscot Bay. Volume I leaves off at Rockland, the next harbor south of Rockport. Don first gives you an overview of Penobscot Bay, perhaps Maine's most popular cruising area. Then he starts with the islands offshore from Penobscot Bay, moves into the Bay circumnavigating it clockwise north along the west shore and south along the east shore. There are side trips to cover all the islands and their anchorages and harbors.

Another chapter is devoted to passages east from Penobscot Bay, and islands, towns, harbors and anchorages along these passages. We then circumnavigate Blue Hill Bay, again clockwise. This is followed with a description of all the harbors on Mount Desert Island and in Frenchman Bay. We then head downeast all the way to the Canadian border.

Though few cruising boats ever go east of Schoodic Peninsula, Don's descriptions will make you want to go there. This also makes it easier for you to enjoy some marvelous cruising—Eastern Bay and Moosabec Reach, Roque Island, and many delightful little-known harbors en route to Lubec and Eastport. The Maine coast deserves this kind of treatment, and has never had it before.

Though the title of the book indicates that coverage stops at Eastport, Don does cover all surrounding bays and waterways to the St. Croix River, including Campobello Island and some other shores of New Brunswick.

Included are large scale reproductions of segments of NOAA NOS charts, marked to indicate additional navigation information, and exact locations of marine facilities and points of interest ashore. The author has drawn several original sketch charts to supplement navigational information. There's a street map of Belfast and several sketches and diagrams to indicate things ranging from stone carvings to lobster larval stages. Cruising sailors find these charts good guides to places of interest ashore. This is what they're intended for. They are not intended for navigational use. We recommend that you carry the latest editions of NOS charts, listed starting on page 8.

Because of the deeply indented configuration of the Maine coast, few of our harbor charts can give proper orientation to a skipper not familiar with this coast. This is true, even though most of our chart segments are 8½" x 11" and even 11" x 17". Because of this, we have included two big folded general charts, printed both sides, inside the front and back covers. These show the entire area covered by this book and are numbered to indicate coverage in each chapter. Locations of most launching ramps are also shown on this chart, even though ramp locations are also shown on the harbor charts all through the book. Loran-C and GPS waypoint coordinates are also shown on these big folded charts, and latitude and longitude given for each waypoint.

These large general charts are cut in two, with a photographic overlap. Those in front of the book add up to 37⅞" x 56" and are on a scale of 1:80,000, reduced approximately 11%. They take you from Penobscot Bay to Petit Manan Island. Those inside the rear cover go from Petit Manan Island to West Quoddy Head on a scale of 1:80,000, reduced approximately 11%, thence to the St. Croix River on a scale of 1:40,000, reduced approximately 11%. Although these large folded charts add cost and bulk, we believe they make the book more useful.

We have also included 13 regional charts, some covering more than one chapter. Eleven of these are on a scale of 1:80,000, but two had to be 1:378,000 to show all of Penobscot Bay on one chart and to show Penobscot Bay and passages east all on one chart. Some of these regional charts include locations of facilities and points of interest now shown on harbor charts. In the text, cross references are made to the proper charts so that readers can refer back as necessary. A complete list of charts, sketches, maps and diagrams is included starting on page 7.

Appendix I is a Maine Charter List, designed to help sailors from other parts of USA and Canada to enjoy Maine cruising. Many well-travelled skippers rate this among the world's best.

Appendix II lists weather and radiofax broadcasts, Coast Guard stations, radiotelephone communications, and RDF beacons.

Appendix III describes Maine's Coastal Public Parks, both State and National, and locates them on an overall chart on page 294. These are described in detail in relevant chapters throughout the book.

At the end of the book, you'll find a place name index.

# CHAPTER 1

## WEATHER

New England weather in general, and Maine weather in particular, is known for its rapid change and variable character. An oft quoted phrase is "if you don't like the weather, wait 10 minutes, it will change." This is not an altogether unfounded attitude, yet there are general, overall patterns to Maine weather, governed by Maine's geographical position and by major weather systems.

### WINDS

During winter, the New England coast is under the influence of the North American continental high pressure system and the Icelandic low. This produces winds which are predominantly from the west to north quadrant. Cold, polar air brought into this area is moderated as it passes over the relatively warm water of the Gulf of Maine and the much warmer Atlantic Gulf Stream. This contrast of surface temperatures creates a condition for storm formation. Frequent and rapidly progressing low pressure cells moving from the west toward the east produce periodic storms. In late spring and early fall, corresponding with a shift in the upper atmosphere jet stream, these lows track down the St. Lawrence River Valley, generating southeast gales, or track out to sea over Cape Cod, producing gales from the northeast. They may also enter from southwest, with the center of the low offshore from the northeast coast.

A northeast gale brings the worst possible combination of elements, cold polar air with much moisture in it due to its long passage over water, and high velocity winds.

No one who has experienced it will forget such a gale as occured on Feb. 2, 1976. Winds of 65-75 miles per hour created waves that engulfed the top of Matinicus Rock, an island that rises 40 feet above sea level. Granite boulders the size of an average house room were rolled around as if they were mere pebbles. The Coast Guard personnel stationed on Matinicus Rock to man the lighthouse felt that their entire island was about to be swept away. The lighthouse structure of heavy granite construction trembled and the men feared for its imminent collapse. In the midst of this maelstrom, they had to constantly keep chipping ice away from the lenses of the light, an additional 50 feet from the base of the lighthouse, where salt spray kept freezing. Farther east, at Grand Manan, gusts at high as 108 mph were recorded, and in Eastport, Maine, only 12 miles away, almost all the waterfront structures and wharfs were destroyed. This storm has subsequently always been referred to as the Ground Hog Day storm. Fortunately, these intense weather systems are infrequent during the warm summer months.

In late spring and early summer both the Continental high and Icelandic low weakens. Correspondingly, the Bermuda high intensifies, shifting toward the Azores and expanding in area. It is then called the Azores high. Wind flows in a clockwise direction, outward from the center of a high pressure system, and as Maine is situated in the northwest quadrant of this large Azores high, the prevailing winds during the summer months are southwesterly.

These then, are the summertime sailing conditions found in coastal Maine. Predominating winds are from the southwest, generally 10-15 knots. This pattern is subject to periodic variations by migratory fronts which pass through, causing the wind to shift to the northwest, temporarily bringing with it cooler, drier air. If there can be said to be a "normal" pattern, it would be southwest winds with increasing buildup of cloud cover over a period of about five days, and then a cold front passing through which produces precipitation, followed by clear, dry air from the northwest. This northwest wind is frequently stronger and gusty, lasting for about one and a half days before moderating. Wind from the southeast always means trouble, bringing with it either fog or a miserable rain.

Overlaid on this pattern is a smaller, daily pattern of land breeze and sea breeze. At the end of the day, the land starts to cool off after sunset and a new breeze will spring up. This breeze, off the land at about 5 knots, will hold through the night and into the morning hours, lasting until the land again warms and the true sea breeze comes up. Thus, you can almost always depend upon being gently propelled downwind out of a harbor or sound toward open water. Here the land breeze dies and the sea-breeze takes over. This true wind, from the southwest, generally comes up around 10:00 a.m. in early June. It is progressively delayed as the summer continues, until about mid-August when it might be delayed until noon or 1:00 p.m. But come up it will, and there will be a fine breeze for the rest of the day.

I remember many times setting sail in Round Pond of Muscongus Sound with the gentle land breeze driving me down the sound. Glancing astern I saw the last of this wind, while advancing toward me the beginning of the true sea-breeze, sometimes with a calm spot between the two, of no more than a few hundred feet. As the sun sets, the sea-breeze diminishes until you are just ghosting into a harbor. Then the daily pattern repeats itself.

## THUNDERSTORMS

Thunderstorms in Maine are a relatively rare occurrence, only 3 or 4 per month during July and August. Their number and severity are lessened when over the sea. It is not unusual to be sailing just a few miles off the coast with clear skies and fair wind, while on shore ominous dark thunderheads are building and displaying their fury. It is almost as though there was an impentrable barrier preventing them from moving out over the water. Weather radio NOAA does a good job of predicting potential thunderstorms. This coupled with the ease of always finding a secure anchorage nearby, practically eliminates the risk of being caught unawares.

## HURRICANES

It is very seldom that hurricanes reach as far north along the eastern seaboard as Maine. Usually they turn out to sea, following the warm waters of the Gulf Stream. Even if one does hit, it most likely would have already dissipated much of its energy.

However, when sailing late in the season, the potential for a hurricane's approach should be kept in mind. Fortunately, it is always easy to find a hurricane hole nearby. The coast abounds in innumerable coves and nearly land-locked bays in which you can quickly take shelter. Rather than recommending any specific harbors, my suggestion is to ask around and find out where the other boats are headed—then keep away from that spot. I am not being facetious. A superior hurricane hole, crowded with boats seeking protection, can place you in a more dangerous position than an adequate one with only a few boats present. Once a single boat breaks loose from its mooring or anchor, or drags, movement of that boat through the rest of the fleet is totally uncontrollable. Remember too, that more boats are lost or damaged in a storm by failure to provide adequate chafing gear to the anchor or mooring line, than by breaking free from the bottom.

## AIR TEMPERATURES

Summer in Maine is beautiful, and nowhere else will you find better sailing. But the summer does begin later and end sooner than anywhere else on the eastern seaboard. You can be fairly sure of the danger of snow being past and the advent of warm wether by June. However, the winds will have not yet settled down to their usual summer pattern, being still variable in direction and frequently gusty. July and August are the two most popular months for sailing, although concomitant with the warm weather is the associated higher frequency of fog. The average, normal air temperature for these two months is around 68 degrees F at Portland, with daytime highs in the upoper 70's and night time lows in the mid 50's. This average temperature is 62 degrees F at Eastport, Maine. By September the temperature drops 6-10 degress, but this cooler weather brings consistently good wind and a greater number of fog-free days. By October, the feel of winter is already in the air and winter gales are beginning. The only year Maine did not have a summer was in 1816. At that time, there was a late frost in July, and the first snowfall began in August.

What this means in being prepared for cruising in Maine is to have along warm clothing. Wool shirts and heavy sweaters will be necessary for your comfort. Even though there may be a period in August when the temperatures can climb up into the 90's on land, once you are on the water, just a mile offshore, the air temperature is considerably lower. I can remember one day in mid-August, sailing by Mt. Desert Rock Island, and the irony of hearing weather radio NOAA saying "well folks, it's going to be another one of those hazy, lazy summer days, with the temperature going up to 98 degrees," while we on the boat had to wear our long winter underwear, as well as wool sweaters to keep warm enough.

## WATER TEMPERATURE

Surface water temperatures are cold. Like the tidal currents along the Maine coast, there is a marked change between the lower section of coast from Cape Ann to Cape Elizabeth, and the eastern section. In fact, there is a direct correlation between the currents and the distribution of water temperatures. On the lower coast, where the currents are weakest, the surface water temperature is higher and less saline. Due to the lack of mixing of the surface and bottom waters, there is a high degree of stability. This allows the surface water to be warmed by the summer sun, which in turn, increases the stability. But in the northeastern section of coast, particularly from Penobscot Bay eastward, there is a strong **vertical** mixing between the bottom and surface waters, hence a much colder surface water. In July and August, the surface water in Portland averages 59.7 degrees F, while at Eastport, it is 49.9 degrees F. In the winter, this pattern is reversed. The colder surface waters being the westerly ones as they are chilled by the cold winter air—and warmer surface water in the northeast section, where it is moderated by the vertical mixing with relatively warmer bottom water.

Thus, east of Portland, a bathing suit is one of the least likely needed items of apparel to bring along, unless you enjoy swimming in the same arctic water with the harbor seals! Even for going overboard to free a fouled propeller from lobster pot-warp or to check the knotmeter impeller, you wouldn't want to wear a bathing suit. At these temperatures, hypothermia sets in quickly. If you must go in for these tasks, it is best done wearing a wet suit. If you have none, wear long pants and long-sleeved shirt, tied off at the cuffs, to retain as much body heat as possible.

There are advantages to this cold water. Marine growth is much slower in accumulating on your boat bottom, so it needs less frequent scrubbing and painting. In the absence of an icebox or refrigeration aboard, you can use the bilge as a naturally built-in area for storage of perishable food. Margarine or butter that comes in plastic tubs will keep for weeks. Even cheese and some fresh meats will last for days and it is an effective place for cold soft drinks or beer. Just don't forget at the end of the sailing season that you put them there. Also retain them in some manner to prevent their rolling into an inaccessible part of the bilge.

## FOG

Fog is a reality of Maine cruising that you will have to come to terms with. I don't think anyone actually enjoys fog sailing, but the dread of anticipation is often worse than the actual experience. When you are deprived of the dominant sense of sight, the feeling of isolation and the vagaries of the unknown seem to overwhelm you. Yet, with reasonable care and precaution, you will have few problems.

The most common type of fog is advection sea fog. This occurs when moist, warm air is cooled in its passage over the cold water of the sea. The cold water of the Gulf of Maine is born in the Arctic. The Nova Scotia Current, a branch of the Labrador Current, sweeps down along the southern coast of Nova Scotia and enters the Gulf. Here is roughly parallels the coastline, trending southwest, until it is deflected to the east by Cape Cod. Warm water of the Gulf Stream is effectively blocked from entrance to the Gulf of Maine by Georges Bank and Browns Bank. When the wind is south to southwest, the predominant summer pattern, conditions are set up for fog formation. It can come suddenly without warning and sometimes lasts for weeks.

At the interface of the Gulf Stream and the Labrador Current, far offshore, dense fog banks are produced. A wind from the southeast will move this bank of fog into the Maine Coast, and there it will stay until the wind shifts to the northwest.

At the mouth of bays or in rivers, it can sometimes be clear of fog, but this is not to be depended upon. Also, you will generally find less fog on the north-facing sides of islands or in bays. For this reason, early farm settlements on islands are found facing north to protect the crops from the cold, damp salt air.

The farther east you travel, the greater number of days that fog will be encountered. Nowhere along the entire New England coast will you find more fog than at Petit Manan. Here, on the average, there are 75 days of fog during the year, and in June, one day out of three will be fog. Compare this to 15 days per year of heavy fog in Nantucket. July and August are the peak months for fog, unfortunately during the best sailing weather. Normally, winds accompanying fog are light, as a strong wind will tend to disperse it. After a cold front passes through, and the wind has shifted to the northwest quadrant, everything will be sparkling clear again.

When you are at anchor, and wake up in the morning to find yourself enveloped in this white world without dimension, the question is, "Will it burn off?" There is no ready answer to this question. Frequently, by midmorning, it will dissipate and you can be on your way again. But, while waiting, you will be tantalized a hundred times with the prospect of its lifting. "There it is, I can see the bell buoy at the entrance of the harbor," you say, and you rush up on deck eager to hoist sail and be under say, and lo, that presage of hope will have again disappeared. Over and over again this will be repeated until you completely doubt your senses.

Finally, you either decide to set out, fog or no fog, or succumb to a leisurely day of reading, exploring the harbor by dinghy, or going ashore for a long walk. If you give into this, you can begin to appreciate the beauty of the fog; how all the normally sharp outlines of stone and tree are softened, while the smell of seaweed, spruce and roses are suspended in each minute droplet of moisture, accentuated for your enjoyment. In the words of Shakespeare, "the gentle air doth nimbly and sweetly recommend itself unto thine senses."

### Navigating in Fog

Even if you never deliberately set out in a fog, fog may envelope you while you are sailing. Here are some helpful hints for fog navigation.

I have read of a system of fog sailing described as "potato navigation," wherein a person is stationed up forward with a sack of potatoes and periodically throws one ahead of the bow. If there is no splash, then it's time to tack! Although this is facetious, it does have two main elements of truth. One is that coastal water in Maine is mostly deep water and full draft can often be carried to within a few feet of the steeply rising shore. At times, you can practically put your bowsprit into the trees before coming about. The other is the importance of sound. Most dangers are well marked by gong, bell, and whistle buoys. These are also placed at the entrance to harbors and thorofares. Although they are extremely valuable as an aid, they should not be solely or explicitly relied upon. Fog can do strange things to the strength of an audible signal, and to the apparent direction of its source. Also the exact position of these buoys, as indicated on the chart, may have changed due to winter storms.

Other audible clues make the presence of land known, the sound of surf breaking on the shore, and cries of gulls or land birds. With the sense of sight deprived, your other senses will be sharpened. Sometimes, it can be the sound of crickets that lets you know you are close to land. Listen not only to the sounds, but to what the sounds may mean. As lobsters are "fished" in the rocky bottom, shallower water, the intermittent sound of engines of the lobster boat hauling its traps, lets you know of your approach to these lesser depths.

See additional notes on Maine navigation in Chapter 2.

# CHAPTER 2

# GENERAL NOTES AND RECOMMENDATIONS

## ANCHORING

In all the major yachting harbors, slips and dock space are available to a limited extent. As you travel farther east along the Maine coast, these facilities become increasingly scarce. The probability of finding a mooring is also lessened. You will have to increasingly rely on anchoring. Good ground tackle and an adequate rode are required. A dinghy becomes a necessity to get ashore and to carry supplies.

Although a Danforth anchor tends to become accidently tripped when the boat swings with the change of tidal current, I still find it the easiest and most useful for the majority of harbors on the Maine coast. However, it will not pierce the tough, leathery leaves of kelp, and it is of little use in those harbors with a rocky bottom. Under these conditions, you need the traditional Fisherman's anchor or some such variation as the Herreshoff anchor. The CQR, or Plow, anchor is excellent as an all around type. Its only faults are that it is cumbersome to handle, and it does not dig in as quickly as other anchors. It will sometimes slide along the surface of a very hard, mud bottom or on kelp, before setting. As yet, I have little information as to how well the highly acclaimed Bruce anchor does in kelp.

To help determine your choice of anchor, I have described the kind of bottom and holding quality of each harbor. Do not assume that the holding ground of a harbor will remain unchanged. You may find that your favorite anchorage, which previously had little or no kelp in it, has subsequently sprouted the growth. This is an increasing problem with many Downeast harbors, and is due to the lack of strong storms in the past few years, which usually keep the harbors cleaned out.

I have visited most of these harbors many times under varying conditions of tide and wind, so generalizations made are fairly accurate. There always remains the possibility of a particular combination of factors that changes the evaluation entirely. An example of this is Deer Isle Thorofare opposite Stonington. I have never had any problems in the past anchoring there, using either a Danforth or a CQR. But last year, I put down my Fisherman's anchor when the wind was blowing straight down the length of the Thorofare at 30-40 MPH. My Fisherman's anchor has very small flukes for greater effectiveness in rock, and it slowly pulled through the mud. I now realize the bottom is of a softer consistency than I previously thought. You need an anchor with broad flukes. The Danforth or Plow, with enough chain to lower the catenary curve, will bury itself in soft mud until it digs in.

Fortunately, the holding ground is excellent in most harbors and along much of the coast. Most often it is composed of sticky, black mud in which the anchor sets quickly and holds firmly. I still am often surprised that in even the smallest coves, where the shore is boldly surrounded by granite, that the holding ground is so good. Where the few exceptions are encountered, they are indicated in our harbor descriptions. Kelp and other seaweed becomes more prevalent the farther east you travel.

In certain places where the tide flows through a gut and scours the bottom, the holding may be poor. You may encounter an anchorage where the bottom is uneven, alternating in patches of rock with mud or sand. Our harbor descriptions note these conditions. If you anchor with a trip-line and float, you will be able to retrieve your anchor by pulling it out backwards with the dinghy if the flukes are caught in rock.

In some harbors where the currents are erratic, it may be necessary to set two anchors to hold your position. In other harbors there may be a rapid reversal of current direction, increasing the chance of the anchor being tripped out. When there is risk of the boat being taken by the current and riding over the anchor, it is best to set out two anchors Bahamian style. Both are led from the bow, with one anchor set forward of the boat and the other aft, as shown in our sketch. This allows the boat to pivot with the current, holding its position, with the strain on either one or both anchors at all times. Although infrequent, there will be times when it is necessary to put out a bow anchor and a stern anchor. An example of this is the narrow harbor of Horseshoe Cove, where it is necessary to limit the swing of the boat, keeping it along the axis of current flow.

You must also consider the effects of tidal range when anchoring. Even in the western section of coast, the average mean tidal range is about 10 feet. Anchoring in 15 feet of water at low tide, with 60 feet of rode gives you a scope of only 4:1. With the additional 10 feet of water at high tide, that ratio changes to 2.4:1, hardly a safe margin if there should be any strong wind. Conversely, if you anchor at high tide, as the tide goes out, the radius of swing would increase by 4 feet.

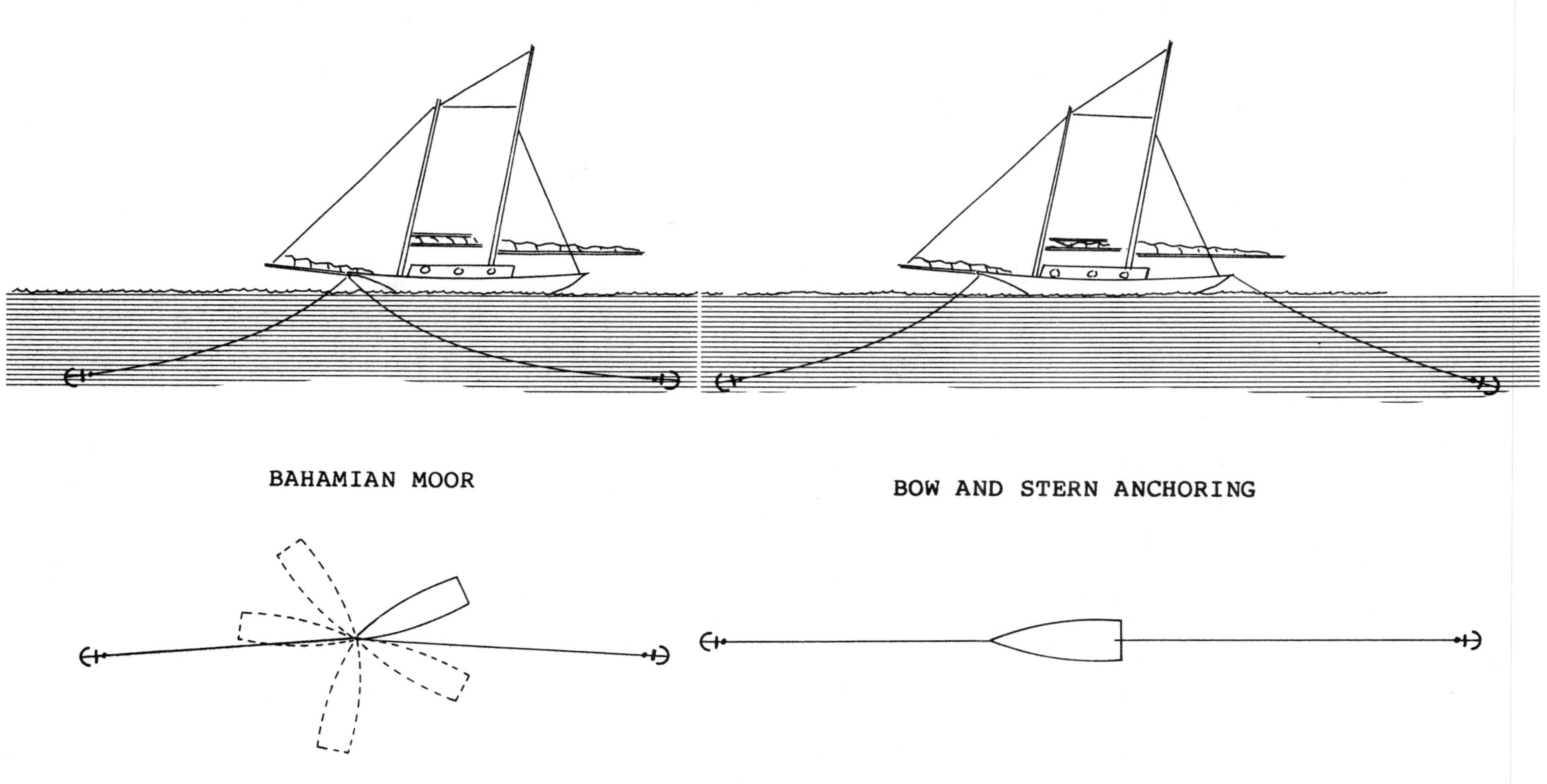
BAHAMIAN MOOR
BOW AND STERN ANCHORING

Hazards or boats previously out of reach of being bumped, could conceivably be within range with this increased radius at low tide. The range of the other boats is increasing also. You can appreciate how much greater these effects are when dealing with 15 to 30-foot tides farther up the coast. To compound the difficulty, as increased tide range makes anchoring more complex farther east, there are also fewer opportunities to find moorings or floating docks.

## FISH WEIRS

East of Schoodic Head, you are likely to encounter fish weirs. These become more common the farther east you travel. The weir, pronounced *ware*, is present in almost every cove.

Each weir is built in shallow water and comprises a roughly heart-shaped enclosure of stakes and twine netting with an opening, usually on the landward side. One or more leaders of stakes and netting or brush are built from the shore or off-lying ledge and serve to guide fish into the opening. The weir relies upon the natural behavior of herring for its operation. At high tide, herring schools move into shallower water and are carried by the currents along the shore. When they sense the leader of the weir, they turn offshore towards deeper water and thus swim into the opening of the enclosure. The heart-shape of the weir inhibits them from swimming out. Fishermen "tend" their weirs each morning at about dawn. If fish are in the weir, another piece of netting called the "drop," is rigged across the opening.

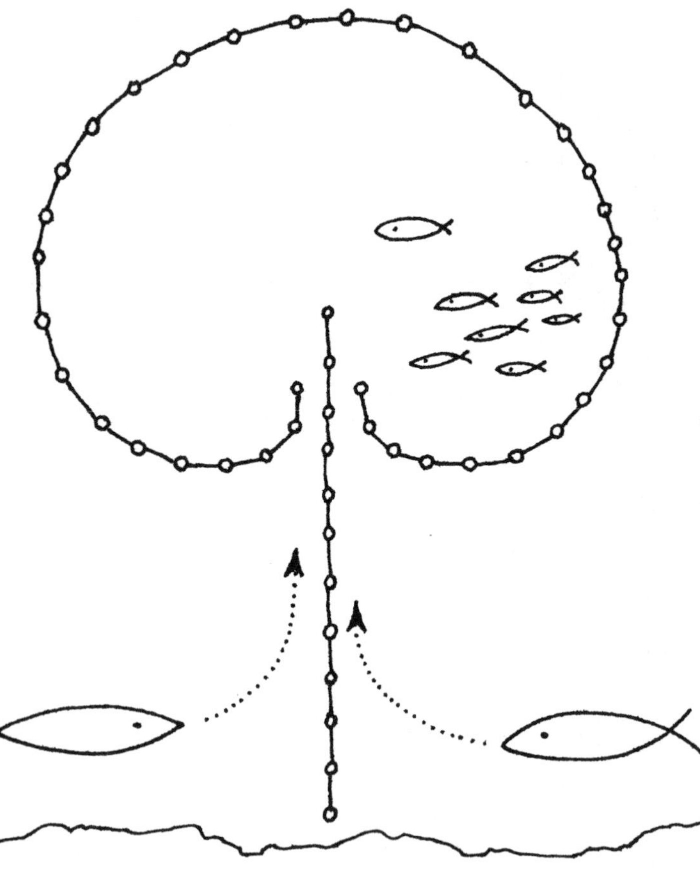

DIAGRAM OF FISH-WEIR

Some weirs have additional enclosures built on. This allows fish to be herded so that the weir can continue to "fish" while the fisherman waits for a market opportunity for his catch. When the sale of fish is arranged, a specially rigged vessel called a pumper, and others called carriers, approach the weir usually near low tide. A seine net is run around the inside of the weir and the fish brailed up into a small area. Fish are pumped into the carrier, while salt is added to preserve them. The pumping operation is cleverly arranged so that the agitation strips the scales off the herring, while a series of screens allow only the herring into the hold of the carrier. The water is caught in plastic buckets with fine saw-cuts in the sides. The scales are thus collected and sold to make iridescent jewelry, and the waste water flows over the side.

Skilled fishermen can estimate how many fish are in a weir by sounding it with a lead plumb-bob on a piano wire. The vibration of fish bumping into the wire is proportional to the number of fish. This is important. because the cost of pumper and carriers must be justified by the number of fish to be transported. There is also no point in sending more carriers than needed for a small catch. The process of seining a weir is well worth watching.

The weir is easily discernible at low tide, but during high tide, the tops of the stakes may be difficult to see, particularly if the weir has not been well maintained. One advantage to yachtsmen is that most weirs have a mooring nearby for making fast a seine boat. These moorings are usually available, but if the weir is being "worked," you must be prepared to move. Do not make fast to the stakes or twine.

A variation of the weir is the "shutoff." Fishermen who detect a school of fish in a cove or embayment, may run a length of netting across the mouth of the cove, thus shutting off the fish inside. Shutoffs are seined in the regular manner. If you are leaving a cove, or approaching the entrance from outside, it may not be possible to see the net and floats. However, the activity of dories on both sides of the opening should alert you to the possibility of shutoff fishing. Give the fishermen time. Usually they will drop a section of the net to let you pass through.

## TIDES AND TIDAL CURRENTS

Anyone sailing the Maine coast, particularly Downeast, is immediately aware of the tides and their resultant currents. Velocities at the strength of full ebb and flood tide are so great in some areas, and the range between high and low water so impressive, they completely dominate all other considerations in coastal navigation. Awesome as they may be, with care and preparation, few problems, will ever be encountered.

Government publications of *Tide Tables* and *Tidal Current Tables* contain a wealth of indispensable information. But they cannot replace judgement and they do not present all the local variations. Equally important is a general knowledge of the systems of currents and the principles of their behavior in order to navigate effectively and sail safely.

Whenever possible, I have expressed current velocities in knots, either as stated in the National Ocean Survey *Tidal Current Tables,* or from personal observation. These are given at strength at mid-tide. Frequently the direction of set is also included. This will enable you to make the necessary corrections in your course if you have to navigate in fog.

## Gulf of Maine

Contained within the Gulf of Maine is a pattern of circulation operating independently of other tidal systems. This current, or drift, is generally weak, about 0.3 knots, except in specific local areas such as Georges Bank. The pattern is a large elliptical, counter-clockwise circulation. Eddies occasionally develop along the edge of this current, but are not significant. In the winter the center of this flow shifts northward and becomes more diffuse. Several major factors contribute to the generation of this current.

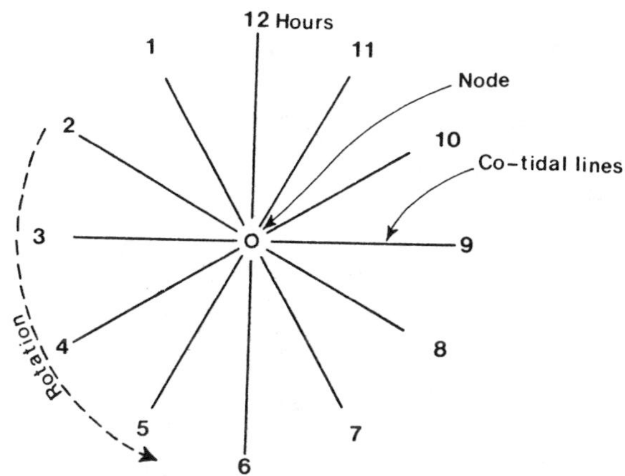


ROTARY CURRENTS

Slope water of the continental shelf of Nova Scotia, augmented by a branch of the Labrador Current, the Nova Scotia Current, enters the Gulf of Maine and trends westward. In the spring, this is amplified by the considerable runoff from the St. Lawrence River. Maine's coastal rivers add to this flow. This mass of incoming water along the shore is higher and less saline than the lower offshore water and therefore, by gravity, flows "downhill." With the spinning of the earth eastward, this water is given a push to the west and southwest along the coast. Confined by the land mass boundaries, when it reaches the southern part of the Gulf it is driven east by Cape Cod. Georges Bank and Nantucket Shoals, as an extension of the East Coast Shelf, and Brown Bank, a part of the Scotian Shelf, act to confine this volume of water at the "open" end of the Gulf. In its flow eastward, some water spills out over the far eastern edge of Georges Bank and through Northeast Channel. But for the most part, this current is contained within the Gulf and continues northward, completing the pattern of flow. The continual oscillation of tides within this mostly enclosed basin further augments this counter-clockwise movement of water, due to the rotational effect of the earth.

## Coastal Tidal Current

For the cruising yachtsman, tidal currents along the shore are of greater importance than those farther out in the Gulf of Maine. Progressing north and eastward along the Maine coast, the amplitude of tide, as well as the velocity of current, increases dramatically. North of Cape Cod the range is 7-10 feet, while in Penobscot Bay, the range of Spring tides is about 12 feet. But by the time Eastport and Passamaquoddy Bay are reached, the tides have attained a height of 28 feet. This increase finally culminates in Minas Basin of the Bay of Fundy, where the perigee Spring tide has reached a height of 55.1 feet, making it the highest recorded tide in the world. Tidal currents created by the movement of such a volume of water, especially in narrow and constricted channels, are correspondingly greater the farther east you sail. They need not be feared, but they certainly must be given a great deal of respect. This is especially true with the prevalence of fog.

Along the entire coast of Maine, and extending up into the Bay of Fundy, the semi-diurnal type of tide, having two high tides and two low tides in 24 hours is the predominant type. These tides are produced by the gravitational effect of the sun and the moon upon the water. During a new moon (when the moon is in conjunction with the sun) and during a full moon (when it is in opposition to the sun) the alignment of these two bodies with the earth produces the high tides called Spring tides. When the moon is at quadrature, that is, when it is at right angles to the sun and the earth, the result is a smaller tide, called Neap tide. This is because the gravitational effects of the sun and moon partially cancel each other out. There are other factors creating fluctuation in the height of tides. Declination of the sun and moon (north or south of the celestial equator) produce unequal high tides between the two daily tides. For a more detailed description, refer to the chapter on Tides in Volume I of our Cruising Guide to Maine.

The maximum possible high tide occurs when perigee Spring tides coincide with perihelion and the moon and sun have zero declination, while the moon, sun and earth are on a common axis. This indeed produces an enormously high tide, but the last time such a combination occured was in the year 1433 AD, and the next time won't be until 3800 AD!

If it were just the relative position of the sun and moon as they orbit around the earth, the tidal wave created would be a progressively moving standing wave.

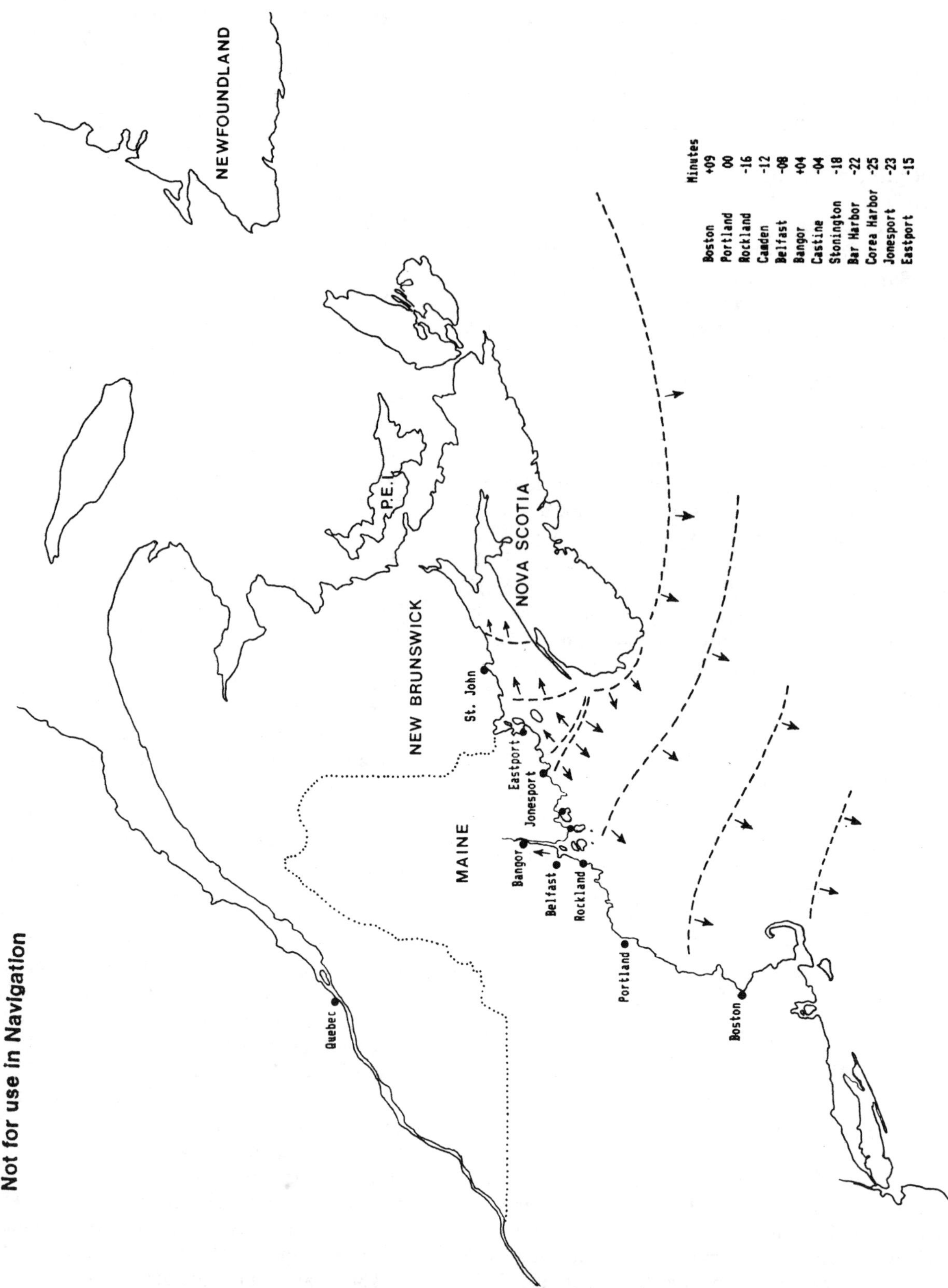


But the major ocean basins are complex in shape and interrupted by land masses. Acting upon these bodies of water is the Coriolus force, created by rotation of the earth. This causes a high water crest to move continually in a counter-clockwise direction around a central, or nodal, point. These are called **rotary** currents and are the major, offshore tidal currents. See diagram.

In the North Atlantic Ocean, tides oscillate around one major node located south of Greenland. It is this rotary tide that is responsible for the tidal action upon Maine's coast. In the Gulf of Maine, however, as well as in many other parts of the North Atlantic, there are smaller, more localized rotary currents. Their presence and location are generated by the particular nature of the basin of water and the topography of the ocean floor.

This wave from the rotary current off Greenland, sweeps along the Atlantic cost of Nova Scotia, reaching the Maine coast. Moving in its counter-clockwise direction, it progresses from **east** to **west** down the coast. Thus high water takes progressively longer to arrive, the farther down the coast it travels towards Portland and Boston. The line of tide also pivots around the southwest corner of Nova Scotia and progresses from **west** to **east** up the Bay of Fundy. The division point of these two, different directions of movement is at the mouth of the Bay of Fundy, somewhere about Jonesport, Maine.

As this crest of high water sweeps along, the phenomena at shore is observed as a reversing current, flooding and ebbing out of the bays, sounds and rivers. Along the coast the flood tide sets approximately in an easterly direction and the ebb tide in a westerly direction. The velocity of these currents, particularly west of Mt. Desert is not strong and will not be troublesome, other than a chop that will be encountered when a strong wind is against the current. East of Petit Manan the strength of current increases considerably.

Sailing along the shore, particularly in thick weather, keep in mind the set of tidal current in and out of the bays and rivers. A good example of the results of the neglect of this can be seen in the two wrecks on the eastern shore of Monhegan Island. Even though this island is 10 miles off-shore, the flood and ebb from the St. George River exert considerable influence. Tide set should also be taken into account when approaching headlands.

For specific direction and velocity of tidal currents, refer to the National Ocean Survey *Tidal Current Tables* In some instances, my own personal experiences do not match conditions stated in the *Current Tables.* An example of this is in Penobscot Bay. The Tables state flood 0.3 k, ebb 0.6 k, I have found current strength to be 0.5k stronger than this, particularly on the ebb tide. The current also runs stronger through Muscle Ridge Channel than it does through Two Bush Channel. As much of your sailing in Penobscot Bay involves criss-crossing it, it will be important in fog to always know the state of the tide and the strength of the current to make appropriate corrections in your course. Other discrepancies are mentioned in the appropriate chapters.

## NAVIGATION HINTS

In Chapter 1, we gave some tips on fog navigation. Here are more, which apply to navigation in Maine, fog or no.

The most important aid to your safety and that of your boat is always knowing your exact position. Have NOS charts for the area you are sailing and make sure you keep them updated. At times, the Coast Guard adds or removes buoys and changes the numbering.

If you keep the chart in a plastic envelope handy to the helmsman, and a china-marking pencil available, you can immediately note your position from hand-bearing compass sights when the fog starts to come in. Don't delay, thinking you have time to make it to your intended harbor, for the fog can rush upon you with unbelievable swiftness, obsuring all landmarks before you even have a chance to point them out to others on the boat. Remember, also, to place several registration marks for the chart on the plastic envelope to guard against error caused by the chart shifting inside. Keep a running, written plot from mark to mark, don't trust to memory. Know at all times the state of the tide and make appropriate corrections for the current set.

Crossing bays, sounds and thorofares, your depth sounder is of limited use. Ledges and individual rocks rise abruptly from the bottom, and the warning of this from the depth-sounder can be concommitant with the cruching sound your keel makes on contact.

However there are places, particularly Downeast, where the depthsounder is an invaluable aid to navigating. In fog, long stretches of coastline can be safely followed along the 10 or 20 fathom curve. This lets you avoid dangers and maintain your proper course. The 20 fathom curve off Great Wass Island and Head Harbor Island is a good example. This technique can also be useful in locating buoys in fog. For instance, Bell Buoy "LR", off Little River, Cutler, lies just inside the 20 fathom curve. Following it will lead you to the buoy.

If your compass is corrected for deviation and you have previously calibrated the percentage of error in your knotmeter/log, you can sail with added peace of mind.

Loran C and radar are great comforts along the Maine coast, increasingly valuable the farther east you go. During the more than usual foggy summer of 1986, I finally broke down and bought a Loran C for "Nakomis." It proved most useful.

### Course Headings

Throughout the book, all reference to course headings is given in degrees Magnetic, rather than degrees True. This is not the usually accepted procedure, but I feel it has great validity. All the coastal charts of Maine, including no. 13260 covering The Bay of Fundy to Cape Cod, have a Magnetic compass rose as well as degrees True, so direct readings may be made from the chart. More importantly, your sailing course and bearings are made with the boat's compass. Keeping everything in degrees Magnetic eliminates changing from degrees True to Magnetic. The slight annual change, along the westernmost part of the coast, is only a decrease of 1 minute of arc per year.

## LOBSTER BUOYS

Lobstering is a major industry in Maine and in some areas innumerable lobster buoys are encountered. You'll know if you've caught one while under way, for even in a really good breeze, suddenly you are not getting anywhere and the boat will refuse to answer the helm. Lobster boats have a welded, metal basket around their propeller to avoid entanglement while under power, so they needn't worry. It is best for you to dodge them.

To make matters more difficult, many lobster traps employ a toggle arrangement. Usually, pot-warp rising from the trap is attached directly to a buoy float. Being a single, vertical line, this does not present a problem. Some traps, however, have an additional line from the buoy to a smaller toggle float. These toggle floats are generally of styrofoam or cork and are not brightly colored as is the main buoy. This 10-15 ft. long horizontal line is just below the water surface and difficult to see. It makes it easier for lobstermen to catch the line with a boathook to haul the traps, but it also makes it easier for a sailboat to become entangled.

On the one hand the plethora of traps is an annoyance, on the other hand they can serve as an excellent navigational aid. First of all, the presence of buoys alerts you to the depth of water. Generally, they are placed along the rocky edge of a shallowing slope or the outer limits of ledge and rocks. Also they are a perfect indicator of the strength and direction of tidal current. The toggle floats are particularly responsive, even in the slightest current.

## LOBSTER HATCHERIES

As a result of concern by lobster fishermen over the dwindling catch of lobsters, there are now four lobster hatcheries in operation along the coast of Maine. Their mission is to reverse this trend of diminishing supply. The Cutler station, funded in part by the Maine Department of Marine Resources, the Maine Lobsterman's Association, the University of Maine and by private donations went into operation in the spring of 1986. Other stations are located at Stonington, Walpole (near South Bristol) and Five Island, Maine. All are somewhat different in their organization and means of funding, but are generally alike in their techniques and goals.

Female lobsters, carrying eggs, are brought in by fishermen and placed in tanks. The newly hatched larvae are placed in tanks of aerated, heated sea-water, and fed with algae-enriched brine shrimp. In a matter of 12-14 days, the larvae pass through several successive stages of development to attain a size of about ½″ in length. At this size (Stage IV) they are benthic (bottom-dwelling) individuals and no longer free-swimming, becoming easy prey for predators. In a natural environment this process, to reach Stage IV, takes up to 45-60 days and has a 99.999% mortality rate. By protecting the earlier larval forms in the tank environment the mortality rate drops to 65-80%. After their release, it will take an additional six to seven years for the lobster to reach maturity and a legal size for "harvesting."

No one has yet been able to **prove** that the program will significantly add to a commercial catch. There is no practical way of tagging the released lobster to differentiate the mature hatchery raised specimen from any other lobster. Yet everyone agrees that it is better to be taking some sort of positive action than to stand by fatalistically watching the death of an industry so important to Maine's economy.

If the technique being attempted at the Ira C. Darling Center hatchery in Walpole, Maine is successful, there will indeed be proof of the efficacy of the program. They have obtained an adult male and female lobster, both royal blue in color, and will breed them. This coloration is a genetic rarity, occuring only once in every 3-4 million lobsters. If a blue lobster mates with a normal colored lobster, the blue color is masked, but if bred pure with another blue individual, the color trait is passed on. If the hatching and release program is successful, and there should be a dramatic upsurge in the number of blue lobsters caught, this would be definite proof of the efficacy of the program. We're told that blue lobsters taste just as good!

## DANGEROUS MARINE ANIMALS

With the exception of a few beaches on the lower coast, there is little swimming because the water is just too cold. Sharks, although not common, are sometimes present. It is not true that they are found only in warm water. Every so often, from as far as Penobscot Bay, a large shark is brought up in a fisherman's net. In the summer of 1988, a 37-foot long shark was caught near Jonesport and brought into Beals Island by local fisherman Avery Kelly for all to see. If you do swim, you will not encounter any sea nettles, those stinging jellyfish that are such a scourge in Chesapeake Bay, nor are there any Portuguese Man-O-War or aquatic snakes.

## INSECTS

Fortunately, by the time of good sailing weather, the major hatches of insect pests are completely over. Except in a few, isolated areas, mainly in the western section of coast, you will seldom be bothered throughout the summer at all, even by mosquitos.

## FORAGING

One of the pleasures of cruising the Maine coast is the opportunity for partaking in different activities. You can explore an island and pick wild strawberries, raspberries or blueberries, depending on the season. Clams are available for the digging and mussel beds are plentiful. Mussels are particularly accessible and no special tools are needed, only a bucket to put them in. At low tide you can wade in knee-deep water and pick to your heart's content. To clean them, add some oatmeal to the bucket of mussels and water, and in a few hours they will be plump and clean. Or keep them in a nylon mesh bag, such as scuba divers use, and hang them over the side of the boat to clean themselves.

Occasionally "red tide" is present. In some years, tiny poisonous plankton are found in coastal waters. When ingested by shellfish the toxin does not affect the shellfish, but it makes them poisonous to eat. Ask al-

## LARVAL STAGES OF LOBSTERS

Courtesy of Cutler Marine Hatchery

Lobster eggs

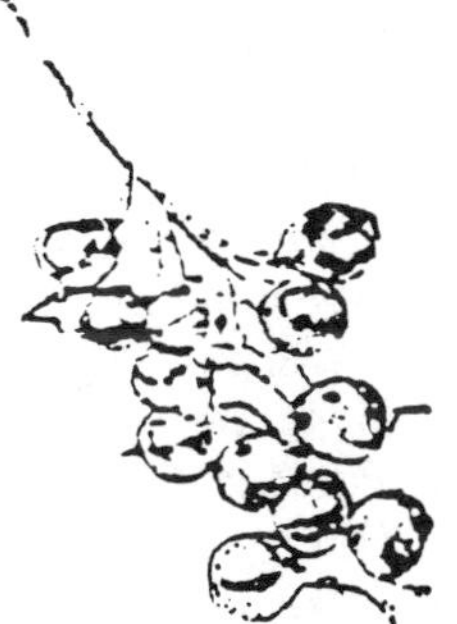

Eggs showing embryos

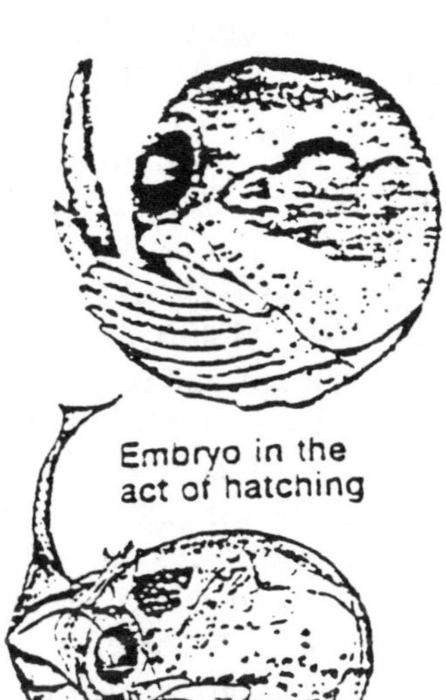

Embryo in the act of hatching

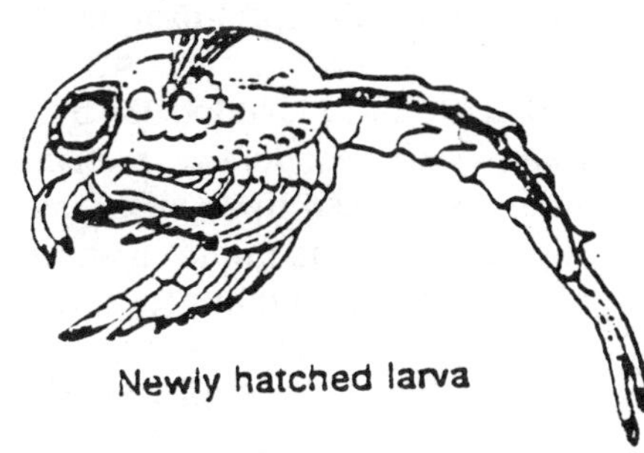

Newly hatched larva

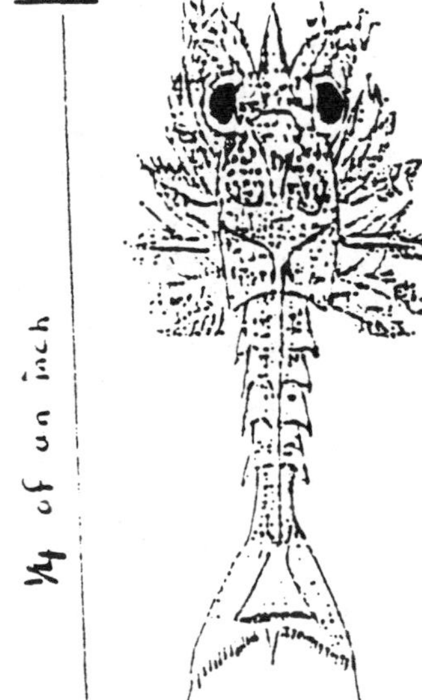


First larval stage

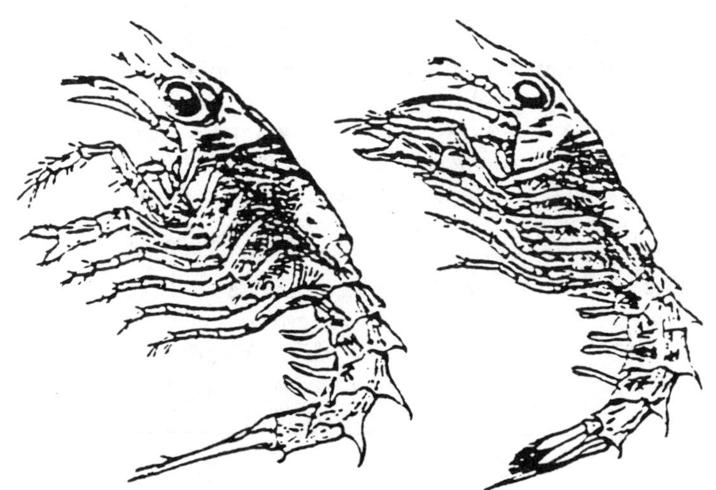

Second larval stage

Third larval stage

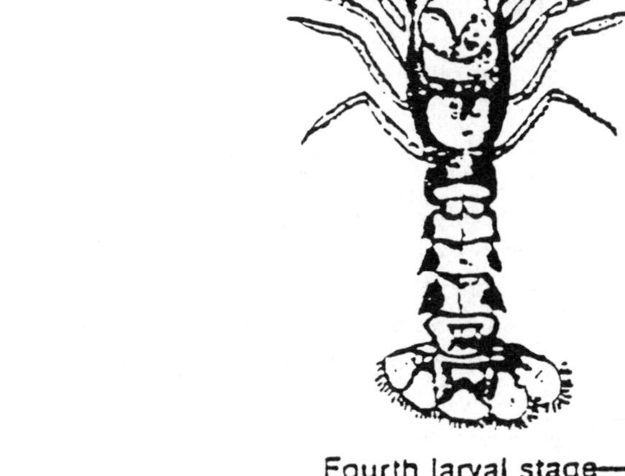

Fourth larval stage—about ½ inch long

most anyone before digging your own clams or mussels, and they'll tell you if "red tide" has affected that particular area. Areas closed to taking shellfish are announced regularly on Radio NOAA Weather broadcasts. "Red tide" has absolutely no effect on lobsters!

•

It is illegal to take lobster by any means other than traps. Don't even dive near a fisherman's traps as it will surely be looked upon with suspicion. If there is the slightest confirmation for assuming that you are taking a lobster, the resultant action can be quite unpleasant.

## FISHING

Ordinarily, I don't believe in mixing fishing and sailing. I would much rather keep them as two separate sports, giving each my undivided attention. I make one exception, when mackerel are running. Mackerel lures, available almost everywhere, are simply five flies or plastic worms tied onto a length of nylon leader. Attach the lure to a spool of line, add a small weight, and merely trail over the side. No rod is needed, it does not take up any space, there is nothing to tangle with sheets or rigging, and there is no bait or mess. I keep a plastic bucket in the cockpit and when sailing through a school of mackerel frequently bring in five at a time. It is a lot of fun for children. They can handle it without your help. It doesn't interrupt or hinder the sailing at all and it provides a great fresh fish dinner.

## FUEL

Diesel fuel and gasoline and generally available everywhere along the coast. This is true even in areas where marinas are absent, as there is almost always a dock with fuel to supply the lobster boats.

## ICE

Ice may be obtained in the more populated areas, but don't count on its availability as you travel farther east along the coast. However, the need for ice correspondingly diminishes with the cooler climate.

## FIRES

Although many of the islands are uninhabited, they are owned either by private idividuals, or various preservation societies. Usually there is no problem in temporarily using this land to explore or to picnic, provided there is proper respect for the property and the rights of privacy of the owner are not infringed. Whenever possible, you should first get permission from the owner or caretaker. When building a fire for cooking, keep it small and definitely keep it below the high tide mark. This way you can be sure no ember will rise again after you douse the fire and leave, to become a fire hazard. Fires can burn in the sub-surface peat for months before erupting into a blaze. Once a fire has started on an island, there is no way to bring fire fighting equipment to it, and the fire cannot be controlled. By thoughtful and considerate use of this land, it can continue to be enjoyed by everyone.

## CUSTOMS AND IMMIGRATION

Foreign-flag pleasure boats (yachts), upon their arrival in U.S. waters, will have to report to a U.S. Customs and Immigration Office to fill out the appropriate forms and obtain a cruising license. This license is required for all boats 30 feet in length and over and is good for one calendar year. There is a fee of $25.

American pleasure boats must also report to the nearest customs office if they are returning from a foreign port. Obviously, this is hardly a concern for most of the yachtsmen cruising coastal Maine, but for those who sail way Downeast, it will eventually become a necessity. Eastport, Lubec and portions of Passamaquoddy Bay are all in U.S. territorial waters. Once you have arrived here, you will undoubtedly want to sail over to St. Andrews, N.B., visit Campobello Island and go through the reversing falls at St. John New Brunswick. These are all in Canadian waters, so even if your stay is for a brief few hours, your return to the U.S. will be considered to be from a foreign port, and you must immediately report to Customs and Immigration.

***Editor's Note:*** *If you're at Eastport, by all means take a few days to explore Passamaquoddy Bay. You get all that wind and no waves! You could sail up there for a week and never repeat a harbor, but high spots for me were St. Andrews, a beautiful tourist town with a marvelous hotel and an active hospitable yacht club, and Campobello Island, with a popular museum. This is where President Franklin Delano Roosevelt vacationed, and if you explore there you'll see why.*

The following information is quoted directly from the booklet titled "Pleasure Boats" provided by the U.S. Customs Service.

### "Cruising Licenses

Cruising licenses exempt pleasure boats of certain countries from formal entry and clearance procedures—filing manifests and obtaining permits to proceed, and from the payment of tonnage tax and entry and clearance fees—*at all but the first port of entry.* They can be obtained from the district director of Customs at the first port of arrival in the United States. Normally issued for no more than a one-year period, a cruising license has no bearing on the dutiability of a pleasure boat. Vessels of the following countries (subject to change) are eligible for cruising licenses (these countries extend the same privileges to American pleasure boats):

| | | |
|---|---|---|
| Argentina | Federal Republic of Germany | Jamaica |
| Australia | Greece | Liberia |
| Bahamas Islands | Honduras | Netherlands |
| Bermuda | Ireland | New Zealand |
| Canada | | Norway |
| | | Sweden |

Great Britain (including Turks and Caicos Islands St. Vincent [including the territorial waters of the Northern Grenadine Islands] the Cayman Islands, the British Virgin Islands and the St. Christopher-Nevis-Anguilla Islands).

### American Pleasure Boats

American pleasure boats not documented by the United States Coast Guard but owned by citizens residing in the United States must comply with Federal laws relating to identification numbers issued by a State, Puerto Rico, the Virgin Islands, Guam, American Samoa, and the District of Columbia. The master of any American pleasure boat must (immediately) report upon arrival from a foreign port or place to Customs and must also report foreign merchandise aboard his boat that is subject to duty. The report may be made by any means of communication and should include the name of the boat, its nationality, name of the master, place of docking, and arrival time. If an inspection is required, the Customs officer will direct the vessel to an inspection area.

No notification to Customs is required when the boats depart for foreign ports or places.

### Immigration Requirements

U.S. citizens should carry proof of their citizenship, such as a passport, birth certificate or voter registration card. Canadian citizens do not need a visa, but must present proof of their citizenship. If a Canadian citizen is arriving from a country outside the Western Hemisphere, he must present a valid Canadian passport.

### Stay on Board!

If your boat has anchored or tied-up, you are considered to have entered the United States. No person shall board or leave the boat prior to completion of Customs processing without permission from the Customs officer in charge, except to report arrival. If it is necessary for someone to leave the boat to report arrival to Customs, he must return to the boat after reporting and remain on board. No one who arrived on board the boat may leave until the Customs officer grants permission to go ashore. Violations may result in substantial penalties and forfeiture of the boat." Remember, this is also true of U.S. citizens entering Canada!

### "Boarding Charges and Overtime

There is no charge for Customs inspection during official business hours, 8:00 a.m-5:00 p.m., Monday through Saturday, except holidays. After hours and Sunday/holiday inspection service will be provided at *pro rata* overtime rates, not to exceed $25 per boat."

Additional information is available in the pamphlet titled "Pleasure Boats," available at Customs ports. Further details may be obtained from the U.S. Customs Service, Washington, DC 20229 (ATTN: Carrier Rulings Branch).

Matinicus Island Harbor, Chapter 4

# CHAPTER 3

## PENOBSCOT BAY

*BRIGHT MOSAIC OF ISLAND AND SKY*

### INTRODUCTION TO PENOBSCOT BAY CHART NO. 13260

Sailing broad Penobscot Bay, no matter which direction you turn your gaze, everywhere the view is most rewarding. In an account by Samuel Adams Drake in 1891, he said, "Taken as a whole, the scenic features of this bay are graceful rather than bold, suggestive of calm rather than riotous commotion. You will not see the full play of ocean as you would along the more exposed coasts, or find here those long levels of gleaming sands that echo to the mighty tread of the free Atlantic; but you will always have green islands, noble mountains, and inviting harbors on every hand—the sea shorn of its terrors, the land divested of its harsh and hideous features." This is as true today as it was then.

Always in the background, the majestic Camden Hills are there to help fix your position in this constantly changing vista of land and water that beckons and entices you to explore ever further.

The earliest explorers of the coast of Maine were wont to giving descriptions full of glowing praise for what they had seen, usually full of exaggeration and discrepancies of the grossest order. But here, in Penobscot Bay, the adulation was well founded and not overdone. The sailors who first came to these shores were fishermen of such diverse origin as France, England, Portugal and Holland. All came to catch fish that swam so thickly "one could scarce plough their way through them." These men were fishermen, not explorers of new territory, nor writers of chronicles. Little remains to remind us of their presence.

The first written report about this region comes from Verrazano, in his voyage of 1524 for Francis 1 of France. In it he gives a fairly detailed description of the coast and its inhabitants. Shortly thereafter, in 1539, the historian Ramusio published a manuscript in which the sea captain, Jean Parmentier of Normandy, describes Penobscot Bay. He is the first to give it the name of *Norumbega*, asserting that the name was of Indian origin, and was the name used by the Indians. In 1555, Andre Thevet, a French gentleman, and Chaplain to Catherine de Medicis, undertook a voyage to Brazil. His return passage to France brought him up the North American Coast as far as Newfoundland. In his publication the following year, entitled *The Singularities of Antarctic France, otherwise called America,* he describes Penobscot Bay and the Penobscot River. He too, refers to it as Norumbega. It seems that at first, the name referred to an area that reached all the way from Florida to Cape Breton. The territory of this name was finally contracted to encompass only Penobscot Bay and its river.

Some historians assert that Norumbega isn't even Indian in origin but is related to the name of Nuremberg, the city in Bavaria, meaning "only one mountain." The Spanish form of this is Nuromberga, and the Latin or Italian form, Norimberga. A map of 1561 uses the name Nurumberg for this region.

Whatever the name given or the origin of that name, one thing that remains consistent is the knowledge of the geographuy of the area. From the earliest 16th century maps of the east coast of North America, no matter how crudely drawn or undiscernable the details, two features are constant and always unmistakable—the hook of Cape Cod, and Penobscot Bay with its many islands.

Part of the appeal of sailing this Bay comes from the great variety of choices available to the sailor. The outermost portion, in the wide mouth of the Bay, is completely exposed to the full forces of the open Atlantic. Here you can have ocean sailing, making fairly long passages betweeen landfalls, even with a chance to practice celestial navigation. Looking to seaward, there is nothing but the open sea between here and Portugal, and you may be tempted to cross!

The air carries the sharp tang of salt which seems to heighten awareness of all your senses. At the end of the day "out at sea," when you approach your harbor, suddenly there is a switch from a sea breeze to a land breeze and you catch that first whiff of land—an elixir of spruce, beach roses and meadow grass. As you slowly sail into the harbor on the last of the dying breeze, you know that here you have the best of both possible worlds.

Within the Bay numerous islands afford protection against the heaviest seas and you can sail with ease and comfort. There is a wide choice of beautiful and protected harbors, no matter what the wind direction.

Fog is not nearly so common here as farther downeast, but if it comes, there is invariably a safe anchorage nearby. All the ledges and rocks are well marked and and the islands are generally bold and easily seen when approached in fog.

If you want isolation and the chance to observe nature around you in peace and quiet, you'll find lonesome anchorages in innumerable coves, bights and harbors throughout the Bay. You may be the only boat present, feeling you have dropped anchor in the time slot of a bygone century. On the other hand if you want to step ashore to restaurants, shops, concerts, etc., there are places like Camden Harbor.

## GENERAL INFORMATION
## CHART NOS. 13260, 13302

Penobscot Bay is divided by a string of islands down its middle into Western Penobscot Bay (1) and Eastern Penobscot Bay (2). The southern extremity of the Western Bay (on its western side) is further divided by another string of islands separating Muscle Ridge Channel (3) and Two Bush Channel (4). These channels, and the group of islands separating them, are described in full detail in Volume I of our *Cruising Guide to Maine.*

The southernmost part of Eastern Penobscot Bay, which lies between Vinalhaven Island. (5), Deer Isle (6), and Isle au Haut (7), is called Isle au Haut Bay (8). The Penobscot River (9) empties into the head of the Bay. Cast far out from the mouth of the Bay is a group of widely separated islands, the most well known being Monhegan Island (10) and Matinicus Island (11).

### Approaches

**Easterly Approaches.** From the east, Penobscot Bay can be entered through Eggemoggin Reach (12), Deer Island Thorofare (13), Merchant Row (14) or Isle au Haut Bay (8). The light on Saddleback Ledge (16) (Fl 6 sec 54 ft 11M) marks the entrance from seaward to Isle au Haut Bay. Aids to navigation in these passages are colored and numbered for passage north and west.

**Westerly Approaches.** From the west, entry is via Muscle Ridge Channel (3) or Two Bush Channel (4), both marked by lighthouses. Muscle Ridge Channel light (Occ G 4 sec 75 ft 14M) is on Whitehead Island (17). Two Bush Channel light (18) (Fl. 5 sec 65 ft 21M) is on the island of the same name. Both lighthouses have foghorns.

A note of caution here about entering Penobscot Bay from the west. If you are using chart no. 13301 (labeled Muscongus Bay) and switch to chart no. 13305 (Penobscot Bay) to continue your course, it appears that there is a complete overlap of the charts at the entrance to Muscle Ridge Channel. However, this is not so! It is **almost** a complete overlap—what is missing is a very important outer "corner" of the string of islands bounding the channel; namely, Crow Island, Crow Island Ledges, Two Bush Island (18), Two Bush Reef and Stallion Ledge. They are south of Pleasant Island and east of Whitehead Island (17). To include these in proper relationship to the other islands, don't neglect to use the intermediate chart no. 13303 (Approaches to Penobscot Bay). All three charts have the same scale, 1:40,000.

Heading up the Bay from the west, your choice is whether to use Muscle Ridge Channel (3) or Two Bush Channel (4). Each has its own advantages. Muscle Ridge Channel is a shorter run, particularly if starting from Tenants Harbor. The savings in distance is not significant if the route is from Burnt and Allen's Islands, or even Port Clyde. Regardless of the direction of the wind, the inner passage (Muscle Ridge Channel) is more protected and has calmer water. It may also have less fog than the outer passage. It is narrow in places, but very well marked with buoys and daybeacons, making navigation easy. Navigation aids are colored and marked for passage northward. There are no sound buoys in Muscle Ridge Channel.

Tidal current does run stronger through Muscle Ridge Channel than Two Bush Channel, reaching a velocity of 2.0 knots, or greater. Although this is not of great concern when making the passage under power, under sail, with the wind against you, it can be difficult, since in most places there is little room to tack. In this case, it would be best to use Two Bush Channel where there is much more maneuvering space. Even in fog, the numerous buoys in the inner channel are close enough together, and the tidal current runs with the channel, so you cannot go too far off course. However, with an ebb tide and a light, southwest wind, better time can be made taking the outside route where the current is less strong.

Within Muscle Ridge Channel there are several places where you can drop anchor to wait out a fair tide, better weather or the lifting of fog: Seal Harbor, False Whitehead Harbor, Home Harbor (19) and Dix Harbor. These are all described in detail in Volume I of our *Cruising Guide to Maine.* In choosing Two Bush Channel, once past Home Harbor (19) (difficult to enter in fog), you are committed to continuing for the full route. In fog, Two Bush Channel is made easier by the large, black and white, mid-channel buoys with their gong or whistle. These mid-channel buoys are in line for a major part of the course on a heading of 360 degrees true. There is some commercial traffic in Two Bush Channel, tankers that go up to Searsport (81a) and Bucksport (81b) at the head of the Bay, but they are infrequently encountered.

Headed south, along the outside edge of the string of islands separating the two channels, there is a decided set to the ebb current pulling into Muscle Ridge Channel. In thick weather this must be carefully watched and a compensatory correction made in your heading. Fisherman Island passage (20), connecting Muscle Ridge Channel to Western Penobscot Bay, has a strong tidal current set towards the SW on the ebb tide.

### Tides and Tidal Currents in Penobscot Bay

Within the main part of the Bay, the set of tidal currents, both the ebb and flood, are on an axis with the main channels. However, it has been my experience that current strength is about 0.5 knot faster, particularly on the ebb tide, than that indicated (flood 0.3 k and ebb 0.6k) in the *Tidal Current Tables.* Of no particular consequence when going up or down the Bay, **in crossing**, it can make a considerable difference in your course correction.

Tidal currents within Penobscot Bay are not strong, particularly if you are accustomed to downeast tides.

Patterns are predictable and can be assumed from an examination of the charts. The only place where the currents attain any velocity is where there is a constriction in a channel. Locations of these will be mentioned in subsequent, pertinent chapters. Additional, detailed information is available in the *Tidal Current Tables* published by the National Oceanic and Atmospheric Administration. Mean tidal range is 10 feet near the entrance to about 12 feet at the head of the Bay.

See chart no. 13302. Ebb currents along the south shore of Vinalhaven Island are swept along parallel to the shore as they come out of Eastern and Western Penobscot Bays. Thus, opposite the White Islands (21), ebb tide current sets SSE. As it continues along the shore toward "The Breakers" (22), it becomes more southeasterly in direction. From the R "2A" Bell Buoy marking Old Horse Ledge (23), to a point south of Otter Island (24), it is almost due east. By the time it reaches this position, the strength of current is much diminished. Near south of Otter Island (24), the ebb current is met with that coming out of East Penobscot Bay which sets toward the southwest.

In the east-west passage, called Oak Island Passage (25), north of North Haven Island (26), tidal currents swirl around in all directions. They are not excessive, and ordinarily are of little problem, but in fog or with a light wind, they should be dealt with carefully. This passage (25) is between Oak Island, Burnt Island and Bald Island, and Sheep Island. Details on this passage are to be found in Chapter 7, North Haven Island and Vinalhaven.

Within Fox Islands Thorofare (27), another east-west passage, currents are generally weak. The only place where they attain any strength is at the constriction near Iron Point (28). The flood tide enters from both ends of the thorofare and the ebb tide similarly exits from both ends. When there is a strong wind from either the west or the east, currents are apt to be stronger, and cause eddies at Iron Point (28).

Now refer to chart no. 13260 this chapter. Tidal currents south of Isle au Haut (7) have a pattern similar to those of Vinalhaven. As the tide ebbs from East Penobscot Bay, the current follows the shoreline in a southeasterly direction until it weakens and is met by the water emptying out of Jericho Bay (29) in a southwesterly direction. In the area between Eastern Ear Ledge and Colt Ledge, the ebb current runs at about 0.75-1.0 knots at a heading of 260 degrees magnetic. However, south of Marshall Island (32), this heading is 180 degrees magnetic, at a velocity of 0.75-1.0 knots. Refer to charts in Chapter (8) on Isle au Haut.

## ENVIRONMENTAL CHANGES FROM PENOBSCOT BAY, EAST

Just as Cape Elizabeth marks the boundary of a major change in topography from that of flat shore and beach, to rocky headlands and numerous, long, parallel islands, Penobscot Bay also is a boundary for a change in geology and ecology.

The islands now are small and dome-shaped, instead of long and narrow. This is due to the change in rock formation from that of bedrock of mountain folds to one of granite as a result of volcanic activity. This is in evidence from the mouth of Penobscot Bay, eastward. Granite, which is "frozen" molten rock, was pushed up by this volcanic activity, the result of collisions of tectonic plates. At one time, two-thirds of the coast of Maine was "literally a ring of fire." The presence of granite is more than mere academic interest only to the geologist, but was of great economic importance in the history of this part of Maine. Granite quarrying was the major industry from the mid-1800's until the beginning of the 20th century, when reinforced concrete replaced granite as an architectural medium.

From Penobscot Bay east, another major change is that of **vertical** mixing of water. A long narrow band of water, immediately offshore, extends from Grand Manan Island to Matinicus Island at the mouth of Penobscot Bay. Here, a vertical circulation, or upwelling of water is brought about by the collision of bottom currents and the topography of the sea floor. The strong-running tide creates much turbulence, moving around and past the irregular shoreline with its many obstructions such as islands and ledges. This, plus the movement over a broken, rough bottom topography, brings the cold bottom water to the surface. As a result, the waters in the eastern and northern edge of the Gulf of Maine differ from the rest of the Gulf in three ways, temperature, salinity and nutrients.

Bottom waters are frequently more nutrient-rich because there is less plant growth (due to reduced sunlight) to deplete the nutrients. Nutrients accumulate from settling of decaying plant and animal remains from the upper layers. The more saline water is found at the bottom due to its greater density. Thus, the upheaval of water brings these nutrients and saltier water to the surface. The cooler bottom water is also brought to the surface, and this continual mixing eliminates any stratification of temperature. The biologic significance of this is a marine environment, in shallow water, approximating that of the far north. To the tourist it means that swimming in water temperatures that are tolerable in the western part of Maine is no longer possible here.

The manifestation of these changes, as experienced by the cruising yachtsman, is cooler air and water temperatures. There is a resultant increase in the frequency and duration of fog as the moist, warm, southerly air piles over this colder water. With the change in water environment, there is a visible change in marine life. Now, harbor seals are frequently seen. Atlantic Puffins, Arctic Terns and other more northerly species of birds and plants are present. The farther east you travel, the more sub-arctic the environment becomes.

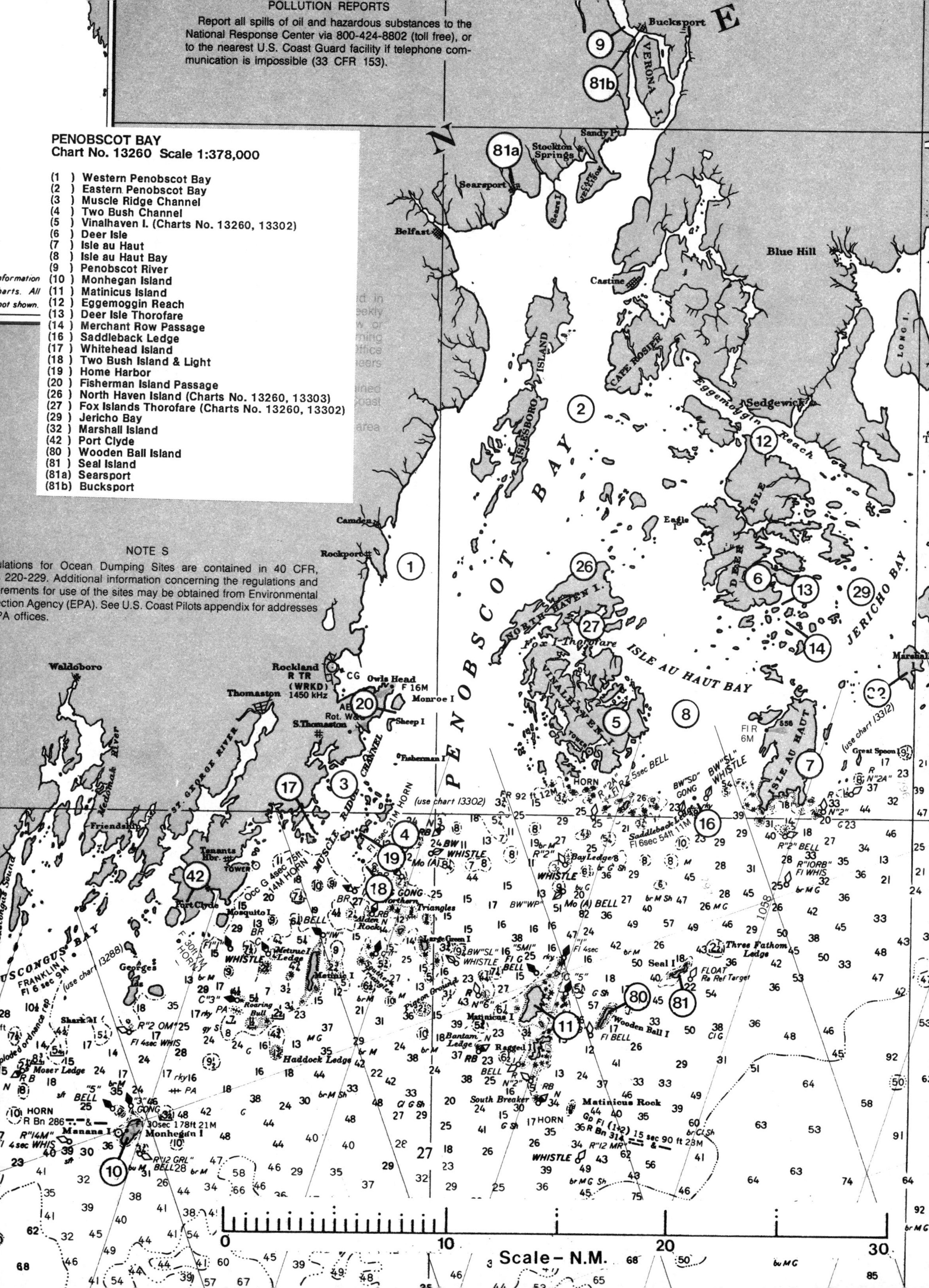
POLLUTION REPORTS
Report all spills of oil and hazardous substances to the National Response Center via 800-424-8802 (toll free), or to the nearest U.S. Coast Guard facility if telephone communication is impossible (33 CFR 153).
PENOBSCOT BAY
Chart No. 13260 Scale 1:378,000
(1 ) Western Penobscot Bay
(2 ) Eastern Penobscot Bay
(3 ) Muscle Ridge Channel
(4 ) Two Bush Channel
(5 ) Vinalhaven I. (Charts No. 13260, 13302)
(6 ) Deer Isle
(7 ) Isle au Haut
(8 ) Isle au Haut Bay
(9 ) Penobscot River
(10 ) Monhegan Island
(11 ) Matinicus Island
(12 ) Eggemoggin Reach
(13 ) Deer Isle Thorofare
(14 ) Merchant Row Passage
(16 ) Saddleback Ledge
(17 ) Whitehead Island
(18 ) Two Bush Island & Light
(19 ) Home Harbor
(20 ) Fisherman Island Passage
(26 ) North Haven Island (Charts No. 13260, 13303)
(27 ) Fox Islands Thorofare (Charts No. 13260, 13302)
(29 ) Jericho Bay
(32 ) Marshall Island
(42 ) Port Clyde
(80 ) Wooden Ball Island
(81 ) Seal Island
(81a) Searsport
(81b) Bucksport
NOTE S
ulations for Ocean Dumping Sites are contained in 40 CFR, s 220-229. Additional information concerning the regulations and irements for use of the sites may be obtained from Environmental ection Agency (EPA). See U.S. Coast Pilots appendix for addresses PA offices.
Bucksport
VERONA I.
Stockton Springs
Sandy Pt.
Searsport
Sears I
CAPE JELLISON
Belfast
Blue Hill
Castine
CAPE ROSIER
ISLESBORO ISLAND
PENOBSCOT BAY
Eggemoggin Reach
Sedgewick
DEER ISLE
Eagle I
LONG I.
JERICHO BAY
Camden
Rockport
NORTH HAVEN I.
Fox I. Thorofare
VINALHAVEN I.
ISLE AU HAUT BAY
ISLE AU HAUT
Marshall
(use chart 13312)
Great Spoon I
Waldoboro
Rockland
R TR (WRKD) 1450 kHz
CG
Owls Head
F 16M
Monroe I
Thomaston
S.Thomaston
Sheep I
Fisherman I
MUSCLE RIDGE CHANNEL
(use chart 13302)
ST. GEORGE RIVER
Medomak River
Friendship
Tenants Hbr.
Port Clyde
Mosquito I
MUSCONGUS BAY
FRANKLIN I Fl 6 sec 9M
(use chart 13288)
Georges Ids
Shark I
Moser Ledge
Metinic I
Southern Triangles
Northern Triangles
Large Green I
Pigeon Ground
Roaring Bull
Haddock Ledge
Matinicus I
Bantam Ledge
Ragged I
South Breaker
Matinicus Rock
Seal I
Three Fathom Ledge
Wooden Ball I
Saddleback Ledge
Bay Ledge
Manana I
Monhegan I
Scale – N.M.
0 10 20 30

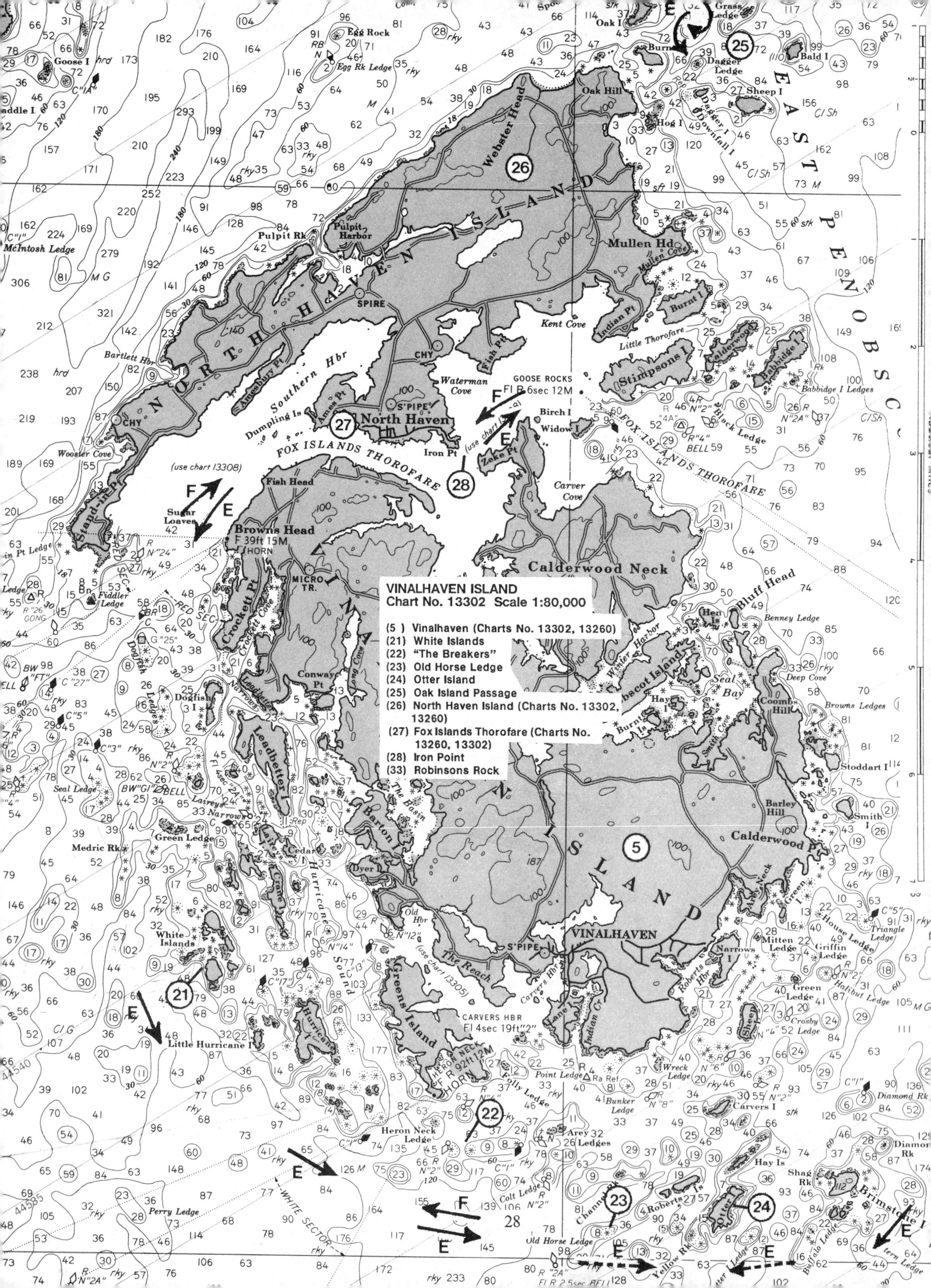
VINALHAVEN ISLAND
Chart No. 13302 Scale 1:80,000
(5 ) Vinalhaven (Charts No. 13302, 13260)
(21) White Islands
(22) "The Breakers"
(23) Old Horse Ledge
(24) Otter Island
(25) Oak Island Passage
(26) North Haven Island (Charts No. 13302, 13260)
(27) Fox Islands Thorofare (Charts No. 13260, 13302)
(28) Iron Point
(33) Robinsons Rock
NORTH HAVEN ISLAND
VINALHAVEN ISLAND
EAST PENOBSCOT
FOX ISLANDS THOROFARE
North Haven
VINALHAVEN
Calderwood Neck
Browns Head
Southern Hbr
Pulpit Harbor
Webster Head
Mullen Hd
Stimpsons I
Greens Island
Hurricane Sound
Little Hurricane I
Heron Neck Ledge
Carvers Hbr
White Islands
Leadbetter I
Crockett Pt
Seal Bay
Bluff Head
Calderwood Pt
Goose Rocks
Iron Pt
Zeke Pt
Sugar Loaves
(use chart 13308)
(use chart 13305)

# CHAPTER 4

# ISLANDS OFFSHORE FROM PENOBSCOT BAY

## MONHEGAN ISLAND—CHART NO. 13301

One of the earliest voyagers in 1590 described Monhegan Island [(10) on Penobscot Bay chart no. 13260 Chapter 3], "Like a sleeping whale," and Manana Island, the small lump of rock nearby, "the nursling." With its 150 ft. high bluffs, the island has served as a beacon to sailors approaching our shores. Flung out far from the mainland, Monhegan Island along with Matinicus (11) and Ragged Islands, guard the outer approach to Penobscot Bay. For an overall view of Penobscot Bay, and how these islands relate to it, refer to chart 13260 in Chapter 3, and to the folded chart inside the front cover.

### History

Some historians believe that Monhegan Island was visited by the Irish monk, St. Brendan, in his exploration of the Atlantic in 560 A.D. Others incline toward crediting the Norsemen as being the first visitors here in 900-1100 A.D. For evidence of this, they point to a group of markings visible on the rocks at Manana Island as being a Viking inscription. These marks (see sketch) are cuneiform, or wedge-shaped, about 45 inches long by 6½ inches high. However, no one has been able to decipher their possible meaning, and it is even questioned as to whether they are man-made or an accident of nature, perhaps caused by glacial scraping during the ice age when it pushed across this area.

In more recent and documented history, Monhegan Island was described by Giovanni da Verrazano, an Italian navigator in the service of France, when he explored this coast in 1524. Captain George Weymouth, English commander of the ship "Archangel," anchored here May 18, 1605. He was much pleased with the appearance of the island and named it Saint George, after the tutelary saint of England. The next day he moved his anchorage to one of the closer inshore islands, present-day Allen's Island, to be more convenient to the mainland. The purpose of his visit was to map the region and suggest possible sites for colonization by the English. Captain Weymounth's accounts spurred the formation of the new Plymouth Company.

Captain John Smith landed here in April, 1614 to fish for cod and explore the coast. In his map of the island, made two years later, Monhegan is laid down as Barty Isle.

However, long before the visits of these and other illustrious seafarers to this region, Monhegan and the nearby waters of Matinicus Island, Damariscove Island and Boothbay were visited by fishing ships, for it was discovered that this was the area of inshore winter breeding ground of codfish. Here, the fish fattened during the summer, could be caught during the late winter and early spring, dried by September, and shipped back to Europe before the catches of the Grand Banks fishermen of Newfoundland.

The first permanent occupation of the island was by Abraham Jennens in 1622. He acted as an intermediary between England and the Pilgrim colony. With the Indian wars in the 1670's many communities west of Kennebec River were deserted, Monhegan Island, among them. Shortly after the American Revolution it was resettled.

Today, Monhegan Island has a year-around population and is still primarily a fishing community, at least during the winter months. Lobstering is the dominant activity. During the summer months, tourism is the island's economic mainstay.

### Approaches

The principal dangers surrounding the approach to Monhegan Island are Duck Rocks (33), Eastern Duck Rock (34), and Gull Rock Ledge (35). They are all well marked by bell or gong buoys. The main harbor (36), with its fleet of moored fishing boats, lies in the cut between Monhegan and Manana Islands. It may be approached from either north or south. Entering from the south, favor the Manana side of the harbor for the deepest water. From the north, access is between Smutty Nose (37) and Monhegan Island. Smutty Nose is a patch of rock northeast of Manana Island.

In clear weather, Monhegan Island is an excellent mark for a landfall approaching from far offshore. Its bold, high cliffs are visible a long way off, and at night the 178-ft. lighthouse, is visible for 21 miles.

In fog, using Monhegan Island as a beacon is not desirable. The horn signal is on nearby Manana Island. Approaching from the east, the sound is blocked by the height of Monhegan. Also, the light on Monhegan Island is obscured within 3 miles of the island between west and southwest. In foul weather, it would be best to keep to the west of the island or preferably use Matinicus Rock Island Lighthouse, with its powerful horn and light as a beacon. Approaching from any direction, these are readily heard and seen. For the relationships between Monhegan and Matinicus Islands, refer to chart no. 13260 in Chapter 3 and the folded chart inside the front cover.

## Marginal Anchorage-Sketch Chart

The pier (38) in the harbor serves the two ferry boats from the mainland, the "Laura B." out of Port Clyde and the "Balmy Days" from Boothbay Harbor. If it is necessary to tie up here, be sure it is for the shortest possible time, only along the sides and not the front face of the pier. Anchorage within the harbor is not possible due to the limited space, but you can anchor (39) north of Smutty Nose, between Nigh Duck Rock (40) (called Inner Duck Rock on the chart) and Monhegan. Unfortunately the bottom is rocky and fouled with chain and other debris. A trip-line and buoy on your anchor is recommended when anchoring here. The tidal current, which sets into and out of the St. George River, runs surprisingly strong through the harbor and past the islands. While at anchor, during the change of tide, your boat will be swung erratically in different directions, and you may also find yourself rolling uncomfortably beam-on to the swell.

Evidence of disastrous effects of the tide are visible at the south end of the island. You can still see the remains of the tugboat "D.T. Sheridan" (41) which went aground in February, 1950. Although she was running south of the island, the northward set of the tidal current caused her to hit a rock at the southern extremity of the island, and she was pounded to pieces by the surf. Little remains now of a yacht which met a similar fate here in 1956. None of this sounds very enticing, but you should not let it deter you from visiting Monhegan, one of Maine's most spectacular and beautiful islands!

If arriving in your own boat, plan to stay for the day and then be off to the mainland for a secure anchorage at night, or leave your boat at anchor or mooring in Port Clyde (42) (refer chart no. 13206 Chapter 3) and take the ferry "Laura B." over. That way you can take as many days as you want to explore this beautiful island. During the height of the summer tourist season reservations on the ferry and at the inns may be necessary. Contact Capt. James Barstow, P.O. Box 238, Port Clyde, ME 04855 or call (207) 372-8848. The boat leaves daily (including Sunday) at 10:30 a.m. and 2:30 p.m., returning from Monhegan at 12:00 noon and 4:00 p.m. The harbormaster at Monhegan is Steve Rollins, phone (207) 594-9585. You may contact him through the Camden Marine Operator, KQU 620, VHF Channels 26 and 84. Make initial contact on Channel 16.

The likelihood of finding a fisherman's mooring empty is slim indeed. The lobstering season, within a 2-mile limit of Monhegan, starts on the first day of January! The event at the start of the season is known as "Trap Day." No one starts to set his traps until everyone is ready. If a boat has mechanical trouble or if one of the men is ill, they will all wait until they can start together—everyone stands an equal chance. The season lasts until June 25th, with no lobstering done during the summer. Thus you can see why the moorings are nearly always occupied in the summer.

## Exploring Monhegan Island

What brings so many people here year after year, is the fantastic natural beauty of the place, for the most part completely unspoiled by the touch of man, and the great diversity of wildlife—both birds and plants. For keeping two-thirds of this island perpetually wild land, we can thank Theodore Edison, son of the discoverer of electricity. In 1954, he helped organize the non-profit Monhegan Association. Through Edison's donation of a large section of the island, along with additional donations and contributions, the Association has been able to attain the goal of preserving the natural beauty of the land.

The only roads on the island are limited to a short section within the village, used by a few small pickups to cart baggage and other heavy goods to the inns and private houses. No other vehicles may be brought over to the island. To reach the numerous scenic sites, there are 15 miles of trails criss-crossing the island. These are marked by name and/or number, inconspicuously attached to a tree. Our sketch chart is modified from the Monhegan Association map, that identifies some of the major trails. A more complete and detailed map is available in most of the island's inns or stores. Monhegan's main activity is walking and observing. There are trails through a deep forest called Cathedral Woods (43) and to spectacular, high rocky bluffs. Over 600 species of wildflowers are found on Monhegan Island, only 7/10 mile wide and 1-7/10 miles long. A principal stopover point for birds during spring and fall migrations, Monhegan is much frequented by observers from the Audubon Society. During these times, it is often possible to see 50-100 species in a single weekend.

Artists have come here to paint and photograph since the early 1900's. The best known are Rockwell Kent and James Wyeth. Many other artists live on the island throughout the summer. Most open their houses to visitors to view their works at specified scheduled times. These are either posted outside the house or on bulletin boards at the island businesses. Artwork may also be viewed at the Plantation Gallery (44).

Some of the residents lead nature walks and wildflower walks during the summer. Ask around as to what is available and when.

The lighthouse (45) is at the land's summit. Built in 1824, it is now fully automated, not open to the public. The former light keeper's house has been turned into a museum where photographs of Monhegan's wildflowers and birds are displayed, and the geology and history of the island is depicted. It is open daily July 1st through Labor Day, 11:30 a.m. to 3:30 p.m. Admission is free, but donations are suggested.

## Supplies

A number of inns and private houses offer accommodations for either an overnight stay or by the week or month. A list of these may be obtained from the postmistress. Restaurants are few. Some of the inns,

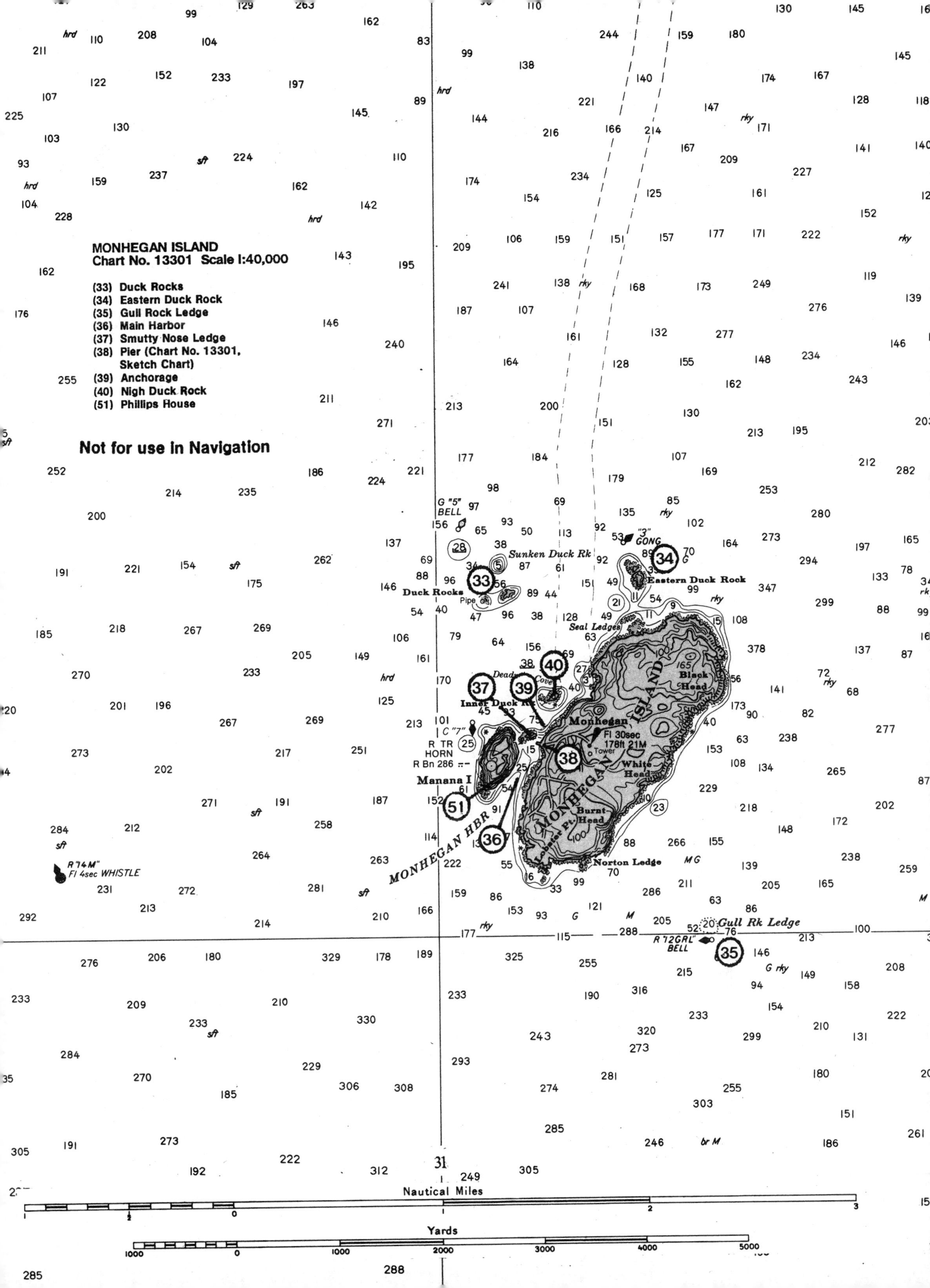
MONHEGAN ISLAND
Chart No. 13301 Scale 1:40,000
(33) Duck Rocks
(34) Eastern Duck Rock
(35) Gull Rock Ledge
(36) Main Harbor
(37) Smutty Nose Ledge
(38) Pier (Chart No. 13301, Sketch Chart)
(39) Anchorage
(40) Nigh Duck Rock
(51) Phillips House
Not for use in Navigation
G "5" BELL
Sunken Duck Rk
"3" GONG
Eastern Duck Rock
Duck Rocks
Pipe
Seal Ledges
Dead Cove
Inner Duck Rk
Monhegan
Fl 30sec 178ft 21M
Tower
MONHEGAN ISLAND
Black Head
White Head
C "7"
R TR HORN
R Bn 286
Manana I
MONHEGAN HBR
Lobster Pt.
Burnt Head
Norton Ledge
R "14M" Fl 4sec WHISTLE
Gull Rk Ledge
R "12GRL" BELL
Nautical Miles
Yards

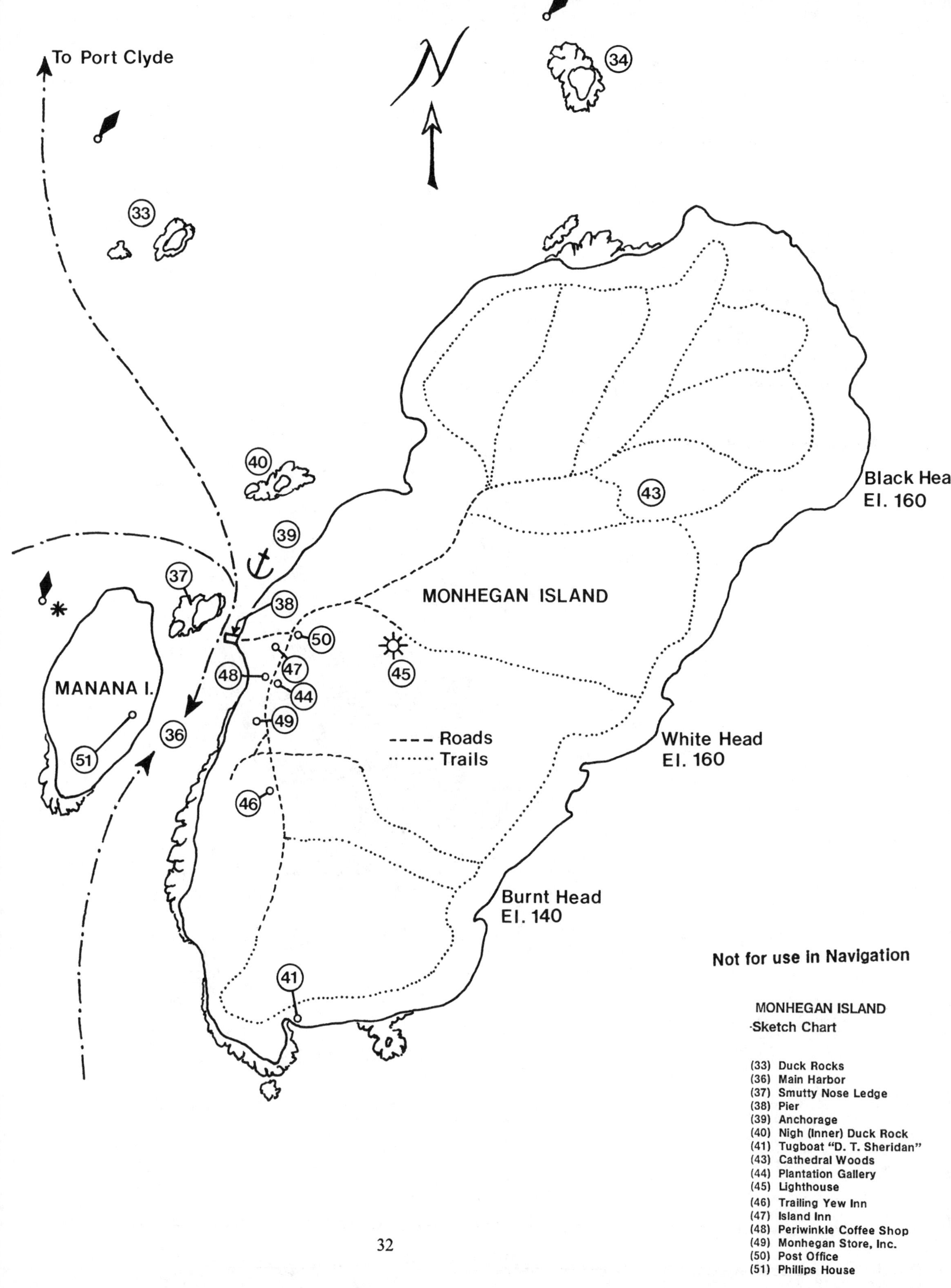
To Port Clyde
N
34
33
40
39
37
38
50
47
48
44
45
49
36
51
46
41
43
MONHEGAN ISLAND
MANANA I.
Black Head
El. 160
White Head
El. 160
Burnt Head
El. 140
Roads
Trails
Not for use in Navigation
MONHEGAN ISLAND
Sketch Chart
(33) Duck Rocks
(36) Main Harbor
(37) Smutty Nose Ledge
(38) Pier
(39) Anchorage
(40) Nigh (Inner) Duck Rock
(41) Tugboat "D. T. Sheridan"
(43) Cathedral Woods
(44) Plantation Gallery
(45) Lighthouse
(46) Trailing Yew Inn
(47) Island Inn
(48) Periwinkle Coffee Shop
(49) Monhegan Store, Inc.
(50) Post Office
(51) Phillips House

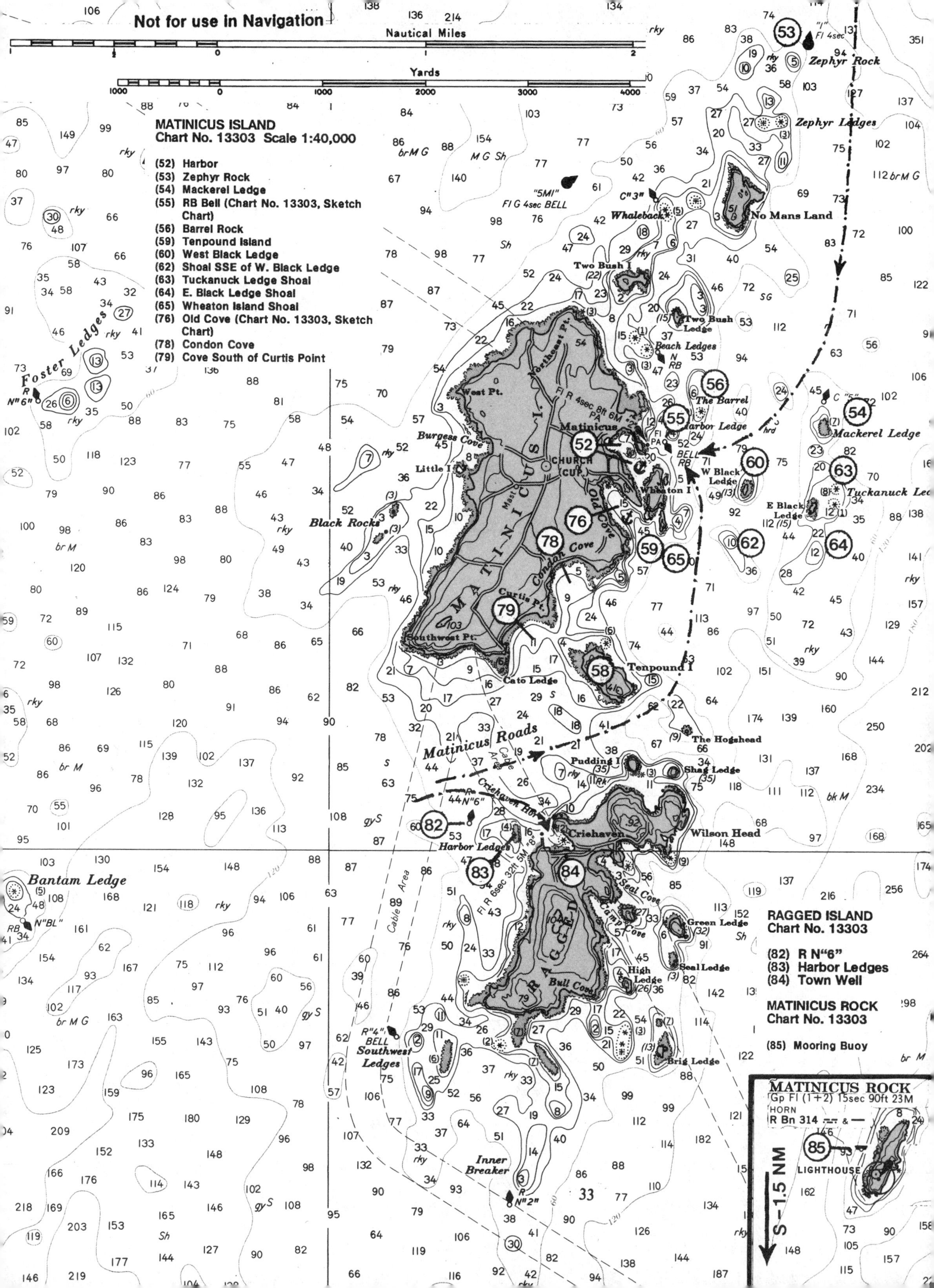

Not for use in Navigation
Nautical Miles
Yards
MATINICUS ISLAND
Chart No. 13303 Scale 1:40,000
(52) Harbor
(53) Zephyr Rock
(54) Mackerel Ledge
(55) RB Bell (Chart No. 13303, Sketch Chart)
(56) Barrel Rock
(59) Tenpound Island
(60) West Black Ledge
(62) Shoal SSE of W. Black Ledge
(63) Tuckanuck Ledge Shoal
(64) E. Black Ledge Shoal
(65) Wheaton Island Shoal
(76) Old Cove (Chart No. 13303, Sketch Chart)
(78) Condon Cove
(79) Cove South of Curtis Point
Foster Ledges
Zephyr Rock
Zephyr Ledges
No Mans Land
Whaleback
Two Bush I
Two Bush Ledge
Beach Ledges
The Barrel
Harbor Ledge
Mackerel Ledge
W Black Ledge
E Black Ledge
Tuckanuck Ledge
West Pt.
Northeast Pt.
MATINICUS I.
Matinicus
CHURCH (CUP)
Burgess Cove
Little I
Black Rocks
Wheaton I
Old Cove
Condon Cove
Curtis Pt.
Southwest Pt.
Cato Ledge
Tenpound I
The Hogshead
Matinicus Roads
Pudding I
Shag Ledge
Criehaven Hbr
Criehaven
Wilson Head
Harbor Ledges
Bantam Ledge
Seal Cove
Camp Cove
Green Ledge
Seal Ledge
High Ledge
Bull Cove
RAGGED
Brig Ledge
Southwest Ledges
Inner Breaker
Cable Area
RAGGED ISLAND
Chart No. 13303
(82) R N"6"
(83) Harbor Ledges
(84) Town Well
MATINICUS ROCK
Chart No. 13303
(85) Mooring Buoy
MATINICUS ROCK
Gp Fl (1+2) 15sec 90ft 23M
HORN
R Bn 314
LIGHTHOUSE
S–1.5 NM

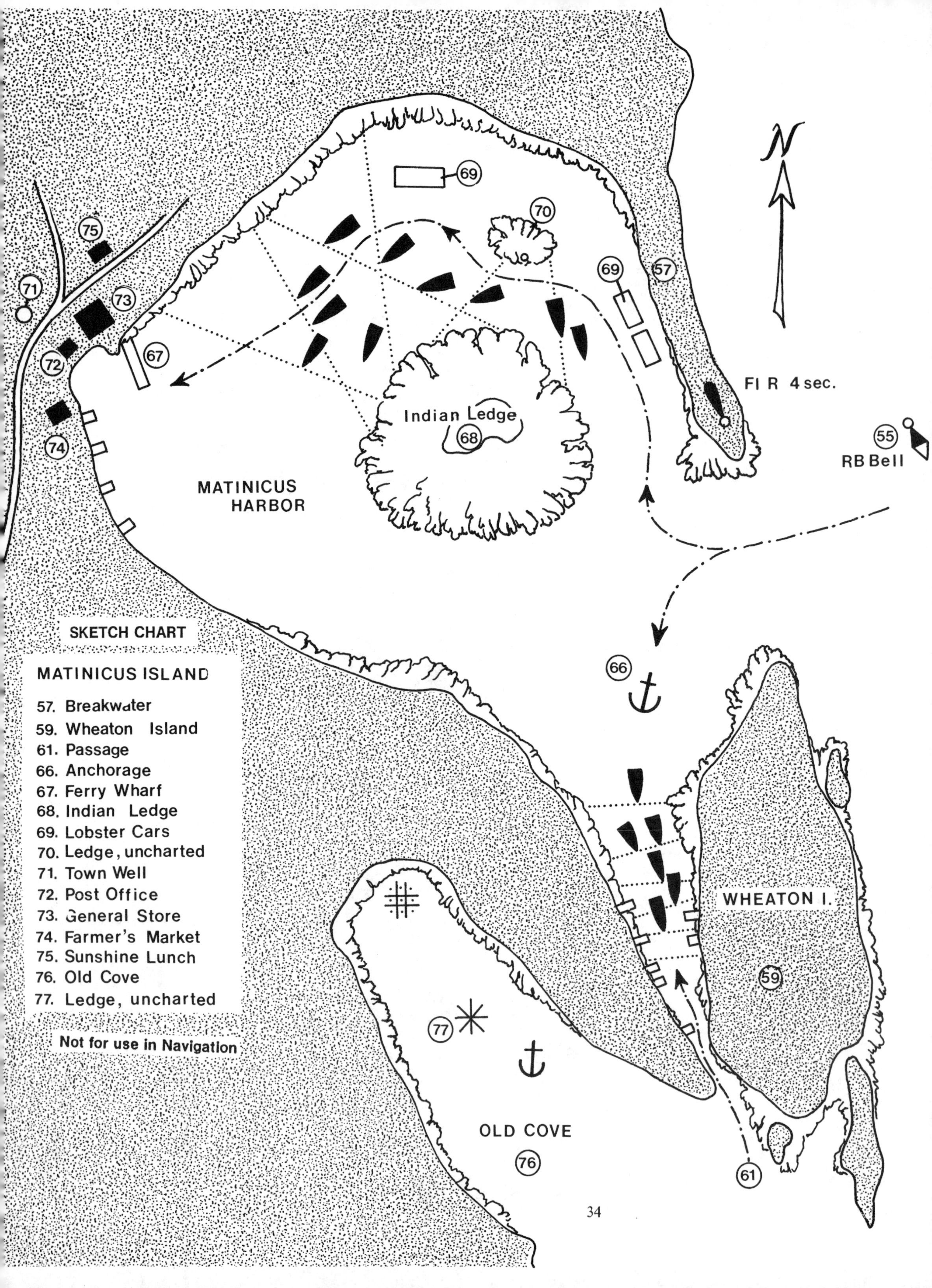

N
69
70
69
57
67
75
71
73
72
74
Indian Ledge
68
Fl R 4 sec.
55
RB Bell
MATINICUS
HARBOR
SKETCH CHART
MATINICUS ISLAND
57. Breakwater
59. Wheaton Island
61. Passage
66. Anchorage
67. Ferry Wharf
68. Indian Ledge
69. Lobster Cars
70. Ledge, uncharted
71. Town Well
72. Post Office
73. General Store
74. Farmer's Market
75. Sunshine Lunch
76. Old Cove
77. Ledge, uncharted
Not for use in Navigation
66
WHEATON I.
59
77
OLD COVE
76
61

like the Trailing Yew (46) and the Island Inn (47) will provide meals to others besides their own clients. The Periwinkle Coffee Shop (48) offers three daily meals. The Monhegan Store Inc. (49) can provide fresh fruit, vegetables, meat etc., as well as sandwiches and hot take-out dinners. The post office (50) is just up the head of the road from the ferry landing.

## MANANA ISLAND
### CHART NO. 13303 and Sketch Chart

Acoss the harbor from Monhegan Island is the small, unprepossessing island of Manana. A granite outcropping with only a sparse covering of grass, it was used at one time for pasturing sheep. The rambling structure, with its many additions, clinging to the side of the hill (51), was once the abode of Ray Phillips who tended sheep. Although always referred to as "the Hermit" he was a sociable hermit. He never minded people visiting him and enjoyed taking the time to chat. The sheep had free run of the house, and would enter during these visits. They all had names. "Hi Rosie," he would say, and the sheep would sometimes stay to listen.

Many visitors regret Phillips' passing away in the mid 1970's. A children's book about the Hermit of Manana, with many photographs about him and his island is available in bookstores in Rockland and Camden.

## MATINICUS ISLAND
### CHART NO. 13303 and Sketch Chart

Refer to chart no. 13260 in Chapter 3 and folded chart inside front cover.

Seventeen miles southeast of Owls Head, Matinicus Island, like Monhegan Island, forms part of the outermost range of coastal islands. It shares the same sense of isolation and insularity as Monhegan. Here too, lobstering is the principal activity. But despite the many similarities, the character of this island is quite different from Monhegan. Here you do not have here the dramatic, high headlands and bluffs, or the rugged harshness. Instead, the landscape has a more gentle feel to it, with open fields and pasture visible from the sea.

At one time Matinicus was as much a farming community as it ws a fishing community, with 200 people living here throughout the year. Now the winter population is down as low as 32 people. In contrast to Monhegan Island, this island does not depend on tourism for summer income. In fact, there are no accomodations whatsoever for visitors. There is no inn or bed and breakfast establishment, no restaurants, and the Maine State Ferry lands only once a month. Also, there are no gift shops or taxis. Mail comes in by plane. Inevitably, though, as the fishing goes down, this will have to change. Meanwhile, it remains a working community of people proud of their independence and appreciative of the natural beauty of their surroundings. For a complete, detailed history of the island, read *Matinicus Isle, Its Story and Its People* by Charles A.E. Long.

### Approaches

Around Matinicus are seven islands, Ragged Island, Matinicus Rock, No Mans Land, Seal Island, Wooden Ball Island, Tenpound Island and Two Bush Island, plus numerous other rocks and ledges. We show course lines on chart 13303 this chapter, showing the two main approaches to the harbor (52), located on the east side of the island. In fair weather there is no difficulty using either of these approaches. But it must be cautioned that in fog, the east sides of both Matinicus and Ragged Islands are bad places to be. Tidal currents make a course unpredictable, and identification of ledges and rocks may be difficult or come too late. A particularly bad tide hole with strong, erratic currents is near Zephyr Rock (53).

An approach from the north would be used by sailors who either have been working their way west along the coast from downeast or by sailors who are departing from Vinalhaven. It is a pleasant daysail from Vinalhaven. Make for Zephyr Rock, staying east of it and continue southward, approaching closely west of C"5" marking Mackerel Ledge (54). Then swing west for the red and black bell at the harbor entrance (55).

**MANANA ISLAND—INSCRIPTION ON ROCK**

Following this course, you can easily identify surrounding ledges and you will be clear of Barrel Rock (56). This rock, 300 yards northeast of Harbor Ledge does **not** show at full high water. If there is any wave action, you may see a curl of white around it, but it does not begin to show until the tide has dropped about 2 feet. A 450-foot breakwater (57) protects the northeastern side of the harbor. See sketch chart of Matinicus Island, this chapter. It has a light at the end, Flashing Red, 4 sec., visible for 6 miles. This light is not at the extreme tip of the breakwater, but is about 100 feet in from the end. If you are coming in at night, give the light a good berth for some of the rocks of the breakwater will be just under the surface at high tide. There are inner passages between Matinicus and Two Bush Island, but these are best left to fishermen with local knowledge.

From the west, approach the harbor using Matinicus Roads between Matinicus and Ragged Islands. Turn north, staying east of Tenpound Island (58), then go between Wheaton Island (59) and West Black Ledge (60), and head for the red and black bell buoy (55).

There is a very narrow passage (61) at the southern part of the harbor between Matinicus and Wheaton Island. It is dry at low tide, but at half-tide or better, it is sometimes used by the lobster boats. The Matinicus shore must be hugged closely (no more than 5 feet from shore) to avoid a ledge in mid-channel. It is best to leave this passage to those who know exactly where they are going.

Many of the shoal areas around Matinicus will break in heavy weather, for they are completely exposed to the full sweep of the open sea. A bad shoal (62) (marked 10 feet) is about 500 yards SSE of W. Black Ledge. Bad shoals are also around Tuckanuck Ledge (63) and south of E. Black Ledge (64). The ledge east of the southern tip of Wheaton Island, marked 4 and 7 feet (65), will also break in heavy weather. When it is really rough, the shoal extending north of Barrel Rock (56) will break for a considerable distance toward Two Bush Ledge.

### Anchorage and Landing

Anchorage (66) in the harbor is inside the breakwater, and west of the north tip of Wheaton Island, in about 26 feet depth. Use a trip-line and buoy as the bottom is patchy with sand and rock. Unless you find the sand, you will need the trip-line to retrieve your anchor. The harbor is quite well protected, and the anchorage is calm, unless there is a strong easterly blow. Do not try to anchor elsewhere in the harbor than where indicated on our diagram. The bottom is mostly rock and you would be fouled on mooring chains. Rather than individual moorings, the fishermen use communal mooring chains. These are strung from shore to shore and the boats are tied to these chains. Not all of the ground lines are chain. Some are heavy polypropylene, particularly in the harbor portion between Wheaton Island and Matinicus. When the wind is strong, the pull on the boats will cause these ground lines to lift off the bottom where you are in danger of catching them in the propeller of your boat. Last summer, a local entrepreneur laid a line across the harbor bottom and attached moorings marked "rental." Pick one up if it's available, and pay for it when he comes around early in the morning.

The preferred route to the Ferry Landing Wharf (67) is around to the north of Indian Ledge (68), a large patch of ledge that sits pretty much in the middle of the harbor. A small portion of this, 2 feet high, shows at high tide. Follow along the breakwater and go between the boats and the lobster cars (69) moored north and west of them. When you start to swing around to the west, keep as close to the moored boats as possible to avoid a second patch of ledge (70), north of Indian Ledge, not shown on the chart no 13303. There is a lobster buoy near the southern part of this ledge, but it is small, fouled with weed and very difficult to see.

None of the wharfs in this harbor have floats. Access is by ladder only. The best place to land and tie your dinghy is at the eastern face of the Town Dock (Ferry Wharf) (67) or to beach it at the head of the harbor. No fuel or ice is available. A limited water supply can be pumped from the town well (71) across the road from the post office. Bring your own containers.

### Supplies

The post office (72) is at the foot of the wharf. Adjacent is the General Store (73), open 12:00 noon - 4:00 p.m. Monday through Friday, and 8:00 a.m. to 12:00 noon on Saturday. It has groceries, fresh fruit, vegetables and meat.

A Farmer's Market (74) at the head of the harbor is open 11:00 a.m. to 1:00 p.m. only Mondays and Fridays. Don't miss it if you are there at these times. All the fresh vegetables and fruit offered are grown right on the island. They are the choicest, picked within ½ hour of when they are brought to the Farmer's Market. Be sure to arrive early for a good selection, for most are purchased almost immediately. There are also fresh baked goods and homemade preserves. Sunshine Lunch (75), across the road from the general store, is a lunch wagon with picnic tables and they serve hamburgers and hot dogs etc., from 11:00 a.m. to 3:00 p.m. The Anchorage is a modest restaurant, ice cream, and sandwich shop, with a deck overlooking the harbor. They serve lobster, and the ice cream is made on Matinicus.

As with many of the other islands, there is no way of disposing of trash. They have enough of a problem with their own trash without the added burden brought to the island.

### Old Cove

Of the three coves on the southeast side of Matinicus, only Old Cove (76) is worth considering as an anchorage. The west side of Old Cove is rocky, but the east side is sandy and you can anchor there. About halfway up into the cove is an uncharted ledge (77) (see sketch chart). This prevents access farther north. Stay outside of where the chart shows 15 feet, anchoring in about 30 feet of water. Condon Cove (78) has poor holding ground because of rocks and the cove south of Curtis Point (79), although it has a sand bottom, is too exposed to be a good anchorage.

### Seal Island

Both Wooden Ball Island (80) and Seal Island (81) (refer chart no. 13260 Chapter 3) east of Matinicus are low, treeless and featureless, totally unappealing. There are no harbors and the only reason to know about their presence is to avoid hitting them.

In the past, Seal Island was used for target practice by the military and there are still a lot of unexploded munitions on the island. Four or five years ago, picnickers set the island on fire with sparks from their campfire. A fire-fighting crew was put on the island but the fire had gone down into the ground and started setting off some of the ammunition. The stuff is still alive!

## RAGGED ISLAND—CHART NO. 13303

Barely a mile south of Matinicus is Ragged Island, but no one calls it that. They always say, "I'm going over to Criehaven." The name is used to denote the village, the harbor and the island. The eleven fishermen who summer here to do their lobstering lead an even more quiet and isolated existence than those on nearby Matinicus Island. For here there is no telephone service, no general store and not even the once a month State Ferry. As on Matinicus, electricity is provided by generators. This harbor is beginning to be visited by yachtsmen with much greater frequency because of its simple beauty, quiet and charm. Added to this is the hospitality and friendliness of the fishermen.

### Entry

The harbor offers protection from all directions except northwest. Entry is easy under all conditions. Refer to the course line on chart no. 13303, this chapter. Stay north of red buoy N"6" (82) and head for the entrance north of the breakwater, but **do not make a straight line** towards it. Curve toward the north until past Harbor Ledges (83), then head for the entrance. A straight line between N"6" and the north end of the breakwater would bring you right over Harbor Ledges which uncovers at 4 feet. At the end of the breakwater is a light 32 feet high, Fl Red, six seconds.

A problem could arise approaching Ragged Island at night from the east. The light at the end of the breakwater could be mistaken for that of Matinicus Harbor, which also is a flashing red. The timing sequence of the two is close, Fl R 6 sec on Criehaven breakwater, Fl R 4 sec at Matinicus. There is a narrow isthmus of land between Criehaven on the west side and Seal Cove on the east side. Because the land here is low, it is possible to see the Criehaven breakwater light from the **eastern side** of the island.

### Mooring

Once within the harbor, ask a fisherman which mooring might be available. Generally there are several that can be used. Last time we were there, six yachts were thusly accommodated. Anchoring is not possible, for the bottom is smooth granite and the anchor would most certainly be fouled on one of the communal mooring chains which cover the harbor bottom. The system is the same as at Matinicus.

A solitary rock which shows as being in the middle of the harbor is really a large patch of ledge, and more on the northeastern side than in the middle. It bares at low water. Immediately west of it, there is a small toggle float which marks its presence. However, it is so weighted down with kelp that it barely shows about ½ inch above the water surface. If you keep to the middle of the harbor or favor the southern edge of it you will have no problem. The ledge as shown on the chart at the south end of the harbor pretty well displays itself during most of the tide.

Fuel is not available and there are no stores for provisioning, nor are there any inns or restaurants. Water may be obtained at the town well (84), but bring your own containers. It is on the south side of the road on the south shore.

### History

Criehaven gets its name from Robert Crie who married and settled there with his wife in 1849. At that time it was called South Matinicus. They had 5 children. All of them stayed, making the running of the island very much a family affair. Then there was a general store, post office and both a fish and lumbering business. The gravestone of Robert Crie is on the island, with the inscription, "Gone but not forgotten."

## MATINICUS ROCK—CHART NO. 13303

Refer also to folded chart inside the front cover.

This 39-acre dome of granite, 1½ miles south of Ragged Island, is Maine's farthest lighted outpost. Treeless and scantily covered with a thin layer of peat and grass, it is hard to believe the wealth of bird life that it supports. You will find many species of pelagic (oceanic) birds. Among them, Leach's Storm Petrels, Shearwaters, Guillemots, the Razorbill Auk, Arctic Tern and the bird that has recently captured public fancy, the Atlantic Puffin, "clown of the sea."

### History

Matinicus Rock has had its full share of maritime history. Until 1924, when the north tower was dismantled, there were two lights on the island. Originally these were wooden towers built in 1827, but were replaced in 1848 by two granite towers. The only other site on this coast to have this unusual feature was the Cape Elizabeth light.

Today, as with nearly all coastal lights, the station is automated. No longer is anyone present to feel and record the power of the sea on this lonely windswept isle.

When a severe storm struck in 1856, the lighthouse keeper was on the mainland at the time and his 17 year old daughter, Abbie Burgess, kept the light burning throughout the gale, thus earning her spot in lighthouse service history. Waves more than 40 feet high washed completely over the island, flooding the keeper's house and she took refuge in the tower. The "Groundhog Day storm" of February, 1978 was of similar violence. The land is 42 feet high and huge 10 ton boulders were rolled around as though they were pebbles. In the strong wind, the tower trembled and its total collapse seemed possible. To keep the light visible, the men had to chip ice off the lens from the water which froze there, 90 feet from sea-level! Now the only visitors to the rock are the occasional visitors to observe the bird life and the Coast Guard for periodic maintenance.

### Mooring and Landing

There is no anchorage, as there is deep water up to the very edge of the rocky shores. However, there is a mooring buoy (85) on the west side of the island which may be used. It is a tall nun buoy, painted light gray. Be prepared with your own mooring line to reeve through the bull-nose at the top of the buoy. You can land your dinghy at the skidway at the Coast Guard boathouse directly east of the buoy. At best this can be difficult, and it can be downright dangerous if there is any sea running. Be sure to pick a calm day for making a landing. The current, even this far out from shore, runs strong past the island on both the flood and ebb. Basically it flows in a north-south direction.

### Birding

If your purpose for landing is to get a close look at the birds, you will find it easier to do this from the water, and it's safer for the birds. Deep water surrounds the island, particularly on the southeast side where most of the Puffins are. You will be able to get closer to the birds as they are catching their food, than you could by land. Furthermore, you don't run the risk of inadvertently stepping on eggs or crushing the nest of the Leach's Petrels, which are made in burrows under the grass. You will see this bird easily, as with its butterfly-like flight it hovers over the water while feeding.

The Shearwater, belonging to the same order of birds as the Albatross and the Stormy Petrels, is occasionally seen here. Most Shearwaters breed on only one island in the South Atlantic, Tristan da Cunha at 60 degrees south latitude! They come to the Gulf of Maine to "winter" during our summer. The Arctic Tern is another species found here that makes such an immense migratory passage, a 25,000 mile round-trip flight to and from their breeding grounds. At one time they were almost wholly eliminated from this coast by collectors of feathers for the millinery trade. They survived on Matinicus Rock and a few other islands due to the protective efforts of the lighthouse keepers.

The Razorbill Auk, Puffins and the Guillemots belong to the same family, called Alcids. For all, the offshore islands of Maine are their southernmost limits. These birds are the Northern hemisphere equivalent of the penquin. Their short, stubby wings, which make them awkward in flight, enable them to "swim" well under water to catch fish. The Razorbill Auk spends its winter at sea, returning to land only to breed. It is the rarest of the Alcids to be found in Maine, at last count, only about 40 pairs. The most common Alcid is the Guillemot. Sometimes called a sea pigeon, these small, black birds with a white wing patch are seen floating on the water. They will be encountered with greater frequency the farther east you travel.

The Puffin is the bird everyone wants to see. Looking life a cross between a penguin and a parrot, they have an immediate appeal. These are found at only three places on the Maine coast, Matinicus Rock, Machias Seal Island, and Eastern Egg Rock at the mouth of Muscongus Sound. Puffins were recently re-introduced on Eastern Egg Rock in the hopes that they will continue to return and to breed there. You will see Puffins diving for fish, resurfacing with several hanging out of their beaks. Usually not content to eat as they catch, they go back down again to increase the number they hold. To do this without losing the ones they already have must not be easy, especially since they may have as many as 28 fish. It is a totally ludicrous sight!

**Matinicus Island Harbor**

# CHAPTER 5

## ROCKLAND TO CAMDEN, WEST SHORE OF PENOBSCOT BAY

### CLAM COVE— CHART NO. 13302

From the chart, it would appear that Clam Cove (1), on the west shore of Penobscot Bay, would be a useful anchorage. Such is not the case. The inner half dries out completely to unattractive mud flats, and the shoreline in the outer half is all privately owned. There are no docks to land, and no yachtsman's services available near. Clam Cove is situated only 2 miles north of Rockland Harbor and 2 miles south of Rockport Harbor. Either of these would be a more logical destination.

### ROCKLAND HARBOR—CHART NO. 13302

Rockland Harbor is described in full detail in Vol. I of our *Cruising Guide to Maine*, and should be referred to for complete information. Here a few additional notes about the harbor. In the portion of harbor near the public landing (2), the City of Rockland now has eleven free guest moorings. In the information building at the landing, public restrooms and shower facilities are available.

An excellent anchorage (3) is near the foot of the breakwater. The holding-ground is good, with mud bottom right up to the very edge of the rip-rap of the breakwater. A float and ramp on the breakwater are privately maintained by the Samoset Inn (4) on Jameson Point. This makes access to the Inn, with its several fine restaurants, most convenient to yachtsmen.

### ROCKPORT HARBOR
### CHARTS NO. 13302, 13307

It is obvious why the early name for this harbor was "Deep Cove" for the water is quite deep and clear of obstructions right up to the very head of the harbor. The only exception is Porterfield Ledge (5) at the harbor entrance. There are no problems in entering under any conditions and the shelter is good for all but southeasterly winds.

#### Approaches

Refer to chart no. 13302, this chapter. Three prominent landmarks on the west shore of Penobscot Bay are helpful to determine your position and the location of Rockland, Rockport and Camden Harbors. One is the light (Fl 5 sec) (6) at the end of the Rockland Breakwater. Another is the movie screen (7) near the entrance to Rockport Harbor. This large square of white, the painted backside of the screen, stands out clearly. The

Rockport Apprenticeshop Boatworks

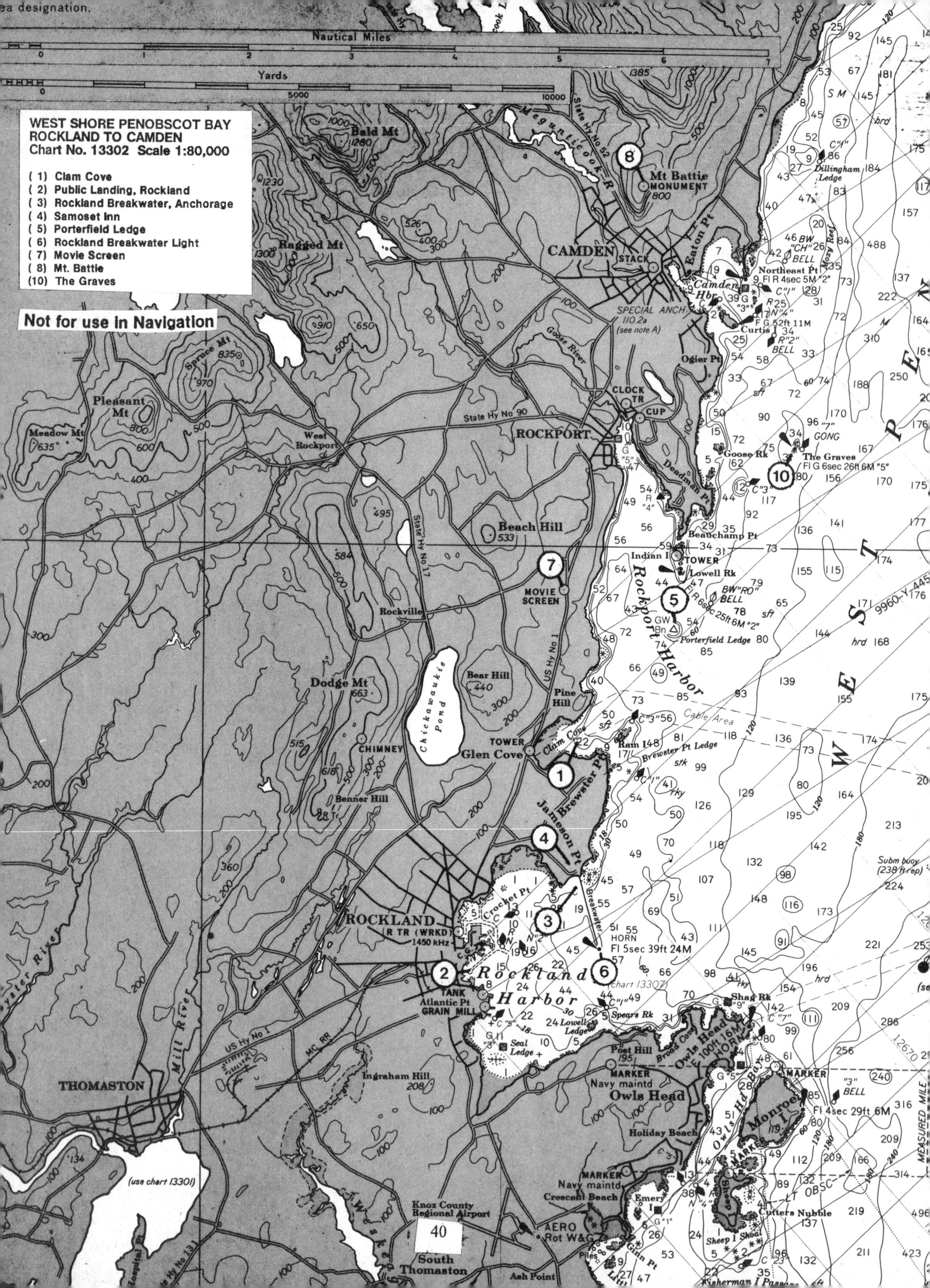

ea designation.
Nautical Miles
Yards
WEST SHORE PENOBSCOT BAY
ROCKLAND TO CAMDEN
Chart No. 13302 Scale 1:80,000
( 1) Clam Cove
( 2) Public Landing, Rockland
( 3) Rockland Breakwater, Anchorage
( 4) Samoset Inn
( 5) Porterfield Ledge
( 6) Rockland Breakwater Light
( 7) Movie Screen
( 8) Mt. Battie
(10) The Graves
Not for use in Navigation
Bald Mt
Mt Battie MONUMENT
Megunticook R
Ragged Mt
CAMDEN
Camden Hbr
Northeast Pt
Curtis I
Ogier Pt
Spruce Mt
Pleasant Mt
Meadow Mt
West Rockport
ROCKPORT
Goose Rk
The Graves
Beauchamp Pt
Indian I
Lowell Rk
Rockport Harbor
Porterfield Ledge
Beach Hill
MOVIE SCREEN
Rockville
Dodge Mt
Bear Hill
Chickawaukie Pond
Pine Hill
Glen Cove
Clam Cove
Ram I
Brewster Pt Ledge
Brewster Pt
Jameson Pt
Benner Hill
Crocket Pt
Breakwater
ROCKLAND
Rockland Harbor
Atlantic Pt
Spears Rk
Lowell Ledge
Seal Ledge
Owls Head
Broad Cove
Shag Rk
Ingraham Hill
THOMASTON
Mill River
Monroe I
Holiday Beach
Crescent Beach
Emery I
Sheep I
Cutters Nubble
Knox County Regional Airport
(use chart 13301)
South Thomaston
Ash Point
Ginn Pt
WEST PENOBSCOT
MEASURED MILE

third is the round, granite tower on top of Mt. Battie (8), behind Camden Harbor.

Now refer to chart no. 13307, this chapter. The two aids for the entrance to Rockport are the black and white bell buoy "RO" (9), which may be taken to either side, and Porterfield Ledge (5). This ledge, almost entirely submerged at high tide, has upon it a four-sided granite, pyramidal structure with a truncated top. It is about 30 feet high, surmounted by a green and white **checkerboard** daybeacon. Porterfield Ledge could be confused with "The Graves" (10), a similar appearing ledge 4 miles northeast. The Graves, about half-way between Rockport and Camden Harbors, has the same type of granite pyramid on it and a green daybeacon. Approaching either of these ledges in fog, the two can be distinguished by several means. The daybeacon on The Graves is solid green, not checkerboard, and it has a flashing green light. Furthermore, there is a black gong buoy ("7") close to the Graves on its eastern side.

The lighthouse tower (11) at the south end of Indian Island is clearly visible from all directions, as there are no trees on the island to obstruct it. The lighthouse is no longer in use, but there is a light (Fl R 6 sec) (12) on Lowell Rock, 300 yards south of the lighthouse.

Within the harbor the only two dangers present are both marked by a daybeacon. Seal Ledge (13) marked by a red daybeacon, is about 0.7 miles north of the light. The other ledge is almost at the head of the harbor, its position is indicated by a green daybeacon (14). Both ledges are so close to the shore that they are not a navigational hazard.

As you approach the head of the harbor, you will see Rockport's buildings, the church with its clock-tower, and numerous yachts on moorings. It is a fairly well protected harbor as long as the wind stays south, or west of south. If weather should come up strong from the southeast, quite a roll can develop, for the fetch is all the way from Europe. Fortunately, a southeast wind is infrequent during the summer and radio NOAA gives sufficient advance warning for you to make preparations or to seek alternate shelter.

Rockport is a crowded harbor and unless you are prepared to put out hundreds of feet of anchor rode and be a considerable ways out toward the entrance, you will need to lie on a mooring. There is a marked fairway down the center of all the moored boats to facilitate access to the dock area.

## Marine Facilities

The docks and float on the east side of the harbor are those of Rockport Marine (15), with 12 feet of depth alongside at low water. They welcome transients, have 5 slips and 30 moorings, diesel fuel, gasoline, water, ice, showers (small fee), complete engine and hull repairs and a restaurant. Additional moorings are available from Mr. Kimball. His dock is the first major dock on your port side as you enter the harbor. At low tide, take your dinghy in to his dock, for there is insufficient water for your boat to lie alongside.

Recently, the entire basin at the head of the harbor has been dredged by the Army Corps of Engineers to provide a MLW depth of 12 feet. There is now 12 feet at the Town Dock floats and 10 feet at the Rockport Boat Club.

There are three floats at the Town Dock (16) at the head of the harbor on the west shore. You'll spot the town dock easily by the nearby flagpole flying American, Canadian and State of Maine flags. The harbormaster is usually there. Free tie-up is limited to 2 hours. If you remain at the floats overnight there is a $10.00 fee. There are public toilet facilities, and a concrete launching ramp with a modest charge for nonresidents.

The Rockport Boat Club (17) is on the east side of Goose River where it empties into the head of the harbor.

## Supplies

Within the town of Rockport proper, there are no places for provisioning. The closest available source is the Market Basket, at the intersection of U.S. 1 and Highway 90; a 15-minute walk from the head of the harbor. They have the best and freshest vegatables, locally grown. They also stock the makings for Indonesian, Japanese, Chinese and other exotic cuisines, and they have a good variety of wine and cheese. The Market Basket also has German delicacies from Schaller and Weber in New York. If you don't know what to do with all this, the store has a large cookbook section and provides a counter and chair for you to read and copy recipes. For other general supplies and meats, it will be necessary to travel to Camden or Rockland. North across the road is the Bohndell Sail Loft (60) with capability for sail repair, replacement and rigging work.

## History and Sightseeing

West of the town dock is the Municipal Marine Park (18), maintained by the Rockport Garden Club. At the back edge of the park are the remains of some of the lime kilns of Rockport. One of the principal industries for which Rockport was known was the quarrying of lime and lime burning, used to make mortar and plaster. The kilns are now protected by a wooden shed and some restoration work is going on. A plaque at the site tells you that "throughout the 19th century Rockport, and other area towns were the major suppliers of lime to East Coast Markets." The output of lime from Rockport in the single year of 1889 amounted to 337,000 casks. "The kilns you see were originally housed in wooden buildings, most of which were damaged or destroyed in the great fire of 1907. The local lime industry never recovered. The kilns are the last remaining evidence of Rockports' industrial past."

A map of the area is available at the Municipal Marine Park, and a succinct description of the history of Rockport is given. "The area was first discovered and described by Capt. George Weymouth in 1605 and was settled permanently in the early 1770's. The village of Rockport was made an historic district in the mid-

1970's and there are 127 buildings listed in the inventory. Among them is the H.L. Sheperd house, Queen Ann style—of about 1875, the Rockport Opera House, Colonial Revival—1891 and the Alexander Pascal house, Greek Revival—1859.

"Rockport became an important seafaring community where shipbuilding and the manufacture of capstans, windlasses, bricks, boots and shoes was carried on. There was also ice shipping, and most importantly the making and shipping of lime. Economics and changes in technology, plus the devastating fire of 1907 brought an end to this era."

The Park is dedicated to the honor of Andre the seal and there is a life-size sculpture of him carved in granite. Andre passed away in 1986. He was the local celebrity in Rockport, a harbor seal (Phoca vitulina), the only species found regularly in New England waters. Born on Robinsons Rock in Penobscot Bay in 1961, he was abandoned at birth and found, raised and trained by Harry Goodridge of Rockport. During the summer there were daily performances by the seal, for which he was awarded with many herring. Children loved to watch him. In the fall he was trucked or flown down to the Mystic, Connecticut aquarium where he spent the winter. In the spring he was released into nearby waters and swam the many miles to return to Rockport. His timing was watched with interest and there was a contest as to the exact time of his arrival. Andre will be missed in Rockland, but his granite sculpture will remain.

Andre is not the only animal for which Rockport is famous. The nearby Aldemere Farms (19) raises and breeds a type of cattle known as the Belted Galloway. They are distinctive in appearance with their short, cropped hair and black body with a narrow band of white around the middle. This breed is reputed to be the oldest breed of cattle in the world today. They originated in the mountains of southwest Scotland, and those of Aldemere Farms have won many prizes.

The red, clapboard-sided building adjoining Rockport Marine is the Sail Loft Restaurant (20). Over the years it has maintained an excellent deserved reputation, for serving first class cuisine. An added benefit is the magnificent view of the harbor from the dining room, open daily 11:30 a.m. to 2:30 p.m., and 5:30 p.m. to 9:00 p.m. Sunday brunch is served 12 noon to 2:30 p.m. The Rockport Corner Shop (21), in the granite bulding on Main Street. seves breakfast and lunch, open Monday-Friday 6:30 a.m. to 3:00 p.m., Saturday and Sunday 7:00 a.m. to 2:00 p.m.

The red brick building north of the Sail Loft Restaurant houses the Maine Photographic Workshop (22). This workshop has now been expanded to include a Film and Television Workshop. Here, amidst the visually stimulating surroundings of Penobscot Bay, a resident faculty plus guest photographers of world reknown, teach photography as an art, a career and a profession. The Workshop is a year-round art school with courses leading to career certificates and college degrees. Besides the classrooms, there is a gallery with exhibitions of photography, a library and a retail store selling equipment and supplies.

Another institution, well known to all in the boat building trade, is the Rockport Apprenticeshop (23). Founded by Lance Lee, who is still guiding its helm, it was formerly associated with the Maine Maritime Museum in Bath. It is now a completely independent organization. The education of their apprentices through building traditional small boats is unexcelled anywhere. Not only is craftsmanship and ability to produce a finished product taught here, but also the total history of our maritime heritage. They build traditional working, sailing vessels of the Atlantic Coast that may have originated anywhere from Newfoundland to the Bahamas. Sizes range from 8 feet to 40 feet. Included are such unique and beautiful vessels as the Tancook Whaler, Maine Pinky, Nomans Land Boat and Muscongus Sloop. For more information on their program, write to Rockport Apprenticeshop, Box 539, Sea Street, Rockport ME 04856. Visitors are welcome to Rockport Apprenticeshop, no set hours, and no admission charge. If Director Lance Lee isn't available, then one of the instructors or a student will show you around. You should ask to see any of the fine boats they built that may be on moorings in the harbor.

There's a lovely view of the harbor from the Mary-Lea Park (27). Here, in a terraced garden, you can sit and enjoy watching harbor activities.

The Rockport Opera House (28) is more than of mere historical interest. It plays a major role in the musical life of the community throughout the year. During the summer, the Bay Chamber Concert Series, featuring the Vemeer Quartet, provides concerts on Thursday and Friday evenings beginning at 8:15 p.m. Frequently, there are other guest artists and programs, including popular folk music. Check the bulletin board outside the Opera House to find out what is currently being performed.

The Harkness Preserve, north of Rockport (closer to Camden), is 5 acres that include a dense stand of American chestnut trees. Chestnut blight has nearly eliminated these stately long-leafed trees, but Harkness Preserve has over 50 healthy American chestnuts. It's owned by the Nature Conservancy who works with scientists at the Maine Bureau of Forestry and the University of Maine to monitor the health of these trees.

Visitors are not allowed into the Harkness Preserve for fear of damage or tree infection, but you can see the chestnut trees from Spruce Street in Rockport, without going into the Preserve.

## CAMDEN

***Where the Mountains Meet the Sea***

**CHART NOS. 13302, 13307, and SKETCH CHART**

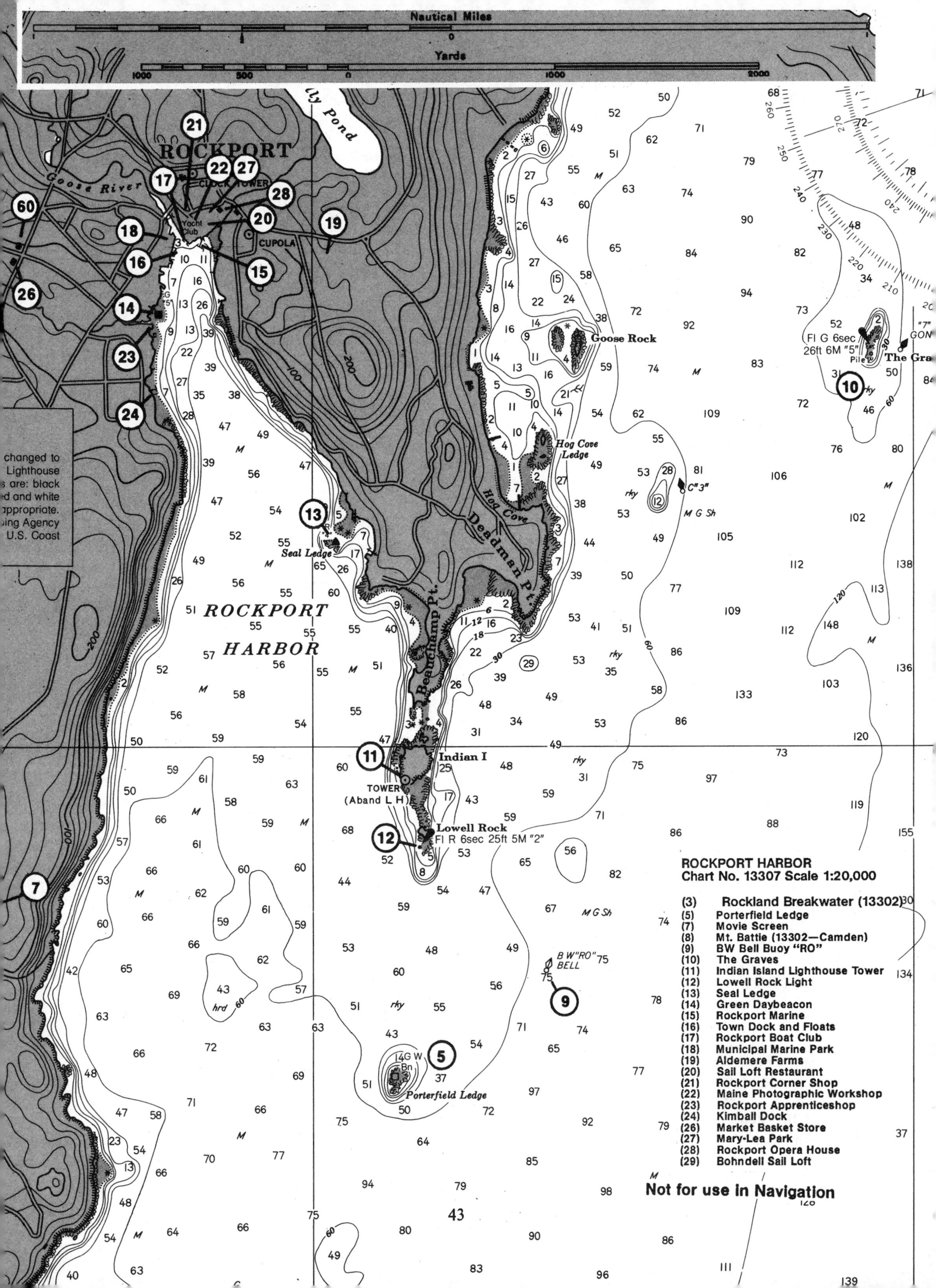
Nautical Miles
Yards
ROCKPORT
Goose River
CLOCK TOWER
Yacht Club
CUPOLA
Goose Rock
Hog Cove Ledge
Hog Cove
Deadman Pt.
Beauchamp Pt.
Seal Ledge
ROCKPORT HARBOR
Indian I
TOWER (Aband L H)
Lowell Rock
Fl R 6sec 25ft 5M "2"
BW "RO" BELL
Porterfield Ledge
The Graves
Fl G 6sec 26ft 6M "5"
ROCKPORT HARBOR
Chart No. 13307 Scale 1:20,000
(3) Rockland Breakwater (13302)
(5) Porterfield Ledge
(7) Movie Screen
(8) Mt. Battie (13302—Camden)
(9) BW Bell Buoy "RO"
(10) The Graves
(11) Indian Island Lighthouse Tower
(12) Lowell Rock Light
(13) Seal Ledge
(14) Green Daybeacon
(15) Rockport Marine
(16) Town Dock and Floats
(17) Rockport Boat Club
(18) Municipal Marine Park
(19) Aldemere Farms
(20) Sail Loft Restaurant
(21) Rockport Corner Shop
(22) Maine Photographic Workshop
(23) Rockport Apprenticeshop
(24) Kimball Dock
(26) Market Basket Store
(27) Mary-Lea Park
(28) Rockport Opera House
(29) Bohndell Sail Loft
Not for use in Navigation

Camden Harbor is high on everybody's list of places to visit when cruising the Maine coast. Its popularity is justified as it offers almost everything of interest for the cruising yachtsman. Approaches to the harbor are moderately clear of outlying dangers. The few dangers are well marked and it is easy to enter the harbor under any weather condition. There are complete marine facilities and all kinds of supplies and provisioning are available, and there is worthwhile sightseeing.

Megunticook River cascades down to the head of the harbor, while the Camden Hills provide an impressive backdrop to the natural beauty of the area. Whether you stay a while by choice or by necessity (provisioning, fog, etc.) there are many activities to keep all members of the family occupied and entertained. This is a very busy harbor and important yachting center, and you will seldom find such a collection and variety of classic wood boats. These range from the numerous Camden Schooners of the windjammer fleet, to cruising boats of other countries.

There have been times while I was moored there for several days without even going ashore, content just to sit on deck and view the other boats and watch the cormorants (shags, as they are locally called) dive for fish. How pleasant to see the sun go down behind the Camden Hills. At the precise moment of sunset, the Yacht Club fires its cannon as a signal to lower all colors and ensign to the deck, a nice touch of sailing formality, all but forgotten. The surroundings are so idyllic, that even the incessant, and usually annoying, slapping of halyards against metal masts sounds like the gentle singing of Japanese wind bells.

## Approaches

Most likely, your first approach to Camden will be from the south, coming up Western Penobscot Bay by way of Muscle Ridge Channel or Two Bush Channel. The first major mark in approaching the harbor will be "The Graves" [(10) chart no. 13302], a high pile of rocks with no vegetation, upon which is a structural steel light (Fl Green 6 sec.) at its south end, and a black gong "7" to the east of it. You can take "The Graves" to either side, day or night, but in fog I would prefer to stay east of it. Do not get close, as submerged rocks stand out some distance from those which are visible.

From there keep a north by west heading (about 350 degrees magnetic) until Curtis Island (29) (formerly called Negro Island) is clearly identified. It is heavily wooded and somewhat higher than might be expected from the chart. It has a white, stone lighthouse (Fixed Green light) in a clearing of the trees in the center of the island. When it is visible, alter course to head directly for the island, entering the harbor staying north and east of the island. Then make for the black can "7" (30). In fog, head due north from "The Graves" for the red bell buoy "2" (31). This is moderate size and has a loud enough bell in all but the calmest seas. After positive identification, a course of 310 degrees magnetic can be set for can "7". The buoys N"4", N"6" and C"1" mark a pair of inner and outer ledges which set off from Northeast Point (32). At high water these ledges are not visible. Nevertheless, danger exists and they should be kept clear. At low water or in heavy weather, seas break on these ledges. Regardless of your draft, do not enter between Curtis Island and Dillingham Point, as the water in this passage is shoal and foul.

Approaching from the east, having departed from the Fox Islands, aim for Mount Battie [(8) chart no. 13302)] on the western shore. Its bold mass is prominent, with a round stone tower at the summit, and you can carry this landmark all the way in until identifying the harbor buoys. In crossing the Bay, particularly in fog, keep track of the ebb or flood tide to make appropriate course corrections. The set in both directions is on an axis with the channels of the Bay. However, it has been my experience that the strength of the current is about ½ knot faster, particularly on the ebb tide, than that indicated in the *Tidal Current Tables* (flood 0.3 and ebb 0.6 knot). The whistle buoy R"8" marking the south end of Robinsons Ledge [(33) chart no. 13302, Vinalhaven Chapter 7)] is fairly quiet, no matter what the sea-state, and should not be relied upon for an auditory signal.

Approaching Camden from the north, make for the black and white bell buoy "CH" (34). There is an alternate channel for entering and leaving Camden Harbor, labeled on the chart as NE Passage. If the wind is from the north to northwest, you may elect to enter on a more favorable tack through this channel between Northeast Point and the green daybeacon G"2". Favor the side closer to the point. where the water is deeper. A white, painted, skeleton tower 20' high (Fl R, 4 sec.) is at the end of the point. In fog, or at night, it would be prudent to proceed from "CH" buoy to the bell R"2" to enter the harbor.

Camden Harbor is divided into an inner and outer harbor. Sherman Cove (35) is a deep indentation in the northern part of the outer harbor. There is no anchorage available in the inner harbor and anchorage is so limited in the outer harbor as to be virtually non-existent. However, once past C"7", numerous moorings are available at a nominal rate and you may find room to anchor in Sherman Cove.

A fairway channel leading into the inner harbor is marked by small ball floats with triangular pennants. These do not mark a deep water channel, but are there to provide a passageway clear of all moored and anchored boats. The mean tidal range is 9.6 feet. Although currents within the harbor are not strong, they swirl around with enough force so that they should be taken into account when picking up a mooring. It can be gusty in the harbor the day after a cold front has passed through. Moderate to strong winds from north to northwest will be accentuated due to down-drafts from the mountains.

## Marine Facilities

Moorings marked by large, round, red floats,

CAMDEN HARBOR
Chart No. 13307 Scale 1:20,000
(8 ) Mt. Battie
(10) The Graves (Chart 13302)
(26) The Marketbasket (Chart No. 13307-Rockport Harbor)
(29) Curtis Island
(30) Black Can "7"
(31) Red Bell Buoy "2"
(32) Northeast Point
(33) Robinsons Ledge (Chart 13302-Vinalhaven)
(34) Black & White Bell Buoy "CH"
(35) Sherman Cove
(36) Wayfarer Marine
(38) Harbor Square
(39) Willey Wharf
(40) Camden Yacht Club
(41) Town Landing
(42) Town Launching Ramp
(43) Harborside West
(45) I.G.A. Foodliner Supermarket
(52) Camden Hbr. Inn
Not for use in Navigation
Mt. Battie
MONUMENT
CAMDEN
STACK
SHERMAN COVE
CAMDEN HARBOR
Eaton Pt.
Northeast Pt
Mouse I
Dillingham Ledge
Inner Ledges
NE Passage
NE Ledge
Outer Ledges
Curtis I.
Dillingham Pt.
Ogier Pt.
FG 52ft 11M
Fl R 4sec 20ft 5M "2"
B W "CH" BELL
R "2" BELL
310° M
To: 45, 26, 59
MAGNETIC
Nautical Miles
Yards

primarily east of the fairway, belong to Wayfarer Marine (36), whose office and facilities are prominent on Eaton Point, extending along the northeast side of the inner harbor. Wayfarer Marine Corp. has 20 slips, moorings, gasoline, diesel fuel, ice, water from a mountain lake, complete engine and hull repairs, two marine chandleries, mail service, telex service, and monitors VHF Channels 9 and 16. They are Volvo Penta dealers and can repair just about anything including electronics. This is a large competent yard. Heading into Wayfarer Marine's fuel dock, keep clear of Eaton Point and the small stretch of shore at the northwestern side of the outer harbor until you are inside the inner harbor, as shoal water and rocks extend out from Eaton Point.

With the popularity of Camden's picturesque harbor, transient facilities are limited. Moorings and slip space are available from Wayfarer Marine (36), P.G. Willey (39), Sun Yacht Charter and Harborside West (43). There are also a few moorings put out by the town of Camden, labeled "TC." To find out about the town moorings, you must contact the harbormaster. He may be found either on his boat (white with buff trim lobster boat) tied up at the Town Landing, or in his office which is on one side of the Chamber of Commerce & Information building in the parking lot at the head of the harbor.

Each year the harbor is filled with more and more moorings, but this still cannot keep up with the demand. If you wish a mooring or slip space, it would be best to call ahead on VHF to any of the above-mentioned places before entering the harbor.

If you have a choice, the preferred moorings are those farthest in and on the southwest side of the harbor, where calmer water is provided by the protection of Curtis Island and the shore. Since Camden Harbor is open and exposed to the wind and sea from the south through the northeast, you can expect some rolling, particularly on the outer moorings. However, even under the strongest weather conditions your boat will be safely secured. If you are leaving your boat unattended for any period of time, it is best to put chaffing gear on the mooring pendant.

Willey Wharf (39) has 140 feet of dock space, 21 moorings, gasoline, diesel fuel, propane, ice, showers and marine hardware.

Space for tie-up, even for dinghys, at the Town Landing is at a premium. There are six vessels using one of the public floats for private charters, four sailing vessels and two motor launches.

Visiting yachts are requested not to tie up to the floats at the Camden Yacht Club (40). The Club is a conspicuous two-story red brick building surrounded by a veranda, and there's a flagpole on the front lawn. The club has launch service at a small fee.

Public floats for dinghy tie-up are provided at the Town Landing (41) at the very head of the inner harbor. In the Town Parking Lot, behind the Town Landing, is a snack bar, ice machine, public telephones and public rest rooms. The rest rooms are in the red brick building. If these floats are too crowded, as they can be at the height of the season, an alternative landing is the Town Launching Ramp (42) on Eaton Point. There is no float, but you can haul your dinghy up on the beach. From there it is a pleasant walk around the harbor to the center of town.

Harborside West (43) has some space to tie dockside, moorings, Texaco gasoline, ice, complete engine and hull repairs, good selection of marine supplies, and is a Johnson Outboard dealer.

Sun Yacht Charters on the west side of the harbor, between Willey Wharf (39 and Harborside West (43), has a well established fleet of bareboat charters, both sail and power. These include over 60 sailboats, 27 to 43 ft., and they give sailing instructions. Sun Yacht Charters also has 120 ft. of dock area, 15 moorings, accomodates transients, and monitors VHF Channel 16.

An excellent place to careen your boat for inspection or to do bottom work is along the stone wall at the south edge of Camden Yacht Club's (40) lawn. At high tide you can come alongside. Stay as close as possible to the finger float setting off at an angle from the main floats, to avoid several large rocks near the shore, exposed at low tide. The wall is marked for the center-line of the boat and she will settle down on a nice, even, sand shelf. Tie-down rings are set into the lawn for attaching mast-head lines to make sure that your boat leans towards the wall. If you cannot find these, ask someone at the Yacht Club to point them out. The Club understandably asks that you please do **not** tie your lines to the support posts of the clubhouse veranda and of course, to leave the area as neat and tidy as you found it.

## Supplies, Sightseeing, and Cultural Attractions

The most convenient grocery shopping is French & Brawn (44 on our sketch chart). They are on Elm St., (U.S. Route 1) immediately at the head of the harbor. Southwest on Elm St. is the I.G.A. Foodliner (45), a major supermarket. Continuing southwest about 2 miles to the intersection of U.S. 1 and Route 90, you will find The Marketbasket (26—Rockport chart no. 13307). This is just west of Rockport and is described in detail earlier in this chapter under Rockport. If you have transportation, it's worth the trip.

Ayer's Fish Market (46) on Main St. in Camden, has been in business since 1859, and is an excellent source for fresh, locally caught seafood. You can buy lobster bodies and and knuckles, 12 for $1.25. These are the remains after the meat from the tail and claws have been removed. After careful and diligent picking, you will find enough meat to prepare a hearty lobster chowder for four persons. They also have homemade fish chowder for takeout.

Along the length of Bayview St. and on Main St. are numerous gift shops, clothing and book stores. "The Owl and Turtle" bookstore (53) has a fine selection. The lower level features marine subjects, and a special

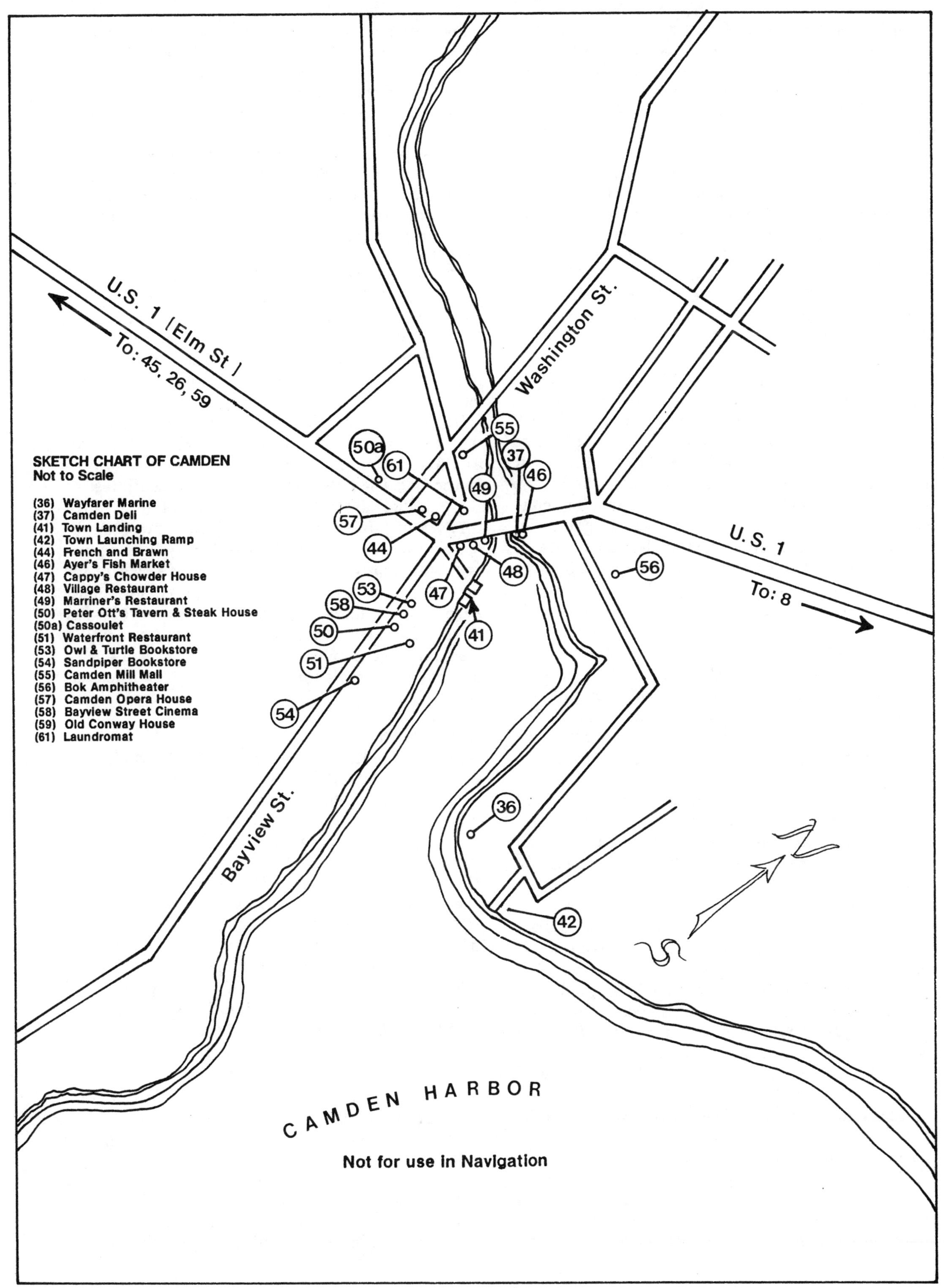

U.S. 1 (Elm St)
To: 45, 26, 59
Washington St.
U.S. 1
To: 8
Bayview St.
SKETCH CHART OF CAMDEN
Not to Scale
(36) Wayfarer Marine
(37) Camden Deli
(41) Town Landing
(42) Town Launching Ramp
(44) French and Brawn
(46) Ayer's Fish Market
(47) Cappy's Chowder House
(48) Village Restaurant
(49) Marriner's Restaurant
(50) Peter Ott's Tavern & Steak House
(50a) Cassoulet
(51) Waterfront Restaurant
(53) Owl & Turtle Bookstore
(54) Sandpiper Bookstore
(55) Camden Mill Mall
(56) Bok Amphitheater
(57) Camden Opera House
(58) Bayview Street Cinema
(59) Old Conway House
(61) Laundromat
50a
61
55
37
46
49
57
44
48
56
53
47
58
50
41
51
54
36
42
N
S
CAMDEN HARBOR
Not for use in Navigation

room for childrens' books, and a reading area with comfortable chairs. They're an NOS chart agency. Another well-stocked bookstore is the ABCDEF Book Shop (54) at 23 Bayview St. in Harbor Square (38). Other craft and specialty shops are at the Camden Mill Mall (55), one block west from the harbor on Washington and Mill Streets.

Here you will find the Wine Emporium Gourmet Food and Wine Shop. They have one of the most extensive collection of wines, including rare vintage wines, to be found anywhere along this coast. There is also a good selection of cheeses, patés, homemade salads and caviar. The caviar is the real thing—Caspian Beluga caviar. If that's too much for your budget, why not try their fresh Maine sea urchin roe, or the flying-fish roe at $33.50 per pound!

Camden always has entertainment of some kind. During the summer, the Camden Shakespeare Company, a repertory group, gives outdoor performances at the Bŏk Amphitheater (56). Evening performances are not to be missed in this beautifully landscaped set of terraces, located behind the library. During the day, it is a pleasant spot for a picnic or to watch the harbor fleet. Other musical and and drama programs are presented in the Camden Opera House (57) on Elm St. These may be presented by the Camden Civic Theater, or by other guest artists and groups. The Bay Chamber Concerts are given in the Opera House at nearby Rockport. The Bayview St. Cinema (58) shows classic as well as current films. Schedules for all events in the area are available in many of the shops in town.

Mt. Battie (8) (chart no. 13302) is not the highest of the Camden Hills which form such a magnificent backdrop to this harbor. That honor goes to Mt. Megunticook, with an elevation of 1380 feet. Mt. Battie is one of the most accessible, and well worth the time and effort to climb to the summit.

Mt. Battie is part of the Camden Hills State Park comprised of 6,500 acres of the Megunticook Mountain Range. The park includes many campground sites and picnic areas, and 25 miles of marked trails. To reach it, you must go about a mile and a half out of town, north on Route 1. Maps of all the trails are available from the park gate-house at the entrance. It is possible to drive up to the top of Mt. Battie, but the trail is infinitely more rewarding. For the most part, the trail parallels the road. The climb is easy, more of an uphill walk than mountain climbing, and takes about 45 minutes.

The panoramic view from the top makes all the effort worth while. Laid out before you is all of Penobscot Bay from Owls Head and beyond, to the east side with the mountains of Isle au Haut, to the head of the Bay and back to the miniature village of Camden and its harbor at your feet. The islands of the Bay are "strewn about as emeralds set in necklaces of foam on a great ruffled plain of sparkling topaz." If the visibility is good, it is possible to see the mountains of Mt. Desert Isle, 45 miles away. Many poems, articles and paintings have been inspired by the view from here. The best known of them is the poem "Renasence" by Edna St. Vincent Millay, who composed it while atop Mt. Battie. She had lived in Camden as a child.

The round tower at the summit of the mountain was built in 1921, designed by one of the summer residents of Camden. It is nearly an identical copy of the round tower in Newport, R.I., which some say was built as part of a medieval Norwegian round church, perhaps when the Norsemen made their voyages to this area. The Camden tower was dedicated in opening ceremonies to Camden men who served in the World War, 1914-1918.

This was not the first building to be built on top of Mt. Battie. In 1897, a carriage road was built to the top and a hotel was open to the public in 1898. Shortly after it was remodeled and turned into a clubhouse, becoming the social center of Camden. Being economically unproductive, the building was eventually torn down and the present tower erected.

Other interesting attractions and walking tours are the annual Camden-Rockport Open House and Garden Tour, in mid-July, and a visit to the Old Conway House (59). The latter is less than 1 mile southwest on Route 1. Built around 1770, it is a beautifully restored complex of house, barn and museum, now administered by the Camden Historical Society. The permanent collection in the museum includes much of the historic past of Camden and Rockport. This homestead and museum are open afternoons, Monday through Saturday during July and August. To complete the setting, the Camden Garden Club has landscaped the grounds with plantings common to New England at that time.

### Restaurants

Many Camden restaurants serve excellently prepared food. The following few that I mention are consistently good and have remained in business for many years, whereas some of the others open and close within a season or two. Approaching Main St. from the Town Landing, the first restaurant on the right is Cappy's Chowder House (47). Their specialty is fish chowder but a wide range of burgers, sandwiches and full meals are also available. Cappy's has a raw bar, makes up box lunches, and monitors VHF Channel 16, open daily from 7:30 a.m.- 1:00 a.m. Next door is the Village Restaurant (48), more formal dining and tables with views overlooking the harbor. Several doors down, at 35 Main St., is the Marriner's Restaurant (49), homemade meals at family prices. They are also the earliest to serve breakfast, starting at 6:00 a.m.

From the head of the harbor, southeast on Bayview St., is Peter Ott's Tavern and Steak House (50). They have been around for 10 years and are open 7 nights a week, serving from 5:30 p.m. to midnight. They have built their reputation on a congenial atmosphere and good cuisine. Beyond this, also on Bayview St., is the Waterfront Restaurant (51), open 11:30-2:30 and 5:00-10:00 p.m., dining either indoors or on the outdoor deck under an awning to enjoy the full view of the harbor activities. Lunch features salads, Mexican food and sandwiches. Another 5 minute walk down Bayview St. brings you to the Camden Harbor Inn (52), just past the Yacht Club. This fine old 19th century Inn serves a wide range of gourmet meals in elegant surroundings. In their Thirsty Whale Tavern, you can get smaller meals and enjoy live entertainment presented Monday through Saturday. There may be folk music, sea chantys, or on my last visit, most enjoyably, a string trio playing classical music.

### Windjammers

There are two aspects of Camden Harbor that your eye is inexorably drawn to and held by, the backdrop of mountains dropping precipitously to the edge of the water, and the forest of masts in the harbor, those of the Camden schooners in particular. Although Maine's fleet of "windjammers" is not limited to Camden as their home harbor, it is from here that the practice of chartering week-long sails on the schooners began, and it is from here that the greatest number of schooners can be seen. Most are in the range of 90-100 feet LOA and have been converted to pleasure use from their original workboat origin.

The "Stephen Tabor," the oldest documented vessel, has seen continuous service since she was built in 1871. Her appearance and beauty is up there with the best of them. The "Adventure" was a Grand Banks fishing schooner out of Gloucester. Her sister ship, the "Roseway" started as a private yacht and later saw service as a fishing boat and a harbor pilot. Others were used as coasting schooners, carrying pulpwood, codfish or sardines.

*Mattie* last sail rites, Autumn Equinox, Camden Harbor

# CHAPTER 6

# HARBORS AND ISLANDS IN PENOBSCOT BAY

## ISLESBORO ISLAND
## CHART NOS. 13305, 13305/13309

From Camden you may sail up West Penobscot Bay to the head of the Bay and the Penobscot River, or strike boldly out across the Bay towards Islesboro (60) or North Haven Island (61). Refer to folded chart inside the front cover.

Islesboro, really includes a cluster of islands extending it as far south as a point due east of Rockport Harbor. It was called Long Island until 1789. Islesboro Island is nearly cut in two, narrowed to a width of only a few hundred yards, creating several harbors and dividing the island into a northern and southern portion. At its lower half, the main island, along with Warren Island, Seven Hundred Acre Island and Job Island forms Gilkey Harbor (71) large, and shaped like a lobster claw. Extending farther south are the islands of Lime, Lasell (68), Saddle (66) and Mark (63) in the order named. This entire string of islands, from Turtle Head Promotory [(5) on chart no. 13302, this chapter] at the north tip of Islesboro, to Robinson Rock (62) divides the upper portion of Penobscot Bay into West Penobscot Bay and East Penobscot Bay.

### Passages South of Islesboro Island

Crossing one portion of the Bay to the other, you can take several possible channels, the choice depending on wind, tide and visibility.

The southernmost passage is south, around Robinson Rock (62) and whistle buoy R "8" which marks the ledge extending from it. The whistle buoy is invariably quiet regardless of the sea state, and should not be relied upon for an auditory signal.

North of this is a frequently used passage close to Mark Island (63). The island is dome-shaped, high and prominent. The ledge and daybeacon at the south end of it is very close to the shoreline and will not be a navagation problem even in fog. A course of 150 degrees magnetic and its reciprocal of 330 degrees can be used from and toward the monument atop Mt. Battie (64). From the red bell buoy "2" at the outer entrance to Camden Harbor (65), a course of 146/326 degrees magnetic takes you around the south end of Mark Island (63). Going around the south end of Mark Island is preferable to the north end, as you avoid the two rocks north of the island.

Mark Island (63) is a Nature Conservancy Preserve. They ask that you do not land between April 1 and August 15, when blue herons and eagles nest and breed there. Osprey also nest there. There were about 80 blue heron nests on Mark Island in 1979, but most of them left when the bald eagles came in 1982. 36 acre Mark Island is the only island in Penobscot Bay that has a large hardwood forest. There's a band of spruce and fir around the shores, but the interior has impressive stands of yellow birch, red oak, giant sugar maple, and American beech. Lower down are dogwood, American yew and other shrubs.

Saddle Island (66), approached from either west or east, is indeed saddle-shaped and easy to identify. Our course line between the south edge of it and East Goose Rock (67) will keep you clear of all dangers.

Lasell Island (68), 1.2 miles northeast of Mark Island is high, wooded and the largest of the group. Passing south of it and Goose Island (69), favor the north side of the passage for the best water. The ledges and group of rocks northeast of East Goose Rock (70) do no show at high water and they are unmarked. But even if the tide sets you off course and fog limits your visibility, you will know of your approach to this shallow region by the sudden appearance of a great number of lobster-trap buoys.

### Gilkey Harbor

Although Gilkey Harbor (71) at the south end of Islesboro is large, it has numerous coves that provide good protection from any weather. It also has an advantage that few other harbors have, you can enter or leave from two different directions. Thus, you can choose your passage and your anchorage according to the direction of the prevailing wind.

**Approaches.** Approaching the harbor from southward, the main channel (72) is between Job Island to the east and Ensign Islands to the west with bell buoy "1" (Fl 4 sec.) as the outermost mark. Proceed directly up the channel, favoring the west side (toward Seven Hundred Acre Island) to avoid Minot Ledge. An alternate entrance from the south is Bracketts Channel (73), east of Job Island. This channel is narrow, crooked and unmarked, making it much more difficult than the main channel. Deeper water is found on the east side of the channel. Beware of the 2-foot spot (which I have encircled on the chart) in mid-channel.

The north entrance (76) to Gilkey Harbor, past Grindel Point (85), is difficult to see because of the

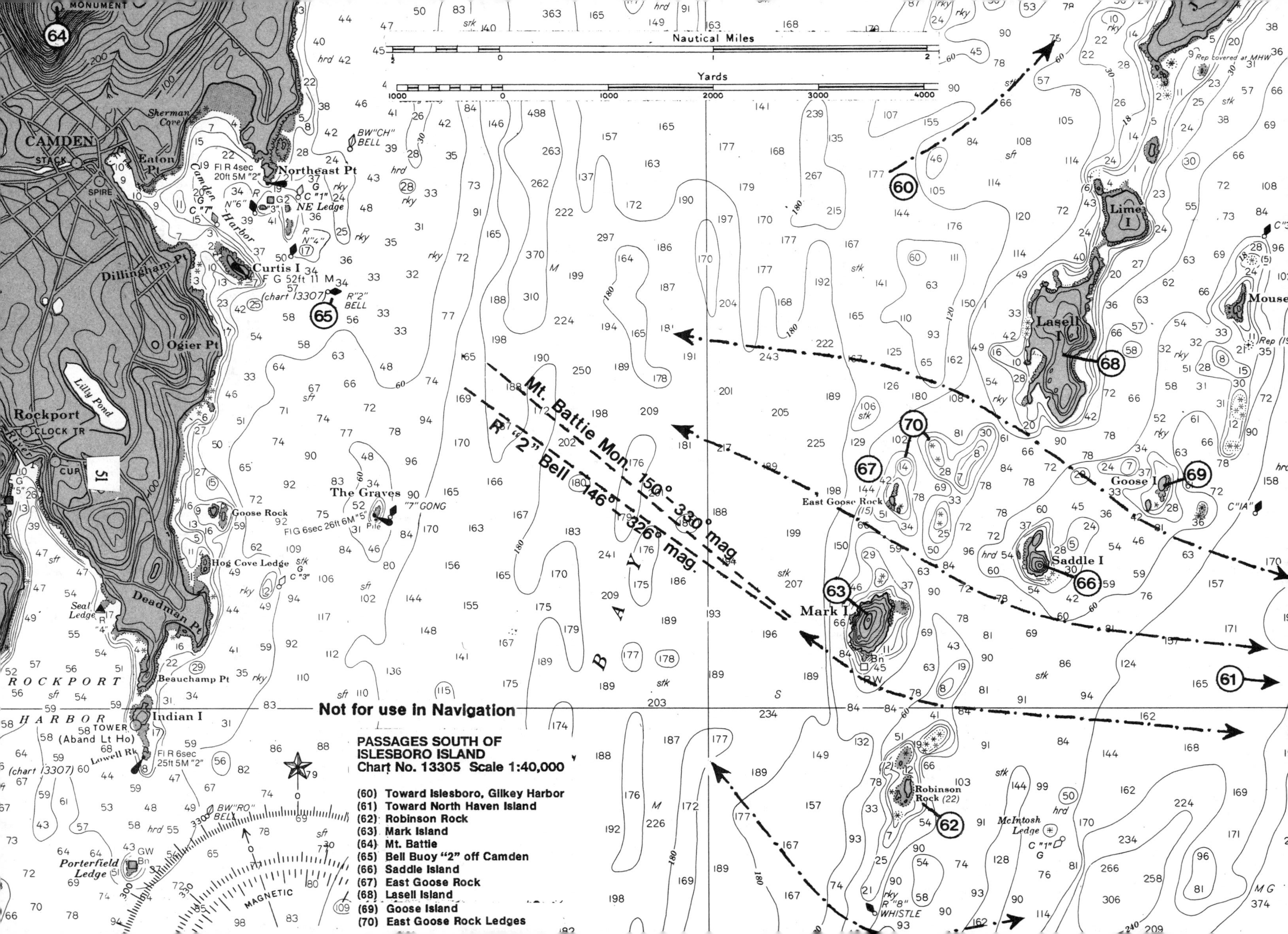

PASSAGES SOUTH OF
ISLESBORO ISLAND
Chart No. 13305 Scale 1:40,000
(60) Toward Islesboro, Gilkey Harbor
(61) Toward North Haven Island
(62) Robinson Rock
(63) Mark Island
(64) Mt. Battie
(65) Bell Buoy "2" off Camden
(66) Saddle Island
(67) East Goose Rock
(68) Lasell Island
(69) Goose Island
(70) East Goose Rock Ledges
Not for use in Navigation
Mt. Battie Mon. 150° – 330° mag.
R "2" Bell 146° – 326° mag.
Nautical Miles
Yards
CAMDEN
Camden Harbor
Rockport
ROCKPORT HARBOR
Lilly Pond
Northeast Pt
NE Ledge
Curtis I
Dillingham Pt
Ogier Pt
Goose Rock
Hog Cove Ledge
Deadman Pt
Beauchamp Pt
Indian I
Seal Ledge
Porterfield Ledge
The Graves
"7" GONG
Lasell I
Lime I
Mouse
Goose I
Saddle I
East Goose Rock
Mark I
Robinson Rock
McIntosh Ledge
MAGNETIC
51

overlapping land masses, but several marks identify its position. Approaching this entrance from the south, you will see three closely spaced vertical white rectangles on Grindel Point (85), each of successive height, the farthest east being the highest. All show quite clearly against the unrelieved dark green of the shore and are visible a long way off, practically from Camden. These show up best in the afternoon when the sun directly strikes the white painted surfaces. The tallest rectangle is the light tower, the next is the lighthouse, and finally a boatshed. Red bell buoy "2" marks the outer entrance (Fl R 4 sec). The characteristic of the Grindel Point Light is Fl G 4sec. Once you are past the entrance, the well marked channel is easily followed.

**Anchorages.** From the south entrances, the first available anchorage is in Ames Cove (74) on the east side of the harbor. The clubhouse and dock of the Tarratine Yacht Club (75) is conspicuous on the east side of the cove. An approach to their dock, which has 4 feet of water alongside, is safely made within the sector of 094 to 138 degrees magnetic. Anchorage in 9 feet depths will be found at the outer edge of the moored boats. The club has no guest moorings and they request you not pick up an empty mooring without the owners' prior consent.

Pendleton Yacht Yard, (75A) on the north shore of Ames Cove, has moorings, some dock space, gasoline, complete engine and hull repairs, marine supplies, and monitors VHF Channel 16.

Within Gilkey Harbor, you are bound to keep company with the Camden Schooners, particularly on Fridays. From here they can be sure to be back in home port by Saturday noon. An attractive anchorage is north of Thrumcap Island (77), with good holding ground of soft mud. The Islesboro Inn (78) is prominent on the east shore. It has a float at its dock where you may land your dinghy and their restaurant and cocktail lounge are open to the public. The Inn has transient moorings by reservations, phone 734-2221. Yachtsmen can use their coin-operated washer and dryer, and for a small fee, the shower facilities.

On the west side of the Gilkey Harbor, another lovely anchorage is in Cradle Cove (79), on the northeast side of Seven Hundred Acre Island. Dark Harbor Boat Yard (80) on the south shore of the cove has a floating dock with depth of 7 feet alongside at low water, 24 moorings, gasoline, diesel fuel, ice, water, showers, laundromat, complete engine and hull repairs, and marine supplies. They are boat builders and can haul boats up to 65 ft. and 3 tons, and monitor VHF Channel 16. Approaching the dock, be sure to come straight toward it instead from either side. Although it may not appear so from the chart, ledges on either side of the dock extend a considerable distance north into the cove. The farthest limit of each of these ledges is marked by privately maintained aids, encircled on our chart. The western ledge (81) has a spindle, topped with a red highway cone, while the eastern ledge (82) is marked by a yellow barrel. The most frequently made mistake is cutting inside the barrel marker when approaching the dock from the southeast.

Warren Island (83), north of Seven Hundred Acre Island, is a State Park. It is one of the few places in this chain of islands where camping is permitted. A pier (84) with 4 feet alongside is on the east side of the island, and several free guest moorings are provided by the State. If you want one, plan to arrive early.

Grindel Point (85) is the ferry terminus to the island. The ferry departs from Lincolnville Beach (86) on the mainland (almost directly across West Penobscot Bay) and makes 9 daily round-trips during the summer. For latest information on schedule and fares, write to Maine State Ferry Service, P.O. Box 645, 517A Main St., Rockland, ME 04841, tel. (207) 594-5543.

At Lincolnville Beach, there's a free public asphalt launching ramp and a float for short term tie-up, near the ferry landing (86). Just north of the ramp is the Lobster Pound Restaurant and cocktail lounge. They have ice, and a guest mooring. There's no protection here from any winds between southwest and southeast. It would be good in winds, between west and northwest, but this must be considered a marginal anchorage.

Next to the State Ferry slip at Islesboro Island is a municipal dock and floats (87) with 12 feet depth at low tide. The lighthouse tower is no longer in use, the light (Fl G 4 sec.) being displayed from an 18 foot high white, skeletal tower at the end of Grindel point. The lighthouse keeper's cottage is now a Sailor's Memorial Museum (88) and exhibits relics and information of the history and maritime heritage of Islesboro. It is open 10:00 a.m. to 4:00 p.m. Tuesday through Sunday, free admission. Picnic tables and a small snack shop are adjacent to the museum. East of the dock and floats is an asphalt launching ramp.

Since the late 19th century, Islesboro has been a resort area for wealthy summer residents. Their large estates are spread throughout the island, many in the Dark Harbor area. Coasting along its shores will give you a glimpse of some of these magnificent "cottages." The island is definitely not oriented towards tourism, being kept very much a private colony. There is no central village on the island and there are only two grocery stores, both quite far from the public landing at the ferry dock. The nearest is Leach's Market located near the middle of the island near the post office (89). Do your provisioning beforehand at Camden or Rockland. The most accessible restaurants are the Blue Heron (90), within walking distance from Ames Cove and the Islesboro Inn (78) near Thrumcap anchorage.

## SEVEN HUNDRED ACRE ISLAND
## CHART NOS. 13305, 13309

Access to Philbrook Cove (91) on the west shore of the island is easy and the cove provides a pleasant anchorage with privacy. Holding ground is good and protection is adequate in fine, settled weather. Favor the east shore of the harbor for deeper water. At half-tide

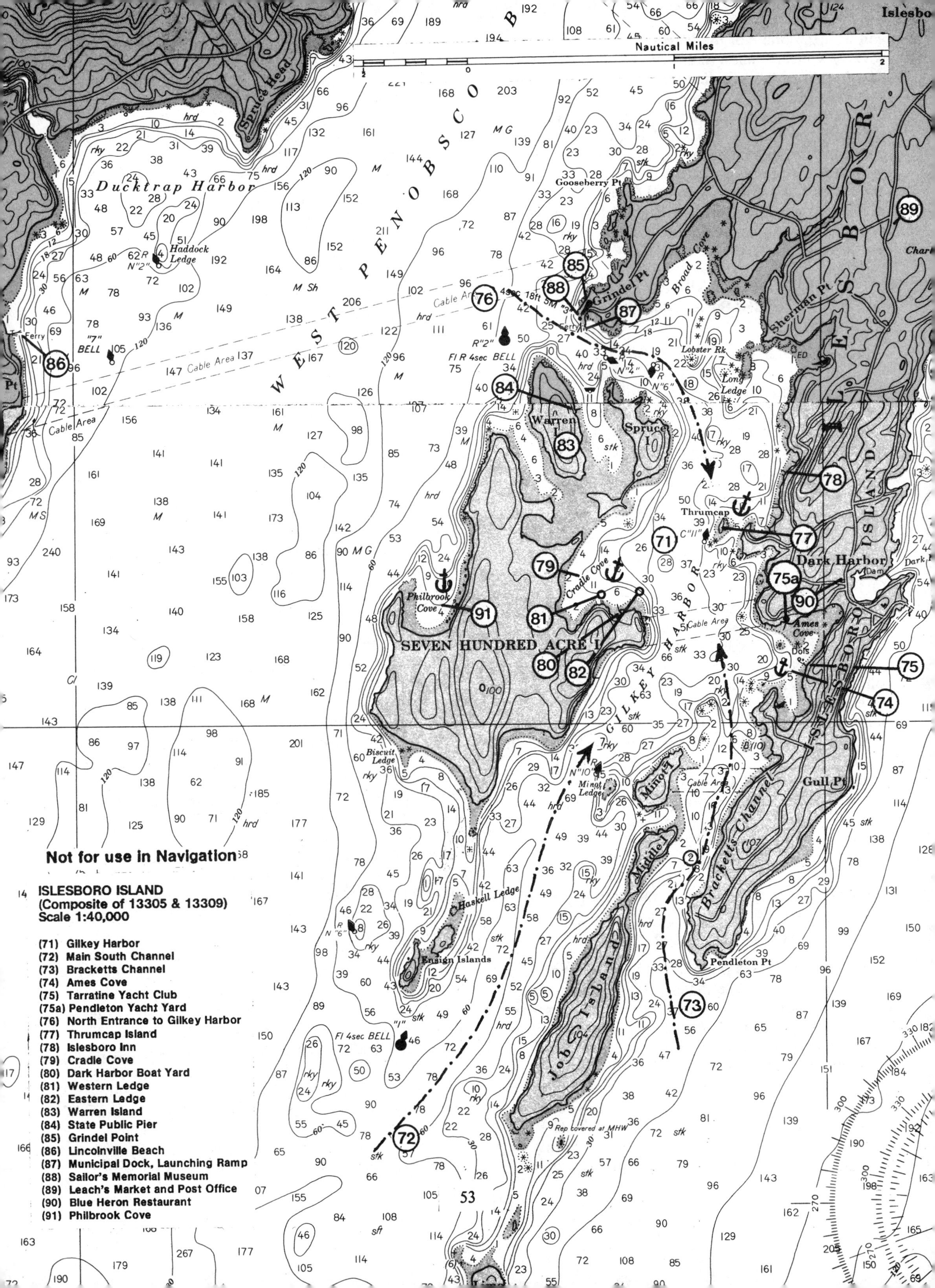

Nautical Miles
Spruce Head
Ducktrap Harbor
Haddock Ledge
WEST PENOBSCOT BAY
Cable Area
Gooseberry Pt
Grindel Pt
Broad Cove
Lobster Rk
Long Ledge
Sherman Pt
Warren I
Spruce I
Thrumcap
Dark Harbor
Cradle Cove
Philbrook Cove
SEVEN HUNDRED ACRE I
GILKEY HARBOR
Ames Cove
Biscuit Ledge
Minot Ledge
Minot I
Middle I
Bracketts Channel
Gull Pt
Haskell Ledge
Ensign Islands
Job Island
Pendleton Pt
ISLESBORO ISLAND
Not for use in Navigation
ISLESBORO ISLAND
(Composite of 13305 & 13309)
Scale 1:40,000
(71) Gilkey Harbor
(72) Main South Channel
(73) Bracketts Channel
(74) Ames Cove
(75) Tarratine Yacht Club
(75a) Pendleton Yacht Yard
(76) North Entrance to Gilkey Harbor
(77) Thrumcap Island
(78) Islesboro Inn
(79) Cradle Cove
(80) Dark Harbor Boat Yard
(81) Western Ledge
(82) Eastern Ledge
(83) Warren Island
(84) State Public Pier
(85) Grindel Point
(86) Lincolnville Beach
(87) Municipal Dock, Launching Ramp
(88) Sailor's Memorial Museum
(89) Leach's Market and Post Office
(90) Blue Heron Restaurant
(91) Philbrook Cove

and less, the limits of the ledges on both sides of the cove very clearly show themselves either by the exposed rocks or the kelp floating on the surface, so the water you see is the water you have. No docks or services are available, all the shore being privately owned. On the other side of the island is Cradle Cove (79) which is described above under Gilkey Harbor.

Most of the island is privately owned by descendents of Charles Dana Gibson who had a large estate on the island and summered here from 1904-1944. He is famous for his drawings of the "Gibson Girl" which graced many magazine covers.

## NORTH ISLESBORO ISLAND
## CHART NO. 13302

### Crow Cove

Proceeding up West Penobscot Bay, the next available anchorage on Islesboro Island is Crow Cove (92), 2.4 miles northeast of Grindel Point. It is small, but pleasant and well protected. Entering, favor the north shore to avoid the rock at the south side of the constriction at the entrance.

### Seal Harbor

Seal Harbor (93), north of Crow Cove, is too open and exposed to the prevailing southwest winds of summer to be of much use. It would be a good refuge in winds between north and southeast.

### Turtle Head Cove

Turtle Head Cove (94) is a large bight at the north end of Islesboro Island. The shelter is fine for winds from all directions except north to northwest and even then, the most you will experience is an uncomfortable roll. Land is close enough so that there's not enough fetch to produce big waves. The bottom is soft mud and holding is good. Keep to the east edge of the cove to avoid the rocks and shoal areas north of Marshall Point. Although there are no docks or any services available nearby, it is a good spot with picturesque surroundings, to spend a summers' evening. There is a short strip of sand beach at the head of the cove and the area is well known for the large Blue Heron rookery.

## GENERAL INFORMATION ON THE UPPER REACHES OF PENOBSCOT BAY
## CHART NOS. 13302, 13309

In the northernmost portion of Penobscot Bay, there are a number of possible routes to choose from, all offering good sailing amidst beautiful surroundings. You are not caught in a cul-de-sac where the only option is to retrace your course, beating back into the wind.

You may elect to enter Belfast Bay (95) and anchor or moor near the city of Belfast, which has provisioning and yachting services available. Or you may sail up the Penobscot River (96), with the wooded high steep shores close-to, and visit the seaport towns of Bucksport and Winterport. Another option is to enter

### LEGEND FOR CHART ON ADJACENT PAGE

**PENOBSCOT BAY—UPPER REACHES**
**Chart No. 13302 Scale 1:80.000**

(95) Belfast Bay Entrance
(96) Penobscot River Entrance
(97) To Castine and Bagaduce River
(98) To Eggemoggin Reach
(99) To Deer Isle, Western Shore
( 1) East Penobscot Bay
( 2) Mack Point, Fuel Tanks
( 3) Radio Tower
( 4) Steels Ledge Light
( 5) Turtle Head
( 6) Dice Head
( 7) Searsport Harbor
( 8) Long Cove
( 9) Stockton Harbor
(10) Sears Island
(11) Fort Point Cove
(12) Public Pier
(13) Fort Pownall
(14) Town Dock, Searsport
(15) Penobscot Marine Museum

**NORTH ISLESBORO ISLAND**
**Chart No. 13302 Scale 1:80,000**

(92) Crow Cove
(93) Seal Harbor
(94) Turtle Head Cove

the area of historic Castine and the Bagaduce River (97) with its labrynthine waterways and innumerable coves and harbors. While you're up there, if time allows, explore the whole area. It's beautiful!

Refer to folded chart inside the front cover.

After going around the north end of Islesboro Island, you may exit Penobscot Bay altogether through the entirely protected route of Eggemoggin Reach (98), or you may continue for a short way south to sail the west shore of Deer Isle (99), discovering its fine harbors, ultimately exiting Penobscot Bay by way of the Deer Island Thorofare or Merchant Row Thorofare.

Finally, there is the option of going down the east side of Islesboro to sail East Penobscot Bay (1) and all the harbors of North Haven, Vinalhaven and Isle-au-Haut. You can then leave Penobscot Bay to continue your travels farther east by going around the south end of Isle-au-Haut. All the choices are equally rewarding. Each has its own unique "flavor" and appearance. You could spend the whole summer up here exploring the entire area. If you don't have that kind of time, keep coming back, exploring one part at a time.

A word of caution about the passage around the south end of Isle-au-Haut. If you look at the chart for Isle au Haut (facing page 86), you will see two nun buoys on the western side of the island toward the southern end, N "4" (71) marking T Rock and N "2" (86) south of The Washers. These two buoys are positioned specifically for marking these rocks only. They are **not** course buoys. Any attempt to set a course line directly from one to the other would place you in danger of being set upon the numerous and scattered rocks of The Brandies. It may seem obvious from inspection of the chart, but when you are out there on the water,

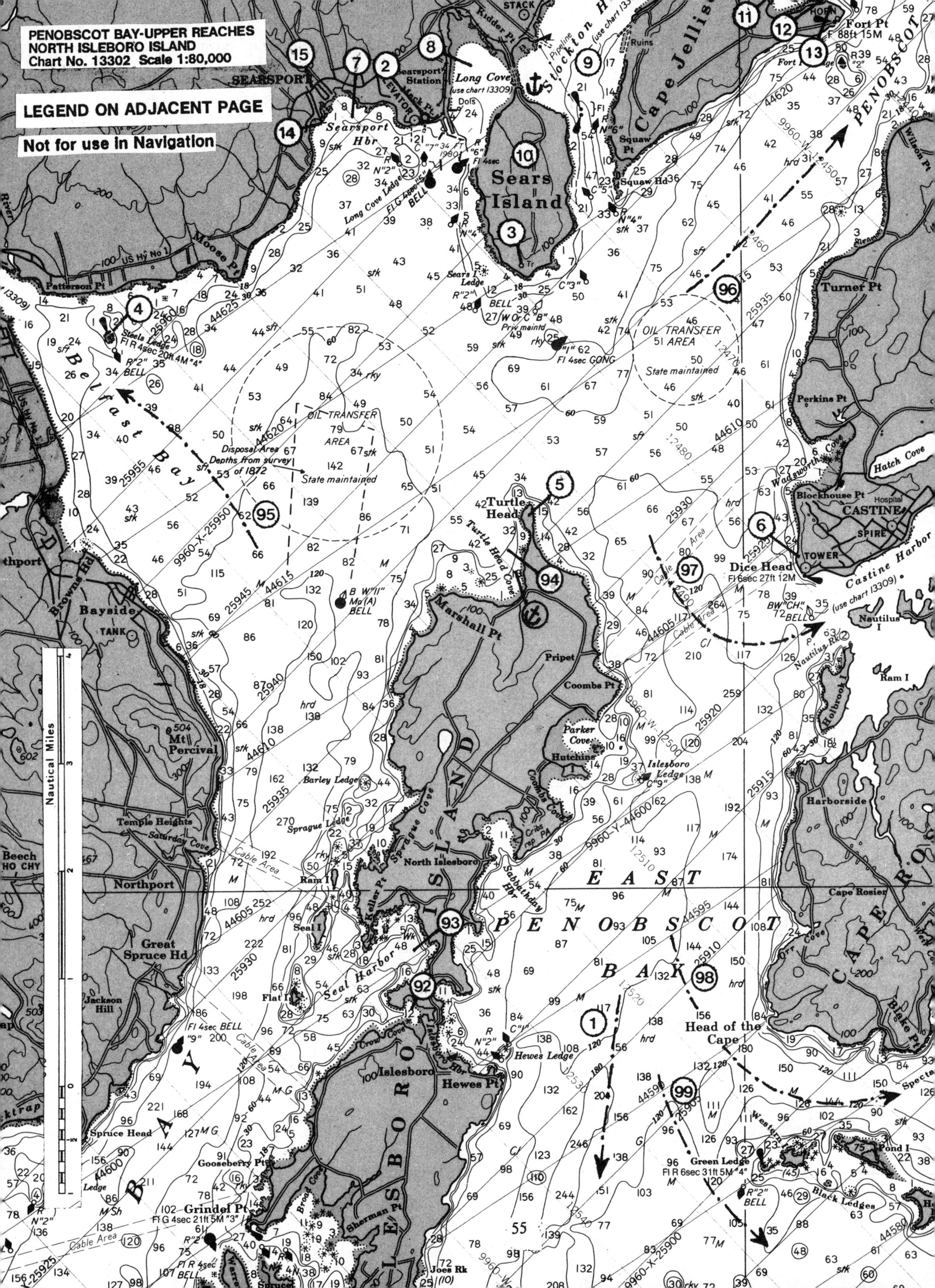

PENOBSCOT BAY-UPPER REACHES
NORTH ISLEBORO ISLAND
Chart No. 13302 Scale 1:80,000
LEGEND ON ADJACENT PAGE
Not for use in Navigation
SEARSPORT
Searsport Station
Searsport Hbr
Long Cove
Stockton H
Cape Jellis
Sears Island
Squaw Pt
Squaw Hd
Fort Pt
PENOBSCOT
Moose Pt
Patterson Pt
Steels Ledge
Belfast Bay
OIL TRANSFER AREA
State maintained
Disposal Area Depths from survey of 1872
Turtle Head
Turtle Head Cove
Marshall Pt
Pripet
Coombs Pt
Parker Cove
Hutchins
Coombs Cove
Islesboro Ledge
Turner Pt
Perkins Pt
Wadsworth Cove
Hatch Cove
Blockhouse Pt
CASTINE
Dice Head
Castine Harbor
Nautilus I
Holbrook I
Ram I
Harborside
Cape Rosier
CAPE ROSIER
Browns Hd
Bayside
Mt Percival
Temple Heights
Saturday Cove
Northport
Great Spruce Hd
Jackson Hill
Barley Ledge
Sprague Ledge
Sprague Cove
North Islesboro
Sabbathday Hbr
Ram I
Seal I
Keller Pt
Seal Harbor
Flat I
Crow Cove
Hewes Ledge
Hewes Pt
Islesboro
ISLESBORO ISLAND
EAST PENOBSCOT BAY
Head of the Cape
Green Ledge
Black Ledges
Pond I
Spruce Head
Gooseberry Pt
Grindel Pt
Broad Cove
Sherman Pt
Joes Rk
Cable Area
Nautical Miles

especially with poor visibility, the inadvisability of this course is not so apparent.

In the northern section of Penobscot Bay, there are several prominent landmarks useful in fixing your position. When the whole north shore is just a thin bluish line lost in the haze, two fuel tanks on Mack Point (2) east of Searsport stand out clearly. Although not marked on the chart, these tanks are adjacent east to the conveyer tower, marked elevator. The tower at the south end of Sears Island is a tall thin radio tower (3). Steels Ledge Light (4), at the entrance to Belfast is a convenient landmark, as are the bold bluffs of Turtle Head (5) at the north end of Islesboro Island, and Dice Head (6) at the entrance to Castine. The lighthouse tower at Dice Head is abandoned and virtually lost in the trees.

## NORTH SHORE HARBORS

There are several harbors on the north shore, but for the yachtsman they may be looked upon more as harbors of necessity than desirability. Searsport (7) is completely open and exposed to the prevailing wind and waves from the southwest as they come up the full length of the Bay. The same is true for Long Cove (8) west of Sears Island. Long Cove and Stockton Harbor (9) have the added disadvantage of heavy commercial traffic and unpleasant, industrial surroundings. Searsport is described in detail further on in this chapter, worth a visit for its Penobscot Marine Museum.

Mack Point (2) has Searsport's commercial docks. There are piers, warehouses and conveyers to handle traffic in potatoes, petroleum, coal and dry bulk commodities. Sailing this area of Penobscot Bay at night, or in the fog, keep a sharp lookout for these freighters and tankers on their way to Searsport and Belfast. Searsport is also the ocean terminus for the Bangor and Aroostook Railway and its connections with the Maine Central Railroad and the Canadian National Railway.

### Stockton Harbor—Chart No. 13309 (Searsport)

Stockton Harbor, with its piers, mooring facilities and chemical plant, is little different than Long Cove and Mack Point. But at least here, if need be, protection from winds from **all** directions can be obtained by anchoring north of Sears Island.

Construction on Sears Island (10) as a major, deep-water cargo port is being decided in the Federal Courts. The island has been designated by the State as one of three where industrial development should be concentrated and work has already begun on building a causeway to connect the island to the mainland. Now, the bar connecting it to the mainland shows only at low tide. Sierra Club representatives argue that such development will have a significant effect on the environment, i.e., the clam flats, marine life, waterfowl and tidal flows. They contend that even if the proposed plans would not materially affect the quality of the environment, that completion would lead the way to further industrial development that would most certainly have a deleterious effect.

With court's refusal for an injunction by the Sierra Club, it appears that Sears Island will finally become a deep-water cargo port. Although the Club has filed another injunction, construction of the facility has already started. These issues are always complex and difficult to resolve.

### Fort Point Cove— Chart No. 13309 (Searsport)

Only a few miles northeast, Fort Point Cove (11) provides good protection, good holding ground **and** beautiful, unspoiled surroundings. There is a State Park at the end of the point with a 200 foot pier (12) available to the boating public. You may tie up there with 12 feet depth at low tide. In a strong north wind, this anchorage may become rough, but then you can move to anchor in the northern part of the cove to gain protection.

A considerable amount of water from the Penobscot River and its drainage basin rushes out. When forced to pass through constrictions, such as Fort Point, the current can attain some velocity, here anywhere from 3.5 to 5.0 knots. Plan to sail up the river on a **flood** tide, for if the wind is strong from the southwest, not only would you have the strong current to contend with, but short steep standing waves. When wind and tide are with you, no problem!

The remains of Fort Pownall (13), built in 1759, can be explored. The strategic importance of the fort at the mouth of the Penobscot River was not to prevent attacks from seaward, but to prevent invasions southward by the French. Along with the Indians, the French controlled much of the interior regions. They could move south by way of the Hudson, Penobscot and St. John Rivers. The fort was proposed by Thomas Pownall, Governor of Massachusetts, to keep the French inland, and "it would take possession of the finest Bay in North America for large shipping just at the mouth of the Bay of Fundy and would be advancing the frontiers of his Majesty's Dominions."

Barely two months after its completion, the fort was of little use, as the French Empire in North America fell with the surrender of Quebec to General Wolfe. A continental regiment partially demolished the fort in 1775 to make sure it could not be used by the British. But during its short lifespan, it did serve a useful function by encouraging settlement in the area by Anglo-Americans.

## BELFAST HARBOR
## CHART NO. 13309

Anyone who has previously sailed the upper reaches of Penobscot Bay and entered Belfast Harbor lately will find the recent changes here to be astounding. The residents of Belfast are to be lauded for effecting a major improvement on the waterfront, and in the image of the town as a whole.

At one time Belfast was a major seaport and a thriving shipbuilding community with eleven boatyards on

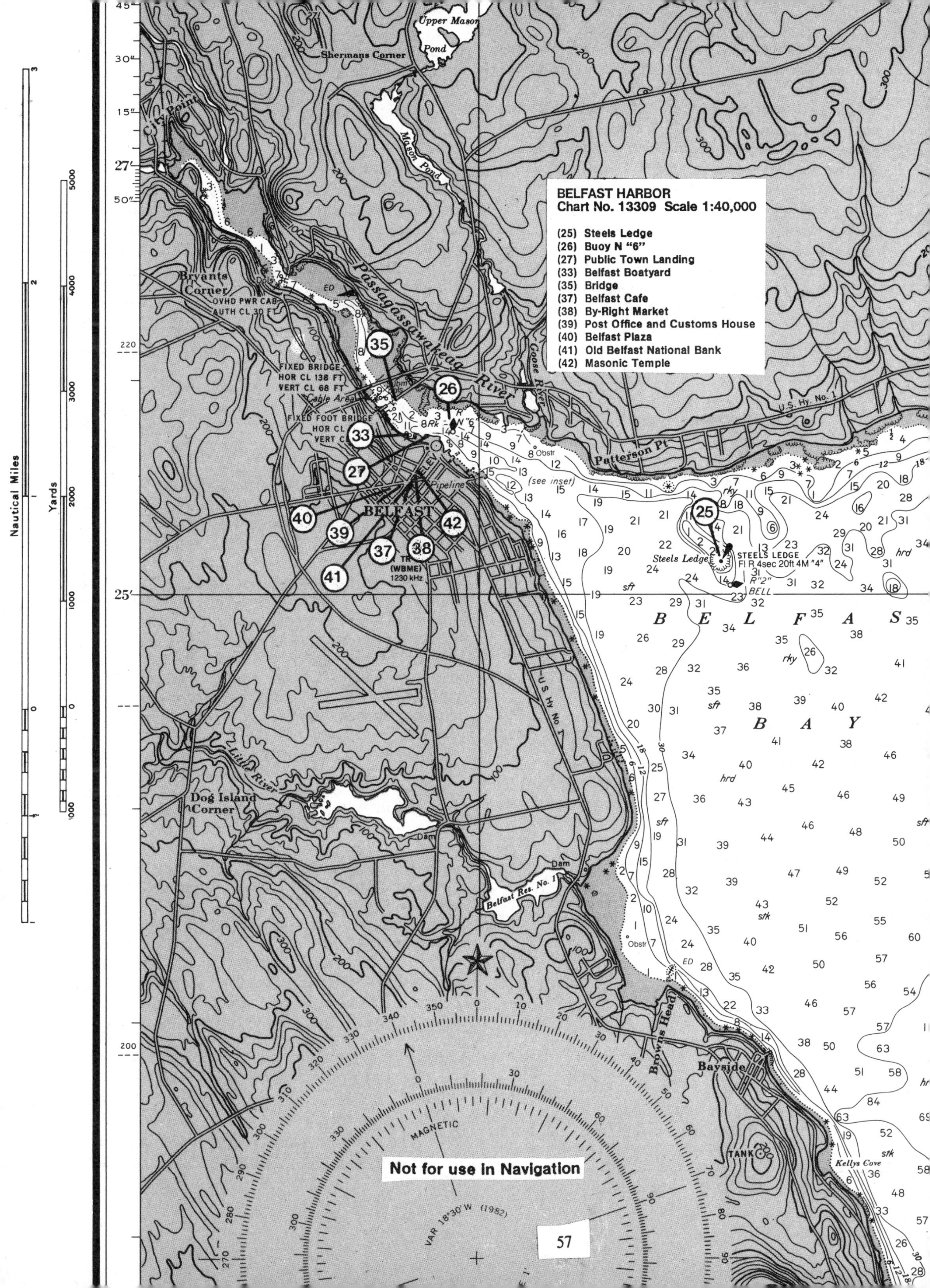
BELFAST HARBOR
Chart No. 13309 Scale 1:40,000
(25) Steels Ledge
(26) Buoy N "6"
(27) Public Town Landing
(33) Belfast Boatyard
(35) Bridge
(37) Belfast Cafe
(38) By-Right Market
(39) Post Office and Customs House
(40) Belfast Plaza
(41) Old Belfast National Bank
(42) Masonic Temple
Not for use in Navigation
Nautical Miles
Yards
Upper Mason Pond
Shermans Corner
City Point
Mason Pond
Passagassawakeag River
Goose River
Bryants Corner
OVHD PWR CAB AUTH CL 30 FT
FIXED BRIDGE HOR CL 138 FT VERT CL 68 FT
Cable Area
FIXED FOOT BRIDGE
BELFAST
TR (WBME) 1230 kHz
Pipeline
(see inset)
Patterson Pt
U.S. Hy. No. 1
Steels Ledge
STEELS LEDGE
Fl R 4sec 20ft 4M "4"
R "2" BELL
BELFAST BAY
Little River
Dog Island Corner
Belfast Res. No. 1
Dam
Browns Head
Bayside
TANK
Kellys Cove
US Hy No 1
MAGNETIC
VAR 18°30'W (1982)

its shores. With the expanding development of industry and manufacturing, Belfast changed to rail and truck for shipping their products. Through neglect, many of the piers fell into ruins. One of the largest industries was poultry processing, and the sea became a means of getting rid of the by-products. When you sailed up Belfast Bay on the swan-bosomed waves, it was neither sea-foam on the crests, nor was it swan feathers—just plain old chicken feathers! It didn't help either to see chicken parts floating past you.

All this is changed now. These practices no longer occur. The water has been cleaned up, and to make the waterfront once again attractive and useful to the boating public, a new waterfront complex has been constructed.

## Harbor Entry

Entry to the harbor is easy under all conditions. Following the western shoreline funnels you directly to the head of the harbor. There are no obstructions. Steels Ledge Light (25) at the outer entrance, is a prominent feature visible for four miles in clear weather. It is a 20 foot, white cylinder on top of a square stone structure, surrounded by rip-rap. The light (Fl R 4 sec.) has a higher intensity beam oriented down the Bay. It is a good radar target. There is also a bell buoy, R "2", immediately south of the ledge.

Because of the land contour, waves that are generated by the southwest summer winds, move northeast up Penobscot Bay and are reflected along the western shore. By the time they reach Belfast Bay, they are headed northwest. The same is true for the winds. The southwest breezes in the upper part of Penobscot Bay do not remain from the southwest. They follow in a direction parallel to the shore and by the time they reach Belfast they are from the southeast. Thus, when you are in Belfast Harbor, you are not in the calm, protected water you might expect. It is equally exposed to strong winds from the southwest as much as from the southeast. Also, for what looks like a river of insignificant size, there are fairly strong currents on both flood and ebb tide into and out of the Passagassawakeag River.

There are no navigation aids beyond N "6" (26). The channel at this point curves sharply toward the western shore and as long as you closely follow the shoreline there is plenty of water. Be careful not to wander too far over toward the eastern shore at the head of the harbor. Every summer, a number of boats get hung up on the drying patch of rocks (43) extending far into the river from the eastern shore. If you follow the sketch diagram on page 59 you will have no problems.

## Marine Facilities

The Public Town Landing (27) is just past N "6" (26) on the south shore. A granite breakwater (28) extends into the harbor shielding 400 ft. of floats west of it from the major force of the currents. Tie-up at the town floats is permitted without fee for a short period of time, but there is a charge of 50 cents per foot (with a $15 minimum) for any overnight stay. There is 6 foot depth alongside, and water and electricity are provided. At the floats, you can also get gasoline and diesel fuel. Showers and restrooms (29) are available beyond the parking lot at the dock, and are open from 7:00 a.m. to 8:00 p.m. The dock attendant will loan you a key to get into the facilities after 8:00 p.m.

So popular has this harbor become in the last few years, that while formerly there was only a handful of moorings in the harbor, there are now 240. At that, during the height of summer, it may be difficult to get one for the night. Check with the Harbormaster, James Richards, whose office (30) is in the small shed in the parking lot at the landing, about the availability of a mooring. The city has a number of moorings at a $10 fee for the night. Free City moorings are a thing of the past.

A small park behind the public landing has picnic tables and a restaurant. A free concrete and asphalt launching ramp (31) is between the granite pier and the Town Landing. This entire waterfront complex is called the City Boat Landing.

West of the Town Landing is the Towage Co. Wharf (32) where several large tugboats are usually tied. Farther west is the Belfast Boatyard (33), owned and operated by Alex Turner. You will find him to be a great help providing assistance and information.

Belfast Boatyard facilities, in keeping pace with the growth of the harbor, now has dockage (10 feet alongside) for about 12 boats. There are 15 moorings, plus 6 floats, which gives tie-up space for 12 more boats. They have stack and rack service for small boats as well as a marine railway and hydraulic trailer, both with 25 ton capacity. They have sheds for storage of large boats. Their riggers are as good as any you can find along the coast.

Chance Along Inn, about 2 miles south of town on Belfast Bay, has 2 guest moorings and showers.

Young's Lobster Pound is on Patterson Point, on the north side of Belfast Bay. They have 200 ft. of dockage, 2 moorings, ice, a snack bar, and a free concrete launching ramp.

You cannot proceed beyond the bridge (35) in any but the smallest boats because of the fixed, 9-ft. vertical clearance.

The Weathervane Restaurant (36) at the public boat landing serves modestly priced meals in a dining room overlooking the harbor. They also have a retail seafood store with an extensive selection of fresh fish and shellfish. There are several small cafes along both sides of Main St. The Belfast Cafe (37) at 90 Main St. has an appealing and wide range of entrees. The Bi-Right Market (38) on Main St. is open 7 days a week 9:00 a.m.-5:00 p.m. and has general groceries, meat, beer and wine. On Belmont Ave., west of the Post Office and Customs House (39), is the Belfast Plaza (40). This includes a large IGA Supermarket (open Monday-Saturday 8:00 a.m.-9:00 p.m., liquor store, drug store and bank.

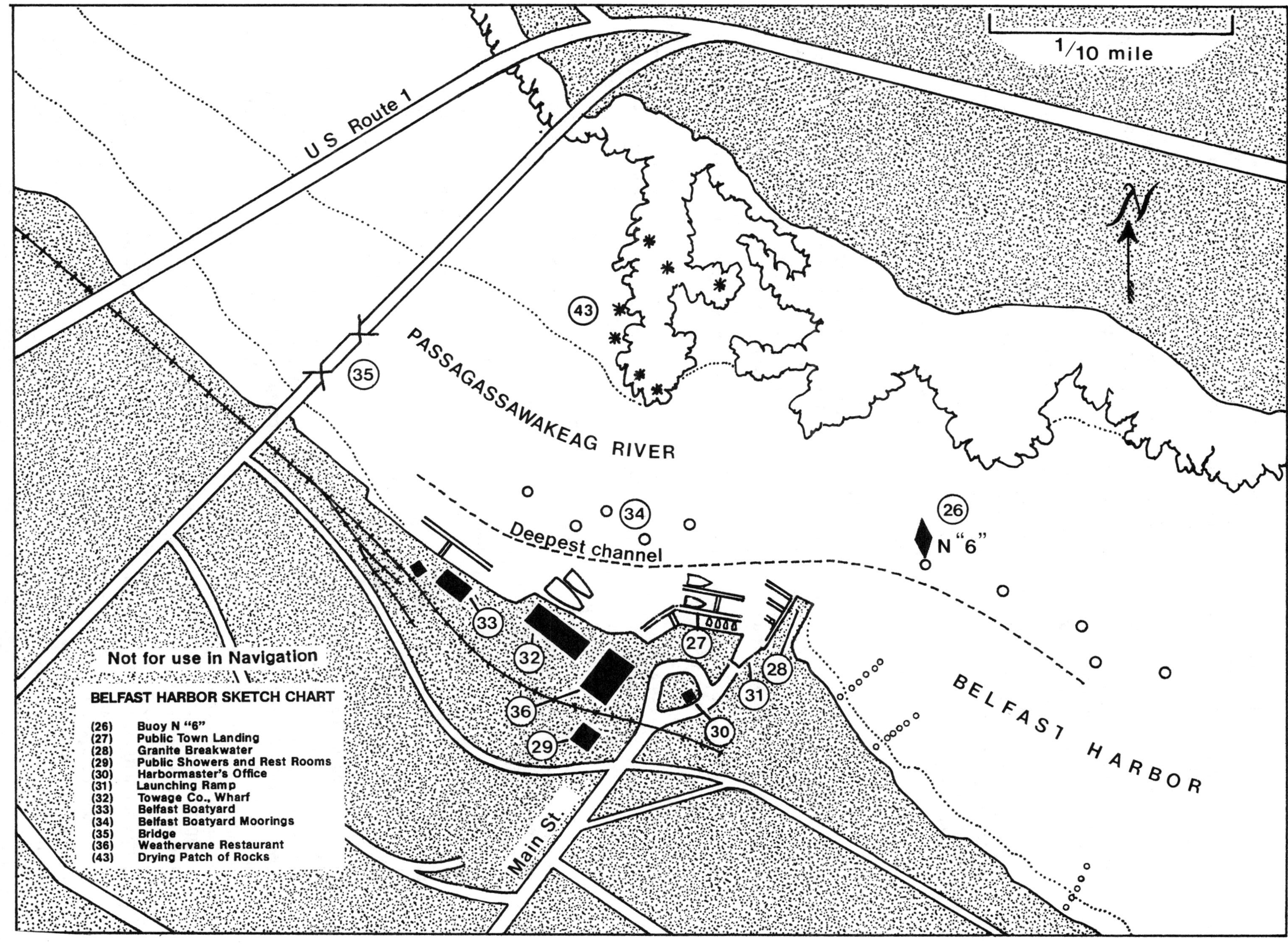
1/10 mile
N
U S Route 1
PASSAGASSAWAKEAG RIVER
Deepest channel
N "6"
BELFAST HARBOR
Main St.
Not for use in Navigation
BELFAST HARBOR SKETCH CHART
(26) Buoy N "6"
(27) Public Town Landing
(28) Granite Breakwater
(29) Public Showers and Rest Rooms
(30) Harbormaster's Office
(31) Launching Ramp
(32) Towage Co., Wharf
(33) Belfast Boatyard
(34) Belfast Boatyard Moorings
(35) Bridge
(36) Weathervane Restaurant
(43) Drying Patch of Rocks

### Sightseeing

After two disastrous fires in 1865 and 1873, much of the downtown section of Belfast was destroyed. Rebuilt with brick, most of the "new" waterfront section is now on the National Register of Historic Buildings. Two of the most fascinating are the old Belfast National Bank (41) built in 1878, and the Masonic Temple (42) built in 1879. These are in the style of High Victorian Gothic. In the residential districts you'll find superb examples of Greek Revival, Federal and Romanesque Revival buildings. To facilitate a walking tour of all these historic buildings, we have reproduced a map published by the Belfast Chamber of Commerce, with their kind permission. The Belfast Historical Museum is on Belmont Ave., near the junction with Main St.

## SEARSPORT—CHART NO. 13309

If for no other reason than to visit the Penobscot Marine Museum, a stay at Searsport is well worth your while. See Additional notes on Searsport under North Shore Harbors earlier in this chapter.

The view from this harbor commands all the northern half of Penobscot Bay and is truly magnificent. However, you may find the anchorage to be a bit rolly in the afternoon (from 1200-1700), particularly with a strong SW breeze. By evening it will settle down a bit. Holding ground is excellent in soft mud. Two guest moorings are available, both without charge. One is owned by the City, and has a 10 ton weight with a 2″ nylon hawser. The other, a 2 ton mooring, is owned by the Penobscot Marine Museum. For use of either, call in advance.

If the anchorage is uncomfortably rough, and traffic at the Town Dock (14) is not too busy, the Harbormaster will allow boats to tie to the inner face of the dock overnight. There you will be completely protected from the waves. Check with him.

There are two floats, with a ramp, attached to the town dock where you may land your dinghy. They have a depth of 4 feet. The outer face of the Town Dock has 7-8 foot depth, while the inner face has about 6 feet at low water.

At low water, a deep draft vessel should keep away from the west side of the dock. At one time, a dock was there and some of the rock piles used for its support still remain. These are immediately adjacent west to the present dock. There is no fuel or water at the Town Dock. There is a free asphalt launching ramp. Restaurants, provisions, laundromat and marine supplies are all available nearby in town, reached by a short, pleasant walk.

In addition to the Camden Schooners, there is a new Maine Windjammer operating out of Searsport. She is a 55′ on deck New England Pinky Schooner called "Summertime." A portion of each fare is donated to the Penobscot Marine Museums and the Searsport Historical Society. For information and reservations call (207) 548-2529, Extension 10.

In the last century, the Penobscot Bay region was the center of activity on the Maine coast for shipbuilding and trade. In all, 23 towns along the shores of this Bay built "Down-Easters," square-rigged cargo ships which carried Maine's products to all the world's ports. Lumber was shipped from Bangor, lime from the kilns of Rockland and Rockport and granite from the quarries in Stonington and Vinalhaven. Blocks of ice insulated with sawdust were shipped to the Caribbean, India and China in specially adapted vessels. On return voyages, these ships brought back sugar, rum, rice and all manner of products from ports as far away as Australia, Chile and Peru. From the 1780's through the 1890's, there was a brisk trade in furniture, china, lacquer, ivory and other artifacts from the Far East. It was through this trade that so much of New England received the influence of Far Eastern culture.

Of all the more than 3,000 Down-Easter ships built in this area, one out of every ten was built in Searsport. More than 250 sea captains made their homes in Searsport. In the single year of 1889, Searsport had 77 deep-water captains. 33 of them commanded vessels that rounded Cape Horn.

Most of these fine homes remain today, serving as Bed & Breakfast establishments. So if your plans include a night ashore, this would certainly be the town in which to do it. Nowhere else will you find such a wide choice of distinguished dwellings.

Ordinarily, you tend to think of these captains braving the seas on long voyages while their wives and family remained at home anxiously waiting for their return. But some wives sailed with their husbands and many a birth at sea was recorded on the birth certificate by latitude and longitude only. One Searsport family had 35 members born at sea.

With such a vast and impressive maritime history, it is only fitting that Searsport be the home of the Penobscot Marine Museum (15). Housed in a complex of seven different buildings (that formed part of the original town) are exhibits, displays and photographs of this heritage of Maine, and particularly of the role that Searsport played in it. A special room is devoted to navigational charts used by Searsport captains. In the Educational Building, you can view a film made in 1929 about a sea voyage made around Cape Horn.

This film, produced by the Mystic Seaport Museum, contains the most exciting footage you will ever see of a massive square-rigger rounding Cape Horn. Filmed in 1929 and narrated by Capt. Irving Johnson, the voyage of the four-masted Bark "Peking" in its 11,000 mile voyage, has a compelling sense of immediacy. Her 32 sails provided over an acre of canvas to the wind. They drove the vessel through the worst storm of the century in the North Sea—a storm that caused the wreck of 68 ships along the coasts of Holland, Belgium and Germany. You get a chance to view this storm, as well as the rounding of the Horn, from the vantage point of the yard of the topsail as sail is taken in; a height equivalent to that of a 17 story building. Waves are so great as to completely wash over the ship.

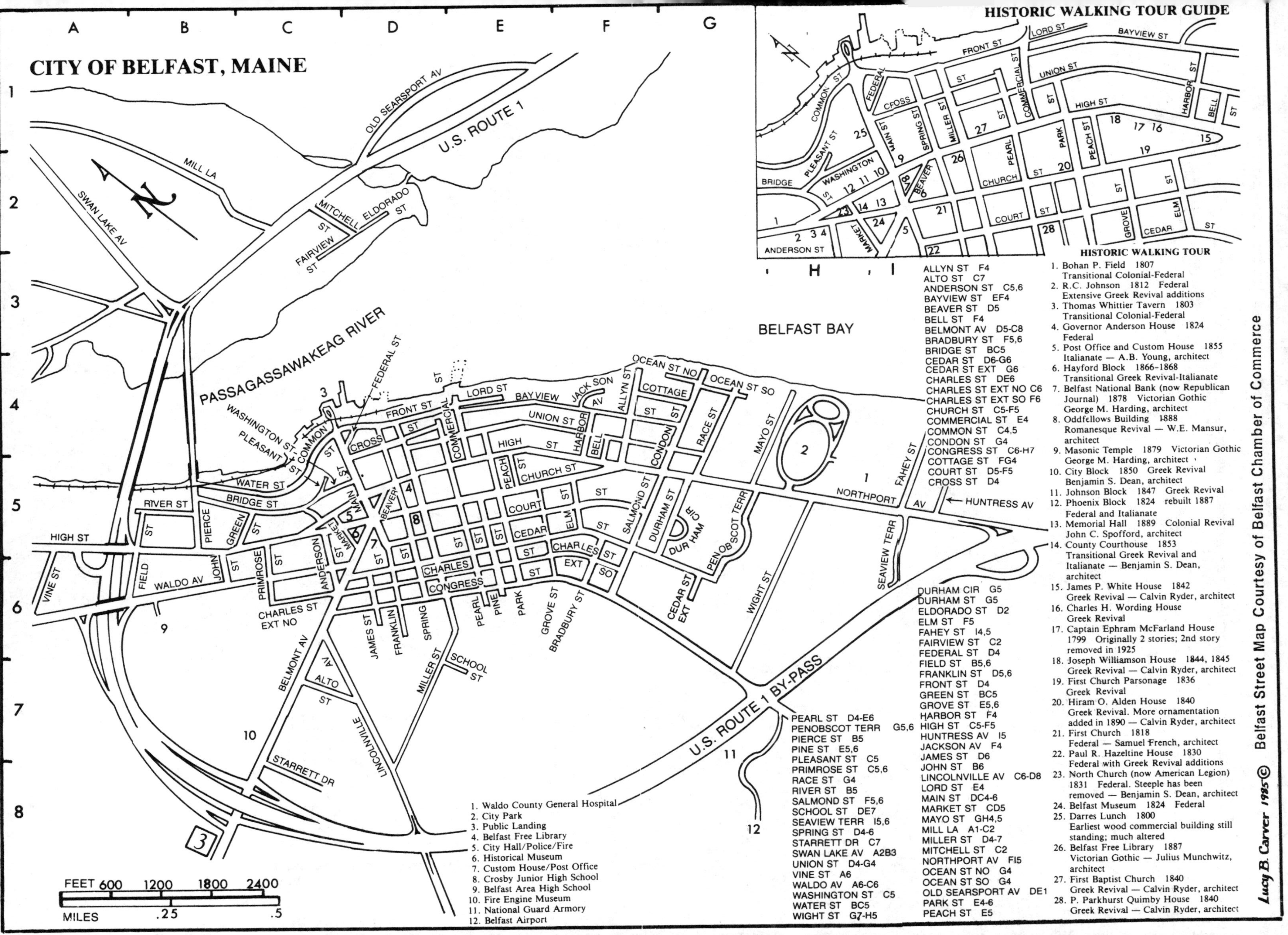
CITY OF BELFAST, MAINE
HISTORIC WALKING TOUR GUIDE
PASSAGASSAWAKEAG RIVER
BELFAST BAY
U.S. ROUTE 1
U.S. ROUTE 1 BY-PASS
1. Waldo County General Hospital
2. City Park
3. Public Landing
4. Belfast Free Library
5. City Hall/Police/Fire
6. Historical Museum
7. Custom House/Post Office
8. Crosby Junior High School
9. Belfast Area High School
10. Fire Engine Museum
11. National Guard Armory
12. Belfast Airport
FEET 600 1200 1800 2400
MILES .25 .5
PEARL ST D4-E6
PENOBSCOT TERR G5,6
PIERCE ST B5
PINE ST E5,6
PLEASANT ST C5
PRIMROSE ST C5,6
RACE ST G4
RIVER ST B5
SALMOND ST F5,6
SCHOOL ST DE7
SEAVIEW TERR I5,6
SPRING ST D4-6
STARRETT DR C7
SWAN LAKE AV A2B3
UNION ST D4-G4
VINE ST A6
WALDO AV A6-C6
WASHINGTON ST C5
WATER ST BC5
WIGHT ST G7-H5
ALLYN ST F4
ALTO ST C7
ANDERSON ST C5,6
BAYVIEW ST EF4
BEAVER ST D5
BELL ST F4
BELMONT AV D5-C8
BRADBURY ST F5,6
BRIDGE ST BC5
CEDAR ST D6-G6
CEDAR ST EXT G6
CHARLES ST DE6
CHARLES ST EXT NO C6
CHARLES ST EXT SO F6
CHURCH ST C5-F5
COMMERCIAL ST E4
COMMON ST C4,5
CONDON ST G4
CONGRESS ST C6-H7
COTTAGE ST FG4
COURT ST D5-F5
CROSS ST D4
DURHAM CIR G5
DURHAM ST G5
ELDORADO ST D2
ELM ST F5
FAHEY ST I4,5
FAIRVIEW ST C2
FEDERAL ST D4
FIELD ST B5,6
FRANKLIN ST D5,6
FRONT ST D4
GREEN ST BC5
GROVE ST E5,6
HARBOR ST F4
HIGH ST C5-F5
HUNTRESS AV I5
JACKSON AV F4
JAMES ST D6
JOHN ST B6
LINCOLNVILLE AV C6-D8
LORD ST E4
MAIN ST DC4-6
MARKET ST CD5
MAYO ST GH4,5
MILL LA A1-C2
MILLER ST D4-7
MITCHELL ST C2
NORTHPORT AV FI5
OCEAN ST NO G4
OCEAN ST SO G4
OLD SEARSPORT AV DE1
PARK ST E4-6
PEACH ST E5
HISTORIC WALKING TOUR
1. Bohan P. Field 1807
Transitional Colonial-Federal
2. R.C. Johnson 1812 Federal
Extensive Greek Revival additions
3. Thomas Whittier Tavern 1803
Transitional Colonial-Federal
4. Governor Anderson House 1824
Federal
5. Post Office and Custom House 1855
Italianate — A.B. Young, architect
6. Hayford Block 1866-1868
Transitional Greek Revival-Italianate
7. Belfast National Bank (now Republican Journal) 1878 Victorian Gothic
George M. Harding, architect
8. Oddfellows Building 1888
Romanesque Revival — W.E. Mansur, architect
9. Masonic Temple 1879 Victorian Gothic
George M. Harding, architect
10. City Block 1850 Greek Revival
Benjamin S. Dean, architect
11. Johnson Block 1847 Greek Revival
12. Phoenix Block 1824 rebuilt 1887
Federal and Italianate
13. Memorial Hall 1889 Colonial Revival
John C. Spofford, architect
14. County Courthouse 1853
Transitional Greek Revival and Italianate — Benjamin S. Dean, architect
15. James P. White House 1842
Greek Revival — Calvin Ryder, architect
16. Charles H. Wording House
Greek Revival
17. Captain Ephram McFarland House
1799 Originally 2 stories; 2nd story removed in 1925
18. Joseph Williamson House 1844, 1845
Greek Revival — Calvin Ryder, architect
19. First Church Parsonage 1836
Greek Revival
20. Hiram O. Alden House 1840
Greek Revival. More ornamentation added in 1890 — Calvin Ryder, architect
21. First Church 1818
Federal — Samuel French, architect
22. Paul R. Hazeltine House 1830
Federal with Greek Revival additions
23. North Church (now American Legion)
1831 Federal. Steeple has been removed — Benjamin S. Dean, architect
24. Belfast Museum 1824 Federal
25. Darres Lunch 1800
Earliest wood commercial building still standing; much altered
26. Belfast Free Library 1887
Victorian Gothic — Julius Munchwitz, architect
27. First Baptist Church 1840
Greek Revival — Calvin Ryder, architect
28. P. Parkhurst Quimby House 1840
Greek Revival — Calvin Ryder, architect
Lucy B. Carver 1985©
Belfast Street Map Courtesy of Belfast Chamber of Commerce

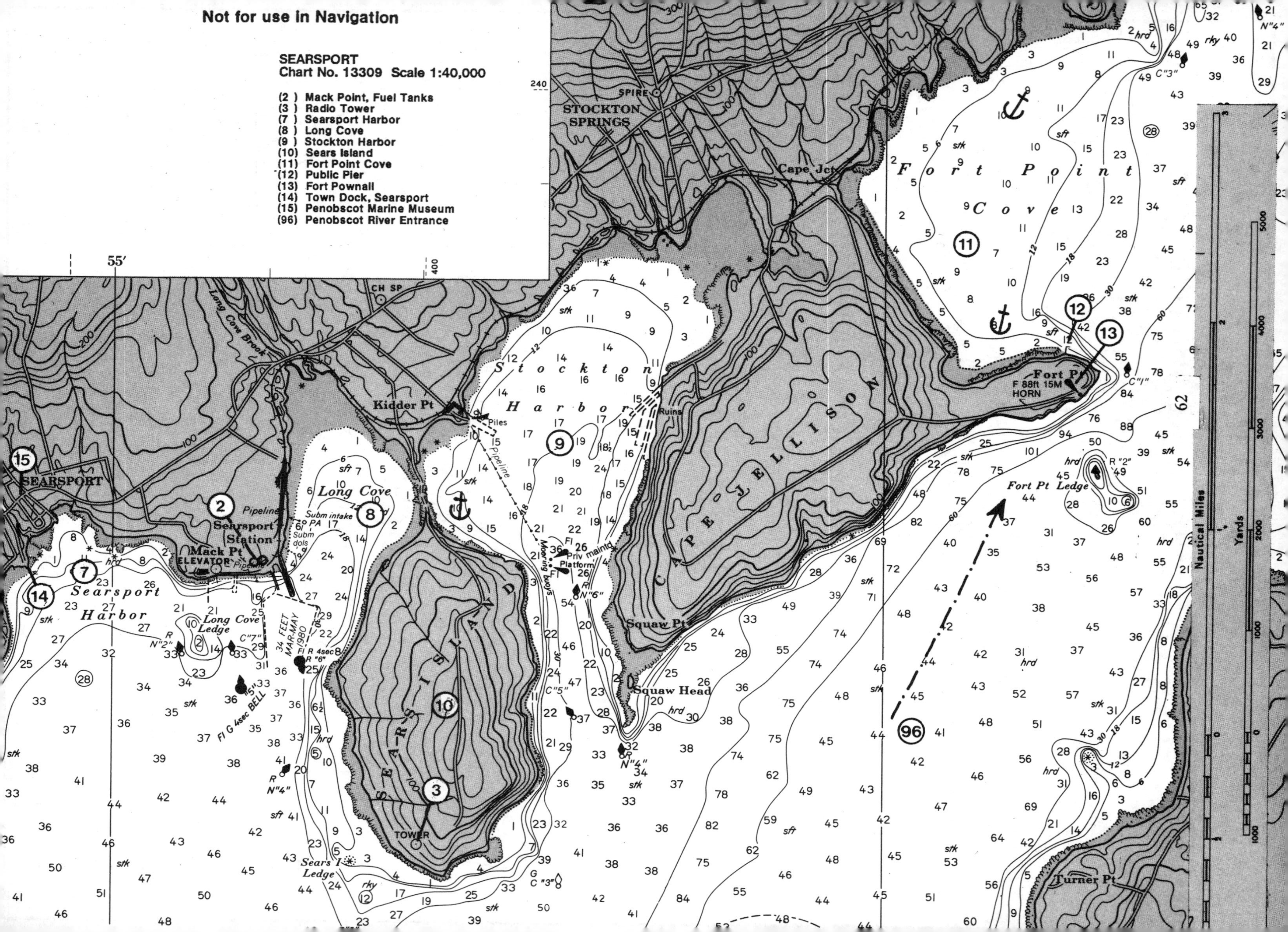

Not for use in Navigation
SEARSPORT
Chart No. 13309 Scale 1:40,000
(2) Mack Point, Fuel Tanks
(3) Radio Tower
(7) Searsport Harbor
(8) Long Cove
(9) Stockton Harbor
(10) Sears Island
(11) Fort Point Cove
(12) Public Pier
(13) Fort Pownall
(14) Town Dock, Searsport
(15) Penobscot Marine Museum
(96) Penobscot River Entrance
STOCKTON SPRINGS
SEARSPORT
Searsport Harbor
Long Cove
Stockton Harbor
SEARS ISLAND
CAPE JELLISON
Fort Point Cove
Kidder Pt
Mack Pt
Searsport Station
Squaw Pt
Squaw Head
Fort Pt
Fort Pt Ledge
Turner Pt
Sears I Ledge
Long Cove Ledge
Cape Jct
Nautical Miles
Yards

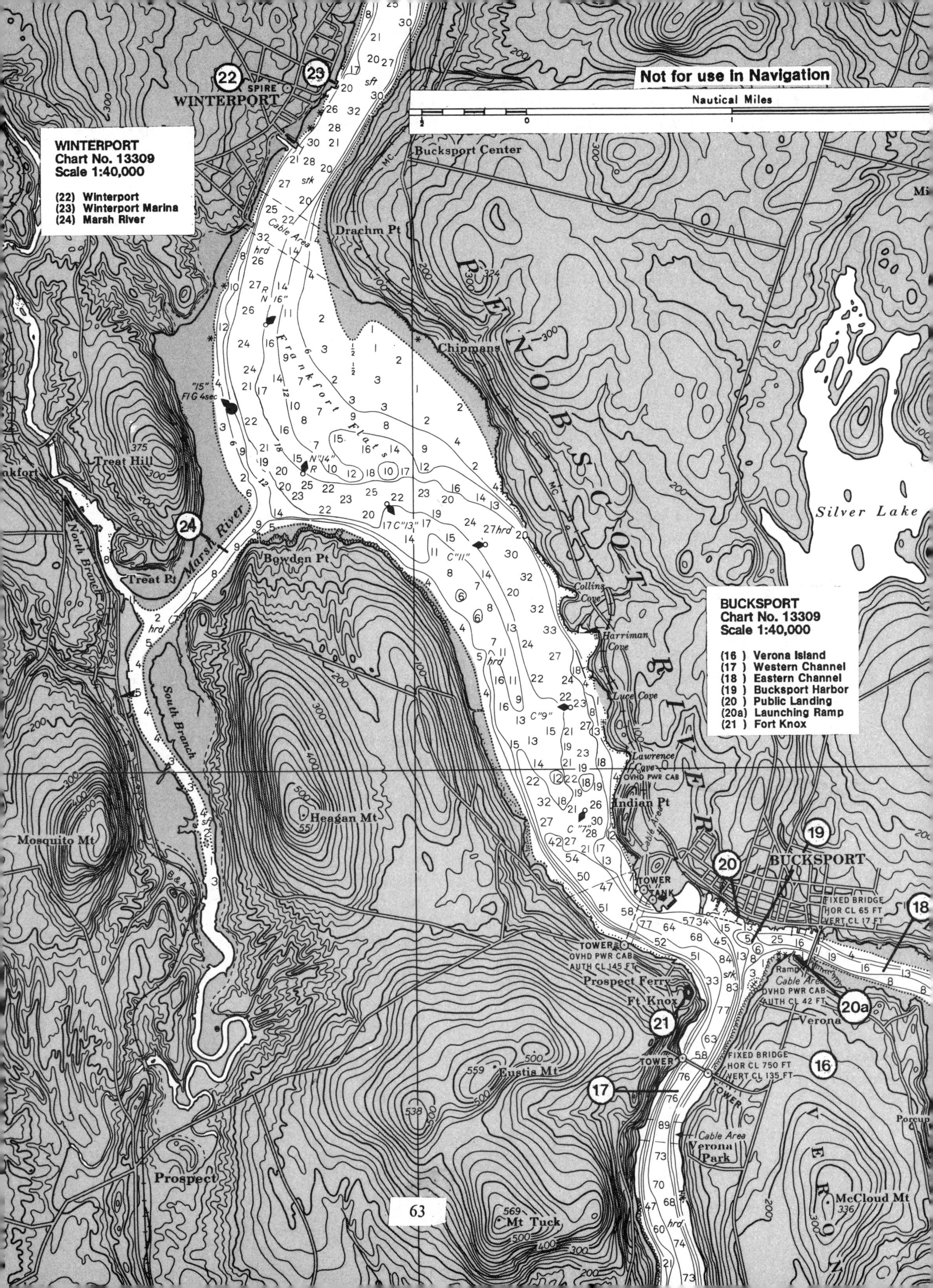
Not for use in Navigation
Nautical Miles
WINTERPORT
Chart No. 13309
Scale 1:40,000
(22) Winterport
(23) Winterport Marina
(24) Marsh River
BUCKSPORT
Chart No. 13309
Scale 1:40,000
(16 ) Verona Island
(17 ) Western Channel
(18 ) Eastern Channel
(19 ) Bucksport Harbor
(20 ) Public Landing
(20a) Launching Ramp
(21 ) Fort Knox
WINTERPORT
SPIRE
Bucksport Center
Drachm Pt
Cable Area
Frankfort Flats
Chipmans
PENOBSCOT RIVER
Silver Lake
Treat Hill
Treat Pt
Marsh River
North Branch
Bowden Pt
Collins Cove
Harriman Cove
Luce Cove
Lawrence Cove
OVHD PWR CAB
Indian Pt
South Branch
Heagan Mt
Mosquito Mt
BUCKSPORT
TOWER
TANK
FIXED BRIDGE
HOR CL 65 FT
VERT CL 17 FT
TOWER
OVHD PWR CAB
AUTH CL 145 FT
Prospect Ferry
Ft Knox
Ramp
Cable Area
OVHD PWR CAB
AUTH CL 42 FT
Verona
FIXED BRIDGE
HOR CL 750 FT
VERT CL 135 FT
Eustis Mt
Cable Area
Verona Park
Prospect
Mt Tuck
McCloud Mt

The "Peking" is still afloat, and is now at the South Street Seaport Museum in New York City. ***Editor's Note:*** *You can go aboard her at South Street and see this exciting film. Irve Johnson was a young man at the time Peking rounded the Horn in 1929. South Street is a great floating museum, and the adjacent area has developed into one of New York's greatest tourist attractions.* Captain Johnson presently resides in the town of his birth, Hadley, Massachusetts.

The Penobscot Marine Museum's library contains an extensive collection of 19th century documents, as well as rare books, journals and photographs. Children, as well as adults, will find their attention captivated for many hours at this museum, open 9:30 a.m.-5:00 p.m. daily, 1:00p.m.-5:00p.m. on Sunday. There is a small admission fee.

Searsport bills itself as the "antique capital of Maine." Many coastal Maine towns have antique shops, but Searsport does have quite a concentration.

## BUCKSPORT—CHART NO. 13309

About 2.2 miles north of the Port Point Light, the Penobscot River is divided by Verona Island (16) into a Western Channel (17) and an Eastern Channel (18). Bucksport (19) is north of Verona Island where the two channels rejoin. Proceed upstream with the tidal current in your favor, using the Western Channel. U.S. Highway 1 crosses both channels by bridge, but there is only 17 ft. clearance under the Eastern Channel bridge. The bridge over the Western Channel has a vertical clearance of 135 feet.

A public landing float (20) with 10 feet depth alongside is next to a large petroleum handling berth. There is 40 ft. of dock space and 6 moorings at this Bucksport Municipal Dock. You can't miss finding the dock, for the nearby fleet of moored boats is directly in front as you approach from downriver. Markets and marine supplies are nearby. There's a free concrete launching ramp (20a) at the north end of Verona Island, just west of the Route 1 bridge.

Of the many famous ships built on the Maine coast, one of the most notable, the "Roosevelt," was built here on Verona Island. Upon its completion, the "Roosevelt" sailed under Admiral Perry with his expedition to the North Pole in 1909.

Fort Knox (21), directly across the river, impressively commands the entire harbor. It is named after Major General Henry Knox, America's first Secretary of War and General George Washington's Commander of Artillery in the American Revolution. The famed Fort Knox in Kentucky is also named after him.

Granite for its construction was quarried at nearby Frankfort, Maine and brought downriver by barge. It took over a million dollars and 20 years of building (from 1845-1865) to create this fort, designed to protect the Penobscot Valley from naval attack by the British. Built to mount 137 guns, it is one of America's largest and most impressive forts, with its awesome dimensions of 350 x 250 feet and granite walls 20 feet high and 40 feet thick.

Guided tours are available and the fort is open daily from May 1 to Nov. 1. Within the center of the fort, you can see the parade ground, officer's quarters, barracks, and stables. There are many fascinating details to explore, such as the granite spiral staircases, moats, and cannon casements.

Unfortunately, the total scene from the harbor is somewhat marred by the surrounding paper mills, industrial buildings and oil docks.

## WINTERPORT—CHART NO. 13309

Continuing another 4.5 miles upriver from Bucksport, you arrive at Winterport (22). No longer the major seasport that it once was, Winterport still is an attractive town and has good facilities for yachtsmen.

Winterport Marina (23) has dockage with 15 feet depth alongside, berths with electricity and water, guest moorings. diesel fuel, gasoline, ice and complete engine and hull repairs. Being only 11.9 miles from Bangor (Maine's third largest city), Winterport is a convenient crew change port. Bar Harbor Airlines and other major carriers service the Bangor Airport. Restaurants, provisioning and all other necessities are nearby in town.

Few yachtsmen penetrate as far as this into the interior, thus missing this pastoral countryside, much of which has remained relatively unchanged. Particularly pleasing to the eye is the whole area of Marsh River (24), both its North and South Branches. Marsh River invites dinghy exploration.

## CASTINE HARBOR—CHART NO. 13309

Castine has unrivalled appeal, with its fine, natural harbor, surroundings of picturesque beauty and rich historical background. Situated on a bold peninsula, it's bounded on the west by the Penobscot River and on the east by the Bagaduce River. Here you can enjoy amenities ashore or find anchorage surrounded by a wild, natural landscape with complete seclusion. The high, knobby hills and labryinthine waterways give the area the feel of a bit of Scotland.

### Approaches

Approaches to Castine Harbor are easy, for the coast is high and clear of outlying dangers. Dice Head (19) and Blockhouse Point (20) are prominent and easily discernible from most of the northern portion of Penobscot Bay. The fairway buoy "CH" (21) at the mouth of the Bagaduce River, has a bell, helpful in fog. At night the light tower (22) (Fl 6 sec.) at Dice Head will guide you in. This is a skeletal tower, 27 feet high with a red and white diamond-shaped daymark. The abandoned lighthouse tower, higher up the hill, is now all but lost in the trees.

A considerable volume of water enters and leaves through the Bagaduce River and basins. When forced through the narrow channels, it attains a velocity of 3-4 knots on both the ebb and flood tide. Tidal current is strongest in the section near the Maine Maritime Acad-

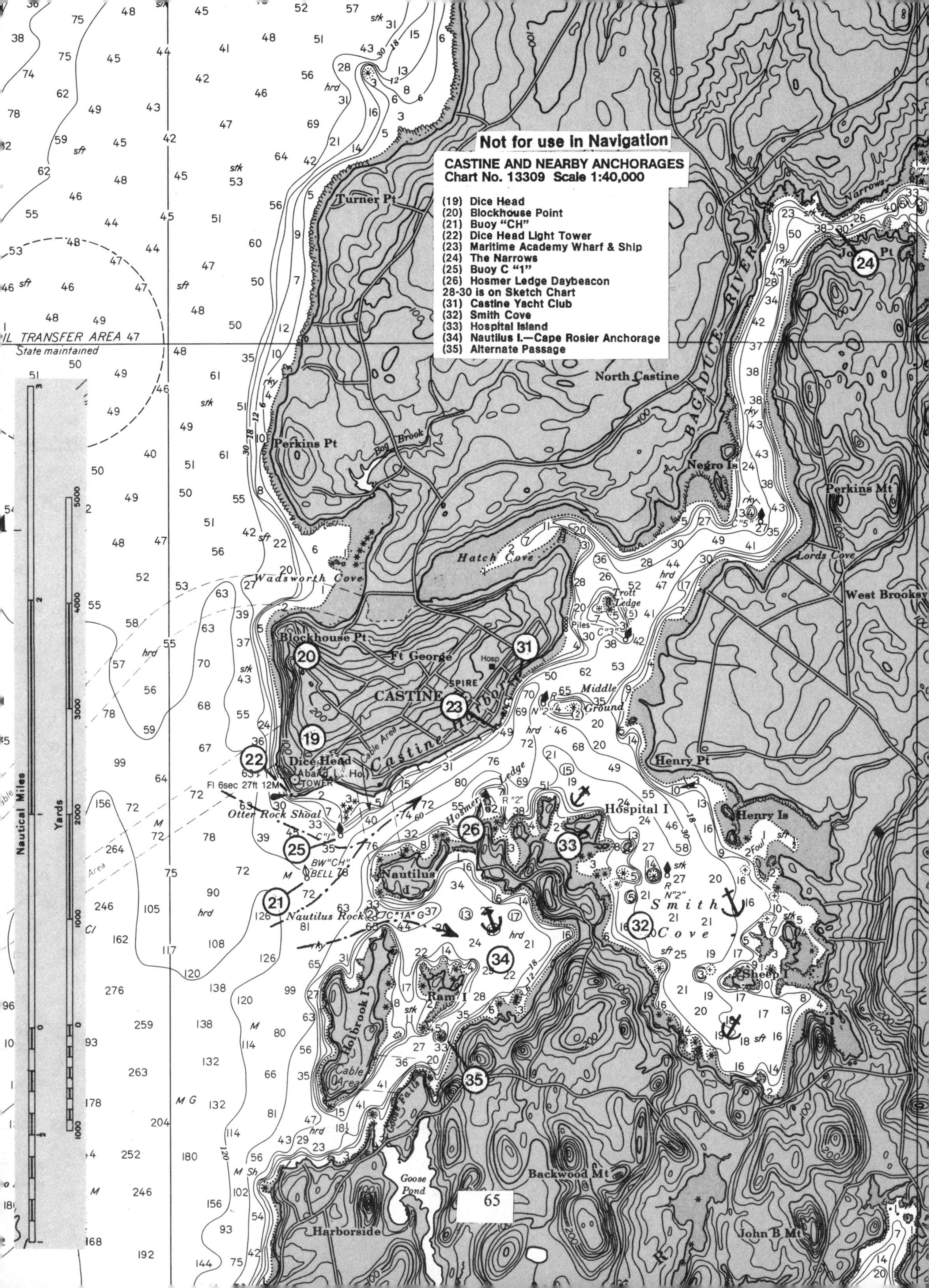

Not for use in Navigation
CASTINE AND NEARBY ANCHORAGES
Chart No. 13309 Scale 1:40,000
(19) Dice Head
(20) Blockhouse Point
(21) Buoy "CH"
(22) Dice Head Light Tower
(23) Maritime Academy Wharf & Ship
(24) The Narrows
(25) Buoy C "1"
(26) Hosmer Ledge Daybeacon
28-30 is on Sketch Chart
(31) Castine Yacht Club
(32) Smith Cove
(33) Hospital Island
(34) Nautilus I.—Cape Rosier Anchorage
(35) Alternate Passage
Turner Pt
Perkins Pt
Bog Brook
North Castine
BAGADUCE RIVER
Negro Is
Perkins Mt
Hatch Cove
Lords Cove
West Brooksv
Wadsworth Cove
Trott Ledge
Blockhouse Pt
Ft George
CASTINE
Castine Harbor
Middle Ground
Dice Head
Otter Rock Shoal
Hosmer Ledge
Hospital I
Henry Pt
Henry Is
Nautilus I
Nautilus Rock
Smith Cove
Sheep I
Ram I
Holbrook I
Cable Area
Goose Falls
Goose Pond
Backwood Mt
Harborside
John B Mt
Nautical Miles
Yards
State maintained

emy training ship (23) and upstream at The Narrows (24), where velocity is as much as 5 knots. At strength of ebb tide, when there's a strong southwest wind, a short steep chop is created, particularly near the mouth of the harbor. By hugging either shore closely, you can avoid the maximum strength of current. Do not let the above description of currents keep you away from one of the loveliest parts of Penobscot Bay. The velocities given are at their maximum; under most conditions they will give you no trouble.

A group of rocks extend south from Dice Head and are marked by buoy C "1" (25). It is a small can buoy, and when approached from the northwest appears to be way over toward the southeastern shore. When approaching from this direction, be sure to give Dice Head sufficient clearance to stay south of that green can. The only other danger is Hosmer Ledge on the south side of the channel, marked by a red daybeacon (26).

### Marine Facilities

As you near Castine, you will be struck by the incongruous and overwhelming appearance of a merchant ship tied to a pier (23). This ship is the "State of Maine" and is used as a training vessel by the Maine Maritime Academy in Castine. Public tours are conducted aboard this vessel every half hour.

East of the Academy training ship is the Town Dock (28), recognizable by the small pavalion in its center. Tie-up is allowed here for a limited time at the two floats with 12 feet depth alongside. Farther east is a private pier, followed by Dennett's Wharf (29), having 6 slips, showers, a cocktail lounge and a restaurant featuring seafood. Included among the more usual offerings are oysters, sea urchins and periwinkles.

Farther east is the wharf and floats of Eaton's Boatyard (30), 4 slips, 2 guest moorings, gasoline, diesel fuel, water, ice, marine supplies and a 20-ton marine railway capable of handling boats up to 45 feet long for hull or engine repairs. The harbormaster, K. Eaton, is usually at this dock. They monitor VHF Channels 9 and 16, and usually have lobsters for sale. There's 8 ft. depth at mean low water at their floats.

The easternmost major pier of the group is the Castine Yacht Club (31), 16 feet depth along the front face of the float. Dinghys may be tied at the inside corner of the dock. The club maintains three guest moorings with a 24-hour time limit, identified by red circles painted on top of the pink ball floats. Shower and toilet facilities in the clubhouse are open from 8:00 a.m. to 8:00 p.m. The club allows visiting boatmen to use their kitchen facilities.

### Nearby Anchorages

In Castine Harbor, anchoring in the channel is not recommended due to very deep water and strong currents. There is anchorage nearby in Smith Cove (32) in excellent holding ground, and plenty of room for everyone. There's good protection from all winds.

Anchorage east of Hospital Island (33), is good, but is apt to be crowded with the large number of moored craft.

Another cove (34) providing excellent anchorage is bounded by Holbrook Island, Nautilus Island and Cape Rosier. Entry is north of Holbrook Island, staying south of C "1A". An alternate entry (35) to this harbor is from the south, between Ram Island and Cape Rosier, but it is difficult and recommended only with local knowledge. There is one mooring here, marked by a lobster buoy, privately maintained and available for use by visiting yachtsmen.

The scenery certainly is beautiful, but tempting as it might be, it is recommended that exploration of the Bagaduce River be limited to that portion **below** The Narrows. Currents are swift, and contrary to what is shown on the chart, there are no navigation buoys beyond that of The Narrows, to indicate the channel, and the complex ledges and rock outcroppings. Best to take as your cue the absence of even any lobster boats up there.

### History

Throughout its history, Castine has been held by five nations: Indian, England, France, Holland and American. During these shifts in allegiance, Penobscot Bay served as neutral territory between the two main protagonists, England and France. The outer defensible limit of the British territory was Fort Pemaquid, on the western shore of Penobscot Bay. Castine, on the eastern shore, was the beginning of French Acadia, a territory which stretched to the St. Croix River far to the east.

Castine occupied a key position on the border between these two territories and through eminent domain, proclamation, battle and treaty, ownership changed hands 33 times!

The first recorded description of Castine was by Samuel de Champlain during his explorations in 1604. He sailed up the Penobscot River, and according to his narrative, found it "pleasant and agreeable." When Captain John Smith explored the Penobscot ten years later, he did not have such praise for the area. He described the coast as "nothing but such high Craggy Cliffy Rocks and Stony Isles that I wondered such trees could growe upon so hard foundations. It is a Countrie rather to affright than delight one."

By 1629, a trading-post was established by Issac Allerton under the auspices of the Plimoth (sic) Plantation. However, the first agent at this post, Edward Ashley, was sent back to England to be imprisoned, for Governor William Bradford would not countenance his trading of powder and shot with the Indians.

The name Castine came from Jean Vincent de l'Abadie, Baron de Saint-Castine, an officer in the French army. When his regiment was disbanded, he was given a grant of land as an inducement to stay in the colony. Arriving in 1667, he enlarged the fort built earlier by the French traders and married an Indian princess. The trading-post did not prosper and eventu-

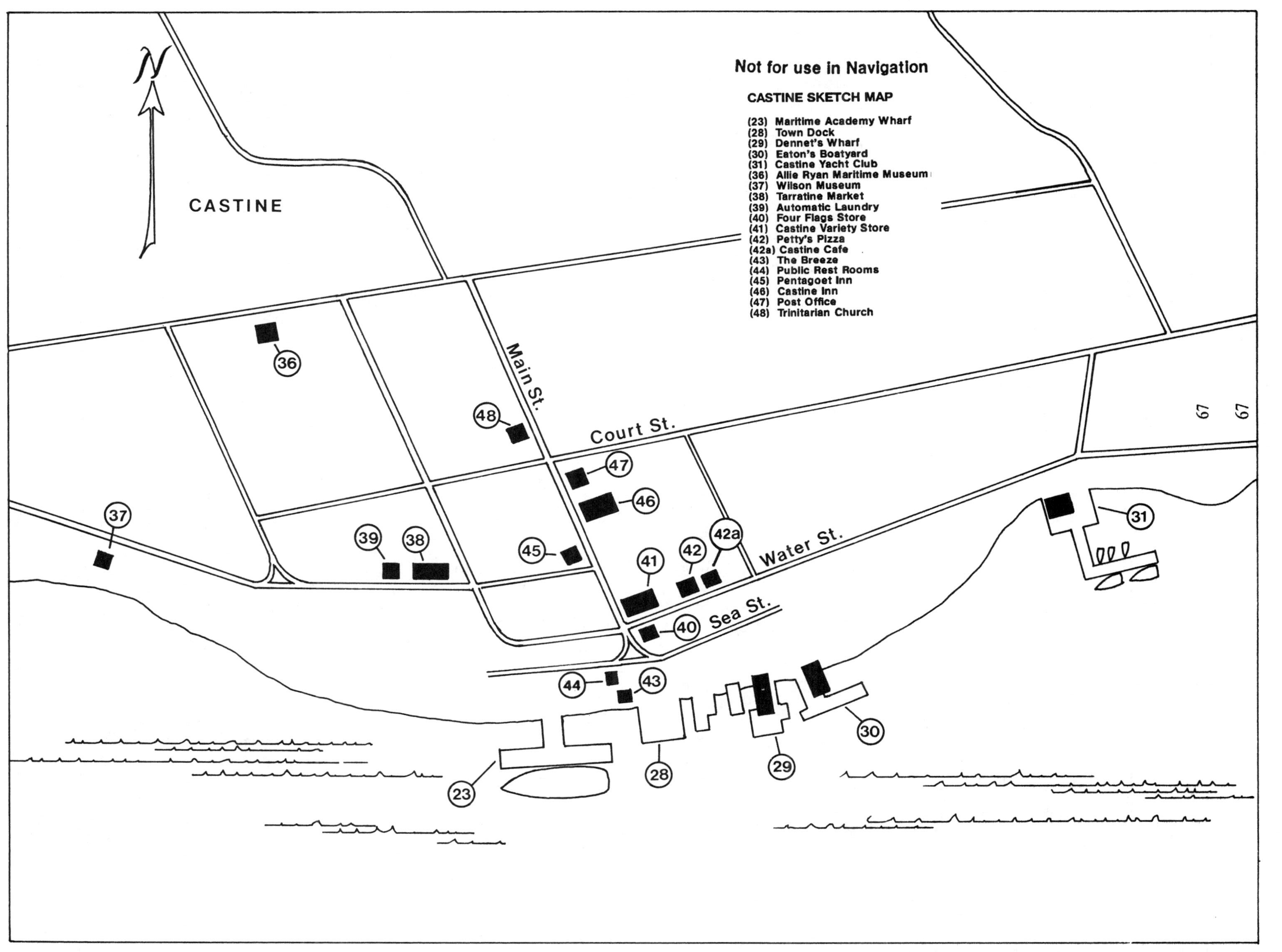
Not for use in Navigation
CASTINE SKETCH MAP
(23) Maritime Academy Wharf
(28) Town Dock
(29) Dennet's Wharf
(30) Eaton's Boatyard
(31) Castine Yacht Club
(36) Allie Ryan Maritime Museum
(37) Wilson Museum
(38) Tarratine Market
(39) Automatic Laundry
(40) Four Flags Store
(41) Castine Variety Store
(42) Petty's Pizza
(42a) Castine Cafe
(43) The Breeze
(44) Public Rest Rooms
(45) Pentagoet Inn
(46) Castine Inn
(47) Post Office
(48) Trinitarian Church
CASTINE
N
Main St.
Court St.
Water St.
Sea St.
36
48
47
46
37
39
38
45
42a
42
41
40
44
43
31
30
29
28
23


67

ally he returned to France.

During the American Revolution, the area saw an influx of Tory refugees, mostly from Boston and Portland, Maine. The sentiment was not sympathetic toward the revolutionary cause and the Tory settlers felt that this peninsula would remain British. After the Treaty of Paris (1783), when Castine again reverted to French dominion, the Loyalist population was forced to move once more.

This time, the more than 40 families, with all their personal belongings and livestock, moved to a new site on Passamaquoddy Bay. They chose a spot at the mouth of the St. Croix River, where they founded the town of St. Andrews, New Brunswick. Some Loyalists even dismantled their houses and floated them on barges up the Bay of Fundy to their new home, where they were reassembled. Some of these, such as the Robert Pagan house, still survive, as do others originally built in the new town. St. Andrews became a seaport and ship-building center and developed a brisk trade in lumber and fish. Thus, the histories of Castine, Maine and St. Andrews, New Brunswick are inextricably linked.

The role of the Dutch in Penobscot Bay was brief, but interesting. Holland's claim here came from Captain Henry Hudson's voyage in 1609 on the ship "Half Moon." Although an English navigator, at that time he was under the service of the Dutch East India Company. He also explored Chesapeake Bay, Delaware Bay, and the Hudson River. We know that the "Half Moon" put into Penobscot Bay to get a new mast before her return voyage to Holland.

The various discoveries made were not for the purpose of colonization, for indeed, Holland had a little surplus population to effect this. Nor was it to provide a haven for religious minorities, as Holland was known for its tolerance in this. The Pilgrims first went from southeast England to Leyden, Holland before deciding to move to America. In Governor William Bradford's original manuscript on the *The History of the Plimoth Plantation*, he says, "it is true, the affections and love of their brethren at Leyden was cordial and entire towards them." The voyages had entirely an economic aim, the search for the northwest passage and a sea route to Asia for the purpose of trade and commercial power.

Whatever small influence the Dutch had in this region was reduced by the Declaration of Breda in 1667. In the war of England against Holland and France, land was given to France through the Declaration, through specific boundaries were not given. In 1676, a Dutch man-of-war captured the French fort at Castine, Fort Penagoet, and held it for a few days, until it was again retaken by the French.

According to some accounts, the attempt of the American forces, under Naval Commander Dudley Saltonstall and Lieutenant Colonel Paul Revere (in charge of ordinance) to roust the British was a campaign fought with bravery and gallantry and lost only by the vagaries of fate. The prevailing account now held is that it was an unmitigated disaster due to cowardice and insubordination.

The British, under Colonel Francis McLean, occupied the peninsula in 1779 to provide support and protection to the Loyalists living there, and as a base for attacks against American privateers. The strategic position of Castine, at the mouth of the Penobscot River, guaranteed access to the vast timber resources inland needed for the King's ships and masts. When Commodore Saltonstall's ships, 18 armed vessels and 24 transports arrived to fight the British, he did nothing but procrastinate, while trying to decide a course of action. Nothing was done for three weeks, until they saw British reinforcements arrive in a squadron of five ships, whereupon the American forces fled up the Penobscot River without firing a shot and destroyed their own ships to prevent capture. As a result, Commodore Saltonstall was court-martialed and dismissed from the Navy and Paul Revere ended his military career in disgrace.

### Sightseeing

Every street and dwelling in this town speaks of its fascinating and complex history. Along all the streets and at various buildings, signs describe the events that have taken place there. A walking tour of the town is a most enjoyable way to take this all in. Guide maps, available in most stores, are provided by the Castine Historical Society. Of all the 16 fortifications built since 1635, five remain in good condition and are open to the public.

There are two museums in Castine, The Allie Ryan Maritime Collection (36) at the Maine Maritime Academy and the Wilson Museum (37). The Allie Ryan Maritime Collection exhibits prints and paintings relating to the period of steamships which plied the New England Coast and Rivers. It is open Tuesday-Saturday from 9:00 a.m.-12:00 noon, and 1:00 p.m.-4:00 p.m. The Wilson Museum has displays of anthropological and geological specimens from North and South America, as well as the Pacific and Africa. Museum hours are Tuesday-Sunday from 2:00 p.m.-5:00 p.m.

### Supplies

On shore, all the services you may require are available, most within one block of the Town Dock. Tarratine Market (38), on the corner of Main St. and Water St,. has complete provisioning including liquor, open 7:00 a.m.-10:00 p.m. Monday-Saturday and 9:00 a.m.-10:00 p.m. on Sunday. Adjacent west is an automatic laundry (39). Four Flags gift shop (40) stocks nautical charts and has a small selection of marine supplies. Across the street is the Castine Variety Store (41). East of it is Petty's Pizza (42). Next to Petty's Pizza is the Castine Cafe (42a). Behind the Town Dock (28) is a snack bar called "The Breeze," (43), where fried clams, hamburgers, ice cream, etc. is available. The brick building north to it houses the public rest rooms (44). Lafferty's, near the Town Dock (28) is a cocktail lounge and restaurant. Several inns in town serve meals in a more formal setting. The Pentagoet Inn (45) and the Castine Inn (46) usually require reservations. The Post Office (47) is a short distance up Main Street.

There is more to see in Castine than historical monuments, museums, forts and buildings of superb and diverse architectural style. Various forms of entertainment are also available. The Castine Chamber Music Series gives frequent summer performances in the historic Trinitarian Church (48) on Main St. For information call 326-9203 or 326-9008. Castine's resident theater is called Cold Comfort Productions, Inc., tel. 326-9041.

# CHAPTER 7

# NORTH HAVEN ISLAND, VINALHAVEN ISLAND DEER ISLE AND ISLE au HAUT

## NORTH HAVEN ISLAND
## CHART NOS. 13302, 13305, 13309

### History

In June, 1603, Martin Pring landed at Monhegan Island. He then proceeded to make a survey of the coast and of the larger rivers. His two ships, "The Speedwell" and "The Discover," entered Penobscot Bay loaded with goods to trade with the Indians for furs and sassafras. On one of the large islands, a number of silver-grey foxes were observed, thus leading to naming North Haven and Vinalhaven Islands and the smaller surrounding islands "Fox Islands." The Indians inhabiting the islands kept them from settlement by others for the next 150 years. The name Fox Islands remained during the 1700's until in 1789 they were incorporated under the name of Vinalhaven.

North Haven became independent from Vinalhaven in 1846. The early economic basis of support for the island was farming and fishing. It never developed the granite quarry business that dominated in Vinalhaven. Like Islesboro Island, from the late 1800's onward, North Haven Island became a private summer retreat for the wealthy and the famous. Many socially prominent families have their estates here. It is also similar to Islesboro Island in that tourism plays a minor role in the activity of the island, even though there's easy and frequent ferry service from Rockland. Unlike Islesboro though, North Haven does have a central community, the village of North Haven on the north shore of Fox Islands Thorofare.

### Oak Island Passage—Chart No. 13305

Oak Island Passage, north of North Haven Island, is frequently used going from West Penobscot Bay to East Penobscot Bay. Generally, the Passage is between Oak (74) and Burnt (75) Islands, then between Bald (76) and Sheep Islands (77). This is the route delineated by our course line on the excerpt from chart no. 13305. However, the route may be varied considerably, for there is deep water around all the islands. Although there are no buoys, the scattered ledges all show, even at high water. The following descriptions will help you identify various islands.

Oak Island (74) is fairly low and mostly grass covered with some widely scattered trees on it. Burnt Island (75) is higher and entirely tree covered except for the little nubbin of grassy land on the northwestern end. All the ledges north of Oak Island show clearly. Bald Island (76) has an equal distribution of grass and trees, whereas Sheep Island (77) is larger and heavily forested. Dagger Ledge (78) is a long and thin ledge, showing clearly at high tide. When approached from southwest, Spoon Ledge (79), does indeed look like an inverted spoon with a bowl and long handle. Dagger Island (80) is entirely grass covered, with the exception of a solitary large tree on it.

Sheep Island (77) is owned by the Nature Conservancy. Visitors are allowed on its 25 acres. There's a small gravel beach at the west end of Sheep Island, the only place to land a dinghy on this rugged shoreline. The shoreline features unusual formations of North Haven greenstone, moved around and weathered by

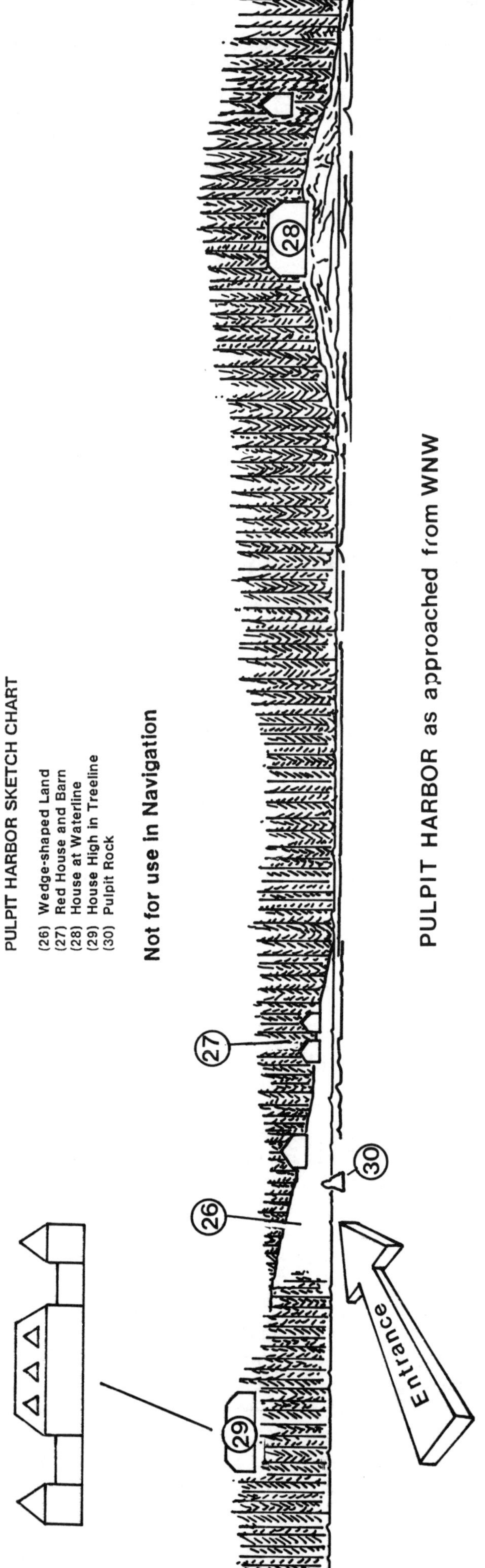


hundreds of years of easterlies. Don't try to land in easterly seas, but on good days it's easy enough. There are no trails, but you can hike around the shore. The interior can be rough going because of raspberry bushes.

At strength of ebb tide the currents in this passage are erratic in direction, with considerable swirls and eddies. They are not violent and normally are little problem but in fog, try to gage the set to correct your course.

On the east end of North Haven Island there are several coves which provide good anchorage in settled weather. The degree of protection from northerly winds varies depending on the cove selected. They are all extremely attractive, though there are no facilities on shore at any of them. These are: Marsh Cove; the cove north of Mullen head; Mullen Cove; the anchorage between Calderwood Island and Stimpsons Island; and the anchorage between Calderwood Island and Babbidge Island. These are all shown by anchor symbols on our Oak Island Passage chart excerpted from chart no. 13305.

## Pulpit Harbor—Chart No. 13308, Sketch Chart

Pulpit Harbor on the north shore of North Haven Island is one of the most popular in Penobscot Bay. It offers scenic surroundings, good holding bottom, excellent protection from any wind direction, and is large enough that despite its popularity it never feels crowded. There is always room for one more.

**Entry.** Finding the entrance is difficult, that is, until you know what you are looking for. No matter what direction you approach it from, the overlapping land masses obscure any hint of a harbor behind.

If your approach is from Camden, across the Bay, you may use any of the passages described in chapter 6 under "Passages South of Islesboro Island." From the south end of Mark Island, the course toward the entrance is 114 degrees magnetic. The primary visual landmark that you will be aiming for is a long, low, spear-shaped wedge (26) that is a pale yellow-green color. It shows up clearly at the waters' edge against the dark green of the spruce trees behind it. The tip of the wedge points toward the south. This slope is a combination of lawn and fields mown for hay. Referring to our sektch chart of the profile for this approach, the features described correspond in numbering with those same features indicated on our except from chart no. 13308, Pulpit Harbor. As you come closer, you will see at the tip of the slope, a red house and barn (27). Southwest of the harbor entrance is a large white house (28), which sits quite close to the waterline. Northeast of the entrance is another large house (29), high in the tree line. Closer to the entrance, you will finally see Pulpit Rock (30). This jagged tooth of granite sticks vertically straight out of the water. Give Pulpit Rock a berth of 100 yards and enter, keeping in mid-channel, north and east of the rock on a southerly course.

If you are approaching Pulpit Harbor from the northeast, the large house (29) high in the treeline is an

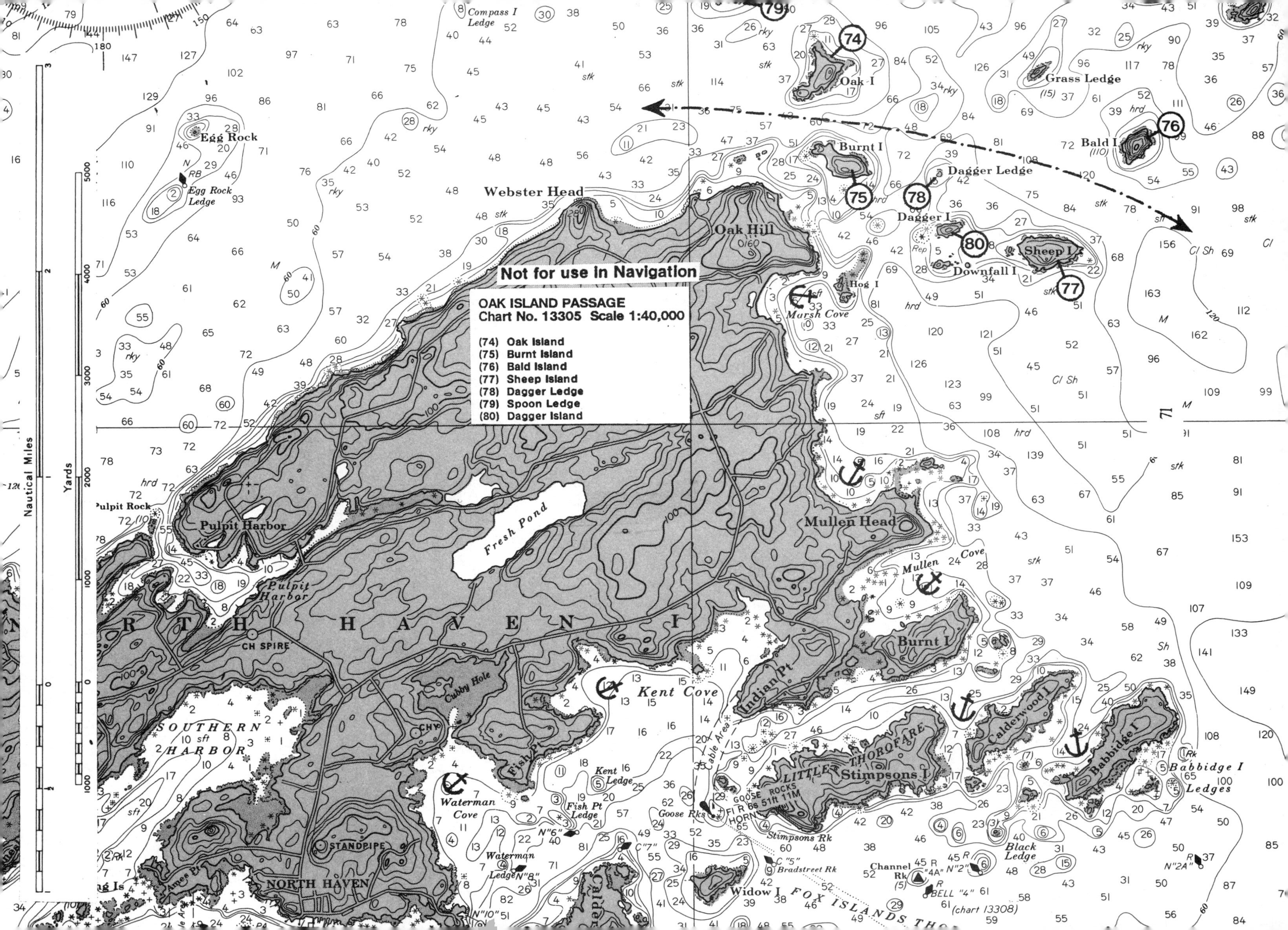
Not for use in Navigation
OAK ISLAND PASSAGE
Chart No. 13305 Scale 1:40,000
(74) Oak Island
(75) Burnt Island
(76) Bald Island
(77) Sheep Island
(78) Dagger Ledge
(79) Spoon Ledge
(80) Dagger Island
Nautical Miles
Yards
Compass I Ledge
Egg Rock
Egg Rock Ledge
Webster Head
Oak Hill
Oak I
Burnt I
Grass Ledge
Bald I
Dagger Ledge
Dagger I
Downfall I
Sheep I
Hog I
Marsh Cove
Pulpit Rock
Pulpit Harbor
Fresh Pond
Mullen Head
Mullen Cove
CH SPIRE
Cubby Hole
Kent Cove
Indian Pt
Burnt I
SOUTHERN HARBOR
Waterman Cove
Fish Pt
Kent Ledge
Fish Pt Ledge
Waterman Ledge
Goose Rks
GOOSE ROCKS
LITTLE THOROFARE
Stimpsons I
Calderwood I
Babbidge I
Babbidge I Ledges
Stimpsons Rk
Bradstreet Rk
Channel Rk
Black Ledge
STANDPIPE
Ames Pt
NORTH HAVEN
Cable Area
Widow I
FOX ISLANDS
(chart 13308)

indication that you're nearing the harbor entrance. Identification is unmistakable. The main central part of this house has three dormer windows, and there is a breezeway at each end with connecting wings set at right angles to the main house. From here, being less than ½ mile away, you need only follow the shoreline around to the entrance. By this time you will probably see the masts of several boats moored in the southwest prong of the harbor.

**Anchorages.** Several coves and indentations invite you to anchor. The very first one is in the southwest prong (31) where there is usually a small group of moored boats. You may anchor almost anywhere within the harbor. The only place to avoid is the first small cove (32) on the northeast side, where the chart shows a road crossing. It is filled with patches of ledge and rock. The south cove (33) is fine, but don't get too far up the cove for not only does it shallow, but some kelp there makes it difficult to properly set your anchor.

The town landing (34) is at the head of the southeastern cove. Although the *Coast Pilot* says three feet depth at this dock, when I was there I sounded depths in excess of 5 feet along the full length of the float at dead low water. Fuel is not available, but there is a water hose to fill your tanks, a public telephone, and a large map of the island giving distances from the dock in walking time. The village of North Haven is about 2 miles southwest.

For those who enjoy foraging, an excellent bed of large mussels (35) shows itself at low tide between the town landing and the bridge at the head of the cove. If you prefer elegant dining, Pulpit Harbor Inn (36), is a 20 minute walk from the town landing. It is a recently renovated, classic 19th century farmhouse with 5 rooms of accommodations. Their restaurant is open to the public for lunch and dinner, excellently prepared using vegetables grown in their own garden. Call ahead for dinner reservations. Visitors from cruising boats, can rent bicycles, and use their showers and laundry.

### Bartlett Harbor—Chart No. 13308

Bartlett Harbor, two miles south of Pulpit Harbor is seldom frequented. However, it is a pleasant harbor, easy to enter and has good holding ground. It provides greater protection from weather from the southwest than might be supposed from the chart, becoming untenable only in a strong westerly. Give the north shore a berth of 250 yards to avoid the long ledge that makes out from there at the entrance. The rock covered with 9 feet of water near the middle of the entrance is a problem only in heavy weather. There are no public docks, but the owner of the small, private dock (37) at the head of the harbor will allow you to tie your dinghy there. A road connects this harbor to the village of North Haven, but it's about 4 miles away.

### Fox Islands Thorofare
### Chart Nos. 13302, 13305, 13308

Refer to excerpt from chart no. 13302 in this chapter on page 72..

Although the name "Fox Islands" is no longer used for the two islands, it has been retained for the thorofare between them. More than merely a means of getting from West Penobscot Bay to East Penobscot Bay, it is a cruising goal in itself. A sail through the Thorofare offers exceptional scenic vistas, wooded land of spruce and birch interspersed with gentle slopes of hayfields and pastures. In the eastern half of the Thorofare are several coves to anchor and appreciate the surroundings in quiet solitude. The village of North Haven (39), with its well kept houses and carefully tended gardens, is on the north shore of the Thorofare. It is a summer resort and yachting center where you can provision and tend to any boat needs.

Throughout the entire length of the Thorofare all navigation aids are colored and numbered as travelling from east to west. Therefore, keep in mind when entering from the west that nun buoys will be kept to your **port** side. All dangers are well marked. The flood current enters from both ends of the Thorofare and exits from both ends. The strength of current is minimal. The only point where there is any velocity is at the constriction (40), between Iron Point and Zeke Point particularly if there are strong east or west winds. Mean tide range is 9.5 feet.

No matter how thick the fog may be in Penobscot Bay, Fox Islands Thorofare invariably remains clear, kept so by the two large land masses on either side. Coming in from the west, by the time you reach Browns Head Lighthouse (41), the fog will have diminished considerably. Prior to last summer, I would have gone so far as to say there **never** is fog in the Thorofare. Then, I was heading for the eastern enterance expecting to find relief from the disappearing world of Isle au Haut Bay, only to find it was just as bad in the Thorofare. But by the time we reached Calderwood Point (42), it had already begun to dissipate.

Approaching the Thorofare from the west, the primary visual reference mark will be the beacon on Fiddler Ledge (43), a large, square granite shaft with a pyramidal top. The name for this ledge was probably supplied by one of the many stone cutters from Ireland who worked in the nearby quarries during the mid-1800's. In Celtic lore, Fiddlers are associated with Faeries and sailors who die, particularly if they die at sea, are said to go to Fiddlers' Green. This is an underworld elysium, a paradise of wine, women and song, the antithesis of Davy Jones' Locker, a place of the devil and hell where "bad" sailors end up.

This discussion won't take you through the Thorofare but to complete the etymological discourse on names, consider that of Davy Jones. Sailors, being superstitious by nature, would not call upon or speak of the devil, preferring the close enough corruption of Deva, Davy or Taffy. Any person aboard ship who was suspected of causing misfortune due to wind or weather, or causing any other kind of bad luck, was called a Jonah. Jonahs were often called Jonas (1612) and from there it became Jones. The original Jonah was the biblical Hebrew prophet —*"So they took up Jonah, and cast*

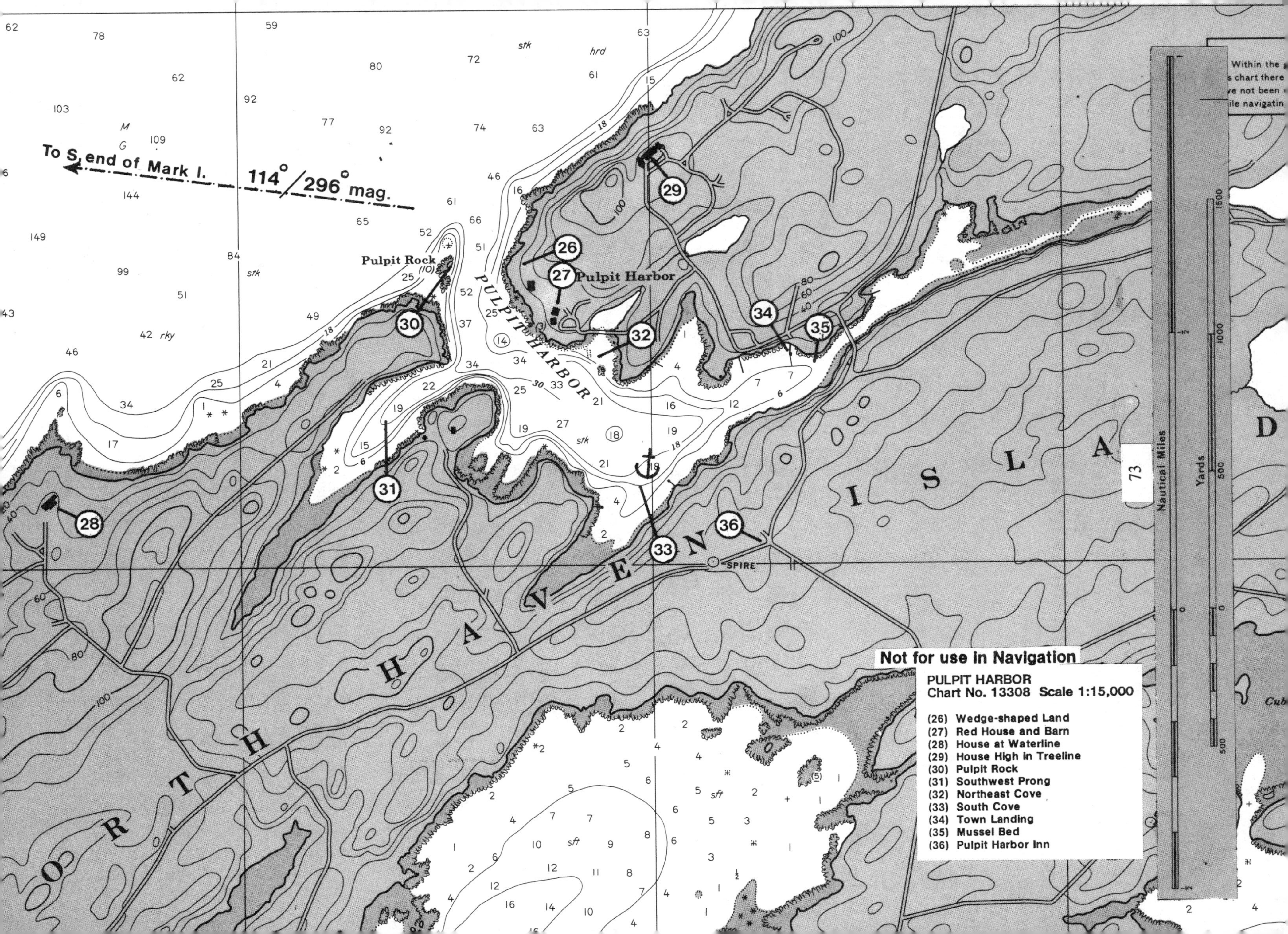
To S. end of Mark I. 114°/296° mag.
Pulpit Rock
PULPIT HARBOR
Pulpit Harbor
NORTH HAVEN ISLAND
SPIRE
Not for use in Navigation
PULPIT HARBOR
Chart No. 13308 Scale 1:15,000
(26) Wedge-shaped Land
(27) Red House and Barn
(28) House at Waterline
(29) House High in Treeline
(30) Pulpit Rock
(31) Southwest Prong
(32) Northeast Cove
(33) South Cove
(34) Town Landing
(35) Mussel Bed
(36) Pulpit Harbor Inn
Nautical Miles
Yards

*him forth into the sea; and the sea ceased her raging."* His locker was a whale. The combination of the two names produced Davy Jones, the mariner's evil angel, or devil. Tripping your keel on Fiddler Ledge could send you to Fiddlers' Green!

Two other reference marks for the west entrance are the large, mid-channel bell buoy "FT" (44) and the lighthouse tower at Browns Head (41). In the fog, gong buoy R "26" (45) and the bell buoy "FT" (44) will help you enter. At night, the white sector (flanked by red sectors) of the Brown Head light (050-061 degrees) shows the extent of clear passage into the Thorofare. The Sugar Loaves (46), a small group of islands about 600 yards northwest of Browns Head Light, are high and prominent, looking much like Sugar Loaf Mountain in Rio de Janiero Harbor.

Approaching from the east, 5 ft. high Channel Rock, with its red daybeacon, and bell buoy "4" (47) alongside, are good reference points. Less than a mile west is Widow Island (48), with a small house near the peak on the southwest side. North of the island is Goose Rocks Light Tower (49). At night the white sector of the light (301-304 degrees) guides you safely into the Thorofare.

Goose Rocks is an especially attractive lighthouse of the cassion type, a white conical tower rising directly out of the water on a black cylindrical foundation.

## North Haven Village—Chart No. 13308

Anchorage for the town of North Haven may be on either side of the channel, the holding ground equally good. Most boats prefer anchoring on the north side to be closer to town, but if it is too crowded there, you always have the other option. Take care not to anchor in the cable area near the ferry landing (50).

All the businesses and facilities are clustered around the large wharf for the ferry boat from the mainland. The wharf has a small white shed on posts at the outer end and pilings beyond to facilitate landing the ferry boat. You cannot tie up here at all. The clapboard and red brick building at the foot of the wharf is the ticket office. Three daily round-trips are made to Rockland with the schedule posted on the office building. For the most up-to-date information on the schedule and rates contact Maine State Ferry Service, P.O. Box 645, 517A Main St., Rockland ME 04841 (tel. 207-594-5543). There are public restrooms in the office. Outside the building is a public telephone and trash containers.

**Marine Facilities and Supplies.** The dock immediately east of the ferry landing is the Town Dock (51), the best place for dinghy tie-up.

East of the parking lot at the ferry landing is the Waterman & Co. Market (52), the major store on North Haven Island for groceries, provisioning and general supplies, open 7:30 a.m.-12:00 noon and 2:00-4:30 p.m. Monday through Saturday. Sundays they're open 7:30-9:30 a.m. and 3:50-5:00 p.m. Waterman is a pleasant, old-fashioned market, fun to shop in with its rambling structure of various levels and additions. Most notices about activities in North Haven are posted outside the store. Across the street is Roman's Fish Market (53), fresh fish and lobsters, and a snack bar serving pizza, hamburgers, hot dogs and ice cream. Usually they do not begin business until the beginning of July. There is no restaurant in the village, the closest being the Pulpit Harbor Inn described above in this chapter, about 1½ miles up the road. A taxi service is available in town. The Almon H. Ames Inn (54) on Browns Cove serves gourmet dinners, but only to guests who remain there overnight. They are open year-round and reservations are necessary (tel. 207-867-4853).

West of the ferry landing is the wharf and floats of the North Haven Yacht Club (55). At the outer end of their wharf is a small, cedar-shingle building, and on shore the main clubhouse with its veranda and porches. You may tie-up your dinghy at the innermost float, but guests are requested not to bring cruising boats to the float except for a short time. There are no shower or toilet facilities and no trash containers. The Yacht Club maintains two guest mooring, identified by the letters N H Y C on small, orange ball floats, Across the road from the yacht club is the post office and library (56). Several gift and craft shops are on Main Street, along the waterfront.

The wharf and float east of the Town Dock is J.O. Brown and Son (57). Established in 1888, the boatyard is still in operation, now by Jim Brown, the grandson of the founder. Dock depth is 5 feet and the largest berth 45 feet. They have 60 ft of dock space, 10 moorings, gasoline, diesel fuel, water, ice, showers, a marine supply store with a large stock, complete engine hull, and prop repair, and they monitor VHF Channel 16. Foy Brown, the Harbor Master, may be contacted through the J.O. Brown Boat Yard.

Now refer to our excerpt from chart no. 13302 on page 72 in this chapter.

## Seal Cove (58), North Shore of Vinalhaven Island

With the rocky areas, shoaling, cable areas and moored boats fairly well filling the cove, this is not a desirable anchorage. Furthermore, most of the shoreline is fringed with private residences making land access difficult.

## Perry Creek (59), North Shore of Vinalhaven Island

A narrow arm west of Seal Cove, the anchorage is good, but much of the shoreline on the north edge dries out to unattractive mud flats. There are no docks for landing and no nearby services.

## Southern Harbor (60), South Shore of North Haven Island

Open and exposed to the southwest, and shallow and rocky near the head of the harbor, this is seldom used. There are no docks and no nearby services.

Now refer to our excerpt from chart no. 13308, showing the east part of Fox Islands Thorofare.

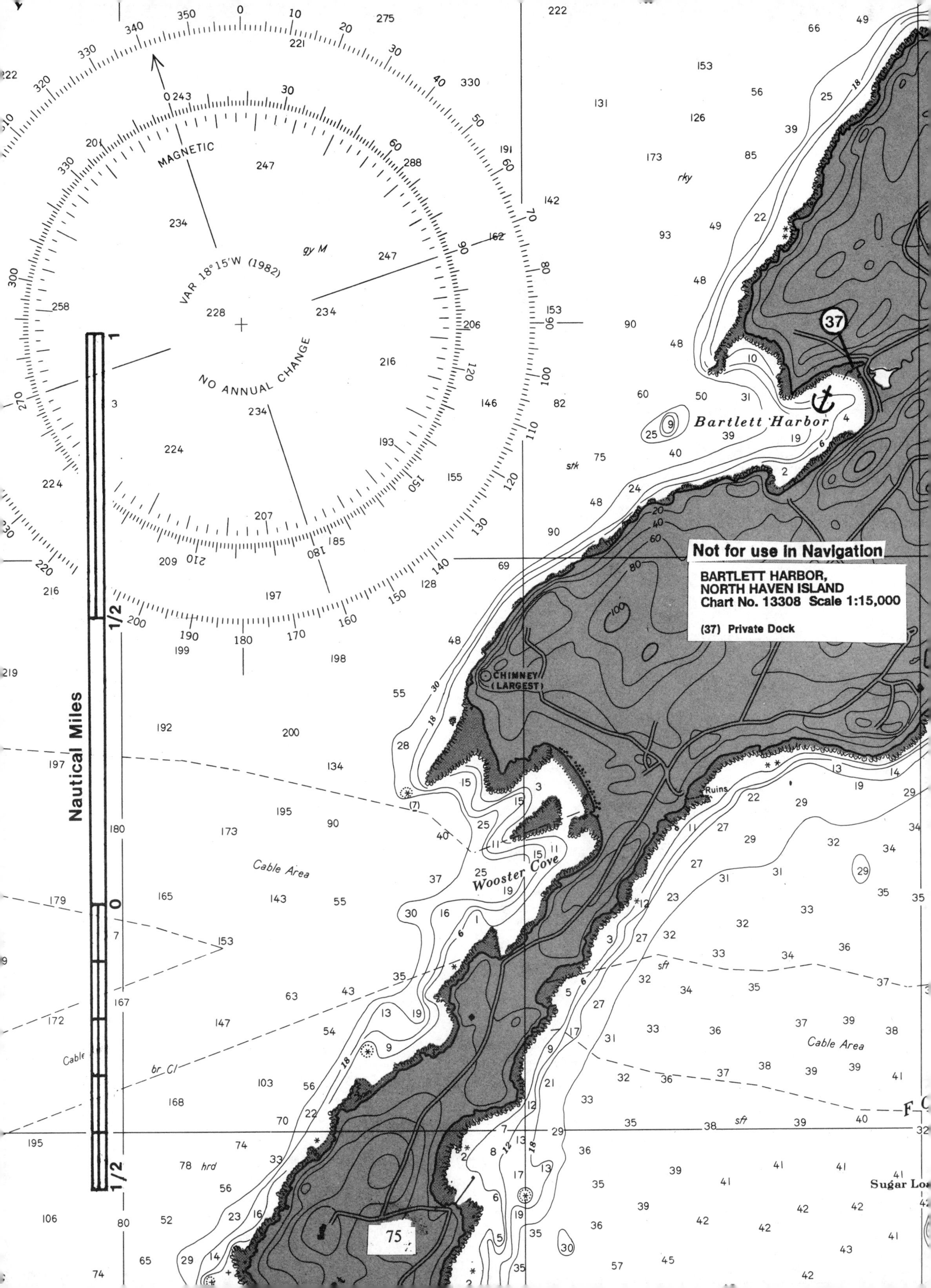
Not for use in Navigation
BARTLETT HARBOR,
NORTH HAVEN ISLAND
Chart No. 13308 Scale 1:15,000
(37) Private Dock
Bartlett Harbor
Wooster Cove
CHIMNEY (LARGEST)
Ruins
Cable Area
MAGNETIC
VAR 18° 15'W (1982)
NO ANNUAL CHANGE
Nautical Miles
Sugar Loa

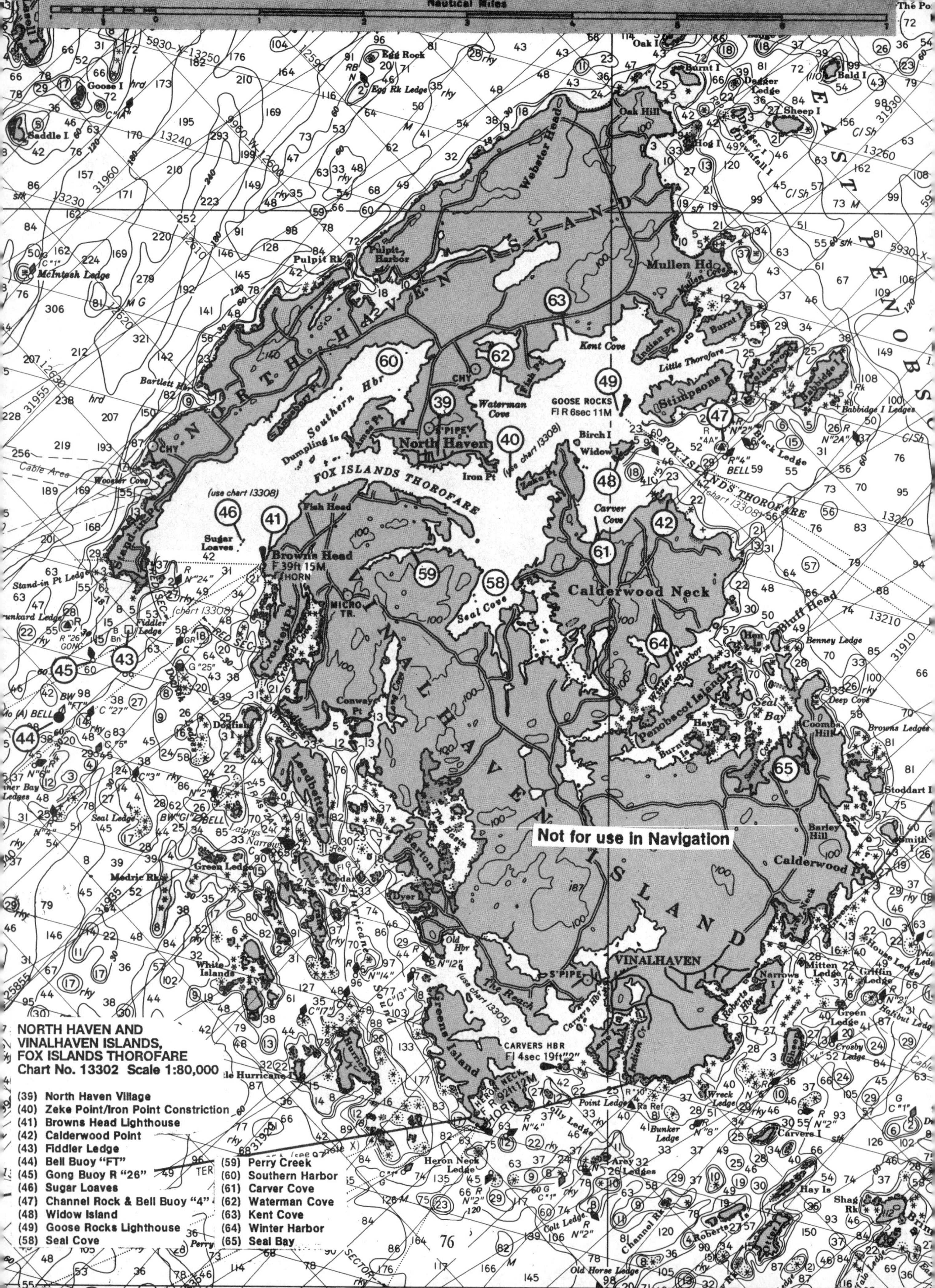
Nautical Miles
NORTH HAVEN ISLAND
VINALHAVEN ISLAND
FOX ISLANDS THOROFARE
EAST PENOBSCOT
Not for use in Navigation
GOOSE ROCKS
Fl R 6sec 11M
Browns Head
F 39ft 15M
HORN
CARVERS HBR
Fl 4sec 19ft "2"
HERON NECK
F R 92ft 12M
HORN
North Haven
VINALHAVEN
Calderwood Neck
Southern Hbr
Kent Cove
Waterman Cove
Seal Cove
Carver Cove
Mullen Hd
Webster Head
Pulpit Harbor
Pulpit Rk
Stimpsons I
Widow I
Birch I
Iron Pt
Zeke Pt
Sugar Loaves
Crockett Pt
Leadbetter I
Greens Island
The Reach
Seal Bay
Penobscot Island
Winter Harbor
Bluff Head
Calderwood Pt
Barley Hill
Coombs Hill
Dumpling Is
Fish Head
Conway Pt
Dyer I
Old Hbr
White Islands
Hurricane I
Green Ledge
Medric Rk
Seal Ledge
Stand-in Pt Ledge
Fiddler Ledge
McIntosh Ledge
Saddle I
Goose I
Egg Rock
Oak Hill
Hog I
Burnt I
Sheep I
Bald I
Babbidge I Ledges
Black Ledge
Benney Ledge
Browns Ledges
Stoddart I
Smith I
Mitten Ledge
Griffin Ledge
Green Ledge
Crosby Ledge
Heron Neck Ledge
Colt Ledge
Arey Ledges
Channel Rk
Carvers I
Hay Is
Shag Rk
Old Horse Ledge
Point Ledge
Bunker Ledge
Wreck Ledge
(use chart 13308)
(use chart 13305)
NORTH HAVEN AND
VINALHAVEN ISLANDS,
FOX ISLANDS THOROFARE
Chart No. 13302 Scale 1:80,000
(39) North Haven Village
(40) Zeke Point/Iron Point Constriction
(41) Browns Head Lighthouse
(42) Calderwood Point
(43) Fiddler Ledge
(44) Bell Buoy "FT"
(45) Gong Buoy R "26"
(46) Sugar Loaves
(47) Channel Rock & Bell Buoy "4"
(48) Widow Island
(49) Goose Rocks Lighthouse
(58) Seal Cove
(59) Perry Creek
(60) Southern Harbor
(61) Carver Cove
(62) Waterman Cove
(63) Kent Cove
(64) Winter Harbor
(65) Seal Bay

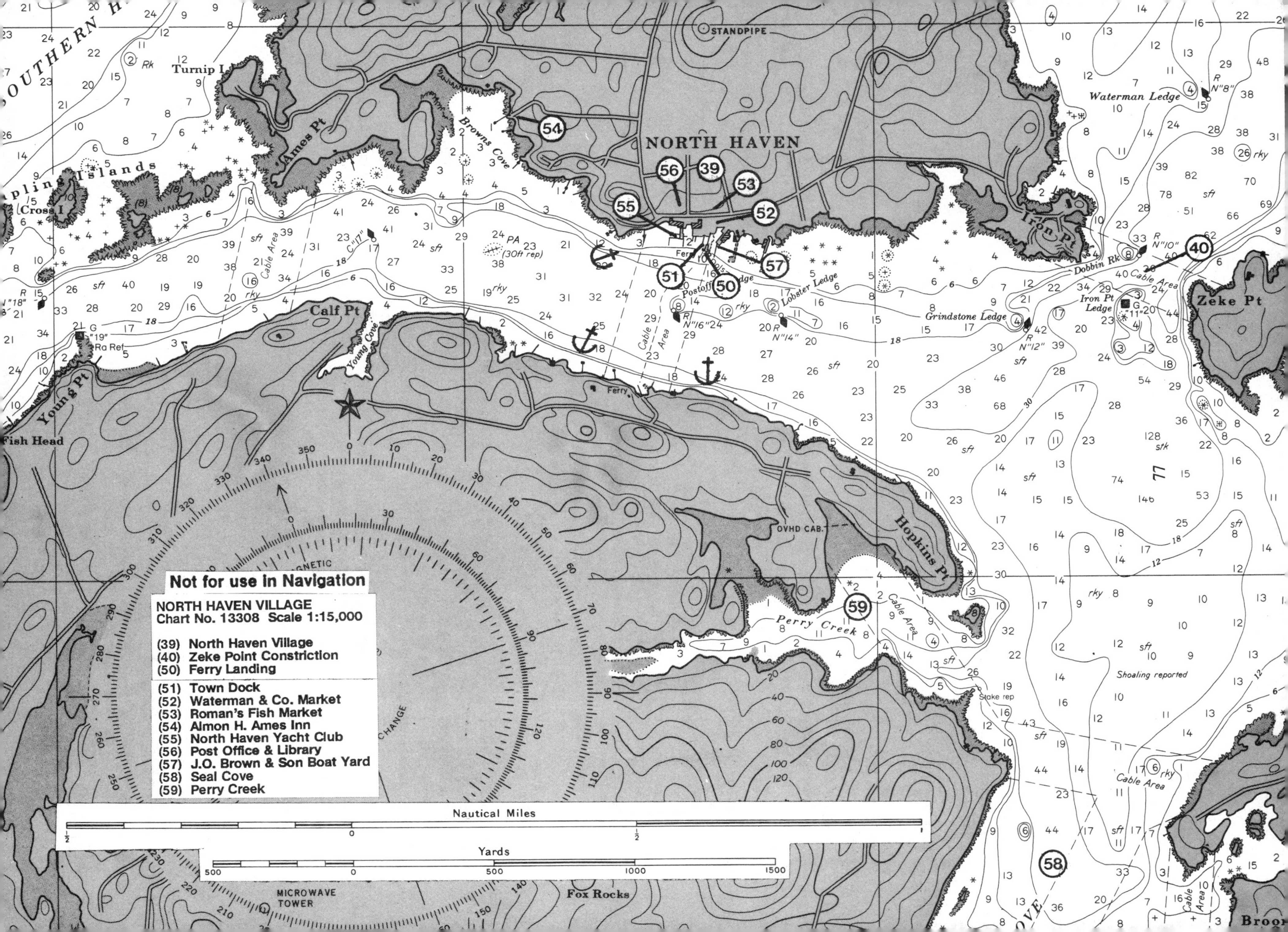
Not for use in Navigation
NORTH HAVEN VILLAGE
Chart No. 13308 Scale 1:15,000
(39) North Haven Village
(40) Zeke Point Constriction
(50) Ferry Landing
(51) Town Dock
(52) Waterman & Co. Market
(53) Roman's Fish Market
(54) Almon H. Ames Inn
(55) North Haven Yacht Club
(56) Post Office & Library
(57) J.O. Brown & Son Boat Yard
(58) Seal Cove
(59) Perry Creek
NORTH HAVEN
STANDPIPE
Turnip I
Ames Pt
Browns Cove
Cross I
Calf Pt
Young Cove
Young Pt
Fish Head
Iron Pt
Waterman Ledge
Dobbin Rk
Iron Pt Ledge
Grindstone Ledge
Lobster Ledge
Zeke Pt
Hopkins Pt
Perry Creek
OVHD CAB.
Cable Area
Shoaling reported
Stake rep
MICROWAVE TOWER
Fox Rocks
Nautical Miles
Yards

### Carver Cove (61), North Shore of Vinalhaven Island

Not to be confused with Carvers Harbor at the south end of Vinalhaven Island, this cove provides excellent anchoring. The holding ground is good, the surroundings are scenic, and there are beatiful views to the north. Complete protection is provided in all but northeast winds, that rarely occur during the summer sailing season. There is deep water right up to the very edge of the shores. It is never crowded here, and it's a good overnight anchorage.

### Kent Cove (63), Chart no. 13308, South Shore of North Haven Island

Kent Cove (63) has two beautiful and well-protected anchorages. The westernmost cove would get some sea in strong southeast winds, which are not prevalent summertime. Under these conditions, you'd find good shelter in the eastern cove. Holding ground is good all over Kent Cove. No landing, no services,but this is a lovely gunkhole.

### Waterman Cove (62) South Shore of North Haven

On the north side of the Thorofare east of the town of North Haven, there is good anchorage in Waterman Cove. No docks for access to land and no services available nearby, nonetheless, it is a lovely spot to spend the evening and watch the parade of sailboats passing through the Thorofare. It is always calm and there are no currents to contend with.

## VINALHAVEN ISLAND

Refer to the excerpt from chart no. 13302 Fox Islands Thorofare, that shows Vinalhaven Island in its entirety.

Some harbors on the north shore of Vinalhaven Island have been described previously in this chapter in the section on Fox Islands Thorofare.

### Winter Harbor, Vinalhaven Island Chart Nos. 13305, 13308

The popularity of harbors is subject to cycles. At present, Pulpit Harbor and Roque Island are high on the list of favorites, whereas Winter Harbor (64) and adjacent Seal Bay (65) on the east side of Vinalhaven Island are seldom visited at all. Now refer to our excerpt from chart no. 13308 showing details of these two harbors. There is no real reason for the emptiness of Winter Harbor and Seal Bay, as there is little difficulty entering either one if you follow the chart closely. Once inside you are amply rewarded for the effort.

Approaching from East Penobscot Bay or Fox Islands Thorofare, the first mark is Bluff Head (66), prominent and easily identified. As you get closer, Hen Islands (67) and other landmarks sort themselves out.

For the full length of Winter Harbor, the water is deep right up to the shore, with two exceptions. One hazard is (68) near the entrance, and the other (70) is south of the 163-foot high hill (69). Both hazards are rocks covered 2 feet at MLW. I have circled these on chart no. 13308. From looking at the small scale chart no. 13305, it would appear that the 2-foot spot (68) at the entrance is in the middle of the channel. This is not so. It is decidedly closer to the north shore as can been seen on chart no. 13308. You can proceed up the middle of the channel, favoring slightly the south shore toward Hen Islands as shown on our course line, without having to worry about this rock.

The high hill (69), halfway down the harbor, rises dramatically as a vertical cliff straight out of the water, and divides Winter Harbor into an outer and inner portion. Most people try to anchor at the base of this hill, but they meet with little success. Holding ground is poor and the boart invariably drags anchor. A much better spot is directly across, on the opposite shore, northeast of the little cluster of islands. Here you will be out of the main current and the holding ground is fine.

You can also go past the cliff to anchor in the inner portion of the harbor. The 2-foot spot (70) can be avoided by closely following the northern shoreline, keeping no farther than 60 feet out. Once past the tip of land, you must swing south to remain in deepest water. There may be more water around the southeast side of the rock, but the problem is finding it. A long bar makes out towards the rock (70) from the Penobscot Island shore, narrowing any passage south of the rock. When this bar is under water, the deep water south of the rock is hard to find.

Going beyond the indicated anchorages to the very head of the harbor is difficult without local knowledge. The channel is sinuous and unmarked. Not that it can't be done, for at one time coasting schooners negotiated the course to load with granite which was quarried from both shores of this harbor. A granite pier (71), as well as evidence of the quarry operations (72), is still present. Explore these fascinating sites by dinghy.

### Seal Bay— Chart No. 13308

Summarily dismissed by the *Coast Pilot* as "not safe for a stranger to enter," this Bay offers beautiful anchorages in well protected water, surrounded by an untouched and unspoiled shoreline. You will most likely have this very appealing place entirely to yourself.

There are two means of entry to Seal Bay. By following the chart closely, you should not have any problem with either one. Identify Bluff Head (66), which can be distinguished by its steeper, bolder configuration than Hen Islands (67) and follow along the north shore of Hen Islands as though you were entering Winter Harbor. Immediately past the second Hen Island, turn southeast into Seal Bay, keeping very close to the southwest shore of Hen Islands. This will keep you clear of the cluster of rocks (73) northwest of Penobscot Island. At half-tide or less, these rocks show themselves as large smooth mounds of granite.

The other entrance is between Bluff Head and Hen Island. Stay close to the west shore of Bluff Head until

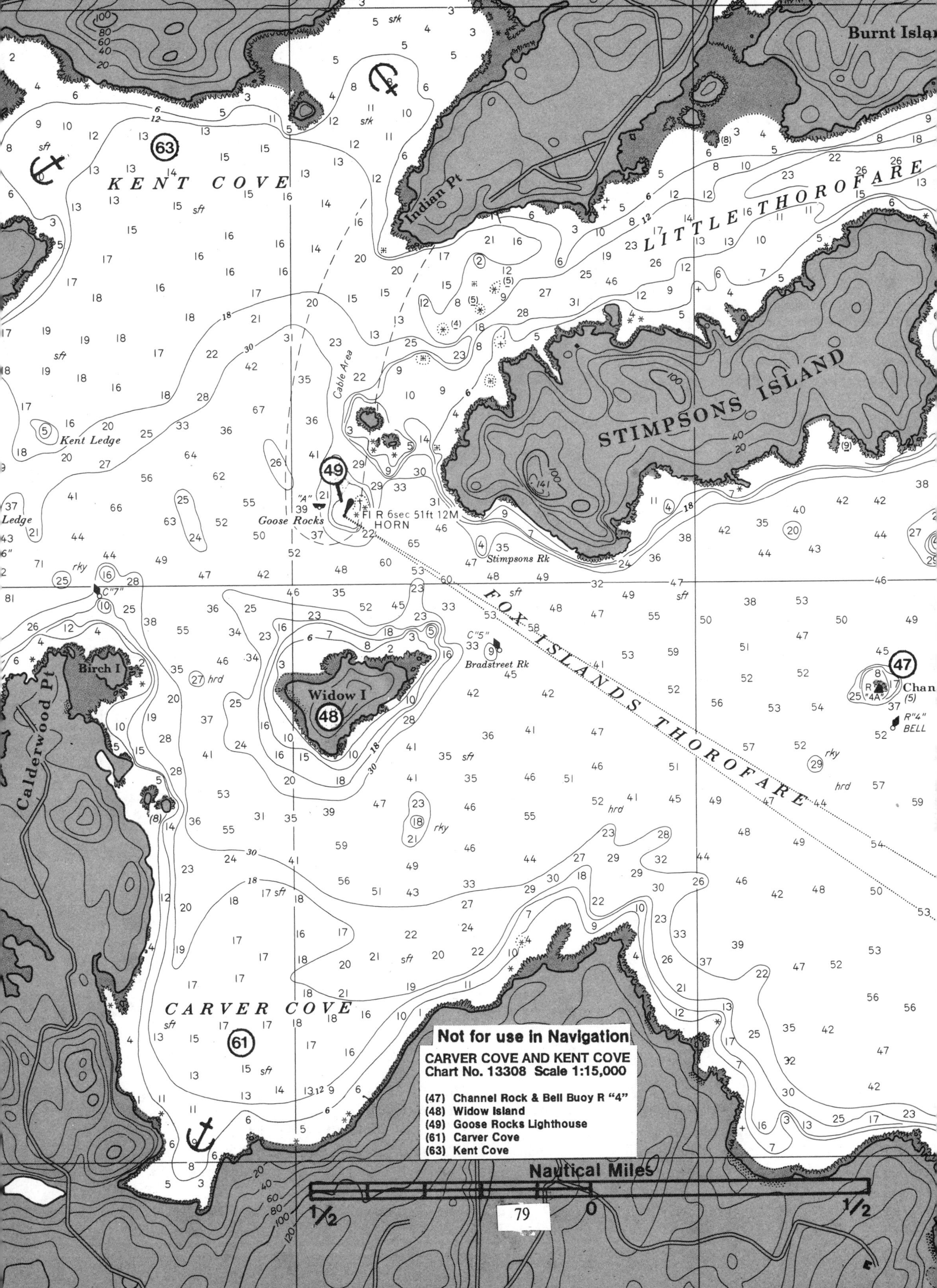
Not for use in Navigation
CARVER COVE AND KENT COVE
Chart No. 13308 Scale 1:15,000
(47) Channel Rock & Bell Buoy R "4"
(48) Widow Island
(49) Goose Rocks Lighthouse
(61) Carver Cove
(63) Kent Cove
KENT COVE
CARVER COVE
LITTLE THOROFARE
FOX ISLANDS THOROFARE
STIMPSONS ISLAND
Widow I
Birch I
Calderwood Pt
Indian Pt
Goose Rocks
Kent Ledge
Stimpsons Rk
Bradstreet Rk
Cable Area
Fl R 6sec 51ft 12M
HORN
Nautical Miles

past the ledges and rocks at the southeast end of Hen Island and turn southwest to enter the main channel. We have shown courselines for both entries to Seal Bay, on our excerpt from chart no. 13308.

Within the Bay you can anchor almost anywhere you please avoiding the very shallow spots, which are rocky. We have indicated on the chart only two of the many possible delightful anchorages.

## Carvers Harbor, Vinalhaven Town
### Chart No. 13305 and Inset

Carvers Harbor, the main harbor of Vinalhaven Island, and the harbor for the Town of Vinalhaven, is truly picturesque and active, filled with fishing vessels, draggers, seiners and lobster boats. This is in contrast to the Thorofare and North Haven where yachts predominate.

**Approaches.** There are three approaches to the harbor. First, (81), directly from the open sea, south of Vinalhaven Island. Second, (82), following the coastline from the east side of Vinalhaven Island into the harbor. Third, (83), an inner, protected route along the west side of the island through Hurricane Sound and The Reach. We have traced course lines for all three approaches on our Carvers Harbor excerpt from chart no. 13305.

In clear weather, good landmarks are the standpipe (85) on the hill behind the harbor and the lighthouse (86) on Heron Neck of Greens Island. Both are visible from as far south as Matinicus Island, 10 miles away. From the south, the outermost mark is bell buoy R "2A" (84). At buoy R "2A," a course of 007 degrees magnetic (reciprocal 187 degrees) will guide you through the line of buoys and safely past the ledges and rocks to the light tower on Green Ledge (87). If navigating in fog, keep in mind that the current set in this area is east by south on ebb and west by north on the flood tide. We have marked directions of the tidal current on both the ebb and flood, on our excerpt from Chart 13305. From Green Ledge it is but a short distance through the "gate" of N "4" and C "5" (88) into the harbor proper. See inset, Carvers Harbor and Approaches from chart no. 13305.

The second approach (82) along the east shore, is very well marked, the buoys being no farther than one mile apart. But in dense fog, this whole south and southeast section of Vinalhaven can be difficult, for while the channel itself is well buoyed, there are numerous rocks, ledges and islands surrounding it. It would take very little current to offset your course and place you near these dangers. The colors and numbers of all the buoys in this east to south quadrant of Vinalhaven are as proceeding toward Carvers Harbor, red even numbers to starboard, and green odd numbers to port. The system is the reverse south of Calderwood Point (89). Halibut Ledge (90) is marked by a **nun** buoy on the outside of the ledge, whereas Triangle Ledge (91) is marked on the outside by a **can** buoy. From Triangle Ledge, the course is marked as though you were headed **north** toward Fox Islands Thorofare.

Smith Island is about 0.4 mile north northeast of Calderwood Point (89). Owned by the Nature Conservatory, its 8 acres are open to the public. Best dinghy landing is in the bight on the southwest shore, where there's a small beach. If it's not blowing from the east, you can land at another small beach on the east shore in the bight near the south end. Both beaches are cobble. The rest of the shore is rocky.

Gulls and cormorants nest on the southeast tip but other birds are scared off the island by a sizeable mink population. You'll see many birds in the vicinity such as common and arctic terns, eider ducks, and black guillemots. Smith Island is all open moors, with high grass and shrubs, including blueberries and raspberries.

The third approach (83), through Hurricane Sound and The Reach, is also well buoyed and presents no problem. Buoys are only about 400 yards apart. Heading toward Carvers Harbor through The Reach, **red** is **kept to port** and **green to starboard** until you reach the "gate" of N "4" and C "5" where the system reverts to the normal pattern.

**Anchorage** Just about every square foot of Carvers Harbor is occupied by boats, and spare moorings are hard to find, but chances are that if you arrive after 5:00 and find an empty mooring, it will be alright to take it. State law forbids lobstering after 4:00 p.m. and on Sundays. By 5:00 p.m., any boat that is going to be in, would already be there. Check with harbormaster Howard Chilles after picking up a mooring to confirm its availability. You can phone him at 863-2216. If he is on his boat, call for "Harbormaster Vinalhaven" on VHF Channel 6. A **small** portion of the southeast part of the harbor is free of moorings, and you can anchor there. I have indicated this on the chart. The bottom is very soft mud with much seaweed, so the holding is not exceptionally good. Fortunately, the harbor is so well protected and the currents minimal, that the chances of dragging anchor are slight.

**Marine Facilities.** The Calderwood Store (92) is the large yellow shingled building near the head of the harbor. This makes it easy to pick out from all the piers and wharfs. It has a wharf with floats where you can tie your dinghy, diesel fuel, gasoline, water, ice, and a large general supplies store with limited groceries, beverages, marine hardware, and bottled gas, open Monday-Saturday, 7:00 a.m.-9:00 p.m., Sunday noon to 5:00 p.m.

Hopkins Boat Yard, near the head of the harbor, has a marine railway with 50 ft. and/or 10 ton capacity, complete engine and hull repairs, and marine hardware.

The Public Boat Ramp and dock (99), has a concrete launching ramp. Dinghies may be tied at the floats here. There is only 3 feet depth at low tide.

Toward the mouth of the harbor is the fish-plant (93), a large corrugated metal building. Farther south-

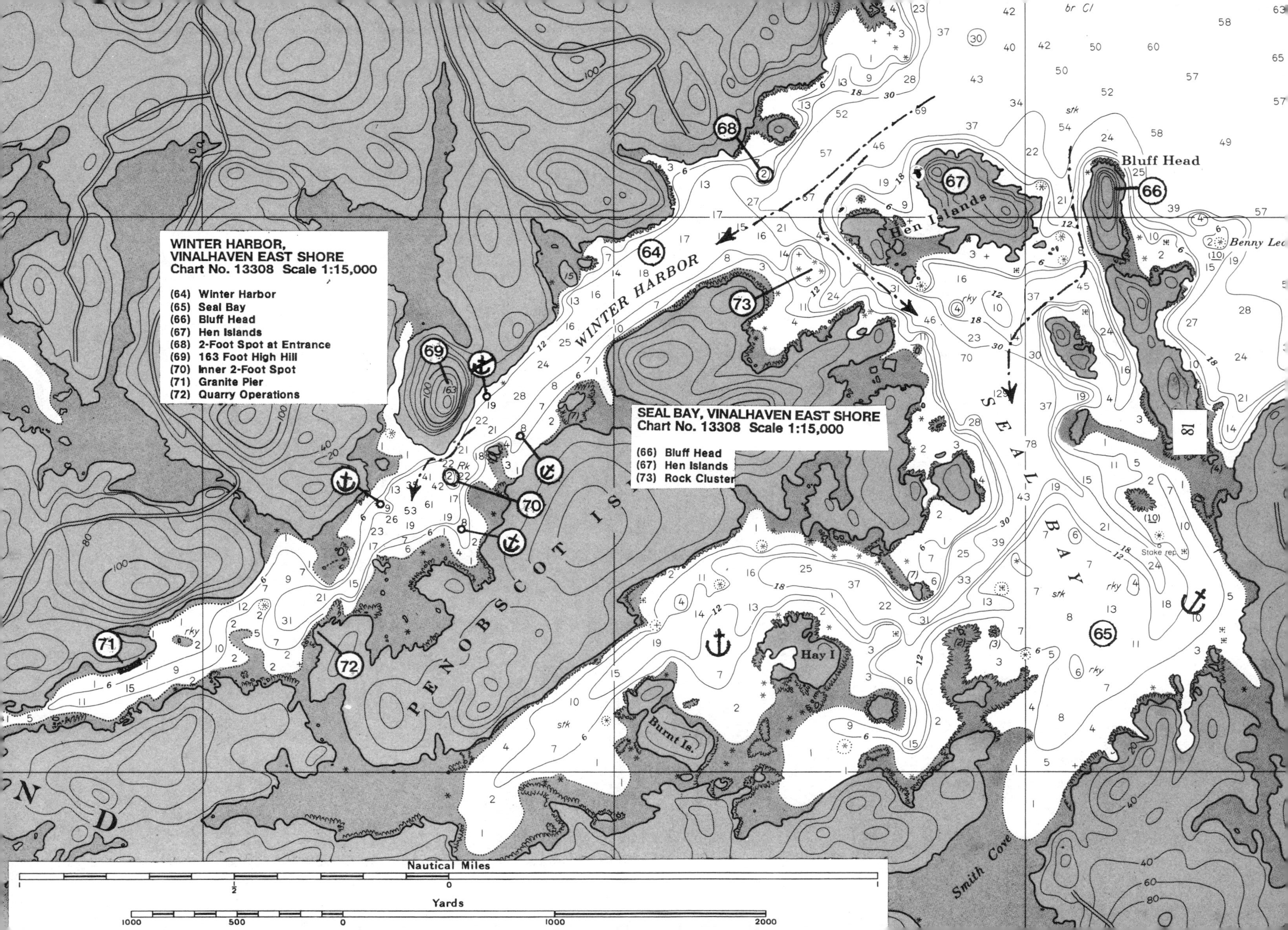
WINTER HARBOR, VINALHAVEN EAST SHORE
Chart No. 13308 Scale 1:15,000
(64) Winter Harbor
(65) Seal Bay
(66) Bluff Head
(67) Hen Islands
(68) 2-Foot Spot at Entrance
(69) 163 Foot High Hill
(70) Inner 2-Foot Spot
(71) Granite Pier
(72) Quarry Operations
SEAL BAY, VINALHAVEN EAST SHORE
Chart No. 13308 Scale 1:15,000
(66) Bluff Head
(67) Hen Islands
(73) Rock Cluster
WINTER HARBOR
SEAL BAY
PENOBSCOT IS
Bluff Head
Hen Islands
Hay I
Burnt Is.
Smith Cove
Benny Led
Stoke rep.
Nautical Miles
Yards

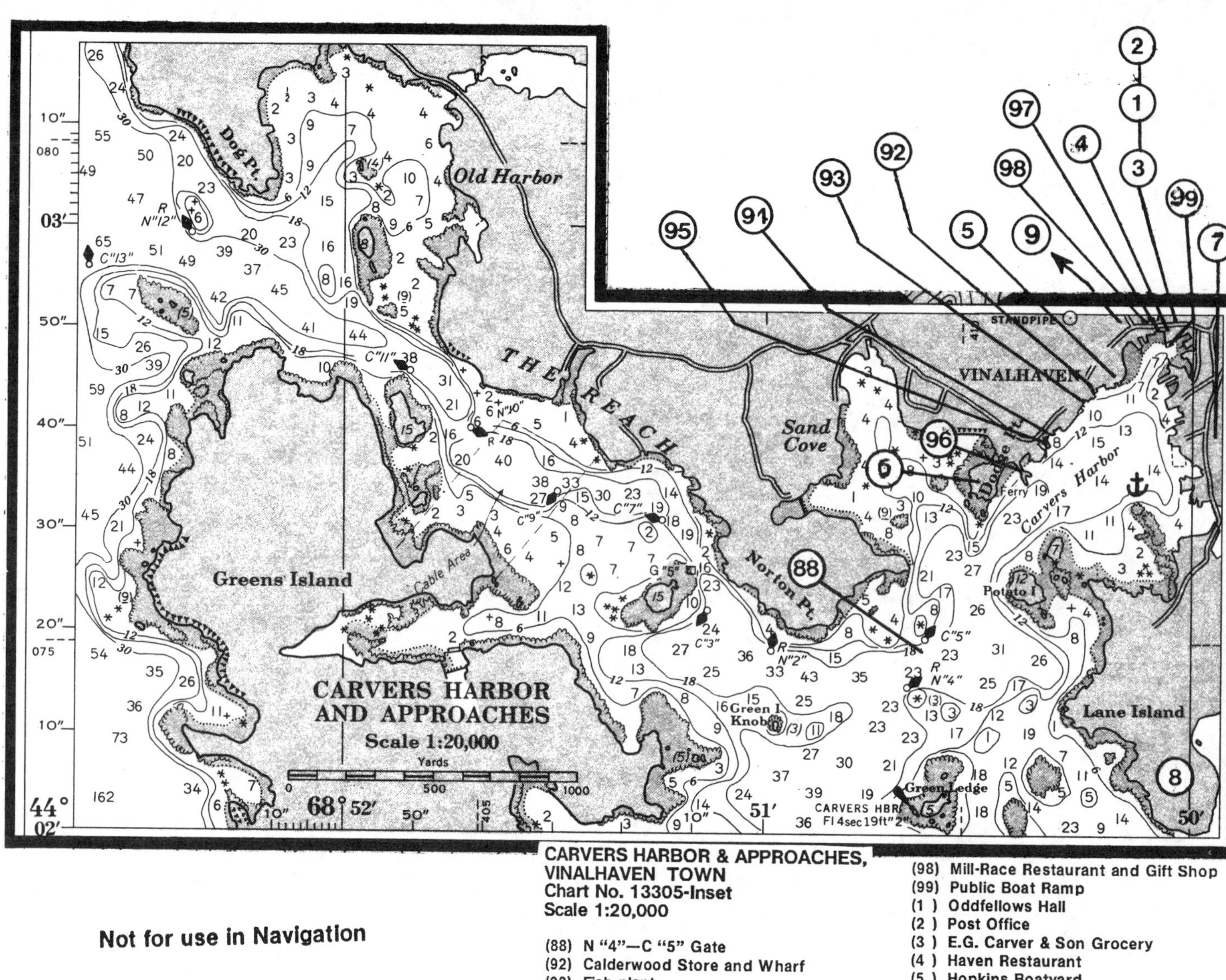


CARVERS HARBOR & APPROACHES, VINALHAVEN TOWN
Chart No. 13305-Inset
Scale 1:20,000

**Not for use in Navigation**

(88) N "4"—C "5" Gate
(92) Calderwood Store and Wharf
(93) Fish-plant
(94) Town Pier
(95) Vinalhaven Fishermans Co-op
(96) Ferry Landing Wharf
(97) Tidewater Motel
(98) Mill-Race Restaurant and Gift Shop
(99) Public Boat Ramp
(1 ) Oddfellows Hall
(2 ) Post Office
(3 ) E.G. Carver & Son Grocery
(4 ) Haven Restaurant
(5 ) Hopkins Boatyard
(6 ) Grimes Park
(7 ) Ambrust Hill
(8 ) Lane's Island Preserve
(9 ) Vinalhaven Historical Society

west is the town pier (94), but there is no dock or floats. Big fishing boats lie alongside this. Across the road is the Burger Ped II where you can buy hamburgers, sandwiches and soft drinks or rent Mopeds to explore the island. The next wharf southwest has a long white shed. This is the Vinalhaven Fishermens' Coop (95), where you can purchase fresh fish and lobster, diesel fuel, and gasoline. The ferry landing wharf (96) is near the harbor entrance. The ferry leaves from Rockland, three round-trips daily..

**Shopping and Sightseeing.** Gift and craft shops, other stores and restaurants are on Main Street which parallels the harbor. The location of Carvers Pond does not show on our inset, but shows very well on chart no. 13305, Carvers Harbor. Carvers Pond, north of Main St., empties out into the harbor through a mill-race under the road. Some of the shops and the Tidewater Motel (97) are built directly over this. The Mill-race Restaurant and Gift Shop (98) are on the north side of the road and they're open for breakfast, lunch and dinner.

Across the road from the Public Boat Ramp (99) is a large square buiding with a Mansard roof and flags flying from the four corners, dominating the scene, visible from anywhere in the harbor. This is one of the old historic buildings in town, the original Oddfellows Hall (1), now a private residence. West of this is the Post Office (2) and east is E.G. Carver and Son Grocery (3). Established in 1894, they are the major suppliers of meat, groceries, fish and provisions, open from 8:00 a.m. to 7:30 p.m., Saturday closing at 5:30 p.m. Across the street from the grocery is the Haven Restaurant (4), open for breakfast, lunch and dinner.

Great ocean overlooks, offering the full sweep of the open sea can be enjoyed by short walks to one of the several nearby parks. Grimes Park (6), near the ferry landing, has two small beaches and picnic facilities. Ambrust Hill (7) has marked and maintained trails with wonderful views. Here granite was first quarried on Vinalhaven, and the remains of this activity can still be seen.

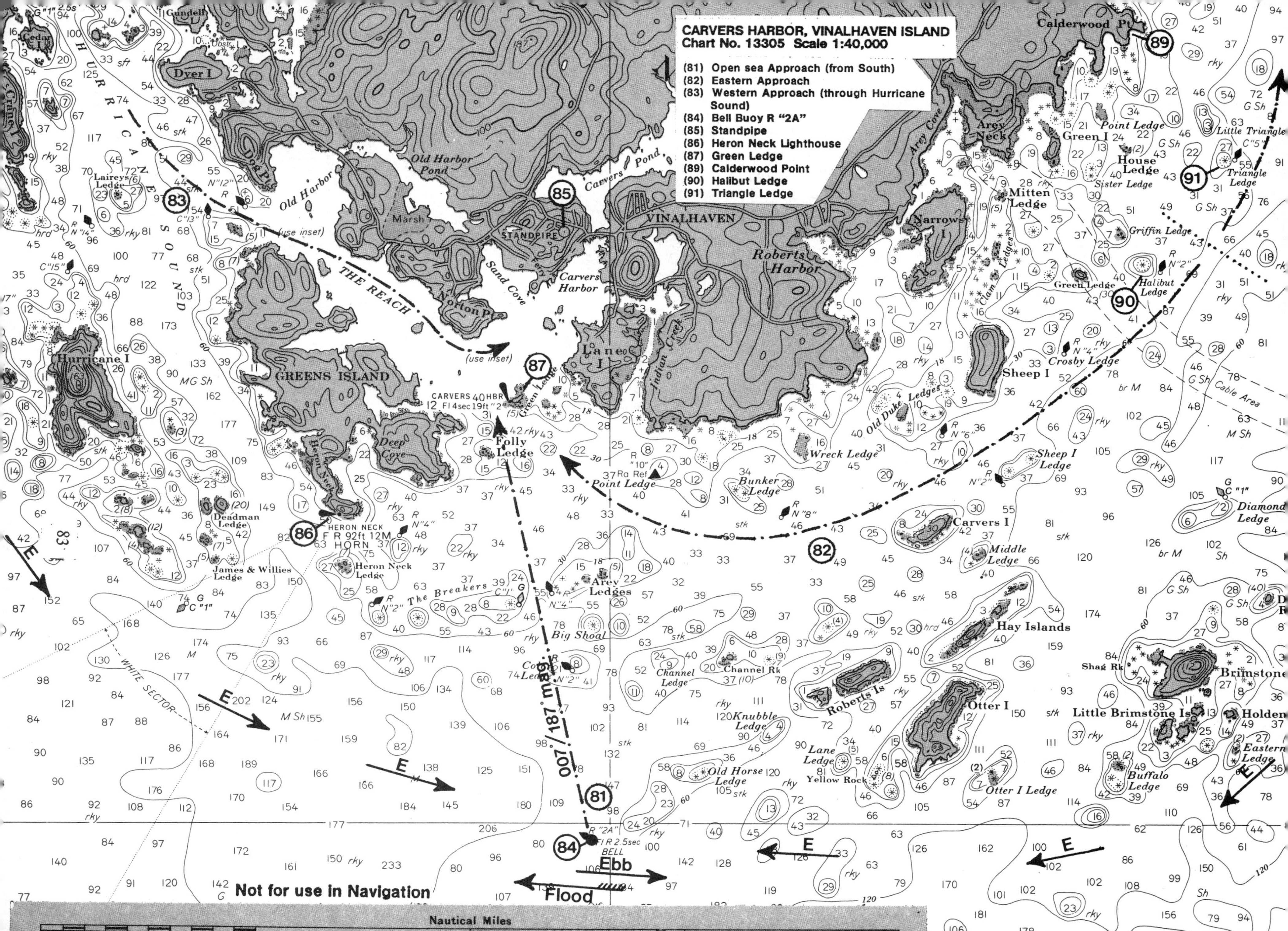
CARVERS HARBOR, VINALHAVEN ISLAND
Chart No. 13305 Scale 1:40,000
(81) Open sea Approach (from South)
(82) Eastern Approach
(83) Western Approach (through Hurricane Sound)
(84) Bell Buoy R "2A"
(85) Standpipe
(86) Heron Neck Lighthouse
(87) Green Ledge
(89) Calderwood Point
(90) Halibut Ledge
(91) Triangle Ledge
VINALHAVEN
GREENS ISLAND
HURRICANE SOUND
THE REACH
Carvers Harbor
Roberts Harbor
Hurricane I
Dyer I
Lane I
Sheep I
Carvers I
Hay Islands
Otter I
Roberts Is
Brimstone
Little Brimstone Is
Heron Neck
Calderwood Pt
Arey Neck
Narrows I
Green I
Old Harbor
Old Harbor Pond
Carvers Pond
Sand Cove
Norton Pt
Deep Cove
Indian Creek
STANDPIPE
Folly Ledge
Green Ledge
Mitten Ledge
Crosby Ledge
Halibut Ledge
Griffin Ledge
Point Ledge
House Ledge
Sister Ledge
Triangle Ledge
Little Triangle
Old Duke Ledges
Wreck Ledge
Bunker Ledge
Sheep I Ledge
Middle Ledge
Diamond Ledge
Arey Ledges
Big Shoal
Channel Ledge
Channel Rk
Knubble Ledge
Old Horse Ledge
Lane Ledge
Yellow Rock
Otter I Ledge
Buffalo Ledge
Eastern Ledge
Holden
Shag Rk
The Breakers
Heron Neck Ledge
James & Willies Ledge
Deadman Ledge
Laireys Ledge
Clam Ledges
Point Ledge
HERON NECK F R 92ft 12M HORN
CARVERS 40 HBR 12 Fl 4sec 19ft "2"
R "2A" Fl R 2.5sec BELL
007°/187° mag
Ebb
Flood
WHITE SECTOR
Cable Area
(use inset)
Not for use in Navigation
Nautical Miles

Lane Island Preserve (8) is a 45-acre tract of land donated to the Nature Conservancy, open to the public. Indian settlements on Lane Island are believed to date back to 4000 BC. It's mostly open moors but several trails criss-cross the Preserve, some leading to the rugged shore, where the surf breaks in spectacular fashion on a windy day. Lane Island is connected to the mainland by a causeway, only a 15 minute walk from Main Street in Vinalhaven Town. You'll see seaducks and shorebirds, and there are bayberry, raspberry, low-bush blueberry and blackberry bushes along with the usual shoreside vegatation. The Preserve occupies the south end of Lane Island, about 60% of the island. The annual Town of Vinalhaven Fourth of July Picnic is held in the field near the north entrance to the Lane Island Preserve.

The Vinalhaven Historical Society (9), where there are exhibits of quarrying tools, quilts and a general history of the island through photographs, is open 11:00 a.m. to 3:00 p.m.

Be sure to take a leisurely walk up the hill and to both sides of Carvers Pond for views of the harbor and to see the many fine old New England homes. Impeccably maintained, and with their lovely gardens, they make Vinalhaven one of the prettiest villages along the Maine Coast. As in almost every community in Maine, the waterfront is being developed with condominium housing, but here they seem to blend in with the surroundings and the older buildings, not conflicting or obtrusive.

## Hurricane Sound— Chart Nos. 13305, 13308

***Sweet odors and bright colors swiftly pass—***
**Swiftly as breath upon a looking glass.**

Being familiar with the entire Maine coast, I am frequently asked, "what is your favorite harbor?" That is a difficult question. It is much like a parent being asked to name his favorite child. I have a number of favorites, depending on the circumstances and what I need from a harbor at the time. I can say though, that one of my favorite passages for an enjoyable afternoon sail is through Hurricane Sound. This area, southwest and west of Vinalhaven Island, is the last segment of our circumnavigation of Vinalhaven and North Vinalhaven Islands. Though last, Hurricane Sound and sourrounding waters and islands, is far from least.

**Approaches.** Whether you approach Hurricane Sound from south or north, try to have both the wind and tidal current in your favor, preferably with a gentle breeze so you can leisurely savor the delights of this passage. You will glide through the Sound with hardly a ripple on its surface, so protected is it from the open sea. The scene constantly changes before your eyes. Each island has its own character. Some are heavily wooded, with dark spruce and fir coming down the waters' edge amidst a tumble of granite boulders. Others are more of a gentle, pastoral nature. Occasionally you catch a glimpse of a salt-water farm or a summer house discretely tucked into the landscape. In these quiet surroundings you will hear the song of birds on shore.

We've drawn course lines on both chart excerpts, one from chart no. 13305, the other from chart no. 13308. Neither of these shows the detail of The Reach, the inside passage to Carvers Harbor and Vinalhaven town. You will find a detail of The Reach in the inset from chart no. 13305 earlier in this chapter.

There are two places along the route where you may exit if you wish. One (10) is north of Hurricane Island (17) and the other through Laireys Narrows (11). Laireys Narrows is the route used by the ferry boat between Rockland and Carvers Harbor. Laireys Ledge (12) is a yellowish, smooth lump of granite, always visible, even at high tide. It may be passed either side.

At the north end of the Hurricane Sound passage, pay particular attention to C"1" buoy (13) north of Leadbetter Island (18). On the small scale chart no. 13305, it appears that the buoy is very close to Leadbetter Island. Actually it is much closer to the shore of Vinalhaven Island as shown on chart no. 13308. Stay north of C "1." even through this appears to be an improbable course. The tide pulls quite strongly through the narrow part of the channel so be sure your passage is with the flow in your favor.

The three rocks (14) shown on the chart between Dogfish Island and Crockett Point are in reality two small ledges plus a scattering of several rocks. The southernmost ledge always shows 2 feet at high water, the middle ledge uncovers at 10 feet and the rest of the rocks are not visible, even at low water. Keep close to the Dogfish Island shore and you will avoid them all. The northernmost exit through Leadbetter Narrows (118) leads to continuing the passage through Fox Islands Thorofare or up Penobscot Bay.

**Long Cove.** No more delightful and secluded anchorage can be found than in Long Cove (15). I have been told that Joshua Slocum, first world circumnavigator, once put in here with his ship, the "Spray."

Head northeast between Fiddlehead Island and the small unnamed island NNW of it, keeping in mid channel all the way into the cove. We've drawn a course line on our excerpt from chart no. 13308. The entrance is only 300 feet wide, but there is deep water to the very edge of land. Do not be misled by the apparent indication of a 3-foot spot in the middle of the cove, as shown on Chart 13305. It is really 13 feet, the first digit lost in the contour line. Anchor anywhere. Holding ground is excellent in sticky mud. There are no facilities or docks, other than a private float and house (16) on the east shore. When courteously requested, the owners have been quite generous in allowing visiting dinghies to tie up here. There is a trail through the woods for about ¾ mile to a paved road where you may be able to hitch a ride to the town of Vinalhaven. It is a beautiful quiet secluded spot.

**History.** The history of this entire region is the history of granite quarrying. The islands were ideally suited for the quarrying operation. With deep water access, the stone could easily be loaded into the holds of granite schooners and transported to market. The first

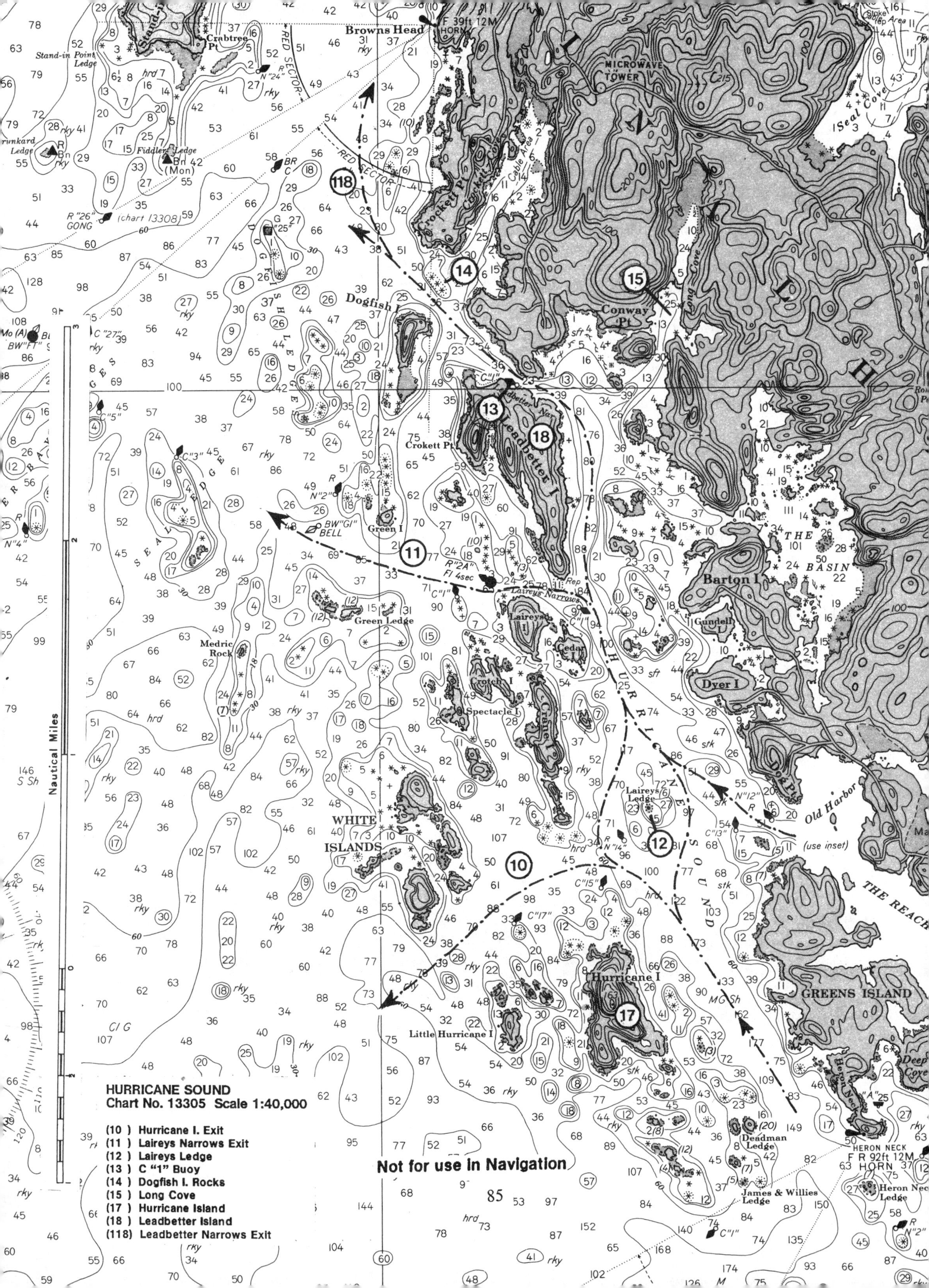

HURRICANE SOUND
Chart No. 13305 Scale 1:40,000
(10 ) Hurricane I. Exit
(11 ) Laireys Narrows Exit
(12 ) Laireys Ledge
(13 ) C "1" Buoy
(14 ) Dogfish I. Rocks
(15 ) Long Cove
(17 ) Hurricane Island
(18 ) Leadbetter Island
(118) Leadbetter Narrows Exit
Not for use in Navigation
Nautical Miles
Browns Head
MICROWAVE TOWER
Crabtree Pt
Stand-in Point Ledge
Fiddler Ledge
RED SECTOR
Dogfish I
DOGFISH LEDGES
Crockett Pt
Conway Pt
Long Cove
Leadbetter I
Leadbetter Nar
Crokett Pt
Green I
SEAL LEDGE
Laireys Narrows
Laireys I
Cedar I
Green Ledge
Medric Rock
Crotch I
Spectacle I
Crane I
WHITE ISLANDS
HURRICANE SOUND
Laireys Ledge
Barton I
THE BASIN
Gundell I
Dyer I
Dog Pt
Old Harbor
(use inset)
THE REACH
GREENS ISLAND
Hurricane I
Little Hurricane I
Deadman Ledge
James & Willies Ledge
Heron Neck
HERON NECK
F R 92ft 12M HORN
Heron Neck Ledge
Deep Cove
Seal Cove

comercially quarried stone was cut in Vinalhaven in 1826. By the mid to late 1800's, at the height of the era, there were 33 quarries along this part of the Maine coast. Many were on the islands of Muscle Ridge Channel and Hurricane Sound.

Hurricane Island (17), a major site, had a population of 600, its own post office, bank, general store and numerous boarding houses and cottages. It was even under its own administration, having separated from Vinalhaven Island in 1878. All this on an island of no more than a ½ mile long. In 1846, a quarry was also in operation on Leadbetter Island (18).

Some of the granite was used in a rough-cut state for paving blocks, other for the construction of breakwaters, lighthouses and forts. The first paving stones were used in New York, Philadelphia and Boston. In 1845, 126.5 tons of these blocks were shipped from Thomaston to New Orleans at the rate of $1.62 per ton.

Granite from this part of the coast took well to cutting and polishing, and the product of this labor is found in the columns of the Cathedral of St. John the Divine in New York City, the Metropolitan Museum of Art, New York Public Library, Philadelphia Post Office and other major public and federal buildings throughout the country. With the emergence of concrete as a prime construction material, all this activity came to an abrupt halt, and Hurricane Island, as well as most of the other quarry sites, was abandoned. Today Hurricane Island is home-base to The Outward Bound School, a summer sailing and survival school.

Some of the White Islands, on the north side of passage (10), just northwest of Hurricane Island (17), constitute the Big Garden and Big White Islands Preserves of the Nature Conservancy, and are open to the public. Though all four islands are shown on chart no. 13305 as "White Islands," the two northernmost are locally called Big Garden Island, and Little Garden Island southeast of it. These two are almost connected by ledges. The two southernmost of the group are called Big White Island, and Little White Island east of it. These two groups are separated by deep water, but the whole area is reef strewn and there's no passage through to the west. Stay south of these islands as shown on our course line (10), where you have a buoy to help you.

Little Garden Island and Little White Island are privately owned. Stay off them. The west shore of Big Garden Island extends south, and is called South Garden Island. The best dinghy landing is on a cobble beach on the east side of this extension, in the bight between Big Garden and South Garden. Big Garden and South Garden were both donated to the Nature Conservancy by Charles and Anne Morrow Lindbergh in 1967. Most of Big Garden is dense forest of spruce and fir, but there is some salt marsh. Blueberries and other shore vegatation is supported on rock outcroppings. Big Garden is known for its offshore clam flats. Big Garden has long sloping rock ledges on shore, and was extensively quarried 100 years ago. Few traces remain.

Many seabirds and songbirds nest on all these islands, and osprey nest on Big White. There are no trails on Big White Island, and vegatation is dense, which will confine your exploration to the shore. Best landing there is on the east shore of the ledge extending north from the island, again on a cobble beach. Don't land on any of these islands if there are any seas. You'll enjoy these typical small Maine deserted islands, forever preserved in the wild, if sea conditions are benign.

Carvers Harbor, Vinalhaven

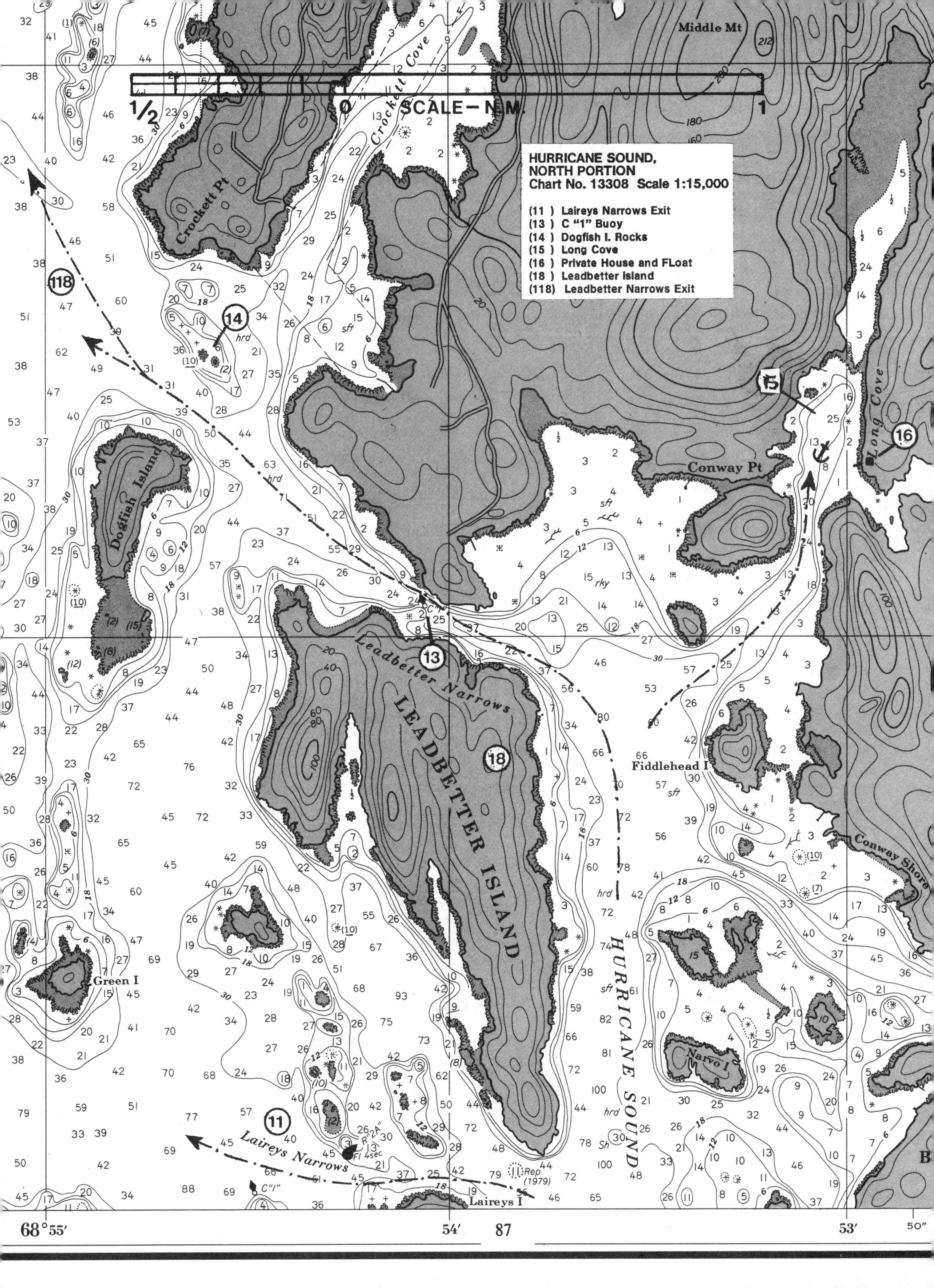
HURRICANE SOUND,
NORTH PORTION
Chart No. 13308 Scale 1:15,000
(11 ) Laireys Narrows Exit
(13 ) C "1" Buoy
(14 ) Dogfish I. Rocks
(15 ) Long Cove
(16 ) Private House and FLoat
(18 ) Leadbetter Island
(118) Leadbetter Narrows Exit
SCALE—N.M.
Middle Mt
Crockett Pt
Crockett Cove
Dogfish Island
Leadbetter Narrows
LEADBETTER ISLAND
HURRICANE SOUND
Conway Pt
Long Cove
Fiddlehead I
Conway Shore
Green I
Narvo I
Laireys Narrows
Laireys I
68°55′
54′
53′
50″

# CHAPTER 8

# ISLE AU HAUT AND WEST SHORE OF DEER ISLE

## ISLE AU HAUT— CHART NO. 13313

This long, sloping mountain, rising steeply from the sea, forms the eastern limit of Penobscot Bay. Aptly named "High Island" by Champlain when he first sighted it in 1604, its crest at 543 feet dominates all of the eastern half of the Bay.

There are several harbors on the west shore, none on the east side and only one, of little use, on the south. The main harbor (68) is in Isle au Haut Thorofare on the northwest side of the island.

Chart no. 13313 shows all of Isle au Haut. See the folded chart inside the front cover for relation of Deer Isle and Isle au Haut to the rest of Penobscot Bay.

### Isle au Haut Thorofare—Chart No. 13313

**Approaches.** The lighthouse (Fl R, 4 sec) on Robinson Point (69) stands out clearly and marks the entrance to the Thorofare. Approaching Isle au Haut from the south, keep a minimum distance of 1.25 miles offshore to avoid the numerous unmarked rocks on the west shore. The outermost of these, called The Brandies (70), consists of a pair of rocks. The southern one shows 4 feet above water at high tide, while the northern one is barely awash. They are unbuoyed and in fog, or with any kind of seas running, they may be difficult to see.

In following this western shore, be certain your position is beyond the outermost of the Brandies rocks. Above all, do not follow a course line directly between buoy N "2" (86) and N "4" (71). These buoys mark the position of nearby rocks and are not intended to be taken as a safe approach from the south to the Isle au Haut Thorofare. This may appear to be quite evident when looking at the chart, but when you are out there on the water and all you see is the two offshore buoys, the inadvisability of such a course is not so apparent. Heading north, once you are past N "4" at Rock T (71), you can safely move in to more closely parallel the shoreline.

Green daybeacon "3" (72) marks a ledge that makes out from the Kimball Island shore. Stay south of it. Undoubtedly, as in many past years, ospreys will have built a large nest atop this daybeacon. Off the Isle au Haut shore is a fish-weir (73) that extends west into the channel but it is quite visible even at high tide. Once past the constriction forming the entrance to the harbor, where the chart shows 15 feet, you may anchor anywhere.

**Anchorage.** The bottom is mud and the holding is good, although there is some scattered, bottom debris. Be sure your anchor is well dug in and that you have plenty of scope. I never had any trouble anchoring here before, but the last time we tried to anchor with a Danforth, we had to reset it 3 times. Each time the flukes were fouled with small debris of brick, wood etc., causing us to drag anchor. After we put down the CQR anchor instead, there was no problem. At the change of tide, currents swirl around in all directions and you want to be sure that they don't cause your anchor to become tripped out.

The solitary rock (74) in the harbor is covered at all but extreme low tide. It has a small, privately maintained spindle on it, but at high tide this may not show. You are safely out of range of this rock if you can still see the green daybeacon (72) at the entrance to the Thorofare. If the point of land on Kimball Island at the entrance to the harbor cuts out the view of the daybeacon, you are in danger of being on the rock (74).

Much of Isle au Haut Island is part of Acadia National Park. Though 2860 acres of a total land area of 5,500 acres is parkland, Isle au Haut has comparatively few visitors, primarily because there is no access by car. The ferry boats used for mail and passengers do not carry vehicles. The privately owned sector is mostly in the northern half of the island with the majority of the population centered around the village of Isle au Haut.

### Isle au Haut Village

The Town Wharf (75) has a float with 6 ft. depth alongside, where you may land and tie your dinghy. Don't tie your boat at the wharf as it is in frequent use, not only by local fishermen, but by the mailboat service out of Stonington and two excursion boats, the "Miss Lizzie" and the "Mink," also out of Stonington. There are several other privately owned piers in the harbor. The wharf at the General Store (76) can be used only at high tide, during which there is 5 feet depth.

Water and fuel are not available at Isle au Haut, other than a few gallons for emergency purposes, carried in your own containers from the General Store in the Village. Stonington, 10 miles distant at Deer Isle, is the nearest place to tank up with fuel and water. The General Store, a short walk up the road, also serves as the Island Post Office and is run cooperatively by the island residents. Meat, produce and groceries are available.

There is but a single inn and restaurant on the island. Called "The Keeper's House" (69a) it occupies the former keeper's house (hence its name) of the Robinson Point light. They have a dock where you may tie up your boat, and their food is reputed to be superb.

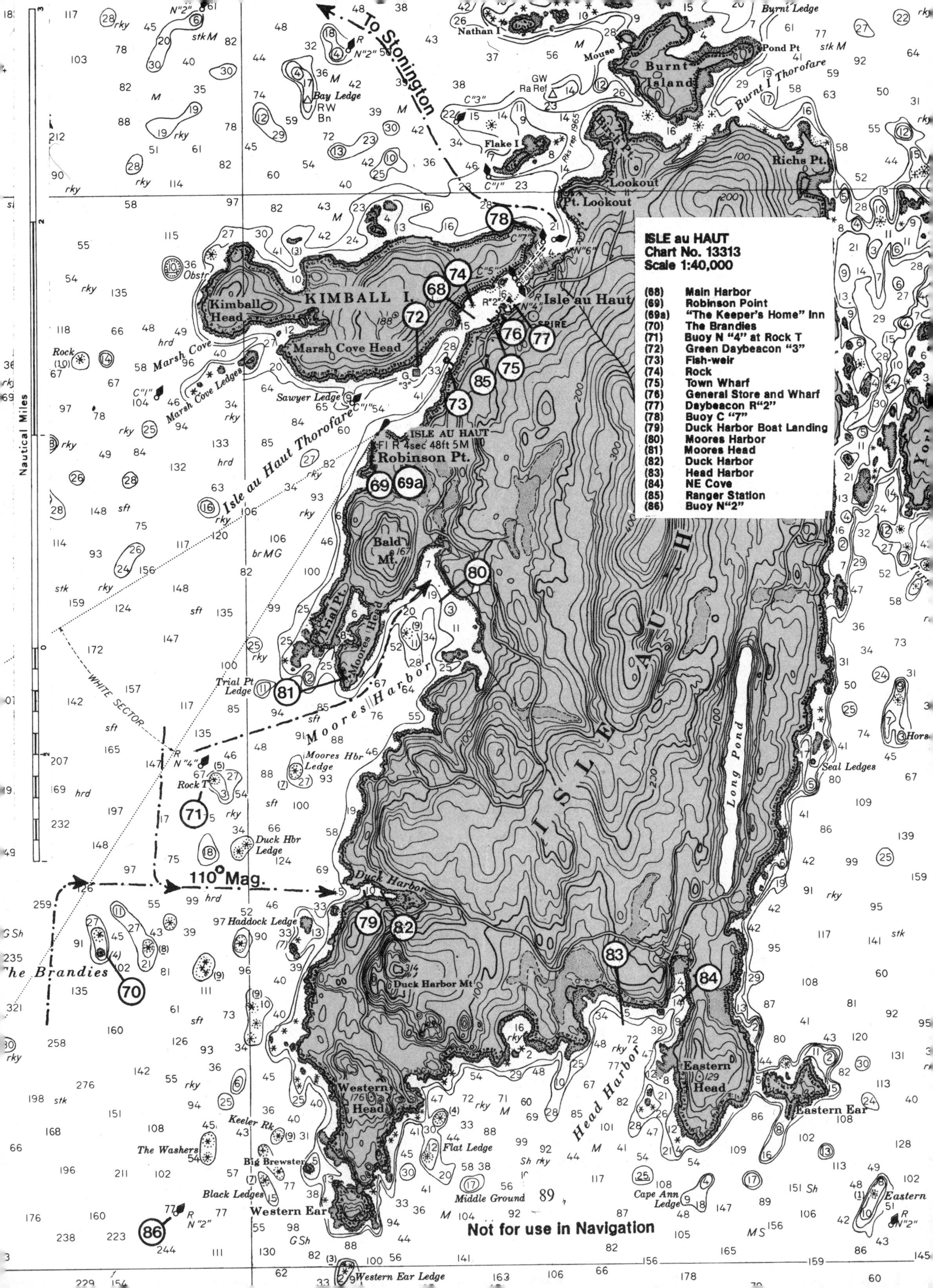
ISLE au HAUT
Chart No. 13313
Scale 1:40,000
(68) Main Harbor
(69) Robinson Point
(69a) "The Keeper's Home" Inn
(70) The Brandies
(71) Buoy N "4" at Rock T
(72) Green Daybeacon "3"
(73) Fish-weir
(74) Rock
(75) Town Wharf
(76) General Store and Wharf
(77) Daybeacon R"2"
(78) Buoy C "7"
(79) Duck Harbor Boat Landing
(80) Moores Harbor
(81) Moores Head
(82) Duck Harbor
(83) Head Harbor
(84) NE Cove
(85) Ranger Station
(86) Buoy N"2"
To Stonington
Nautical Miles
Burnt Ledge
Nathan I
Mouse I
Burnt Island
Pond Pt
Burnt I Thorofare
Bay Ledge
Flake I
Birch Pt.
Richs Pt.
Lookout
Pt. Lookout
Kimball Head
KIMBALL I.
Marsh Cove Head
Marsh Cove
Marsh Cove Ledges
Sawyer Ledge
Isle au Haut
Isle au Haut Thorofare
ISLE AU HAUT
Fl R 4sec 48ft 5M
Robinson Pt.
Bald Mt.
Trial Pt
Moores Head
Trial Pt Ledge
Moores Harbor
Moores Hbr Ledge
Rock T
Duck Hbr Ledge
110° Mag.
WHITE SECTOR
Duck Harbor
Haddock Ledge
The Brandies
Duck Harbor Mt
ISLE AU HAUT
Long Pond
Seal Ledges
Western Head
Keeler Rk
The Washers
Big Brewster
Black Ledges
Western Ear
Flat Ledge
Middle Ground
Head Harbor
Eastern Head
Eastern Ear
Cape Ann Ledge
Western Ear Ledge
Not for use in Navigation

Reservations are necessary, so best to call in advance from Stonington (tel. 367-2261).

As on all the islands, refuse disposal here is a major problem. Usually it has to be hauled to the mainland, so you can imagine how unwelcome additional trash contributed by the short-time visitor is to the permanent residents. A good supply of large, strong plastic bags will take care of your refuse problem until you reach a place where it can be properly disposed of. When refuse starts to build up, we place the filled bags in the dinghy even though this may make you feel that the dinghy is a trailing garbage scow!

**North Channel.** A dredged channel leads out through the north end of Isle au Haut Thorofare, the route used headed toward Stonington, the Deer Islands Thorofare or toward Merchant Row. Controlling depth at low water is 3½ to 4 feet, with a width of about 90 feet. Post a lookout forward as you pass through, for there are scattered boulders in the channel and the limits are poorly defined.

Due to the growth of mussel beds, this dredged channel is becoming more shallow and more difficult to negotiate each year. There are places that all but dry out at low tide. The *Coast Pilot* warns that the ledge marked by daybeacon R "2" (77) extends so close to the 16-foot spot that boats run aground on it. Give this daybeacon a generous berth, keeping well out toward the middle of the channel. At the north end, closely hug buoy C "7" (78), for its opposing buoy, N "6" is set directly over a rock! Fortunately, the water is clear, and all dangers are visible.

### Acadia National Park

The opportunity to explore this large wilderness tract of mountain, woods and bogs, with its great natural beauty and quiet solitude, is the appeal that draws people to Isle Au Haut. It is a paradise for the avid hiker, photographer or bird-watcher. To provide help and information to visitors about the trails and the wildlife of the area, the National Park Service has a full-time ranger and a naturalist on the island during summer. You will find them at the Ranger Station (85) a short 10 minute walk south of the village. or at the boat landing at Duck Harbor (79). The Park Service has a printed pamphlet describing the island, including a map showing the major trails, obtainable at the ranger station (85). It can also be obtained by writing to Acadia National Park, U.S. Dept. of Interior, P.O. Box 177, Bar Harbor, ME 04609.

A more detailed map prepared by Wm. Stevens shows all the trails, as well as the extent of marshy land and location of all dwellings. This is available at the General Store (76) in Isle au Haut village and several bookstores in Stonington, Deer Isle. Both maps give the length of each trail in miles to help in planning the walking time required. One road circles the island and has alternate paved and dirt sections. Twenty-five trails criss-cross the island, going to every point of interest, totalling 33 miles in length. All are marked. A hike to the top of Mt. Champlain, the highest peak on the island, should provide an excellent view of Penobscot Bay, but unfortunately overgrowth at the top blocks the view.

### Moores Harbor— Chart No. 13313

The protection afforded by this harbor (80) on the west shore of Isle au Haut is better than what might be surmised from the chart. Although it is large and open to the southwest, you can tuck into coves and indentations on either side of the harbor to keep out of any wind and waves. Surroundings are attractive and the view across Penobscot Bay is magnificent. Moores Harbor is large, but is quiet and secluded and it shouldn't be overlooked, particularly in fine, settled weather.

Approach the harbor keeping north of N "4", which marks Rock T (71), and head for the tip of Moores Head (81). From there, closely follow the west shore of the harbor until well up toward the head, thus avoiding the rock in the middle which uncovers at 9 feet. We've shown a course line on our excerpt from chart no. 13313.

### Duck Harbor— Chart No. 13313

This narrow inlet (82), 0.8 miles south of Moores Harbor is well sheltered in all but westerlies. A dock on the south shore (79) has several floats where you can land your dinghy to go ashore. The dock, with 5 feet depth is used by excursion boats from Stonington and the Acadia Park Service. There may be a spare mooring available, maintained by the Park Service. You can confirm this by asking the Park Ranger who is usually at the landing. If you are anchoring, watch the depths carefully, taking into account the 10-foot tide range. If you go too far east toward the head of Duck Harbor, you'll have no water under your keel at low tide.

Approaching from the south, proceed north 0.25 miles past the northernmost rock of The Brandies (70) until you can see east down the length of the harbor. Then turn east toward the harbor. This will bring you in at a course heading of 110 degrees magnetic. From the north, proceed south for 0.55 miles past N "4" (71), enabling you to clear Duck Harbor Ledge. Then make your turn when you can see into the harbor. The course heading will be the same, 110 degrees magnetic, and in both instances you will be kept clear of the rocks and ledges to either side. We've shown course lines for both approaches on our excerpt from chart no. 13301.

•

Currents south of Isle au Haut have a pattern similar to those of Vinalhaven Island.You'll see all this best on the folded chart inside the front cover. As the current ebbs out of Isle au Haut Bay, the direction of current follows parallel to the shoreline of Isle au Haut Island, trending generally in a southerly direction. South of the island, the set is more easterly and gradually weakens until it is met by water emptying out of Jericho Bay, east of Isle au Haut, in a southwesterly direction. Between Eastern Ear Ledge and Colt Ledge, the ebb current runs about 0.75-1.0 knot at a heading of 260 de-

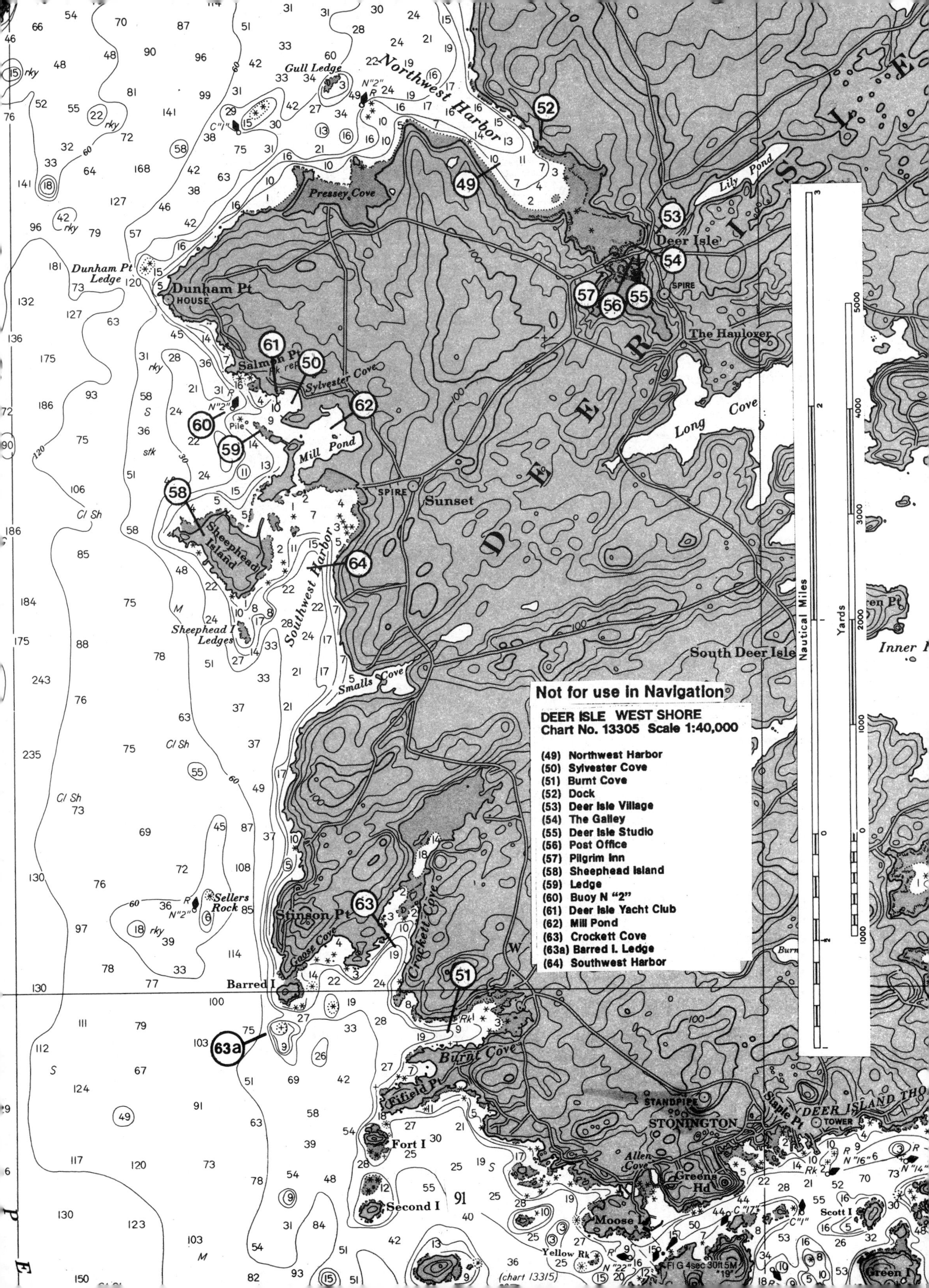

Not for use in Navigation
DEER ISLE WEST SHORE
Chart No. 13305 Scale 1:40,000
(49) Northwest Harbor
(50) Sylvester Cove
(51) Burnt Cove
(52) Dock
(53) Deer Isle Village
(54) The Galley
(55) Deer Isle Studio
(56) Post Office
(57) Pilgrim Inn
(58) Sheephead Island
(59) Ledge
(60) Buoy N "2"
(61) Deer Isle Yacht Club
(62) Mill Pond
(63) Crockett Cove
(63a) Barred I. Ledge
(64) Southwest Harbor
Nautical Miles
Yards
Northwest Harbor
Gull Ledge
Pressey Cove
Lily Pond
Deer Isle
The Haulover
Long Cove
DEER ISLE
Dunham Pt Ledge
Dunham Pt
Salmon Pt
Sylvester Cove
Mill Pond
Sunset
Sheephead Island
Sheephead I Ledges
Southwest Harbor
Smalls Cove
South Deer Isle
Sellers Rock
Stinson Pt
Goose Cove
Crockett Cove
Barred I
Burnt Cove
Fifield Pt
Fort I
Second I
STANDPIPE
STONINGTON
Allen Cove
Greens Hd
Moose I
Yellow Rk
Scott I
Green I
Staple Pt
DEER ISLAND THO
Inner
(chart 13315)

grees magnetic. On the ebb south of Marshall Island, the set is about 180 degrees magnetic, also about 0.75-1.0 knot velocity.

### Head Harbor—Chart No. 13313

Most of Head Harbor (83) is of little use for it is hardly more than a deep bight on the south shore. Completely exposed to the south and southwest, it offers little protection. Unless the wind is strong out of the southwest, you can find some measure of security by going as far as possible up into the cove in the northeast corner of the harbor (84). The ledges and rocks west of Eastern Head help to break up any large seas and keep them from entering the cove. The cove is used by a few fishermen. The bottom is generally rocky, mixed with clay in some areas, and sandy up in the cove. At the head of the cove are a few summer houses, but no docks for landing. No supplies are available. The loop road comes down to the head of the cove and it may be possible to hitch a ride to Isle au Haut village.

## W. SHORE DEER ISLE—CHART NO. 13305

Most of the coves on the west side of Deer Isle are not much use to yachtsmen. Either they are exposed to weather from the south and/or shoal and fouled with rocks and ledges. Others have obstructed entrances. The exceptions are Northwest Harbor (49), Sylvester Cove (50) and Burnt Cove (51). Harbors on the east and south sides of Deer Isle are described in Chapter 9.

### Northwest Harbor—Chart No. 13305

Although this harbor (49) on the northwest side of Deer Isle is easy to enter and provides good protection from all but northwesterly winds, it is usually empty of any boats. The harbor east of the constriction is completely dry at low tide. Do not anchor east of the dock (52) on the north shore, for the harbor has silted in considerably and it shallows rapidly.

Northwest Harbor was formerly a port of entry with a dredged channel to the head of the harbor. Coasting schooners came here, lay alongside the docks, to change cargo, grounding at low tide. It was the main important port on Deer Isle before Stonington, at the south end of Deer Isle, was developed. The original site of Stonington was the cove east of Greens Head and the town was called Greens Landing.

One advantage of Northwest Harbor is its proximity to Deer Isle Village (53), where at high tide you can come by dinghy for supplies. At the head of the harbor is The Galley (54), a store with groceries, produce, meat, beer, and wine. Across the street is Deer Isle Studio (55) where photographic supplies are available. Adjacent west is the Post Office (56). The Pilgrim Inn (57) serves lunch and dinner.

Bradbury Island is a 180 acre Nature Conservancy Preserve two miles west of Northwest Harbor. You can land there on a calm day. Don't try it if there are heavy seas. There's a good landing area on a small cobble beach in the westernmost bight on the south shore. You could land on a similar beach on the north shore about 250 yards east from the northwest point. Be careful approaching because tidal currents swirl around Bradbury Island.

Most of the central portion is hardwood growth, maple, beech, and birch, with spruce on the steeper slopes. There are cliffs along the west shore, as high as 164 ft., with lower cliffs along the south shore and the east end. A bog area is near the center. Bradbury Island has small streams feeding this bog, and supporting a deer population. You'll see a few osprey nests along the shore. The island was inhabited only from 1850 to 1880. Sheep were grazed there during the 1940's.

### Sylvester Cove— Chart No. 13305

Sylvester Cove (50), south of Dunham Point, offers better protection than might appear. Sheephead Island (58) and a long line of ledge which bares at half-tide (59) helps keep out seas from the south and southwest. Entering the cove, be sure to stay north of buoy N "2" (60) to avoid rocks which extend beyond the reef. On the north shore is a large dock on stone piers with a float belonging to the Deer Island Yacht Club (61), 9 ft. depth alongside at low tide. The club maintains a guest mooring for visiting yachtsmen, marked D.I.Y.C. Guest. There is no club house, nor any facilities. We found members of this club to be extremely helpful, going out of their way to provide information and even to drive us to Deer Isle Village to obtain fuel and provisions.

There is 10 feet depth everywhere within the harbor. Mill Pond (62) has a mill-dam in disrepair across it and is not navigable. It is, however, a beautiful spot to explore by dinghy. From Sylvester Cove, you'll have spectacular views of the islands north of North Haven and across Penobscot Bay to the Camden Hills.

The cove is an old community, based on four families that have been here since the middle of the 19th century. The descendents of the original families regularly return to spend the summer. Fifty years ago Sylvester Cove was mainly a fishing cove for half a dozen boats. In 1927 one of the summer residents had a Friendship Sloop, originally a work boat, which he made over into a yacht. She was the first large boat in the cove to be used strictly for pleasure. There were also some catboats and sailing dorys. Eventually a cruising fleet of other large yachts started to build up and today there are 15-20 cruising sailboats.

### Burnt Cove— Chart No. 13305

Burnt Cove (51), near the south end of Deer Isle, offers protection from all winds except westerlies. You will see a few boats moored here. The inner half of the harbor is shallow and rock strewn, but if you keep to the outer half you will find good anchoring in mud bottom. There are no supplies.

If you are headed into Burnt Cove or Crockett Cove to the north, be sure to give Barred Island a generous berth. Extending south of this island is a long ledge (63a), shown on the chart as a rock and a 9 foot spot. The rock is exposed at half-tide. But there is less than

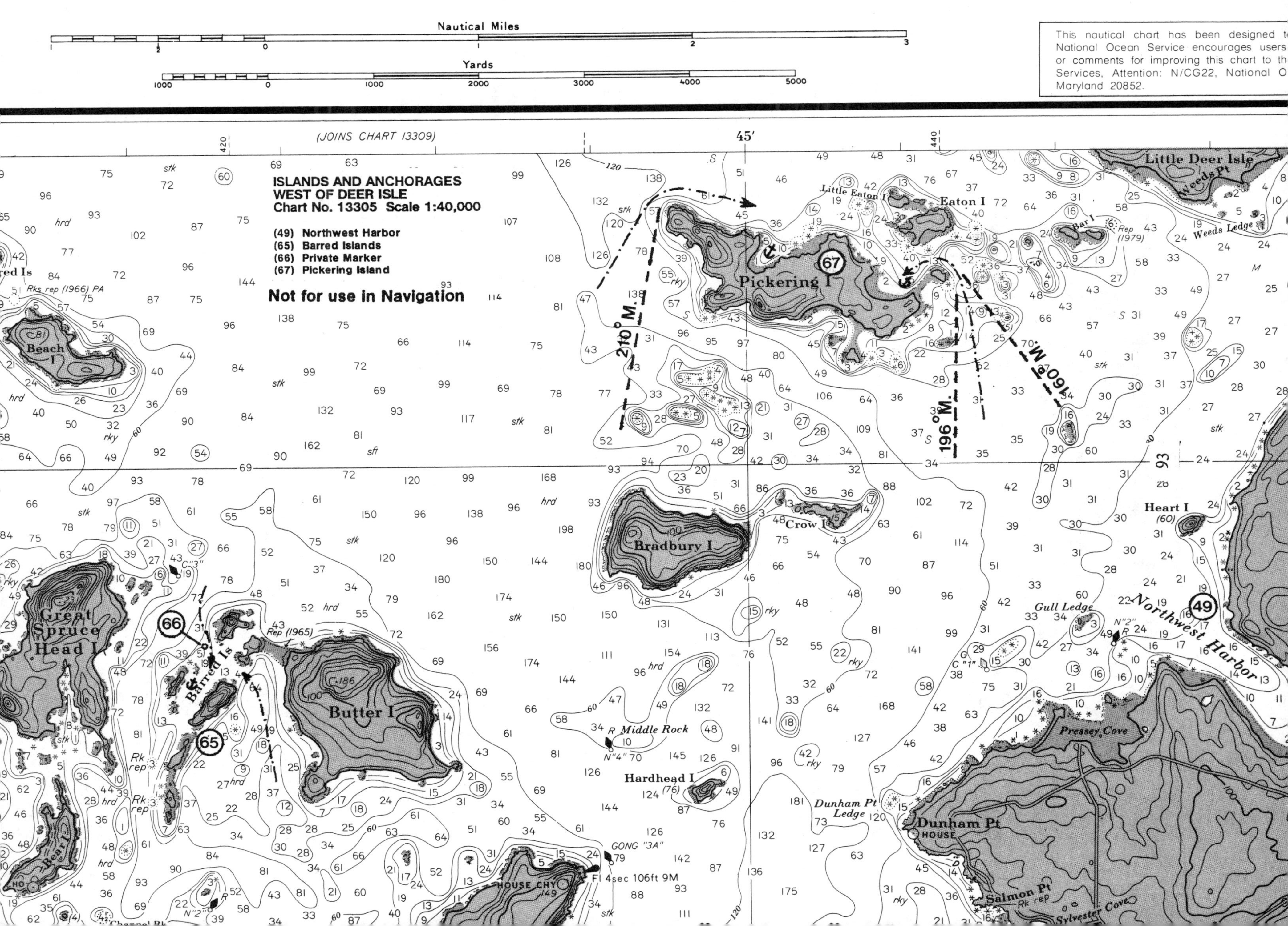
Nautical Miles
Yards
This nautical chart has been designed t
National Ocean Service encourages users
or comments for improving this chart to th
Services, Attention: N/CG22, National O
Maryland 20852.
(JOINS CHART 13309)
ISLANDS AND ANCHORAGES
WEST OF DEER ISLE
Chart No. 13305 Scale 1:40,000
(49) Northwest Harbor
(65) Barred Islands
(66) Private Marker
(67) Pickering Island
Not for use in Navigation
Little Deer Isle
Weeds Pt
Weeds Ledge
Little Eaton I
Eaton I
Bar I
Pickering I
210° M.
196° M.
160° M.
Beach I
Bradbury I
Crow I
Heart I
Great Spruce Head I
Barred Is
Butter I
Middle Rock
Hardhead I
Gull Ledge
Northwest Harbor
Pressey Cove
Dunham Pt Ledge
Dunham Pt
HOUSE
Salmon Pt
Sylvester Cove
Bear I
HOUSE CHY
GONG "3A"
Fl 4sec 106ft 9M

the indicated 9 feet of water to the south of it, for at low tide, it is barely awash and has caught the keel of more than one boat.

### Crockett Cove

Crockett Cove (63), to the north, is unacceptable for an overnight anchorage as it is completely exposed. On a calm day you could anchor there to enjoy nearby nature preserves.

Barred Island and Crockett Cove Woods are two Nature Conservancy Preserves, easily accessible from Crockett Cove (63) or Burnt Cove (51). Barred Island should not be confused with Barred Islands further north off the west shore of Deer Isle, shown on chart no. 13305, Islands and Anchorages West of Deer Isle. This Barred Island is shown on chart no. 13305, Deer Isle, off the south tip of Stinson Point, west of Crockett Cove (63). The best place to land is on the sand bar at the north end of the island. This bar connects Barred Island to the mainland at low tide. You'll find shells on this bar, whelks, periwinkles, limpets, razor clams, but in your eagerness to find them, watch out that you don't step on the sea urchins which are also present.

There are no trails on Barred Island. Vegetation is mostly spruce and fir, though there's a large raspberry thicket covering most of a burn that destroyed trees in part of the interior. Most visitors confine themselves to exploring the shore, extensive rounded granite ledges, with the usual shoreside vegetation and a few small small tidal pools.

Crockett Cove Woods is 100 acres lying inland from the east shore of Crockett Cove (63) and extending nearby to the north shore of Burnt Cove (51). The Preserve doesn't touch any shore, so you'd have to cross private property to reach it. Don't do this without asking permission. You can walk to Crockett Cove from Stonington, (described in Chapter 9). Go about 2 miles west along the Shore Road to Whitman Road, which continues about 0.3 mile west. At the end, make a right turn onto a dirt road, and you'll see the parking lot on your right.

A self guided trail leads through Crockett Cove Woods, through dense spruce woods, with some cedar and tamarack in wet parts. There's a corduroy planked trail across sphagnum moss, and you'll see many birds, and some beard lichen hanging from trees.

**Southwest Harbor (64)**, 2 miles north of Stinson Point, is also too exposed for an overnight anchorage. It was formerly the town harbor and had a dock, but now it is considerably silted in at the north end, besides being exposed.

### Barred Islands— Chart No. 13305

In addition to the harbors on Deer Isle, fine anchorage may be had on the lee shore of some of the smaller, nearby islands to the west.

A beautiful secluded anchorage may be found here west of Deer Isle between Great Spruce Head Island and Butter Island. Barred Islands (65) lie between these two larger islands. The anchorage can be approached from south or north. To facilitate entry from the north, a privately maintained red marker (66) is east of the 5-foot spot. Come around close east of it and then head south. There is deep water within the cove and good holding ground. Approaching from the south, you may need some tide help to cross a 4-ft. spot at the bar. We've shown course lines on our excerpt from chart no. 13305.

### Pickering Island— Chart No. 13305

Two coves on the north side of Pickering Island (67) provide excellent anchorage with good holding ground amid scenic surroundings. In a southerly, you will be protected from any seas. You can enter from around either the east or west ends of the island. Entry from the west is somewhat easier. We've shown course lines on our excerpt from chart no. 13305.

Approaching the west end from the south, aim for the westernmost tip of the island on a course heading anywhere west of 210 degrees magnetic. This will clear the rocks south of the island.

Approaching the east end from the south, aim for the small islet set off northeast from the main island, keeping within the arc of a heading of 160 to 196 degrees magnetic to clear all dangers. Then pass between the small unnamed islet and Eaton Island, following the shore around southwest into the cove. Pickering Island is privately owned. Don't go ashore without requesting permission.

•

This completes our circumnavigation of Penobscot Bay, one of Maine's most spectacular cruising grounds, and one of the most spectacular anywhere. Now let's continue our cruise down east.

Deer Island Thorofare near Stonington

# CHAPTER 9

# PASSAGES EAST FROM PENOBSCOT BAY, WEST SHORE OF DEER ISLE AND NEARBY HARBORS

## PASSAGES EAST FROM PENOBSCOT BAY

### CHART NOS. 13260, 13302, 13316, 13313-A

Refer to our excerpt from chart no. 13260 Passages East from Penobscot Bay. Heading east from Penobscot Bay, there are four alternate passages; Eggemoggin Reach (1), Deer Isle Thorofare (2), Merchant Row (3) or open water around the south end of Isle au Haut (4). Determine your choice according to your starting position, your destination, and visibility (fog).

### Eggemoggin Reach

If you have worked your way toward the head of Penobscot Bay and wish to proceed to Blue Hill Bay (5) or any of the harbors on Mt. Desert Island (6), then Eggemoggin Reach will be the most direct. Because it is oriented on a northwest-southeast axis, you'll have a beam-reach both ways with the prevailing southwesterly summer wind. For the most part, the passage is clear of dangers, with deep water close to shore. Hazards are mostly near each end, and all ledges and rocks are well marked by buoys and daybeacons. Along the length of Eggemoggin Reach are fine harbors, providing protection and supplies. Like Fox Islands Thorofare (Chapter 7), Eggemoggin Reach is generally fog-free due to the mass of land of Deer Isle on one side and the mainland on the other.

Currents within Eggemoggin Reach are minimal, seldom attaining the strength of 1.0 Knot. Direction of ebb and flood tide is dependent on the wind. With prevailing summertime winds from the southwest, flood tide enters the Reach from both its eastern and its western ends, meeting somewhere in the middle in the vicinity of Deer Island Bridge. Correspondingly, ebb tide flows out from both ends of the Reach. However, if there is a strong easterly wind, the flood will run from east to west throughout the entire length of the Reach, meeting the flood tide as it comes up Penobscot Bay, in the region of Bell Buoy "ER" (8) southeast of Cape Rosier. Refer to our Chart No. 13302.

**West Entrance.** Entrance marks for the western end of Eggemoggin Reach are the bold high bluffs, thickly wooded, of the southern end of Cape Rosier (7) and the red and white fairway buoy labeled "ER" (8). Refer to our excerpt from chart no. 13302. Cape Rosier was named in honor of James Rosier, the journalist of Weymouth's voyages. An additional aid is the lighthouse on Pumpkin Island (9), at the southeast side of the entrance. Although the lighthouse is abandoned, the house and white tower are highly visible.

**East Entrance.** Refer to our excerpt from chart no. 13316B. At the eastern entrance to Eggemoggin Reach is a fairway bell buoy labeled "EE" (10). Devils Head (11), a high, rocky promontory at the south end of Hog Island, stands out clearly and helps determine your position.

Now refer to our excerpt from chart no. 13260 titled Penobscot Bay and Passages East.

The east end of Eggemoggin Reach empties out at the upper end of Jericho Bay (12). From there you can proceed on an easterly course through Casco Passage (13) toward Mt. Desert Island, or turn north to enter Blue Hill Bay.

### Deer Island Thorofare—Chart No. 13313A

Passage east may also be made south of Deer Isle, through Deer Island Thorofare (2). This passage, and Merchant Row (3) south of it are the most direct routes east from the mid-region of Penobscot Bay. Buoys and daybeacons in both these passages are colored and numbered for traveling north and west. So bear in mind when headed east through them to keep **red** to port.

Refer to our excerpt from chart no. 13302. Approaching Deer Island Thorofare from the west, all the islands and ledges are either large enough to be seen when approached or they are well marked by buoys. One of the outermost dangers is a solitary rock called "The Brown Cow" (14). It is located 1.3 miles southwest of the lighthouse on Mark Island (15) and marked by whistle buoy, "2BC." For some unknown reason this buoy sits in 120 feet depth, fully ½ mile south of the danger it marks. Although the rock does show 3 feet at high tide, it is difficult to see at night, in dense fog, or in seas of any height. Last year, the "Brown Cow" has caused the loss of a sardine carrier which ran into it.

West Mark Island Ledge (16), another solitary rock, is 0.7 miles northwest of the light on Mark Island and is

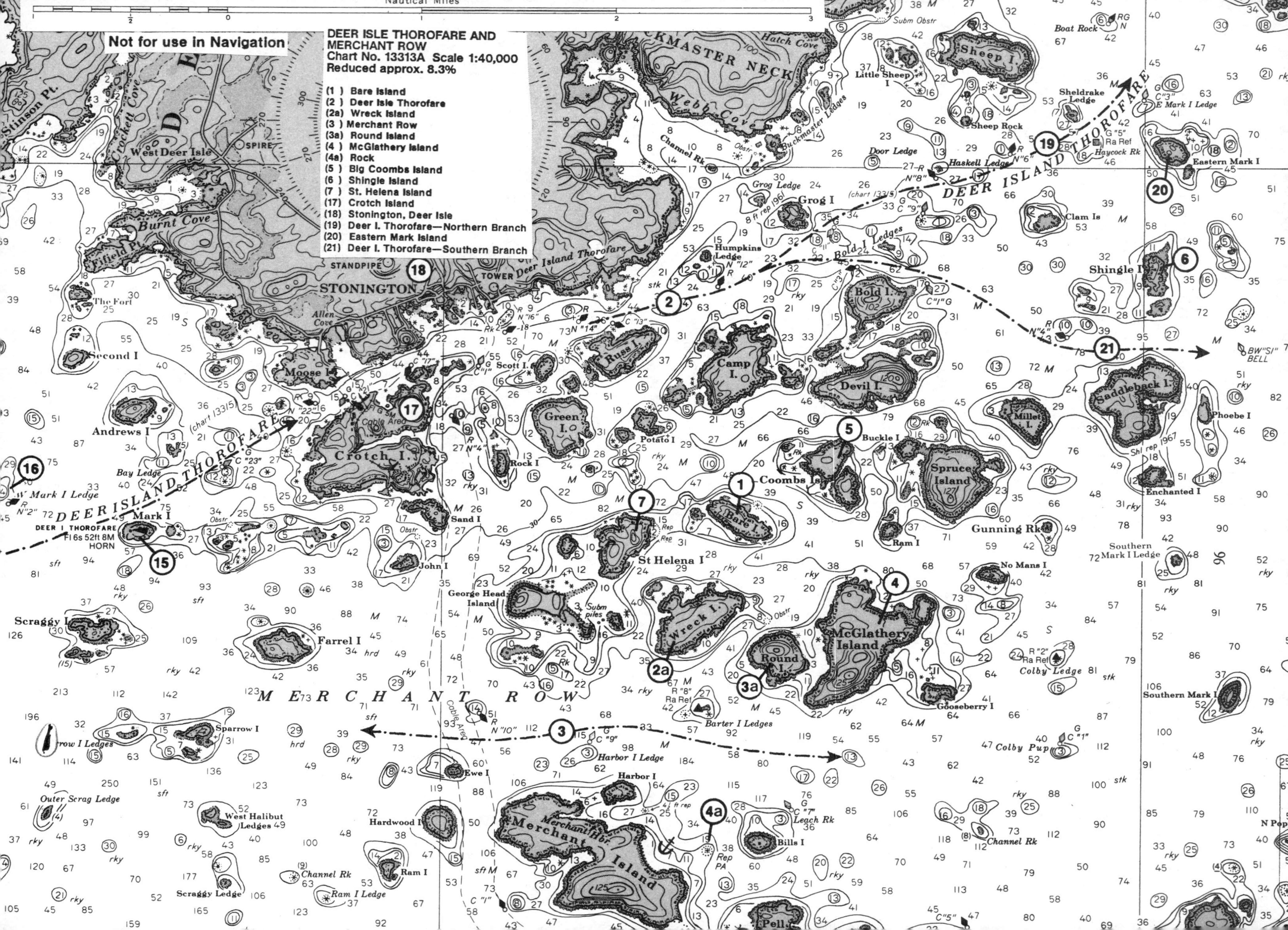
Nautical Miles
Not for use in Navigation
DEER ISLE THOROFARE AND
MERCHANT ROW
Chart No. 13313A Scale 1:40,000
Reduced approx. 8.3%
(1 ) Bare Island
(2 ) Deer Isle Thorofare
(2a) Wreck Island
(3 ) Merchant Row
(3a) Round Island
(4 ) McGlathery Island
(4a) Rock
(5 ) Big Coombs Island
(6 ) Shingle Island
(7 ) St. Helena Island
(17) Crotch Island
(18) Stonington, Deer Isle
(19) Deer I. Thorofare—Northern Branch
(20) Eastern Mark Island
(21) Deer I. Thorofare—Southern Branch
STONINGTON
DEER ISLAND THOROFARE
MERCHANT ROW
Deer Island Thorofare
West Deer Isle
Crockett Cove
Burnt Cove
Fifield Pt
Stinson Pt.
The Fort
Second I
Andrews I
Moose I
Crotch I.
Green I.
Russ I.
Camp I.
Devil I.
Bold I.
Saddleback I.
Shingle I
Sheep I.
Little Sheep I
Eastern Mark I
Buckmaster Neck
Webb Cove
Hatch Cove
Mark I
Sand I
John I
St Helena I
Bare I.
Coombs Is
Buckle I
Spruce Island
Millet I.
Phoebe I
Enchanted I
Gunning Rk
Ram I
George Head Island
Wreck I.
Round I.
McGlathery Island
No Mans I
Gooseberry I
Farrel I
Scraggy I
Sparrow I
Harbor I
Merchant Island
Bills I
Hardwood I
Ewe I
Ram I
West Halibut Ledges
Scraggy Ledge
Outer Scrag Ledge
Southern Mark I
Southern Mark I Ledge
Colby Ledge
Colby Pup
Barter I Ledges
Harbor I Ledge
Leach Rk
Channel Rk
Ram I Ledge
Grog I
Grog Ledge
Humpkins Ledge
Bold I Ledges
Door Ledge
Haskell Ledge
Sheep Rock
Sheldrake Ledge
Haycock Rk
E Mark I Ledge
Boat Rock
Clam Is
Potato I
Rock I
Scott I.
Bay Ledge
W Mark I Ledge
DEER I THOROFARE
Fl 6s 52ft 8M
HORN
STANDPIPE
TOWER
SPIRE
Allen Cove
96

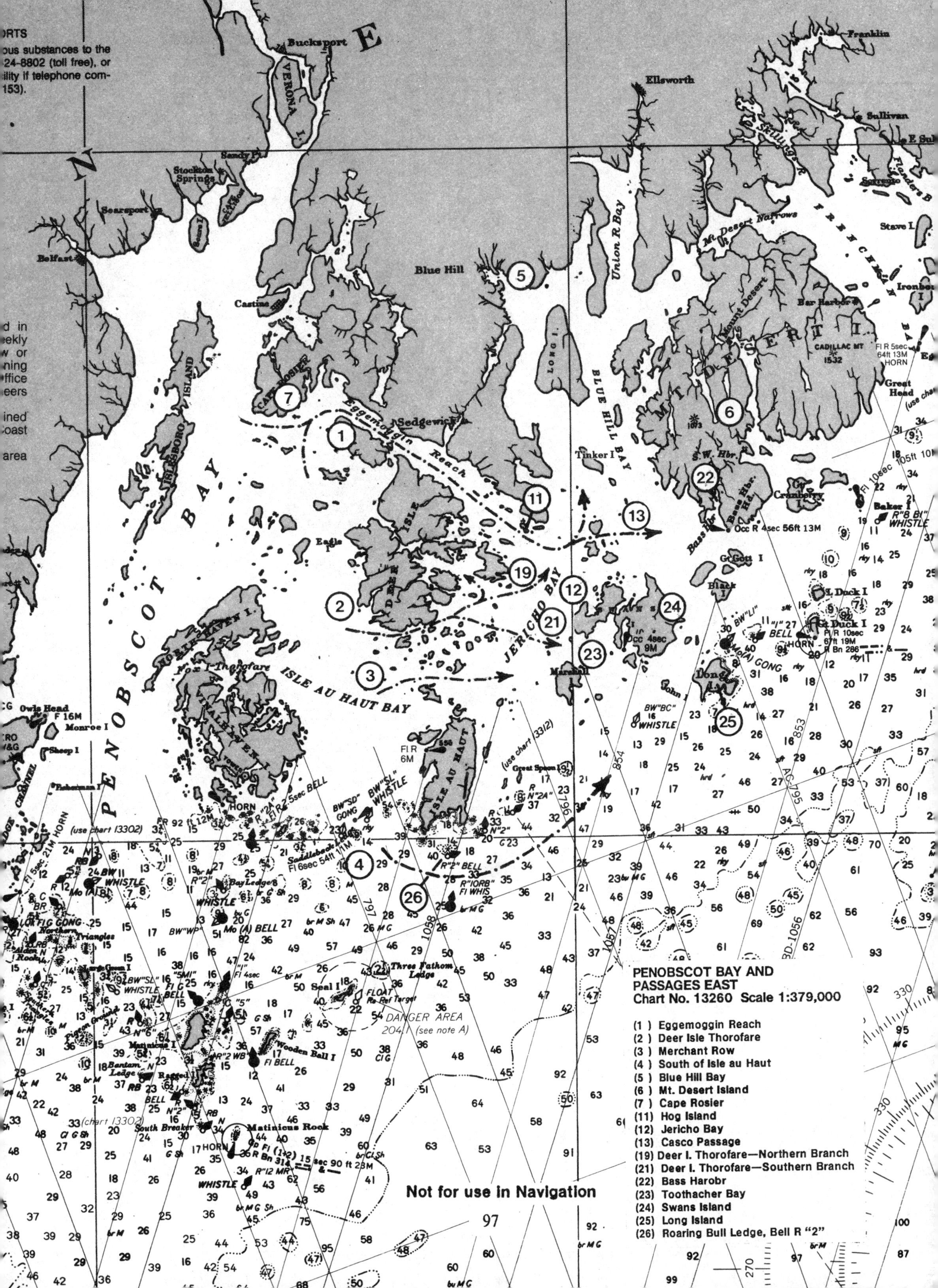

PENOBSCOT BAY AND
PASSAGES EAST
Chart No. 13260 Scale 1:379,000
(1 ) Eggemoggin Reach
(2 ) Deer Isle Thorofare
(3 ) Merchant Row
(4 ) South of Isle au Haut
(5 ) Blue Hill Bay
(6 ) Mt. Desert Island
(7 ) Cape Rosier
(11) Hog Island
(12) Jericho Bay
(13) Casco Passage
(19) Deer I. Thorofare—Northern Branch
(21) Deer I. Thorofare—Southern Branch
(22) Bass Harobr
(23) Toothacher Bay
(24) Swans Island
(25) Long Island
(26) Roaring Bull Ledge, Bell R "2"
Not for use in Navigation
PENOBSCOT BAY
ISLE AU HAUT BAY
JERICHO BAY
BLUE HILL BAY
Eggemoggin Reach
Bucksport
Ellsworth
Franklin
Sullivan
Blue Hill
Castine
Sedgewick
Belfast
Searsport
Stockton Springs
Sandy Pt.
Owls Head
Matinicus Rock
Seal I
Three Fathom Ledge
Wooden Ball I
DANGER AREA
Bar Harbor
CADILLAC MT
Great Head
Baker I
Tinker I
Marshall
Long I.
Mt. Desert Narrows
Union R. Bay

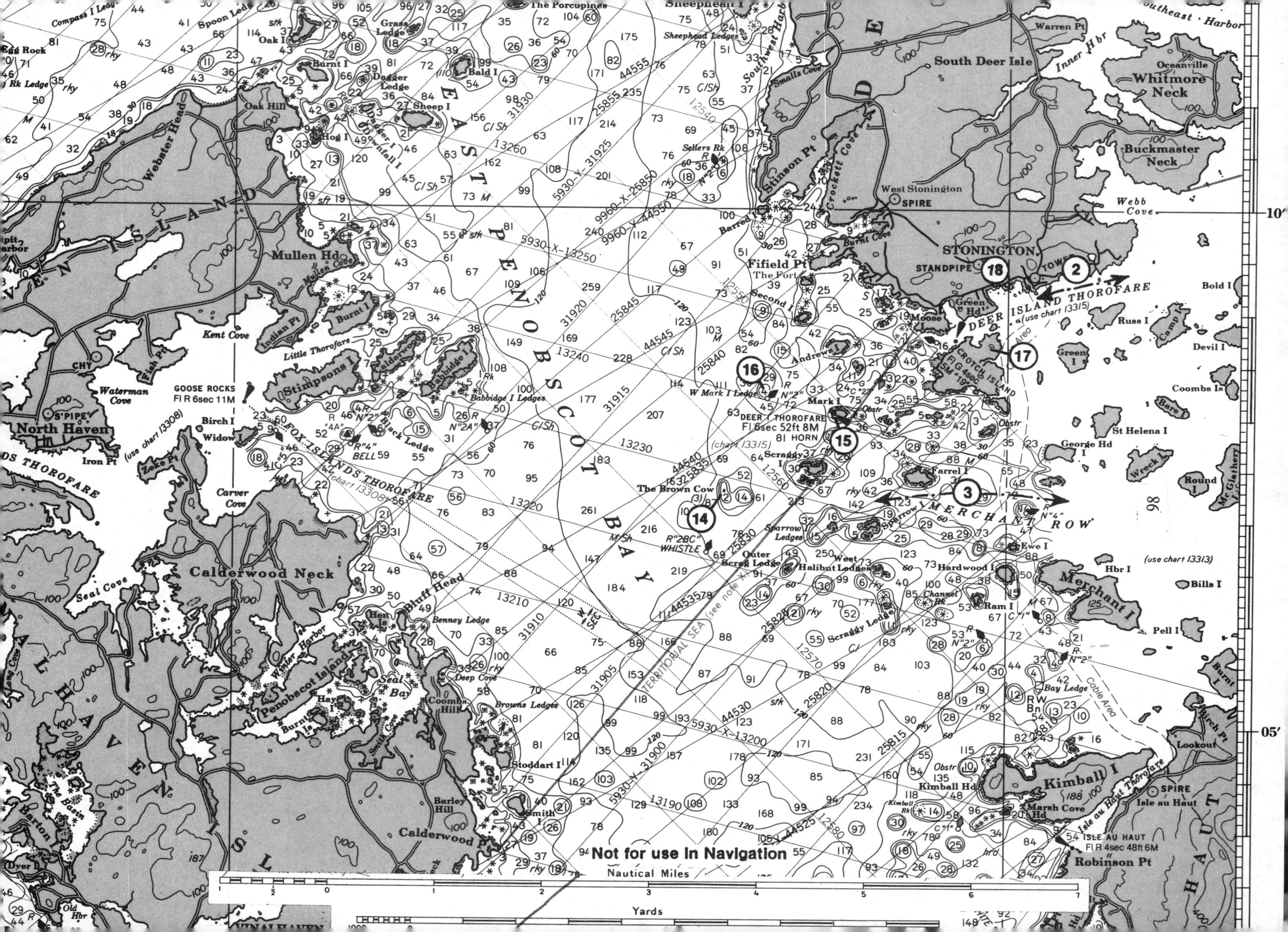

EAST PENOBSCOT BAY
VINALHAVEN ISLAND
DEER ISLE
ISLE AU HAUT
MERCHANT ROW
DEER ISLAND THOROFARE
FOX ISLANDS THOROFARE
Calderwood Neck
Stonington
Webster Head
Crockett Cove
South Deer Isle
Whitmore Neck
Buckmaster Neck
Kimball I
Merchant I
Stinson Pt
Southwest Harb
GOOSE ROCKS FI R 6sec 11M
DEER I THOROFARE FI 6sec 52ft 8M 81 HORN
ISLE AU HAUT FI R 4sec 48ft 6M
TERRITORIAL SEA (see note X)
(use chart 13308)
(use chart 13315)
(use chart 13313)
Not for use in Navigation
Nautical Miles
Yards
05'
10'

98

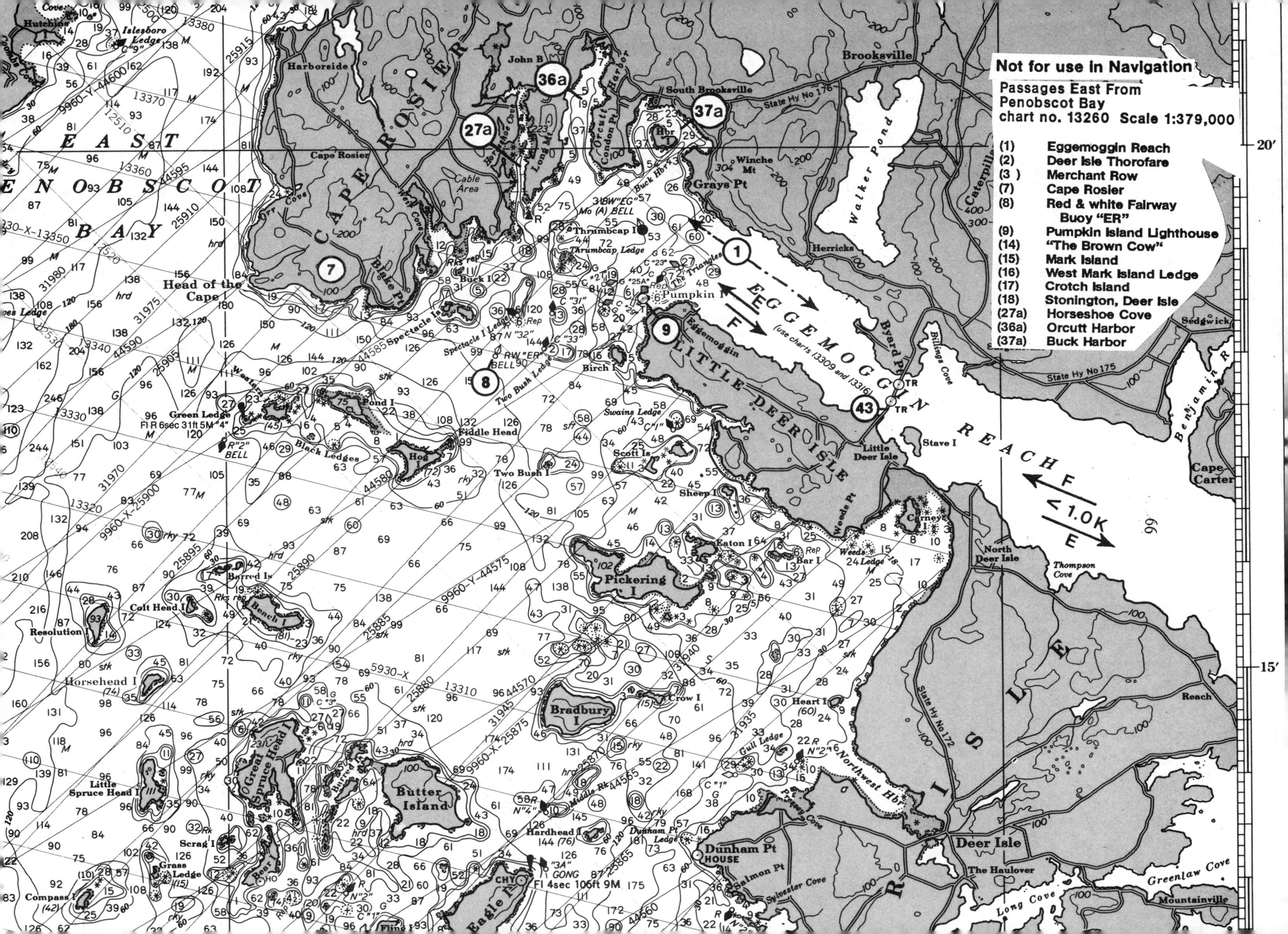
Not for use in Navigation
Passages East From
Penobscot Bay
chart no. 13260 Scale 1:379,000
(1) Eggemoggin Reach
(2) Deer Isle Thorofare
(3 ) Merchant Row
(7) Cape Rosier
(8) Red & white Fairway
Buoy "ER"
(9) Pumpkin Island Lighthouse
(14) "The Brown Cow"
(15) Mark Island
(16) West Mark Island Ledge
(17) Crotch Island
(18) Stonington, Deer Isle
(27a) Horseshoe Cove
(36a) Orcutt Harbor
(37a) Buck Harbor
EAST PENOBSCOT BAY
CAPE ROSIER
EGGEMOGGIN REACH
LITTLE DEER ISLE
DEER ISLE
(use charts 13309 and 13316)
Head of the Cape
Harborside
Brooksville
South Brooksville
Walker Pond
Herricks
Grays Pt
Pumpkin I
Thrumbcap I
Thrumbcap Ledge
Spectacle Is
Birch I
Pond I
Hog I
Fiddle Head
Two Bush I
Scott Is
Sheep I
Pickering I
Eaton I
Bar I
Bradbury I
Crow I
Butter Island
Great Spruce Head I
Little Spruce Head I
Beach I
Colt Head I
Resolution I
Horsehead I
Compass I
Grass Ledge
Scrag I
Eagle I
Hardhead I
Dunham Pt
Dunham Pt HOUSE
Salmon Pt
Sylvester Cove
Heart I
Gull Ledge
Northwest Hb
Deer Isle
The Haulover
Greenlaw Cove
Mountainville
Long Cove
North Deer Isle
Thompson Cove
Reach
Carney I
Weeds Pt
Little Deer Isle
Stave I
Billings Cove
Byard Pt
Sedgwick
Benjamin R
Cape Carter
Caterpillar
State Hy No 176
State Hy No 175
State Hy No 172
Cable Area
Black Ledges
Green Ledge
Islesboro Ledge
Hutchins
Swains Ledge
Middle Rk
Winche Mt
20′
15′

covered with only 4 feet of water at low tide. But here buoy N "2" marking it is very close.

The light on Mark Island (15) is the principal mark entering Deer Island Thorofare. It is a 52 foot high, white, square tower, Fl 6 sec., and has a fog horn. Mark Island is high and domed-shaped, easily distinguished at a great distance from other islands nearby. Another excellent landmark for locating the entrance to Deer Island Thorofare are the crane and derricks on Crotch Island (17). These tall spidery metal legs are visible from all directions, and are particularly useful in crossing Isle au Haut Bay from Fox Islands Thorofare. These are the remnants of the once active granite quaries on the island and can be picked out even before Mark Island and its light are recognized.

The advantage of Deer Island Thorofare (2) over Eggemoggin Reach (1) is the ease and convenience of stopping for provisioning at Stonington (18) on the south shore of Deer Isle. Also, with its many islands, Deer Island Thorofare has greater scenic variety. The main channel is well buoyed, and if you pay close attention to the chart, you should have no problems. However, in fog, with a complete lack of visual references, it is not easy a passage as Eggemoggin Reach. Currents are not strong in Deer Island Thorofare, achieving a maximum velocity on both the flood and ebb tide of 0.6 knots. The current runs in a line with the channel, the flood tide setting east and the ebb west. The wind exerts considerable influence on this current. During a strong easterly, both ebb and flood tide will set west. Conversely, a strong westerly wind will cause both ebb and flood tide to set to the east.

Refer to our excerpt from Deer Island Thorofare and Merchant Row, chart no. 13313A. The east end of Deer Island Thorofare bifurcates into a northern and a southern branch. The north branch (19) passes between Eastern Mark Island (20) and Sheep Island. Just as the western entrance has a Mark Island to identify the approach, so too has the eastern entrance, with Eastern Mark Island (20). The southern branch (21) passes between Saddleback Island and Shingle Island (6). A black and white bell buoy at the east entrance is labeled "SI."

Now refer to our excerpt from chart no. 13260, Penobscot Bay and Passages East. The northern branch of Deer Island Thorofare (19) is more convenient than the southern branch for entering the coves and harbors on the east side of Deer Isle, or any of the passages continuing to the east or north; to Eggemoggin Reach, Blue Hill Bay or through the York Narrows and Casco Passage (13) toward Bass Harbor (22) on Mt. Desert Island (6). The southern branch (21) more conveniently leads to Toothacher Bay (23) southwest of Swans Island (24).

### Merchant Row

Now refer to our excerpt from chart no. 13133A Deer Island Thorofare and Merchant Row. Merchant Row Passage (3) lies south of the group of islands of Merchant Row. It is wider than the Deer Island Thorofare, allowing more room to tack if the wind has an unfavorable slant. Its dangers are all well buoyed, marked and colored for heading west. In Merchant Row there is no place to obtain fuel, water or other supplies, but there is good anchorage with most pleasant surroundings on the lee side of almost any of the islands. Like Deer Island Thorofare, this passage also exits at its eastern end into Jericho Bay. Now refer to our excerpt from chart no. 13260 Penobscot Bay and Passages East. You can either continue eastward to Swans Island (24) or Long Island (25) or turn north towards Blue Hill Bay or Mt. Desert Island (6).

### Passage South of Isle au Haut Island

The passage around the south end of Isle au Haut Island is the shortest and most direct route from the south end of Penobscot Bay. The principal dangers southeast of Isle au Haut are Roaring Bull Ledge (26), Eastern Ear Ledge, and Colt Ledge. They're all buoyed, but only Roaring Bull Ledge (26), with its bell buoy R "2", is a sound buoy. The only disadvantages of this route are its full exposure to the open sea, and the relatively long distance between snug harbors. In fine summer weather it is just as delightful a sail as any of the other passages.

•

East of Penobscot Bay, you will encounter two conditions that are generally not found to the west, the presence of kelp and of fish-weirs. Both become more prevalent the farther east you go. See notes on Anchoring and Fish Weirs in Chapter 2.

## HARBORS AND ANCHORAGES IN EGGEMOGGIN REACH

All the harbors in Eggemoggin Reach are on the north shore, but throughout its length the bottom is mud and you can make use of numerous coves to anchor on either side, to provide a lee shore according to wind direction. Currents are weak, generally about 0.5 Knot. All navigational aids are colored and numbered for traveling from east to west.

### Horseshoe Cove
#### Chart No. 13309 and Sketch Chart

Horseshoe Cove (27a) is not nearly as difficult to enter as it might appear from the chart. Pay strict attention to the marks, and you'll be amply rewarded. Not only is Horseshoe Cove a relatively untouched, unspoiled area of great natural beauty, but there is the opportunity for adventure for the whole family. The cove penetrates deeply into Cape Rosier, terminating in a large pool (36). There's no water in The Pool at low tide but it's great for dink exploration. Taking advantage of the tides and currents, you can get a free ride to The Pool and back. This is why most people come to Horseshoe Cove.

At the entrance to the cove a long line of ledge extends south from the point on the east shore. The south

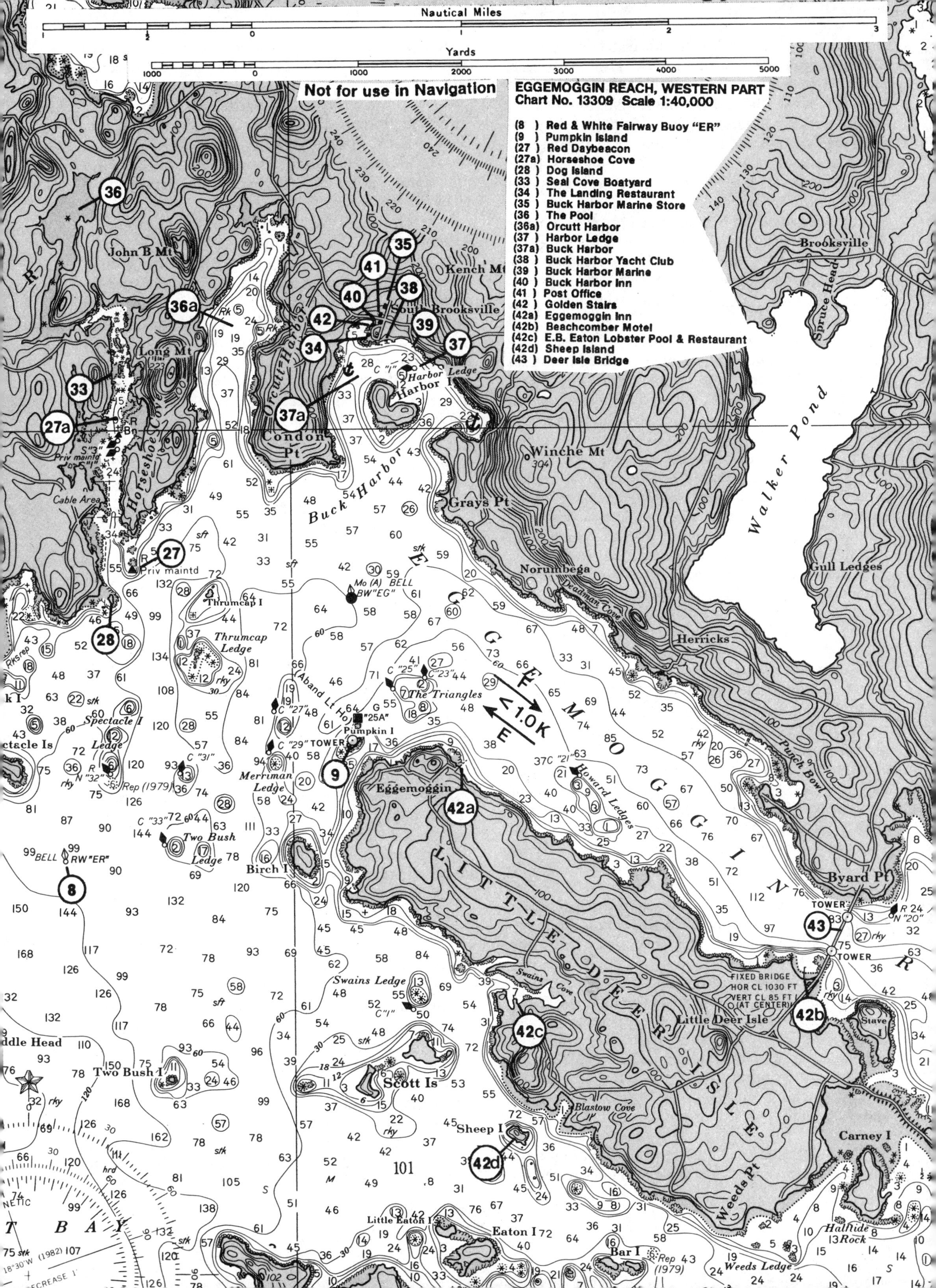

Nautical Miles
Yards
Not for use in Navigation
EGGEMOGGIN REACH, WESTERN PART
Chart No. 13309 Scale 1:40,000
(8 ) Red & White Fairway Buoy "ER"
(9 ) Pumpkin Island
(27 ) Red Daybeacon
(27a) Horseshoe Cove
(28 ) Dog Island
(33 ) Seal Cove Boatyard
(34 ) The Landing Restaurant
(35 ) Buck Harbor Marine Store
(36 ) The Pool
(36a) Orcutt Harbor
(37 ) Harbor Ledge
(37a) Buck Harbor
(38 ) Buck Harbor Yacht Club
(39 ) Buck Harbor Marine
(40 ) Buck Harbor Inn
(41 ) Post Office
(42 ) Golden Stairs
(42a) Eggemoggin Inn
(42b) Beachcomber Motel
(42c) E.B. Eaton Lobster Pool & Restaurant
(42d) Sheep Island
(43 ) Deer Isle Bridge
John B Mt
Long Mt
Horseshoe Cove
Orcutt Harbor
Condon Pt
South Brooksville
Kench Mt
Harbor I
Harbor Ledge
Buck Harbor
Winche Mt
Grays Pt
Brooksville
Spruce Head
Walker Pond
Gull Ledges
Norumbega
Deadman Cove
Herricks
Punch Bowl
Byard Pt
Cable Area
Priv maintd
Thrumcap I
Thrumcap Ledge
Spectacle I Ledge
Spectacle Is
Two Bush Ledge
Merriman Ledge
Birch I
Pumpkin I
(Aband Lt Ho)
The Triangles
Howard Ledges
Eggemoggin
EGGEMOGGIN REACH
LITTLE DEER ISLE
Little Deer Isle
Swains Cove
Swains Ledge
FIXED BRIDGE
HOR CL 1030 FT
VERT CL 85 FT
(AT CENTER)
TOWER
Stave I
Scott Is
Sheep I
Blastow Cove
Weeds Pt
Carney I
Halftide Rock
Weeds Ledge
Little Eaton I
Eaton I
Bar I
Two Bush I
Saddle Head
BELL RW "ER"
Mo (A) BELL BW "EG"
Rep (1979)

end of this ledge is marked by a privately maintained red daybeacon (27). A small rock, always exposed, marks the westernmost limits of this ledge. On the west shore is a small island, Dog Island (28). Refer to our sketch chart of Horseshoe Cove. Enter midway between the daymark and Dog Island and proceed up the middle of the cove. After passing the small rock, favor the eastern shore. This will bring you in on a course of about 020 degrees magnetic.

There are two privately maintained black spar buoys (29). Keep these close to port and pass between the second spar buoy, S "3", and the red daybeacon (30). Note that the solitary rock just north of the red daybeacon is farther west into channel than the daybeacon. Edge over towards the west shore to clear this rock, then head for the string of moored boats.

Proceed down through the center of the boats to find a mooring. There are about 12. Boats fairly well fill all the deep water, so you do not want to wander either side of them. This does not leave any room to anchor. There's a private dock (31) on the west shore. Shortly beyond it is the last mooring and then two rocks (32) in line east and west in the middle of the channel. Do not go any farther than the last mooring. the two rocks are the higher peaks of a ledge that completely dries out at low tide across almost the entire width of the harbor. This all sounds complex, but as you can see from our sketch chart, it's easy enough, just **observe the buoys.** Every summer, 2 or 3 boats do get into trouble by failure to keep to the proper side of the buoys. They just look at them and say "the channel can't be that narrow"—but it is!

If all the moorings are taken, there are several spots to anchor. A quick mast count as you approach will let you know even before you go all the way up. Refer to our sketch chart which shows anchorages east and south of the spar buoys. Holding ground is good, but it is important either to put out two anchors Bahamian style, or set a bow and stern anchor. With a single anchor, you are likely to ride up over the anchor and break it out when the tide changes.

Up until the Fall of 1988, moorings were provided free of charge by the Seal Cove Boatyard. However, due to regulation of moorings and increased cost of maintenance, a nominal charge is now requested. This is on an honor basis. A note attached to the mooring buoy will indicate the presence of a collection can on the dock.

The Seal Cove Boatyard (33) is farther up Horseshoe Cove, but do not attempt to reach it on your own. Many try, but very few succeed. Instead, pick up one of the moorings and row over to the yard. They will have someone act as pilot to guide you in. There is room for 3 or 4 boats at the dock, 6 feet depth at low tide, electricity and water, but no fuel. Seal Cove Boatyard does complete rebuilding and restoration work on both wood and fiberglass boats, and they have complete engine and hull repairs, a complete line of marine electronics, and are Volvo Penta dealers. Winter storage is a large portion of their business. Last year, 134 boats were hauled out, many of them stored under cover in large sheds.

Do not depend upon the availability of provisions here. The former Horseshoe Cove Market is now closed. Buck Harbor Marine Store (35) at South Brooksville is also closed. The next nearest place for provisioning is the B & L Grocery in Sargentville, 4 miles distant, reachable only by auto.

To reach the pool at the north end of the cove (36), wait until about 2 hours before the top of the flood tide. This way you will be nicely propelled by the current and need only use oars to occasionally guide your direction. At the several constricted portions, the 4-5 knot current will shoot you through a set of rapids. This is not dangerous white water, as there will still be 4 feet of water over the rocks. The dinghy will pretty well take care of itself, giving you a swift and exciting ride. There are rocky shores on the east side of the pool where you can have a pleasurable picnic lunch and wait for the ebb tide to carry you back to your boat.

### Orcutt Harbor— Chart No. 13309

Orcutt Harbor (36a), east of Horseshoe Cove, is large, open and completely exposed to the prevailing summertime southwest winds. Thus, it is seldom used. However, the holding ground throughout is good and some measure of protection can be obtained by anchoring behind the small island on the western shore.

### Buck Harbor Chart No. 13309

Buck Harbor (37a), not to be confused with Bucks Harbor much farther east, is located at the northern end of Eggemoggin Reach. This harbor is quite popular and often crowded. Enter either side of Harbor Island, which occupies the center of the harbor and provides protection from seas resulting from southerlies. Harbor Ledge (37) extends north from the northwest tip of the island and is marked at its far end by a small green can buoy. Do not pass between the island and the buoy—go all the way around, staying east and north of the buoy.

Buck Harbor Yacht Club's clubhouse and docks (38) are prominent on the north shore. At the front face of their 130-ft. long dock, there is over 20 feet depth at low tide. Tie-up is limited to 30 minutes and fresh water is available. They request that it **not** be used for washing down your boat. Dinghy landing is at the back side of the float. They have two guest moorings available for visiting yachtsmen, labeled BHYC.

East of the club is Buck Harbor Marine (39), with 18 feet depth dockside, 100-ft. of dock space, 9 moorings, diesel fuel, gasoline, water, ice, showers (small fee), marine supplies, engine repairs, and they monitor VHF Channels 16 and 9. They have boats for charter and run excursion boats.

Trash disposal is an increasing problem everywhere along the coast. There is no place on the islands for it, so trash must be hauled by boat to the mainland. Even on the mainland, costs are high to have it trucked to a

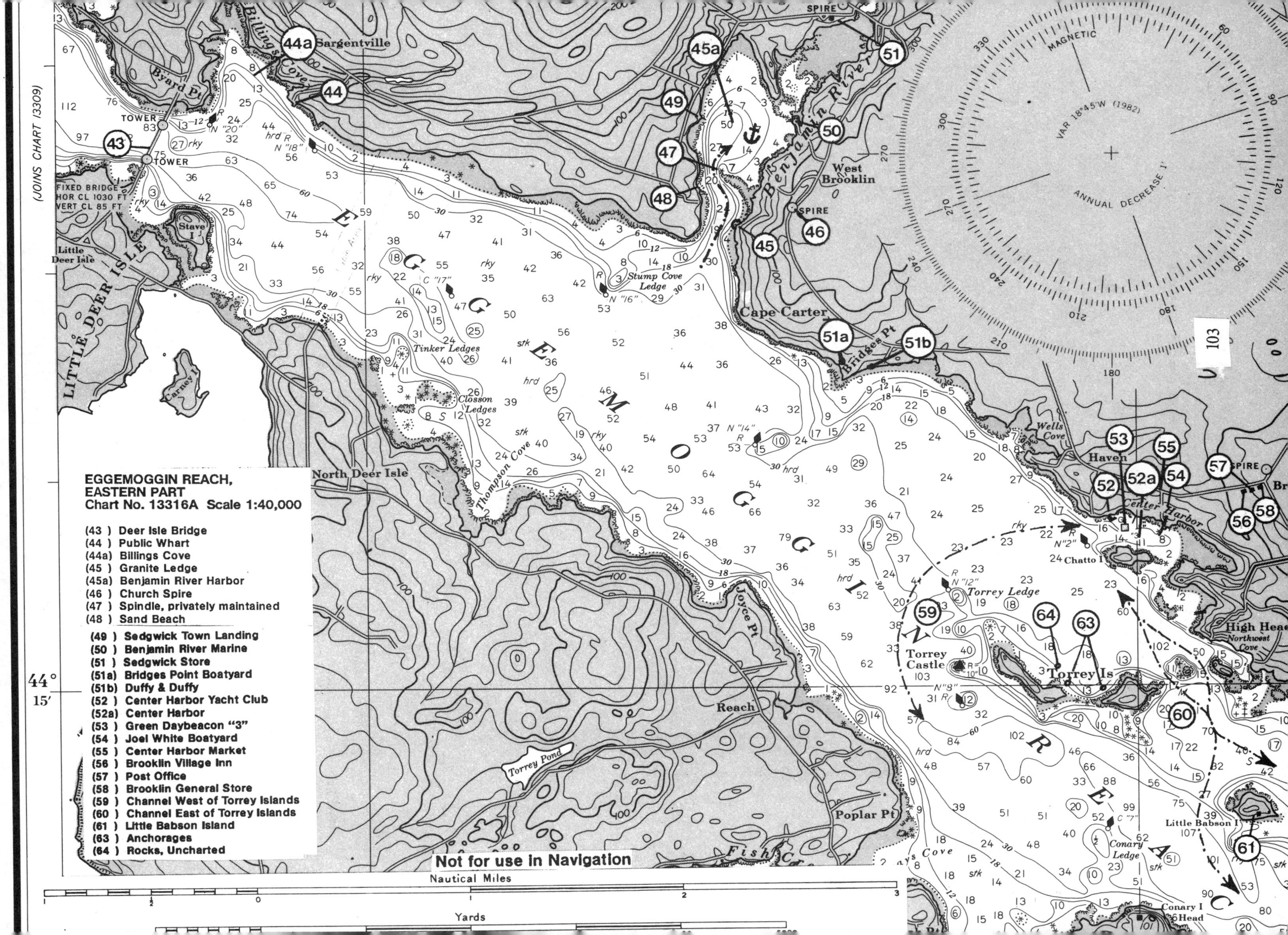

(JOINS CHART 13309)
EGGEMOGGIN REACH,
EASTERN PART
Chart No. 13316A Scale 1:40,000
(43 ) Deer Isle Bridge
(44 ) Public Wharf
(44a) Billings Cove
(45 ) Granite Ledge
(45a) Benjamin River Harbor
(46 ) Church Spire
(47 ) Spindle, privately maintained
(48 ) Sand Beach
(49 ) Sedgwick Town Landing
(50 ) Benjamin River Marine
(51 ) Sedgwick Store
(51a) Bridges Point Boatyard
(51b) Duffy & Duffy
(52 ) Center Harbor Yacht Club
(52a) Center Harbor
(53 ) Green Daybeacon "3"
(54 ) Joel White Boatyard
(55 ) Center Harbor Market
(56 ) Brooklin Village Inn
(57 ) Post Office
(58 ) Brooklin General Store
(59 ) Channel West of Torrey Islands
(60 ) Channel East of Torrey Islands
(61 ) Little Babson Island
(63 ) Anchorages
(64 ) Rocks, Uncharted
Not for use in Navigation
Nautical Miles
Yards
LITTLE DEER ISLE
Little Deer Isle
Stave I
Carney I
FIXED BRIDGE
HOR CL 1030 FT
VERT CL 85 FT
TOWER
Byard Pt
Billings Cove
Sargentville
North Deer Isle
Tinker Ledges
Closson Ledges
Thompson Cove
Stump Cove Ledge
Cape Carter
Bridges Pt
Benjamin River
West Brooklin
SPIRE
EGGEMOGGIN REACH
Torrey Pond
Joyce Pt
Reach
Poplar Pt
Torrey Castle
Torrey Ledge
Torrey Is
Chatto I
Wells Cove
Haven
Center Harbor
High Head
Northwest Cove
Little Babson I
Conary Ledge
Conary I
Head
MAGNETIC
VAR 18°45'W (1982)
ANNUAL DECREASE 1'
44°
15'

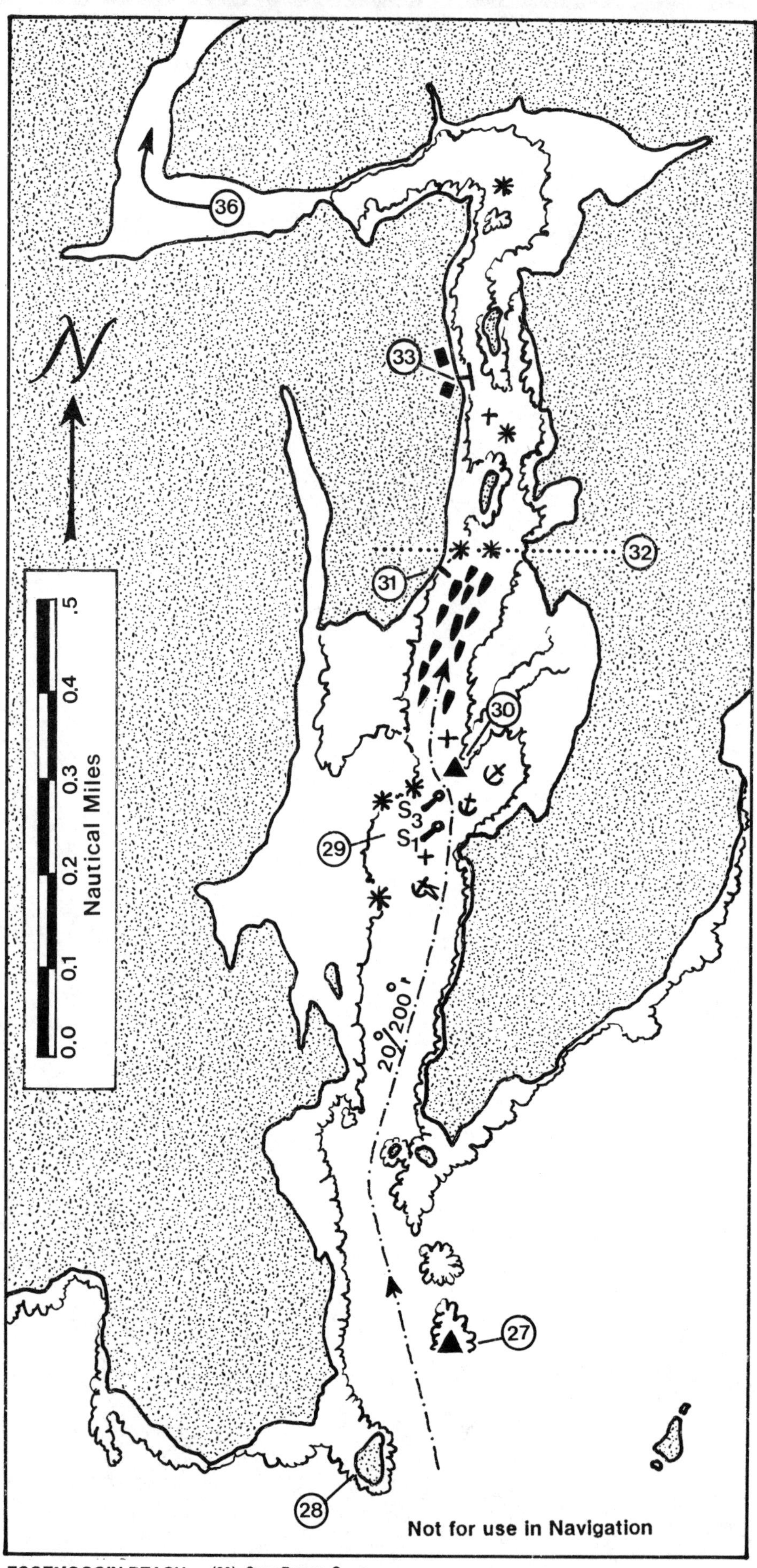


EGGEMOGGIN REACH,
HORSESHOE COVE
Sketch Chart

(27) Red Daybeacon
(28) Dog Island
(29) Spar Buoys, $S_1$, $s_3$
(30) Inner Red Daybeacon
(31) Private Dock
(32) Mid-Channel Rocks
(33) Seal Cove Boatyard
(36) The Pool

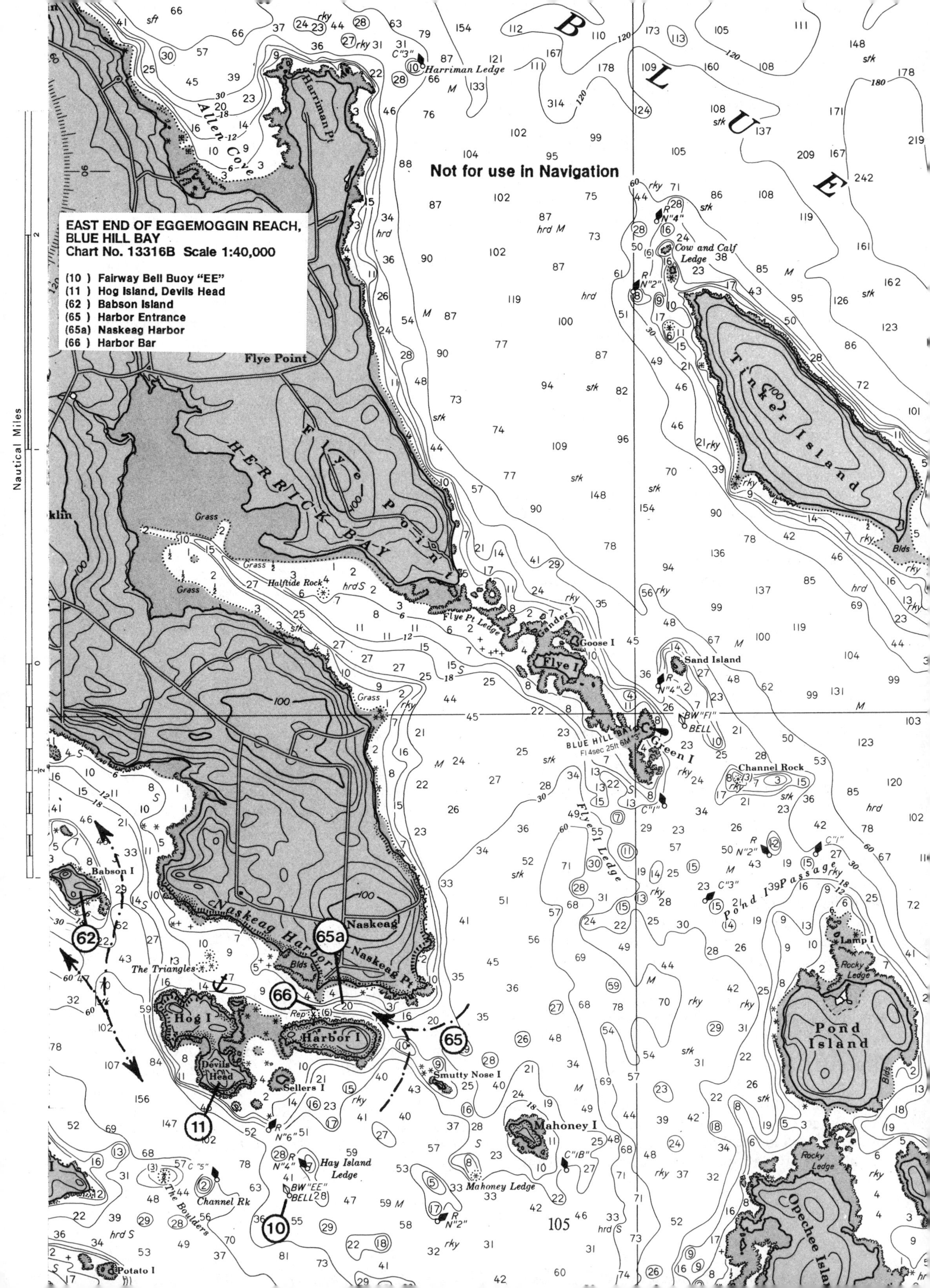

**Not for use in Navigation**

**EAST END OF EGGEMOGGIN REACH, BLUE HILL BAY**
**Chart No. 13316B Scale 1:40,000**

(10) Fairway Bell Buoy "EE"
(11) Hog Island, Devils Head
(62) Babson Island
(65) Harbor Entrance
(65a) Naskeag Harbor
(66) Harbor Bar

disposal site. To help offset this cost, the trash dumpster at Buck Harbor Marine now has a sign requesting a fee of $1.00 per bag of trash deposited. However, a season dock fee includes the trash fee. This may be paid at the office.

Although holding ground is excellent in Buck Harbor, anchoring space is severly limited due to the number of moored boats. The best spot for a protected anchorage is in the small cove at the east end of the harbor where there is 15-20 feet depth. You could also anchor on the west side of the harbor, but this is less desirable because of its exposed position.

A 2-minute walk north up the road brings you to the main intersection in South Brooksville. On the southwest corner is the Buck Harbor Inn (40), known for fine dining. Reservations are required and should be made before 11:00 a.m., tel. 207-326-8660. "The Landing Restaurant" (34), is a few hundred yards west of the Yacht Club.

On the northwest corner is the Post Office (41), a yarn shop. West down the road is "Golden Stairs" (42). It is on two levels with a gift shop upstairs, and selling marine supplies and nautical charts on the lower level.. Golden Stairs has two moorings and are a Johnson outboard dealer and do outboard repairs. They have a dock but there's water only at half tide.

### Little Deer Isle—Chart No. 13309

The western part of Eggemoggin Reach is borderd by Little Deer Isle. It doesn't have any harbors in the Reach, and those on the south shore of Little Deer Isle are not as attractive as those described in Chapter 8, under the West Shore of Deer Isle.

However, there are a few points of interest to cruising yachtsmen. The Eggemoggin Inn (42a) has three moorings, and motel rooms ashore. The Beachcomber Motel (42b), just west of the Deer Isle Bridge, has a restaurant. On the south shore of Little Deer Isle is E.B. Eaton Lobster Pool & Restaurant (42c). They have a dock for tie-up while dining, one guest mooring, and they sell lobsters.

Sheep Island (42d) is only 5 acres, off Blastow Cove on the south shore of Little Deer Isle. Sheep Island is a Nature Conservancy Preserve. Landings are permitted but can be difficult. The best possible landing is in the bight on the north shore where there's a small stony beach. There are few trees and sparse shrubby vegation that includes juniper, raspberries, blueberries, bayberry, and speckled alder. Osprey nest on Sheep Island, and eiders like the the offshore ledges southeast. Much of Sheep Island is exposed bedrock. There's a thunder hole on the west end where spray comes up. The cliffs there are 60 ft. above the water.

### Deer Isle Bridge— Chart Nos. 13309, 13316A

It wasn't until the 1930's that Deer Isle was connected to the mainland by bridge (43) and road. Prior to that, the only access was by boat. As you pass under the bridge you will notice that it fairly bristles with devices for measuring wind-speed, wind direction and other forms of motion. They are all there to monitor this very "lively" bridge.

The design is similar to that of the former Tacoma Narrows Bridge in Washington State. And like the Tacoma Bridge, which self-destructed only 4 months after its completion, this bridge too wants to become airborne when high winds pass under it. I am sure some of you will remember, as I do, watching newsreels of the Tacoma Bridge as it writhed and contorted like a giant serpent caught in some struggle; until finally in one convulsive tormented lurch, it crashed, plummeting portions of the bridge and the autos on it into the water.

The Deer Isle Bridge seemed destined to follow the fate of its predecessor, having exhibited oscillations of as great as 12 feet. Part of the problem is in the initial design of the lightweight suspension bridge and part in the construction techniques used to reduce costs as much as possible. Adding to the problem was the subsequent stretching of the limits of the design by increasing the vertical clearance in the center part of the bridge from 85 feet to 105 feet, creating a steeper grade. Also, the width of the span was increased. Furthermore, the solid steel panels of which it is constructed and the solid concrete roadbed does not allow wind to pass through. The addition of diagonal stay cables, vertical cables to the stiffening plates and many other modifications have helped. Things are calmer now but with strong winds, everyone is wary. The problem of how to stabilize the bridge continues to be studied, but the solution is yet forthcoming.

The center of the span with the greatest elevation is marked by a green light which is flanked by a red light on both sides of the channel.

### Billings Cove— Chart No. 13316A

Billings Cove (44a), on the north shore of Eggemoggin Reach near the Deer Isle Bridge, is attractive in appearance but limited in usefulness by being so exposed from the southeast. In a strong blow, the mile long fetch of waves can cause a boat to jump around uncomfortably. All the shoreline is privately owned and the only access to land is the Public Wharf (44) at the far eastern end of the cove. No supplies are available in the immediate area.

### Benjamin River— Chart No. 13316A

Located on the north shore of Eggemoggin Reach 2.5 miles east of the bridge, Benjamin River (45a) provides excellent anchorage and protection. However, entering is not as straightforward as it might seem. Although not shown on the chart, the water is quite shoal and rocky on the west side of the entrance. This necessitates favoring the east shore when entering the harbor. Proceed pretty much up the middle, continuing to favor the east shore, until you are opposite a large, dome-shaped, smooth granite ledge (45) sloping upward out of the water. On the hill behind this is a hayfield, and finally, all but lost in the trees, is the church spire (46) marked on the chart.

At this granite ledge, swing over toward the west shore to avoid the long, submerged ledge extending west into the harbor from the east shore. At the far end of the ledge is a rock, but neither the ledge nor the rock show at half-tide. Sometimes a privately maintained marker, a spindle with a small, red pennant attached (47), is present at the end of the ledge. The ledge extends a few feet beyond so do not cut this marker too close. There may also be one or more brush stakes on the ledge marking mussel beds, so take care not to confuse these for the spindle at the end of the reef.

Once past the bar, swing back northeast again. You will have made a large, gentle "S" shaped course. Most people have a problem, not with the reef itself, but in going so far toward the west shore in order to be sure they have cleared the reef that instead they run aground on another bar than extends out from the west shore. This other bar is near the small sand beach (48).

In the past several years, the Coast Guard has placed temporary buoys, two red and one green, to mark the channel entrance to Benjamin River. These are small, styrofoam buoys which are removed in the fall. Whether they will continue this practice in future years is uncertain.

Once within the harbor, there is plenty of room to anchor with good scope. The water is quiet and the harbor is not crowded. Surroundings are that of a rural farm community rather than a resort or summer residence area.

The Sedgwick Town Landing (49) on the west shore has a wharf and float landing with 8 feet depth alongside. No fuel or water is available but there are trash barrels. On the east side, near the head of the harbor, is the Benjamin River Marine (50). Their dock can be reached only at high tide as it completely dries out at low water. They have 5 moorings, complete engine and hull repairs, marine hardware, 15-ton capacity marine railway, and are boat builders.

Supplies are easily fetched by dinghy from the Sedgwick Store (51) in town, but this can only be accomplished at or near high tide. Even then, proceed with caution when using an outboard motor, for the whole area beyond the narrows at the boatyard is randomly strewn with large boulders. At the time of this writing, you have to land your dinghy behind the store, pulling it up on shore, but the owner of the store assures me that by next summer there will be a dock and float for visitors. Sedgwick Store is well stocked with groceries, fruit and meat, open 6 a.m.-6 p.m. Monday-Saturday, closed Sunday. They sell wine and have a superb selection of imported beer. Gasoline and kerosene are sold here, but you must bring your own containers.

Just west of Bridges Point is the Bridges Point Boatyard (51a). They have two moorings, marine hardware, are boat builders, and offer some hull repairs. East of Bridges Point is Duffy & Duffy (51b) also boat builders.

### Center Harbor— Chart No. 13316A

Center Harbor (52a) is completely open and exposed from the northwest or west. It would be untenable in weather from these directions, but for the usual summer weather, it is fine. This is a popular harbor and usually quite crowded with a large fleet of moored pleasure boats. Entrance and exit to this harbor is only from the west, as there is insufficient water, even for shoal draft boats, to pass east of Chatto Island. The only available anchorage is near the harbor entrance.

The first dock is the Center Harbor Yacht Club (52). Their float has 8 feet depth alongside and they maintain one or two guest moorings. A string of sailing dinghies are moored in a line from the end of the float parallel with the shore. Just beyond the last dinghy is a rock, not shown on the chart, which is exposed at low tide. The green daybeacon "3" (53) is on a large mound of rock almost in the middle of the harbor and should be given a berth of at least 30 feet at high tide and 45 feet at low tide. Always pass south of this rock and daybeacon. The rest of the harbor has 8-10 ft. depths and a good holding mud bottom. East of the yacht club, there's a private dock, followed by the dock near the head of the harbor owned by the Joel White Boatyard (54), 5-6 feet depth at their float landing, 10 moorings, marine hardware, complete engine and hull repairs, 12-ton capacity marine railways, 25 ton travel-lift, sail loft, and they are boat builders, specializing in building and repair of wooden boats.

Taking the road north from the J. White Boatyard brings you to a "T" intersection and the Center Harbor Market (55). This is the nearest place for supplies, but the selection is very limited. Open Monday through Saturday 8:00 a.m.-6:00 p.m. Center Harbor Market has a fuel dock on the harbor with Texaco gasoline, diesel fuel, and ice.

The road east leads to the village of Brooklin about ½ mile from the harbor. The Brooklin Village Inn (56) there serves dinner from 6:00 to 9:00 p.m. Coffee shop hours are 7:00 a.m. to 2:00 p.m. They are closed Mondays. The Post Office is at (57). The Brooklin General Store (58) has groceries, meat, produce, ice, snacks, sandwiches, and pizza. The walk is pleasant, providing nice views of the harbor.

### Torrey Islands— Chart Nos. 13316A and 13316B

The main channel at the east end of Eggemoggin Reach passes west of the Torrey Islands (59). This is well marked by buoys and beacons. There is a smaller secondary channel (60) east of the Torrey Islands but it's safer to detour around south and west of Torrey Islands. If you do use the narrow east pass, you can pass either side of the bare rock east of the most eastern island, where depths are at least 15 feet. Be prepared for the tidal current to pull strongly through the shallow constricted part of this passage.

If you are headed east, you can then elect to re-enter the main channel west of Little Babson Island (61) or continue east of Little Babson and Babson Island (62) (see excerpt from chart no. 13316B East End of Eggemoggin Reach and Blue Hill Bay). Coming from the east, Little Babson Island (61) is readily identified by the large house with a bright red painted shingle roof, situated on the south side of the island. The ledge extending from the southeast end of Babson Island (62) clearly shows itself, even at high tide. Several boulders are always exposed and there are half a dozen good-sized trees growing out of the fissures of the rock.

A pleasant anchorage (63), popular as a picnic area, can be had on the north side of either of the Torrey Islands. Here a bar, partially rock and partially sand, stretches between the two islands at low tide. Be careful near the eastern tip of the western island, for there, where the ledge extends north, are three rocks (64) not indicated on the chart. They are approximately at the "T" and "O" of the Torrey Islands legend on the chart. They are an extension of this ledge and they don't show, even at low water but there is only 2 feet of water covering them.

### Naskeag Harbor— Chart No. 13316B

As crowded as Center Harbor (65a) is with pleasure boats, so is Naskeag Harbor, but with fishing boats. Fifteen to 20 boats moor here leaving very little room for anchorage. The harbor is entered from the east (65), as the combination of the bar extending south from the mainland, and the rock north of Harbor Island, effectively closes the western end (66). There is a small open channel through the bar, but it is best left for local fishermen. The harbor is completely open and unprotected from the east.

## HARBORS AND ANCHORAGES— EAST SIDE OF DEER ISLE CHART NO. 13313B

The east side of Deer Isle presents the picture of a crumpled mass of land wherein the debris is scattered about in the form of a multitude of islands. Between these bits of land, a complex system of waterways and coves is created, providing many good anchorages quite accessible from Deer Island Thorofare. There are very few buoys, facilities and services are virtually non-existent, but with an increased boating population, these coves are now seeing greater use.

### Webb Cove— Chart No. 13313B

Webb Cove (67) is the closest harbor to Stonington. Except for Channel Rock in the middle of the harbor entrance, entrance is straightforward. You can pass either side of Channel Rock. Once past Channel Rock, head over toward the north shore and follow closely along it to enter the completely protected inner harbor. This course will avoid the fish-weir (68) about 500 yards northwest of the rock. The wier (68), which stretches almost all the way across the harbor, is shown on chart no. 13315 but not on no. 13313B where I have drawn it in. At the constriction between the inner and outer harbor there is 16 feet depth. The northeastern shore is high and bold. Webb Cove's inner harbor is a lovely, quiet secluded spot. The ruins of a granite quarry and dock and a one-time boatyard are the only remaining evidence of the long-ago commercial use of Webb Cove.

### Southeast Harbor— Chart No. 13313B

Entrance to Southeast Harbor (69), between Sheep Island and Stinson Neck, is easy. The water is deep and the only two dangers, Whaleback Ledge and Boat Rock, are both marked with buoys. Both Billings Cove (70) and Pickering Cove (71) in the outer part of the harbor, present no difficulties. Both have good protection with pleasant surroundings and good holding ground. Eaton's Fishing Pier (70a) on the south shore of Billings Cove, has some dock space, 15 moorings, a gravel launching ramp, and sells seafood.

Deer Isle Sailing Center (71a) has some dock space, 15 moorings, showers, a restaurant, a stone launching ramp, charter fishing boats, and sailboats for charter.

If you proceed farther west into Southeast Harbor, hug the north shore closely until you pass the ledge in the middle of the channel. This is shown clearly on the chart. The Southeast Harbor is shaped like a "T" lying on its side. You may anchor either where the shaft of the "T" meets the crossbar, or work your way toward the ends of the crossbar. The south end, leading down to Inner Harbor (72), has a narrow but deep channel and is usually devoid of boats.

Some boats do go all the way up into Long Cove (73) at the end of the northern branch. To do this, keep the eastern shore **close aboard** until passing the small island south of the 15-foot spot on the chart. There is 12 feet depth in this narrow channel, after which it suddenly opens up into Deep Hole (74) with 102 feet depth! Turn west and anchor in 10-11 ft. depths. You will find only a few summer houses, no docks to land or places to replenish supplies.

There are two lobster docks on the northeast shore of Stinson Neck. Curtis Heanssler (74a) will sell you gasoline, diesel fuel, lobsters, has some marine hardware, and monitors CB Channel 20 and VHF Channel 70. Conary Cove Lobster Co. (74b) is run by Basil Heanssler, and offers gasoline, diesel fuel and lobsters. These are reef-strewn waters. If it's your first time in the area, take the dinghy in to buy lobsters, then get directions for approaching these docks.

### Greenlaw Cove— Chart No. 13313B

Greenlaw Cove (75), north of Greenlaw Neck, may be used as an anchorage, but seldom is. Perhaps this is because by the time you're this close to the entrance of Eggemoggin Reach, there are other more desirable anchorages nearby. Certainly the east shore of Deer Isle offers a wide choice of lonesome anchorages.

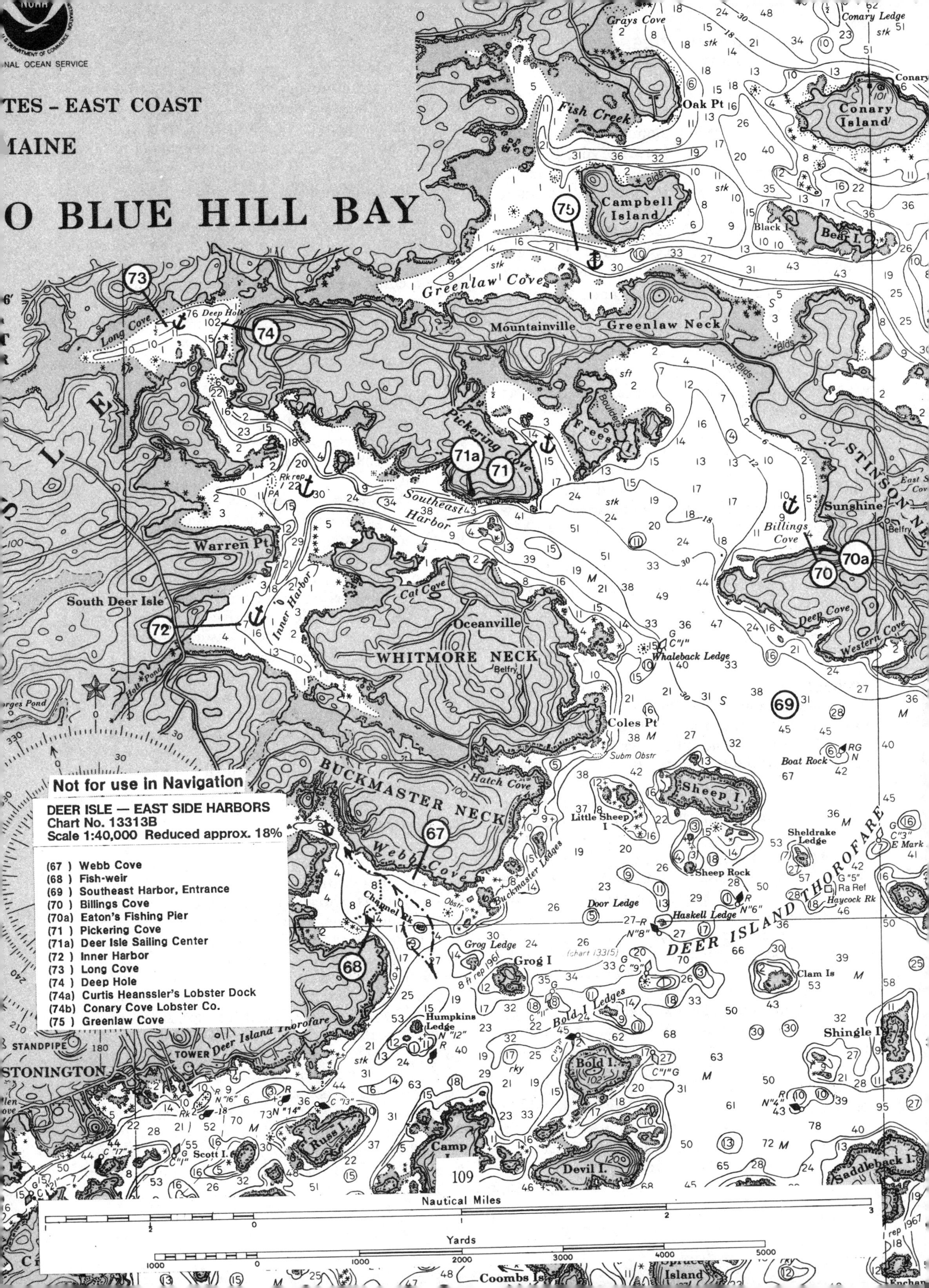

NATIONAL OCEAN SERVICE
TES - EAST COAST
MAINE
O BLUE HILL BAY
Not for use in Navigation
DEER ISLE — EAST SIDE HARBORS
Chart No. 13313B
Scale 1:40,000 Reduced approx. 18%
(67 ) Webb Cove
(68 ) Fish-weir
(69 ) Southeast Harbor, Entrance
(70 ) Billings Cove
(70a) Eaton's Fishing Pier
(71 ) Pickering Cove
(71a) Deer Isle Sailing Center
(72 ) Inner Harbor
(73 ) Long Cove
(74 ) Deep Hole
(74a) Curtis Heanssler's Lobster Dock
(74b) Conary Cove Lobster Co.
(75 ) Greenlaw Cove
Grays Cove
Conary Ledge
Fish Creek
Oak Pt
Conary Island
Campbell Island
Black I
Bear I.
Greenlaw Cove
Long Cove
Deep Hole
Mountainville
Greenlaw Neck
Pickering Cove
Frees I.
Stinson Neck
Southeast Harbor
Sunshine
Billings Cove
Warren Pt.
South Deer Isle
Inner Harbor
Cat Cove
Oceanville
Whitmore Neck
Whaleback Ledge
Deep Cove
Western Cove
Coles Pt
Holt Pond
Hatch Cove
Buckmaster Neck
Webb Cove
Buckmaster Ledges
Little Sheep I
Sheep I.
Sheep Rock
Boat Rock
Sheldrake Ledge
Haycock Rk
Door Ledge
Haskell Ledge
Deer Island Thorofare
Channel Rk
Grog Ledge
Grog I
Clam Is
Humpkins Ledge
Bold I Ledges
Bold I.
Shingle I.
Standpipe
Tower
Stonington
Deer Island Thorofare
Scott I.
Russ I.
Camp I.
Devil I.
Saddleback I.
Spruce Island
Coombs Is
Nautical Miles
Yards

## STONINGTON, DEER ISLE
## CHART NO. 13315

As with most Maine coastal towns, the early economic base was built on fishing, shipbuilding and coastal trade. By the 1850's, Stonington was a major fishing port, second only to Gloucester. Along with the fishing, came the development of a canning industry for lobsters, clams and sardines. But it was the granite quarries that begun around 1870 that made Stonington famous and brought it to the height of its prosperity.

As evidence of the high esteem held for Stonington granite, it was used in the supports of the Brooklyn, Triborough, George Washington and Manhattan bridges, and was supplied for construction of Rockefeller Center, the New York County Court House and the John F. Kennedy Memorial at Arlington National Cemetery. All that remains of this once thriving industry is a very modest amount of quarrying done on nearby Crotch Island (78).

The canning activity is survived by only a single plant and the fishing is much reduced. However, Stonington is still a town full of activity and promise. Its new fish pier and improved related facilities has brought a resurgence of the fishing industry. Like Carvers Harbor on Vinalhaven, this is very much a working fishing harbor, filled with draggers, seiners, gill-netters and lobster boats. Stonington is also home port to the mail and passenger ferry to Isle au Haut, and to several excursion boats.

### Approaches

The various approaches to Stonington are well buoyed. If you pay close attention to the chart and navigation aids, there are no difficulties in entering. The main approach is the east-west channel of Deer Island Thorofare. The western entrance (76), from Isle au Haut Bay, is described at the beginning of ths chapter, under Passages East from Penobscot Bay. The large storage sheds and other buildings of the Billings Boatyard (77) on Moose Island are highly visible a long ways off, as are the cranes and derricks of Crotch Island (78). These, along with the navigation buoys, aid in setting your course from the west.

From Jericho Bay and the east (79), the approach is similarly well-buoyed, colored and numbered for passage from east to west, and easily followed. North of Russ Island (80), ½ mile east of Stonington, the channel narrows considerably. The south side is marked by buoy C "13." Stay close to it, to avoid rocks and ledge extending into the channel. Dow Ledges on the north side of the channel have a privately maintained spindle with a "5 MPH speed limit" sign on it. This spindle (81) is on the most southerly rock of the ledge.

The approach from the south (82) is used by vessels from Isle au Haut Island and closely follows the eastern shore of Sand Island and Crotch Island.

### Anchorage

All the wharf space is occupied by commercial fishing vessels. Moorings too, are all filled with work boats. Fortunately, the main channel is not deep, the currents are weak and there is good protection from any seas. Most visitors anchor right within the channel in front of town. The bottom is soft mud and the holding is adequate only if there isn't a strong wind. The mud is quite soft, and a strong wind will cause your anchor to drag. Normally, it is fine to anchor just outside the line of moored boats and spend a few hours on shore for shopping, provisioning and touring Stonington. For a more secure anchorage (83) for the night, it is best to move over to the area between Scott Island and Green Island south of the Thorofare. Holding is excellent here and protection from winds and seas is much greater. Give the western end of Scott Island a generous berth when rounding it. Although not indicated on the chart, the whole section labeled with depths of 5 and 6 feet is a massive ledge with a jumble of granite. It is not a comfortable feeling to be sailing over it and have your depth sounder showing a mere 12 inches under your keel.

As with many other islands in the region, Scott Island was once quarried, and the remains of this activity in the form of exposed shelves and cut blocks are still visible. The island is not inhabitated and is a perfect place to explore. Mostly grass covered, there is no tangled cover of underbrush to hamper climbing around, and its height is sufficient to provide wonderful views in all directions. During their seasons, you will find wild strawberries, raspberries, blueberries, and cranberries for the picking. On the west shore, a small portion of ledge is always exposed, just below the "t" in the Scott Island legend. This connects to Scott Island by a gravel bar, forming a little cove. This makes an excellent spot to land your dinghy, and the cove has a good mussel bed for those who wish to forage for luscious, fresh blue mussels for dinner.

### Marine Facilities

Stonington Harbor has two places to land your dinghy. One is at the foot of the large brown shingled building, Colwell Bros. (84), a large wholesaler in lobsters and clams, who also sells retail. Colwell Bros. has gasoline, diesel fuel, some marine hardware, a free stone launching ramp, and monitors VHF Channel 9 and 70; and CB Channels 11 and 17.

The other float where you can land your dinghy is Stonington Lobster Co-op (86), which has a reported depth of 7 feet, gasoline, diesel fuel, ice, some marine hardware, seafood, and monitors VHF Channel 68.

The Stonington Canning Company (85), has diesel fuel and gasoline at their float. Tie-up is limited to only the length of time necessary to take on fuel as it is a busy wharf, in constant use by fishing boats.

Docks and floats (87) north of the Co-op are used by the mail and passenger ferry boat "Miss Lizzie" and the excursion boat "Palmer Day II." Visiting boats are

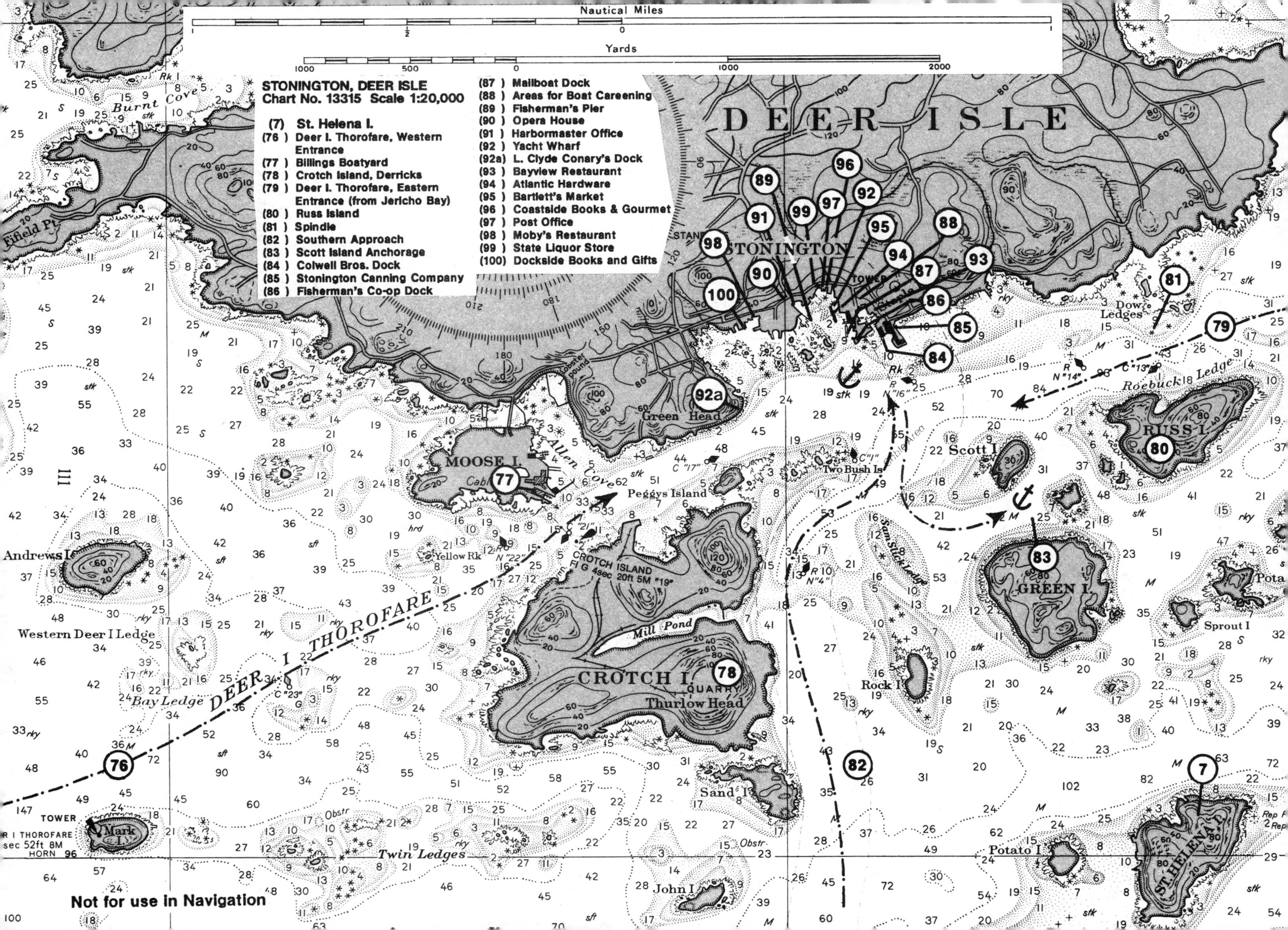
Nautical Miles
Yards
STONINGTON, DEER ISLE
Chart No. 13315 Scale 1:20,000
(7) St. Helena I.
(76) Deer I. Thorofare, Western Entrance
(77) Billings Boatyard
(78) Crotch Island, Derricks
(79) Deer I. Thorofare, Eastern Entrance (from Jericho Bay)
(80) Russ Island
(81) Spindle
(82) Southern Approach
(83) Scott Island Anchorage
(84) Colwell Bros. Dock
(85) Stonington Canning Company
(86) Fisherman's Co-op Dock
(87) Mailboat Dock
(88) Areas for Boat Careening
(89) Fisherman's Pier
(90) Opera House
(91) Harbormaster Office
(92) Yacht Wharf
(92a) L. Clyde Conary's Dock
(93) Bayview Restaurant
(94) Atlantic Hardware
(95) Bartlett's Market
(96) Coastside Books & Gourmet
(97) Post Office
(98) Moby's Restaurant
(99) State Liquor Store
(100) Dockside Books and Gifts
DEER ISLE
STONINGTON
Burnt Cove
Fifield Pt
Green Head
MOOSE I.
Allen Cove
Peggys Island
Two Bush Is
Scott I
RUSS I.
Roebuck Ledge
Dow Ledges
CROTCH ISLAND
CROTCH I.
Mill Pond
Thurlow Head
QUARRY
Sam Slick Ledge
GREEN I.
Rock I
Sprout I
Andrews I
Yellow Rk
Western Deer I Ledge
Bay Ledge
DEER I THOROFARE
Twin Ledges
Sand I
John I
Potato I
ST. HELENA I.
Mark I.
TOWER
Not for use in Navigation

requested not to use this dock (87). If you need to careen your boat for any work or inspection, there are two excellent spots (88) near these docks.

The large new wharf and float west of these docks is the Commercial Fisherman's Pier (89). This is easy to pick out, for behind it is a high slate-gray building (90) with the words OPERA HOUSE painted on its side in 3 foot letters. The Harbormaster's house (91) is a small cedar shingled structure at the foot of this pier. Both the pier and its float are solely for use of commerical vessels and at that they can only stay long enough to unload their catch and take on ice, fuel and supplies.

To accommodate the increased number of pleasure boats visiting Stonington, a new pier and floats has been constructed (92). The portion of the harbor where they are located shows on the chart as having 2 feet of water, but this has been dredged to now provide a controlling depth varying between 8 and 11 feet. Beyond the public landing, the basin shallows and dries rapidly, with navigable limits of the basin extending to about 40 feet north of the dock. These limits are defined by a cloth line with plastic floats strung across the harbor. Water and electricity are available at the dock.

Anchorage is permitted in the main, outer channel, which runs east/west, but in the north/south, inner channel it is prohibited. This is clearly marked.

L. Clyde Conary's dock (92a) is at Greens Head, west of Stonington Harbor. They have gasoline, diesel fuel, marine hardware, seafood, and monitor CB Channel 11, and VHF Channels 6 and 77.

If berthage, moorings or any kind of marine service is required, go to Billings Diesel Marine Service, Inc. (77) on Moose Island, 0.8 miles west of Stonington. This is a full-service yard, the largest in the area, capable of hauling boats up to 250 tons on one of their 4 marine railways and 30 tons on the travelift. Controlling depth to their docks and alongside is 10 feet. They have 800 feet of dockage, moorings, gasoline, diesel fuel, ice, showers, laundromat, complete engine and hull repairs, machine shop, marine supplies, lobsters, clams, are builders of sailboats, power boats and commercial vessels, are dealers for Detroit Diesel, Caterpillar, Lister, Westerbeke, and Volvo-Penta, and they monitor VHF Channel 16.

### Stonington Village

The village is picturesque, with multi-colored houses on the terraced hill behind the waterfront. Sitting on foundations of the pink granite for which Stonington is famous, surrounded by gardens, they add a cheerful countenance to the busy harbor.

The shops, restaurants and inns are almost all located along the several blocks of Main St., which parallels the water. The road leading northeast from Colwell Bros. Co. (84) is Sea Breeze Ave. where you will find the Bayview Restaurant (93) for fine dining on the harbor. They are open 6:00 a.m. to 10:00 p.m. seven days a week. One block over is Atlantic Ave. From the Co-op wharf (86) at the foot of Atlantic Ave., it is only a few hundred yards to Atlantic Avenue Hardware (94), dealing in marine supplies, housewares and general hardware. Bartlett's Market (95) is a large supermarket that can supply all your provisioning needs. Located at the intersection of Atlantic Avenue and Main St., they are open seven days a week. The village has placed trash barrels between Atlantic Avenue Hardware and Bartlett's Market.

Walking west along Main St. from Atlantic Ave. and Main St., you'll find Coastside Books and Gourmet (96), a bookstore with maps, tea, coffee and cheese. Farther west is the Post Office (97). Next is the State Liquor Store (99) and then the Opera House (90), now used as a movie theater. Across the street from the liquor store is Moby's Restaurant (98), serving pizza, subs and other sandwiches. Dockside Books and Gifts (100) specializes in Maine and marine books as well as local handcrafts. They also are suppliers of nautical charts. Stonington's streets, with gift shops, antique shops and other interesting stores interspersed along the way, provide a pleasant walk ashore.

It's about a 40 minute walk west to Crockett Cove Woods, an interesting Nature Conservancy Preserve with a self guided trail. This is described in Chapter 8, under Crockett Cove, including walking directions from Stonington. If that's too long a walk for you, take a taxi.

## MERCHANT ROW
## CHART NO. 13313A

Refer to our excerpt from chart no. 13313A, Deer Island Thorofare and Merchant Row, earlier in this chapter.

One of the great pleasures of sailing the Maine coast is the opportunity to anchor in some secluded cove after a good day's sail and be able to walk the shore, uncluttered with the detritus of civilization. You'll hear the wind in the spruce, the surf breaking against the granite cliffs, the song of birds without the overlay of strident, man-made sounds. You'll smell that wonderful elixir of beach rose, spruce and salt air. You'll appreciate with all your senses, nature in a free and wild state. The numerous islands of Merchant Row, south of Deer Isle, afford ample opportunity for this.

Place names along the Maine coast have been acquired in various manners. Some are descriptive terms of the physical appearance of the land or island, while others take their name after those who first settled there. Still others are derived from original Indian names. However, some names always seem to elude their origin. One such name is Merchant Row.

From an examination of the nautical chart, and in reading the *Coast Pilot*, you're uncertain whether this name refers to the string of islands south of Deer Isle, or if it is applied to the channel between them. Actually, neither is correct.

The true story behind this name was revealed to me through reminiscences of one of the local residents whose family has lived in the area for many generations.

The Merchant family, the first being Anthony Merchant, came from Canada in the very early 1800's to settle in eastern Maine. Most of the Merchant descendents were stone cutters and quarrymen. They started in the Jonesport area, and from there, spread out, settling and working in the granite quarries around Deer Isle, Stonington, and Somes Sound.

Robert Merchant married the daughter of Robert Alley, who had settled in "The Cows Yard" on Head Harbor Island, near Jonesport. They moved to what is now called Merchant Island, north of Isle au Haut. Robert was known to be rowdy, and a very mean person. His meaness accounted for the deaths of two of his own children. One was sent off on the low tide bar to an adjoining island to tend the cows, even though Robert knew full well the tide was coming in. The kid, coming back, got washed off and was drowned. He beat the other so bad that he died. Robert was so mean, that when he left the island to go fishing he would put his foot in the flour barrel, leaving a big footprint from his boot. This way he would have known when he came back if anyone had taken any flour.

His wife took all this as long as she could. Finally, one day when he was away, and had left the dory on the island, she told the children she had enough of this treatment, they were going back to live with their grandfather. She put them in the dory, along with what personal items she could gather, and she started rowing east. She rowed until a vessel sighted her. They put her on deck with the kids and the dory and gave them a ride to Head Harbor Island where her father lived. And that is how the name came to be, from Mrs. Merchant's row to freedom. Robert Merchant never did come to get her.

## History

Most of the islands are uninhabited now, and have been so for the last 50 to 100 years. In the past they have been used for farming, lumbering and sheep raising, which accounts for some of the islands being open and grassy while others are densely wooded. There were many advantages to raising sheep on islands. There was no need for time-consuming building and maintaining of fences, the sheep could forage for their own food, which included seaweed, and they could get the necessary water from dew and from rain which accumulates in small granite pockets. Furthermore, sheep were not subject to infestation of parasitic worms that was a constant problem on the mainland. The conditions of island living also produced a wool which was of higher quality and brought a higher market price.

Although sheep are notorious for eating so close to the roots that they kill plants, it was not totally the result of the grazing which accounts for the bareness of these islands. The common practice of periodically burning the islands to stimulate new growth also hampered new growth. This did provide nitrates that fertilized the roots of the undamaged plants, but most of the nitrates were washed into the sea by rainfall, eventually leaving the soil sterile.

## Exploring Ashore

In Merchant Row, Bare Island (1) and the interior portion of Wreck Island (2a) owe their grassy fields to the effects of sheep raising. For a visitor, there are advantages to this openess. It is much easier to climb around, unhindered by dense growth of trees and brush, there are excellent views of the sea and surrounding islands which would otherwise be blocked, and the increased sunshine favors the growth of strawberries, raspberries and blueberries. Some of the islands still contain sheep. Sheep trails make it easier for you to explore the island, but remember in following these trails, that the interests and goals of sheep may not always coincide with your own.

Though the islands are uninhabited, most are either privately owned or are under the auspices of various conservation groups. Wreck Island (2a) and Round Island (3a) are owned by the Nature Conservancy, while nearby McGlathery Island (4) is owned and managed by the Friends of Nature organization. These preserves are open to the public, but under the following regulations:

* Use of Preserves is limited to such passive recreational activities as hiking, bird-watching, photography, nature study, and the like.
* The Preserves are open during daylight hours only.
* Stay on designated paths. Avoid wet spots by walking on rocks or logs.
* Build no fires.
* Leave pets at home (or on boat).
* Remove no rocks, plants or animals, from the Preserves.
* Leave no litter.
* Keep group size small.

If we all keep these rules in mind and leave no litter, those who follow us will have the same opportunities.

We show anchorages on the north side of 80-acre Wreck Island (2a). South of the westernmost you'll see a Nature Conservancy sign at a small beach where you can land your dinghy. There are also two small gravel beaches where you can land, in the two small bights on the southeast shore. Wreck Island was once actively farmed, grazing both sheep and cows. You'll find foundations of homes long gone, and a granite pier on the southeast shore.

Land your dinghy on the southeast shore of 46-acre Round Island (3a), where you'll find a small sand and mud beach. A dense stand of spruce nearly covers the island, though there are some oak, poplar, and alder. The north shore has granite cliffs, rising to 101 ft. The southeast side is lower and more open, with raspberries and blueberies. Fishermen used the cabin near the shore.

Big Coombs Island (5) and Shingle Island (6) are privately owned, but are protected from future development by conservation easements. These properties are **not** open to the public.

## Anchorages

A lee shore, providing good holding and protection may be found near any of the islands. One of my favorites is the area formed by a triad of Wreck Island, St. Helena Island (7) and Bare Island (1), where I have indicated particularly good anchorage spots on chart no. 13313A. Although chart no. 13315 shows the islands of Merchant Row in larger scale and greater detail, I prefer no. 13313 with its smaller scale, for it shows all the islands and ledges on both sides of the channel as well as the more distant approaches to the groups.

St. Helena Island (7) is privately owned, the house being quite visible on the east side of the island. If you wish to go ashore, you should ask permission first. I have found the owners to be quite accommodating to reasonable requests. The point of land at the southwest end of St. Helena Island is a gravel and small boulder bar, from which there is a superb sunset view. Another good anchorage is off the northwest side of McGlathery Island (4).

Another pleasant, well protected anchorage is to be found off the beach on the northeast side of Merchant Island. Watch out for the rock (4a) "reported" halfway between Merchant Island and Bills Island. It most definately does exist, as attested to by the dozens of sailboats that have run aground on it. At low tide, it is barely covered by inches of water.

Stonington, Deer Isle (18), only 2 miles north is a convenient supply port. Then if you want a lonesome anchorage, you can easily retire to the isolation of Merchant Row. This does not take you out of the way to continue passage east or west.

Eggemoggin Reach, Buck Harbor

# CHAPTER 10

# CASCO PASSAGE, SWANS ISLAND, LONG ISLAND

## CASCO PASSAGE & YORK NARROWS
## CHART NOS. 13312, 13313A, 13315

Refer to our excerpt from chart no. 13312, Casco Passage and York Narrows. Casco Passage (8), north of Swans Island (8a), provides a protected inland route between Jericho Bay and the south end of Blue Hill Bay. It is the most direct route between the east end of Deer Island Thorofare or Eggemoggin Reach, and Mt. Desert Island. It is shaped like a "Y" lying on its side, with the stem at the east end and the two branches (York Narrows and Casco Passage) at the west end.

Entrance from the east is marked by the black and white bell buoy "CP" (9). The channel is fairly wide until 0.7 mile to the west where it divides into two branches at buoy C "1". The northern branch is the continuation of Casco Passage and is the most convenient sailing to or from Eggemoggin Reach. The course from the black and white entrance buoy "EE" at the lower end of Eggemoggin Reach, to buoy N "10" (10) at the west entrance of Casco Passage is 142 degrees magnetic (reciprocal 322 degrees M).

The southern branch is called York Narrows (11) and is marked at its west entrance by red bell "8" (Fl R 4 sec.). From Deer Island Thorofare (12), either branch may be used as there is no appreciable difference in distance. However, York Narrows Passage is narrower and the tidal current flows with greater velocity than in Casco Passage. In both passages the ebb tide sets west and the flood tide sets east. In Casco Passage current velocity is 0.7 knot, but this may be greatly influenced by strong winds.

From the eastern entrance fairway buoy "CP" (9), the course to the entrance of Bass Harbor on Mt. Desert (13) is 083 degrees magnetic (reciprocal 263 degrees M). To the black and white gong "EB" at the Bass Harbor Bar Channel (14), the course is 093 degrees M (reciprocal 273 degrees M). Bear in mind that there may be a marked set on these courses due to the tidal flow in and out of Blue Hill Bay. Be particularly cautious in fog. At Staple Ledge (15a), near the northeast corner of Swans Island, the current velocity is a maximum of 2.0 knots. When the wind direction is opposed to the tide, you'll encounter nasty, short, steep seas.

All the dangers through Casco Passage and York Narrows are well buoyed, colors and numbers marked for passage west. Both channels have narrow spots where there is little margin for error.

### Anchorages

Now refer to our excerpt from chart no. 13315, Casco Passage. Several nice anchorages off to the side of the passage provide good protection and holding ground. One is (15), between Phinney Island, Round Island and the Triangles. Another (16) is west of Phinney Island, between it and Orono Island. Favor the Phinney Island shore. A third anchorage is in Buckle Harbor (17) between Buckle Island and Swans Island, easily accessible from York Narrows. Entering this harbor, favor the east shore of Buckle Island.

Now refer to our excerpt from chart no. 13313A, Swans Island. On the north side of Casco Passage, a good anchorage (18) during fine weather is between Black Island, Opechee Island and Sheep Island. None of the above anchorages have any dock for landing and there are no services or supplies available. They are all attractive anchorages and have good holding ground.

## SWANS ISLAND
## CHART NOS. 13312, 13313A,B,C,D

Swans Island, named after Colonel James Swann, an early settler and promoter of the island, is separated from Mt. Desert Island by only 4 miles. Fishing, lobstering and summertime residents are the backbone of the economy. These activities are carried on in a setting of pastoral serenity in complete contrast to the nearby mainland. For an area measuring 6 miles across and containing 7,000 acres, the summer population, 750, is still comparatively low. But unfortunately, even Swans Island cannot entirely resist the changes to the times. Several large-scale land and residential developments are now underway.

The island has two excellent harbors, Mackerel Cove (19), on the north shore, and Burnt Coat Harbor (20), on the south shore. Other harbors and numerous coves are fine only in settled calm weather, due to their exposed position, or are too shoal and foul to be of much value in any weather.

### Winds and Tidal Currents

Refer to our excerpt from chart no. 13312, Casco Passage and York Narrows, in this chapter.

As close as Swans Island is to Mt. Desert, it still is far enough out to sea that it can have its own wind pattern, completely different from that of adjacent Blue Hill Bay. Frequently, near the island there will be a strong

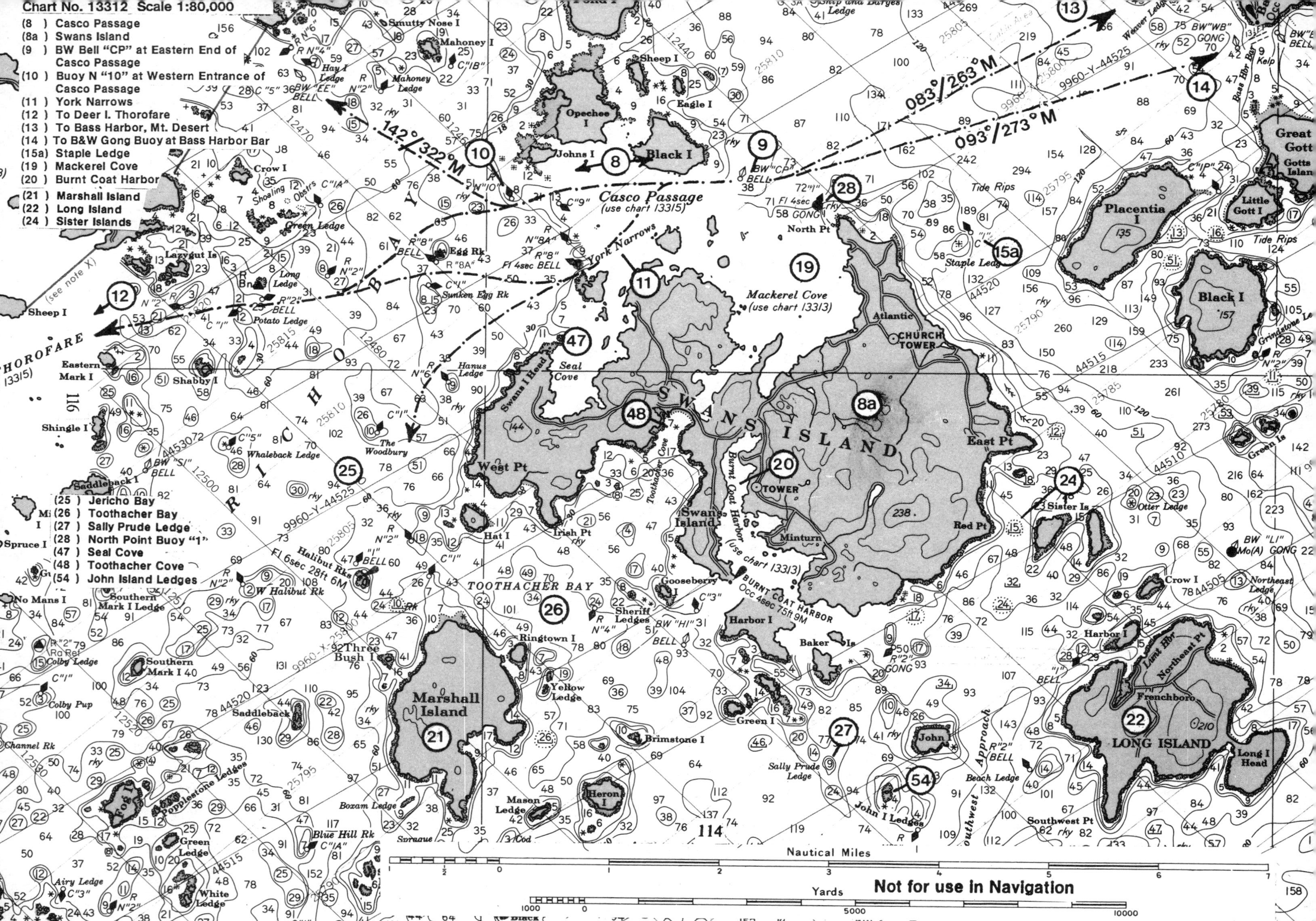
Chart No. 13312 Scale 1:80,000
(8 ) Casco Passage
(8a ) Swans Island
(9 ) BW Bell "CP" at Eastern End of Casco Passage
(10 ) Buoy N "10" at Western Entrance of Casco Passage
(11 ) York Narrows
(12 ) To Deer I. Thorofare
(13 ) To Bass Harbor, Mt. Desert
(14 ) To B&W Gong Buoy at Bass Harbor Bar
(15a) Staple Ledge
(19 ) Mackerel Cove
(20 ) Burnt Coat Harbor
(21 ) Marshall Island
(22 ) Long Island
(24 ) Sister Islands
(25 ) Jericho Bay
(26 ) Toothacher Bay
(27 ) Sally Prude Ledge
(28 ) North Point Buoy "1"
(47 ) Seal Cove
(48 ) Toothacher Cove
(54 ) John Island Ledges
083°/263° M
093°/273° M
142°/322° M
Casco Passage
(use chart 13315)
Mackerel Cove
(use chart 13313)
Burnt Coat Harbor
(use chart 13313)
SWANS ISLAND
JERICHO BAY
TOOTHACHER BAY
LONG ISLAND
Marshall Island
Placentia I
Black I
Opechee I
Nautical Miles
Yards
Not for use in Navigation

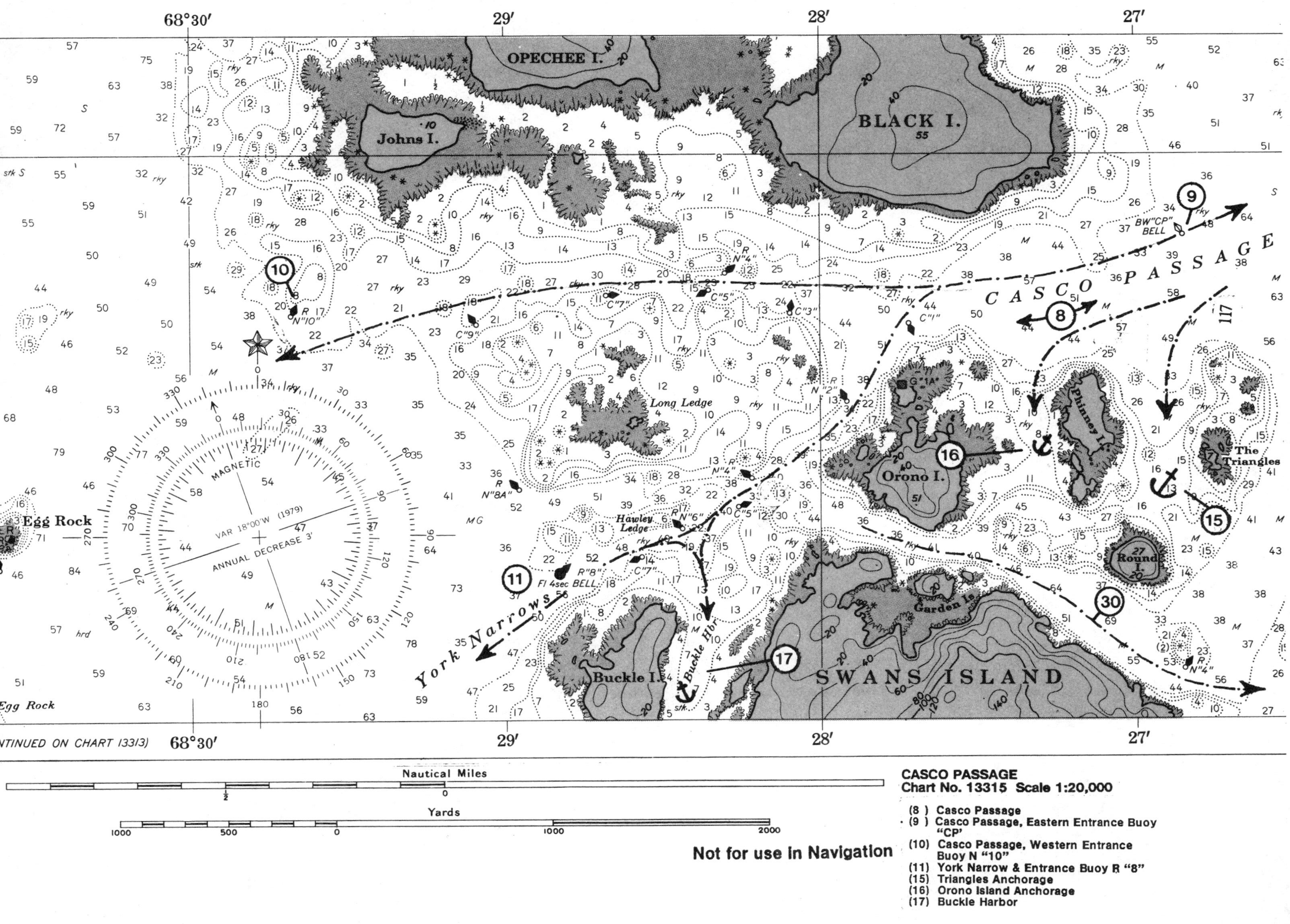
OPECHEE I.
Johns I.
BLACK I.
Long Ledge
Hawley Ledge
Orono I.
Phinney I.
The Triangles
Round I.
Garden Is.
Buckle I.
Buckle Hbr
SWANS ISLAND
Egg Rock
York Narrows
CASCO PASSAGE
BW"CP" BELL
Fl 4sec BELL
MAGNETIC
VAR 18°00'W (1979)
ANNUAL DECREASE 3'
68°30′
29′
28′
27′
CONTINUED ON CHART 13313
Nautical Miles
Yards
Not for use in Navigation
CASCO PASSAGE
Chart No. 13315 Scale 1:20,000
(8) Casco Passage
(9) Casco Passage, Eastern Entrance Buoy "CP"
(10) Casco Passage, Western Entrance Buoy N "10"
(11) York Narrow & Entrance Buoy R "8"
(15) Triangles Anchorage
(16) Orono Island Anchorage
(17) Buckle Harbor

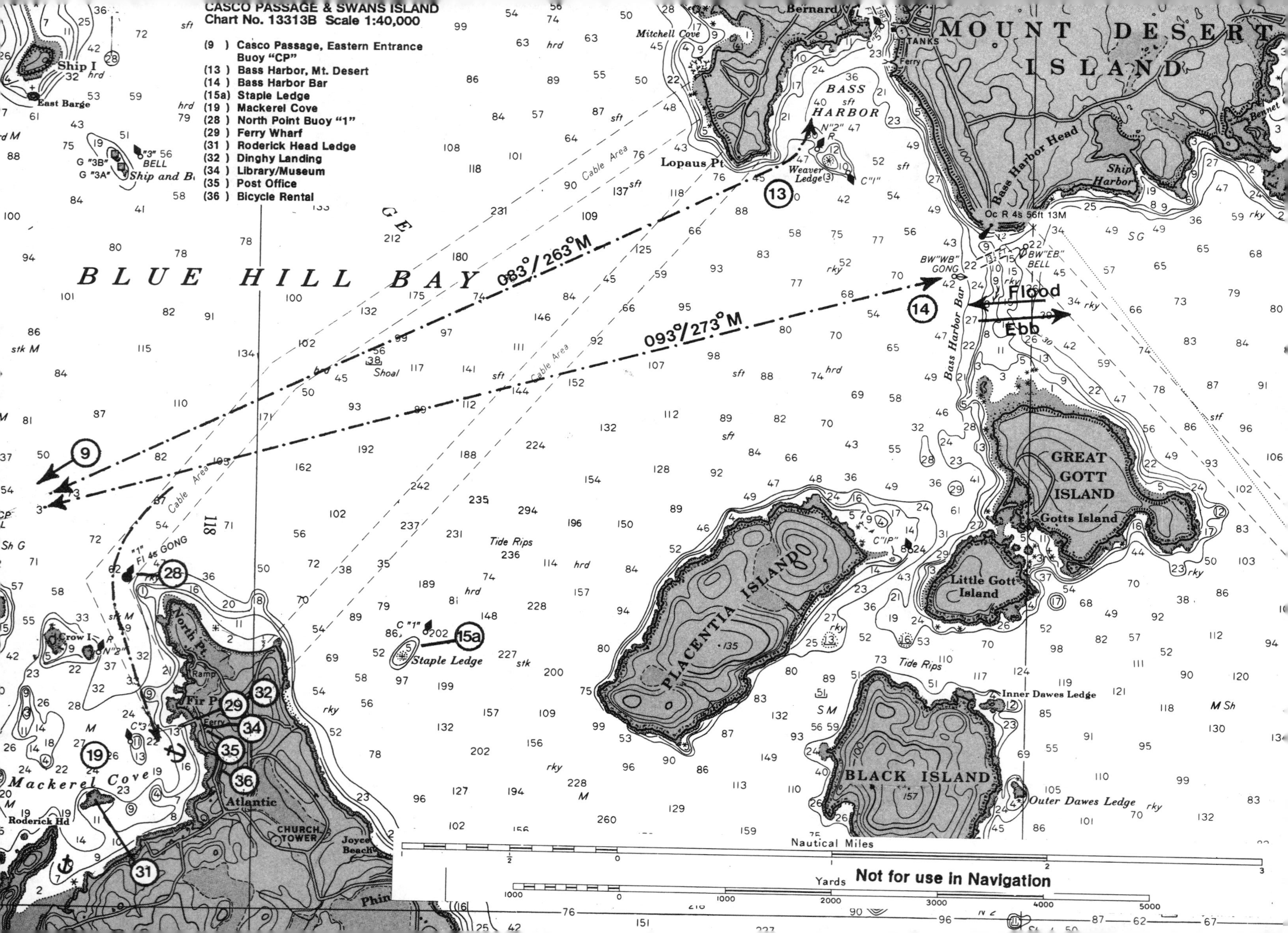
CASCO PASSAGE & SWANS ISLAND
Chart No. 13313B Scale 1:40,000
(9 ) Casco Passage, Eastern Entrance Buoy "CP"
(13 ) Bass Harbor, Mt. Desert
(14 ) Bass Harbor Bar
(15a) Staple Ledge
(19 ) Mackerel Cove
(28 ) North Point Buoy "1"
(29 ) Ferry Wharf
(31 ) Roderick Head Ledge
(32 ) Dinghy Landing
(34 ) Library/Museum
(35 ) Post Office
(36 ) Bicycle Rental
MOUNT DESERT ISLAND
BLUE HILL BAY
083°/263°M
093°/273°M
Flood
Ebb
Bass Harbor Head
Bass Harbor Bar
BASS HARBOR
Lopaus Pt
Mitchell Cove
Bernard
Ship Harbor
Weaver Ledge
GREAT GOTT ISLAND
Gotts Island
Little Gott Island
PLACENTIA ISLAND
BLACK ISLAND
Inner Dawes Ledge
Outer Dawes Ledge
Staple Ledge
Tide Rips
Shoal
Cable Area
Ship I
East Barge
North Pt.
Fir Pt
Ferry
Ramp
Atlantic
CHURCH TOWER
Joyce Beach
Mackerel Cove
Roderick Hd
Crow I.
Nautical Miles
Yards
Not for use in Navigation

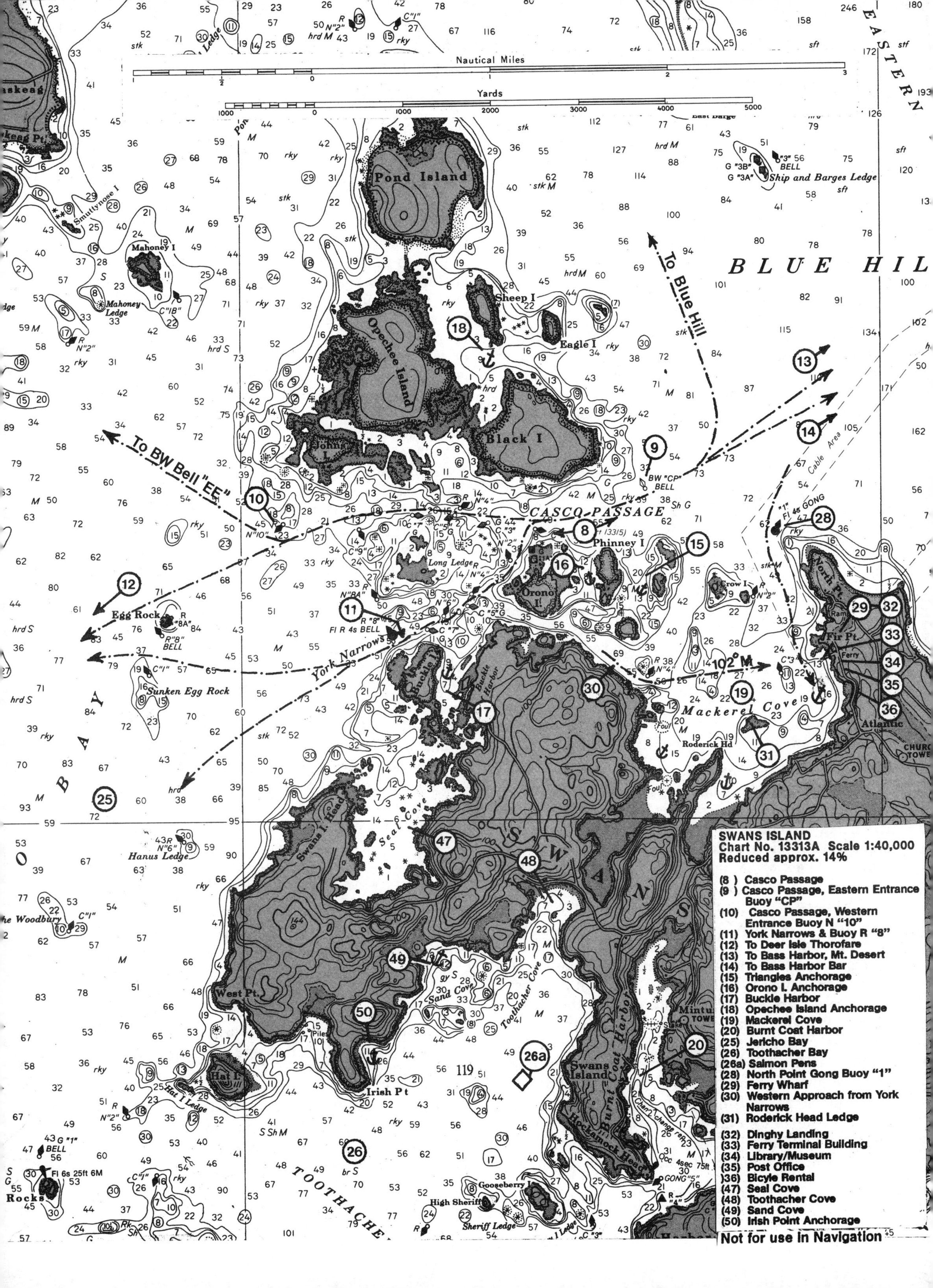
SWANS ISLAND
Chart No. 13313A Scale 1:40,000
Reduced approx. 14%
(8) Casco Passage
(9) Casco Passage, Eastern Entrance Buoy "CP"
(10) Casco Passage, Western Entrance Buoy N "10"
(11) York Narrows & Buoy R "8"
(12) To Deer Isle Thorofare
(13) To Bass Harbor, Mt. Desert
(14) To Bass Harbor Bar
(15) Triangles Anchorage
(16) Orono I. Anchorage
(17) Buckle Harbor
(18) Opechee Island Anchorage
(19) Mackerel Cove
(20) Burnt Coat Harbor
(25) Jericho Bay
(26) Toothacher Bay
(26a) Salmon Pens
(28) North Point Gong Buoy "1"
(29) Ferry Wharf
(30) Western Approach from York Narrows
(31) Roderick Head Ledge
(32) Dinghy Landing
(33) Ferry Terminal Building
(34) Library/Museum
(35) Post Office
(36) Bicyle Rental
(47) Seal Cove
(48) Toothacher Cove
(49) Sand Cove
(50) Irish Point Anchorage
Not for use in Navigation
Nautical Miles
Yards
Pond Island
Opechee Island
Black I
Sheep I
Eagle I
Johns I
Phinney I
Orono I.
Long Ledge
CASCO PASSAGE
To Blue Hill
To BW Bell "EE"
BLUE HILL
EASTERN
Egg Rock
Sunken Egg Rock
York Narrows
Buckle I
Buckle Harbor
Mackerel Cove
Roderick Hd
Crow I
North Pt.
Fir Pt.
Ferry
Atlantic
102° M
Seal Cove
Swans I. Head
SWANS
West Pt.
Sand Cove
Toothacher Cove
Irish Pt
Hat I.
Hat I Ledge
Swans Island
Burnt Coat Harbor
Hockamock Head
Gooseberry I.
High Sheriff
Sheriff Ledge
TOOTHACHER
Hanus Ledge
Smuttynose I
Mahoney I
Mahoney Ledge
Ship and Barges Ledge
Cable Area
B A Y
Woodbury
Rocks
119

sea-breeze out of the southwest, giving vessels a good rail-down sail, while in actual sight of this, boats are drifting on a flat calm sea along the west shore of Mt. Desert or Bass Harbor. these winds may further be amplified by a funneling effect between Swans Island and the other nearby islands. For example, the passage between Swans Island and Marshall Island (21), Swans and Long Islands (22) or between Marshall Island and Isle au Haut to the southwest. On a very warm summer day, there can be a belt of calm on the south side of Swans Island. You'll have to go several miles out to find the true sea-breeze. Sometimes there can be a calm spot west of Long Island (22).

Now refer to our excerpt from chart no. 13313D, Long Island, Frenchboro.

The passageway on the east side of Swans Island, between Swans Island, and Long Island can be exceedingly uncomfortable if there is a strong wind from the southwest in opposition to the ebb tide. This can be particularly bad in the channel between the Sister Islands (24). Here the full sweep of the open sea suddenly meets a constricted and shallow ground. The ebb tide pulls strongly out of Blue Hill Bay on the east side of Swans Island, up to 2.0 knots at Staple Ledge and also out of Jericho Bay (25), (chart no. 13313A) towards Isle au Haut, 1.0+ k along the west side of Swans Island. This can markedly affect your course and should be watched carefully, particularly when sailing in fog.

Now refer to our excerpt from chart no. 13313C Marshall Island and south shore of Swans Island.

Southeast of Hat Island in Toothacher Bay (26) the tidal current runs 0.9 k at maximum flood on a heading of 318 degrees True and 1.3 k on maximum ebb at 124 degrees True. South-southeast of Harbor Island (37) is Sally Prude Ledge (27), a shallow spot with 9 feet depth. Waves break on this ledge in heavy weather or with any large ocean swell.

### Mackerel Cove— Chart No. 13313A

Mackerel Cove (19) is the largest and most popular harbor on the north side of Swans Island. Entry is easy and there's good protection except from a strong norther. The principal entrance mark is the lighted gong buoy "1" (Fl 4 sec) (28) northwest of North Point. Do not cut between the buoy and the point. After rounding "1" (28) follow along the east shore of the harbor, giving it a berth of 300 yards to avoid the ledges making out from Fir Point.

Anchor south of the Ferry Wharf (29) in 13-16 feet depth. The bottom is a sticky mud, excellent holding. One time we anchored there with a 20-25 knot wind blowing. We set the Danforth which dug in immediately and our position remained unchanged throughout our stay. When we hauled the anchor the next morning we found the an 18 oz tin can had been wedged between the shank and flukes, effectively reducing the area of the flukes by a third. Even this made no difference to our holding.

Much more of a problem in Mackerel Cove than the 11-foot spot marked by buoy C "3" are the two 4-foot spots and one 3-foot spot which are unmarked. Two of these shallows are in the center of the harbor north and south of a line between N "4" and C "3". The other is southwest of the anchorage south of the ferry dock. Keep their presence in mind when traversing the harbor anywhere near low tide.

Entrance to the harbor (30) can also be made from the west out of York Narrows. The passage follows closely along the north shore of Swans Island, passing south of Orono Island and Round Island. You have to stay south of buoy N "4", but not too far south. Note another unmarked 4-foot spot only 100 yards south of N "4". From buoy N "4", aim for the Ferry Wharf, keeping buoy C "3" to starboard. This will bring you in on a course of 102 degrees magnetic and will keep you clear of the unmarked dangers. The extensive ledge (31) northwest of Roderick Head has a very small portion showing clear at high tide. While this is not enough to indicate the full extent of the ledge, it will show you its general location.

Anchor far enough away from the Ferry Wharf to allow maneuvering room for the ferry, which plies 5 or 6 times a day between Swans Island and Bass Harbor on Mt. Desert Island. Along the south side of the wharf is Mt. Desert Island. Along the south side of the wharf is a float for dinghy landing (32) and a ramp to the dock. Atlantic, one of three towns on the island, is located south of the ferry dock. It consists only of the ferry terminal building (33), an infrequently open library/museum (34) next to the ferry landing, and the Post Office (35). The rest of the town is made up of widely scattered private residences. There are no stores, services or facilities available. For fuel, water and groceries, you must go to Burnt Coat Harbor on the south side of the island. About ¼ mile down the road from the ferry landing is a place to rent bicycles (36). This is an excellent way to get around the island and to see the sights.

In strong southwest winds, there is sufficient fetch for waves from across Mackerel Cove to cause a small boat to jump around enough to be uncomfortable. Under these conditions, you'd find better shelter on either side of Roderick Head in the southwest corner of Mackerel Cove, where we've drawn anchors.

### Burnt Coat Harbor—Chart No. 13313C

Burnt Coat Harbor (20) is the major harbor on the south side of Swans Island. The village of Swans Island is on the west shore of the harbor, and the village of Minturn on the east shore. Like Atlantic, both these villages consist of a loosely scattered collection of buildings, mostly private dwellings. Burnt Coat, which was once the name of the entire island, is an anglicized corruption of the French Brule-Cote, meaning burnt hill. The reason for this is in dispute by historians. It is attributed to Champlâin during his voyage in 1604 to Mt. Desert, but there is no documentation.

The main entrance to the harbor is from the southwest, between Harbor Island (37) and Hockamock

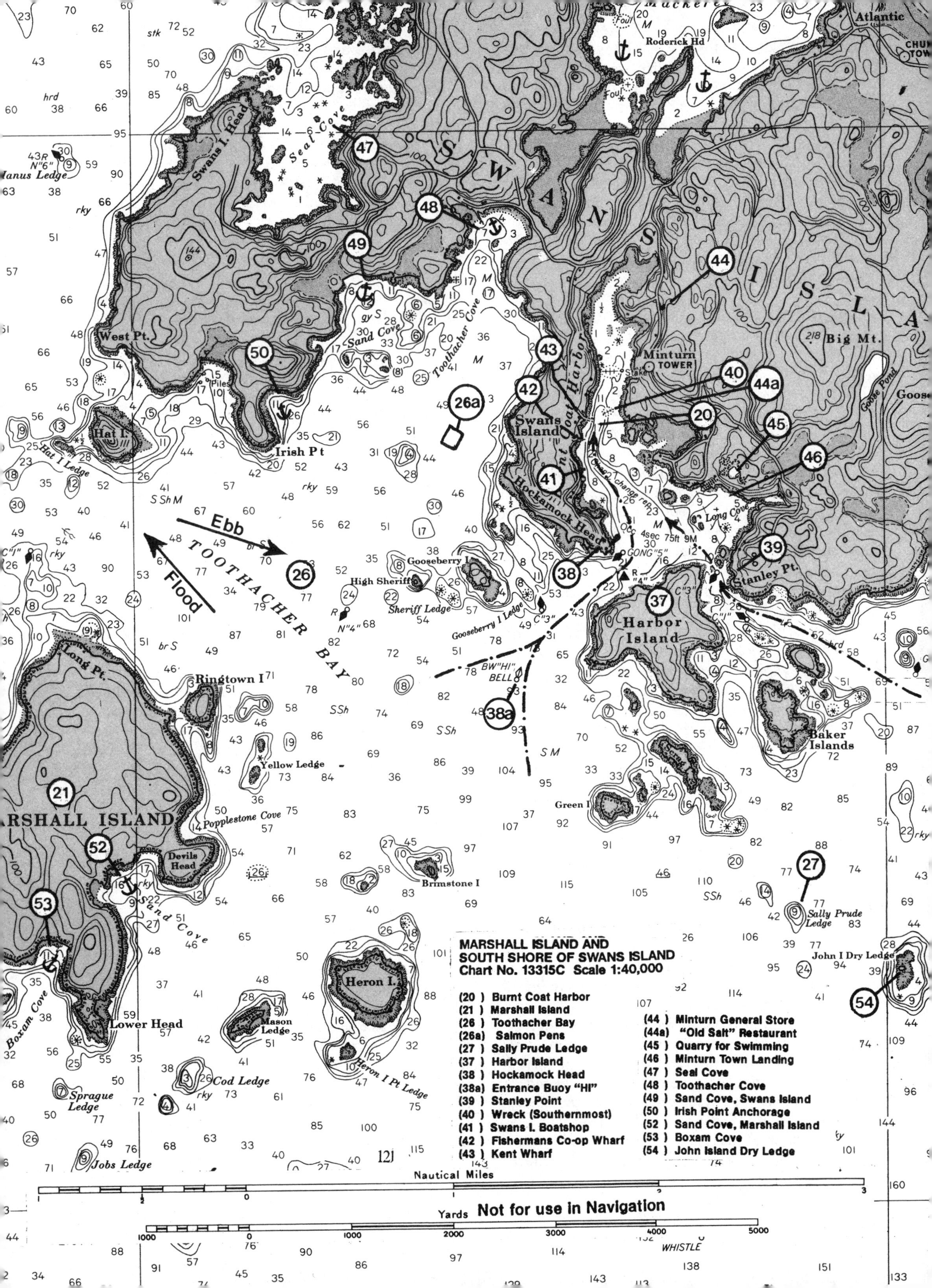
MARSHALL ISLAND AND
SOUTH SHORE OF SWANS ISLAND
Chart No. 13315C Scale 1:40,000
(20) Burnt Coat Harbor
(21) Marshall Island
(26) Toothacher Bay
(26a) Salmon Pens
(27) Sally Prude Ledge
(37) Harbor Island
(38) Hockamock Head
(38a) Entrance Buoy "HI"
(39) Stanley Point
(40) Wreck (Southernmost)
(41) Swans I. Boatshop
(42) Fishermans Co-op Wharf
(43) Kent Wharf
(44) Minturn General Store
(44a) "Old Salt" Restaurant
(45) Quarry for Swimming
(46) Minturn Town Landing
(47) Seal Cove
(48) Toothacher Cove
(49) Sand Cove, Swans Island
(50) Irish Point Anchorage
(52) Sand Cove, Marshall Island
(53) Boxam Cove
(54) John Island Dry Ledge
Nautical Miles
Yards
Not for use in Navigation
SWANS ISLA
Swans I. Head
Seal Cove
West Pt.
Irish Pt
Hat I.
Hat I Ledge
Sand Cove
Toothacher Cove
Swans Island
Hockamock Head
Minturn
TOWER
Big Mt.
Goose Pond
Long Cove
Stanley Pt.
Harbor Island
Gooseberry I.
High Sheriff
Sheriff Ledge
Gooseberry I Ledge
TOOTHACHER BAY
Ebb
Flood
Ringtown I
Long Pt.
Yellow Ledge
MARSHALL ISLAND
Popplestone Cove
Devils Head
Sand Cove
Boxam Cove
Lower Head
Sprague Ledge
Jobs Ledge
Cod Ledge
Mason Ledge
Heron I.
Heron I Pt Ledge
Brimstone I
Green I
Baker Islands
Sally Prude Ledge
John I Dry Ledge
Roderick Hd
Atlantic
Janus Ledge
GONG "5"
BELL
WHISTLE

Head (38). A black and white bell buoy, labeled "HI" (38a) is the outer mark. The light tower, 75 ft high, white, Occ. 4 sec. with a green daymark, is on Hockamock Head. From Bell "HI" steer a course between the light and the red daybeacon marking a ledge off the north side of Harbor Island, keeping south of gong buoy "5". Then proceed north, up the center of the harbor, favoring the west shore.

Some yachts anchor along the north shore of Harbor Island, but this is moderately exposed, open to the southwest. The best anchorage in the harbor is opposite the wharfs on the west shore, outside the line of moored lobster boats.

A secondary entrance is possible from the east, between Harbor Island (37) and Stanley Point (39). It is not as difficult as it appears from the chart. Keep buoy C "3" close to port when entering and keep a close eye out for the ledge. It is best to do this on a rising tide.

The chart shows two submerged wrecks in the harbor. They **are** present and they constitute navigational hazards. For all practical purposes, the position of the most southerly wreck (40), just north of the last large wharf on the west shore, should be considered the head of the harbor. This wreck is the remains of an old steamship that burned at a wharf back in the 30's. At low water you can see its boiler. Yachts anchoring too close have on occasion become hung up on it. The bottom is soft mud, with some kelp in it, so the holding is not the best, but the harbor's excellent protection is a strong compensating factor.

The first dock on the west shore is Swans Island Boatshop (41). They have a float with 5-ft. depth at the outer face, and 12 guest moorings, water, ice, and a restaurant, but no fuel. They can arrange for a scuba diver, or delivery of groceries, or laundry service. They sell lobsters when the dealers are closed. The large, gray structure on steel pilings houses their Bridge Restaurant, open for dinner only. Swans Island is dry, but you may bring your own bottle. The Fisherman's Co-op (42) and Kent's Wharf (43), both have gasoline and diesel fuel.

There are several gift and handcraft shops in Swans Island village, but no place to buy groceries. The one general store that was here previously is no longer in business. To obtain provisions, it is necessary to go to the general store in Minturn (44), across the harbor. There's a public float for dinghy landing at Minturn, and the general store is about 1½ miles from the Minturn Town Wharf (46). They stock groceries, meat, vegetables and drugstore items. About halfway between the Town Wharf and the **General Store** is the Old Salt Restaurant (44a). The entire island is dry, no beer, wine or liquor for sale. As mentioned above, Swans Island Boatshop will arrange for groceries to be delivered.

Until 1929, there was granite quarrying on the island. One of the quarries (45) is now filled with spring water and provides a good spot for swimming in fresh water. Dinghy landing can be made at the nearby Minturn Town Wharf (46).

### Other Coves and Harbors
### Chart No. 13313A, C, D

Seal Cove (47), on the north side of Swans Island, can not be entered very far without running into shoal water with boulders strewn about. It is of little use. Buckle Harbor (17) is good and is described in the section on Casco Passage in this chapter. Toothacher Cove (48), Sand Cove (49) and Irish Point (50), on the south side of the island, are fine to anchor for a limited period of time if you keep an eye on the weather. They are all open and provide no protection from the prevailing summertime southwest winds. As the name implies, Sand Cove has a beach, called Fine Sand Beach. The cove (50) east of Irish Point is attractive with large boulders and high hills.

Toothacher Bay has joined the long list of other coves and harbors along the Maine coast, particularly Downeast, to contain salmon-raising pens (26a). Their approximate position is marked on Chart No. 13313C of Marshall Island and South Shore of Swans Island. These pens have lights at night. Don't let these lights confuse you if you are sailing at night.

## MARSHALL ISLAND—CHART NO. 13313C

Another sand beach, used for frigid swimming, and a pleasant anchorage is on the east side of Marshall Island (21) at Sand Cove (52). For a lunch stop on a nice day, anchor in Boxam Cove (53), on the south side of Marshall Island. This also has a sandy beach.. On the chart, this region looks to be a horror, scattered with unmarked dangers, but it is not as bad as it looks. Waves break on all the ledges so their position is easily located. You can follow close along the shore of Marshall Island, rounding Lower Head to enter Boxam Cove. Beware of the one large rock west of Lower Head.

•

John I. Dry Ledges (54), about 2 miles southeast of Harbor Island (37) is a favorite sunning spot for seals. You can sail quite close on the west side to watch them.

## LONG ISLAND, FRENCHBORO
## CHART NOS. 13312, 13313D, AND SKETCH CHART

Not many towns along the Maine coast have managed to retain their original fishing village character. Frenchboro on Long Island (22) is one of the fortunate few. It's a lesser known offshore island, and its anonymity helps protect it from intrusion of many visitors. There are no inns, hotels or restaurants on the island to serve tourists, and no grocery or general store to provide for the needs of visitors. Without tourists, there are no antique or gift shops. What puts the final touch on the island's insularity is the infrequent ferry service. This Long Island is frequently referred to as "Outer Long Island" to differentiate it from the Long Island in nearby Blue Hill Bay.

For the cruising yachtsman who desires an anchorage amidst gentle and picturesque surroundings, this

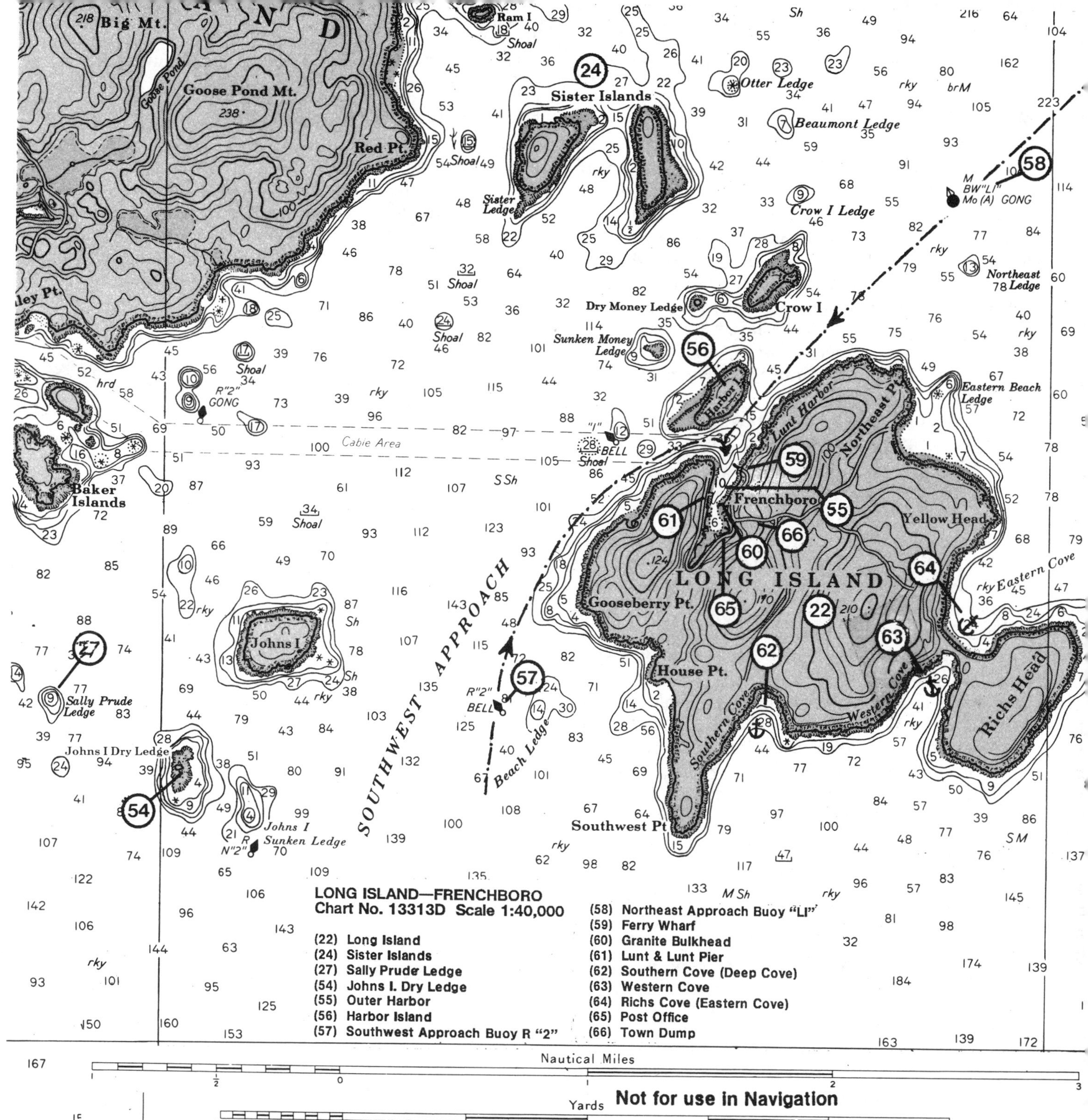


place is ideal, nothing bold, dramatic or unique, but eminently satisfying.

## Approaches

Whether the approach to the island is from the northeast or southwest, entry into Lunt Harbor is straightforward and without problems. In both entries the final approach is between Long Island and the smaller adjacent northwest Harbor Island (56). From the southwest, the major mark is bell R "2" (57) off Beach Ledges. From there follow the northwest shore all the way into the harbor. It is best to stay fairly close to this shore, rather than the Harbor Island side, as a long narrow ledge extends west from the south end of Harbor Island.

From the northeast, the major mark is BW gong buoy "LI" (58). From there head southwest toward the shoreline of Long Island, following it in between the main island and Harbor Island. Anchorage out of tidal current may be found anywhere south of the ferry landing pier (59), on the east side of the harbor. The excellent holding ground is sticky mud. The harbor is well protected from all but northeast winds, which are seldom encountered from this direction during the sailing season.

### Marine Facilities

Lunt Harbor is divided into an outer and inner portion, the two being divided by a constriction about half-way toward the head of the harbor. There is plenty of room to anchor in the outer harbor (55). At the constriction, on the east side of the harbor is a large, granite bulkhead (60). The Lunt & Lunt Pier (61) is the first one on the west shore when entering the harbor. You may temporarily tie up at the float anytime, but there's only 3 ft. depth at low tide. They have 9 moorings, gasoline, diesel fuel, kerosene, water, limited marine supplies, and are a good source for general information.

Refer to our sketch chart, Long Island-Frenchboro this chapter. The inner harbor beyond the granite bulkhead, is smaller and nearly filled with local lobster boats. It has 6 feet depth at mean low tide. Crowded as it may seem, there is sufficient space to anchor. Occasionally one of the Camden Schooners will come into the inner harbor to stay overnight. Long scope is not needed because the holding ground is excellent and the area so well protected.

When entering the inner harbor, you will notice a large space in the center entirely devoid of moorings or boats. Do **not** anchor here! The reason will become quite apparent at low tide when a large patch of rocks thrusts itself up out of the water. They are not indicated on the chart, nor are they marked by any daybeacon, but their position is clearly evident by the absence of any boats in the area. The deepest water in this inner harbor is on the west side.

### Frenchboro

Long Island is moderately hilly, the highest elevation 210 feet. It is densely covered with spruce and fir and almost entirely a natural wilderness. The only public road circles around the harbor. Other roads indicated on the chart are either private roads or fire trails. All the houses for the island's 52 people are along this harbor road. The rest of the island is a portion of the Rockefeller estate and is totally undeveloped.

The Post Office (65) and the now defunct general store are both on the east side of the harbor. It is unlikely that the store will be reopened, so be sure you have sufficient provisions before arriving at Long Island. If you're caught short on an item or two, you might inquire at the Lunt & Lunt pier whether any of the resident fishing boats are making a trip to the mainland for shopping. They may be able to help you out.

There is a town dump (66), something which is not often found on the islands, making it possible to properly dispose of trash. It is on the first dirt road to the east, past the Post Office (65), leading up the hill.

The ferry landing (59) is also on the east side of the harbor. The ferry makes one trip a week, leaving from Frenchboro on Thursday, going over to Bass Harbor on Mt. Desert Island, and returning the following day to Frenchboro.

### Other Harbors—Chart No. 13313D

There are other anchorages at Long Island, all with good holding ground but due to their exposed position, their use is limited to periods of fine settled weather. Southern Cove (62), which is locally referred to as Deep Cove, is ledgey outside, but close-in has a sand bottom. Both Western Cove (63) and Richs Cove (Eastern Cove (64) have a coarse gravel and small rock bottom.

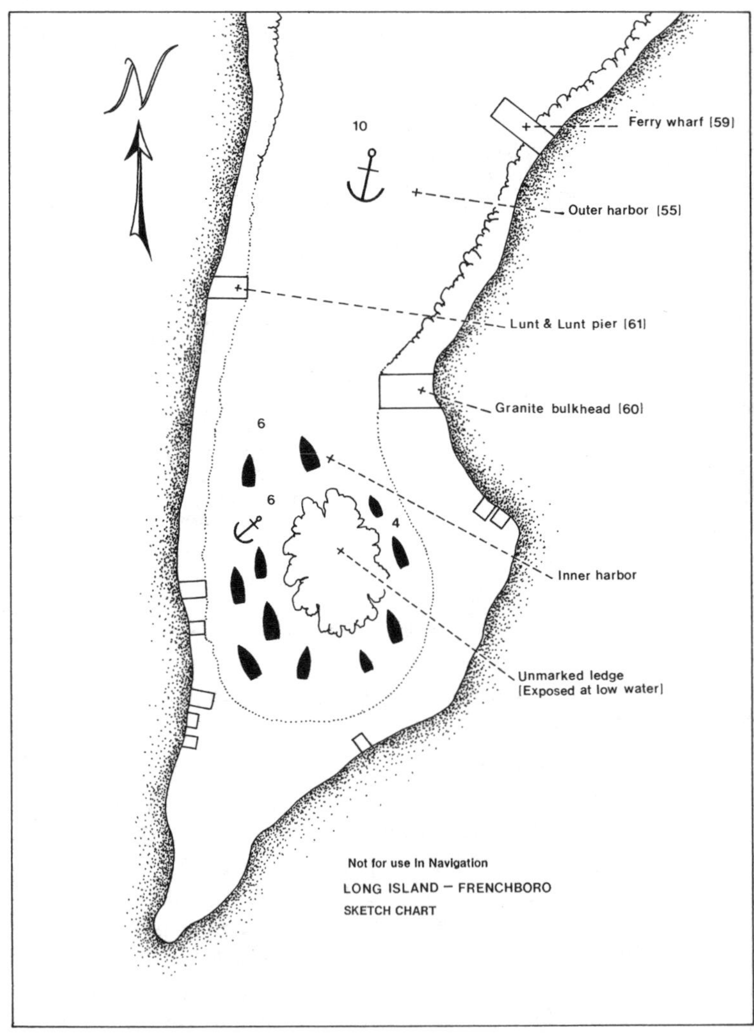

# CHAPTER 11

## BLUE HILL BAY

**CHART NOS. 13312, 13312B, 13316C**

See chart no. 13312B, Upper Portion of Blue Hill Bay, this chapter. Also refer to folded chart inside front cover for an overall chart of the bay and how it relates to surrounding waters.

Blue Hill Bay is a large, well protected body of water offering good anchorage in several fine harbors the most notable being Blue Hill Harbor (84). Numerous islands at the lower end of the Bay take the strength out of any seas from a southerly blow and several very large islands in the middle of the Bay (Long Island) (83) and (Bartlett Island) (7) provide sufficient land mass to help reduce the amount of fog formation. Generally, when it's fogbound outside, you will find Blue Hill Bay free of fog.

Bounded on the west and north by the mainland and on the east by the west shore of Mt. Desert Island, Blue Hill Bay has mostly deep water. The few ledges and other dangers are all well marked by buoys and daybeacons. At the head of the Bay is Union River Bay (6) and the Union River leading north to the town of Ellsworth.

### APPROACHES TO BLUE HILL BAY

All approaches to Blue Hill Bay are made from its southern end. The passage east from Blue Hill Bay to Frenchman Bay leading north of Mount Desert Island through The Mt. Desert Narrows is limited by a fixed bridge with vertical clearance of 25 feet. Furthermore, the channel on either side of the bridge, particularly at the eastern side, is shoal, foul, tortuous and unmarked by any navigation aids. We are not showing this passage north of Mt. Desert Island on our detailed charts, but for orientation you can find it on the large folded chart in the front of the book. Look for Chapter 11 coverage, "Mount Desert Narrows."

#### Approaches from the West

Now refer to chart no. 13316C, Approaches to Blue Hill Bay from the West. You can enter Blue Hill Bay from the west via Eggemoggin Reach through the Flye Island Channel (68) or Pond Island Passage (69). These passages are also used from Deer Island Thorofare and the upper end of Jericho Bay.

**Pond Island Passage.** Note that buoys in Eggemoggin Reach are colored and numbered for travel westward, as are those in Deer Island Thorofare. This system continues through the Pond Island Passage. Thus, heading east, the red buoys are kept to **port.** Technically, the proper route through Pond Island Passage is between the two black can buoys and N "2,", where the depth is 19 feet. But as these buoys respectively mark two 15-foot spots and a 12-foot spot, shallow draft boats can go to either side of them. Any deviation from the correct following of the buoys should not exceed 500 yards in either direction, for there is a ledge (70), extending north of Pond Island, while 0.4 miles east of Channel Rock (71) (3 feet high) is an unmarked ledge covered with 3 feet of water. For the safest route follow the buoys.

**Flye Island Channel.** Flye Island Channel is equally useful for entering Blue Hill Bay but please note that the buoys here are colored and numbered for passage **eastward.** The primary mark is the white tower and house of the now abandoned Blue Hill Bay Lighthouse on Green Island (72). Green Island is low and grassy, so the tower shows up clearly. The light (Fl 4 sec) is displayed from a 25 foot high white, skeletal tower with a green square daybeacon. Green Island is part of a long line of ledge, extending more than a mile southeast of Flye Point. When this ledge is covered at high tide, the position of the lighthouse is deceiving, for it appears to be out in the middle of the Bay and not anywhere near land. Be sure you don't inadvertently pass west of the lighthouse and the ledge. This ledge does not end at Green Island. It continues another ¼ mile south, its farthermost extremity being marked by buoy C "1." After rounding southeast of C "1", you may then proceed to the black and white fairway buoy "FI," thence northwest staying west of N "4" (73).

Now refer to chart no. 13312 Entrance to Blue Hill Bay.

From the south, entrance to Blue Hill Bay is gained by way of Eastern Passage (74) east of Swans Island. The tidal current runs strong here, attaining a velocity of 2.0 knots at Staple Ledge (75). When the wind direction is against the tidal current direction, a short steep chop is encountered.

#### Approaches from the East

From the east, enter Blue Hill Bay by following along the south side of Mt. Desert Island using the channel through Bass Harbor Bar (76). Generally speaking, the tide on the Maine coast sets toward the east and north on the flood and to the west and south on the ebb. However, here at Bass Harbor Bar the pattern is the opposite, flood tide setting **west** and ebb to the **east.** This presents no problem when entering Blue Hill Bay from the east, for the flood tide will continue

ENTRANCES TO BLUE HILL BAY
Chart No. 13312 Scale 1:80,000
(68) Flye Island Channel
(69) Pond Island Passage
(72) Green Island
(74) Eastern Passage
(75) Staple Ledge
(76) Bass Harbor Bar
(77) Western Way
(78) Ship & Barges Ledge
(79) Tinker Island
(80) Fairway Buoy "TI"
(81) Herrick Bay
(82) Allen Cove
Not for use in Navigation
Nautical Miles
Yards
BLUE HILL BAY
Eastern Passage
Casco Passage
(use chart 13315)
Herrick Bay
(use chart 13316)
Southwest Harbor
Bass Harbor
Bass Harbor Head
Tinker I
Pond I
Black I
Placentia I
Great Gott I
Little Gott I
Swans Island
Naskeag Pt
Flye Pt
Bernard
Manset
Dodge Pt
Seal Cove
Bernard Mt
York Narrows
Staple Ledge
Ship and Barges Ledge
Mackerel Cove
Opechee I
Moose I
Trumpet I
Ship I
Bar I
Goose Cove Rk
Dix Pt
Nutter Pt
Lopaus Pt
North Pt
Atlantic
East Pt
Allen Cove
Harriman Pt
Cow and Calf Ledge
Sand I
Flye I
Channel Rk
Smuttynose I
Mahoney I
Hog I
Devils Head
Crow I
Green Ledge
Egg Rk
Johns I
Eagle I
Sheep I
Rumell I
West Tremont
Babson I
Tide Rips
Cable Area
Long Ledge
Horseshoe Ledge
Grindstone Ledge
Shabby I

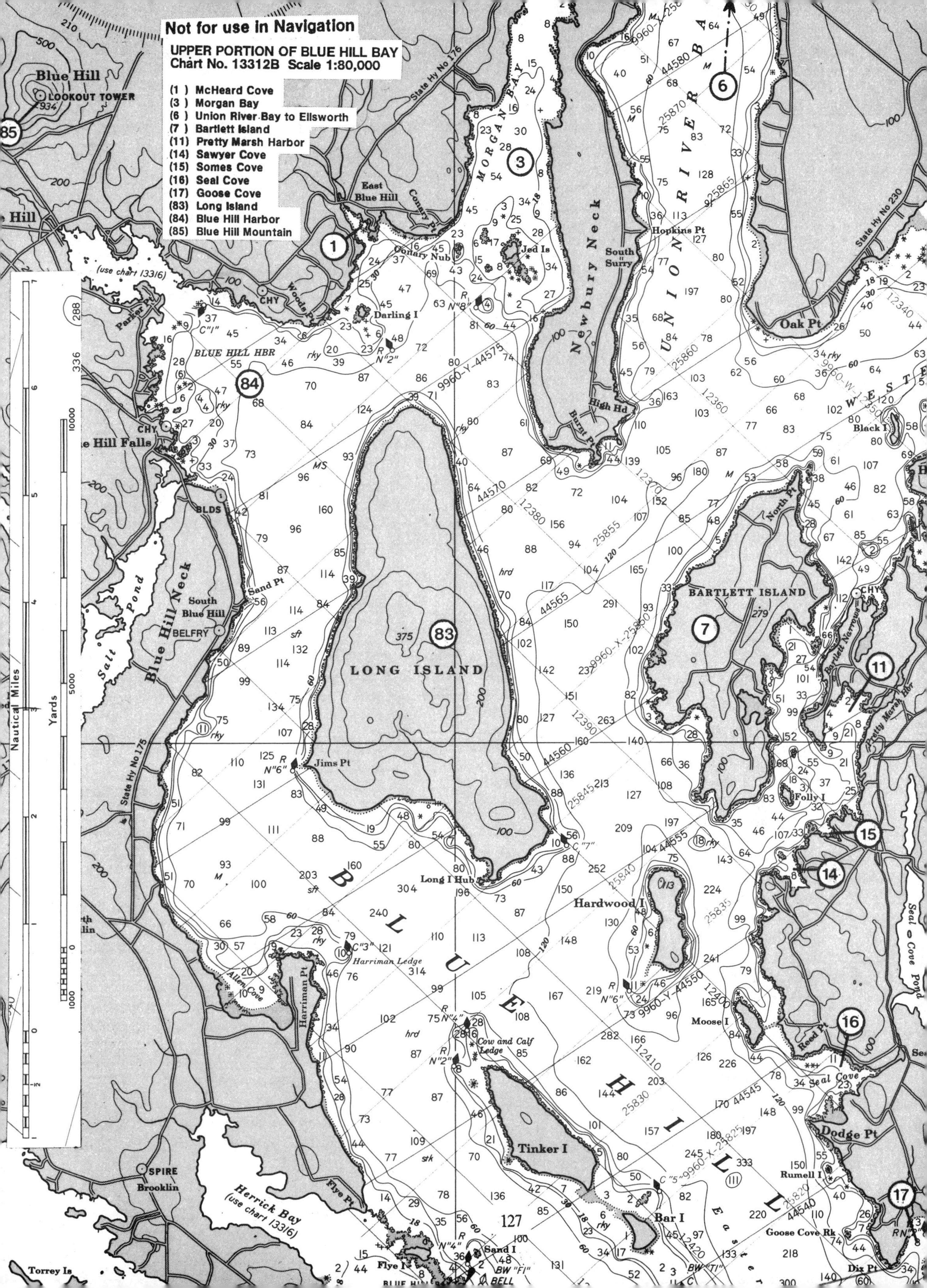
Not for use in Navigation
UPPER PORTION OF BLUE HILL BAY
Chart No. 13312B Scale 1:80,000
(1) McHeard Cove
(3) Morgan Bay
(6) Union River Bay to Ellsworth
(7) Bartlett Island
(11) Pretty Marsh Harbor
(14) Sawyer Cove
(15) Somes Cove
(16) Seal Cove
(17) Goose Cove
(83) Long Island
(84) Blue Hill Harbor
(85) Blue Hill Mountain
Blue Hill
LOOKOUT TOWER
East Blue Hill
Conary Pt
Conary Nub
Darling I
Jed Is
MORGAN BAY
Newbury Neck
South Surry
Hopkins Pt
High Hd
Burnt Pt
UNION RIVER BAY
Oak Pt
State Hy No 176
State Hy No 230
State Hy No 175
BLUE HILL HBR
Parker Pt
Woods Pt
Blue Hill Falls
Salt Pond
Blue Hill Neck
Sand Pt
South Blue Hill
BELFRY
Jims Pt
LONG ISLAND
Long I Hub
BARTLETT ISLAND
North Pt
Bartlett Narrows
Pretty Marsh Hbr
Black I
Folly I
Hardwood I
Moose I
Reed Pt
Seal Cove
Seal Cove Pond
Dodge Pt
Rumell I
Goose Cove Rk
Dix Pt
BLUE HILL
Harriman Ledge
Harriman Pt
Allen Cove
Cow and Calf Ledge
Tinker I
Bar I
Herrick Bay
(use chart 13316)
Flye Pt
Flye I
Sand I
Brooklin
SPIRE
Torrey Is
Nautical Miles
Yards

to give you a favorable push on your course toward the head of the Bay. However, if you are headed east across the Bar, intending to enter harbors on Mount Desert Island through Western Way (77), then no matter how you work it, at one point or another, you will be bucking the tidal current. While the ebb is to the east (in your favor) across the Bar, it is to the south through Western Way, and against you. If you have a choice, it would be preferable to go against the tidal current for the short distance across Bass Harbor Bar, and have it to your advantage through Western Way. A black and white fairway buoy marks the narrow channel at both ends of Bass Harbor Bar. Although you may encounter rough water across the Bar, the distance is short.

The lower half of Blue Hill Bay is divided into west and east portions by a string of low, grassy islands and ledges commencing at the south end with Ship and Barges Ledge (78) and terminating at the north end with Tinker Island (79). To cross from the west side to the eastern side, it is not necessary to go all the way around either end of the chain of land and reefs, for there is a channel north of Trumpet Island, between Trumpet Island and Bar Island Bar. This is marked with a black and white fairway buoy "TI" (80) where there is 17 feet depth at low tide.

## HERRICK BAY—CHART NO. 13316C

Herrick Bay (81), the first harbor encountered on the west side of Blue Hill Bay, is of little use. Large and open, there is no access to shore, and the entire upper half of the bay dries out at low tide.

Flye Point Marine (81a), on the north shore near the entrance, are boat builders, and can do any kind of hull repairs.

## ALLEN COVE—CHART NO. 13316C

Located west of Harriman Point, Allen Cove (82) also has limited usefulness. Its greatest asset is its proximity to the general east/west routes, making it a convenient place to wait out foul weather or an unfavorable tide. It is easy to enter under any condition, the only danger being Harriman Ledge, marked by Buoy C "3" off Harriman Point. The ledge is no danger to small boats, being covered with 10 feet at low tide. Holding ground of mud in Allen Cove is good. Protection is fine for the prevailing summertime winds from the south and southwest, but it is completely exposed to wind and a long fetch of waves from the north. Surroundings are agreeable, composed of farms and hayfields, but the shoreline is foul and there is no access to land. No services, fuel or provisions.

## LONG ISLAND—CHART NO. 13312B

This very large island (83), privately owned, is heavily wooded and almost totally uninhabited. Along with other sizable and high islands, Long Island lends a certain grandeur and majesty to Blue Hill Bay, but for its entire length of shoreline, there are no coves or anchorages.

## BLUE HILL HARBOR
## CHART NOS. 13316D, 13316 INSET, 13312B

Situated in the northwest corner of Blue Hill Bay (84) (chart nos. 13316D and 13312B), this harbor has everything to offer the cruising yachtsman. The harbor is well sheltered, surroundings attractive, and the town has numerous buildings of architectural interest, good restaurants, and stores for provisioning and shopping. The Bay, the Harbor and the Town all take their name from the imposing solitary hill (85) (chart no. 13312B) rising almost 1000 feet above the water. Originally the hill was completely covered with spruce and fir, which from a distance imparted a bluish color, therefore named Blue Hill.

Now refer to chart no. 13316-Inset, Blue Hill Harbor. Blue Hill Harbor is a large, open bight in the northwest corner of the Bay. The enclosed portion, beyond the constriction formed by Parker Point and Sculpin Point (88), is the Inner Harbor (86). However, it is the inner harbor that is ordinarily thought of as Blue Hill Harbor, and it is further divided by Peters Point into an inner and outer portion. Whether by chance, or by design, the outer portion is almost entirely taken over by yachts and pleasure crafts, while the inner portion primarily serves for moorings of lobster boats and other fishing boats.

### Harbor Entry

Surrounding the approach to the harbor are scattered ledges and rocks requiring you to pay close attention to the chart and your position. Middle Ground (87) is a large detached shoal with rocks nearly awash near the entrance to the inner harbor. This shoal has two buoys marking the east end, C "1" and C "3." The correct procedure for entering the harbor is to pass to the east and north of both these buoys and then head for C "5" and N "6" off Sculpin Point (88). Although there is a deep water channel west of Middle Ground, it's not marked.

As you come up the Bay toward Blue Hill Harbor, the Middle Ground buoys are not easily seen until you are quite close. To find them, aim for the flagpole (89) on the north shore on a course slightly west of north. Note that there are **two** flagpoles here. One is near the tip of Sculpin Point (88), the other (89) northeast of buoys C "1" and C "3". The one on Sculpin Point is much more prominent and easily seen from a greater distance. The other (89) is harder to find, being partially obscured by surrounding trees. It is this latter flagpole that you want to aim for to round the buoys and enter the harbor. At mid-tide be prepared for a fairly strong current coursing through the channel. This might be expected from the large body of water west of it, which must enter and leave through this 50-foot wide channel.

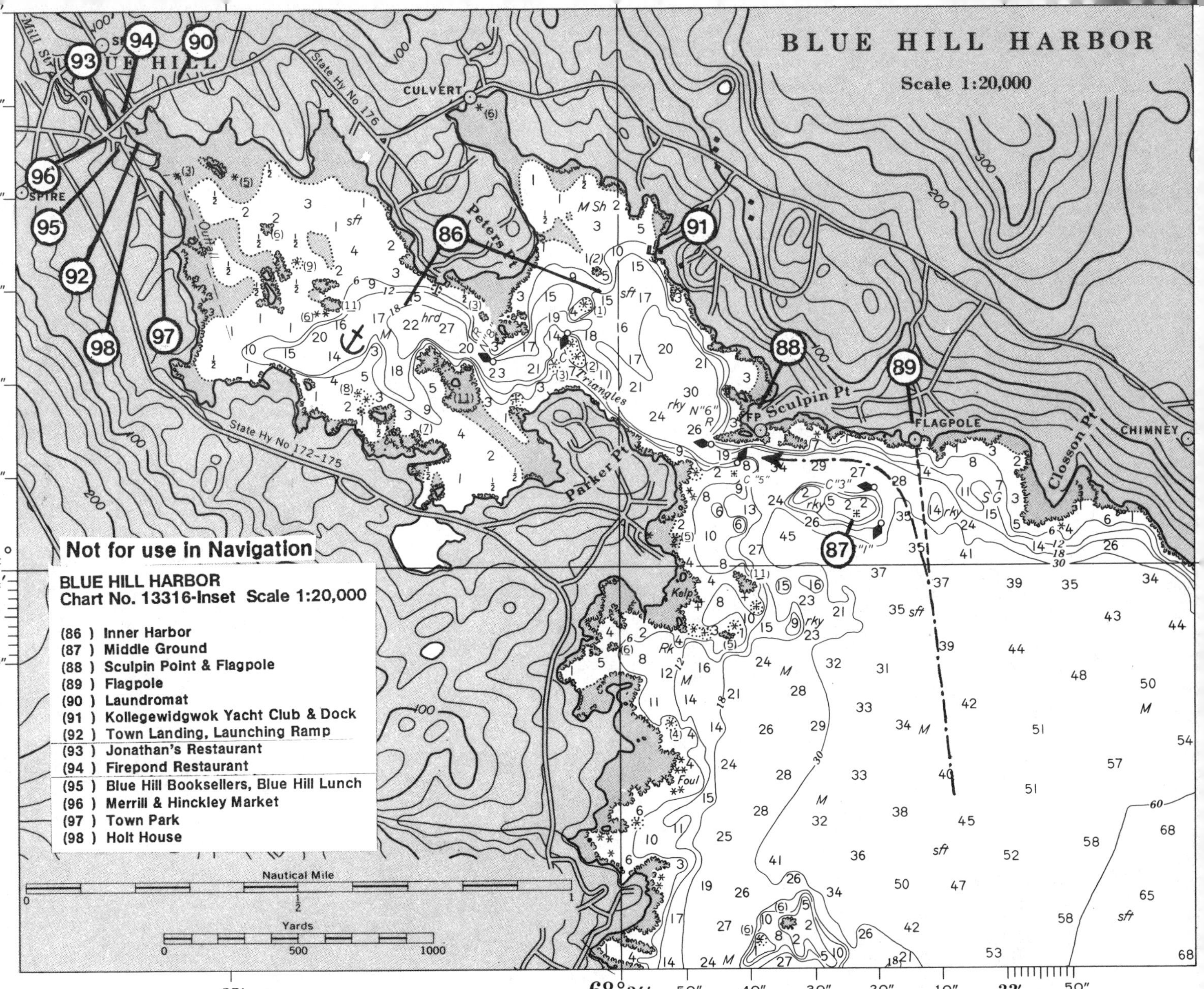


## Inner Harbor

The outer portion of the Inner Harbor is almost entirely filled with private moorings and anchorage space is severely limited. On the east side is the dock and float of the Killegewidgwok Yacht Club (91) where there is 12-16 feet depth at low tide. The south end of the float has the deeper water. At the yacht club float you can get gasoline, diesel fuel, water, and ice in blocks and cubes. There is a ½ hour tie-up limit. They have 5 guest moorings marked KYC, but usually they can accommodate up to 9 or 10 guest boats, with a most generous 4-day limit. The inner face of the float may be used for dinghy landing. Trash disposal is behind the club building.

Entrance to the inner portion of the Inner Harbor is not difficult if you carefully follow the buoys and the chart. The western portion of the Inner Harbor is less congested, with room to swing to an anchor. It would be best to enter and anchor near low tide, for at high tide, once past the channel markers, there is a large expanse of water with few clues to help determine depths and dangers. The bottom is mud and holding is excellent.

## Blue Hill Ashore

The Town Landing (92) is a bulkhead with pilings at the head of the harbor. There is no float or ramp, access to land being by ladder. This upper portion of the harbor dries out completely at low tide and can be approached by dinghy only within one hour of either side of high tide. There is a free concrete launching ramp alongside the Town Landing (92).

There are two very fine rstaurants on Main St., Jonathan's (93) and Firepond Restaurant (94), both offering excellent cuisine in a picturesque setting. Reservations are advisable. Firepond is housed in an old mill and blacksmith shop, and has such enticing items on the menu as scallops of veal with cognac, garden herbs and chanterelles, or veal sweetbreads with oysters and truffles. They serve hors d'oeurves and cocktails in the

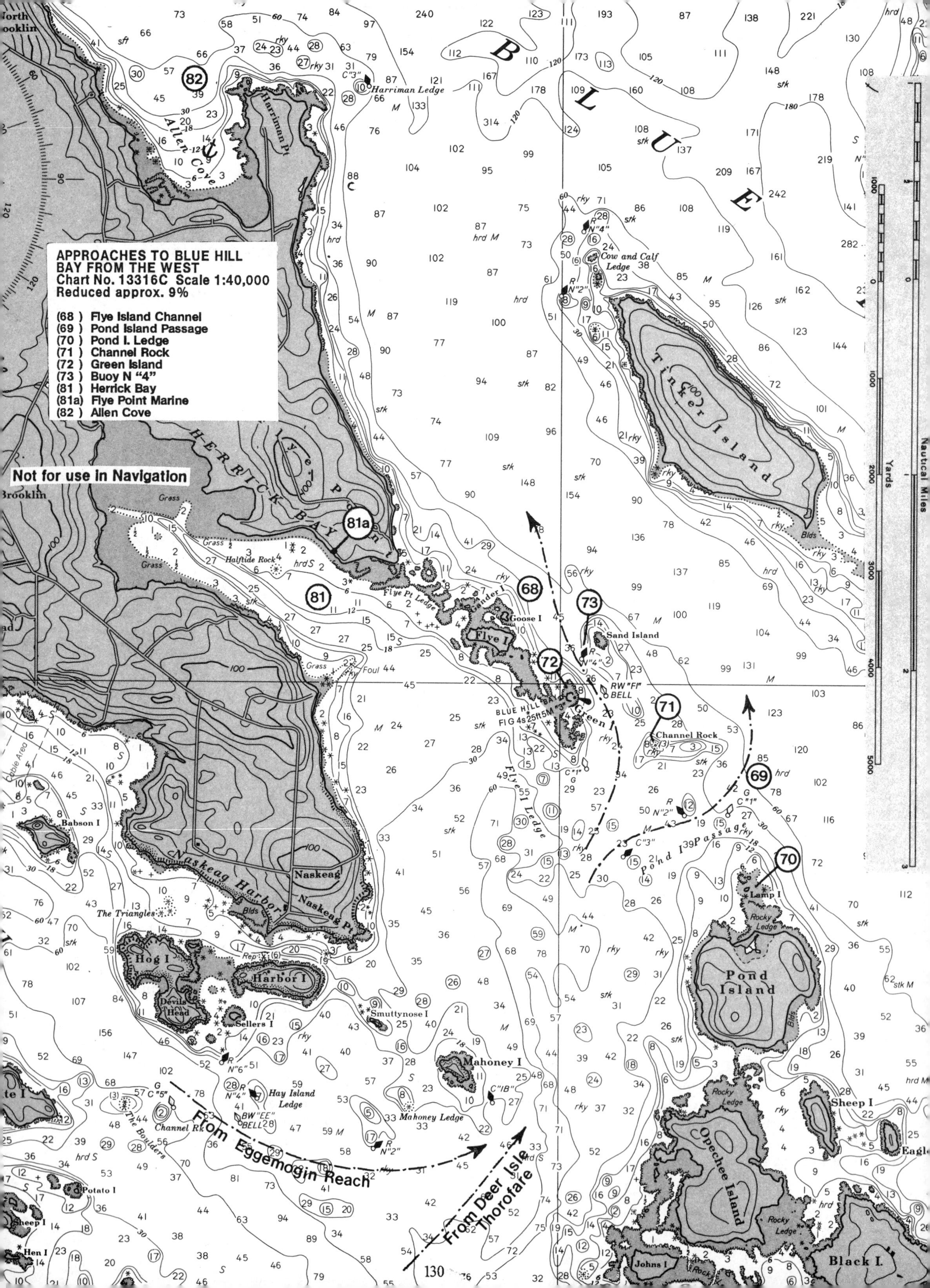

APPROACHES TO BLUE HILL BAY FROM THE WEST
Chart No. 13316C Scale 1:40,000
Reduced approx. 9%
(68 ) Flye Island Channel
(69 ) Pond Island Passage
(70 ) Pond I. Ledge
(71 ) Channel Rock
(72 ) Green Island
(73 ) Buoy N "4"
(81 ) Herrick Bay
(81a) Flye Point Marine
(82 ) Allen Cove
Not for use in Navigation
BLUE
North Brooklin
Brooklin
Allen Cove
Harriman Pt
Harriman Ledge
Herrick Bay
Flye Point
Halftide Rock
Flye Pt Ledge
Goose I
Flye I
Green I
Sand Island
Cow and Calf Ledge
Tinker Island
Channel Rock
Flye I Ledge
Pond I Passage
Lamp I
Rocky Ledge
Pond Island
Naskeag
Naskeag Harbor
Naskeag Pt
Babson I
The Triangles
Hog I
Harbor I
Devils Head
Sellers I
Smuttynose I
Mahoney I
Mahoney Ledge
Hay Island Ledge
Channel Rk
The Boulders
Potato I
Sheep I
Hen I
Opechee Island
Rocky Ledge
Johns I
Black I.
Eagle
From Eggemoggin Reach
From Deer Isle Thorofare
BLUE HILL BAY
Fl G 4s 25ft 5M "3"
RW "Fl" BELL
BW "EE" BELL
Nautical Miles
Yards

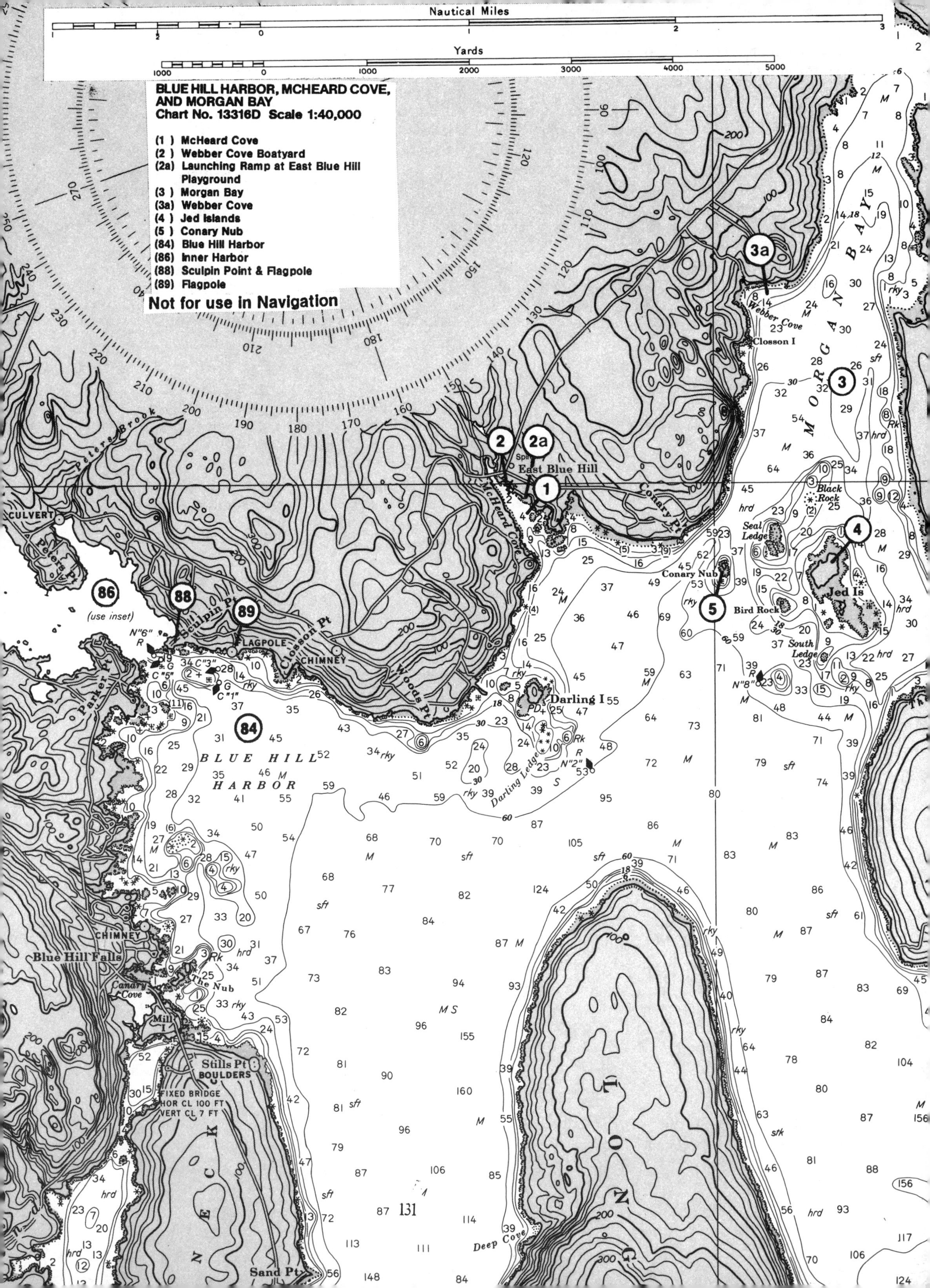

Nautical Miles
Yards
BLUE HILL HARBOR, MCHEARD COVE, AND MORGAN BAY
Chart No. 13316D Scale 1:40,000
(1 ) McHeard Cove
(2 ) Webber Cove Boatyard
(2a) Launching Ramp at East Blue Hill Playground
(3 ) Morgan Bay
(3a) Webber Cove
(4 ) Jed Islands
(5 ) Conary Nub
(84) Blue Hill Harbor
(86) Inner Harbor
(88) Sculpin Point & Flagpole
(89) Flagpole
Not for use in Navigation
Peters Brook
CULVERT
Peters Pt
(use inset)
Sculpin Pt
FLAGPOLE
Closson Pt
CHIMNEY
Woods Pt
McHeard Cove
East Blue Hill
Conary Pt
Webber Cove
Closson I
MORGAN BAY
Black Rock
Seal Ledge
Conary Nub
Jed Is
Bird Rock
South Ledge
Darling I
Darling Ledge
Parker Pt
BLUE HILL HARBOR
CHIMNEY
Blue Hill Falls
Candy Cove
The Nub
Mill I
Stills Pt
BOULDERS
FIXED BRIDGE
HOR CL 100 FT
VERT CL 7 FT
NECK
Deep Cove
Sand Pt

afternoon. Jonathan's features seafood, with an emphasis on Greek and Portuguese specialties, open for lunch and dinner.

At the head of the Town Landing is a red brick building housing Blue Hill Booksellers and Blue Hill Lunch (95). They serve breakfast 7:30-11:30, lunch, and dinner 6:30-8:30. When we visited, the Friday and Saturday evening feature was Japanese Tempura dinner.

Across the road is the Merrill & Hinckly Market (96), hours are 8:00 a.m. - 10:00 p.m. seven days a week. You will find an exceptionally large selection of fresh fruit, produce, cheese, meat and groceries, with many specialty gourmet items and they are the agency liquor store. If you shop there between 8:00 a.m. and 5:00 p.m. on weekdays, they will provide free delivery to the Yacht Club dock.

Kneisel Hall, a summer school for chamber music, gives concerts on Wednesday evenings. Try to visit Blue Hill in late July or early August to enjoy Blue Hill days. They have foot races, other competitions, bagpipe concerts and other entertainment, all on the large grassy lawn of the town park (97) overlooking the harbor.

It's a long walk, but you can climb Blue Hill Mountain (85) on chart no. 13312B. Certainly this has its rewards in a magnificent view of Blue Hill Bay and nearby mountains of Mt. Desert. It is about 2 ½ miles from the Yacht Club to the base of the mountain from where there is a road up to the fire look-out tower at the peak. The Jonathan Parson Fisher House, at the top of the hill toward the west side of town, is one of the early historical buildings. Built in 1814, it has been restored and contains the furnishings, books and journals of its original occupant, Jonathan Fisher, Blue Hill's first parson. He is known to have walked from Blue Hill to Bangor and back to preach services. Besides his religious commitments he found time to teach, farm and write. The house is open on Tuesday and Friday from 2:00 p.m. - 5:00 p.m. and Saturday 10:00 a.m. - 12:00 noon. The Holt House (98) is a Federal style mansion, housing the collection of the Blue Hill Historical Society, open Tuesday and Friday, 1:00 - 5:00 p.m.

Though it's not easy to get ashore, Blue Hill is too good to miss, a good supply port, excellent restaurants, and interesting sightseeing.

## McHEARD COVE—CHART NO. 13316D

McHeard Cove (1) is the kind of harbor that makes cruising in Maine such a pleasure. Here, tucked in among the larger and more popular harbors quite nearby, is the sense of solitude and Downeast flavor that you would expect to find much farther to the east. Seals and osprey abound, and during our last visit, we were treated to the sight of a bald eagle circling the harbor.

This small cove, with the village of East Blue Hill at its head, provides an attractive anchorage, secure to all but a southeast wind. However, if the wind is strong out of the southwest, it may get a bit lumpy near the mouth of the harbor. There is plenty of deep water in the outer half of the harbor, but at low tide, the inner half dries out completely. At extreme low tides, this drying may extend all the way out to where the chart shows 4 feet depth.

Outboard of Mink I. (see Sketch Chart), to the southwest, there are many ledges, which do not always show at high water. Mink I. is wooded, mostly with spruce, and is always visible, although it too has a line of rocks extending into the harbor which are covered at high water. Deepest water, both at the entrance to the harbor, and all the way in toward the boatyard, is to be found on the western shore. As long as you favor the western shore, you will be kept clear of all dangers.

The number of moored boats at the entrance, where there is deeper water, make it impossible to swing to an anchor, but moorings are available from the Webber Cove Boatyard (2) at the head of the cove on the eastern shore. The boatyard was originally located at Webber Cove, hence the name, but has moved here. Their moorings are easily identified as theirs are the only ones with a pole (winter-stick) float. Since the number of moorings is limited (4 altogether), it is best to call in advance. The yard moniters Ch. 16, and on occasion, channels 70 or 6.

Webber Cove Boatyard has facilities for boat building and repair, winter storage and haulout by travel-lift for moderate size boats. Gasoline and water are available at their wharf, which dries out at low tide. Even at high tide, their dock should be approached carefully. Almost directly in front of the dock, about 50 feet out, is a small ledge covered with only 2 feet of water. It is barely discernable by the attached rockweed seen at the surface of the water. To avoid the rock, proceed up the harbor on the western side until you are abreast of the dock, then make a sharp, right-angle turn directly into the dock. Do not cut any corners.

Next to the boatyard is the East Blue Hill town park and playground, where there is a free public launching ramp (2a). Directly behind the boatyard is the post office and the library (2b).

## WEBBER COVE —CHART NO. 13316D

Webber Cove (3a) is even more open and exposed to weather from the south than McHeard Cove, producing an uncomfortable anchorage. This, coupled with a very hard, gravelly, rocky bottom, makes staying here untenable. There are some moorings in the harbor, but they are all privately owned.

## MORGAN BAY—CHART NO. 13316D

Morgan Bay (3), on the north side of Blue Hill Bay, is completely open and unprotected, and has little to offer. Its chief attraction is the group of ledges and Jed Island (4) near the entrance which is a favorite sunning spot for seals. If the weather is calm and pleasant, sail in for close observation of the seals. Entrance can be made to either side of Conary Nub (5), a small rock with some scrub vegetation, but the preferred channel is west of it.

## UNION RIVER BAY—CHART NO. 13312B

There is not much of note here. At the head is Patten Bay and the Union River which continues to the town of Ellsworth (6). However, the channel in the river is dredged and narrow, poorly marked, and with a least depth of 3 feet at the upper end. In spots this has silted up to drying patches. Little is to be accomplished for the effort, and it is a long beat against the prevailing wind to sail back to Blue Hill Bay.

## HARBORS ON THE EAST SHORE OF BLUE HILL BAY, INCLUDING THE WEST SHORE OF MOUNT DESERT ISLAND

Refer to the folded chart inside the front cover. On the northwest shore of Mount Desert Island, fronting on Western Bay, you'll find Indian Point, west of Northwest Cove. The 110-acre Indian Point-Blagen Preserve of The Nature Conservancy lies on the Indian Point peninsula. It's long and narrow, but has about 0.4 mile frontage on Western Bay. There are some gravel beaches, but stay away from the west end of the preserve which is designated as a seal haul-out. There are marked trails, apple orchards, mature forest, deer, osprey and many kinds of birds, but the sight to behold is harbor seals sunning themselves on the small islands and ledges off the west shore of the peninsula.

### Bartlett Island—Chart No. 13316E

Bartlett Island (7) is privately owned but boaters are allowed on shore as long as the owners' right to privacy is respected and no fires are built. Several coves provide attractive anchorages, which may be used in fine, settled weather. My favorites are Dogfish Cove (8), Great Cove (9) and the cove south of Galley Point (10), the best protected of the three. None have any services or supplies.

### Pretty Marsh Harbor—Chart No. 13316E

Pretty Marsh Harbor (11) is a large, open bight on the west shore of Mount Desert Island. Surroundings are attractive and the anchorage is perfectly acceptable in settled weather. However there can be a rather uncomfortable roll in the harbor in strong southerlies. Most of the shoreline is privately owned and there is no access to the shore by dock. A small portion of the east shore, directly opposite the south tip of West Point, is a part of Acadia National Park. a pavilion (12), visible from the water. You can land your dinghy at the steps leading up to the picnic area.

The town of Mt. Desert has a wharf and float (13), but it is on the other side of the cove, in Bartlett Narrows. There is 6 feet of water alongside at low tide and several moorings are available. Arrangement for their use must be made through the harbormaster, reached by telephone at the number posted at the landing.

### Sawyer Cove, Somes Cove
### Chart Nos. 13312B, 13316E

Sawyer Cove (14) is on the west shore of Mt. Desert Island. Somes Cove (15), is ½ mile to the north. Both are excellent anchorages with good protection and good holding ground. The shoreline is privately owned and there are no public docks or landings. Other than the several boats moored and the few summer homes, you will be pretty well have these coves to yourself, to appreciate the tranquility and beauty of the area. The ledge at the mouth of Sawyer Cove is barely awash at high water. It is visible most of the time. By one hour after full high tide it shows itself clearly. To make the exposed portion more highly visible, someone has constructed a small cairn of rocks in the center portion. Even if you have difficulty seeing it, as in the case of fog, you can gain entry to Sawyer Cove by following closely alongshore from either the north or south headlands, for there is deep water close to both shores at the entry.

### Seal Cove, Goose Cove
### Chart Nos. 13312B, 13316E

Seal Cove (16) and Goose Cove (17), one mile south of it, each contain a fleet of fishing boats and small

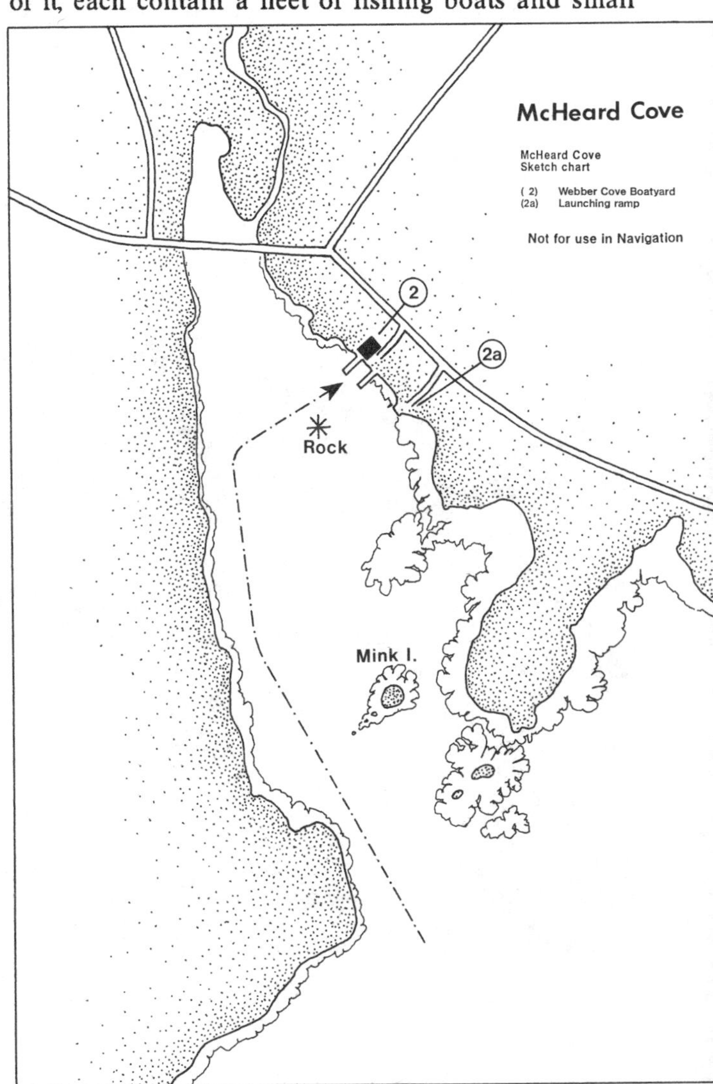

pleasure craft. The holding ground is good, but both coves are open to the prevailing summertime southwesterly winds. Neither one is much frequented by cruising yachtsmen. Besides the inherent drawbacks of these coves, Bass Harbor, much superior in all respects, is only 2 miles southeast of Goose Cove. Bass Harbor is described in Chapter 12.

There's a free concrete public launching ramp (16a), where the road comes down to the shore near the head of Seal Cove.

Bar Island is about 2.3 miles west of Goose Cove (17). It is one of a string of small islands extending southeast from Tinker Island, shown on chart no. 13313B. Others are Trumpet Island, and Ship Island, shown on chart no. 13316F. Together, Bar, Trumpet, and Ship form the Ship Island Group Preserves of the Nature Conservancy. Around 1900 there was a settlement on Bar Island, and fishermen used Trumpet and Ship. The camp on Bar Island is not part of the Preserve. East Barge and West Barge, near Ship Island, are part of the Preserve.

Ship Island is connected to Trumpet Island by a bar, exposed at low tide. A similar bar connects Bar Island to Tinker Island. There is a passage between Bar Island and Trumpet Island marked by black and white buoy "11," a mid-channel marker. Stay close to it if you use this passage. It's safer to go around the north end of Tinker Island, or the south end of Ship Island.

These islands were acquired to protect large nesting populations of common eider ducks. They're also a significant nesting site for herring gulls, greater black-backed gulls, and double-crested cormorants. Therefore public visiting is not allowed, but you'll sure see some birds as you cruise by the entrace to Blue Hill Bay.

Schooner at Anchor, Buck Harbor

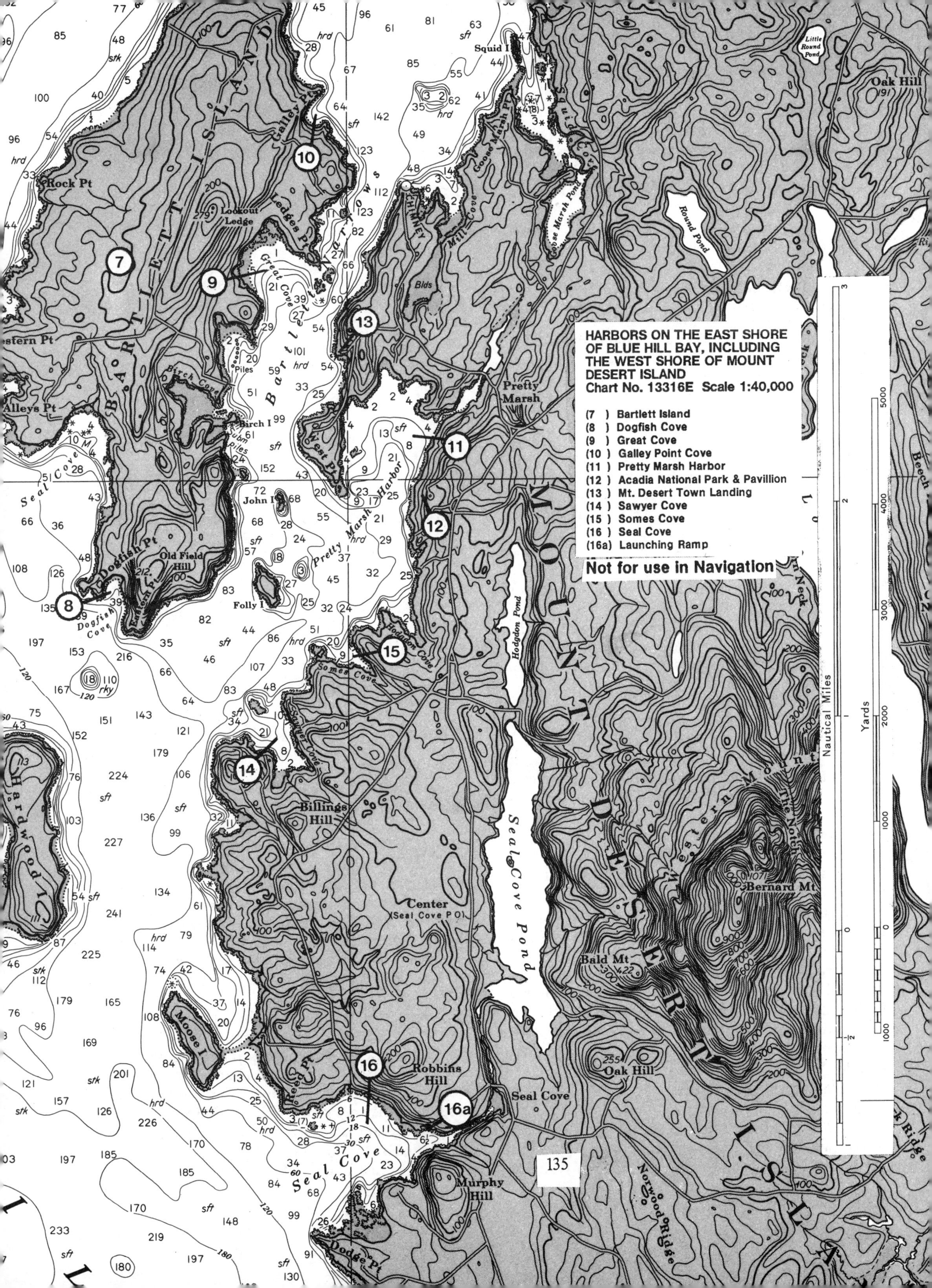
HARBORS ON THE EAST SHORE
OF BLUE HILL BAY, INCLUDING
THE WEST SHORE OF MOUNT
DESERT ISLAND
Chart No. 13316E Scale 1:40,000
(7 ) Bartlett Island
(8 ) Dogfish Cove
(9 ) Great Cove
(10 ) Galley Point Cove
(11 ) Pretty Marsh Harbor
(12 ) Acadia National Park & Pavillion
(13 ) Mt. Desert Town Landing
(14 ) Sawyer Cove
(15 ) Somes Cove
(16 ) Seal Cove
(16a) Launching Ramp
Not for use in Navigation
Nautical Miles
Yards
BARTLETT ISLAND
Rock Pt
Lookout Ledge
Galley Pt
Ledges Pt
Great Cove
Birch Cove
Birch I
Alleys Pt
Seal Cove
Dogfish Pt
Old Field Hill
Eastern Pt
Dogfish Cove
Bartlett Narrows
Squid I
Goose Marsh Pt
Goose Marsh Pond
Mill Cove
Chimney
Little Round Pond
Round Pond
Oak Hill
Pretty Marsh
West Pt
Pretty Marsh Harbor
John I
Folly I
Hodgdon Cove
Somes Cove
Hodgdon Pond
MOUNT DESERT ISLAND
Billings Hill
Center
(Seal Cove P O)
Seal Cove Pond
Western Mount
The Notch
Bernard Mt
Bald Mt
Oak Hill
Hardwood I
Moose I
Robbins Hill
Seal Cove
Murphy Hill
Norwood Ridge
Dodge Pt

# CHAPTER 12

## HARBORS ON THE SOUTH SHORE OF MOUNT DESERT ISLAND

### MOUNT DESERT ISLAND

#### History

For an overall chart of the entire island, refer to folded chart inside front cover.

*"Island of the Barren Mountains"*. . . so it was named by Champlain in his epic voyage with Pierre du Gast, Sieur de Monts, in 1604. Champlain describes in his journal, on the 5th of September, the island as being "very high, notched in places, so as to appear from the sea like a range of seven or eight mountains close together. The summits of most of them are bare of trees for they are nothing but rock. . . I named it *L'Isle des Monts Deserts."*

From the very beginning the French and the English were in conflict over claims of possession. King James I of England had granted this territory to the Virginia Company in 1606. Three years prior, much of this same land was deeded to de Monts in the patent by King Henry the IV of France. The resultant disputes, clashes and treaty reversals of ownership were to continue for the next 150 years.

This new land was called La Cadie or Acadia by the early French explorers who either coined the word or adapted it from a word of the local Abnaki Indians. As early as 1613, French Jesuits tried to settle on the island. This was eight years before the Pilgrims landed at Plymouth and but a scant six years after the colonization of Jamestown, Virginia. The Marquise de Guercheville, during the regency of Marie de Medicis, sought to found a religious colony or mission to serve the heathen of Acadia. It was to be a center for spreading the Jesuits powerful influence. In March, 1613 two Jesuits and 45 colonists sailed for Acadia. Their destination was the head of Penobscot Bay, but dense fogs in the Bay of Fundy near Grand Manan nearly ended the enterprise in shipwreck. Instead, they dropped anchor at The Narrows near the mouth of Somes Sound, by Fernalds's Point (7) chart no. 13318B, on Mt. Desert. The Jesuits decided that here they would stay, as it was evidently the hand of God that decried it so. In gratitude for being saved from disaster at sea, they called this anchorage Saint Sauveur.

The gratitude was short lived, for barely had they started their task when the English, having heard of the project, attacked them, using as justification a clause in the Virginia charter to "remove by force any and all persons who settled without permission within the limits of their province." The battle was brief and the overthrow of the newly started colony complete. Some of the survivors were sent as captives to Virginia, while others made their way back to Port Royal in Nova Scotia. From this point, up until the middle of the 18th century, there was little interest by either power in settling on Mt. Desert.

It is not certain whether the Massachusetts Colony had the valid right to grant ownership of land east of the Penobscot. Boundaries and titles were both vague and complex. Although general opinion at the time conceded it most likely belonged to Nova Scotia, they nonetheless gave title of Mt. Desert to Massachusetts Governor Francis Bernard in 1762. He tried to establish a town at Southwest Harbor, but the effort was not successful. International disputes and conflicts continued until in 1783, at the Treaty of Paris, the eastern boundary of the United States was finally fixed at the Saint Croix River.

**Description of Mount Desert Island**

Now, the fame of Acadia is perpetuated in the name of the National Park that covers 35,000 acres of Mount Desert Island as well as much of Isle au Haut and a portion of Schoodic Peninsula. Acadia National Park is one of New England's treasures, and the second most visited of all the nation's parks. Each year over four million people visit Acadia. The island has five excellent harbors, four of which will be described in this chapter, with other nearby anchorages and passages.

Mount Desert Island is Maine's largest. As you approach from the sea, its mass of mountains with their barren crown of granite holds your eye and is awesome. Towering cliffs and foaming headlands holds you spellbound, while down the mountain gorges the sea-fog "rolls like an invading host, the spires of fir trees piercing the surging vapors like lances in the smoke of battle."

In the northeast corner of the island is famed Bar Harbor (20) chart no. 13318C (not in this chapter. See Frenchman Bay, Chapter 13), while the southwest corner contains Bass Harbor (18) chart no. 13316F. These two are as diametrically opposed in appearance and purpose as they are geographically. Bar Harbor primarily caters to tourists, particularly those who drive onto the island. By the 1880's, Bar Harbor was a retreat for the wealthy and famous who built grand "cottages" for

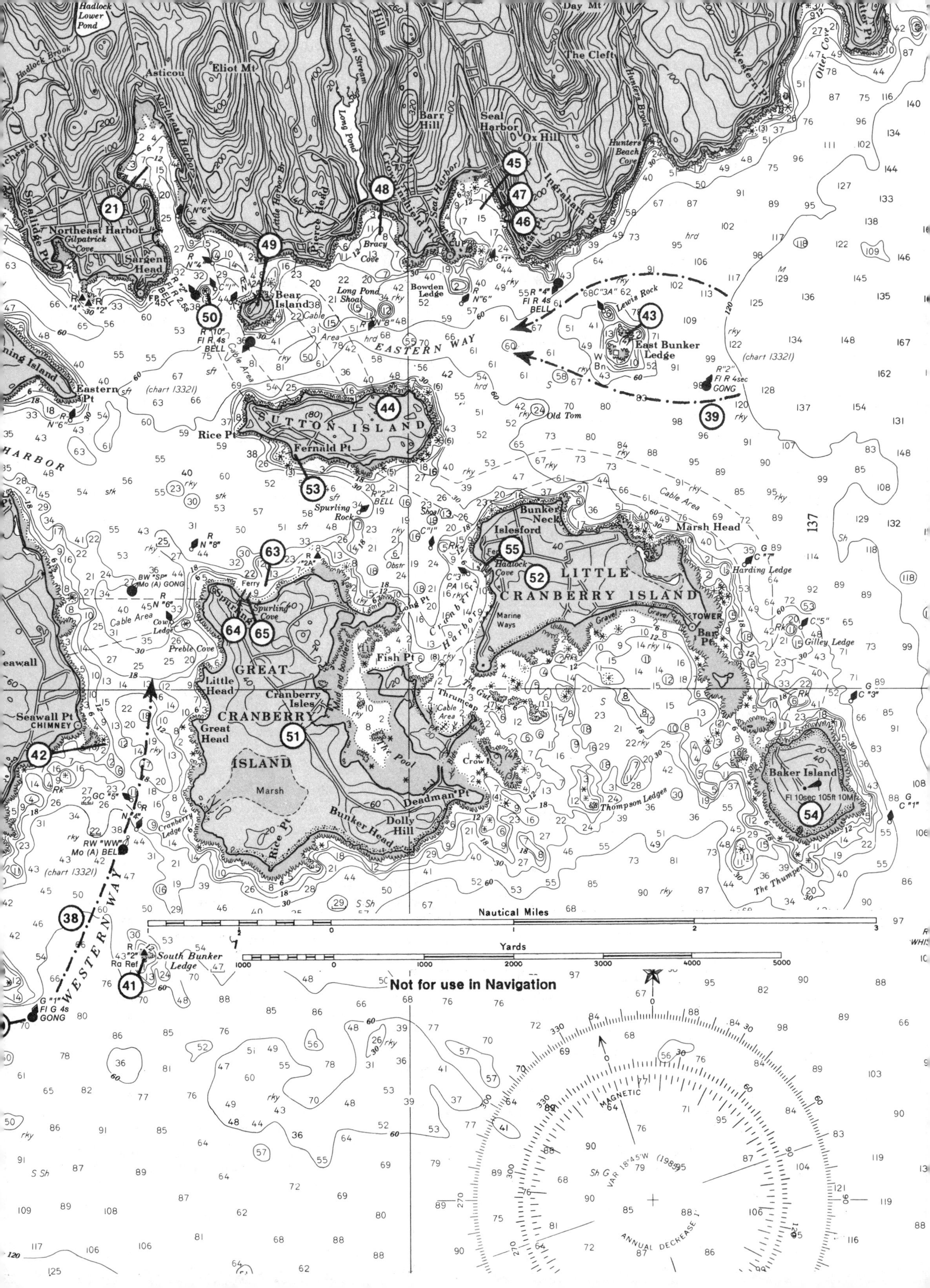

Hadlock Lower Pond
Hadlock Brook
Asticou
Eliot Mt
Jordan Stream
Hills
Day Mt
The Cleft
Hunters Brook
Western Pt
Otter Cove
Barr Hill
Long Pond
Seal Harbor
Ox Hill
Hunters Beach Cove
Northeast Harbor
Manchester Pt
Smallidge Pt
Gilpatrick Cove
Sargent Head
Little Harbor Br
Pierce Head
Crowninshield Pt
Seal Harbor
Ingraham Pt
East Pt
Bracy Cove
Bowden Ledge
Long Pond Shoal
Bear Island
Cable Area
EASTERN WAY
Lewis Rock
East Bunker Ledge
(chart 13321)
R "2" Fl R 4sec GONG
R "4" Fl R 4s BELL
R "10" Fl R 4s BELL
Eastern Pt
Rice Pt
SUTTON ISLAND
Fernald Pt
Old Tom
HARBOR
Spurling Rock
R "2" BELL
Shoal
Bunker Neck
Islesford
Marsh Head
Harding Ledge
Hadlock Cove
LITTLE CRANBERRY ISLAND
TOWER
Bar Pt
Marine Ways
Gravel
Gilley Ledge
BW "SP" Mo (A) GONG
Cable Area
Cow Ledge
Ferry
Spurling
Spurling Cove
Preble Cove
Long Pt
Cranberry Harbor
Obstr
Fish Pt
Mud and boulders
GREAT CRANBERRY ISLAND
Little Head
Great Head
Cranberry Isles
Seawall
Seawall Pt
CHIMNEY
Thrumcap
The Gut
Cable Area
The Pool
Crow I
Marsh
Deadman Pt
Dolly Hill
Bunker Head
Rice Pt
Thompson Ledges
Baker Island
Fl 10sec 105ft 10M
The Thumper
Cranberry Ledge
RW "WW" Mo (A) BELL
WESTERN WAY
South Bunker Ledge
Ra Ref
G "1" Fl G 4s GONG
Nautical Miles
Yards
Not for use in Navigation
MAGNETIC
VAR 18°45'W (1985)
ANNUAL DECREASE

their summer residence. It was the "Newport of the North," containing residences of such notables as Joseph Pulitzer and J.P. Morgan. Although many of the large homes and inns were destroyed in the disastrous fire of 1947 (which consumed over 17,000 acres of the island), Bar Harbor still draws a multitude of visitors. The streets are crowded, and shops for all manner of goods and accommodations compete for tourists' attention. It is as though the town feels the need to proclaim, in one frenzied outburst of activity, its being the final outpost, the edge of civilization abruptly stopping here. Bass Harbor, on the other hand, remains primarily a fishing community, scarcely visited by tourists and a few yachtsmen.

In between the two, on the south side of Mount Desert Island, are the three harbors that cater to and are the mecca to cruising sailors. The overall shape of these waters is like a trident, with Northeast Harbor (21) chart no. 13318B the eastern prong, Southwest Harbor (22) the western prong and Somes Sound (23), as the elongated center prong, penetrating as a deep cleft into the very heart of the island, perhaps the only true fjord in USA. Harbors on the west shore of Mount Desert Island are described in Chapter 11, as they front on Blue Hill Bay.

The town of Mt. Desert is spread over five different communities. Besides Northeast Village, the others are Pretty Marsh, on the west shore of Mount Desert Island, and Somesville, Seal Harbor and Otter Creek, on the south shore. Somes Sound goes so far north into the island that Somesville, at the head of it, is only about 4 miles from Pretty Marsh.

## BASS HARBOR— CHART NO. 13316F

This important fishing port at the southwest end of Mount Desert Island is easy to identify and to enter. Besides the great activity of fishing boats in the area, two water storage tanks (24), high on stilts, unmistakably show the harbor's location. These tanks, near the fish cannery, are visible a long way off. The Ferry Landing Wharf (25) is prominent on the east side of the entrance to the inner harbor. This is the landing for the State Ferry that goes 4 to 5 times a day to Mackerel Cove on Swans Island and to Frenchboro on Long Island.

### Outer Harbor

Approaching the outer harbor, do not confuse the two buoys N "2" and C "1" as channel markers. They are there to indicate the position of Weaver Ledge (26), which exposes itself at 3 feet. If you go between them, you hit the ledge. Enter west of the nun, or east of the can. Although it is fairly open and exposed to the south and southwest, boats anchor in this outer harbor opposite the Ferry Landing. The holding ground is good and if the weather takes a turn for the worse, shelter is nearby in the inner harbor.

South of the Ferry Landing is Bass Harbor Marine (27) with depths of 10 feet at their wharf. They have 25 moorings, gasoline, diesel fuel, water, ice, propane, showers, marine supplies, complete engine and hull repairs, NOS charts, are dealers for Westerbeke and Volvo Penta, and monitor VHF Channels 9 and 16. Hinckley Yacht Charters is based at Bass Harbor Marine. This is a full service yard.

The Bass Harbor Town Landing (28) is north of the Ferry Wharf. Tie-up time at the float is limited to 8 hours. If there is a strong southwesterly, the swell produced can make this an uncomfortable place. The face of the float must be kept open, as this is reserved for a tour boat that takes out National Park tourists. During Monday-Saturday, the space must be available for it to take on and discharge passengers. One other portion of the float is tied up by a diving service, but the rest of the space is open to visitors. This is one of the two places that is convenient to land your dinghy. The other landing is at the small beach (29) next to the cannery.

C.H. Rich Co., north of Bass Harbor Marine, has Texaco gasoline and diesel fuel, ice, and sells seafood.

On the east shore, Power & Robinson, north of the water tanks, has marine hardware, complete engine and hull repairs, and propeller work. If there's anything wrong with your boat, you can get it fixed in Bass Harbor.

### Inner Harbor

To enter the inner harbor, where there is much better protection, first favor the eastern shore until past the two water tanks. This brings you east of buoy C "5" whereupon you swing over toward the western shore, following it in. This entire portion of the inner harbor is dredged, the channel to a depth of 10 feet, and the anchorage basin to the west, 4 ½ feet. It is a very congested harbor, filled with moored lobster boats, so do not expect to find any place to anchor. The many boats make it difficult to see buoy N "6" marking the eastern edge of the north end of the channel, but they fairly well define the edge of the channel, and you can assume that anything outside them is drying mussel flats or rocks. Proceed through the moored fleet, aiming for the small island (30) at the north end of the channel. Here the channel makes a dog-leg turn toward the east. As you get close to the island, you will then see N "6" buoy, as well as the group of sailboat masts at the pier of the Bass Harbor Boat Corporation (31). The channel northeast of there is also filled with moored boats.

There are many lobster cars in the inner harbor, some very close to the channel. They can be a navigational hazard at night or in fog. These large, almost entirely submerged boxes, are poorly marked and difficult to see. They are securely anchored and do not give way if hit.

Bass Harbor Boat Corp. (31) has 8-10 feet depth at their floats and can accommodate boats in slips and at the dock. They have 20 transient slips, 14 moorings, Texaco gasoline, water, ice, complete engine and hull repairs, and are boat builders. Diesel fuel can be obtained at two of the three fish wharfs which line this

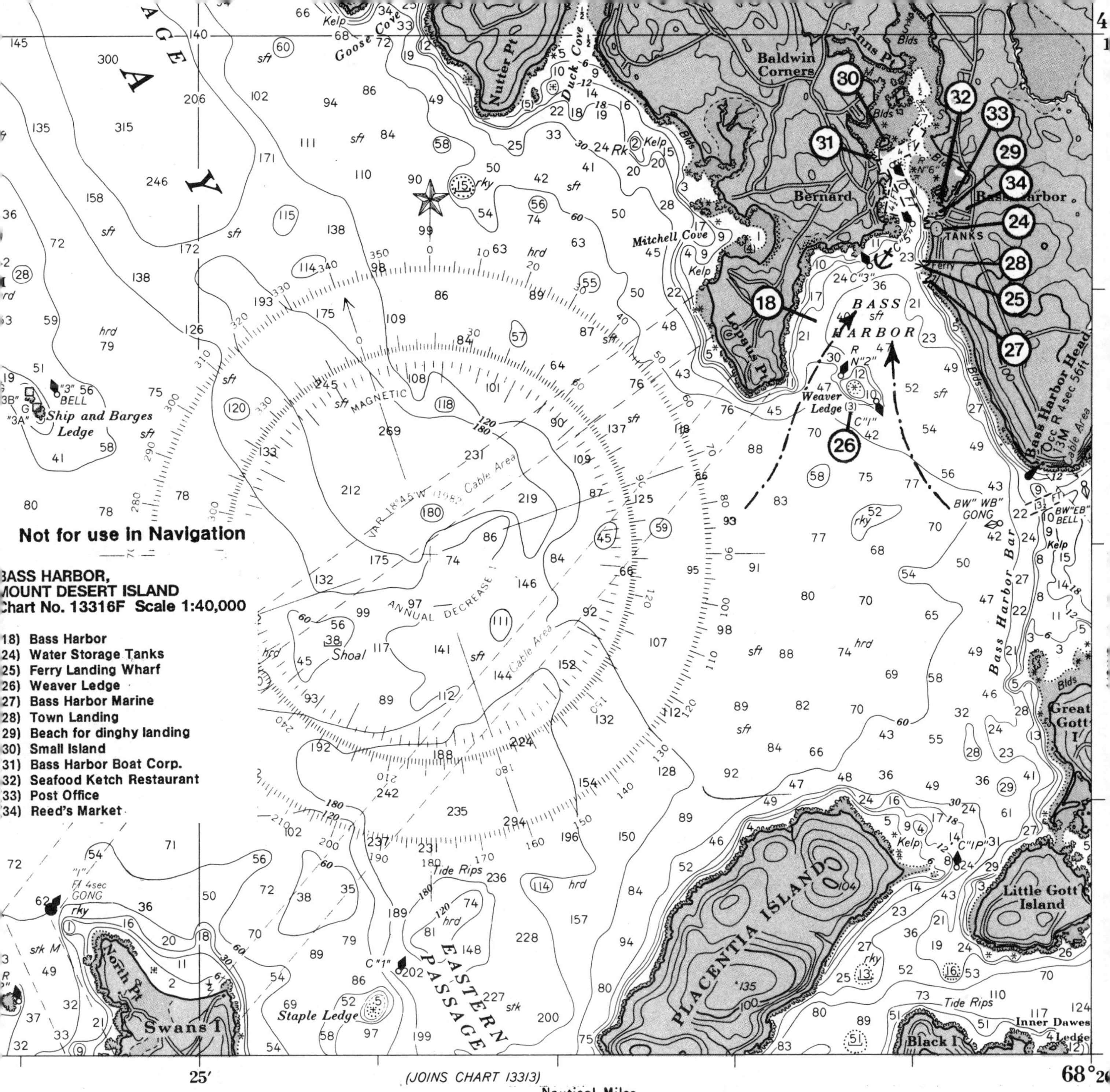


western shore. South to north, these are: Blacks Lobster Pound, snack bar and seafood; F.W. Thurston Co., Texaco gasoline and diesel fuel, some marine supplies, and lobsters, monitors CB Channel 11 and VHF Channel 16; and Damon's Wharf, 1 mooring, diesel fuel, marine hardware, and seafood.

The village of Bernard is on the west side of the harbor and the town of Bass Harbor on the east side. Bernard is primarily residential with several antique and gift shops. All shopping for supplies must be done in Bass Harbor. North of the dinghy landing beach (29) is the Seafood Ketch Restaurant (32), where, as might be expected, the primary emphasis is on seafood, open 7:00 a.m. - 9:30 p.m. Adjacent in the yellow shingled building, is the Post Office (33). Reed's Market (34), a short distance up the hill from the beach is the only store in town for grocery shopping. It is a general store, also dealing in hardware and some marine supplies, open 8:00 a.m. - 8:00 p.m. Monday through Saturday.

## SOUTHWEST HARBOR

### Approaches—Chart No. 13318A

Whether you intend to go to Northeast Harbor (21), Southwest Harbor (22) or Somes Sound (23), the initial approach is the same. From the west, entrance to these harbors is through Western Way (38), between Mt. Desert and Great Cranberry Island (51).

From the east, it is through the passage north of Little Cranberry Island, called Eastern Way (39). Both entrances are well marked by navigation aids for any dangers, and both have sound and light buoys.

Heading east, having come through Bass Harbor Bar Channel toward Western Way, you will want to move farther off shore to avoid Long Ledge which extends 0.5 mile out from the mainland. At high tide, the gong buoy "1" (40), Fl 4 sec, marking this ledge seems an improbable distance out from land, but do not cut west of this gong "1" (40).

South Bunker Ledge (41), at the approach to Western Way, is completely submerged at high tide, uncovering at 4 feet. It is marked by a daybeacon on a tall pole. Care must also be taken to avoid the ledge (42) that extends diagonally southeast from Seawall Point. This narrows the navigable channel considerably. You will find a strong tidal current through Western Way, attaining a velocity of 3 knots, the ebb tide flowing south. Trying to enter against the current in a dying late afternoon breeze can be frustrating. A strong southerly wind against the outgoing tide will create a short, steep chop here. Once over the bar and into deeper water, it will calm down considerably. The tidal current runs less strongly through Eastern Way (39).

East Bunker Ledge (43) at the east end of Eastern Way, is actually two small islets about 4 feet high, each surrounded by an extensive area of ledge. On the southern most of the two is a pyramidal stone structure painted white. A can buoy, C "3A", marks the most northerly extension of ledge (Lewis Rock) of the northern islet. You may pass to either side of these islets. The remainder of the way in is clearly indicated by a succession of red buoys on the north side of the channel and the bold shores of Sutton Island (44) on the south side. At the head of the harbor is Great Harbor Marina (73).

### Southwest Harbor— Chart No. 13321A

Southwest Harbor is a large harbor open to the east, with boating activity of all kinds. It's a great repair and supply port, has excellent restaurants, and the downeast atmosphere that must be experienced. Yachts tend to cluster along the south shore, particularly near the entrance, while work boats of the Island's fishermen and lobstermen congregate along the more commercial north shore. It is a well protected harbor except for winds from the east to southeast, but the most that would be encountered in the usual summer weather is an uncomfortable roll. Room to anchor in this big harbor is severely limited due to all the moored boats. In all, there are over 500 moorings, carefully laid out on a grid pattern. About the only available space left for anchoring is near the very head of the harbor in the southwest corner. I've indicated this on Chart No. 13321A. At present, there are three guest moorings (100) maintained by the town of Southwest Harbor, available on a first come, first served basis. A fee for their use is charged by the town. These moorings are very large rubber floats in the shape of an inverted mushroom, painted bright yellow.

Entrance to the harbor is easy under all conditions. There are no dangers, marked or unmarked and currents are minimal.

Southwest Harbor may be used as a port of entry for customs. Although the customs office (formerly in Bar Harbor) is closed, operations are being coordinated through the Bangor Office. For Canadian citizens using Southwest Harbor as their first port of call or for American citizens returning after a visit in Canadian waters, be sure to contact the customs office at 207-947-7861 and they will come down to meet you. You are requested to remain aboard your boat until the customs official arrives. Between Southwest Harbor and the Canadian border, the only other official port of entry is at Eastport.

**South Shore Facilities (Manset).** The first large dock on the south shore is Henry R. Hinckley Company (70), builders of yachts of the highest quality for over 50 years. Their name is prominently displayed on the building behind the dock and their boats fill the dock space and surrounding moorings. Hinckley has 40 moorings, diesel fuel and water at the dock, ice, showers, propane, marine supplies, complete engine, hull and electronics repairs, rigging service, are boat builders, and monitor VHF Channels 9 and 16. However most of the above-mentioned facilities, including dock space, are available only to Hinckley customers. The exception being moorings, which are available for rental by the day, week or month. If you do intend using their moorings, reservations should be made early, for by the middle of July they are already booked up for the remainder of the summer.

The dock immediately to the west is The Boathouse (71), which has 30 moorings for small boats up to 25 ft., marine supplies, complete engine and hull repairs, and asphalt launching ramp and they monitor VHF Channel 68. Farther west is the Manset Village Town Dock (72) with a depth of 12 feet and tie-up time limited to 8 hours.

A dumpster is present for trash disposal and there are pumpout facilities for holding tanks. If you have any problem with finding a mooring or anchorage, talk to the Harbormaster. He is usually present at one of the three town landings, but if not, may be reached by phone at 244-3908.

Across the road from the Town Dock is the Dockside Motel and Restaurant (74). They are open from 5:00 a.m. through dinner time.

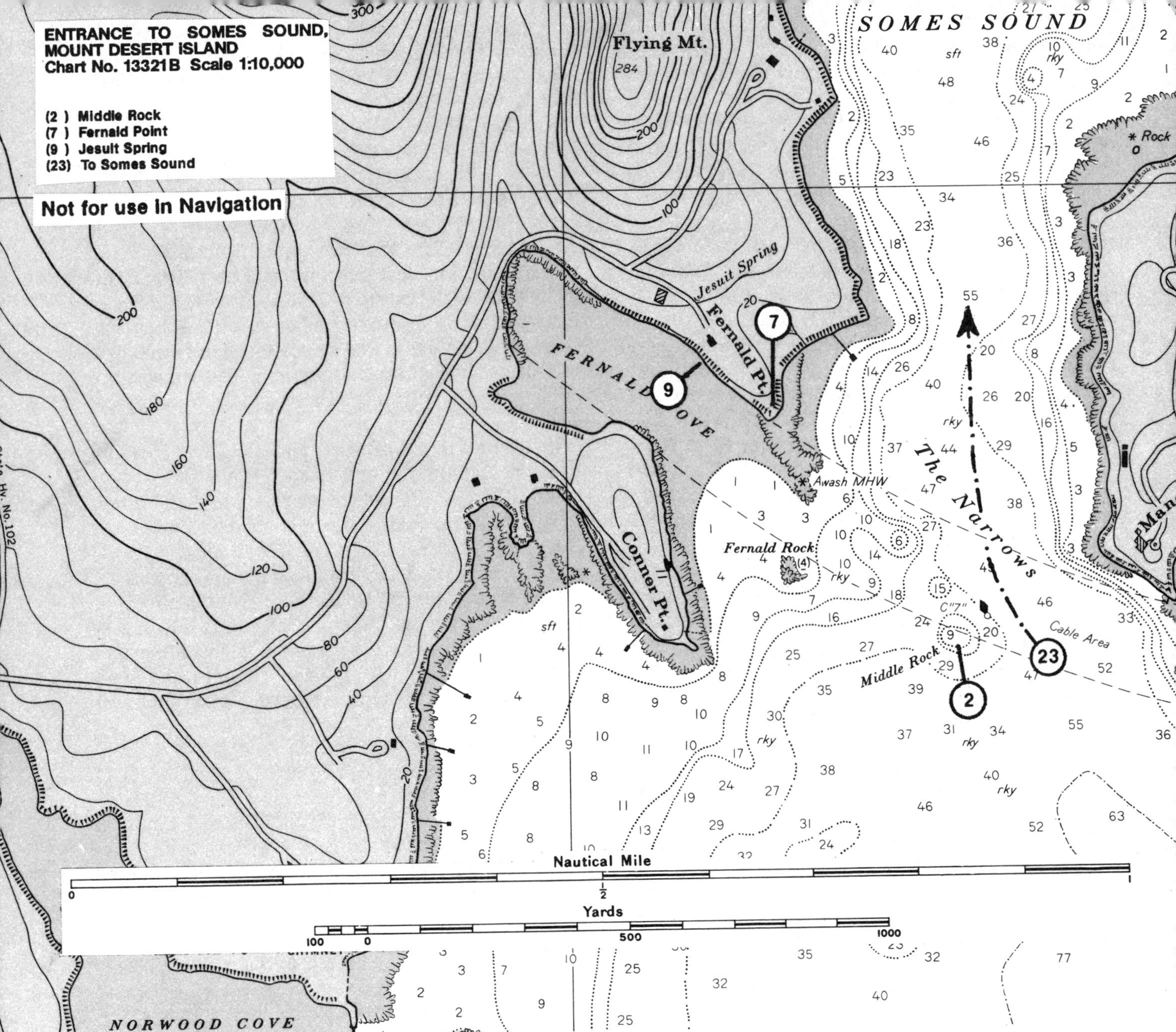


At the head of the harbor is the commercial wharf for the sardine cannery (73). All the rest of the wharfs and float landings on the south shore are privately owned. You can land your dinghy either at the Hinckley float or the Town Landing.

East of the Hinckley Wharf is the Moorings Inn and Restaurant (75). From their dining room, you will have a superb view of the harbor and Somes Sound.

Across the road are many buildings of the Hinckley Boatyard (70a). If you want to see how Henry R. Hinckley & Co. have earned and maintained their fine reputation as builders, you can sign up at the office for their twice daily tours of the plant. Their ship chandlery, called The Ships Store (76), has marine supplies, foul weather gear and clothing. Farther down the road is the Double J. Grocery (78), which will deliver your purchases to the dock. Across from the grocery is another of Mt. Desert's fine boat builders, the Lee S. Wilbur Boatyard (79). A few hundred yards down the road is the Manset Post Office (99).

**West Shore Facilities.** Since the construction of Great Harbor Marina (73), Southwest Harbor now easily accommodates a much greater number of boats. They have slip space for 150 boats, and can handle vessels up to 150 feet in length. There are power pedestals for water, cable TV, 30 and 50 amp hook-ups, as well as shower and laundry facilities, and holding tank pump-out. From here, it is only a 5 minute walk to the village of Southwest Harbor for supplies and restaurants.

**North Shore Facilities.** The north shore has a large Coast Guard Station (80) near the entrance, and numerous wharfs with convenient access to the nearby village of Southwest Harbor. West of the Coast Guard Station is the very busy wharf of Harvard R. Beal &

Sons (81), referred to as Beal's Lobster Wharf. They have 6 transient moorings, gasoline, diesel fuel, water, ice, propane, snack bar, seafood, and they monitor VHF Channel 16. Beal's Wharf now has dock space, as well as 6 moorings for transients, a laundromat, showers, marine hardware store, and an inside dining room—all in addition to the services described above. On Beal's Wharf is The Captain's Galley (82), a restaurant serving chowders, lobsters, steamed clams, sandwiches, etc., with outdoor picnic tables, and a retail fish market with all kinds of fresh seafood. Their summer hours are 9:00 a.m. to 7:30 p.m.

Adjacent west of Beal's Wharf, is the Lower Town Wharf (84), one of the two Town Wharfs of Southwest Harbor. There are 3 floats and a depth of 12 feet at low water. Public restrooms are at the foot of the wharf. The other Town Wharf is called the Upper (or New) Town Wharf (83). Depths at the Upper Town Dock are limited to 4-6 feet, but is the most convenient to use if you are planning to walk up to the village. It has a concrete launching ramp. Both docks have dumpsters for trash disposal.

West of Lower Town Dock is Village Electronics (84a), with sales and service of electronic equipment. They monitor VHF Channel 16. Next toward the head of the harbor, is Downeast Diesel and Marine (85), with complete inboard engine repairs. Their slip is for service only. Southwest Harbor Boat Corp. (86) has no facilities for transients, but can work on boats up to 115 ft. long, has marine supplies, complete engine and hull repairs, a complete machine shop and are boat builders. They monitor VHF Channel 16.

Farther west is Southwest Harbor Lobster Co., Texaco gasoline and diesel fuel, marine hardware, lobsters, and monitors VHF Channels 6 and 80. Doug's Diving & Salvage is next to the Town Dock, and has moorings and monitors VHF Channel 16. Ralph W. Stanley and Morris Yachts, farther west, both have complete hull repairs and are boat builders (77).

The complex of buildings comprising Morris Yachts (77), builders of cruising auxiliaries, also contains Shore Sails. Shore Sails is open 7:30 a.m. to 4:00 p.m., Monday through Friday. They have complete sailmaking service, including repair and winter service.

In town are two grocery stores: Sawyers Market (88) and Walts Food Store (89). Both will deliver to your boat. Restaurants include: The Harbor Deli and Bakery (90), with their own homemade cookies, breads and cakes; The Deacon Seat Restaurant (96), with enclosed porch dining; The Drydock Cafe and Inn (91), with takeout lunches available; and the Clark Point Cafe (92). Don't be misled by the modest exterior and simple name of Clark Point Cafe, for inside you will find an extremely varied and excellent gourmet menu, serving such entrees as Salmon Fettucine with black olives and mustard sauce, or Feta Tiger Scampi (large shrimp sauteed with garlic, tomato, lime, oregano and Feta cheese, served on rice). The Clark Point Cafe is open from 5:00 p.m. on Tuesday through Sunday, closed Monday. Reservations are suggested. All the restaurants serving breakfast are open at 5:00 a.m.; allowing a good early start to your sailing day.

The Post Office (93), Laundromat (94), Hardware (95) and Liquor Store (97) are all located in the center of town, a short walk from the new Town Dock (83). The drug store (101) is on the west side of Main Street. Several doors down from the drug store is a Bicycle Rental Shop (88a). Don't overlook this leisurely mode of transportation for exploring Mt. Desert Island. Although the island is mountainous, its many miles of roads and carriage paths are all quite level, without any steep gradients. Ideas and routes for bicycle trips will be provided by personnel in this and other rental shops on the island (Bar Harbor) where you obtain your bicycles.

Headed north out of town, and but a few doors up from the Harbor Deli and Bakery, is a Visitors Information Center (90a) where you can find out about activities and concerts going on about town and on Mt. Desert Island. Menus from all the restaurants in the area are available, making your dining selection easier.

Next door is the Oz Books store (90b). Not only is there an extensive selection of books on Maine in general, and Mt. Desert I. in particular, including trail maps, but it is the oldest and must complete children's bookstore in Maine. They are open Monday through Saturday, 9:30 a.m. to 5:00 pm.

Even if your boat library is well stocked with reference books on the wildflowers, birds and marine life of Maine, you might want to incorporate a publication (1988), titled "The Geology of Mt. Desert Island," to more fully understand the origin, history, diverse nature and beauty of the geology of Acadia National Park. It is published by the Maine Geological Survey, Department of Conservation.

If you plan to do any hiking, utilizing the extensive trail system, another useful publication is "A Hiking Guide to Acadia National Park." In it, besides maps of all the trails, is a description of the trails, distance, location, hints and facts, plus special points of interest. At a cost of only $2.50, and small enough to be easily carried in your pocket, it is an indispensable aid to climbing. Books like these are almost essential to finding and appreciating all the unique and beautiful features of this island that have made it so famous.

An ideal place to learn about marine environment, so intimately connected with the lives of the people on the Maine coast, is the Mount Desert Oceanarium (98). Situated between the Coast Guard Base and Beal's Lobster Wharf, it is an exciting and stimulating place for children to learn about many aspects of the sea. There are a variety of exhibits on lobsters and lobster fishing, fishing gear, tides and weather. The emphasis is on **involvement** by the viewer, with things to touch, taste and hear. In the whale exhibit you can listen to the "songs" of whales, while in another area you are encouraged to try and taste the difference between sea salt

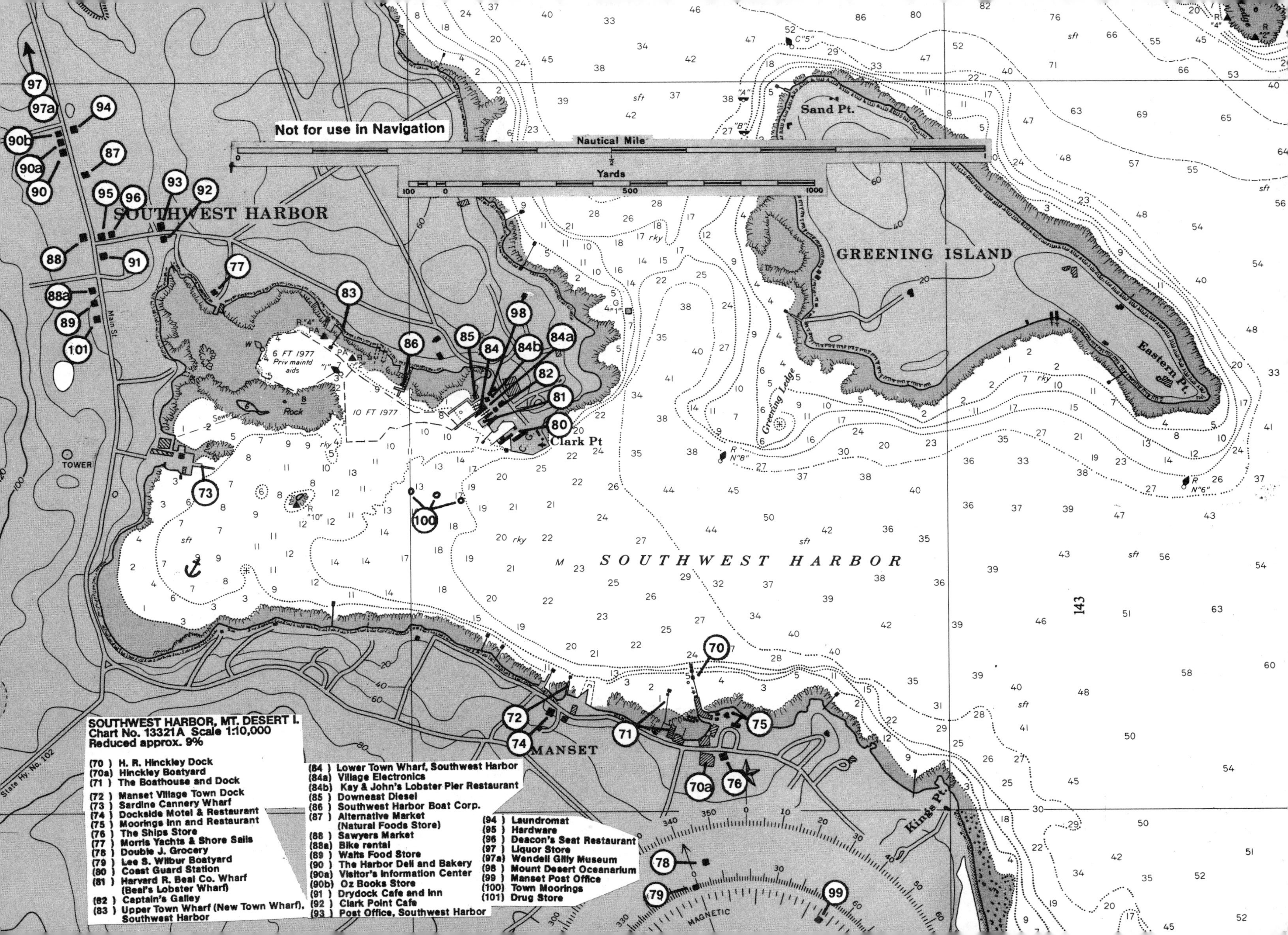
Not for use in Navigation
Nautical Mile
Yards
SOUTHWEST HARBOR
GREENING ISLAND
Sand Pt.
Greening Ledge
Eastern Pt.
Clark Pt
Rock
Kings Pt.
MANSET
TOWER
Main St.
State Hy. No. 102
6 FT 1977 Priv maintd aids
10 FT 1977
MAGNETIC
SOUTHWEST HARBOR, MT. DESERT I.
Chart No. 13321A Scale 1:10,000
Reduced approx. 9%
(70) H. R. Hinckley Dock
(70a) Hinckley Boatyard
(71) The Boathouse and Dock
(72) Manset Village Town Dock
(73) Sardine Cannery Wharf
(74) Dockside Motel & Restaurant
(75) Moorings Inn and Restaurant
(76) The Ships Store
(77) Morris Yachts & Shore Sails
(78) Double J. Grocery
(79) Lee S. Wilbur Boatyard
(80) Coast Guard Station
(81) Harvard R. Beal Co. Wharf (Beal's Lobster Wharf)
(82) Captain's Galley
(83) Upper Town Wharf (New Town Wharf), Southwest Harbor
(84) Lower Town Wharf, Southwest Harbor
(84a) Village Electronics
(84b) Kay & John's Lobster Pier Restaurant
(85) Downeast Diesel
(86) Southwest Harbor Boat Corp.
(87) Alternative Market (Natural Foods Store)
(88) Sawyers Market
(88a) Bike rental
(89) Walts Food Store
(90) The Harbor Deli and Bakery
(90a) Visitor's Information Center
(90b) Oz Books Store
(91) Drydock Cafe and Inn
(92) Clark Point Cafe
(93) Post Office, Southwest Harbor
(94) Laundromat
(95) Hardware
(96) Deacon's Seat Restaurant
(97) Liquor Store
(97a) Wendell Gilly Museum
(98) Mount Desert Oceanarium
(99) Manset Post Office
(100) Town Moorings
(101) Drug Store

and table salt. There are staff members at various exhibits to answer questions.

Not to be missed during your stay at Southwest Harbor is the Wendell Gilley Museum (97a). Founded in 1981, the Museum is an architecturally splendid piece of art. It houses a collection of over 200 carved birds by Southwest Harbor's resident, Wendell Gilley. You will be attracted, not only to the exquisite detailing of the carving of these birds, and their very lifelike poses, but by the extreme care taken in accuracy. Mr. Gilley was as much as first-rate scientist and ornithologist as he was an artist. Bird songs, taped and played on the museum's speaker system, add the final touch of pleasure. In addition to the displays, you can watch a woodcarver at work to see just how these masterpieces were created. If you wish to try your hand at it, courses are offered in woodcarving for both adults and children. The museum is only a short walk out of town and is open every day but Monday, June through October.

## SOMES SOUND—CHART NOS. 13321B, 13318B

For many, the highlight of a visit to Mount Desert Island is a sail up Somes Sound (23).This long arm of the sea, the largest fjord in America, thrusts itself inland for almost 6 miles, walled in by mountains rising steeply from the water.

At the head of the Sound is the town of Somesville (1), site of the first permanent settlement on Mt. Desert Island and named after Abraham Somes, a barrel maker from Massachusetts who landed on this shore with his wife and family in 1761.

It is best to plan your trip up the Sound with the flood tide to help carry you past the rush of tide at the narrow entrance and on up the Sound. The entire way is clear of any dangers and obstructions, the only hazard being a rock (Middle Rock) (2) near the entrance, covered with 9 feet of water and marked by buoy C "7" on its northeast side.

The most dramatic spot in the entire Sound to anchor is Valley Cove (3), on the western shore about one mile above the entrance. Here,, the granite face of St. Sauveur Mountain (4) plummets from a height of 679 feet straight down to the water. Work your way toward the shore as close as possible to anchor, or pick up one of the several guest moorings which are maintained by the National Park Service and provided free of charge. Along the waters' edge is one of the numerous hiking trails on the island. This trail leads to the summit of St. Sauveur Mountain (4) and nearby Acadia Mountain, (5), elevation 681 ft. From here you can take the trail to Echo Lake (6), or over Flying Mountain to the several interesting sites on Fernald Point (7). This is where the French Jesuits first attempted settlement in 1613 (refer to History at the beginning of this chapter).

In Fernald Cove near the high-water mark, approximately 200 yards northwest of the point, is a unique fresh water spring (9). This was used by the Jesuits, and now, nearly 400 years later, it is still flowing, producing clear, sweet water. What makes this all the more remarkable is that the spring is below the high-tide line. At half-tide the spring is accessible and the water drinkable.

### Marine Facilities in Somes Sound

#### Chart No. 13318B

Farther up the Sound, on the west side, is Hall Quarry (10). At one time granite was extensively quarried here. Now, you'll find John M. Williams Co. boatyard with 20 ft. depth at the float landing, moorings, gasoline, diesel fuel, water, marine hardware and complete engine and hull repair. Across the sound is the Bar Harbor Boating Co. (11), with 8 moorings, dock space, ice, some engine and hull repair, sailboat charters, and they monitor VHF Channels 9 and 10.

Near the head of Somes Sound, are two more yards. Henry R. Abel & Co. Yacht Yard (21a) has 16 moorings, ice, complete engine and hull repair, marine hardware, cocktail lounge and Abel's Lobster Pound seafood restaurant. There is no charge for picking up a mooring while dining there. Reservations are suggested, phone 276-5837. Mt. Desert Yacht Yard (22a) has 14 moorings, and complete engine and hull repair.

### Somes Harbor

Entrance to Somes Harbor, at the very head of the Sound, presents no problem. Keep Bar Island (12) to starboard and green can buoy "9" to port.

Most of Somes Harbor is filled with privately owned moorings, leaving limited room for anchoring. There are no public or guest moorings. Plan to arrive in the early afternoon to be sure to find a spot to anchor. The deeper water is on the eastern side and you can anchor either forward of the moored fleet or astern of it. Your best chance of finding an anchorage is close along the shore of Sheep Island (13), going as far north as the three rocks near the head of the harbor. The holding ground is only moderately good. The mud bottom is soft and in really heavy weather the anchor will slide through it. In normal summer weather there should be no trouble. The dock and floats (14) are maintained by an association of Somesville residents. However, visiting yachtsmen are allowed to land there and tie their dinghy at the float.

### Somesville

The village of Somesville is centered near the road junction where you will find the Post Office (15) to the west and an Exxon Station (16) and the A.G. Market (17) to the north. At the market you can do very adequate provisioning, including fresh produce and meat. They are open until 9:00 p.m. Close to the town landing is the A. V. Higgens Market (17a), easily accessible for provisioning of your boat.

The Exxon station (16) can refill liquid propane tanks, and if you bring your own containers, provide gasoline and diesel fuel. For entertainment, try the Acadia Repertory Theater, which performs in the Masonic Hall (18), a short walk south from the landing.

Not for use in Navigation
SOMES SOUND,
MOUNT DESERT ISLAND
Chart No. 13318B Scale 1:40,000
(1 ) Somesville
(2 ) Middle Rock
(3 ) Valley Cove
(4 ) St. Sauveur Mountain
(5 ) Acadia Mountain
(6 ) Echo Lake
(7 ) Fernald Point
(9 ) Jesuit Spring
(10 ) Hall Quarry
(11 ) Bar Harbor Boating Co.
(12 ) Bar Island
(13 ) Sheep Island
(14 ) Somesville Association Landing
(15 ) Post Office
(16 ) Exxon Station
(17 ) A.G. Market
(17a) A.V. Higgens
(18 ) Masonic Hall
(19 ) Sargent Mountain
(20 ) Sawyer Cove
(21 ) Northeast Harbor
(21a) Henry R. Abel Boatyard
(22 ) Southwest Harbor
(22a) Mt. Desert Yacht Yard
(23 ) Somes Sound
Nautical Miles
Yards
Somes Pond
Oak Hill
Echo Lake
Somes Sound
Acadia Mt
St Sauveur Mt
Sargent Mt
Norumbega Mt
Northeast Harbor
Southwest Harbor
Greening Island
(chart 13321)

They have productions at 8:00 p.m. during July and August.

### More Trails

One of the most rewarding features of Mount Desert Island is the extensive system of foot trails and carriage paths for exploring the island and climbing its mountains. There are eighteen peaks in all, with Cadillac Mountain at 1530 feet being the highest. Mt. Cadillac (formerly called Green Mountain) is the highest coastal point north of Rio de Janeiro.

There are over 120 miles of trails in the Park, plus 57 miles of carriage paths. This network of paths was funded and directed by John D. Rockefeller, Jr., from 1913 to 1933. They enable you to see much of the island by foot, bicycle or horseback, without the intrusion or annoyance of automobiles. The foot trails vary widely in ease of climbing, from near level gentle walks to steep difficult climbs where iron ladder rungs are set into the vertical face of granite walls and where drop-offs of 300 to 400 feet are not uncommon. It doesn't take more than a tea-cup full of brains to figure out that trails called The Perpendicular Trail and the Precipice Trail are not for beginners.

Before doing any climbing, you should have with you one of the printed trail maps of the island. These can be obtained from the Park Service or other private sources. The one I use, and particularly like, is the map put out by the Appalachian Mountain Club. It is for sale ($1.20) in stores on the island or may be ordered from the Appalachian Mountain Club, 5 Joy St., Boston Mass. 02108. They also have a companion guide book describing the condition and clearness of all the trails.

The Giant Slide Trail to the top of Sargent Mountain (19), elevation 1373 feet, is easily reached from Somesville. Take the dinghy, or sail over to Sargent Cove (20) on the east side of Somes Sound. A road parallels the shore, and opposite the mouth of the cove, across the road is a small, stone, Episcopal Church. There, a trail marker will point out the trail to the top of Sargent Mountain. It is of moderate difficulty, and 2.4 miles long. This trail is named for its large smooth slope of exposed granite which was used for sliding down cut trees to the water during logging operations. As might be expected, the views from the top are unsurpassed. If you are climbing in late summer, be sure to bring along plastic bags or containers. The upper slopes are covered with wild blueberries. If you can refrain from eating while you pick, you can bring a marvelous treat back to the boat.

Don't leave Mount Desert Island without exploring magnificant Somes Sound.

## NORTHEAST HARBOR—CHART NO. 13321

Bear Island (49), near the entrance to Northeast Harbor, is high and wooded, easily identified by the attractive white tower and house of its now abandoned lighthouse. This is on the west side of the island and shows well in a clearing of trees. South of the island is bell buoy R "10" (Fl 4 sec) which marks the west end of Eastern Way. The only existing danger to entering Northeast Harbor is a rock (50) near the entrance which uncovers at 3 feet. It is marked by buoys on both sides of it. They should **not** be confused for channel markers. Do not go between them. Go west of R "2" bell or east of C "1" can. Red right returning! Beyond this rock, passage is straightforward, with no hindrances. The west side has deeper water close to shore. A buoyed fairway leads you through the moored fleet to the head of the harbor. The dolphins (58), pilings lashed at the top, are just within the boundary of deep water. Do not go beyond them. I have indicated these on the chart.

### Marine Facilities

Northeast Harbor is one of the most important yachting centers in Mount Desert and is always crowded. To accommodate as many as possible, a grid of moorings has been laid out with mathematical precision, covering the entire area. This leaves no room for anchoring.

Even if you do find what seems to be enough space for anchoring, it should not be considered, for it is not permitted by the Harbormaster. Furthermore, the bottom is very soft silt, providing poor holding. There are no free town moorings or guest moorings available. All moorings (about 30), slip space and dockage are assigned by the Harbormaster, Will Boddy, on a rental basis. The Harbormaster, or assistant, is always present at the office at the head of the Municipal Dock (51), and monitors VHF Channels 16 and 68, 24 hours daily from June 15 to Sept. 15. In addition to town moorings, some of the private moorings are sublet when their owners are out cruising. This brings the total number of available moorings to about 60. It is rare that anyone has to be turned away because of unavailability of space, but it's best to call ahead for reservations. All reservations must be reconfirmed by 2:00 p.m. on your scheduled day of arrival, otherwise you will be dropped to the bottom of the wait list. For a complete description of all regulations in Northeast Harbor, as well as a business directory of the area, pick up a copy of the Northeast Harbor Port Directory at the Harbormaster's Office.

Throughout the inner harbor the bottom has been dredged to a depth of 7 feet, while in the channel there is 10 ft. depth at mean low water.

The Northeast Harbor Municipal Pier (51) has 70 slips, ice, showers, a pumpout station (one of the few in Maine), and a concrete launching ramp. As we've noted, they monitor VHF Channels 16 and 68. Besides the slips, there's dockage for large boats. They can take boats up to 200 ft, as long as their draft doesn't exceed the 10 ft. depth prevalent all through the marina.

There is no parking at the municipal launching ramp (56). After launching, you have to move your car and trailer. The showers are in a new building (57), which also contains the heads, an information desk,

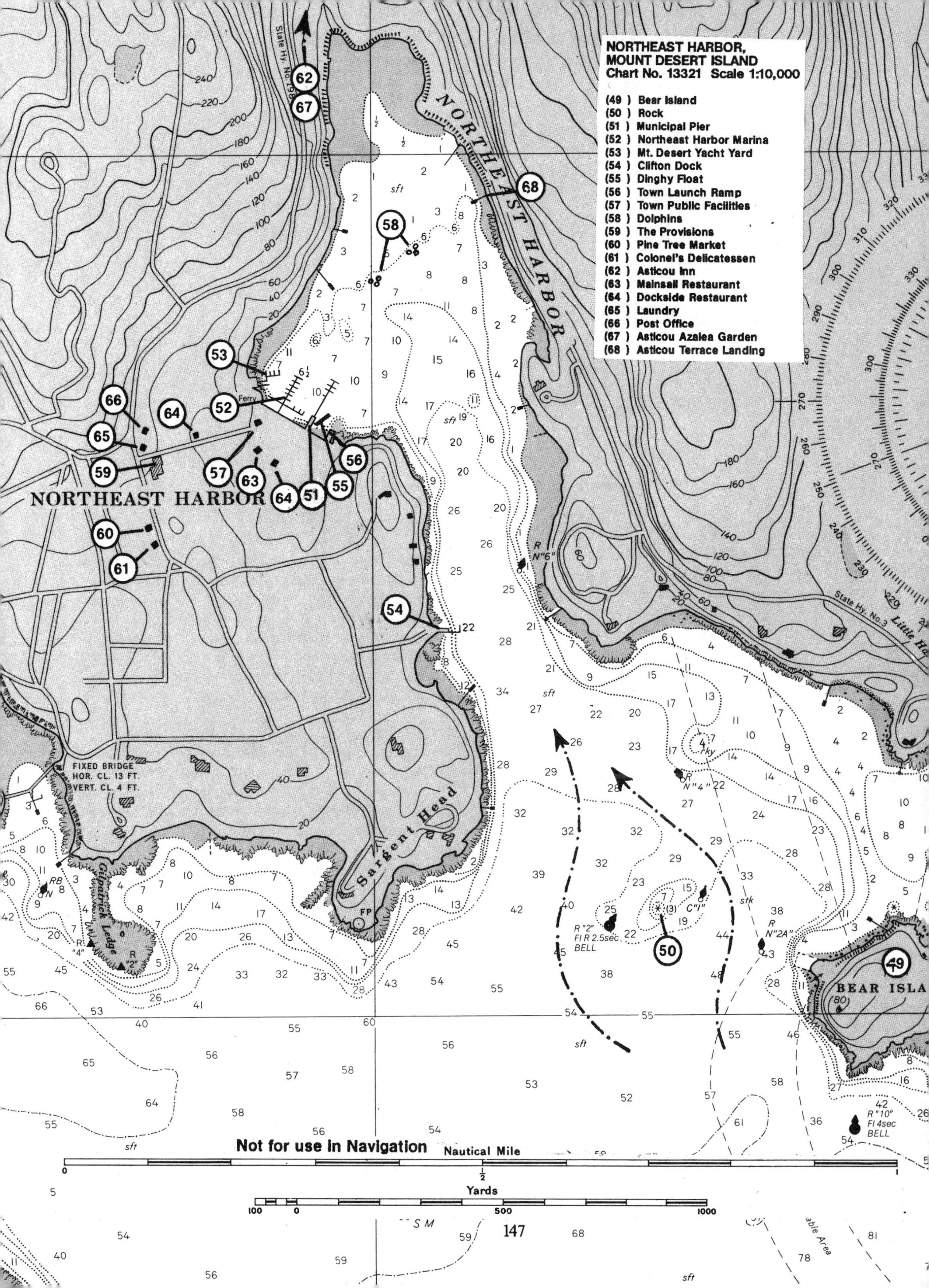

NORTHEAST HARBOR,
MOUNT DESERT ISLAND
Chart No. 13321 Scale 1:10,000
(49) Bear Island
(50) Rock
(51) Municipal Pier
(52) Northeast Harbor Marina
(53) Mt. Desert Yacht Yard
(54) Clifton Dock
(55) Dinghy Float
(56) Town Launch Ramp
(57) Town Public Facilities
(58) Dolphins
(59) The Provisions
(60) Pine Tree Market
(61) Colonel's Delicatessen
(62) Asticou Inn
(63) Mainsail Restaurant
(64) Dockside Restaurant
(65) Laundry
(66) Post Office
(67) Asticou Azalea Garden
(68) Asticou Terrace Landing
NORTHEAST HARBOR
NORTHEAST HARBOR
State Hy. No. 198
State Hy. No. 3
Ferry
FIXED BRIDGE
HOR. CL. 13 FT.
VERT. CL. 4 FT.
Sargent Head
Gilpatrick Ledge
BEAR ISLA
R "2" Fl R 2.5sec BELL
R "10" Fl 4sec BELL
C "1"
R N "2A"
R N "4"
R N "6"
Not for use in Navigation
Nautical Mile
Yards

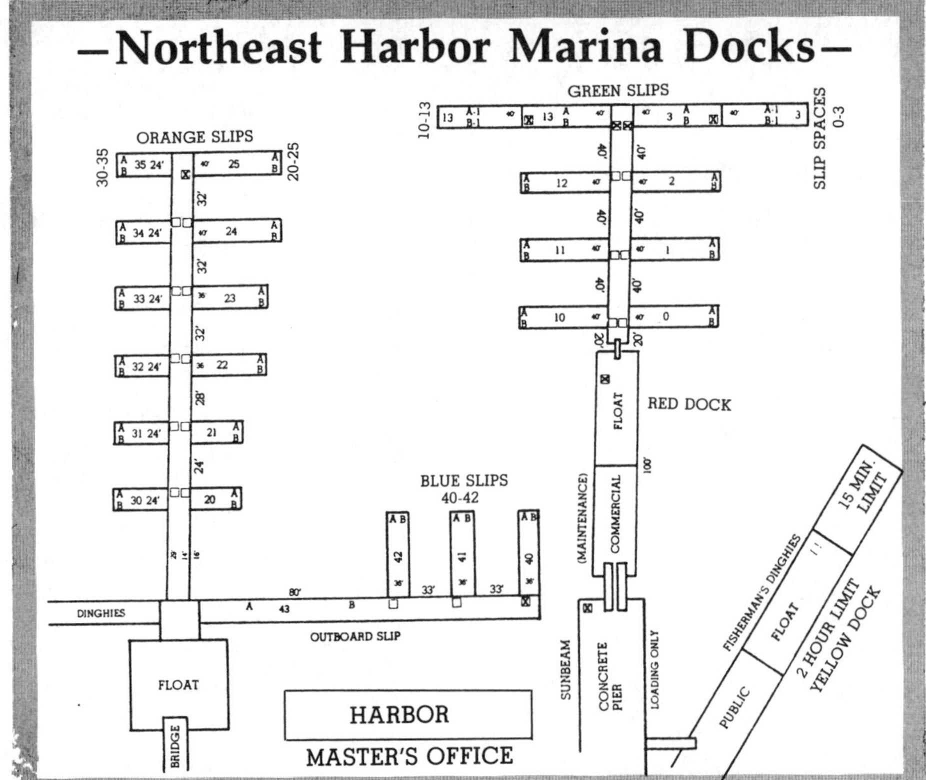


*Courtesy: Northeast Harbor Port Directory*

and a lounge. A dinghy float (55) is on the east side of the Municipal Pier. Consult the Harbormaster for recommendations on master mechanics, electronics repair, compass adjuster, outboard repair or any other marine skills. Northeast Harbor has them all.

Clifton Dock Corp (54), on the west shore at the harbor entrance, has the only fuel dock. They have 25 ft. depth alongside, moorings, gasoline, diesel fuel, block ice, and they monitor VHF Channel 16.

Mount Desert Yacht Yard (53) has 10 slips, 10 moorings, and complete engine and hull repair.

The Town Pier (51) is an active scene, with many tour boats departing from it. Besides the "Sea Queen," providing regular mail boat and passenger ferry to Cranberry Island, and Little Cranberry Island there is a whale watch tour, lobster tour, and daysails on the Friendship Sloop "Blackjack." A 3-hour long historical and nature cruise aboard the "Sea Princess," is accompanied by an Acadia National Park Ranger acting as narrator.

There are so many fine harbors, points of scenic beauty, fine restaurants, and other things to see and do, that it is only natural that you will want to spend a considerable amount of time on this part of Mount Desert Island. The passenger ferry between Northeast Harbor and the Cranberry Isles makes it easy to have your boat in one harbor, while you are off exploring, eating, or meeting friends in another. Check for the schedule at the harbormaster's office. Inevitably, the time will come when you are separated from your boat, and the ferry schedule is either inconvenient, or you've missed the last one for the night. Not to worry—Captain John Dwelley's Water Taxi Service is available 24 hours a day, servicing the harbors of the Cranberry Isles, Northeast Harbor, Southwest Harbor and Seal Harbor. Rates vary according to the time of day, with those between midnight and 6:00 a.m., naturally being the highest. Reservations can be made by calling (207) 244-5724. This service is in operation from May to October, and there is a six passenger maximum.

## More Trails

The Park Rangers participate in various other programs, e.g., seashore walks, woodlands and mountaintop walks, bird walks, and wildflower walks. On the tide pool walks, a Park Service naturalist will point out the different species of plants and marine animals that inhabit this special environment. Schedules for these are posted at the National Park Headquarters (at Hull's Cove near Bar Harbor) and the Park campgrounds. The National Park Service also publishes many maps and information booklets about the island which you will find most helpful. Whatever your interest, fishing (fresh or salt water), climbing, bird watching or scuba diving, there is a booklet for each subject. These can be obtained at the visitor center at the Park Headquarters, or you can get them in advance of your visit by writing to Superintendent, Acadia National Park, Bar Harbor, Maine 04609.

## Supplies

The two grocery stores will deliver to the dock. The Provisions (59) has high quality meat, cheese, produce, etc. The Pine Tree Market (60) has specialties of imported and gourmet items. On Main Street, the Colonel's Delicatessen (61) has a bakery in the front part of the building with a nice selection of cheese and wines, and a restuarant in the back part. This is home-style cooking and it is where most of the locals dine.

Among the many fine restaurants in the village is the Asticou Inn (62), an elegant building from the turn of the century, serving excellent food. Jacket and tie is required and reservations are necessary. The Mainsail Restaurant (63) of the Kimball Terrace Inn serves fine food and is close to the docks. Reservations are recommended. A short walk west is the Dockside Restaurant (64), serving a more simple fare with salads, chowders, steamers and general seafood, plus beer and wine. They have indoor and outdoor picnic tables and take-out service, open from 11:30 a.m.

Various clothing shops, galleries, craft shops and drug store are all south when you reach Main Street. The laundry (65) and Post Office (66) are noth on Main Street. The laundry is not a coin-operated type. You drop it off, they do it and you pick it up.

## Sightseeing

If you are fogged in and wish to explore the town of Ellsworth or other inland areas, Ford Rent-a-Car System is conveniently located behind the marina at the Kimball Terrace Inn.

Mt. Desert Island has a unique geography, providing a great variety of habitats in its range of elevations. The bare mountain tops have species of plants normally found in the higher peaks of New England, while the more moderate coastal climate favors mixed coniferous and deciduous forests. There are bogs, with their uniquely adapted pitcher plants, leather leaf, bog rosemary and Labrador tea. There are salt marshes, ponds, lakes, meadows, all with their own special indigenous plants. The National Park Service provides a list of over 200 species of wild flowers that are commonly found here.

It would certainly take a considerable amount of time to explore the island and search out many of these wild flowers and special plants, but this can be shortened by visiting one of the several Public Gardens on the Island. At Northeast Harbor, there are two such gardens: The Asticou Azalea Garden and the Asticou Terraces and Thuya Lodge. The Azalea Garden (67) is close to the Asticou Inn, near the head of the harbor. This garden was designed by Mr. Charles K. Savage, a well known landscape architect and conservationist. The best time to see the azaleas in bloom is from late May to mid-July.

Asticou Terraces and Thuya Lodge are on the east shore of the harbor. The pier with granite rip-rap and float is the Asticou Terrace Landing (68). You may tie up your dinghy here, but only boats belonging to summer residents or permanent residents of the town may use the other facilites of the Asticou Landing. A path leads to the road from the Landing, where signs direct you to the Thuya Gardens and Lodge.

This is a large park complex of over 215 acres, composed of 5 areas: Asticou Landing, Asticou Terraces, Thuya Lodge, Thuya Garden and all of the west slope of Eliot Mountain. The climb up the hill to the garden is a carefully tended system of paths, stone steps and sheltered rest areas. Along the way is planted a great variety of trees, shrubs and flowers, all kept in a natural setting. Occasionally you glimpse fine views of the harbor. At the top is Thuya Garden, designed in the style of a formal English garden with beds of cultivated flowers and outstanding specimens of trees and shrubs. Most are native species, but there are some imported plants, such as the "dawn redwood," native of China, and many types of rhododendrons, including some from the Caucasus Mountains.

The Lodge was the summer home of Joseph Henry Curtis, who was a Boston landscape architect and the founder of Asticou Terraces. It is a beautifully and tastefully designed and constructed building, well worth the climb to visit. You can spend many enjoyable hours inside perusing the extensive library. There are over 1500 volumes of books on botany, gardening, landscape architecture, etc. and many original floral paintings. Some of the books are quite rare, dating back to the 15th century, and all are available to the general public. The gardens are open from 7:00 a.m-7:00 p.m. throughout the summer and early fall. Thuya Lodge is open from 10:00 a.m.-5:00 p.m. on weekdays and from 12:00 noon-5:00 p.m. on Sundays.

The following succinct history of the property is given by the guide/hostess of Thuya Lodge. Joseph Henry Curtis fell in love with the area while visiting, and in 1880 bought a great deal of property along the water and up the mountain. At the same time, President Eliot of Harvard came up. They were both Bostonians and knew each other. They walked the shores together and President Eliot purchased much of the abutting land, but higher up. Joseph Curtis bought an existing farmhouse on the shore and he summered there for about 6 years. At the age of 45, he married a beautiful French woman who had come over here as a singer. At this point he felt he didn't want to live in this home any longer and built another for his new bride on the road which now leads up to the Lodge. In 1909 he conceived of the idea of using his landscape talents to make a botanical park for the inhabitants of the village. He is responsible for everything you see on the paths coming up to the Lodge, including the shelters. He transplanted many wild shrubs and flowers, bringing them closer to the path.

Mrs. Curtis died in 1915. The following year, Joseph Curtis sold the house and built Thuya Lodge, living there until he died at the age of 87. The Lodge has been open to the public every day of every summer since 1930. Toward the end of 1946, trustee Charles Savage decided to assemble a collection of botanical books and he enlarged the library considerably. This led to the interest of Mr. John D. Rockefeller, Jr., who donated an additional 155 acres of land bordering on the park and the financial support for the Thuya Garden.

Another garden you want to be sure not to miss, although not as conveniently nearby as this, is the Wild Gardens of Acadia (97c). See Chart No. 18818C for location, and section titled Supplies and Sightseeing in Bar Harbor for a description of the gardens.

Though crowded, Northeast Harbor is another must for cruising sailors. Excellent marine facilities, a good supply port, striking natural beauty, and much interest ashore.

## BRACY COVE—CHART NO. 13318A

Only a little over a mile east of Northeast Harbor, Bracy Cove (48) looks like an inviting anchorage. You'll see moored boats, but it has a rocky, uneven bottom and is unfit as an anchorage.

## SEAL HARBOR—CHART NO. 13318A

Numerous private residences line the shores of Seal Harbor (45), making access to land difficult. The harbor is fairly filled with moored boats. The Seal Harbor Town Wharf (46) with 9 feet depth is on the east side of the harbor and has two 40-ft. floats. Farther north is the pier and float landing of the Seal Harbor Yacht Club (47). Although space could probably be found for you by the Harbormaster, other major harbors with their complete facilites and services are conveniently nearby.

## CRANBERRY ISLANDS
## CHART NOS. 13318A, 13321C

This group of islands divides the waters southeast of Mount Desert Island into Western Way (38) and Eastern Way (39). These are the entrances to the major harbors on the south shore of Mt. Desert Island. Of the five islands, only two are of any particular interest to the cruising yachtsman, Great Cranberry Island (51) and Little Cranberry Island (52). Bear Island (49), near the entrance to Northeast Harbor, has no place to anchor and the only pier is privately owned by a summer resident. Much of Sutton Island (44) is also privately owned, with houses and piers lining the shore. However, there is a Town Wharf (53) near Fernald Point, used by the mail and passenger ferry. It should be approached carefully for the passage lies between the two rock ledges. Baker Island (54), with its lighthouse at the peak in the center of the island, has no harbor and no dock. The western half of Baker Island is part of Acadia National Park, with landings by Park personnel made by dory from a private mooring. All the islands are frequently visited by the Islesford Ferry Company boats and other cruise ships out of Northeast Harbor.

Both Great Cranberry and Little Cranberry Islands are relatively low and flat, lacking the bold headlands and steep, granite shores you expect on this part of the Maine coast. They are mostly composed of grassy fields alternating with woods and areas of peat bogs. At one time cranberries were harvested from these bogs, hence the name given to the islands. Most of this is gone now with the draining of the bogs for mosquito control.

### Little Cranberry Island—Chart No. 13321C

Summer residents occupy much of Little Cranberry Island but there is still a year round permanent population of 90-100 people. Although tourists are brought over on the ferrys, their number is comparatively small and they tend to remain near the museum and wharfs at the village of Islesford. The general feel of the island is thus a more leisurely one compared to Mt. Desert Island. The mood of the island is one of pastoral serenity.

### Islesford

Anchorage is in Hadlock Cove on the west shore, off the three piers. The bottom is somewhat rocky, with patches of kelp, so a heavy fisherman's anchor should be used. In anchoring, it is best to stay northwest of the Islesford Dock (55) and green can "1" buoy. To the south there is much grass and kelp, making it difficult for the anchor to dig in. The Little Cranberry Yacht Club maintains two guest moorings for visitors. They are identified by the orange ball floats with the letters LCYC. No fee is required provided your stay is limited to a single night. For any longer duration, there is a user fee. You should check with the Club for availability and approval. Protection is fine for anything from the south due to the shallowing water and ledges, but only moderate in strong winds from west to northwest. Even then, the fetch is not great and the most you would experience is an uncomfortable roll.

The popularity of this anchorage is steadily increasing as other harbors on Mt. Desert Island become more congested. From here, the view of the mountains of Mt. Desert Island is unsurpassed. The sun setting behind them adds a touch of glory. Adding to the appeal is the recent appearance of many more amenities for the cruising sailor.

The three piers are visible from several miles away, for on the northernmost is a long, low building with a corrugated metal roof. When it catches the sun, it acts as a beacon to home in on. This pier (55) is the Islesford Dock. Puddles-on-the-Water (55), a restaurant located at the end of the Islesford Dock, is open for breakfast, lunch and dinner. They also have 3 moorings available for rent and will handle your trash disposal. There is a take-out window for lobster rolls, sandwiches, ice cream, etc., and there are picnic tables on the dock. A gift shop at the foot of the dock features island handicrafts.

You may tie up at any of the three floats at the three docks, 7 feet depth at low tide. Gasoline and diesel fuel, ice and water are available at the Islesford Dock (55). Fisherman's Co-op (56) also has gasoline, diesel fuel, water, sells live lobsters and clams, and monitors CB Channel 11 and VHF Channel 16. The southernmost of the three docks is the Islesford Town Landing (57), used by the mail and passenger ferry.

Most of the merchants on Mount Desert Island will deliver goods by ferry to Islesford. By telephoning, you

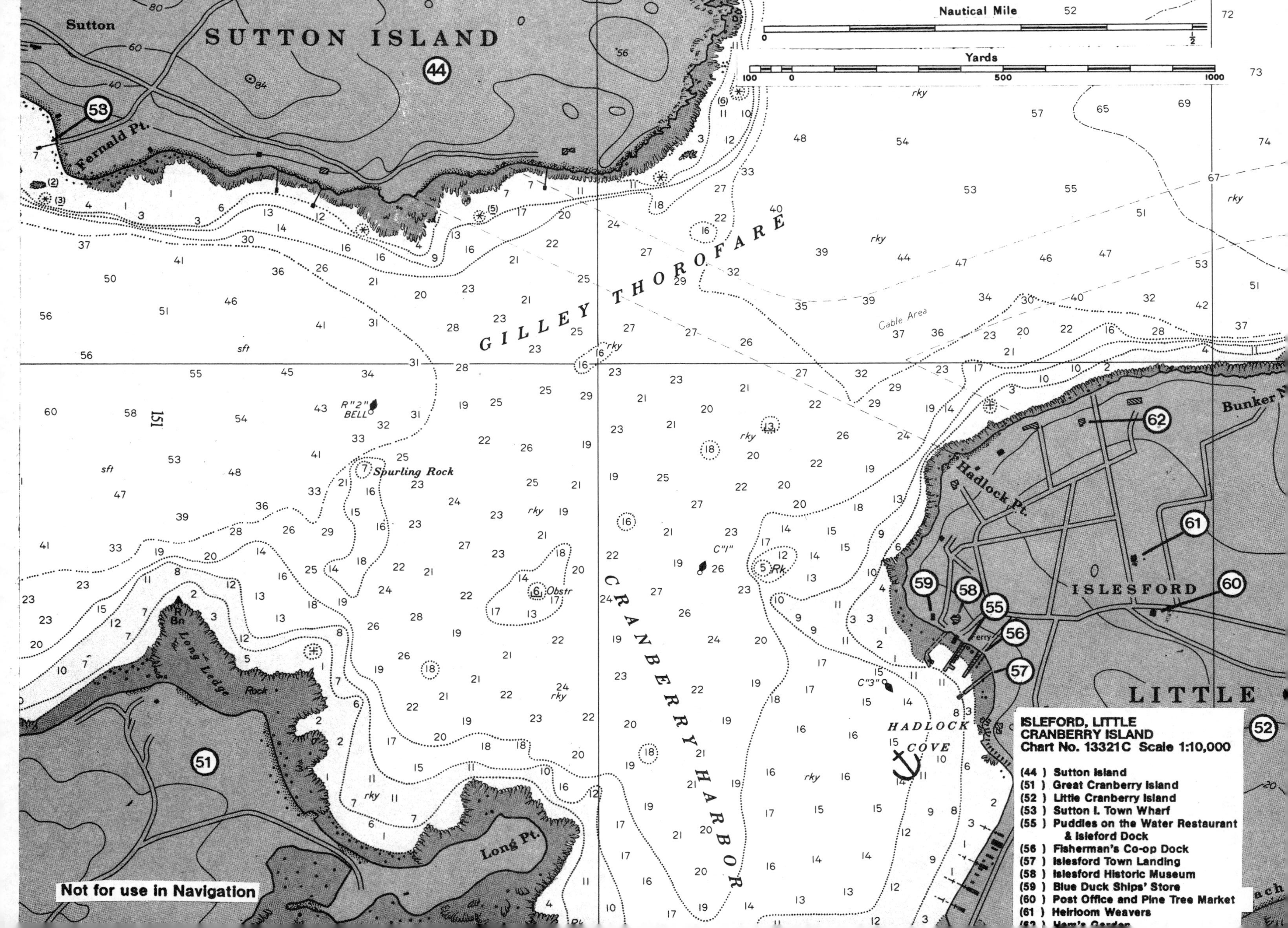

ISLEFORD, LITTLE CRANBERRY ISLAND
Chart No. 13321C Scale 1:10,000
(44) Sutton Island
(51) Great Cranberry Island
(52) Little Cranberry Island
(53) Sutton I. Town Wharf
(55) Puddles on the Water Restaurant & Isleford Dock
(56) Fisherman's Co-op Dock
(57) Islesford Town Landing
(58) Islesford Historic Museum
(59) Blue Duck Ships' Store
(60) Post Office and Pine Tree Market
(61) Heirloom Weavers
SUTTON ISLAND
Sutton
Fernald Pt.
GILLEY THOROFARE
CRANBERRY HARBOR
HADLOCK COVE
Hadlock Pt.
ISLESFORD
LITTLE
Bunker
Spurling Rock
Long Ledge Rock
Long Pt.
Cable Area
Nautical Mile
Yards
Not for use in Navigation

can get just about anything delivered to the ferry landing (57). This includes groceries, hardware, clothing or anything else. They deliver your order to a booth at the end of the ferry landing, with your name on the package or box.

**Sightseeing and Supplies.** The Islesford Historic Museum (58) is in the fine red brick and granite building northwest of the docks. This, and the Blue Duck Ships' Store (59) are a part of Acadia National Park. The wood frame clapboard building of the Blue Duck Store was built in 1850 and was originally used as a ships' chandlery and sail loft, later a general store. Subsequently, it was the home of the exhibits and collection of the Islesford Historical Society. In 1927, when their needs for space outgrew the building, the new Islesford Historical Museum was built. Now the Blue Duck Store is used only for storage, with one end of the building remaining open for public restrooms.

The Museum (58), open 10:00 a.m.-4:00 p.m. daily, no admission charge, houses an extensive collection of original documents, land grants and reproductions of maps of the area in the formative years of Acadia. There are also numerous articles from the activities of the Cranberry Islanders, ships tools and instruments, housewares and other personal possessions, and many photographs of early settlers.

From the displays and the narrative panels in the museum you learn that "the early settlers of Cranberry Islands in 1760 earned their living through commercial fishing. By 1800 they diversified, with schooners trading on both sides of the Atlantic, leaving home port with dried fish, plaster and lumber, often returning with a hold full of salt from the Bahamas. Agriculture was largely subsistence farming, the settlers raising sheep, growing flax, weaving their own cloth and putting down enough food for the winter. There was haying on the island, and of course, the harvesting of the cranberries, for which the island gets its name." Maps of the island, with the various roads, trails and sites of interest are available at the museum.

The road leading east from the docks brings you to the Post Office and the Pine Tree Market (60), which has general supplies, as well as fresh meat, cheese and wine. Summer hours are 7:30 a.m.-5:30 p.m. daily, except Sunday. Heirloom Weavers (61) is a craft shop on Mosswood Road, featuring many fine handwoven items, stoles, ponchos, dresses, etc. Many of them are made of hand-spun wool from Maine Island sheep. All the weaving is done here in the shop. Farther north down the same road is Ham's Garden (62). This is a private residence, whose owner has lavished much care and attention on his garden. It is both a treat and delight to see what can be done during the short growing season here.

Exploring the roads and beaches of the island is the main activity for visitors. At the east end of the island is an interesting rock beach where there is a lot of re-melt of rocks so that they look like big, solid marbles. At the beach south of the docks in Hadlock Cove, sand-dollars may be found at low tide. All the beaches are privately owned, and access to them will remain only as long as the owners right to privacy is maintained and the beaches are not littered or abused.

## Great Cranberry Island—Chart No. 13318A, 13321D

Spurling Cove (63) is in a small bight of land on the north side of the island. Anchorage here is possible, but not particularly attractive, nor is it as sheltered as nearby Cranberry Harbor off Islesford. Two long wharfs make out from the shore, the most westerly being the Village Pier (64), where the mail and passenger ferry lands, the other is the commercial pier of Beal and Bunker (65). Both have floats for dinghy landing and tie-up, with diesel fuel, gasoline and water available at the Beal and Bunker wharf. A grocery called Spurling Cove and a take-out lunch shop, The Islander, are close by.

Alternately, you can enter the harbor called The Pool (65a) on the east side of the island. Here you will find complete protection from all winds and seas. At first glance of the chart it does not seem possible, with most of the water indicated as being only 1 and 2 feet. But remember, these figures are for low tide, and at halftide or better, there is enough water for most cruising boats. Once inside, and into The Pool, there is 7-10 feet, even at low tide. On the western shore are the docks, floats, and sheds of Cranberry Islands Boatyard (65b). Though the dock and floats both dry out at low water, with the proper state of tide, it is still possible to remain here a number of hours. Water is available, but no fuel. The yard builds boats, hauls out for winter storage, and can provide for most of your needs. As the tide falls, you can either anchor in the deeper water of The Pool, or inquire at the boatyard about the availability of a vacant mooring.

To enter The Pool, approach from halfway between Long Point and Fish Point of Great Cranberry Island. When I was there last year, the boatyard had set out privately maintained markers to facilitate entry. They are floating pipes, about 4" in diameter, and painted red or green. Aim for a point about 100 to 150 feet before the end of the long, gravel spur at the western end of Fish Point. Follow along this shore **closely**—30 feet off. There is plenty of water. The critical point is near the very tip of this spur where the channel is narrowest due to a patch of rock. A red buoy also marked this rock. If it is not present when you enter, just keep very close to the spur of land. Maintain your course for another 100 feet beyond the end of the spur to avoid a shallow prolongation; then turn and head directly for the dock.

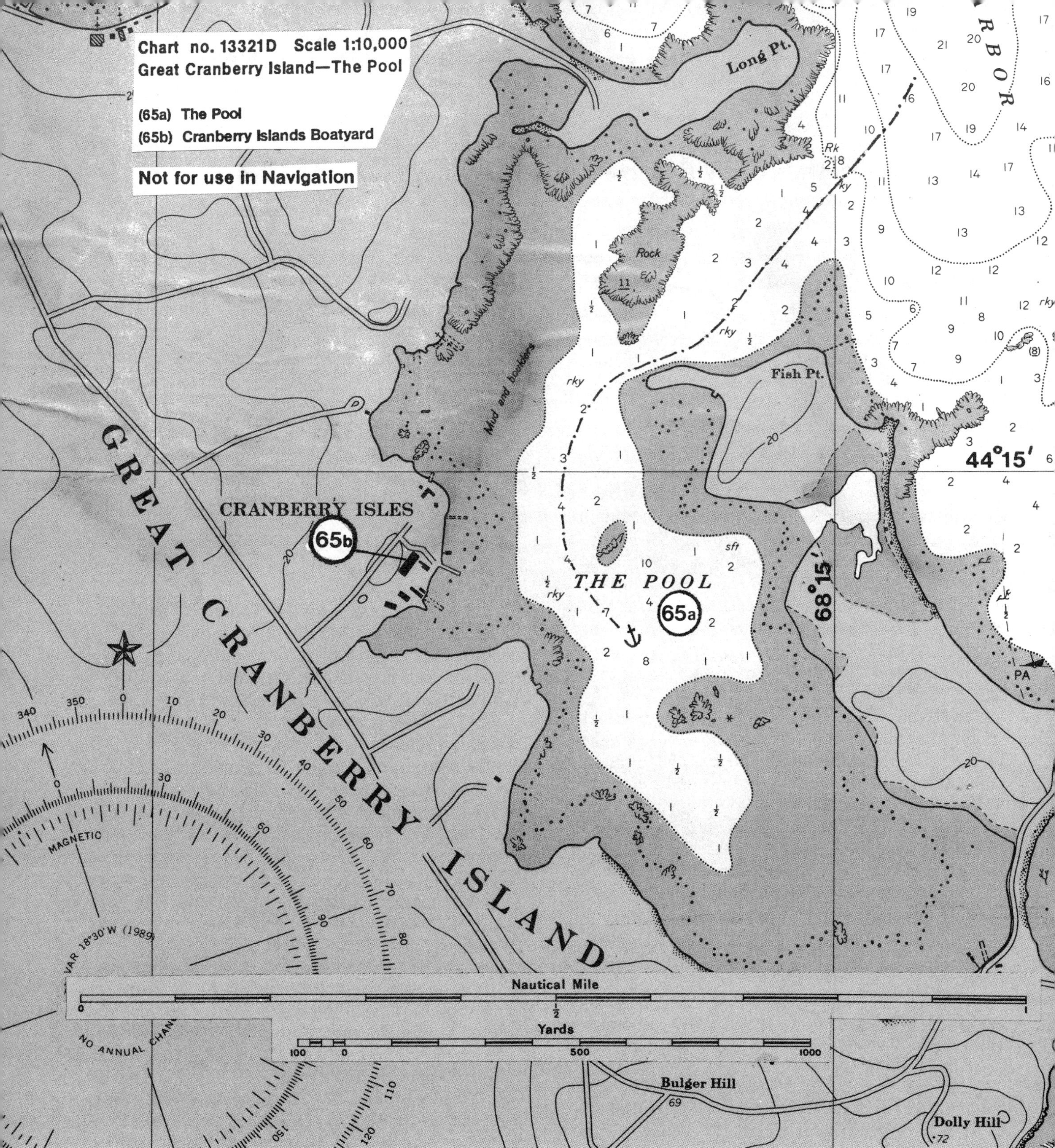
Chart no. 13321D Scale 1:10,000
Great Cranberry Island—The Pool
(65a) The Pool
(65b) Cranberry Islands Boatyard
Not for use in Navigation
Long Pt.
Rock
Fish Pt.
Mud and boulders
CRANBERRY ISLES
65b
THE POOL
65a
GREAT CRANBERRY ISLAND
44°15′
68°15′
MAGNETIC
VAR 18°30′W (1989)
NO ANNUAL CHANGE
Nautical Mile
Yards
Bulger Hill
Dolly Hill

# CHAPTER 13

## FRENCHMAN BAY—CHART NO. 13312A

### GENERAL INFORMATION AND ENTRY

Frenchman Bay is still another of Maine's delightful bays and sounds that make the entire coast a great cruising ground. Bounded by Mount Desert Island on the west, and the Schoodic Peninsula on the east, you could cruise this relatively small area for a week without anchoring in the same harbor more than once.

Frenchman Bay is an easy body of water to sail. There are few navigational dangers and the shores of its islands are high and bold with deep water close to shore. Everywhere, spectacular views of the mountains of Mt. Desert dominate the scene.

Tidal currents are weak, attaining a velocity of 0.3 knot on the flood tide and 0.7 knot on the ebb. These set northwest and southeast in the area between Bar Harbor and Ironbound Island (66). Mean tide range throughout the Bay is 10.5 feet. The chart notation of "Local Magnetic Disturbance" refers to a magnetic variation of 003 degrees from normal in the vicinity of Jordan Island (67).

Several prominent landmarks help you enter Frenchman Bay, and are useful throughout most of the lower half of the Bay for taking bearings. In the middle of the entrance is Egg Rock with the Egg Rock Light, (68) Fl R, 5 sec. This island is a bare rock, scarcely more than 20 feet high, so the 40-ft. white square tower of the light stands out clearly from all directions. It also has a fog signal. One mile south of the light is a whistle buoy, R "4" (69).

The long, mountainous central spine of Schoodic Peninsula culminates at the south end in Schoodic Head (70) at an elevation of 440 feet, and is a great far-off landmark from both east and west. The water storage tank (71) on Big Moose Island is also prominent. Painted a dark green, it is highly visible and a good radar target from offshore.

The name Frenchman Bay was originally given to the Bay of Fundy, but later changed to this body of water. It was in rememberance of the priest, Nicolas Aubry, a member of Sieur deMonts company. While their ship was in St. Marys Bay, Nova Scotia, he had gone ashore, become lost in the woods, and was near starving to death until his companions found him.

### BAR HARBOR
### CHART NOS. 13318C, 13323

Bar Harbor is not truly a harbor, but rather an open roadstead anchorage in Frenchman Bay. Its limited measure of protection, as well as its name, is derived from the mud and gravel bar which forms at half-tide between the land of Mt. Desert Island and Bar Island (72). Additional shelter is provided by the widely scattered group of islands called the Porcupines. They are all high, wooded, without habitation, and have few prominent landmarks. Bald Porcupine (73) is distinguished from the others by its bare rocky lower slopes on the south side of the island. Though close to the busy area of Bar Harbor, several of the Porcupine Islands have eagle nests on them. There is a large nest on Long Porcupine (74), one on Bald Porcupine (73), and a large osprey nest on the north side of Yellow Island (75), near Jordan Island, (see chart no. 13318E, Schoodic Peninsula and Eastern Portion of Frenchman Bay, this chapter.)

Chart no. 13312A shows the whole of Frenchman Bay. Long Porcupine Island (74) west of Bar Harbor, constitutes the Long Porcupine Island Preserve of The Nature Conservancy. Landing is permitted and is best on the east side of the bar northeast of Long Porcupine Island. The Hop is connected to Long Porcupine Island at low tide, but is not part of the preserve. You'll find the interior tough going, all dense second growth after the logging done in 1938. Cliffs near the SW end are 100 ft. high, with a 165 ft. hill behind them. An arch here spans a 10 ft. space 40 ft. above the water, and there's a cave with a 70 ft. ceiling. Don't go near these cliffs unless it's calm, and don't try to enter the cave or the arch at anytime. It's too dangerous. Look from your dinghy, or big boat. The southwest shore is not only high, but depths drop sharply to over 80 ft.

As we mentioned, bald eagles roost on Big Porcupine, and so do osprey, and there are black guillenots on the southwest cliffs, night herons in the interior, and there's a small herd of deer.

Now refer to chart no. 13318C.

A breakwater extending from Bald Porcupine Island toward the east shore of Mt. Desert Island, has a white daybeacon at the far end. This breakwater (76) is submerged at high tide, and except for a small portion where Porcupine Dry Ledge is incorporated, there will be no indication of its presence, either by breaking waves or tide rips. Don't run over the breakwater, stay west of it, or east of Bald Porcupine Island. The west end of the breakwater (76) is marked by a daybeacon.

Entry to the harbor is through the channel (77), between the end of the breakwater and the shore of Mt. Desert Island or through any of the deep water channels (78) between the various Porcupine Islands.

FRENCHMAN BAY
Chart No. 13312A Scale 1:80,000
(19) Turtle Island
(20) Inner Approach, through Halibut Hole
(66) Ironbound Island
(67) Magnetic Disturbance near Jordan I.
(68) Egg Rock Light
(69) Whistle Buoy R "4"
(70) Schoodic Head
(71) Big Moose Island, Water Storage Tank
(74) Long Porcupine Island
Not for use in Navigation
Nautical Miles
Yards
FLANDERS BAY
(use chart 13318)
FRENCHMAN BAY
LOCAL MAGNETIC DISTURBANCE
(see note)
WINTER HARBOR
(use chart 13322)
Hancock Point
Sorrento
Bean I
Preble I
Calf I
Hog I
West Gouldsboro
Jones Pond
Stave I
South Gouldsboro
Stave I Harbor
Yellow I
Jordan I
Halibut Hole
Cod Ledges
Ironbound Island
Winter Harbor
Grindstone Neck
Crow I
Heron I
Ned I
Mark I TOWER
Turtle I
Egg Rock
Fl R 5sec 64ft 13M
HORN
Schoodic
Big Moose I
TANK
Sunken Ledge
Halftide Ledge
Bald Rock
Hulls Cove
Burnt Porcupine I
The Hop
Long Porcupine I
Bar I
Sheep Porcupine I
BAR HARBOR
The Porcupines
Bald Porcupine I
Eagle Lake
Cadillac Mt
Dorr Mt
Champlain Mt
Pemetic Mt
Jordan Pond
NATIONAL PARK
The Thrumcap
Newport Ledge
Cable Area
Schooner Head
Old Whale Ledge
Great Head
Old Soaker
Otter Creek
Otter Cliff
Otter Pt
Seal Harbor
Lewis Rk
TERRITORIAL SEA
State Hy No 3
State Hy No 186
F 0.3K
E 0.7K
(chart 13323)
155

BAR HARBOR, MT. DESERT ISLAND
Chart No. 13323 Scale 1:10,000
Reduced approx. 14%
(72) Gravel Bar
(76) Breakwater
(77) Inside, Breakwater Channel
(78) Outside, Inter-island Channel
(79) Town Pier
(80) Harbormaster Office
(81) Frenchman's Bay Dock
(82) Town Launching Ramp
(83) Don's Shop 'n Save
BAR ISLAND
SHEEP PORCUPINE I.
BAR HARBOR
BAR HARBOR
Breakers
foul
"7" BELL
Por, 1944
mud
gravel
boulders
boulders
mud
Tanks
Ramp
STACK
Breakwater (covered at HW)
Porcupine
Dry Ledge

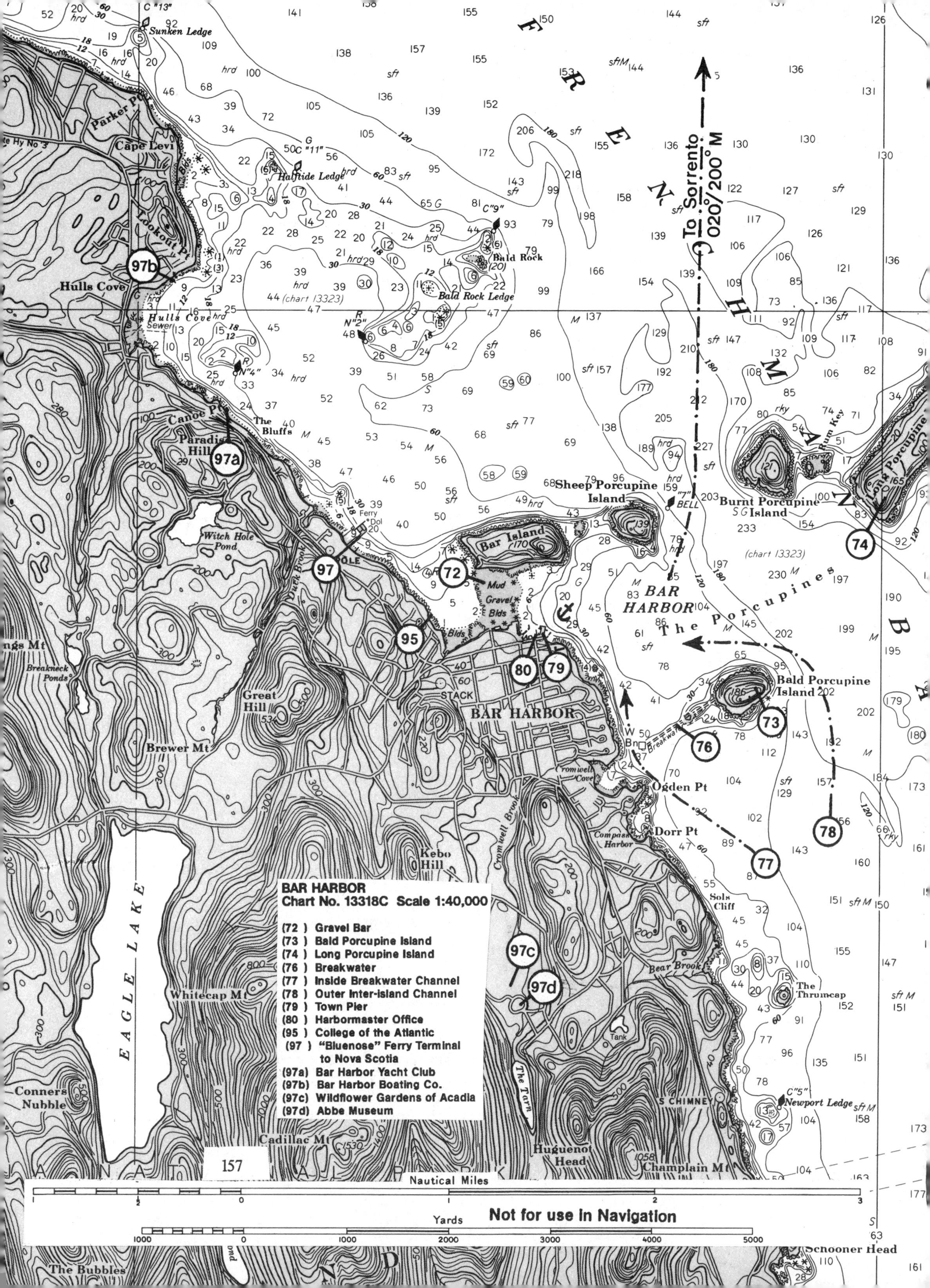

BAR HARBOR
Chart No. 13318C Scale 1:40,000
(72) Gravel Bar
(73) Bald Porcupine Island
(74) Long Porcupine Island
(76) Breakwater
(77) Inside Breakwater Channel
(78) Outer Inter-island Channel
(79) Town Pier
(80) Harbormaster Office
(95) College of the Atlantic
(97) "Bluenose" Ferry Terminal to Nova Scotia
(97a) Bar Harbor Yacht Club
(97b) Bar Harbor Boating Co.
(97c) Wildflower Gardens of Acadia
(97d) Abbe Museum
To Sorrento
020°/200° M
FRENCHMAN BAY
Sunken Ledge
Parker Pt
Cape Levi
Halftide Ledge
Lookout Pt
Bald Rock
Bald Rock Ledge
Hulls Cove
(chart 13323)
Canoe Pt
The Bluffs
Paradise Hill
Witch Hole Pond
Duck Brook
Ferry
Bar Island
Mud
Gravel
Bars
Sheep Porcupine Island
"7" BELL
Burnt Porcupine Island
Rum Key
Long Porcupine
BAR HARBOR
The Porcupines
Bald Porcupine Island
Breakwater
Ogden Pt
Dorr Pt
Compass Harbor
Cromwell Cove
Cromwell Brook
STACK
BAR HARBOR
Great Hill
Brewer Mt
Breakneck Ponds
Kebo Hill
EAGLE LAKE
Whitecap Mt
Conners Nubble
Cadillac Mt
The Tarn
Huguenot Head
Champlain Mt
Sols Cliff
Bear Brook
Tank
The Thrumcap
S CHIMNEY
Newport Ledge
Schooner Head
The Bubbles
Nautical Miles
Yards
Not for use in Navigation

### Anchorage and Marine Facilities

Anchorage can be found east of the Town Pier (79). Holding ground is only moderate to poor. Your boat anchored here should not be unwatched or unattended for very long, particularly if any heavy weather is in the making. With winds from the south and southeast, a swell makes into the harbor. Twelve town moorings are for rent from the Harbormaster, whose office (80) is in the building at the foot of the Town Pier.

The Town Pier (79) is a stone seawall with floats on both sides. It stands out prominently from shore and is actively used by visiting yachts, commercial fishing boats and numerous charter and excursion boats. Depths are 8-10 feet at the floats and 11-15 feet at the front face of the pier. Water and electricity are available at the floats, and there's a free concrete launching ramp (82) east of the Town Pier.

As you approach the Municipal Dock from the east, the two extensions of floats on the near side are for yachts. On the far side of the docks, floats are restricted to use by fishermen only. At the next small dock beyond this, is a nicely arranged bed of sleeper timbers which allows you to comfortably ground out at low tide. At the top are nice big cleats, closely spaced, with which to make fast.

Frenchman's Bay Boating Co., (81) west of the Town Pier, has Texaco gasoline and diesel fuel, ice, and monitors VHF Channel 16. A party fishing boat bases there, and the Town Pier is a base for two excursion boats, a National Park Naturalist Cruise, and cocktail cruises.

Fisherman's Landing, farther west, has gasoline, snack bar, and sells seafood.

North of town, on Route 3, is the Ferry Terminal (97) for the "Bluenose" Ferry to Yarmouth, Nova Scotia.

Bar Harbor Yacht Club (97a) is at Canoe Point, north of town, south of Hulls Cove. Bar Harbor Boating Co. (97b) on the north shore of Hulls Cove, has 8 moorings, ice, and complete engine and hull repairs.

### Supplies and Sightseeing

The village of Bar Harbor is the commercial and recreational center of Mount Desert Island. During summer, streets are thronged with tourists who have arrived by auto, ready to patronize a plethora of gift shops, antique shops, craft shops and galleries. The overall ambience is similar to Boothbay Harbor and Kennebunkport, far to the west. Shops and restaurants in this town, in contrast to most others on the Maine coast, remain open far into the night, seven days a week. With this catering to the great number of summertime tourists, it is difficult to imagine that at one time Bar Harbor was one of Americas' foremost, elite summer resort area. What brings the crowds is Acadia National Park, one of the most spectacular in the East, described in Chapter 12. Bar Harbor is also a customs port of entry, although the office here is now closed. Service is being carried out through the Bangor Office. See Chapter 12 on Southwest Harbor for details.

Restaurants are too numerous to list or even to single out any one in particular. They are on every street in town, many of them close to the waterfront and overlooking the harbor. They range in style from elegant, expensive dining to fast food snack-bars. As might be expected, many feature seafood, but you will also find restaurants of ethnic specialties: French, Italian, Mexican and Chinese.

Two supermarkets are within walking distance of the Town Pier (79), Don's Shop & Save (83) and the H. & H. Red and White Food Store (84), both on Cottage St., one block south from the water. The Red & White store is open daily from 8:30 a.m. - 9:00 p.m. and Sunday 10:00 a.m. - 7:00 p.m. On Main St. is the J. H. Butterfield Co. (85) with specialty and gourmet food items. The Alternative Market (86), also on Main St., is a country market with fresh baked goods, local produce, and a large selection of natural foods. Near the south end of Main St. is the Seafood Market (87) for fresh seafood and home-made chowder to take out. The Cask & Wedge (88), on Cottage St., has chilled wine, cold beer, and over sixty varieties of cheese. The carry 400 labels of imported wines, and 80 kinds of domestic and imported beer, open daily 9:30 a.m. - 11:00 p.m. and Sunday 12:00 noon to 11:00 p.m.

The movie theater (89), is the next to last one on the Maine coast between Mt. Desert Island and Calais, Maine, a distance of 95 miles. The only other along this stretch of coast is in Millbridge. If you arrive in Bar Harbor on a Monday or Thursday, you can listen to the free band concerts given on the Village Green, 8:00 p.m. Numerous other festivals and concerts are given in Bar Harbor, but the groups participating and the schedule changes yearly. Inquire while you're there.

For one of the finest collections of stained glass windows in New England, visit St. Saviour's Church (96a). A great many of these were made by the famed master artist-craftsman, Tiffany. This is still an active parish church, but visitors are welcome and tours are offered daily, free of charge, at 11:00 a.m. and 3:00 p.m. during the summer months.

Bar Harbor is the center to rent bicycles, mopeds or horses to explore the interior of Mount Desert Island. There is the Acadia Bike & Conoe Co. (90), The Bar Harbor Bicycle Shop (91) and Mopeds of Maine (92). For a totally different perspective on Mt. Desert Island and its surroundings, you might want to try soaring over it in a glider. Glider rides are offered at the Bar Harbor Airport (93), just off the island on route 3 (you'll have to take a taxi for this). They are available from 10:00 a.m. until dusk, daily. For reservations call (207) 667-SOAR.

The Jackson Laboratory (94) in Bar Harbor is internationally recognized as a center for mammalian genetics research. Genetically pure and consistent strains of over three million mice are raised here to be used in the study of cancer, heart disease, neuromuscular disorders and a wide range of other diseases. They employ a staff of about 450 people in the disciplines of genetics, cell biology, physiological genetics, immunogentics and developmental biology. An hour-long presentation about the laboratory, with film and slides, is offered to the public on Monday, Tuesday and Thursday at 2:00 p.m., June 17 to August 29.

Just outside Bar Harbor are two other attractions you should not miss; the Wildflower Gardens of Acadia (97c) and the Abbe Museum of Maine Indian Artifacts (97d). Both are located off route 3, south of Bar Harbor, near the Sieur de Monts Spring exit. Explore the gardens, where you'll see flowers, trees, and shrubs, all indigenous to this region. All are displayed in natural groupings and labeled for easy identification.

The Robert Abbe museum has many displays and exhibits on the culture of the early American Indians. Featured are stone tools and other prehistoric artifacts from the surrounding area, and baskets made by the Passamaquoddy and Penobscot tribes. But the museum is much more than a mere series of rooms exhibiting its collection, for it was Robert Abbe's aim to create a museum "....which will be for all time both fascinating and educative for thousands who are not accustomed to visit museums of this sort...." Since 1927, the museum has been actively involved in conducting its own archaeological research, focusing primarily on the Frenchman Bay and Blue Hill area. Education is also an important part of their program. Museum publications are available on the results of their research, and craft demonstrations, speakers programs and tours are all presented to the public. Open May-June & September-October: 10:00 a.m.—4:00 p.m. and July & August 9:00 a.m.—5:00 p.m. A small admission fee is charged.

The nearby College of the Atlantic (95) offers a 4 year program leading to a B.A. degree in Human Ecology, and has a large Natural History Museum. There are over 40 exhibits on the animal, marine mammal, sea birds and plant life of Mt. Desert Island. On display is the skeleton of a 25 foot Minke whale, and much accompanying information on whale biology. One of their most popular programs is participatory, where you are encouraged to fit together the giant jig-saw puzzle of a whale skeleton. Hours are 9:00 a.m. - 4:00 p.m. daily, admission is $1.50 for adults, $0.50 for children.

The collection of the Bar Harbor Historical Society is displayed in the Jesup Memorial Library (96). The history of Bar Harbor is seen through their extensive collection of photographs, including views of the elaborate summer residences, the steamships which frequently called here, and much material on the disastrous fire of 1947 which demolished most of the town. Summer hours are 1:00 - 4:00 p.m., Monday through Saturday, admission free.

## SORRENTO—CHART NO. 13318D

Located in the northern part of Frenchman Bay, Sorrento Harbor (1) provides an appealing anchorage for cruising yachtsmen, offering excellent shelter from wind and seas from all directions. This is enhanced by surroundings of great physical beauty and superb views of Mt. Desert Island.

Although it is not on the direct route for boats travelling east and west along the coast, the distance from Sorrento to Schoodic Point is only 9 miles. With the prevailing summertime winds, it is an easy and lovely sail in both directions.

There are three harbors to choose from at Sorrento. A partially submerged bar connects the middle north side of Preble Island with the mainland. This divides the strait into Sorrento Harbor (1) west of the bar, and Eastern Point Harbor (3), east of the bar. Both are easy to enter and both offer good protection, though Eastern Point Harbor is more exposed to a strong easterly blow.

The approach from the south to Sorrento Harbor and Eastern Point Harbor is without difficulty, even in fog. Dram Island (7), Preble Island (2), and Calf Island (8) are all very high, with bold shores and deep water right up to the very edge of land. There are no offlying ledges, rocks, or shallow spots.

Dram Island (7) is a Preserve of The Nature Conservancy. Landing is permitted, but difficult on the rocky and cliffy shore. The only place to land your dinghy is on the small beach on the east shore. The north shore is all 20 to 30 ft. high cliffs. Osprey nest in the white cedar trees growing among spruce and fir on the west end of Dram Island. Most of the interior is spruce and fir but there are some clearings, one containing a dense growth of American yew.

### Sorrento Harbor

Red and White Bell buoy "SH" (9) facilitates entry into Sorrento Harbor. This is a fairway buoy. Pass either side of it, and then head north mid-way between Dram Island (7) and Preble Island (2).

An alternate, less preferable entrance (10), is around the west end of Dram Island. If you use this west entrance, stay about 100 yards north of Dram Island. This will avoid the ledge that extends south from the north side of this passage.

Sorrento Harbor is quite filled with moored yachts and lobster boats. The Town Landing (11) has 5-6 feet depth at low tide, water, telephone, and trash receptacles. This is used by the Sorrento Yacht Club, which has three guest moorings. If you have any trouble finding a mooring, Harbormaster Willie Bunker will help you find one. He's most helpful and accomodating, usually present at the dock, or easily found nearby.

### Eastern Point Harbor

Eastern Point Harbor is primarily used by fishing boats, and has room available to anchor. At the dock (4) you can obtain gasoline and diesel fuel, but there is only one foot depth at low tide.

### Back Cove

Another anchorage in Back Cove (5), north of Sorrento. This is the least used of the three harbors and there is plenty of room here to swing to an anchor. A large rock in the middle of the entrance is to be

SORRENTO
Chart No. 13318D Scale 1:40,000
(1) Sorrento Harbor
(2) Preble Island
(3) Eastern Point Harbor
(4) Fuel Dock
(5) Back Cove
(5a) Swimming Pool
(6) West Cove Boatyard
(7) Dram Island
(8) Calf Island
(9) Red & White Bell Buoy "SH"
(10) Alternate (western) Entrance to Sorrento Harbor
(11) Town Landing
Not for use in Navigation
Nautical Miles
Yards

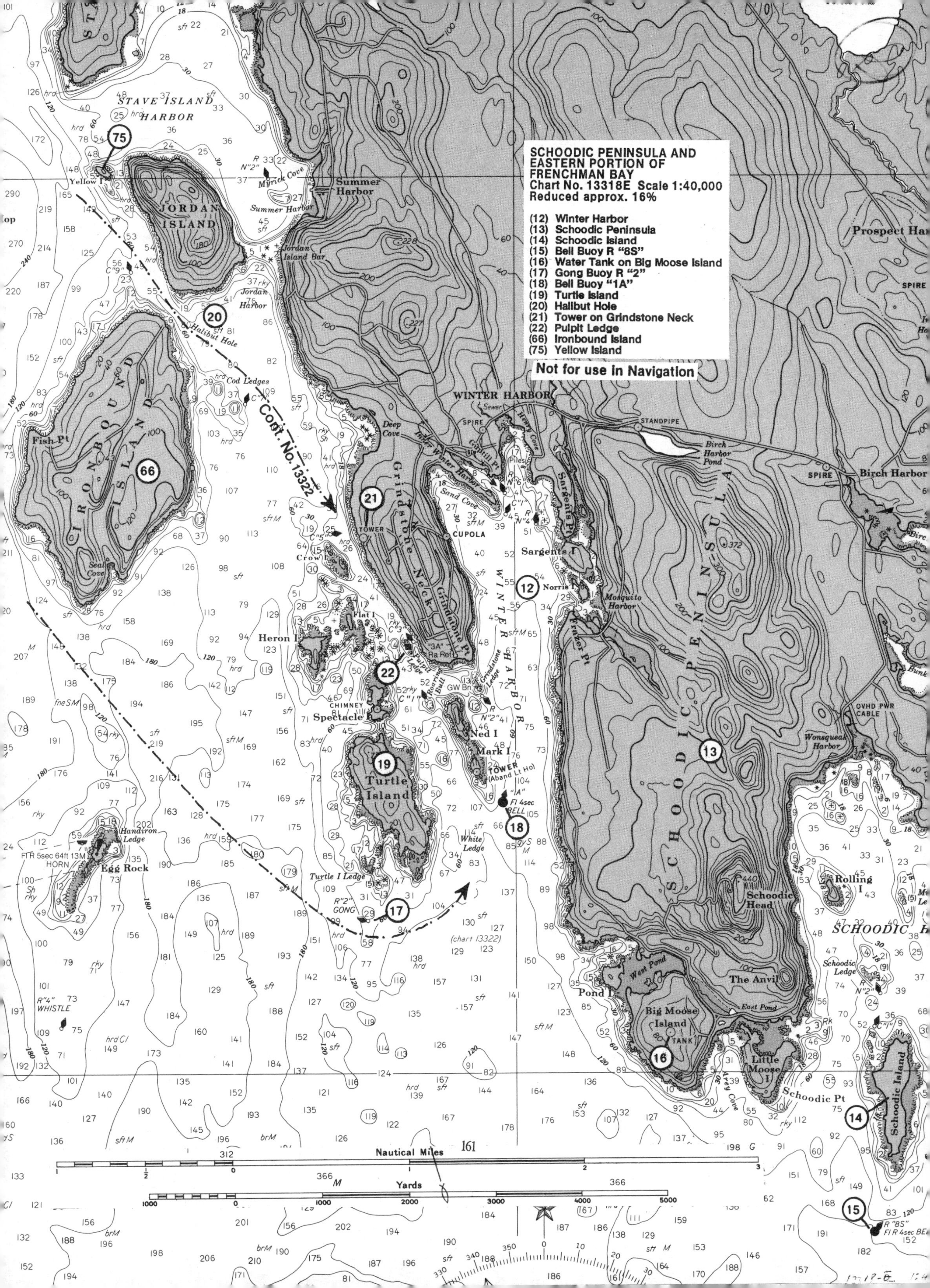
SCHOODIC PENINSULA AND
EASTERN PORTION OF
FRENCHMAN BAY
Chart No. 13318E Scale 1:40,000
Reduced approx. 16%
(12) Winter Harbor
(13) Schoodic Peninsula
(14) Schoodic Island
(15) Bell Buoy R "8S"
(16) Water Tank on Big Moose Island
(17) Gong Buoy R "2"
(18) Bell Buoy "1A"
(19) Turtle Island
(20) Halibut Hole
(21) Tower on Grindstone Neck
(22) Pulpit Ledge
(66) Ironbound Island
(75) Yellow Island
Not for use in Navigation
STAVE ISLAND HARBOR
JORDAN ISLAND
Yellow I
Summer Harbor
Myrick Cove
Jordan Island Bar
Jordan Harbor
Halibut Hole
Cod Ledges
IRONBOUND ISLAND
Fish Pt
Seal Cove
Cont. No. 13322
Deep Cove
Inner Winter Harbor
Grindstone Neck
Grindstone Pt
Sand Cove
Gerrish Pt
WINTER HARBOR
Sargents Pt
Sargents I
Norris
Mosquito Harbor
Frazer Pt
STANDPIPE
Birch Harbor Pond
Birch Harbor
Prospect Har
SCHOODIC PENINSULA
Crow I
Flat I
Heron I
Pulpit Ledge
Roaring Bull
Grindstone Ledge
Spectacle I
CHIMNEY
Ned I
Mark I
TOWER (Aband Lt Ho)
Turtle Island
White Ledge
Turtle I Ledge
R "2" GONG
Fl 4sec BELL
(chart 13322)
Handiron Ledge
Egg Rock
Fl R 5sec 64ft 13M HORN
R "4" WHISTLE
Wonsqueak Harbor
OVHD PWR CABLE
Schoodic Head
Rolling I
SCHOODIC H
Schoodic Ledge
The Anvil
West Pond
East Pond
Pond I
Big Moose Island
TANK
Little Moose I
Arey Cove
Schoodic Pt
Schoodic Island
R "8S" Fl R 4sec BE
Nautical Miles
Yards

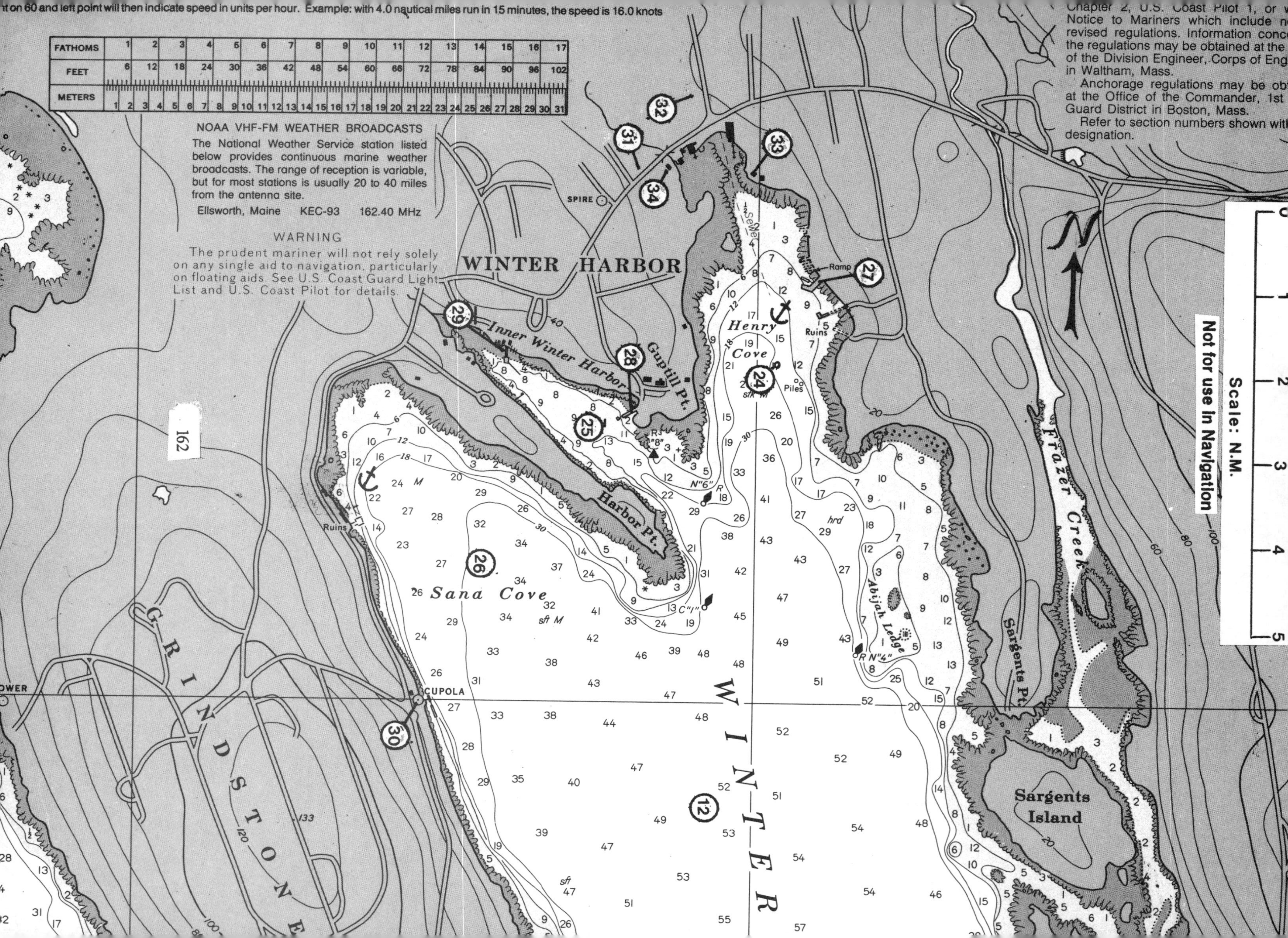

...t on 60 and left point will then indicate speed in units per hour. Example: with 4.0 nautical miles run in 15 minutes, the speed is 16.0 knots
| FATHOMS | 1 | 2 | 3 | 4 | 5 | 6 | 7 | 8 | 9 | 10 | 11 | 12 | 13 | 14 | 15 | 16 | 17 |
| FEET | 6 | 12 | 18 | 24 | 30 | 36 | 42 | 48 | 54 | 60 | 66 | 72 | 78 | 84 | 90 | 96 | 102 |
METERS 1 2 3 4 5 6 7 8 9 10 11 12 13 14 15 16 17 18 19 20 21 22 23 24 25 26 27 28 29 30 31
NOAA VHF-FM WEATHER BROADCASTS
The National Weather Service station listed below provides continuous marine weather broadcasts. The range of reception is variable, but for most stations is usually 20 to 40 miles from the antenna site.
Ellsworth, Maine KEC-93 162.40 MHz
WARNING
The prudent mariner will not rely solely on any single aid to navigation, particularly on floating aids. See U.S. Coast Guard Light List and U.S. Coast Pilot for details.
Chapter 2, U.S. Coast Pilot 1, or w... Notice to Mariners which include n... revised regulations. Information conc... the regulations may be obtained at the... of the Division Engineer, Corps of Eng... in Waltham, Mass.
Anchorage regulations may be ob... at the Office of the Commander, 1st... Guard District in Boston, Mass.
Refer to section numbers shown wit... designation.
Scale: N.M.
0 1 2 3 4 5
Not for use in Navigation
WINTER HARBOR
Inner Winter Harbor
Guptill Pt.
Henry Cove
Harbor Pt.
Sand Cove
Abijah Ledge
Frazer Creek
Sargents Pt.
Sargents Island
WINTER
GRINDSTONE
SPIRE
CUPOLA
Ruins
Ramp
Piles
Sewer

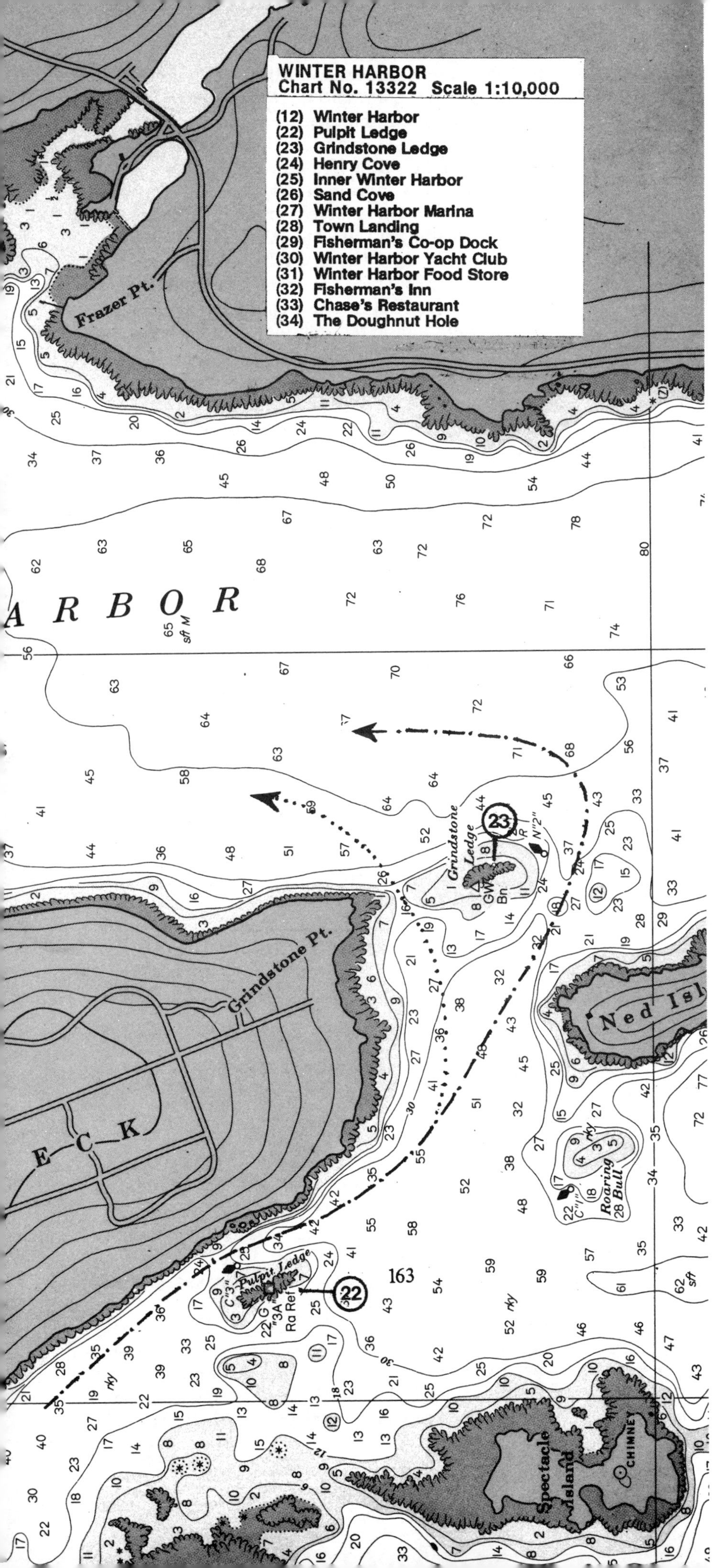

**WINTER HARBOR**
**Chart No. 13322 Scale 1:10,000**

(12) Winter Harbor
(22) Pulpit Ledge
(23) Grindstone Ledge
(24) Henry Cove
(25) Inner Winter Harbor
(26) Sand Cove
(27) Winter Harbor Marina
(28) Town Landing
(29) Fisherman's Co-op Dock
(30) Winter Harbor Yacht Club
(31) Winter Harbor Food Store
(32) Fisherman's Inn
(33) Chase's Restaurant
(34) The Doughnut Hole

Frazer Pt.

ARBOR

Grindstone Ledge

Grindstone Pt.

ECK

Ned Isl

Roaring Bull

Pulpit Ledge

Spectacle Island

CHIMNEY

Thuya Gardens, Northeast Harbor, Chapter 12

avoided. It may not show, even at low tide. The only other danger is the extensive ledge, extending north near the entry, which shows itself at about half-water.

Both these dangers may be avoided by heading north, past the harbor entrance, before turning in. Align the stern of your boat with buoys C "3" and N "4," and the bow with a swimming pool and small, triangular building (5a) which is visible on the north side of the harbor. This will bring you in roughly on a bearing of 110° Magnetic (90°True), and will keep you clear of both the rock and the ledge. Then, follow the eastern shore until you are well into the cove. Due to silting, depths in the cove are not quite as great as the chart shows. Any boat drawing more than 5 feet may ground out at dead low tide. At the head of the cove is the West Cove Boatyard (6) with sheds for storage and a crane capable of hauling boats up to 40 feet for hull and engine repairs. Some boat hardware is available in their chandlery. There is no place for provisioning in Sorrento, no matter which of the three harbors you are in. The nearest store is 4 miles north, at the intersection of route 185 and Route 1, in Sullivan.

## WINTER HARBOR
## CHART NOS. 13318E, 13322

Winter Harbor (12) is a favorite place among yachtsmen making the passage along this part of the coast. It conveniently breaks the distance between anchorages, allowing for an easy day's sail. There are no problems entering whether bound east or west. The few dangers, are well marked. Marine facilities, stores and provisions are conveniently nearby.

### Approaches

From the east, Schoodic Peninsula (13), with its long central mountainous spine, thrusts itself seaward. Aim for the south tip of this land, passing south of Schoodic Island (14), which will separate itself from the land behind it as you approach. A lighted bell buoy, R "8S", Fl R, 4 sec. (15) is great aid at night or in fog. Thereafter, follow the west shore of Schoodic Peninsula north into Winter harbor.

Coming across Frenchman Bay from the southern harbors of Mt. Desert Island, you will be guided by 440 ft. Schoodic Head and the very prominent green water tank (16) on Big Moose Island. Gong buoy R "2" (17) and bell buoy "1A" (18) help lead you past the islands and ledges at the outer part of the entrance. Approaching from the west, Schoodic Island (14) appears to be smaller and farther away from the mainland than it would seem from the chart. The south half of the island is wooded, while the north half low and treeless.

From Sorrento, at the north end of Frenchman Bay, there are two possible routes to Winter Harbor. You may either go around the west side of Ironbound Island (66) and Turtle Island (19) before turning north into the harbor, or you may elect to take a shorter inside passage. If the weather is good, the inside passage provides a very pleasant and scenic sail, not nearly as difficult as it might appear from the chart.

The inside passage leads you through Halibut Hole (20), between the north end of Ironbound Island and Jordan Island. From there, head southeast toward the tower on Grindstone Neck (21). This is a round, grey house which looks like a lighthouse. Then, closely follow the shore of Grindstone Neck. In this passage, the buoys and beacons are marked for travel northward, so in heading south, you will want to keep the green buoys to **starboard**. On the 1:40,000 scale chart it doesn't look possible to pass between buoy C "3" at Pulpit Ledge (22) and the shore, but rest assured there is a passage of 40 yards width and at least 20 foot depth. This shows better on chart no. 13322, scale 1:10,000.

Arriving at the southern tip of Grindstone Neck, you may pass between it and Grindstone Ledge (23), or continue until south of the ledge, turning north after rounding buoy N "2". The latter is the safer route and the one most generally recommended. If you choose to go between the ledge and the point, favor the north side of the passage, where if you are lucky or skillfull, you'll pass through the narrow channel with 16 feet depth. If it is not full low tide, there is a larger margin for error. We draw 4 feet and went through near low tide, slightly to one side of the channel, without problems, but there was only a foot of water under our keel and it wasn't a comfortable feeling. Be safe and go south of N "2".

Turtle Island (19) (chart no. 13312A) is a Preserve of The Nature Conservancy. Visitors are welcome, but it's difficult to get around the interior. Most visitors picnic or walk along the shore of this 136-acre preserve. The only landing area is at the beach on the northeast shore where you'll see The Nature Conservancy sign. Two-thirds of the island is covered by huge old spruce and fir trees, some over 150 years old.

The north end was cut by loggers in the early 1960's and now has raspberry and blackberry thickets, with cherry and grey birch trees. There are tidal pools on the east shore near the south end of Turtle Island. Great blue herons and osprey are found in the interior. You'll see harbor seals sunning themselves on the ledges off the southwest shore.

There are three coves at the head of Winter Harbor where you may anchor or moor: Henry Cove (24), Inner Winter Harbor (25) and Sand Cove (26).

### Henry Cove

Henry Cove (24) is the least sheltered from wind and waves from the south, but there is plenty of room to drop anchor and pay out ample scope. Unfortunately, much of the head of the cove dries out to shallow, unattractive mud flats. But at least there is no longer a sewer pipe outflow to add its effluent, thanks to the new sewage treatment plant.

One advantage of Henry Cove is Winter Harbor Marina (27) with 16 moorings, gasoline, diesel fuel, ice, showers, propane, marine supplies, complete engine and hull repairs, fork lift rack storage, asphalt launching ramp. They can haul out boats up to 25 tons weight, provided the length does not exceed 40 feet. At the dock floats, there is 6 -6½ feet of water at low tide. The closer you get to the head of the pier, the shallower it gets. Winter Harbor Marine is no longer a pumpout station for holding tanks. The nearest place for this service is at Bar Harbor, Northeast Harbor and Southwest Harbor over on Mt. Desert Island. As a courtesy to their customers, Winter Harbor Marine will provide transportation to the nearby grocery store, liquor store and laundromat. Open 5 days a week, they are closed on Saturday and Sunday.

### Inner Winter Harbor

Inner Winter Harbor (25) is the most protected of the three coves being filled with moored lobster boats. It is also the most crowded. You may be allowed to use an unoccupied mooring for the night, or lie alongside one of the lobster cars. Inquire at the Town Landing (28), just inside the entrance on the north side, or at the Fisherman's Co-op Dock (29) at the head of the harbor. Winter Harbor Town Landing (28) has 40 ft. of dock space for which there is no charge. Winter Harbor Fisherman's Co-op (29) has 3 moorings, some dock space, gasoline, diesel fuel, marine supplies, and monitors CB Channels 1, 7 and 18; and VHF Channel 6.

### Sand Cove

Sand Cove is more attractive than Henry Cove and the holding ground, in sticky mud, is excellent. Work your way up toward the head of the harbor, preferably on the south side, to avoid anchoring in too deep water. Winter Harbor Yacht Club (30) on the west shore can be recognized by the prominent cupola and long veranda of the club house. At their floats, there is 20 feet depth and fresh water is available. They maintain 2 guest moorings and allow the use of shower facilities for a small fee.

Moored in front of the dock is a small fleet of handsome class racing boats. These boats are 21 feet on the waterline and 31 feet overall. The Yacht Club commissioned Burgess & Packard of Marblehead, Mass. to design a boat that club members could race in any weather safely. Seven were built in 1906 and two more in 1911. Of these original nine boats, five are still sailing, and an additional one is on its way. The present day membership is as pleased with their sailing characteristics as the original members were.

### Supplies and Sightseeing

The town of Winter Harbor is accessible from Henry Cove or Inner Winter Harbor. Winter Harbor Food Store (31) has a good selection of groceries. There are two restaurants, The Fisherman's Inn (32) and Chase's Restaurant (33). At the Doughnut Hole (34), you can get home-made muffins, doughnuts and breakfast, starting at 5:00 a.m. Lunch is served until they close at 2 p.m.

Try to plan your arrival at Winter Harbor to coincide with their Annual Winter Harbor Lobster Festival and Lobster Boat Races. Even if you aren't interested in power boats or in racing, you can't help but be caught up in the infectious enthusiasm generated by the participants and their families. They arrive early in the morning from miles around, intent on having a good time as they are on winning. This is a short, measured distance race, divided into many categories, e.g., wood, fiberglas, diesel engine, gasoline engine, number of cylinders, etc., to give everyone a fair chance. If Winter Harbor were to completely dry up by a super-low tide, I think there would be enough beer around to float the boats and carry on the race!

When the racing is finished, most come back to participate in other competitions, such as tug-of-war contests between various townships, softball tournaments and craft fairs. The Lobster Festival goes on all day, terminated by a parade and fireworks. Inner Winter Harbor then is wall-to-wall lobster boats. It probably is the only time you will see the normally independent loner-type lobsterman rafted with others, twelve abreast.

Two other important lobster boat races in Maine are at Jonesport on the 4th of July, and at Stonington.

Corea Harbor, Chapter 14

# CHAPTER 14

# SCHOODIC PENINSULA TO PETIT MANAN

## EAST OF SCHOODIC—CHART NO. 13312B

Some points along the Maine coast are either major landmarks themselves, or they indicate a division between regions with distinct differences. For example, Cape Elizabeth heralds the end of the sandy beaches west of it and the beginning of Maine's famous rockbound coast. East of Schoodic Point, you leave behind the security of services provided for cruising yachtsmen and the company of other cruising vessels, and you encounter a lonesome rugged coast with increasing Bay of Fundy tides, currents and fog. Although greater effort and planning is required to sail here, the rewards are much greaer. The effects of civilization are minimal, and the natural order of life is undisturbed. Downeast Maine is a place where you can truly be an explorer, watch the eagles soar and the whales plunge.

Although sailboats are considerably fewer than in western Maine, and Coast Guard Stations are much further apart, there are fishermen and lobstermen about if you need assistance in any real emergency.

Surprisingly, much of the section of coast from Pigeon Hill Bay to Prospect Harbor is low and featureless. Petit Manan Point (35), Dyer Point (36), Cranberry Point (37) and Prospect Harbor Point (38) all blend together, with few distinguishing characteristics, particularly when enveloped in a heavy summertime haze or fog.

Several features will help provide orientation, the most dominant being the Petit Manan Light (39) on its 123-foot tower. North of Cranberry Point is a naval communication station with a group of tall radio towers (40) arranged in a large circle. These are part of the U.S. Navy's Security Group Activity anti-submarine radar net. I have indicated their approximate position on the chart. The light tower on Prospect Harbor Point (38) is not that prominent, but the domed tank (41) immediately behind it, certainly is, as are other surrounding buildings.

Gouldsboro Bay (42) and Dyer Bay (43) are seldom used by yachtsmen, as they are considerably out of the way and there is little reward for the effort. The entrances to both are constricted by a long string of islands, creating narrow channels between them through which the tide rushes strongly. There are many ledges, shallows and tortuous waterways, none of which are marked by any navigational aids. In addition, numerous fish weirs, covered at or near high water, create a hazard.

Most who are making the east and west passage along this section of coast take a course directly between Schoodic Point and Petit Manan Island, but in between these two points are several harbors definitely worth visiting.

## SCHOODIC HARBOR
### CHART NOS. 13312B, 13324

Schoodic Harbor (44) is completely exposed from the south, making it undesirable as an anchorage. Where it isn't too deep to anchor, the harbor is strewn with unmarked ledges and boulders. There are no facilities or conveniences ashore.

## BUNKER HARBOR
### CHART NOS. 13312B, 13324

Bunker Harbor (45) is truly delightful, used almost exclusively by local lobstermen. It is seldom visited by yachtsmen because of of its proximity to the better known Winter Harbor and because of its unjustified reputation of being difficult to enter. True, the entrance to Bunker Harbor is almost totally obstructed by unmarked ledge and rocks. Buoy, C "1" (46) at the outermost limit is of little use, besides being rather low in the water and difficult to see. However, there is a safe and easy way in and out.

### Entering The Harbor

The following directions contradict the *Coast Pilot* but they worked fine for me when, for the first time, I had to enter in the densest of downeast fogs. Later, this procedure was confirmed by local lobstermen who use the same approach. Refer to chart 13324—Harbors East of Schoodic Head.

From the south, head for the black and red whistle buoy (47) off Schoodic Harbor, staying east of it. This buoy's red/black marking is intended for those entering Schoodic Harbor. It is a rather quiet whistle buoy. From here, keep a heading east of 020 degrees magnetic to avoid Brown Cow Ledge (48) until past Spruce Point (49). Then closely parallel the shore, while keeping a depth of 24-30 feet showing on the fathometer. Once you are beyond the point of land at the south side of the entrance and are half-way between both shores, make your turn west to head into the harbor. At full high tide the last portion of land on this southern point is discontinuous with the rest of the point, so that it

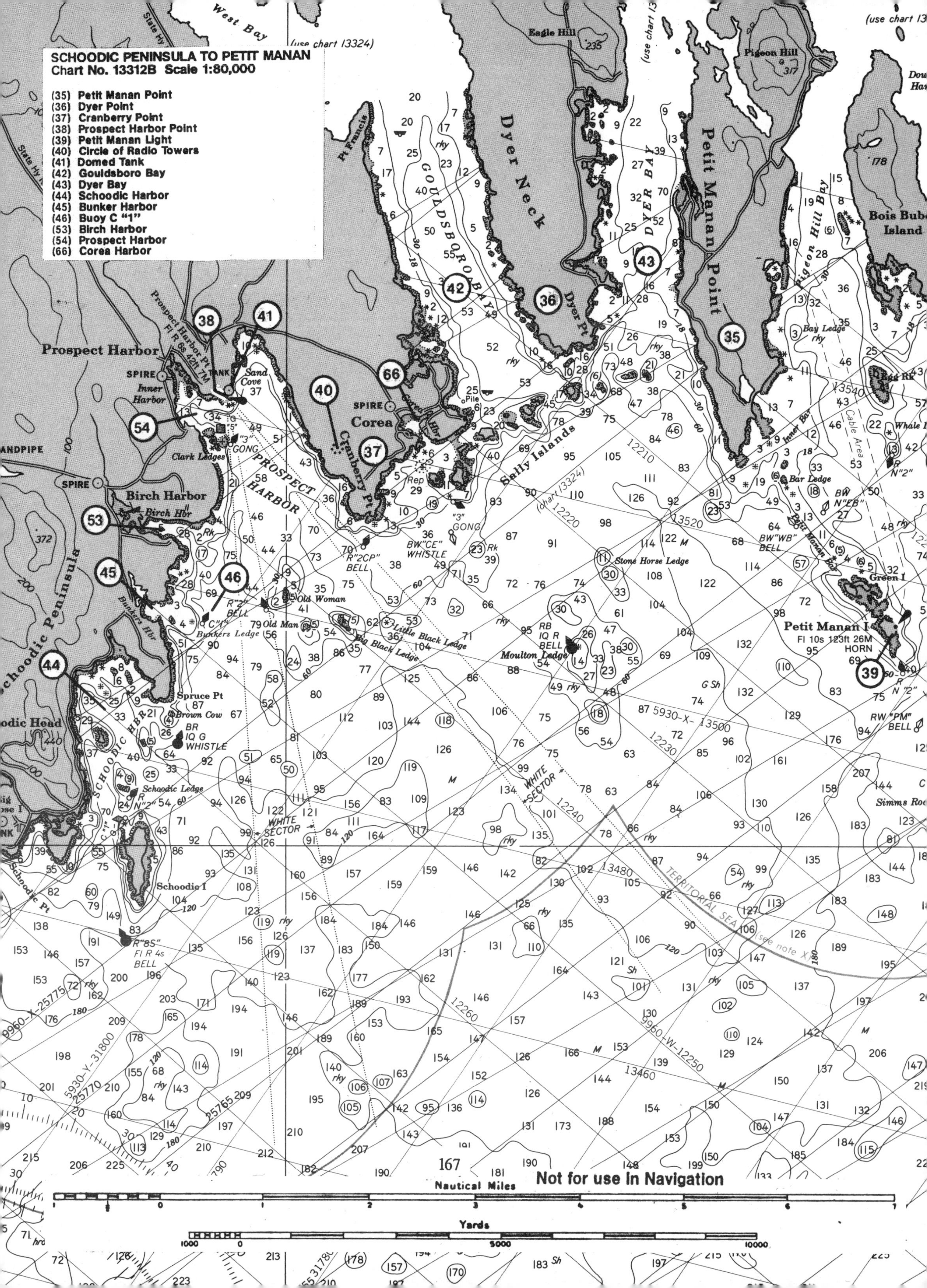
SCHOODIC PENINSULA TO PETIT MANAN
Chart No. 13312B Scale 1:80,000
(35) Petit Manan Point
(36) Dyer Point
(37) Cranberry Point
(38) Prospect Harbor Point
(39) Petit Manan Light
(40) Circle of Radio Towers
(41) Domed Tank
(42) Gouldsboro Bay
(43) Dyer Bay
(44) Schoodic Harbor
(45) Bunker Harbor
(46) Buoy C "1"
(53) Birch Harbor
(54) Prospect Harbor
(66) Corea Harbor
Prospect Harbor
Birch Harbor
Schoodic Peninsula
Corea
Dyer Neck
Petit Manan Point
GOULDSBORO BAY
DYER BAY
PROSPECT HARBOR
Sally Islands
Petit Manan I
Schoodic I
Not for use in Navigation
Nautical Miles
Yards

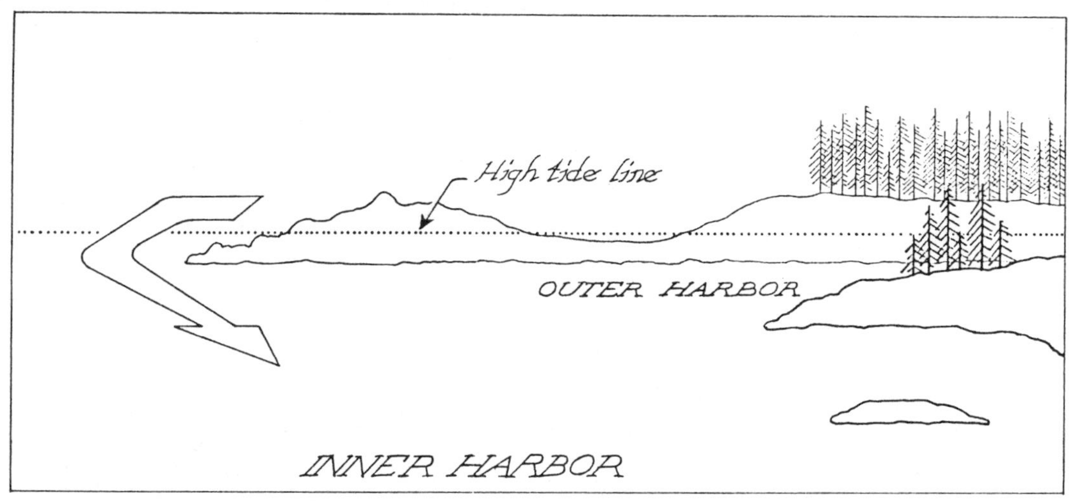


Bunker Harbor—View from Inside the Harbor at About Half Tide

looks like a separate boulder coming out of the water north of the point. Be sure you clear this as well, before making your turn west into the harbor. Refer to sketch chart of this point of land.

The ledge (50), south of the rock exposed at 6 feet, is awash at half-tide. The channel north of all these obstructions may have the deeper water, but the trick is trying to find it!

From the east, aim for a point about mid-way along the Spruce Point Peninsula and follow the preceeding description.

### Anchorage

Bunker Harbor has an outer part which is a perfect punch-bowl shape, and a long narrow inner part. The outer portion has good holding ground, a patchy mixture of mud and sand, and plenty room to anchor with sufficient scope. The protection is fine for everything except a strong southeast to easterly blow. The inner harbor is filled with moored lobster boats and there is no room whatsoever to anchor. You may be able to pick up an unoccupied mooring for the night by asking at any of the fish wharfs.

The very head of the harbor is sealed off with a wall forming a lobster pound behind it. There are two wharfs (51) with approximately 6 feet depth at low tide. Both sell gasoline and diesel fuel. Heading toward the wharfs, stay **closely** along the edge of moored boats, as ledges extend out a considerable distance from both shores.

The nearest groceries available are about a mile north at Chipman's (52) in Birch Harbor

## BIRCH HARBOR—CHART NOS. 13312B, 13324

Birch Harbor (53) has silted in considerably and is seldom used for anchorage. The fact that the usually ever-present lobster boats are not moored here, gives you a clue to its undesirability.

## PROSPECT HARBOR
## CHART NOS. 13312B, 13324

Of all the harbors between Schoodic Point and Petit Manan Island, Prospect Harbor (54) is the easiest to approach and enter under any weather conditions. It is also the least attractive in appearance, its chief merit being the ease of entry and the convenience of its location for stopover while proceeding along the coast.

### Harbor Entry

A collection of mostly unmarked ledges is spread across the outer entrance to the harbor. The only buoy indicating their presence is the bell buoy R "2" (55), which like C "1" off Bunker Ledge (46), is small and difficult to see. Both Old Man Ledge (56) and Old Woman Ledge (57) begin to bare and are awash at mid-tide. Of the two, Old Man Ledge is exposed first. Big Black Ledge (58) has a tiny portion of it showing above high water, while Little Black Ledge (59) is barely awash at high water. At night, the two white sectors from the Prospect Harbor Point Light (60), Fl R, 6 sec., guide you safely past on either side of these ledges. In any thick weather, plan to give them a more than generous berth.

The only obstruction in entering Prospect Inner Harbor are Clark Ledges (61), but these are well marked by a gong buoy and a green daybeacon. After passing east and north of them, proceed into the Inner Harbor. Sand Cove (62), the eastern branch of the harbor, is not used as it is completely open and exposed from the south. Though Inner Harbor is somewhat exposed from the southeast, by working as close as possible to the west shore near the wharfs, you will find good protection. The bottom is mud, and anchor holding quality is excellent. Sardine carriers enter and leave frequently day or night. Keep an anchor light on all night.

### Facilities

The first wharf with the large, green shed behind it is the Stinson Sardine Cannery (63). This is one of the

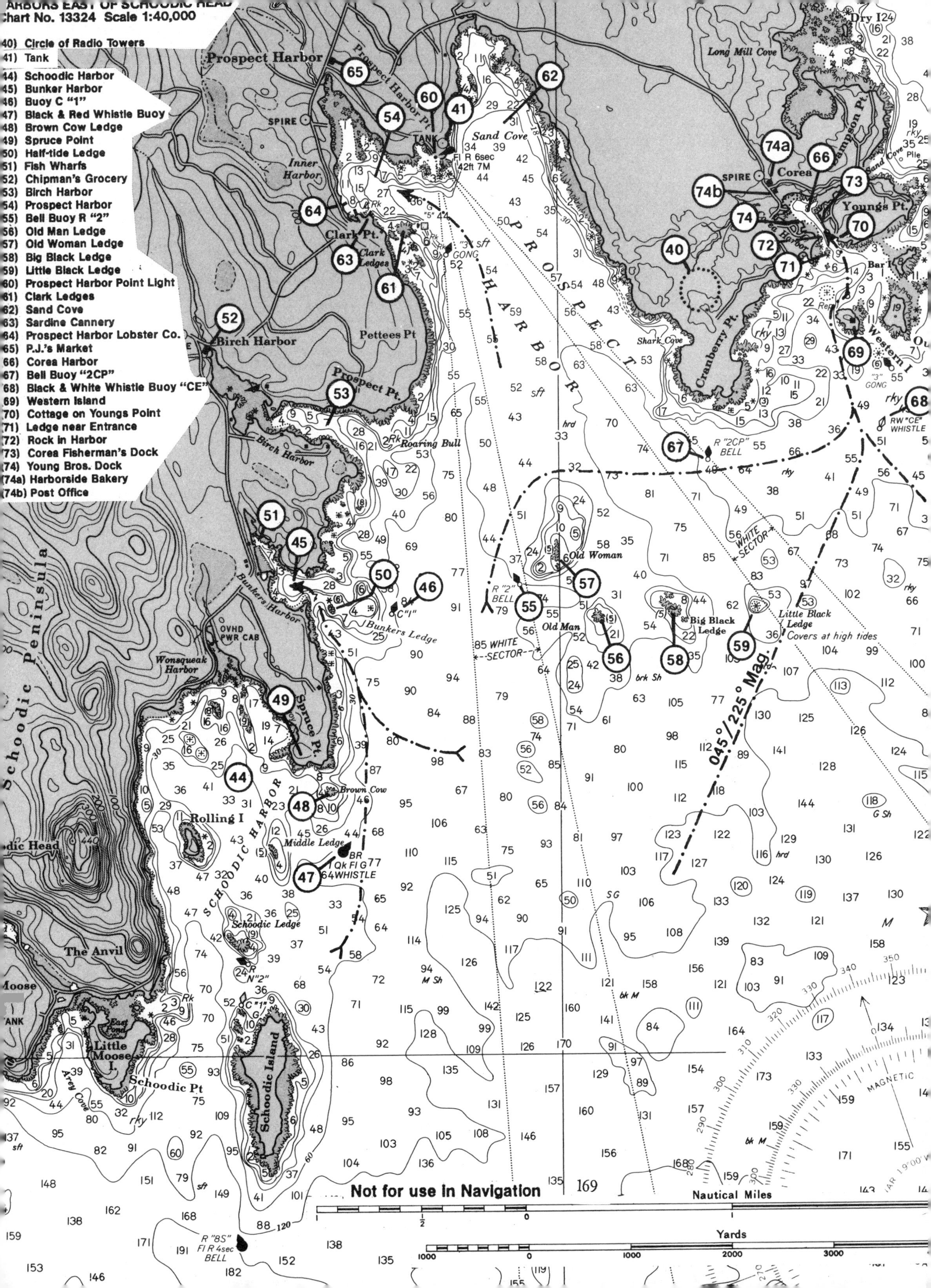

Chart No. 13324 Scale 1:40,000
40) Circle of Radio Towers
41) Tank
44) Schoodic Harbor
45) Bunker Harbor
46) Buoy C "1"
47) Black & Red Whistle Buoy
48) Brown Cow Ledge
49) Spruce Point
50) Half-tide Ledge
51) Fish Wharfs
52) Chipman's Grocery
53) Birch Harbor
54) Prospect Harbor
55) Bell Buoy R "2"
56) Old Man Ledge
57) Old Woman Ledge
58) Big Black Ledge
59) Little Black Ledge
60) Prospect Harbor Point Light
61) Clark Ledges
62) Sand Cove
63) Sardine Cannery
64) Prospect Harbor Lobster Co.
65) P.J.'s Market
66) Corea Harbor
67) Bell Buoy "2CP"
68) Black & White Whistle Buoy "CE"
69) Western Island
70) Cottage on Youngs Point
71) Ledge near Entrance
72) Rock in Harbor
73) Corea Fisherman's Dock
74) Young Bros. Dock
74a) Harborside Bakery
74b) Post Office
Prospect Harbor
Prospect Harbor Pt
Long Mill Cove
Sand Cove
Inner Harbor
Clark Pt.
Clark Ledges
Birch Harbor
Pettees Pt
Prospect Pt.
Roaring Bull
PROSPECT HARBOR
Shark Cove
Cranberry Pt.
Corea
Sampson Pt.
Youngs Pt.
Western I
Bar I
Dry I
Bunkers Harbor
Bunkers Ledge
Wonsqueak Harbor
Spruce Pt.
Schoodic Peninsula
SCHOODIC HARBOR
Brown Cow
Middle Ledge
Rolling I
Schoodic Ledge
The Anvil
Little Moose I.
Schoodic Pt
Schoodic Island
Arey Cove
East Pond
Old Woman
Old Man
Big Black Ledge
Little Black Ledge
Covers at high tides
045°/225° Mag.
WHITE SECTOR
85 WHITE SECTOR
Fl R 6sec 42ft 7M
R "2" BELL
R "2CP" BELL
RW "CE" WHISTLE
"3" GONG
BR Qk Fl G WHISTLE
R "8S" Fl R 4sec BELL
SPIRE
TANK
OVHD PWR CAB
MAGNETIC
Not for use in Navigation
Nautical Miles
Yards

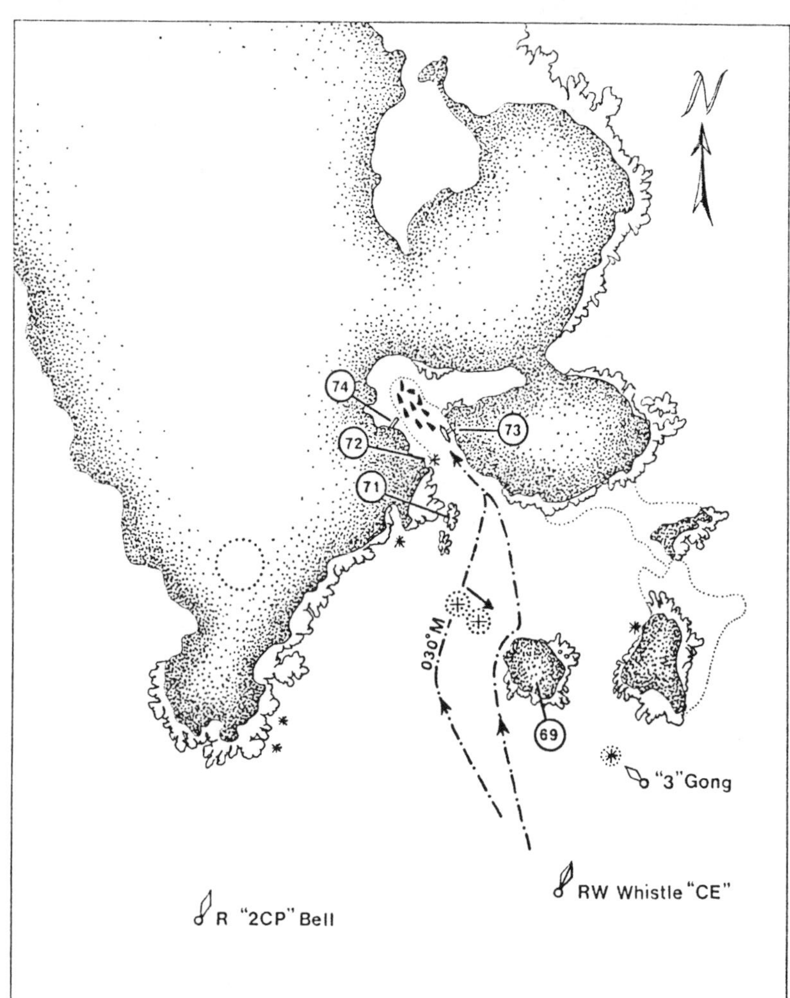


**Corea Harbor**

69. Western Island
71. Ledge near Entrance
72. Rock in Harbor
73. Corea Fisherman's Co-op Dock
74. Young Bros. Dock

note change in position of rock "reported" in mid-channel, closer to Western Island.

**Not for use in Navigation**

12 sardine canning factories now remaining in Maine. At one time, there were as many as 22 factories in the Eastport vicinity alone. The wharf has a depth of 10 feet alongside. Do not tie up here as it is in constant use by commercial vessels. There is a float landing for small boats, but it nearly dries out there are low tide.

Prospect Harbor Lobster Company (64) has a wharf, but at low tide it completely dries out. However, a float moored about 90 feet off the wharf has 4 feet of water alongside at low tide. Gasoline, but no diesel fuel, is pumped from this float. They also sell lobsters, and moniter CB Channel 5. Do not proceed into the northern half of the inner harbor, as it is shallow and filled with rocks and ledges.

Although P.J.'s Market (65) at the head of the harbor is close by, for any extensive provisioning, it would be best to go to Chipman's Supermarket (52) about 1.0 mile southwest, at Birch Harbor. Much larger, and more extensively stocked, they have fresh meat, produce, ice and liquor. Chipman's is open 8:00 a.m.-9:00 p.m. on Monday through Saturday, and 9:00 a.m. to 9:00 p.m. on Sunday. Across the road is a laundromat and a hardware store.

## COREA—CHART NOS. 13312B, 13324

Corea (66) is one of those few places on the Maine coast that has managed to retain its character as purely a fishing village, with very few changes over the years. Many of the lobster boats are fiberglass now and the traps are made of wire instead of wood lath, but the fishermen who work these seas and depend on them for survival, remain unchanged. They are a hard-working, helpful and friendly group, proud of their work and of their community.

### Harbor Entry

From the west, round bell buoy R "2" (55) off Old Woman Ledge (57) and head over toward bell buoy (67) off Cranberry Point. Be sure to give Old Woman Ledge more than enough clearance, for shallow water surrounds it for a much greater distance than you would think possible. The same is true for the very uneven bottom off Cranberry Point. From R "2CP" (67) head east towards the red and white whistle Buoy "CE" (68) before turning north to enter the harbor.

Alternately, you could head directly for buoy 'CE" (68) staying east of all the ledges. A compass bearing of 045 degrees magnetic or an approach anywhere east of this, will clear Little Black Ledge (59).

Whichever approach you make, then head for the northwest shore of Western Island (69) and follow **closely** along it well on to the north side. Next head for the bold yellow ledge and grey shingle cottage (70) on

Youngs Point. Keep close to the east shore all the way into the harbor. The patch of ledge (71) near the entrance to the harbor is just barely awash at high tide, so it is visible throughout most of the tide. The solitary rock (72) shown in the middle of the harbor is unmarked and does not bare until half-tide. It is somewhat closer to the west shore, and will be avoided as long as you remain close to the east shore.

The directions I have just given, which are drawn on Chart No. 13324 (Harbors East of Schoodic Head), have always worked well for me. However, in talking to one of the resident fishermen, I was informed that the rock marked "reported," which is northwest of Western Island, is actually closer to the Island than is indicated on the chart. His method of entry is to head for the northwest end of Western Island, giving it good berth, and when approximately in mid-channel, aiming for Youngs Point. This brings him in on a course bearing of about 030° Magnetic. The sketch diagram shows both the original and this alternate route. Which entry course you choose to follow, remember once reaching Youngs Point, to stick close by to that northeastern shore, for that's where the deep water is.

### Facilities

The harbor is crowded with lobster boats, leaving absolutely no room to anchor. Whatever water you may see between the edge of the fleet and the shore, will dry out completely at low tide. The very first dock, on your starboard as you enter the harbor, is the Corea Fisherman's Co-op. Depth alongside their floats is about 6 feet. Here, you may get gasoline and diesel fuel, but no water. In the channel, almost directly opposite the float, is a large, pink, ball float. This is **not** a guest mooring, though it can be used as one. Actually, it is a mooring for the floats in the event of severe weather. If you do use it for the purpose of mooring your boat, be sure to increase the length of your pennant to it, for it's a bit short at high water. Add 5 or 6 feet of rope to it. Otherwise, inquire at the dock about the possibility of occupying an unused mooring in the harbor.

The channel has been dredged to a depth of 8 feet, and there is 6 feet throughout the rest of the basin. Young Brothers Boatyard (74) farther up the harbor on the southwest shore, has a large dock with floats, 4-5 ft. depth alongside. They are builders of fiberglass lobster boats. Someone there may know of an unoccupied mooring that you may use for the night. All the other docks dry out at low tide.

Sailboats frequently anchor outside the harbor entrance, between Western Island and Youngs Point. This is alright for fine, settled weather, but the bottom here is all sand and its holding quality is poor.

In Corea, the Harborside Bakery sells pies and cakes, and serves breakfast. There are no other stores or places for provisioning in Corea. The nearest grocery is P.J.'s (65) in Prospect Harbor, about 3 miles west.

## PETIT MANAN ISLAND—CHART NO. 13324A

You are truly "downeast" once safely past Petit Manan Island (75). Though more than 2 miles offshore, it is almost connected to the mainland by a series of islands, ledges and shallow bars. Under the best of conditions, passages near Petit Manan can be troublesome, and under the worst, downright dangerous.

### Tidal Currents

The problem lies in the strong and conflicting currents produced here, compounded by the usually prevalent fog. One reason for the nature of these currents is the many Bays in the vicinity which are oriented north and south. On the ebb tide, the large volume of water coming out of these bays meets with the general ebb current moving in a southwesterly direction along the coast, creating much confusion and turbulence. When the wind is against the tide, this condition is worsened.

A second reason for these strong and conflicting currents is the extremely uneven, rough bottom configuration. Pinnacles of rock near Petit Manan Island rise abruptly from the depths. Not all of them are indicated on the chart. Sailing through this area, it is amazing to watch the depth-sounder jump from 130 feet to 13 feet, and then back down again in as little distance as the length of the boat.

The tidal current action on this uneven bottom also results in a thorough **vertical** mixing of water, bringing the cold water of the Bay of Fundy to the top where it meets the warm, moist, surface air. This accounts for the high frequency of fog at Petit Manan. In fact, the Petit Manan Light holds the record for the most hours of fog signal operation of any lighthouse between Cape Cod, Mass. and West Quoddy Head, Maine, 1800+ average hours per year. Petit Manan's maximum one year rate of operaion was 2,941 hours. For June, July and August, the highest fog months, the average rate per month is 256 hours.

Even in the calmest of weather conditions, with the most gentle breeze, there will be patches of over-falls, tide rips and a generally confused sea. With a strong wind against the tide, it can be a miserable experience crossing the area. Fortunately, it is limited to about a 4 mile stretch of water.

The set of the current on the flood tide pulls strongly into Gouldsboro Bay and Dyer Bay, west of Petit Manan. This is particularly felt as you near Moulton Ledge (76). Just south of the Petit Manan Bar, this current shifts to a more easterly direction of about 080 degrees magnetic. At half-tide, the strength of current 0.5 mile east of the Petit Manan bell (77) is about 2.5 knots and sets 075 degrees magnetic. Refer to folded chart inside rear cover. Past Tibbett Rock buoy, east of Petit Manan, the flood current is 035-040 degrees magnetic, setting in toward Pleasant Bay, east of Petit Manan. If sailing toward Cape Split east of Pleasant Bay, the set of the flood current is in the same general direction as your heading and will not materially set you off course.

## Passages

Understandably, the water rushes over Petit Manan Bar with considerable velocity. With the wind against the tide, this will produce very short, steep, standing waves. With a swell, or a heavy sea running, waves will break across the entire length of the bar. There are two channels through Petit Manan Bar. The more northerly one, Inner Bar (78), is unmarked and should not be attempted without the aid of local knowledge. The more southerly one is Outer Bar Channel (79). It is marked by fairway buoys at both ends. These are black and white buoys, and the west one is a bell buoy. Pass closely either side of both buoys. There is 13 feet depth in the channel, but passage through here should be made only when the sea is smooth and visibility is good.

Most vessels prefer to keep south of Petit Manan Island entirely, rather than going across the bar. We have marked this passage (77a). The extra distance in traveling east and west is minimal, and it is less of a problem. Petit Manan and Green Islands are both very low and treeless. With the usual haze or fog enveloping them, you would most certainly run aground before they were even seen, if it were not for the tall and strongly penetrating light on Petit Manan Island. This is visible for a good distance, even in adverse conditions. However, the fog sound signal does not carry nearly as well. You usually must be nearly abeam of the horn before it is even heard. The safest course is to pass outside the bell buoy (77) south of the island. It is now a red and white bell buoy. If the weather is really bad, it would be best to keep south of the whistle buoy R "6A" (78a).

## Petit Manan Light

The Petit Manan tower, built in 1817, stands 123 feet above mean high water, making it the third highest light on the coast of Maine. The highest is Sequin Island Light at 180 feet, followed by Boon Island Light off York, Maine, at 137 feet. Petit Manan Light is probably one of the first prefabricated structures on the Maine seacoast. It was built in Trenton, Maine, where all the blocks of granite were numbered then disassembled, transported and erected once again at its final site on Petit Manan Island.

As one of the most important lights on the coast, it boasted a 2nd order lens, having an inside diameter of four and a half feet. Second order lights mark the secondary points or headlands along the seacoast and entrances to bays and sounds. This particular lens, over 10 feet in height and composed of 2,000 pounds of curved glass panels, may presently be seen on display at the Shore Village Museum in Rockland. The museum, which features a vast collection of Maine lighthouse items, acquired the lens when the tower was automated in 1970. You'll admire the quality of workmanship and the beauty of this lens. To reproduce such a thing today has been estimated to cost over 6 million dollars. The Petit Manan Light, under its present automated state, has as its characteristic one flash every 10 seconds. The original light had a unique characteristic that was both a fixed **and** flashing light. The lamp burned continuously, but there was a panel within that rotated, and as a clear portion passed in front of the lamp, it created a flash of greater intensity.

## Bird Life

Petit Manan and Green Islands are also known for their extensive colonies of Arctic, Common and Roseate terns. At one time this area was the nesting site of the largest tern colonies along the Maine coast. Historical accounts as far back as 1885 mention the vast numbers of these birds. They are easily identified, with their slender bodies, narrow wings and long forked tails.

With the recent, rapid increase in gull population, competition for nesting sites has increased sharply, much to the detriment of the terns. In addition, the gulls raid the tern's nests, killing and eating the young chicks. To try to offset the marked decline in number of terns, a gull/tern management program has been initiated. Under the auspices of the U.S. Fish and Wildlife Service, with the help of the Maine Audubon Society, the National Audubon Society, and The College of the Atlantic, a plan of gull avicide has begun. The gulls are fed a poisoned bread which appears not to affect the other species of birds. It will take several years to determine if this action is a success and the terns will recolonize here. The program is being carefully monitored. If it is successful, it might provide a chance for nesting sites for eider ducks and puffins, who have recently been seen approaching the area, not to mention the possibility of such a program at other important bird nesting sites, e.g., Machias Seal Island or Matinicus Rock.

Isleford Harbor, Little Cranberry Island, Chapter 12

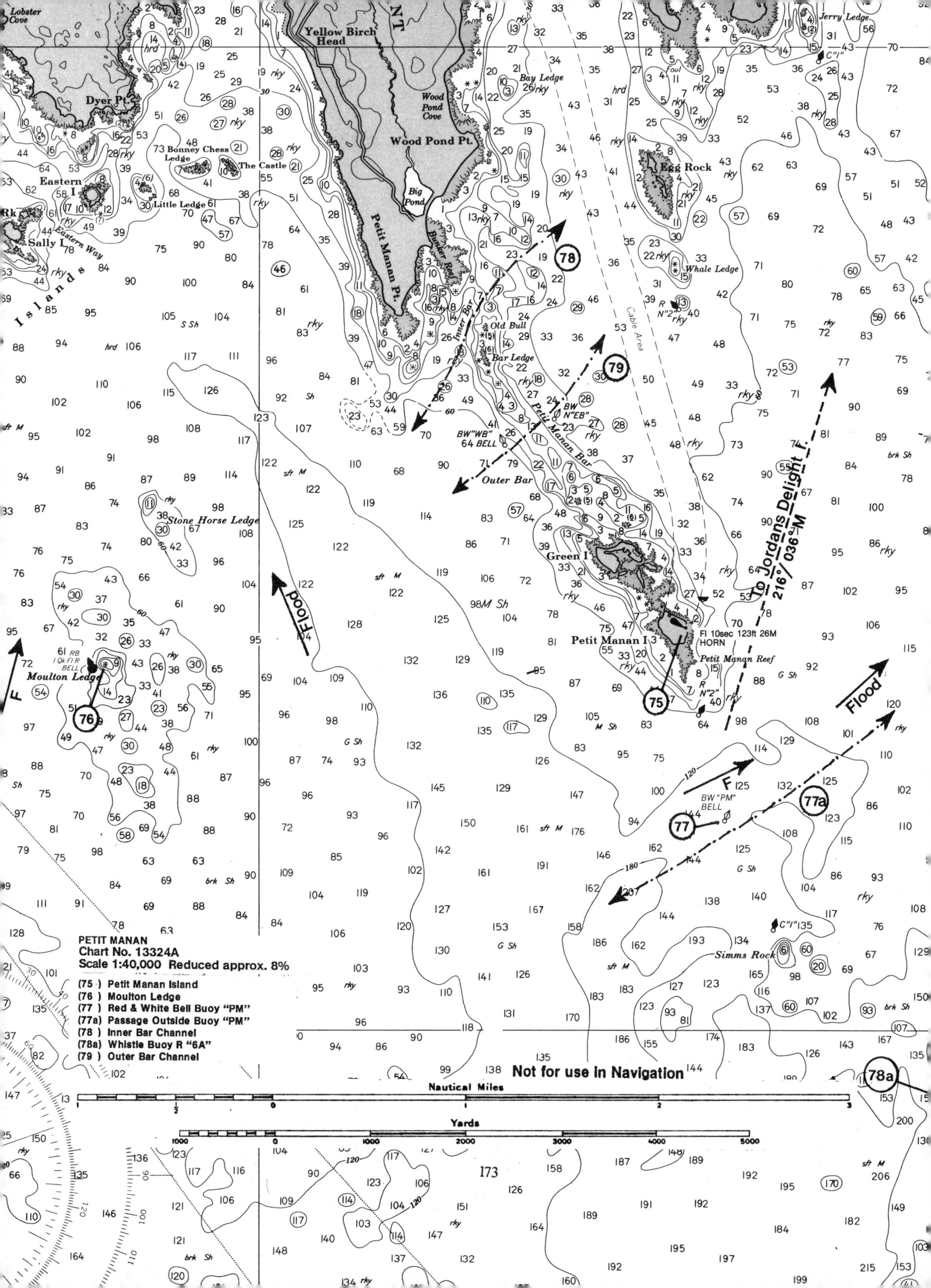
Lobster Cove
Yellow Birch Head
Jerry Ledge
Dyer Pt.
Wood Pond Cove
Wood Pond Pt.
Bay Ledge
Bonney Chess Ledge
The Castle
Egg Rock
Eastern I
Little Ledge
Big Pond
Sally I.
Eastern Way
Islands
Petit Manan Pt.
Bunker Reef
Whale Ledge
Inner Bar
Old Bull
Bar Ledge
Cable Area
BW "WB" 64 BELL
BW N"EB"
Petit Manan Bar
Outer Bar
Stone Horse Ledge
Green I
Flood
To Jordans Delight I.
216°/ 036° M
Petit Manan I
Fl 10sec 123ft 26M HORN
Petit Manan Reef
Moulton Ledge
RB 1 Qk Fl R BELL
F
BW "PM" BELL
Simms Rock
PETIT MANAN
Chart No. 13324A
Scale 1:40,000 Reduced approx. 8%
(75) Petit Manan Island
(76) Moulton Ledge
(77) Red & White Bell Buoy "PM"
(77a) Passage Outside Buoy "PM"
(78) Inner Bar Channel
(78a) Whistle Buoy R "6A"
(79) Outer Bar Channel
Not for use in Navigation
Nautical Miles
Yards

# CHAPTER 15

## NARRAGUAGUS BAY TO JONESPORT

### NARRAGUAGUS BAY—CHART NO. 13324B

#### Approaches

The lower half of Narraguagus Bay is easy to navigate, with deep water, easily recognizable landmarks and buoyed dangers. However, the upper portion of the Bay shallows extensively and is totally unmarked except for the dredged channel to the town of Millbridge (79). At night or in dense fog it is considerably more difficult as there is only a single buoy with light or sound, bell "1" (80), east of Pond Island.

Jordans Delight (81) is an easy landmark from any direction. This rocky grass covered island, 94 feet high, has very steep sides and is completely treeless. It can be approached on a compass course of 036 degrees Magnetic from the buoys south of Petit Manan Island (chart no. 13324A in Chapter 14).

Shipstern Island (82), on the east side of Narraguagus Bay, is also high and craggy, but with a dense crown of trees on top. The appearance of the rocky bluffs on the south end give the island its name, for as you approach it looks like a stern end of a Spanish Galleon. The stratified layers of rock have deep crevices, creating alternating color bands of red, white, brown and black. Approaching Narraguagus Bay from the east, Shipstern Island bears 300 degrees Magnetic (reciprocal 120 degrees) from the Nash Island Light (83) (chart no. 13324C Pleasant Bay and Cape Split this chapter).

Shipstern Island and Flint Island to the east are under the jurisdiction of the Nature Conservancy. These islands are the nesting site of a pair of bald eagles, at least one pair of osprey and for the Leach's Petrel. In good weather (no seas) you can anchor off the northeast shore of 170 acre Flint Island. Landing is permitted, the best areas being on shingle beaches on the west shore and in the bight on the south shore. Most of Flint Island is covered with spruce and fir. There are two areas of open fields and several alder swamps. Most of Flint Island's shore is steep cliffs, a lavender grey color that resembles flint. Seals haul out on the ledges off the north and east shores.

#### Trafton Island—Chart No. 13324B

An excellent anchorage is found in the bight on the northwest side of Trafton Island (84). This large, attractive island is privately owned and the owners are usually on the island during the summer. Please respect their privacy and property rights. It's a pleasant, intermediate point to stay the night instead of going into Cape Split, or for waiting out fair weather and tide before crossing Petit Manan Bar.

Approach to the anchorage is most easily made by going up the east side of the island and anchoring in 8-10 feet depth when you are abeam of the patch of ledge on the island's west side. The bottom is mud with good holding quality, but it is not a desirable anchorage if any heavy weather is expected from the north. Although this is a relatively isolated part of Maine's coast, don't expect complete seclusion here, for Trafton Island, like Roque Island farther east, has been popularized as one of the most beautiful islands on this part of the coast.

#### Millbridge—Chart No. 13324B

The village of Millbridge (79) at the head of Narraguagus Bay is reached by way of a 2.75 nautical miles long dredged channel. It is visited by only 3 to 4 yachts a summer as it is out of the way. The channel is clearly marked and well buoyed all the way to the head of navigation where two bridges cross the river. Take care to keep clear of the ruins of several piers and of a wreck (85) on the west side of the channel between C "13" and C "15". Immediately before the bridge, on the east shore, is a public wharf and float (86) with a free concrete launching ramp north of it. The outer face of the wharf has 8 feet depth at low tide. The two floats on the far side of the wharf can be used as dinghy floats and for boat tie-up, but there is only 4 feet depth here at low tide. Before you reach the last green buoy in the channel, an area has been dredged out for anchorage (87). No fuel or water is available at the dock.

Within town, there are grocery stores, a drug store and restaurants. Millbridge boasts the only movie house between Bar Harbor and Calais.

#### Harrington Bay—Chart No. 13324B

Entrance to Harrington Bay is marked by buoys west of Dyer Island through Dyer Narrows, as well as east of the island through Strout Island Narrows. But contrary to what you might expect, when heading up the bay from Trafton Island, buoys C "5" and C "3" are to be kept to your starboard. C "7", marking the 4 foot spot, can be left to port. Within the bay there are two unmarked ledges, Dry Ledge, and Halftide Ledge. The former is always visible, and can be used to help locate the position of Halftide Ledge when it is submerged. With a mean tide range of 11-12 feet, you can easily sail up into Harrington River and Mill River, at the head of Harrington Bay, when there is half tide or better. At low

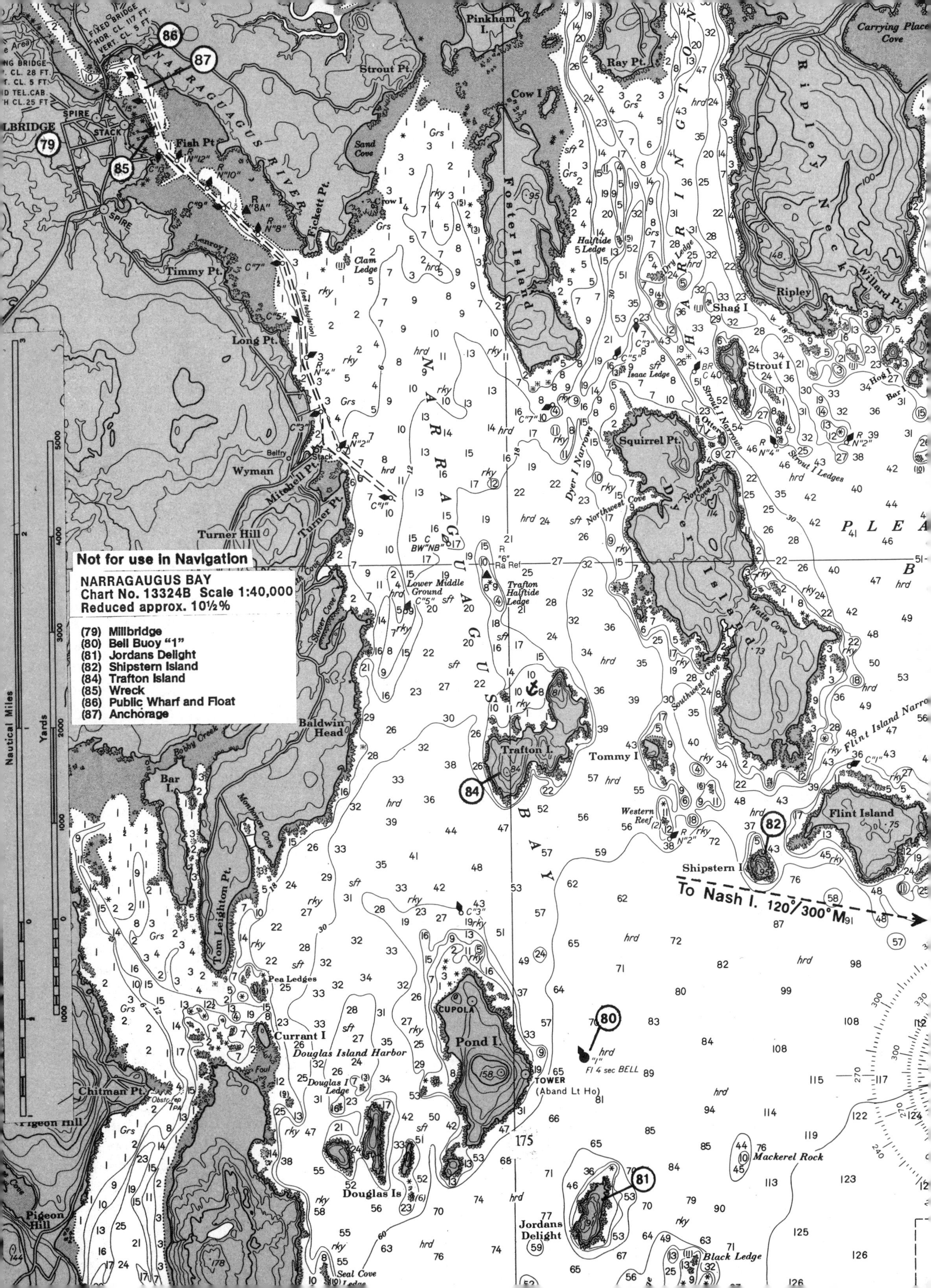
Not for use in Navigation
NARRAGAUGUS BAY
Chart No. 13324B Scale 1:40,000
Reduced approx. 10½%
(79) Millbridge
(80) Bell Buoy "1"
(81) Jordans Delight
(82) Shipstern Island
(84) Trafton Island
(85) Wreck
(86) Public Wharf and Float
(87) Anchorage
Nautical Miles
Yards
NARRAGUAGUS RIVER
NARRAGUAGUS BAY
HARRINGTON
Ripley Neck
Foster Island
Dyer Island
Pinkham I.
Ray Pt.
Carrying Place Cove
Strout Pt.
Cow I
Sand Cove
Fickett Pt.
Crow I
Fish Pt
Timmy Pt.
Long Pt.
Wyman
Mitchell Pt.
Turner Pt.
Turner Hill
Clam Ledge
Halftide Ledge
Dry Ledge
Shag I
Ripley
Willard Pt.
Strout I
Hog I
Bar I
Isaac Ledge
Strout I Narrows
Strout I Ledges
Otter I
Squirrel Pt.
Dyer I Narrows
Northwest Cove
Northeast Cove
Watts Cove
Southwest Cove
Lower Middle Ground
Trafton Halftide Ledge
Trafton I.
Tommy I
Western Reef
Shipstern I
Flint Island
Flint Island Narrows
To Nash I. 120°/300°M
Baldwin Head
Bobby Creek
Bar I.
Tom Leighton Pt.
Pea Ledges
Currant I
Douglas Island Harbor
Douglas I Ledge
Douglas Is
Chitman Pt.
Pigeon Hill
Pond I.
CUPOLA
TOWER
(Aband Lt Ho)
Fl 4 sec BELL
Mackerel Rock
Jordans Delight
Black Ledge
Seal Cove Ledge
SPIRE
STACK
Belfry
FIXED BRIDGE
HOR. CL. 117 FT.
VERT. CL. 5 FT.

tide, the channels are nothing more than an eel-rut. If you run aground, the bottom is mud, and with a short wait, you will be lifted out by the tide.

At the mouth of Flat Bay, almost opposite Oak Point, there are privately-set brush stakes to mark the channel for entering Mill River. You have to look sharply for them, since they are very slender. Near the top of most of them an empty plastic container is tied to mark their position when the stake is covered by high water. In all, there are about 8, stretching pretty much in an east/west line. They are to be kept **close** to your starboard side. Once past Oak Point, the markers end.

At this point, you can see up Mill River to a row of moorings. On the shore opposite Oak Point, a pile of rocks juts out into the entrance. A solitary pole marks this. You have to head for these rocks, and when slightly beyond their outermost limit, make a switch-back turn into the river. Most of the moorings are owned by George Arey of the Petit Manan Yacht Club, and he could probably fix you up with one. From the floating pontoon dock on the western shore is a path to his house. Though the chart says only 3-4 feet in the channel, there is almost always 6-7 feet depth.

## PLEASANT BAY—CHART NO. 13324C

Refer also to folded chart inside rear cover.

Pleasant Bay is pleasing in appearance with little navigation difficulty during daylight and clear weather. All dangers are well marked by buoys, but none are lighted. Do not cruise here at night. There are no harbors offering secure protection, but adequate anchorage may be obtained in the lee of several islands in the Bay.

### Ports Harbor

Ports Harbor (88), on the east shore, is also a good anchorage if the weather is calm and settled. Do not proceed east of the eastern end of John White Island (89) as Ports Harbor becomes quite shallow.

### Upper Birch Island

In the northwest corner of chart no. 13324C, you'll see Birch Islands. The northernmost of the two, 27-acre Upper Birch Island is a Preserve of The Nature Conservancy. Landing is not permitted from February 15 to August 15. This is to protect the substantial great blue heron rookery, about 80 nests in 60 trees. Blue herons are Maine's largest wading birds. Bald eagles also nest on Upper Birch Island. The best landing is on the southeast shore where the land slopes more gradually than the rest of the island's steep ledges. You can cruise close enough to see the birds without landing. Harbor seals haul out on the steep ledges surrounding most of the island.

### Pleasant River

Pleasant River, which empties into Pleasant Bay, has a navigable channel buoyed as far as the town of Addison (90), about 5.0 miles above the mouth of the river. Once within the river you are committed to staying in the channel, for at low tide it dries out on both sides to extensive mud flats fringed with dense thickets of alder. Shoaling has occured in places within the channel and 4 feet should be considered the maximum draft to safely carry as far as Addison. Travel beyond this is prevented by the highway fixed bridge with its vertical clearance of 5 feet. There is a free asphalt launching ramp at the Addison Town Pier, on the east shore of Pleasant River, at Addison.

The charts in this chapter do not show the upper reaches of Pleasant Bay and the rivers that flow into it. These are shown on the big folded chart in the envelope inside the rear cover.

## EASTERN HARBOR (CAPE SPLIT HARBOR) CHART NO. 13324C

Eastern Harbor (91), locally referred to as Cape Split Harbor, is much frequented by cruising boats headed downeast. Approach and entry are easy in all weather and it offers secure protection with scenic surroundings. This is strictly a fishing community, little changed over the years.

Approaching Cape Split from the west, the island of Jordans Delight (81) (chart no. 13324B, this chapter) is immediately recognizable. It rises very steeply out of the water, and with its bold rocky cliffs makes a good landmark. Both Big Nash Island (92) and adjacent Nash Island (93) are low and grassy, lacking any trees. Nash Island is extremely low and not easily seen from a great distance. However the lighthouse on it is highly visible, making identification of the island easy. This light tower no longer is operational, its function being taken by the nearby whistle buoy. A black and white lighted whistle buoy 'NI" (94) is 0.5 mile west of Nash Island.

To enter the harbor, Pot Rock (95) and Ladle Ledges (96) may be passed east or west. If you come from the south, east of Ladle Ledges, make sure your final approach to the entrance is less than 200 degrees Magnetic to avoid the solitary rock east of Ladle Ledges. Pot Rock (95) is only 6 feet high and devoid of any vegetation. Approached from the south, it is dome-shaped on the east side, with a long, low handle-like ledge off the the west. Ladle Ledges is a much higher domed, symmetrical rock 78 feet high and is grass covered.

At the harbor entrance, a pair of buoys, N"2" and C"1", mark the ledge that extends from Marsh Island on the east side and the edge of the deep water channel on the west side. Farther north, N"4" and C"3" mark the limits of the ledges. North of the last black can, before you reach the moored boats, there is a fish weir on the west side.

Within the harbor, the fleet of lobster boats is moored in a line in mid-channel opposite the wharf (97). There is a guest mooring here, courtesy of the Petit Manan Yacht Club. On the outside face of the wharf, where lobsters are landed, there is 4 feet of water at low tide. Immediately north of the wharf is a float with a ramp, where you may tie your dinghy. Anchorage with

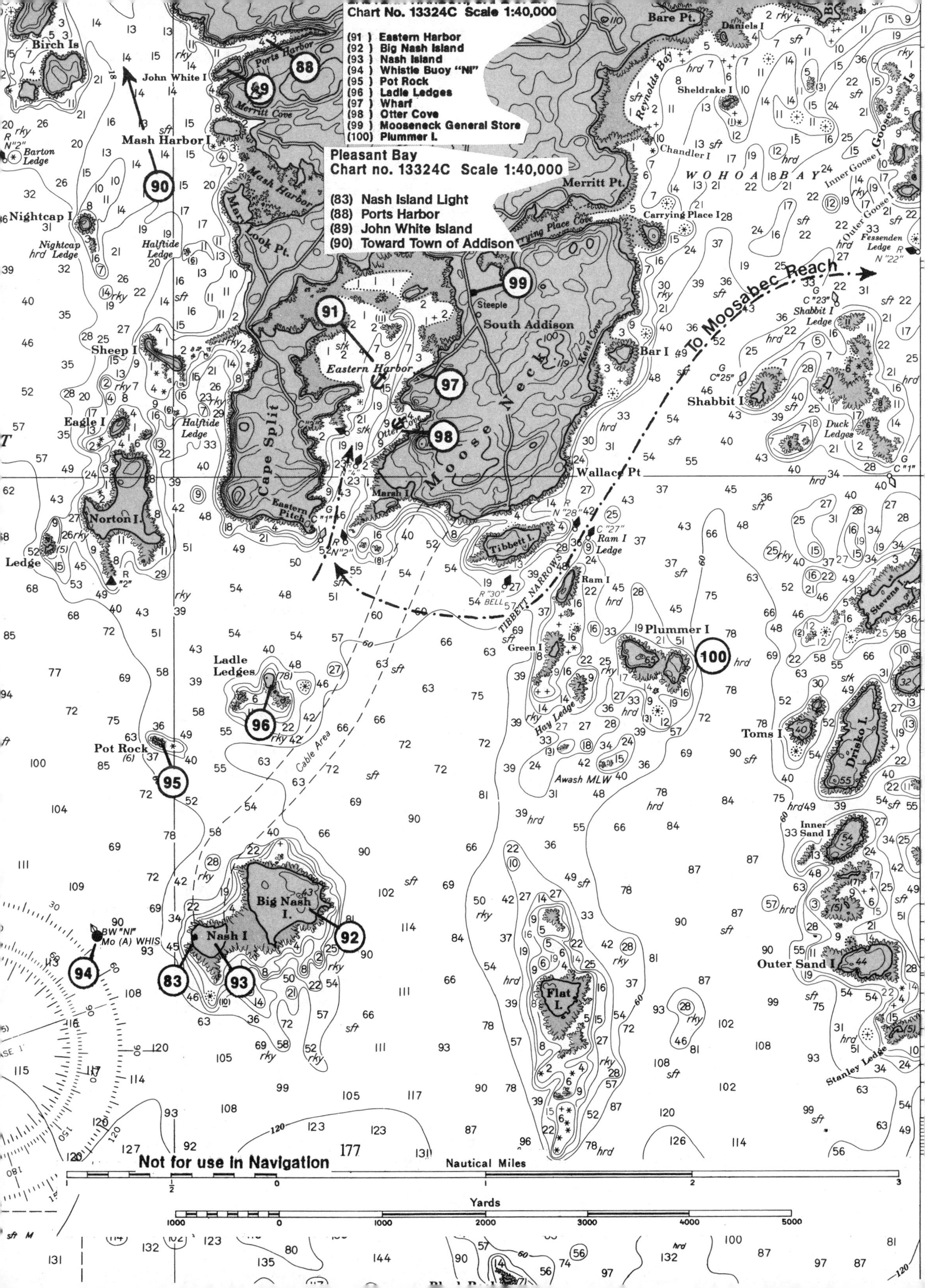
Chart No. 13324C Scale 1:40,000
(91) Eastern Harbor
(92) Big Nash Island
(93) Nash Island
(94) Whistle Buoy "NI"
(95) Pot Rock
(96) Ladle Ledges
(97) Wharf
(98) Otter Cove
(99) Mooseneck General Store
(100) Plummer I.
Pleasant Bay
Chart no. 13324C Scale 1:40,000
(83) Nash Island Light
(88) Ports Harbor
(89) John White Island
(90) Toward Town of Addison
Birch Is
John White I
Ports Harbor
Merritt Cove
Mash Harbor I
Barton Ledge
Nightcap I
Nightcap Ledge
Halftide Ledge
Mark Look Pt.
Mash Harbor
Sheep I
Eagle I
Halftide Ledge
Norton I.
Ledge
Cape Split
Eastern Pitch
Eastern Harbor
Otter Cove
Marsh I
South Addison
Steeple
Moose Neck
Kent Cove
Carrying Place Cove
Merritt Pt.
Bare Pt.
Daniels I
Reynolds Bay
Sheldrake I
Chandler I
WOHOA BAY
Inner Goose I
Outer Goose I
Goose Is
Carrying Place I
Fessenden Ledge
To Moosabec Reach
Shabbit I Ledge
Bar I
Shabbit I
Duck Ledges
Wallace Pt
Tibbett I.
Ram I Ledge
Ram I
TIBBETT NARROWS
BELL
Green I
Plummer I
Hay Ledge
Awash MLW
Stevens I
Toms I
Drisko I.
Inner Sand I
Outer Sand I
Stanley Ledge
Ladle Ledges
Pot Rock
Cable Area
Big Nash I.
Nash I
BW "NI" Mo (A) WHIS
Flat I.
Not for use in Navigation
Nautical Miles
Yards

good holding ground is west of the fleet of lobster boats. Do not proceed much beyond the moored boats as the harbor shallows rapidly, with rocky ledges and mud-flats uncovering at low water. Another good anchorage spot is in Otter Cove (98) on the east side of the harbor beyond N"4". In both locations there is sufficient depth and there is room to swing comfortably on an anchor.

Neither fuel nor water is available at Cape Split, but provisions may be obtained at Mooseneck General Store (99). Just a three minute walk toward the head of the harbor, this small, but well supplied store can take care of most of your needs, including fresh meat and cold beer. Their hours are from 6:00 a.m. to 8:00 p.m., Monday through Saturday, and 8:00 a.m. to 6:00 p.m. on Sunday. Eastern Harbor and South Addison have slowed down.

Plummer Island (100), southeast of Cape Split and Tibbett Narrows, is actually two islands—West Plummer and East Plummer Island, connected by a mud and gravel bar at low tide. 10-acre East Plummer Island is a Preserve of the Nature Conservancy. No landing is permitted as American eagles have nested there since the mid-50's.

## CROWLEY ISLAND (CHART NO. 13325, 13326)

Crowley Island, above the western end of Moosabec Reach, is bounded on the west by West River, and on the east by Indian River. The scenery is beautiful, but as with so much of this part of the coast, sailing will be dependent on the state of the tide. Although the chart doesn't show it, there is a channel at the northern end of the island, allowing complete circumnavigation at high tide. At one time, there was a bridge from the mainland over to Crowley Island. It was washed away. However, if you are going to attempt to go through—approach cautiously. Some of the residents have petitioned to have the bridge rebuilt. Hard to tell if this will come to pass, or how long it will take before it is actually constructed.

## EASTERN BAY AND MOOSABEC REACH
### CHART NOS. 13325, 13326, SKETCH CHART

### Routes

Proceeding along the coast between Cape Split and Cutler, you can choose between a sheltered inside route through Moosabec Reach (1) or (2) going south of Great Wass Island, Steele Harbor Island and Head Harbor Island. The inner route, well buoyed for all dangers, is readily followed in good weather and clear visibility. But unless you are familiar with the passage, it should not be attempted at night because the only lighted buoys are at each end of The Reach. Throughout the entire length of Tibbett Narrows and Moosabec Reach, buoys are marked for travel from **east** to **west**. Another factor in deciding which route to take is the fixed bridge (4) crossing Moosabec Reach between Jonesport and Beals Island. It has a vertical clearance of 39 feet. Mean low tide gives you an extra 11.5 feet for getting under the bridge.

The outside passage is easy under all conditions. A lighted bell buoy, R"6", marks Seahorse Rock (5) at the west end of this group of islands. Stay south of R "6." Seahorse Rock uncovers at 5 feet. The tidal current parallels the edge of the seaward shore of these islands, ebb to the southwest and flood to northeast. However, on the ebb tide, as the current sweeps past Seahorse Rock and nearby Egg Rock, it runs quite strongly, and takes a marked turn towards the north, setting into Western Bay.

You will probably find, as I invariably have, that there is no way of passing this mass of Great Wass Island and Head Harbor Island without having the fog suddenly clamp down on you. It occurs swiftly and with great density, but it need be little cause for concern for you can safely maintain your course by following the 20 fathom curve on the depth sounder. Land may not be seen, and breakers will be heard crashing on the bold shore frighteningly close, but you will be safe from all ledges and dangers.

Following the 10 fathom curve provides the same security, but the 20 fathom line prevents making an unwarranted excursion into Popplestone Cove (6), Cape Cove (7) or Mud Hole Channel (8). Following the 20 fathom curve, you will be brought directly opposite Moose Peak Light on Mistake Island (9) and into the channel entrance of Main Channel Way (10). From here, even in the densest fog, there will be no problem feeling your way into Mistake Harbor. Alternately, with the least amount of visibility, safe anchorage may be reached in The Cows Yard (11) of Head Harbor.

A passage between Head Harbor Island and Great Wass Island allows you to reach Jonesport via Eastern Bay (12) without having to go all the way around to either end of Mossabec Reach. This route is buoyed through Eastern Bay (12) and buoyed in a dredged channel, called Pig Island Gut Channel (13), south of Pig Island. Using this channel should **only** be attempted in fair weather with excellent visibility. There are many unmarked ledges and rocks along the way in Eastern Bay. It is important to be sure you are following in a straight line from buoy to buoy and that the erratic currents have not swept you off course. This is particularly critical in the area (14) half-way between C"5" and N"2". At C"5" the passage divides into a western branch (Pig Island Gut) (13) and an eastern branch (Sheep Island Passage) (15). Both bring you into Moosabec Reach. Refer to our Sketch Chart, and both chart nos. 13326 and 13325.

The buoys along Pig Island Gut Channel are set directly along the edge of the channel, leaving no margin for error in navigation. If you wander but a few feet off course, you will be aground. One buoy in particular, N "10" should be carefully watched. The channel is very narrow at this point. At low tide, the increased length of chain allows the buoy to be displaced too far to the

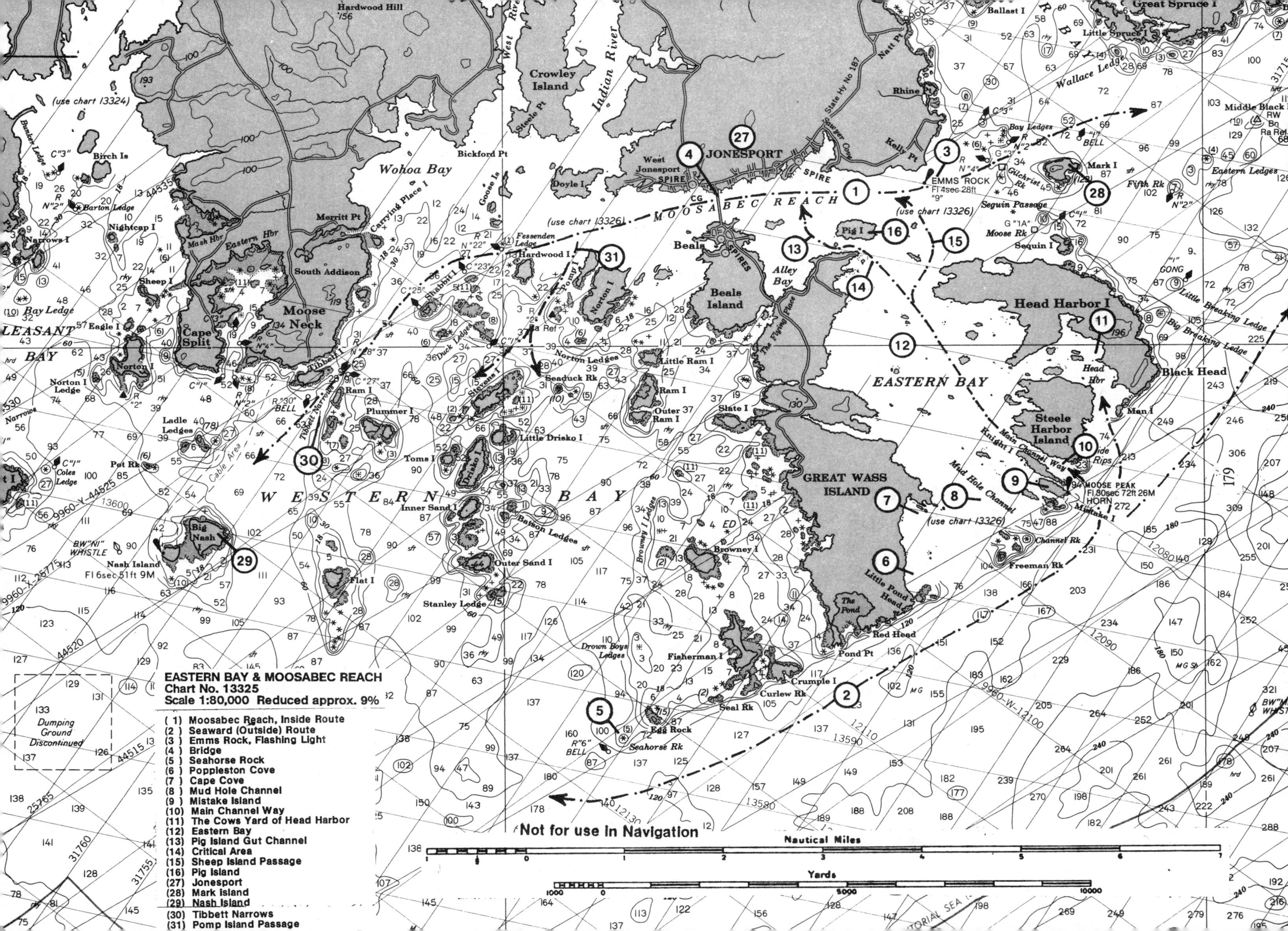
EASTERN BAY & MOOSABEC REACH
Chart No. 13325
Scale 1:80,000 Reduced approx. 9%
( 1 ) Moosabec Reach, Inside Route
( 2 ) Seaward (Outside) Route
( 3 ) Emms Rock, Flashing Light
( 4 ) Bridge
( 5 ) Seahorse Rock
( 6 ) Poppleston Cove
( 7 ) Cape Cove
( 8 ) Mud Hole Channel
( 9 ) Mistake Island
(10) Main Channel Way
(11) The Cows Yard of Head Harbor
(12) Eastern Bay
(13) Pig Island Gut Channel
(14) Critical Area
(15) Sheep Island Passage
(16) Pig Island
(27) Jonesport
(28) Mark Island
(29) Nash Island
(30) Tibbett Narrows
(31) Pomp Island Passage
Not for use in Navigation
Nautical Miles
Yards
Dumping Ground Discontinued
JONESPORT
West Jonesport
Beals
Beals Island
GREAT WASS ISLAND
Head Harbor I
Steele Harbor Island
EASTERN BAY
WESTERN BAY
MOOSABEC REACH
Wohoa Bay
Indian River
Crowley Island
Moose Neck
South Addison
Cape Split
Big Nash I
Nash Island
Fl 6sec 51ft 9M
EMMS ROCK
Fl 4sec 28ft
MOOSE PEAK
Fl 30sec 72ft 26M
HORN
(use chart 13324)
(use chart 13326)

north, thus placing the rocks directly into the middle of the channel. The *Local Notice to Mariners* gives the following information about the channel. The controlling depth from buoy N "2" to C "3" is 5.1 feet; from C "3" to N "8", 5.0 feet; from N "8" to N "12", 6.0 feet; and N "12" to N "14", 5.3 feet. Shoaling to 3.4 feet has occured at the southern limit of the channel near C "3", and to 2.7 feet at the southern end of the channel near N "12". There is a small anchorage basin south of Pig Island (16) which has a depth of 4.3 feet at low water. You may need tide help if you take this passage to Jonesport.

### MISTAKE HARBOR—CHART NO. 13326

The main entrance to Mistake Harbor is through Main Channel Way (10) between Knight Island (17) and Steele Harbor Island (18). In good weather, with care, it can alternately be entered by way of Mud Hole Channel (8). Tide rips may be present at both sides of the entrance to Main Channel Way, but they are not dangerous and should not present any problem. The harbor proper is between the northwest end of Knight Island and black buoy C "1". However, the water is deep and not completely out of the tide-way.

It is preferable to follow around to the west shore of Knight Island (17), giving the ledges on its northwest end a safe clearance. Anchor in water of 10-15 foot depth between Knight Island and Water Island. The bottom is mud and holding is excellent. In general, the holding ground is good, but there is some kelp, so be sure that your anchor is well set down into the mud, and not just tangled in weed. The ledge on the northwestern end of Knight Island has several patches of rock always exposed, so it is easy to determine the outermost edge. A smaller, isolated patch of ledge (19) is submerged at high tide, but there is an iron spike on it, about 12 inches high. Stay west of this ledge with its spike when entering to avoid anchoring in the cable area. In the northwestern part of the harbor are the remains of an old herring weir (20), with 8 very hefty poles about 6 inches in diameter which do not show until half-tide.

In this anchorage you will be completely surrounded and protected by long, granite ridges, which bare themselves like the giant spines of a slumbering dinosaur. In this rugged, beautiful setting, you will be overwhelmed with the profusion and diverse kinds of wildlife. On these apparently lifeless, granite ledges, hidden in the crevices and small patches of green, are an abundance of wildflowers, plants and edible berries. In season, wild blueberries, cranberries, raspberries and beach peas are available. Seals are found by the hundreds, sunning themselves on the ledges during the middle of the day. At night you can hear them snorting, barking, coughing and generally cavorting about. It's a wild and wonderful place, only a little over four miles from Jonesport.

Much of Great Wass Island (21) and all of Mistake Island (9) is a Nature Conservancy Preserve, except for the land around the light owned by the Coast Guard. These islands have many unique characteristics and unusual plant life. Thrust far out to sea, they are dominated by a cold climate of constant fog and salt-spray mist. The effect is an ecosystem of tundra and bog. Many of the plants that thrive here are subarctic and are at the southernmost edge of their range.

To help preserve and protect this unique archipelago as a single unit, the Maine Chapter of the Nature Conservancy has acquired additional property to be under its management. Land was received from the Maine Audobon Society and Maine Coast Heritage Trust. Besides the large acreage on Great Wass Island, plus that on Mistake and Crumple Islands, the Conservancy now administers Man, Outer Man, Little Hardwood, Mark and Black Islands. Conservation easements have also been obtained on Steele Harbor, Head Harbor and Sequin Islands, as well as the 4 islands of the Cow Yard Group.

Fortunately, the relative inaccessibility to these islands has allowed the ecological integrity of the group to remain intact. Many of the rare plant species are still to be found in their original habitat, undisturbed by the intrusion of human activities.

#### Great Wass Island

The Nature Conservancy's Great Wass Island Preserve covers 1,543 acres, including the west shore south of Three Falls Harbor, the east shore south of Mud Hole, and all the shore south to Red Head and Pond Point. Bridges and roads connect Jonesport with the Preserve parking lot near the northwest border.

Two trails lead from there to the east shore. The Mud Hole Trail generally follows the Mud Hole Shore to Mud Hole Point. This may be the closest point that the trail comes near the water, making it accessible by dinghy, but it is difficult leaving your boat here due to an ever-present undertow. Best to anchor in the Mud Hole (43b), row ashore there, and strike inland until you reach the footpath.

The Mud Hole is certainly as protected an anchorage as you could ever hope to find. You have to feel your way in carefully though. Near the entrance is an abandoned weir, the approximate position which I've placed on the chart (no. 13326). It is completely covered at high water. Once past this, hug the south shore of the harbor closely to avoid a patch of ledge sitting directly in the middle. Passing south of the ledge, proceed up the harbor to the pool with 16 feet of water. You will have to negotiate all this with a bit of tide in your favor to get over the 2 foot spot immediately beyond the ledge.

As an alternate anchorage, the Cape Shore of Cape Cove (7) is not too bad a place to lay in a southwester. In a strong southerly though, you might want to reconsider your position.

One of the most handsome spots on the entire island

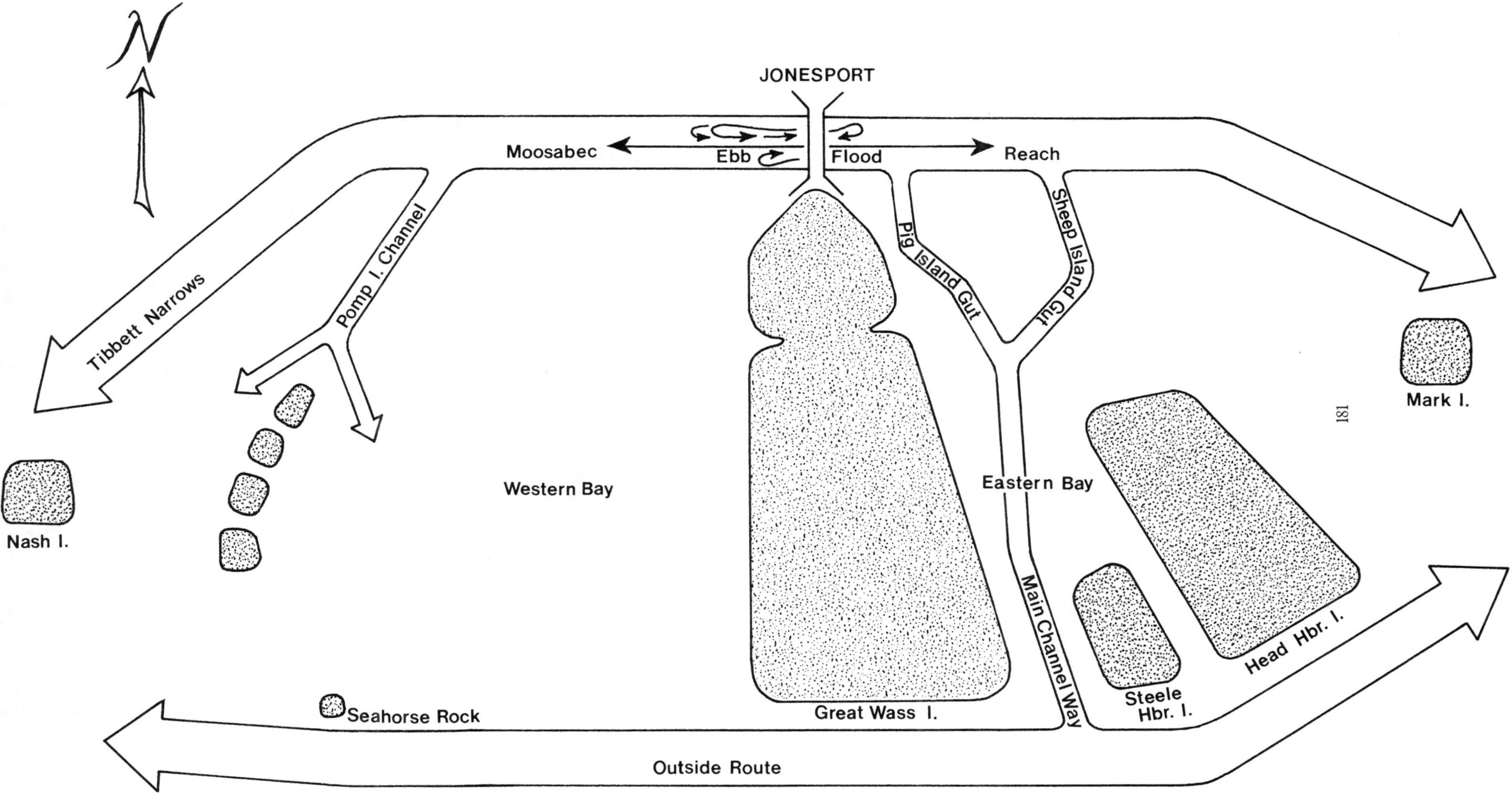


EASTERN BAY & MOOSABEC REACH
SKETCH CHART
Not for use In Navigation

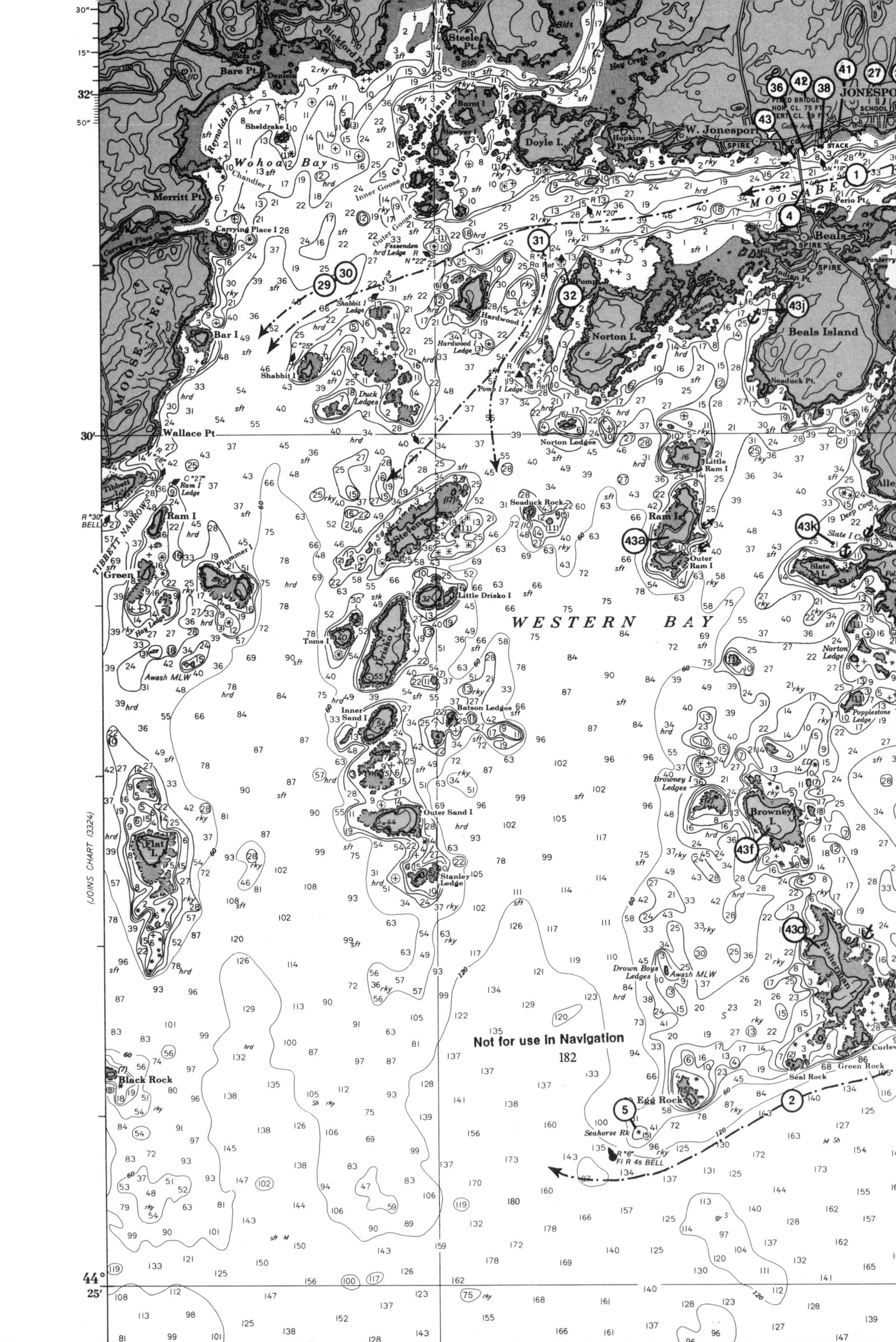

Bare Pt.
Daniels I
Bickford Pt
Steele Pt.
Hay Creek
Reynolds Bay
Sheldrake I
Wohoa Bay
Chandler I
Merritt Pt.
Carrying Place I
Carrying Place Cove
Inner Goose I
Outer Goose I
Goose Islands
Burnt I
Sawyer I
Doyle I.
Hopkins Gut
Hopkins Pt
W. Jonesport
JONESPORT
FIXED BRIDGE
HOR. CL. 75 FT
VERT. CL. 39 FT
SCHOOL
SPIRE
STACK
MOOSABEC
Perio Pt
Beals
Mill Pond
Indian Pt.
Cranberry Cove
Fessenden Ledge
Shabbit I Ledge
Shabbit I
Duck Ledges
Hardwood I
Hardwood I Ledge
Pomp I Ledge
Pomp I
Norton I.
Sheep I
Beals Island
Seaduck Pt.
MOOSE NECK
Bar I
Wallace Pt
Norton Ledges
Little Ram I
Tibbett I
TIBBETT NARROWS
Ram I Ledge
Ram I
Seaduck Rock
Outer Ram I
Deep Cove
Slate I Cove
Slate I.
Green I
Plummer I
Hay Ledge
Awash MLW
Steele I
Little Drisko I
Toms I
Drisko I.
WESTERN BAY
Norton Ledge
Popplestone Ledge
Inner Sand I
Batson Ledges
Outer Sand I
Stanley Ledge
Flat I.
Browney I Ledges
Browney I.
Fisherman I
(JOINS CHART 13324)
Drown Boys Ledges
Not for use in Navigation
Black Rock
Egg Rock
Seal Rock
Green Rock
Curlew
Seahorse Rk
R "6" Fl R 4s BELL

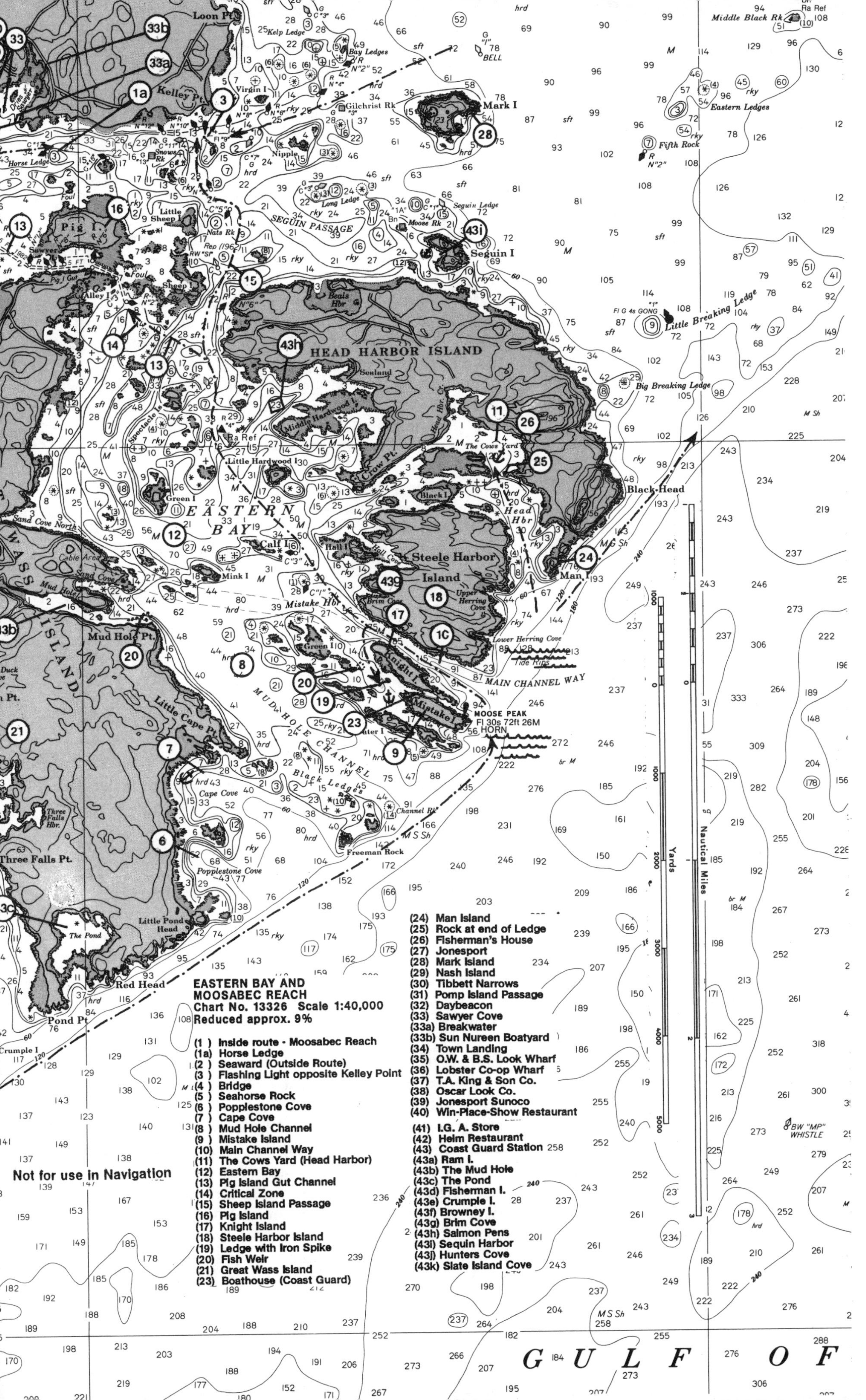
EASTERN BAY AND
MOOSABEC REACH
Chart No. 13326 Scale 1:40,000
Reduced approx. 9%
(1) Inside route - Moosabec Reach
(1a) Horse Ledge
(2) Seaward (Outside Route)
(3) Flashing Light opposite Kelley Point
(4) Bridge
(5) Seahorse Rock
(6) Popplestone Cove
(7) Cape Cove
(8) Mud Hole Channel
(9) Mistake Island
(10) Main Channel Way
(11) The Cows Yard (Head Harbor)
(12) Eastern Bay
(13) Pig Island Gut Channel
(14) Critical Zone
(15) Sheep Island Passage
(16) Pig Island
(17) Knight Island
(18) Steele Harbor Island
(19) Ledge with Iron Spike
(20) Fish Weir
(21) Great Wass Island
(23) Boathouse (Coast Guard)
(24) Man Island
(25) Rock at end of Ledge
(26) Fisherman's House
(27) Jonesport
(28) Mark Island
(29) Nash Island
(30) Tibbett Narrows
(31) Pomp Island Passage
(32) Daybeacon
(33) Sawyer Cove
(33a) Breakwater
(33b) Sun Nureen Boatyard
(34) Town Landing
(35) O.W. & B.S. Look Wharf
(36) Lobster Co-op Wharf
(37) T.A. King & Son Co.
(38) Oscar Look Co.
(39) Jonesport Sunoco
(40) Win-Place-Show Restaurant
(41) I.G. A. Store
(42) Helm Restaurant
(43) Coast Guard Station
(43a) Ram I.
(43b) The Mud Hole
(43c) The Pond
(43d) Fisherman I.
(43e) Crumple I.
(43f) Browney I.
(43g) Brim Cove
(43h) Salmon Pens
(43i) Sequin Harbor
(43j) Hunters Cove
(43k) Slate Island Cove
Not for use in Navigation
HEAD HARBOR ISLAND
EASTERN BAY
SEGUIN PASSAGE
MUD HOLE CHANNEL
MAIN CHANNEL WAY
MOOSE PEAK
Fl 30s 72ft 26M
HORN
Steele Harbor Island
Loon Pt
Kelley Pt
Mark I
Seguin I
Pig I
Sheep I
Green I
Calf I
Mink I
Knight I
Mistake I
Man I
Black Head
Little Breaking Ledge
Big Breaking Ledge
Eastern Ledges
Fifth Rock
Middle Black Rk
Mud Hole Pt
Little Cape Pt
Cape Cove
Popplestone Cove
Three Falls Pt
Little Pond Head
Red Head
Pond Pt
Freeman Rock
Black Ledges
Yards
Nautical Miles
G U L F O F

is down at the southernmost end, near The Pond (43c). Only small, shallow draft boats should attempt to enter here. At the top of the tide, there is about 4 feet of water over the bar stretching across the entrance. Once within, approximately 4 feet of water remains at low tide—with the best spot over toward the eastern side. Once you are in, you needn't worry about dragging anchor, for you are completely protected and the bottom is very soft mud.

The Cape Cove Trail comes out south of Little Cape Point, near where the (7) is on our chart no. 13326. The Mud Hole Trail winds through a white birch forest. The Cape Cove Trail takes you through spruce and fir forests, has an overlook of a bog, passes through ledge with jack pines, and through a swamp. Both trails are worth hiking.

It is possible to walk along the shore to connect the east ends of the two trails, but this is slippery going. No trails lead south. You'd have to hike along the shore to Red Head.

A large population of deer is present on Great Wass Island. Osprey nest there, as do Lincoln sparrows, spruce grouse and boreal chickadees. Bald eagles make frequent visits, although they do not nest there. On the tidal marshes and mud flats, you will see great blue herons and shore-birds feeding.

### Mistake Island

On Mistake Island, all the typical plants of a peat bog are found in the tangled mat of sphagnum moss and accumulation of peat. Ospreys, bald eagles, great blue herons, as well as many species of shore birds are sure to be seen.

Access to Mistake Island is best made by tying the dinghy at the boathouse (23) at the northwestern end of the island. From there, a raised board-walk runs the full length of the island to the light tower. This not only makes it easier to explore the island, but prevents the plants from accidently being stepped on. Stay on the boardwalk or explore along the rocky shore, to protect the fragile plants.

The light is automated now, and the lightkeeper's house has been gone since 1982, but the importance of Moose Peak Light is certainly evidenced by its operation on the average of 1600 hours per year in heavy fog. July and August are the worst months with an average of 276 and 234 hours of operation.

## HEAD HARBOR—CHART NO. 13326

Enter Head Harbor by keeping midway between Steel Harbor Island (18) and Man Island (24) at the south end of Head Harbor Island. The harbor is rather open and exposed, but a most secure and attractive anchorage is in its inner portion, called The Cows Yard (11). Although there are a number of unmarked rocks, passage between them is not as difficult as it may look. They are all fairly close to the shore (except one northwest of the 9 foot spot) and are easily avoided. After gaining entrance to Head Harbor, where the water shallows from 30 to 14 feet, a course heading of 360 degrees Magnetic will bring you safely into The Cows Yard. At the constriction, the long ledge east of the narrow opening has large rock (25) at its outermost end, visible at all states of tide. Be sure that you stay west of this rock. The best anchorage is on the west side near the two islands, where the water is deeper.

The bottom is mud and holding is good, but beware of several patches of kelp. Use a heavy anchor and make sure it is well set and not just tangled in kelp. This harbor has all the elements of charm and beauty to hold your attention. There are high, rocky shores to explore, tree covered islands and tremendous views in all directions are attained from the heights of the larger islands. In contrast, there are also green meadows and abundant birdlife. The security of this anchorage is matched by a sense of tranquility and privacy. Seldom will there be more than one or two other boats here and there are only two dwellings on shore. One of these is hidden from view from the water. The other, seldom occupied, is a fisherman's small house (26) on the east shore of the harbor.

No provisions are available on any of the sourrounding islands, but it is possible to replenish a supply of fresh water from a spring behind the house on the east shore. This is near a small clump of birch, about 200 feet up the hill behind the house. Perhaps you may be as fortunate as we were during our visit here to be able to purchase freshly caught fish or lobster from one of the local fishing boats that use the harbor at times.

## OTHER ANCHORAGES—CHART NO. 13326

Changes have occured in this once-isolated group of islands. Whereas previously you would have found yourself to be the only boat in Mistake Harbor or the Cow Yard, now it is not uncommon to find rafts of 8-10 boats. The largest, most accessible harbors which have already been described, those providing all-weather protection, are the first to fill up. But there are many other anchorages, mostly in the lee of islands, or in smaller coves, where you can be secure during normal, settled, summer weather and find the peace and quiet with which to enjoy this unique and fascinating variety of wildlife.

### Ram Island

Ram Island (43a), in Western Bay, may seem too exposed to be of any value as an anchorage. However, the string of islands that practically encircles it keeps out most of the heavy weather. You may anchor either north or south of Lynn's Ledge—that long line of ledge that sticks out from the southeast corner of the island. With its fine, sand beaches and saltwater pond, it is a pleasant island to explore on foot.

Outer Ram Island, immediately south of Ram Island, contains a jumble of square, granite blocks. This bespeaks of one-time quarry operations here, yet local residents don't recollect any. In the center is a pretty, freshwater pond. You will want to take your dinghy and poke around in Ram Island Gut (that separates the two islands) where there is great clam digging.

### Anchorages Off Fisherman Island and Crumple Island

The lee of Fisherman Island (43d) or Crumple Island (43e) serves as a good anchorage in a southwester, although the closer you are to the southern end, the more of a swell you are likely to encounter. Fisherman I. is treeless and mostly marsh, but what it does have is a great deal of Baked-apple Berry (Rubus chamaemorous), an Arctic species common to Labrador and found in Maine only in certain coastal bogs of Washington and Hancock counties. Cobble beaches and an extensive amount of driftwood all along the shore, makes Crumple Island an interesting anchorage.

•

Forget about Browney Island (43f), for even though it has a pretty beach on the north side, a shipwreck and lots of driftwood, it is pretty hard to lay anywhere around it.

### Brim Cove

Brim Cove (43g), on Steele Harbor Island, doesn't look very large on the chart, but there is enough room for a couple of boats and is a pretty place to anchor.

•

Occasionally, yachts formerly anchored in the cove on the northwest side of Head Harbor Island, just above Middle Hardwood Island, but this is increasingly difficult to do now because of the salmon-raising pens (43h) which are positioned in the 23 foot spot.

### Other Anchorages

Sequin Harbor (43i), Hunter's Cove (43j) and Slate Island Cove (43k) are all potential anchorages. This is by no means an exhaustive list of all the possibilities for anchoring.

However, a word of caution. The tide runs strong and erratically through this complex arrangement of islands and channels. Fog is frequent and dense, and there are literally thousands of unmarked ledges and rocks. It is an area to be explored with prudence, in settled weather and definitely with good visibility. You'll be rewarded for your effort!

## MOOSABEC REACH
## CHART NOS. 13325,13326

See information on Moosabec Reach earlier in this chapter under Eastern Bay and Moosabec Reach.

The approach to Jonesport (27) through Moosabec Reach is well buoyed along the entire length. With good visibility and the tidal current in your favor, there are no problems. From the east, the prominent mark for entrance is Mark Island (28), 123 feet high and heavily wooded. A bell buoy is a quarter of a mile northwest of it. From the west, the guide for entrance is Nash Island (29) with its light tower (Fl 6 sec). It has a whistle buoy, labeled "NI" a quarter mile to the west. From Nash Island, the course is through Tibbett Narrows (30), off Moose Neck, and thence eastward through The Reach. A less frequently used channel between Hardwood Island and Pomp Island is marked for passage (31), and brings you into Moosabec Reach near its western end. The red and black buoy shown west of Pomp Island has recently been replaced by a red daybeacon (32).

The tide sets west on the ebb and east on the flood. Generally, the ebb and the flood are related to high and low water, but this can be influenced by the strength and direction of the wind. Also, the tide changes one hour earlier at the eastern end of The Reach than at the western end, on both ebb and flood tide. According to the NOAA *Tidal Current Tables*, currents atain a velocity of 1.0 to 1.2 knots at maximum in both direction. However, I would judge them to be somewhat higher, about 1.5 to 1.75 knots. On both sides of the fixed bridge a causeway with solid landfill protrudes into the channel, producing a narrowing of the channel and a corresponding marked increase in current velocity in the area. It also has created a condition of strong back currents, particularly on the north side of the channel. On the ebb tide, these extend for a distance of ¼ to ½ mile beyond the bridge. Plan to pass through with the tide in your favor, but be sure beforehand that you have enough clearance under the bridge as there will be no chance for a last minute change of mind.

Moosabec Reach presents no problems if you pay attention to the buoys, keeping to their correct side. Remember, the buoys are marked for passage east to west through the Reach. The most common mistake made in this regard is passing on the wrong side of buoy C "9" marking Horse Ledge (1a). Be sure to stay north of this buoy.

## JONESPORT—CHART NO. 13326

### Anchorage

Finding a good spot to anchor in Jonesport can be difficult. You don't want to anchor in the middle of the channel because the water is deep and Moosabec Reach is in constant use by commercial fishing boats and lobster boats. Nor is it possible to anchor along the narrow edge of shelf out of the channel, as this area is almost completely filled with moored boats of the fishing fleet. Sawyer Cove (33), at the east end of Jonesport used to be about the only place to anchor. It was a quite poor anchorage.

Dredging and a completed breakwater (33a) has transformed Sawyer Cove into a mooring basin. The cove was dredged to a depth of 8 feet in the outer portion and 6 feet in the inner part. A 100 foot wide and 1,000 long, clear channel leads from the end of the Breakwater to the Town Dock. I have drawn the breakwater on our chart. There has been some shoaling at the entrance. When entering or leaving at low tide, stay close to the breakwater, as the western ⅔ of the entrance has less than 5½ ft. depth.

Within this 15 acre cove are 83 moorings. Most are privately owned, but 8 or 9 moorings are reserved for transients—that is, yachtsmen and fishermen from other areas passing through. A fee is charged for the use of these moorings.

At the northern end of the cove, beyond the drying ledge and dredged area, is the former old Frost Shipyard. Owned by Sune Nureen, it is now named the Jonesport Shipyard (33b) and has laundry, showers, haulout, repair, and storage facilities.

### Marine Facilities

A dock with floats is on the north side of Sawyer Cove. This was a State Marina at one time, but now it is the Town Landing (34). No services are available, but there is 60 feet of floating dock space and an asphalt launching ramp. Visiting boats are allowed to tie-up to the dock for a limited time to take on provisions, etc., but no overnight staying is allowed. The commercial wharf west of this is O.W. & B.S. Look (35), gasoline, diesel fuel, lobsters, and they monitor VHF Channel 78. Take care when coming into the wharf, for ledges almost completely block the approach. It is best to wait until half-tide when the ledge begins to bare to be sure of its position. Also, you don't want to wait until full low tide, for at that time there is only 3 feet of water at the dock. Three large fuel storage tanks behind the wharf and a blue shed at its far end make identification easy. Beals-Jonesport Lobster Co-op (36), east of the bridge, has Texaco gasoline and diesel fuel, and marine hardware.

### Supplies and Sightseeing

At the head of the street from the Town Landing is T.A. King & Son Co. (37), with general hardware and some marine supplies. Marine supplies are also available at Oscar Look Co. (38), located in the red brick building next to the large smoke stack. Directly across from T.A. King is Jonesport Sunoco (39), selling groceries, beer and wine. Next to this is Win-Place-Show Restaurant (40), for breakfast, lunch and dinner. For major provisioning, the I.G.A. Store (41) is on Main St. east of the bridge. Tall Barney's Restaurant (42), also on Main St., serves lunch and dinner, fresh seafood, well prepared, generous quantity.

A Coast Guard Station (43) is located immediately west of the bridge. Besides all the usual activities, it is a customs and immigration port of entry.

Undoubtedly, the summer highlight is the annual 4th of July race for determining the world's fastest lobster boat. Then Moosabec Reach is churned to a froth by the competitors vying for this title.

Roque Harbor Sand Beach

# CHAPTER 16

## ROQUE ISLAND TO CUTLER

### ROQUE ISLAND HARBOR—CHART NO. 13326B

For many, the ultimate goal on the Maine coast is Roque Island. To have passed Schoodic Head, that point beyond which the imaginary "true" downeast sailing begins, and to have safely crossed fog-shrouded Petit Manan with its Fundy currents is final proof of sailing ability. Though this is challenging navigation, any prudent reasonably skilled coastal navigator can do it. Roque Island is indisputedly magnificent with its high headlands, towering trees and great sweep of fine white sand beaches. It is even more rewarding to approach it the hard way, from the east, like doubling The Horn. In a "smoky" southwester against the Fundy tide, you can be certain of a boisterous sail. Then to shoot through any of the channels to enter the harbor with its complete protection and placid water is indeed a joy and a fair ending to the day.

Our arrival last June was greeted by an abundance of wildlife activity. In the air, two eagles were fighting with an osprey. The eagles were young, immature birds, not old enough to nest, but they had inadvertently flown too close to the nesting site of the osprey. Not all predatory birds are as protective of their nest as the osprey, and this one was making certain that the eagles learned their territorial limits. On the water were flocks of eider ducks, and horned grebes were diving in pursuit of food. On Seal Ledge (51), several families of seals with young pups were sunning themselves. They quickly slipped into the water when we approached.

Although you can anchor on the north side in Shorey Cove (44), the most popular anchorage is Roque Island Harbor (45) on the east side. The harbor can be entered by any one of five channels, the selection dependent on which has the most favorable wind. The 7-foot spot (46) indicated as "reported" in the channel between Great Spruce Island and Double Shot Island **does** exist. We exited at low tide and saw it quite clearly as our keel passed over. There is plenty of room to enter (47) between Double Shot Island and Anguilla Island and there's a passage (48) between Anguilla and Halifax Island. All the rocks are quite close to the islands and usually are visible. Roque Harbor can be entered from north of Halifax Island (49), the widest passage of the four, but stay well north of Halifax Island to avoid the 5-ft. shallow.

Finally, there is the Thorofare (49a) between Roque Island and Great Spruce Island. Be extremely cautious of the rock that is indicated on the chart as "reported." It **does** exist, sitting just about in the center of the channel. At all states of the tide, it is covered with water, although at low, dreen tide it is no more than 2 feet below the surface. Pass close to the shore on either side until you are beyond it.

The bottom is hard sand, not quite as good holding quality as sticky mud, yet with excellent protection from wind and seas and ample room for good scope. Make sure your anchor is dug in. The best anchorage is in the northern portion of the bight. In the southernmost portion of the harbor are the remains of an old weir (50) which is barely discernible at high tide, but plainly visible at low tide. Kelp appears to accumulate loose on the bottom. Boats not adequately anchored have been blown ashore in strong northwesterly winds. The holding ground is good **providing** your anchor is well set with adequate scope.

Many boats opt for dropping the hook close to the southern end of the beach, where there is calmer water, due to less fetch of the waves from prevailing southwest winds. Time and again I have seen boats enter Roque Harbor and head directly for this spot, apparently completely oblivious to having passed directly over the disused weir (50). At high tide the poles, very large ones indeed, are completely covered, but about 2½ hours from low tide they stick several feet above the surface. Ledge extends beyond the point much farther than may be expected from inspection of the chart. The line of poles begins at the end of this ledge, continuing to the main, circular enclosure. From there, a wing of poles extends at a right angle toward the beach. Last year, two of the poles were privately marked, one with a flag, the other by a white plastic jug (Refer to Sketch Chart).

A choice little anchorage, called Sugarloaves Cove (50a), is west of the Thorofare. It is named such because of the dome-shaped rocks comprising the two, small islands nearby. You can work yourself quite close in and still have 9 feet of water at low tide. On the eastern side of the Thorofare is Money Cove (50b). At one time there was an Indian settlement here, as well as on the western shore of the Thorofare. Some of the clam shells, used as a form of money, and other artifacts of stone are still occasionally found.

Seal Ledge (51), the only obstruction within the harbor, is quite large, more than just a solitary rock as the chart shows. It is barely awash at high tide, so its location can be determined throughout most of the tide. Another weir (52) is between Seal Ledge and the main-

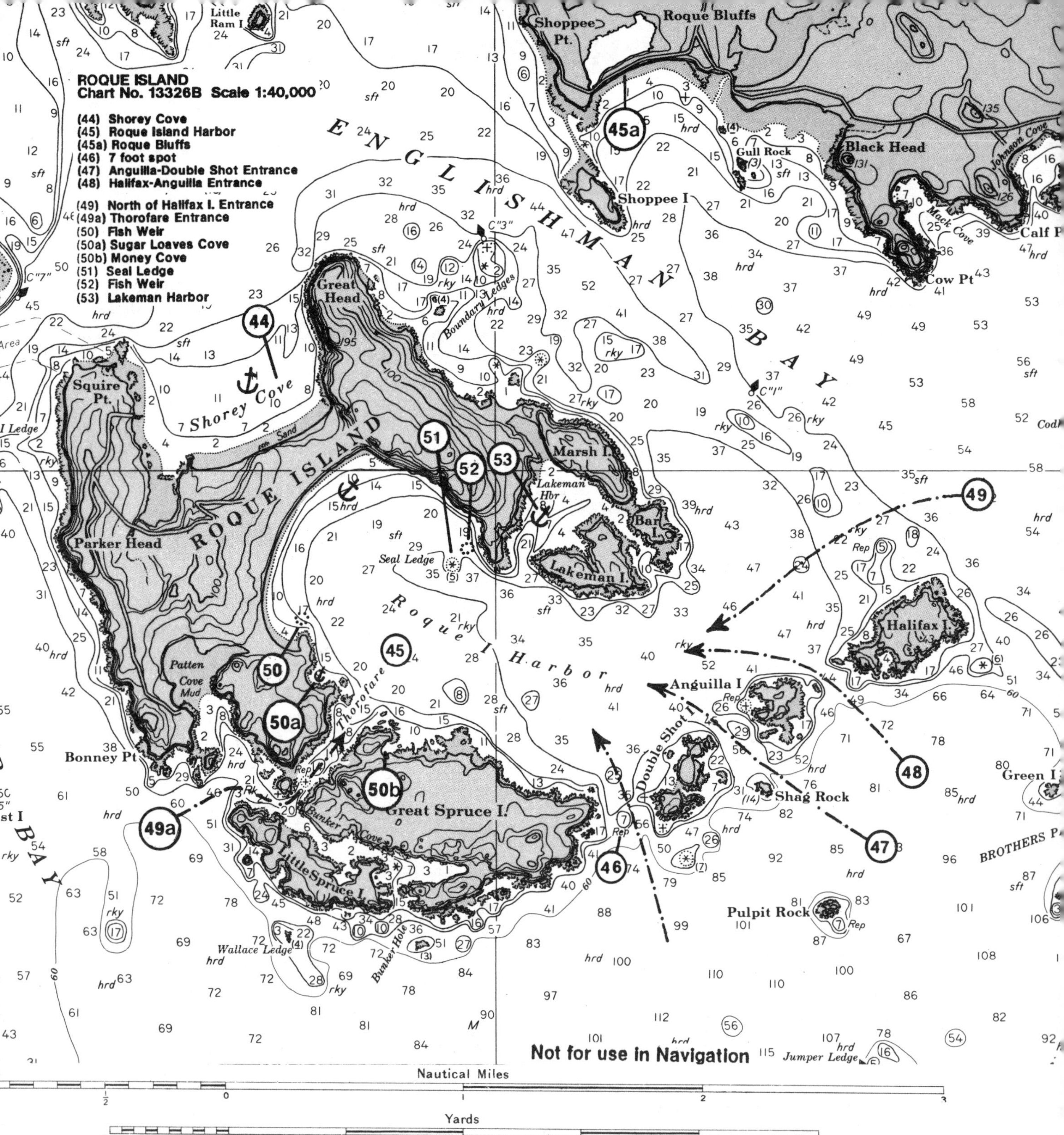


land, so do not try to sail north of Seal Ledge.

All of Roque Island is privately owned by the Gardner family but they allow visitors on shore. They prefer to keep the south portion of the beach private, indicating the limits by a sign. No camping and no fires are allowed above the high tide mark.

The island is an intact coastal ecosystem, harboring a significant number of intact wetlands, and is an important habitat for birds, marine and terrestrial animals, and plants. The owners of the island are trying to maintain it in an undisturbed, natural state, and ask that those visiting it respect this.

Lakeman Harbor (53) formerly was an excellent anchorage, providing good shelter and holding ground. Now it is difficult to get the anchor to set. Last fall, after three failed attempts with our CQR, we gave up and

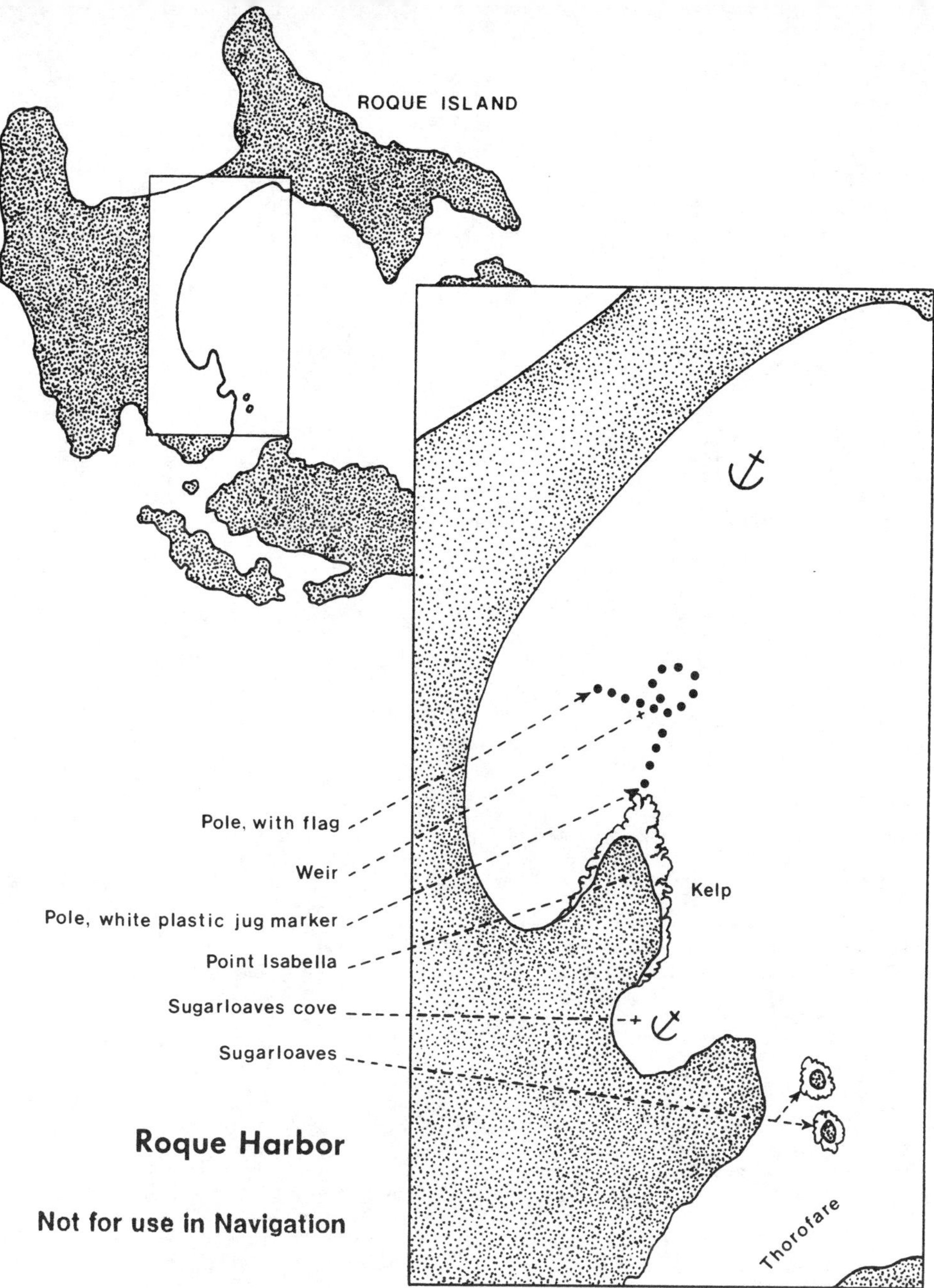


**Roque Harbor**

**Not for use in Navigation**

moved out. Each time the anchor was brought up, tangled in kelp, maidenhair and other seaweed. This rapid growth of kelp and weed is an increasing problem in many Downeast harbors, due to the lack of strong storms in the last few years, which normally keeps a harbor cleared.

There are no stores for provisioning on any of the islands, but you can have a delightful time foraging for your own food, clams and mussels, in the shallows between Lakeman Island and Bar Island.

## MACHIAS BAY—CHART NO. 13325A

Machias Bay (53) is seldom used by cruising yachtsmen. Beyond Avery Rock, (54), the upper half of the bay quickly shallows out into unattractive mud flats, ledges and boulders, all unmarked. The lower half has nearby better harbors in both directions. Shortly beyond Machiasport (55), a bridge with 25 feet vertical clearance across the Machias River prevents passage to the town of Machias. However, there are two good harbors in the lower half on the Bay, Starboard Cove (56) and Bucks Harbor (57).

There is a free asphalt launching ramp and public floating dock at Machias on the north side of the river where it bends southwest, just south of the U.S. Route 1 fixed bridge. The location is shown on the folded chart inside the rear cover. The Machias River is quite deep, over 20 feet, nearly to the bend west, above Machiasport. Controlling depth west of this is 7 feet, but it shallows to 1 to 2 feet just before the bend to the southwest. You may need some tide help if you use this ramp.

The principal landmark at the entrance of Machias Bay is the Libby Islands Light (58). The islands themselves are low, grassy and hard to see, but the light, 91 feet above the water, is visible from 25 miles. In a small wedge of arc to the northeast, the light is obscured. This light, plus the radar dome (59) on the peninsula near

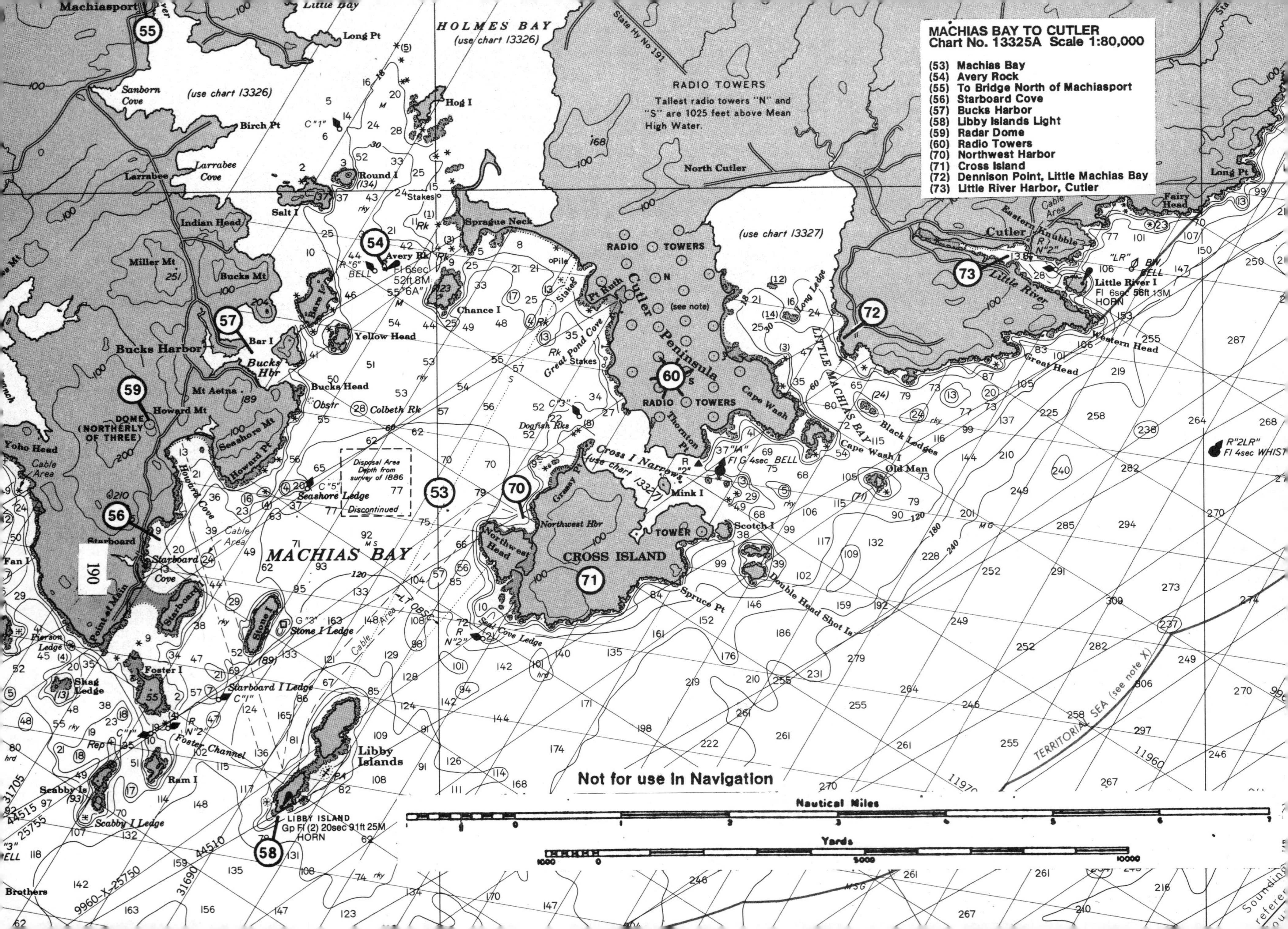
MACHIAS BAY TO CUTLER
Chart No. 13325A Scale 1:80,000
(53) Machias Bay
(54) Avery Rock
(55) To Bridge North of Machiasport
(56) Starboard Cove
(57) Bucks Harbor
(58) Libby Islands Light
(59) Radar Dome
(60) Radio Towers
(70) Northwest Harbor
(71) Cross Island
(72) Dennison Point, Little Machias Bay
(73) Little River Harbor, Cutler
RADIO TOWERS
Tallest radio towers "N" and "S" are 1025 feet above Mean High Water.
HOLMES BAY
(use chart 13326)
(use chart 13327)
MACHIAS BAY
LITTLE MACHIAS BAY
CROSS ISLAND
Cutler Peninsula
Disposal Area Depth from survey of 1886 Discontinued
LIBBY ISLAND
Gp Fl (2) 20sec 91ft 25M
HORN
Little River I
Fl 6sec 56ft 13M
HORN
Machiasport
Cutler
North Cutler
State Hy No 191
Bucks Harbor
Libby Islands
TERRITORIAL SEA (see note X)
Not for use in Navigation
Nautical Miles
Yards

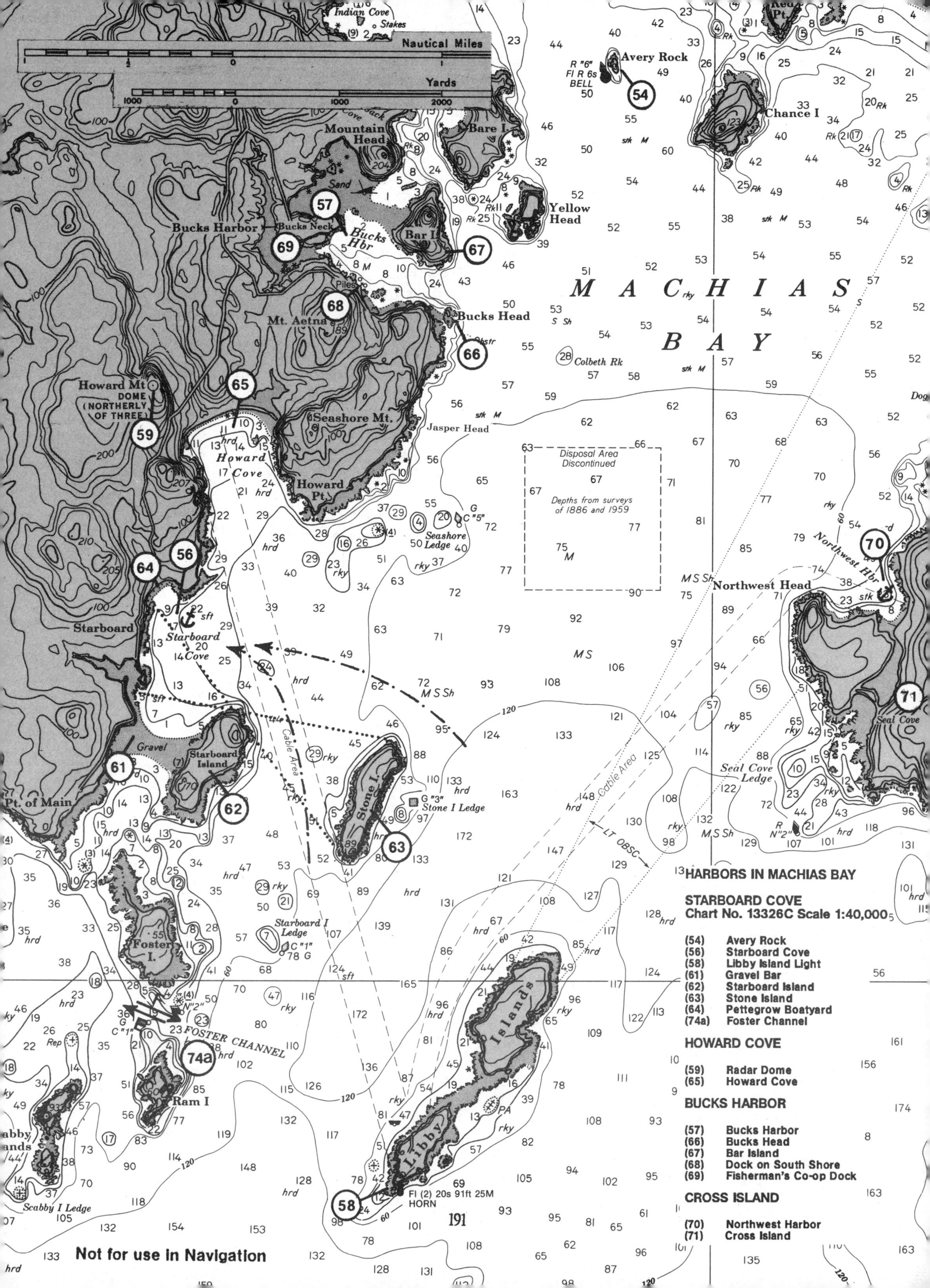
Nautical Miles
Yards
1000
0
1000
2000
Indian Cove
Stakes
Avery Rock
R "6"
Fl R 6s
BELL
Chance I
Mountain Head
Bare I.
Sand
Bucks Harbor
Bucks Neck
Bucks Hbr
Bar I.
Yellow Head
Piles
Mt. Aetna
Bucks Head
Obstr
MACHIAS BAY
Colbeth Rk
Howard Mt
DOME
(NORTHERLY OF THREE)
Seashore Mt.
Jasper Head
Howard Cove
Howard Pt.
Disposal Area Discontinued
Depths from surveys of 1886 and 1959
Seashore Ledge
Northwest Hbr
Northwest Head
Starboard
Starboard Cove
Cable Area
Gravel
Starboard Island
Stone I.
G "3"
Stone I Ledge
Pt. of Main
Seal Cove
Seal Cove Ledge
LT OBSC
Starboard I Ledge
C "1"
Foster I.
FOSTER CHANNEL
Ram I
Islands
Libby
Fl (2) 20s 91ft 25M
HORN
Scabby I Ledge
Not for use in Navigation
HARBORS IN MACHIAS BAY
STARBOARD COVE
Chart No. 13326C Scale 1:40,000
(54) Avery Rock
(56) Starboard Cove
(58) Libby Island Light
(61) Gravel Bar
(62) Starboard Island
(63) Stone Island
(64) Pettegrow Boatyard
(74a) Foster Channel
HOWARD COVE
(59) Radar Dome
(65) Howard Cove
BUCKS HARBOR
(57) Bucks Harbor
(66) Bucks Head
(67) Bar Island
(68) Dock on South Shore
(69) Fisherman's Co-op Dock
CROSS ISLAND
(70) Northwest Harbor
(71) Cross Island

Bucks Harbor, are convenient points for determining your position by cross-bearings. The dome is part of the former Bucks Harbor Air Force Station. Although the station is no longer manned, the radar equipment is still in use. The radar dome is indicated on Chart No. 13325 as being the most northerly of three; but there is only one, the other two having long since been removed.

The radio towers (60) on Cutler Peninsula dominate all of Machias Bay. There are 26 towers, the tallest being 1025 feet high. These belong to the U.S. Navy's Communication Station at Cutler, the most powerful radio station in the world. They are used for transmission to the military fleet, particularly submarines, throughout all of the North Atlantic, Arctic and Mediterranean. They stand out in eerie starkness on this flat, coastal plain. However, they are of little use for determining your position as they all are about the same height, making it difficult to distinguish one tower from another.

From Roque Harbor, you may elect to take a shortcut into Machias Bay by sailing north of Scabby Islands and Ram Island, through Foster Channel (74a). The tide pulls strongly through the channel, flood to the east, ebb to the west. This will affect your heading in the lower part of Machias Bay, being particularly troublesome when sailing in fog.

### Libby Island

A combination of rocky shores, swift currents, and often, thick weather, has produced many shipwrecks along the Maine coast. Libby Island (58), at the entrance to Machias Bay, has claimed its share of vessels. One shipwreck there has an interesting story behind it. It was related to me by Avery Kelly, a fisherman and local historian from nearby Beals Island.

Leander Look was a sea-captain who lived in Jonesport during the early 1900's. His wife, Cora, was always regarded cautiously by other residents. There was nothing dangerous about Cora Look, and she did no harm to anyone. Yet, there was something about her appearance and her manner that created an unease in people. Somehow, she seemed a little different. Most of the kids were scared of her. Some say she was a witch.

One of Coras' favorite activities was playing the ouija-board. She could make a oui-ja-board set on the table and talk to it until it danced right up and down on that table. Leander wouldn't allow one in the house, but she had a friend who had one and Cora visited her friend to ask questions of the board.

She would find out if Leander was chasing any women while he was away at sea. If he was, the board would reveal their names. When he'd come home and be confronted with the information, he would say "there was no way you couldn't get nothing by her. I don't know how she found this out." But he should have known the ouija-board was telling her.

One night while Leander was away, Cora dreamt that he went ashore on Libby Island in a snowstorm and he lost his cook. The cook had gone up in the rigging and Leander went up to get him, but he wouldn't come down, and the cook froze to death in the rigging.

That same night, the boat, loaded with lumber struck Libby Island. The next morning, when they called to let her know her husband was safe, but that they were shipwrecked on Libby Island, she said, "You ain't got to tell me a thing, I know more about it than he does!"

### Starboard Cove—Chart Nos. 13325A 13326C

Starboard Cove (56) is an excellent anchorage, easy to enter under all weather conditions. It provides good protection except from winds from the northeast to east, an infrequent direction during the summer. The bar (61) which extends from the mainland to Bar Island is exposed at 7 feet, or until about 2 hours on either side of high tide, so throughout most of the tide range it is an effective barrier to any seas from the south. Even at full high tide it is sufficiently shallow to cause any waves to break.

Entry is made keeping east of Starboard Island (62) and then rounding west into the Cove. Stone Island (63) may be passed to either side. As long as you can still see the north end of Stone Island past the north end of Starboard Island, you will be clear of the gravel bar. Anchor anywhere north of this, until the southern end of Stone Island is in line with the northern end of Starboard Island. The best anchorage is between these two ranges, as shown on chart no. 13326C.

On the west shore is the Pettigrow Boatyard (64). They have a marine railway for hauling boats and they do engine and hull repairs. The marine supply store, run by his wife Nettie, is well stocked, not only for the needs of fishermen, but yachtsmen also. Conscientious work and dependable service is making this yard a favorite stopping place during the summer, and for winter haulout.

There is no grocery store near Starboard Cove. The nearest place for provisioning is at Machias, a nine mile drive.

Stone Island (63) is a Preserve of The Nature Conservancy. It is one of the most important rookeries for great blue herons, and has nesting osprey. There are over 100 great blue heron nests. There have been eight pairs of osprey in one year nesting in the tall white spruce that rims the island's shores. Because of this, landing is prohibited between February 15 and August 15.

Most of Stone Island is spruce and fir. On the north end there are raspberry thickets, mountain maple, mountain ash, and yellow birch. The southern tip has some arctic species of shrubs, along with lowbush blueberry, alpine cranberry, and crowberry. The east shore has steep cliffs, nearly 90 ft., and piles of boulders. The west shore has a few small cobble beaches where you could land, but stay off during nesting season until August 15.

### Howard Cove—Chart No. 13326C

Howard Cove (65) is not a good anchorage. Not only is it completely exposed, but the holding ground is poor. However, you might want to take your dinghy or walk from Starboard Cove, to beachcomb for the wave-polished pebbles of Jasper quartz that abound in Howard Cove. They are slippery smooth and come in many colors.

### Bucks Harbor—Chart Nos. 13325A, 13326C

Bucks Harbor (57) is attactive, offering good shelter and easy access. Enter midway between Bucks Head (66) and Bar Island (67). This will keep you clear of ledges and the fish weirs on the south shore. Anchor fairly well in the middle of the Cove, favoring the south shore for the deeper water. Bucks Harbor Lobster Company (68) on the south shore, has a 30 foot "T"-head dock and float with 4 to 6 feet depth alongside, gasoline, lobsters, and monitors VHF Channel 16. Bucks Harbor Fisherman's Co-op (69) on Bucks Neck, has a prominent shed at the end of the pier. They have 4 to 6 ft. depth at their float landing, gasoline and diesel fuel.

About 1.4 miles north of Bucks Harbor is Salt Island, shown on chart no. 13325A. The western half of Salt Island, about 40 acres, comprises the Salt Island Preserve of The Nature Conservancy, an American eagle nesting site. No landing is permitted. The island has dense forest and 25 to 30 ft. high cliffs except on the north shore. The eastern half of Salt Island is private property. Clams and periwinkles are harvested on the extensive shallow flats around Salt Island.

### Northwest Harbor, Cross Island
### Chart Nos. 13325A, 13326C

Northwest Harbor (70), the bight on the northwest side of Cross Island (71), is infrequently used as an anchorage, since much better harbors, Starboard, Bucks, and Cutler are nearby. There are no docks. Do not anchor in the south part of the harbor, to avoid the risk of fouling your anchor in the cable area.

One thing in its favor is the large tidal pond extending southward to Seal Cove. Take your dinghy in on a rising tide so as to have the current with you. Current runs rather strong through the narrow opening. Once you are in the major part of the pond, you can walk around in the soft mud in a pair of sneakers or boots. Clamming is excellent here, and best of all, you don't need a clam rake to get them out. To do this, find a clam hole and put your middle finger in it. Once you get used to it you can feel the spurts of water and chase that spout hole right down to the clam. It takes a while to get the knack of it, but when you do, you'll be able to feel the clam right on the side of your finger. Then move your hand over just a whisker, cup the clam in your hand and reverse it right back out. With a bit of practice, you can get yourself a pretty good mess of clams for dinner. And you can get them when the tide is almost high water.

## LITTLE MACHIAS BAY
## CHART NOS. 13325A, 13327

There is not much to recommend here, as inspection of the chart will reveal. But if required as a harbor of refuge, the preferred spot for anchoring is north of Dennison Point (72) where the chart shows 14 feet. The bottom is gravel.

## LITTLE RIVER, CUTLER
## CHART NOS. 13327, 13325A

Little River at Cutler, Maine is an important harbor (73), serving as base to a large fleet of lobster and fishing vessels and recently, greater usage by yachtsmen. The almost landlocked harbor is easy to enter and offers excellent shelter from all winds. From Cutler eastward, there are no other secure anchorages to be found on this section of coast until you reach Head Harbour on Campobello Island or North Head at Grand Manan, both a good day's sail distant. Campobello and Grand Manan are shown on the folded chart inside rear cover.

Little River is easy to locate regardless of weather conditions. Little River Island (74), at the harbor entrance, has a strong light and a fog signal. The light is on a skeletal tower 56 feet above the water on the northeast corner of the island, visible 17 miles, Fl 15 sec. At the mouth of the harbor is a bell buoy "LR" (75), easy to find in fog, for it lies just inside the 20 fathom curve which closely parallels this section of coast. On the most recent chart, this is indicated as being a black & white bell buoy, but it is now red & white. There is a lighted whistle buoy (Fl 4 sec.) R "2LR" (76) about 2.0 miles southeast of the light.

Entrance to the harbor is through the channel north of Little River Island. With care, the channel south of the island may be used, but it has only 6 feet depth at low tide. By keeping 100 yards off either shore of the main channel, all ledges and rocks will be avoided. A ledge (78) which uncovers south of Eastern Nubble is marked by a red buoy, N"2". Beyond this buoy, there are four fish weirs, two on each side of the harbor. They are in a state of disrepair and difficult to see at high tide. By coming down the middle of the harbor they are avoided.

This harbor has not escaped the proliferation of pens for raising salmon that is found in so many other Downeast harbors. Refer to the section on aquaculture in our Introduction at the beginning of this book. You will find several pens on your port side as you enter, just before the the first set of fish-weirs. Fortunately, they are located in an area where they cause no problem to navigation, and do not occupy anchoring space.

There are no guest moorings, but there is plenty of room to anchor near the fleet of moored boats opposite the wharfs. The bottom is mud and holding is good. There are some patches of kelp, so be sure that your anchor is well dug in and that it reaches the mud. The tides of the Bay of Fundy begin to exhibit their strong influence here, the mean tidal range being 13.6 feet with spring tides of 15.5 feet. Allow sufficient scope on your anchor rode to accommodate this range.

The first wharf (79) on the north shore is the Farris Wharf. It has a green painted shingle building on it, and has a float and ramp. You can tie your dinghy here, but make certain that it is tucked well out of the way, as the wharf is much used for unloading fish and lobster. Farris has gasoline and some marine hardware, but no water, and monitors CB Channel 11.

The white building across the road from the wharfs is the Village Store and Restaurant (80) which has groceries. Ray MacKeen is the proprietor and the hours are 7:30 a.m.-12:00 and 1:00-6:00 p.m., closed for lunch hour, Monday through Friday, 7:30 a.m.-5:00 p.m. Saturday, 1:00-6:00 p.m. Sunday. Besides groceries, you may get breakfast, sandwiches for lunch and seafood dinners. The store is open year-round, but the restaurant is open only from May to September, same hours as the store. The red brick building east of the store is the Post Office (81).

You may also anchor off the second group of boats moored farther into the harbor. This is opposite Neil Corbett Lobster Pound, a prominent wharf and float (82) with a Mobil sign. They have a guest mooring, gasoline, diesel fuel, ice, lobsters and some marine hardware. Behind the wharf is a white house, the residence of Neil Corbett. Besides being a lobster dealer, he is the Harbormaster and is most knowledgeable about this section of coast. There is 10 feet depth at the wharf. If the one large guest mooring is taken, ask Neill about the availability of an unoccupied fisherman's mooring. Across the road, the Little River Lodge (83) offers overnight accommodations for guests and has a restuarant. Reservations are required. They also allow the use of their shower facilities for cruising yachtsmen.

The Cutler Lobster Hatchery is located in the basement of the public library, a five minute walk up the road from Neil Corbett's dock (82). It's open to the public and they'll show visitors around and explain what's happening. Refer to Chapter 2 under "Lobster Hatcheries," for more information, including an illustration of larval stages of lobsters.

If you want a feast of plump fresh blue mussels, take your dinghy towards the head of the harbor. Here, at the remains of an old mill-run dam (84a) are large beds of these luscious mollusks, easily picked at low tide.

Captain Barna Norton operates his vessel, the "Chief" out of Cutler (as well as his homeport of Jonesport) taking people to Machias Seal Island, 10 miles out to sea, to view the Puffins and Arctic Terns that nest there. Machias Seal Island was established as a migratory bird sanctuary by the Canadian Wildlife Service. Prior permission for visitors to land on the island is required. Anchorage is both difficult and exposed, so a visit with Capt. Norton who best knows the island and these waters is the easiest way to see this unique bird colony. Machias Seal Island is shown on the folded chart inside the rear cover.

Cutler, Little River

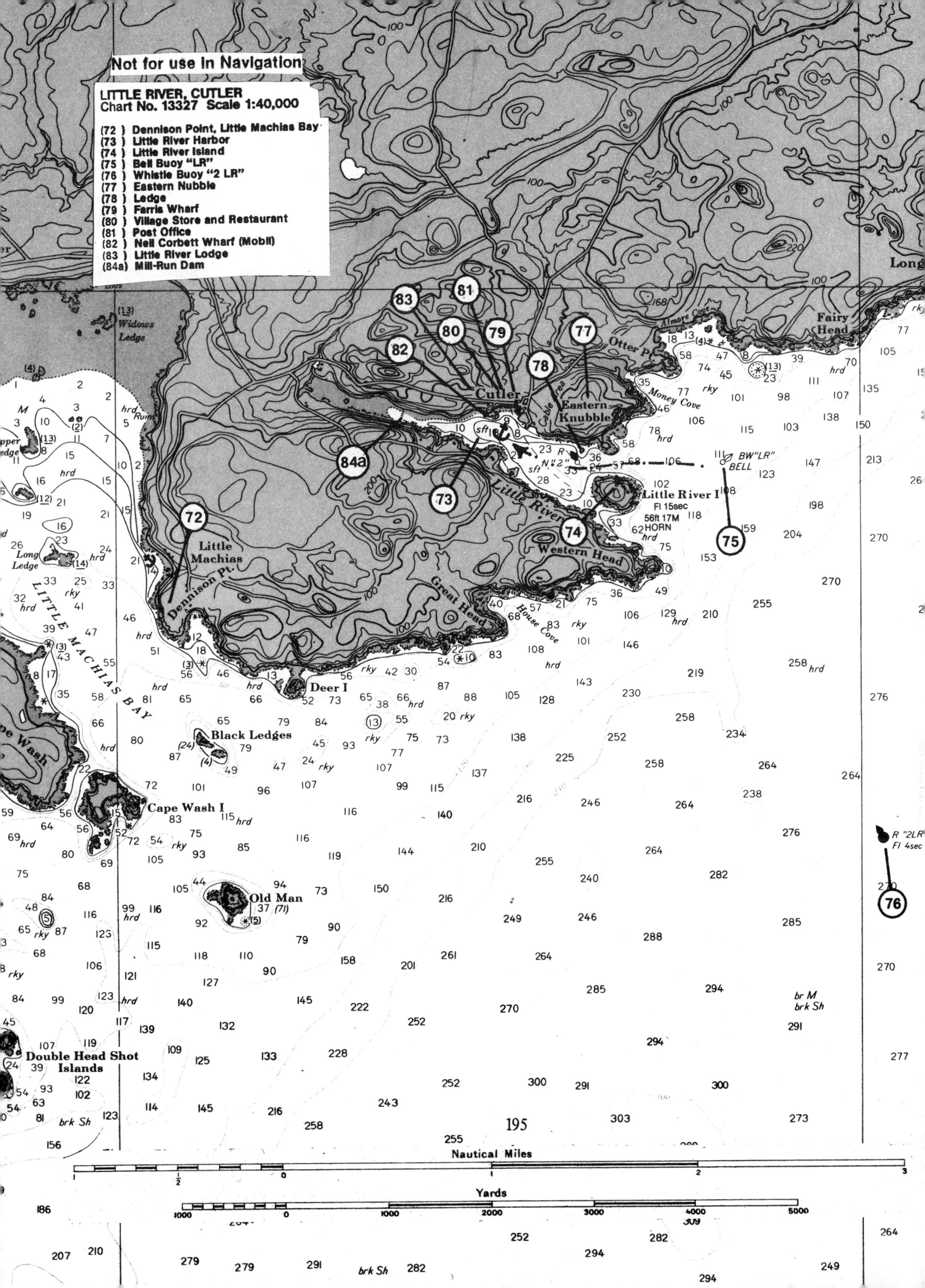
Not for use in Navigation
LITTLE RIVER, CUTLER
Chart No. 13327 Scale 1:40,000
(72) Dennison Point, Little Machias Bay
(73) Little River Harbor
(74) Little River Island
(75) Bell Buoy "LR"
(76) Whistle Buoy "2 LR"
(77) Eastern Nubble
(78) Ledge
(79) Farris Wharf
(80) Village Store and Restaurant
(81) Post Office
(82) Neil Corbett Wharf (Mobil)
(83) Little River Lodge
(84a) Mill-Run Dam
Widows Ledge
Almore Cove
Fairy Head
Otter Pt
Money Cove
Cutler
Eastern Knubble
Little River I
Fl 15sec
56ft 17M
HORN
BW "LR"
BELL
Little River
Western Head
Great Head
House Cove
Little Machias
Dennison Pt.
Long Ledge
LITTLE MACHIAS BAY
Deer I
Black Ledges
Cape Wash I
Old Man
Double Head Shot Islands
R "2LR"
Fl 4sec
Nautical Miles
Yards

# CHAPTER 17

## LITTLE RIVER, CUTLER, TO LUBEC

### MOOSE COVE—CHART NO. 13327A

Moose Cove (84) is large, open and completely exposed to the prevailing summertime winds. Moose River, which empties into it has silted up, so anchorage there is not possible. Eastern Head Ledges (85), at the eastern edge of the entrance are unbuoyed, but there are two bits of rock on it that remain exposed at high tide. They are called Mink Islet and Little Mink Islet. Both are only 6 feet high.

### HAYCOCK HARBOR—CHART NO. 13327A, SKETCH CHART

This small harbor (86), 6.3 miles southwest of West Quoddy Head Light, and approximately halfway between Moose Cove (84) and Baileys Mistake Harbor (87), is difficult to pick out from offshore. The easiest way to find it is to aim for the headland at the east side of the entrance from either the black and red buoy (88) at the mouth of Baileys Mistake, course 236 degrees magnetic; or from the R "2BM" whistle buoy (89), course 257 degrees magnetic.

At the entrance to the harbor, proceed up the middle, favoring the northeast side, until opposite the small gravel beach (90) on the north side. A piling in the outer harbor marks the limits of the ledge on the south shore. Stay north of it. Round the piling, then closely follow along the north edge of the channel to remain in the deepest water.

Immediately beyond the constriction at the beginning of the channel is a deep hole where local lobster boats are moored (92). You can tie-up here to pilings. There are three rows of pilings to which the boats tie fore and aft, thus keeping them aligned with the channel. Approaching the mooring area, watch out for a sunken boat in the middle of the channel. It has been there for several years and although I am told it is to be removed soon, such may not be the case. The boat's dark outline is clearly visible at half-tide or less. Water runs out of the channel rapidly, so be prepared for a strong current and very little maneuvering room. Even at the bottom of the tide, within an hour of slack water, there may be as much as 1.5 knots of current. If you have choice, try to tie up near the outer edge of the pilings, placing you more toward the center of the channel. It's shallow close to the south shore.

There are no services or stores for provisioning. A privately maintained road follows along the north side of the harbor connecting with State Route 191 at The Pool (91). From there you might hitch a ride to the general store (97) in South Trescott, 1.5 miles northeast.

The Pool (91) at the west end of Haycock Harbor can be entered only within 2 hours either side of high tide. It is even smaller than it appears on the chart, which is certainly small enough. There are no wharfs and it is not possible to moor or anchor here for it has so silted up that it completely dries out at low tide. At best, with high water, it can be used as a turning basin or a quiet, protected lunch stop.

If your timing is right, entering The Pool certainly affords a unique experience. Sides of the narrow channel are high and steep, with trees growing right down to the water's edge, providing a veritable tunnel to pass through. Inside, except for the fluctuations of the tidal level, you would scarcely know you were anywhere near an ocean. So calm and protected is this spot that even a gale would hardly ruffle the water.

### BAILEYS MISTAKE—CHART NO. 13327A

Baileys Mistake Harbor (87) is easy to find, even in a thick fog, and the entrance to the harbor is straightforward. Whistle buoy R "2BM" (89) marking the harbor is directly upon the 10 fathom curve which closely parallels the shore line. The three spots of ledge, that uncover at 5 feet obstructing the mouth of the harbor, are marked by a black and red buoy (88). Although you can pass either side, the preferred entry course is to stay east of the black and red buoy. Unfortunately, whatever beneficial qualities the harbor may have are completely negated by its exposed position. Furthermore, the holding ground is poor making it altogether an undesirable anchorage.

If it should become necessary to take shelter, the best anchorage is north of the two small islands (93) in the northeastern part of the harbor. Space is limited here as it is mostly filled by fishing boats on moorings. An alternate anchorage (94) is close to the shore of the high hill on the west side of the harbor, where the chart indicates 16 feet depth.

At high water it is also possible to enter the pool (95) at the extreme northwestern part of the harbor at the town of South Trescott. Access to the pool is through a narrow opening (96) at the south end of that long thin spit of land blocking the entrance. As in other nearby coves, silting has occurred, and in this innermost basin you will ground out at low tide. A general store (97) for limited provisioning, and a Post Office is in the village

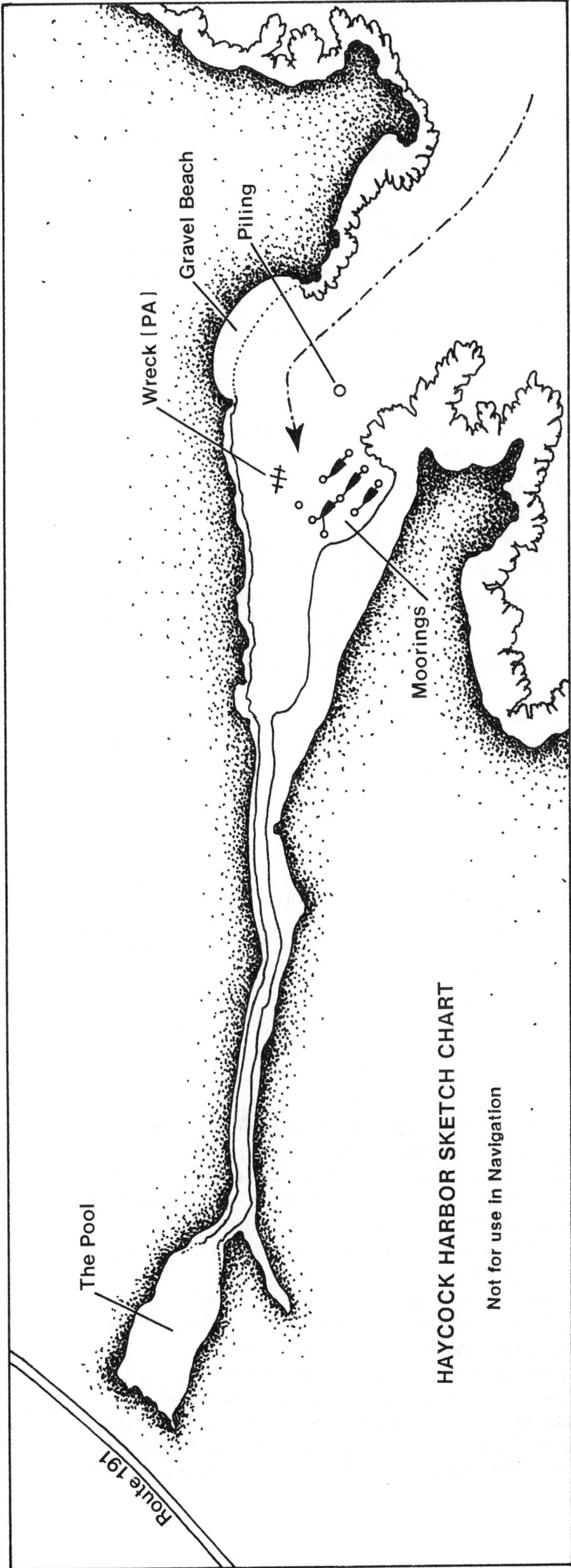


at the head of the harbor. If you take your dinghy up there, don't stay long, because you'll be stranded when the tide goes out.

The name of the harbor fairly begs the question "what was Bailey's mistake?" The story is that a Captain Bailey was bound for Lubec in his 4-masted Schooner. In the fog he misjudged his time and distance and entered this harbor believing he was rounding West Quoddy Head. The crashing of his ship on the rocks made him recognize his error, although much too late. The beautiful surroundings of the area appealed to him and his crew, and they decided to remain and settle here.

## BOOT COVE—CHART NO. 13327A

Of all the small coves and indentations along this portion of the coast, Boot Cove (98) is the most useful for an anchorage. It is pleasant in appearance and provides shelter from winds except those within the quadrant of northeast through southeast. There are several lobster boats on moorings. As in almost every cove and harbor on this part of the coast, watch out for fish weirs. One here stretches from the patch of rock that shows exposed on the northeast corner of the cove, extending diagonally across the cove towards the southwest corner. There is room to tuck in by the shore of Boot Head.

## LUBEC—CHART NO. 13328

### Approaches

The Quoddy Narrows (1) and Lubec Channel (2) provides the most immediate access to Passamaquoddy Bay and the shortest route to the town of Lubec (3).

A lighthouse, strikingly painted in alternating red and white bands, sits high on the east end of West Quoddy Head (4) and guides vessels entering Quoddy Narrows. It's 83 ft. above the sea, group flashing twice every 15 seconds, visible 18 nautical miles, has a fog horn, and a radio direction finding station . — — — — . — & —

Originally built in 1808, the present tower was constructed in 1858 and is situated on the most easterly point of land in the United States. Like so many others along this coast, this familiar landmark with its candy-striped tower has become fully automated. On June 30th of 1988 the 180 year old lighthouse saw the end of an honored tradition of a manned lightkeeper.

Two other aids to navigation are in the outer approach; whistle buoy "1" (5), southeast of Sail Rock (7), and a black and white bell buoy "WQ" (6) at the mouth of the Narrows. The whistle buoy lies directly on the 30 fathom curve, making it easy to find in fog using your depth sounder. A great deal of turbulence is generally found in this region, when at the strength of tide, the outpouring of water at 4.0 knots through the narrows meets with an ebb tide at 2.5 to 3.5 knots coming down the Bay of Fundy.

To avoid this turbulence and reduce the amount of time spent bucking the outgoing tide, local fish vessels and sardine carriers hug the West Quoddy Head shoreline as much as possible before turning in toward Quoddy Narrows, even to the point of passing between West Quoddy Head and Sail Rock (7). Although you may see local boats do this, I would most certainly caution any yachtsman from trying it. Not only are the currents swift, requiring a great deal of power to push through them, but they swirl in an erratic matter, pulling boats onto the rocks.

The flashing green light (8) at the entrance to Lubec Narrows is a prominent lighthouse of the caisson type, 53 feet high, rising straight out of the water, with nothing surrounding it to obstruct the view. The local name, which aptly describes it, is the "sparkplug light."

### Tidal Currents

Lubec Narrows Channel (2) is best used during or near slack water, at which time passage through is very straightforward. Unfortunately, slack water within the Narrows lasts only 5-15 minutes. The Channel is well marked and at slack tide you will have no difficulties. As the channel is narrow and steep sided, it is important to follow the buoys carefully. Any short-cuts or excursions out of line will place you on a mud bank.

The key to use of this passage is the timing of the tidal current. If it's not in your favor, it would be best to go all the way around north of Campobello Island (9) and come down through Head Harbour Passage (10). The *Canadian Sailing Directions for Nova Scotia and the Bay of Fundy* place the velocity of current in Lubec Narrows on the outgoing tide at 8.0 knots and 6.0 knots on the incoming tide. These rates may be higher during spring tides! You will also find cross-currents and strong back-eddies, particularly in the region of the bridge.

Velocity is less in the Quoddy Narrows, where it attains 4.0 knots on both ebb and flood tide. To judge the approximate time of slack water through Lubec Narrows, it is important to remember that the ebb current through the Lubec Channel begins about **1½ hours before high tide at Eastport**, only three miles away. Flood tide begins about **one hour earlier** than low tide at Eastport. Sailors exiting from Passamaquoddy Bay through Lubec Narrows can tieup at the Town Landing (12) and watch the direction of flow past the nearby breakwater to determine the schedule.

### International Bridge and Other Navigational Hazards

The International Bridge (11), connecting Lubec with Campobello Island has a vertical clearance of 47 feet. With the 17.5 ft. mean tide range (20 ft. ranges are not uncommon here), this distance is increased considerably at low tide. The navigable portion of the span is between the two pylons protected with wood planking. This is marked by a fixed green light over the center portion and a fixed red light at each of the outermost limits. Horizontal clearance is 100 ft.

Immediately south of the bridge is an unused underwater electrical cable. Boats that have tried to anchor here have become caught on it. Approaching the bridge in fog, radar is useless to find the pylons at the bridge. There are so many structures on either side of the channel that too much clutter is created on the screen for a meaningful picture.

Two structures, although barely indicated on the chart, are nonetheless prominent as you pass through. On the west side is a breakwater (13) extending into the channel, and on the east shore is the Mullholland Point Lighthouse (14). The lighthouse is abandoned now, but you would never know it from its appearance. A beautiful, octagonal-shaped structure, its cedar shingled sides are well maintained and freshly painted a sparkling white. It's further enhanced by a bright red base and cap. Small, dormer windows encircle the outside of the tower.

### Marine Facilities

As you approach Lubec, the scene is remarkably picturesque. With houses rising to the summit of the hill, crowned by a church spire, Lubec has an almost medieval look to it. Beyond the bridge, on the west shore are a number of piers used for off-loading fish to the sardine canneries and herring smoke-house. These piers are not considered safe, even though they are still in use by commercial fishermen. With the new Municipal Marina (Town Landing) (12) conveniently nearby, there is no need to consider tying up at these cannery and smoke-house piers.

The Municipal Marina is on the north side of town, west of the breakwater. The landing is an "L" shaped series of articulated floats. At the outer face there is normally 10 feet of water, but this may be reduced to 7 feet or less during spring tides. There's 200 feet of float space, and a free concrete launching ramp. It quickly shallows along the stem of the dock, making this portion a poor place to lie alongside. On the ebb tide, a strong current pulls past the front of the dock on the way east past the breakwater. Be sure to take this current into account when approaching the dock and to head into the current. Current eddies, though much weaker, are also present on the flood tide.

Anchorage in hard mud buttom off the Town Landing is quite acceptable. The anchor should be well dug in to this tide-scoured bottom. Use two anchors in a Bahamian moor or bow and stern to prevent the tidal current from tripping a single anchor. Otherwise, you might find yourself making a rapid excursion through the channel!

The concrete pier (15) west of the Town Landing is little used either by fishermen or pleasure-boaters. There are too many complaints about boats being damaged by the strong tides and waves knocking them against the pilings. Furthermore, the float inside the pier has been removed because of substantial damage to it. There are no facilities or services at either of the docks, but diesel fuel will be delivered by truck to the

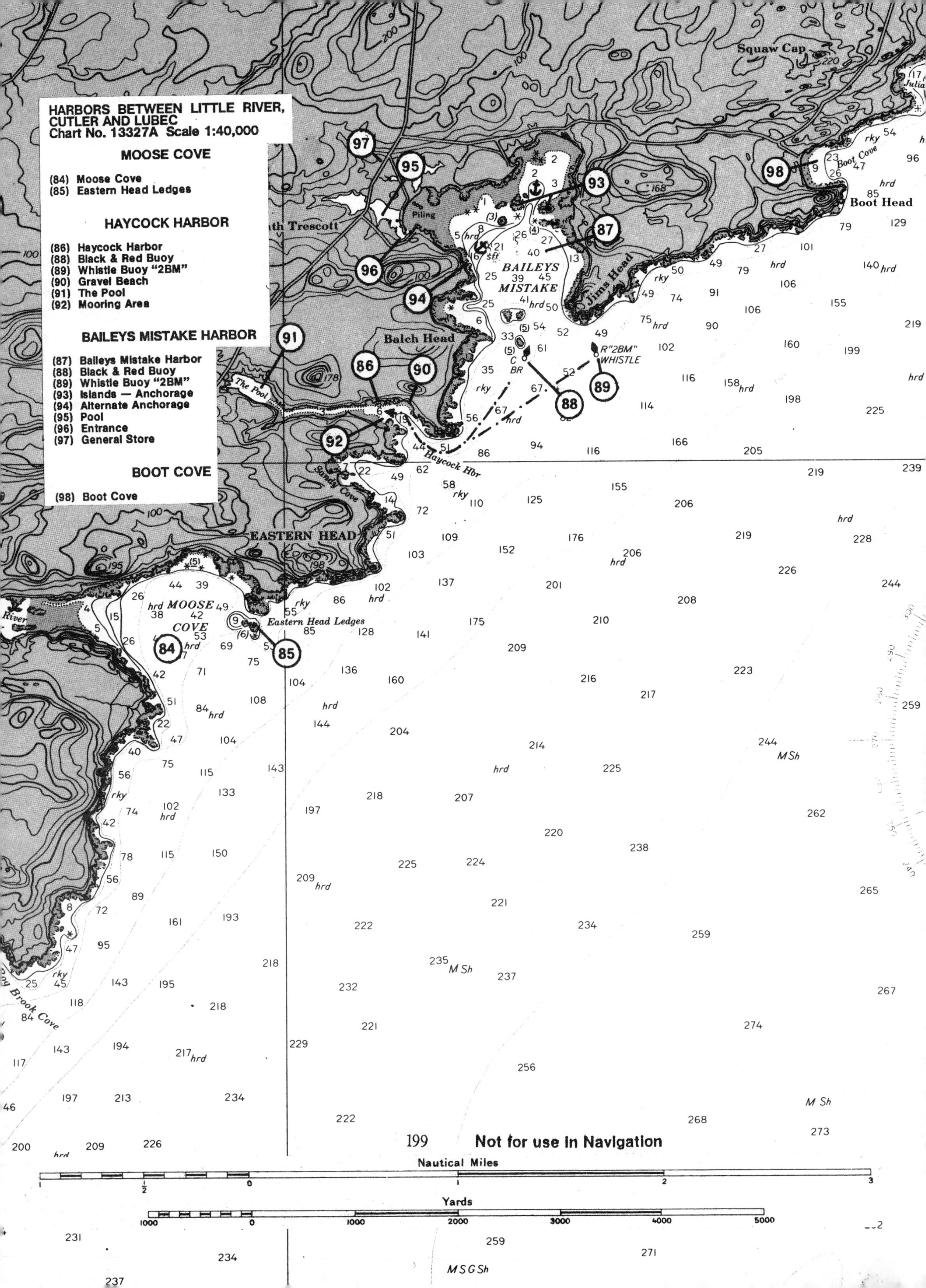
HARBORS BETWEEN LITTLE RIVER, CUTLER AND LUBEC
Chart No. 13327A Scale 1:40,000
MOOSE COVE
(84) Moose Cove
(85) Eastern Head Ledges
HAYCOCK HARBOR
(86) Haycock Harbor
(88) Black & Red Buoy
(89) Whistle Buoy "2BM"
(90) Gravel Beach
(91) The Pool
(92) Mooring Area
BAILEYS MISTAKE HARBOR
(87) Baileys Mistake Harbor
(88) Black & Red Buoy
(89) Whistle Buoy "2BM"
(93) Islands — Anchorage
(94) Alternate Anchorage
(95) Pool
(96) Entrance
(97) General Store
BOOT COVE
(98) Boot Cove
Squaw Cap
Julia
Boot Cove
Boot Head
Jims Head
BAILEYS MISTAKE
Piling
Balch Head
The Pool
R"2BM" WHISTLE
Haycock Hbr
Sandy Cove
EASTERN HEAD
MOOSE COVE
Eastern Head Ledges
River
Brook Cove
Not for use in Navigation
Nautical Miles
Yards

LUBEC,
Chart No. 13328
Scale 1:40,000 Reduced approx. 5%
(1) Quoddy Narrows
(2) Lubec Channel
(3) Lubec
(4) West Quoddy Head
(5) Whistle Buoy "1"
(6) Black & White Bell Buoy "WQ"
(7) Sail Rock
(8) Lubec Channel Lighthouse
(9) Campobello Island
(10) Head Harbour Passage
(11) International Bridge
(12) Municipal Marina-Town Landing
(13) Breakwater
(14) Mulholland Point Lighthouse
(15) Concrete Pier
(16) Tip's Restaurant
(17) Farmer's Red & White Market
(18) Peacock Canning Co.
(19) John McCurdy Smoked Herring Plant
(22) Treat Island
(23) West Quoddy Marine Research Station
(18a) Lubec Packing Co.
Not for use in Navigation
NOTE B
Soundings between the purple limits on the Canadian side of the International Boundary Line in the vicinity of Lubec Channel are referred to Mean Low Water.
FIXED BRIDGE
HOR. CL. 100 FT.
VERT. CL. 47 FT.
CAMPOBELLO
JOHNSON BAY
LUBEC
Lubec Neck
Lubec Channel
Lubec Narrows
QUODDY NARROWS
Mulholland Pt
Charleys Pt
Mowry Pt
Cranberry Pt
Abrahams Plain
FOX HILL
Southern Head
Owen Head
Ragged Pt
Liberty Pt
Liberty Cove
The Boring Stone
Round Rk
Middle Ground
Wormell Ledges
Gravel Bar
Woodward Pt
West Quoddy Head
LOOK TOWER
Porcupine Mt
Sail Rock
Duck Is
Gooseberry Pt
Lower Duck Pond
Upper Duck Pond
Deep Cove
Glensevern Lake
Herring Cove
Eastern Pond
Eastern Head
Red Head
Meadow Brook Cove
Friars Bay
Friars Hd
Snug Cove
Treat I
Dudley I
Gull Rk
Major I
Burial I
Rodgers I
North Lubec
STANDPIPE
Gp Fl (2) 15sec 83ft 18M
HORN
R Bn 308
Fl G 6sec
53ft 6M
HORN
Fl 4sec
WHISTLE
BW "WQ"
BELL
CANADA
UNITED STATES
Nautical Miles
Yards

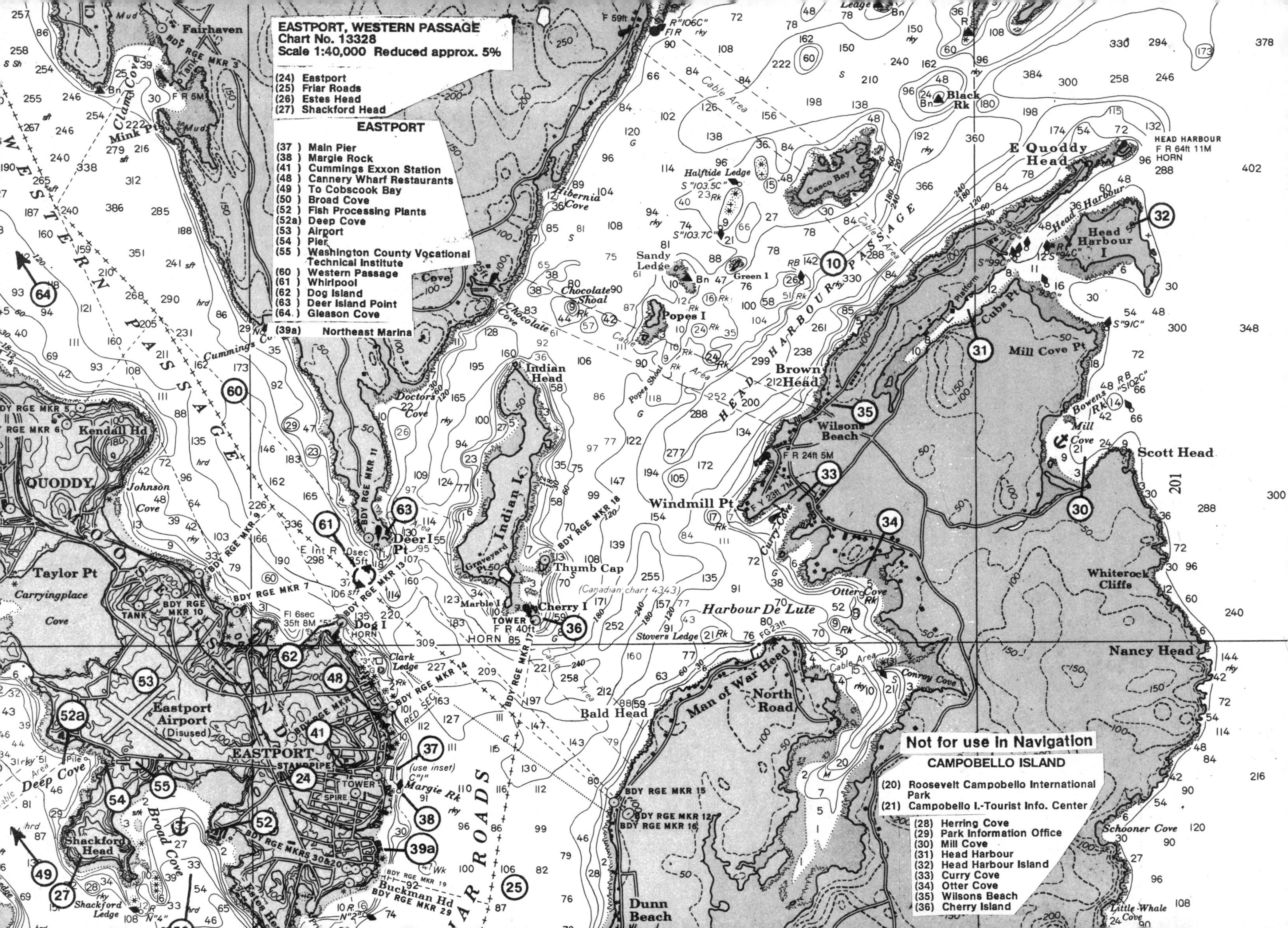

EASTPORT, WESTERN PASSAGE
Chart No. 13328
Scale 1:40,000 Reduced approx. 5%
(24) Eastport
(25) Friar Roads
(26) Estes Head
(27) Shackford Head
EASTPORT
(37) Main Pier
(38) Margie Rock
(41) Cummings Exxon Station
(48) Cannery Wharf Restaurants
(49) To Cobscook Bay
(50) Broad Cove
(52) Fish Processing Plants
(52a) Deep Cove
(53) Airport
(54) Pier
(55) Washington County Vocational Technical Institute
(60) Western Passage
(61) Whirlpool
(62) Dog Island
(63) Deer Island Point
(64.) Gleason Cove
(39a) Northeast Marina
Not for use in Navigation
CAMPOBELLO ISLAND
(20) Roosevelt Campobello International Park
(21) Campobello I.-Tourist Info. Center
(28) Herring Cove
(29) Park Information Office
(30) Mill Cove
(31) Head Harbour
(32) Head Harbour Island
(33) Curry Cove
(34) Otter Cove
(35) Wilsons Beach
(36) Cherry Island
WESTERN PASSAGE
HEAD HARBOUR PASSAGE
Fairhaven
Clam Cove
Mink Pt
Hibernia Cove
Chocolate Cove
Chocolate Shoal
Cummings Cove
Doctors Cove
Kendall Hd
QUODDY
Johnson Cove
Taylor Pt
Carryingplace Cove
Eastport Airport (Disused)
EASTPORT
STANDPIPE
TOWER
SPIRE
Deep Cove
Broad Cove
Shackford Head
Shackford Ledge
Estes Head
Buckman Hd
Margie Rk
Clark Ledge
Dog I
Deer I Pt
Indian Head
Indian I
Graveyard Pt
Marble I
Thumb Cap
Cherry I
(Canadian chart 4343)
Harbour De Lute
Stovers Ledge
Bald Head
Man of War Head
North Road
Dunn Beach
Sandy Ledge
Popes I
Popes Shoal
Green I
Halftide Ledge
Casco Bay I
Black Rk
E Quoddy Head
HEAD HARBOUR F R 64ft 11M HORN
Head Harbour I
Brown Head
Wilsons Beach
Windmill Pt
Curry Cove
Otter Cove
Conroy Cove
Cubs Pt
Mill Cove Pt
Bowens Rk
Mill Cove
Scott Head
Whiterock Cliffs
Nancy Head
Schooner Cove
Little Whale Cove
FRIAR ROADS

concrete fish pier. The Harbormaster is usually found at the Town Landing (12).

### Supplies and Sightseeing

All the shops and a restaurant are conveniently nearby, within a short walking distance. Tip's Restaurant (16) is at the foot of the breakwater. There are some small stores on Water Street, the first street paralleling the water, where simple basic food supplies may be purchased. For more extensive provisioning and a wider selection, you must go a short way out of town to the Farmer's Red & White Market (17). This is at the "Y" intersection of Route 189 where Main St. and Washington St. meet.

Along the waterfront is one of the few remaining survivors of the 23 sardine canning plants that once was a thriving industry and economic mainstay of Lubec. The Peacock Canning Company (18) is open to tours. If a load of sardines (juvenile herring) are in, do avail yourself of the opportunity to watch the process. Automation has never touched this industry. The process is the same as 100 years ago. Women are lined up along a conveyor belt, each with a stack of empty cans near her. As the sardines pass by, each is individually lifted off the belt, its head and tail snipped off with a large pair of shears, and it is carefully placed in the can. The procedure is repeated until the can is filled, when it is then boiled and sealed. The speed and dexterity is truly unbelievable. The movement of fish, shears and fingers, so fast they all melt into one flashing, silvery blur to the eyes.

Still going strong today, is the other remaining factory, the Lubec Packing Company (18a). Located on Commercial Street, it is a descendent of Lubec's golden age of sardine packing. In 1988 they packed 79,000 cases of sardines. From their newsletter (Summer, 1989) we learn much about the early years of this important industry to the area.

"The sardine business in Maine began during the Franco-Prussian War in 1870 when French sardines and other fish products from Europe were difficult to import. The fledgling smoked herring industry in the Eastport-Lubec area attracted the attention of sardine importers and when they saw the volume and quality of the fish in the area, they decided to establish fish canning plants.

The first canning plant in the area was located in Eastport and called the Eagle Preserved Fish Company. It was operated by Wolfe & Reessing and produced canned sardines that were marketed under the Eagle Brand.

In 1875, 60,000 cans of sardines were packed and sold. The product was such a success that by 1880, there were 16 factories operating; one in Lubec and the rest in Eastport. Shortly after the founding of the first factory in Lubec, 22 others were established.

Even though the product that was produced by area factories was well received, the marketers, who were also importers, at first failed to let their customers know that some of their product came from Maine. Since they did not have to worry about "truth in labeling" and the Food and Drug Administration, some of the cans bore labels that were printed in French and on others, there was a small soldered medallion on the cans that said "PACKED IN NANTES, FRANCE." The deception, however, did not last long and soon Maine sardines from Lubec were sold all over the country.

1899 marked the end of the first era of growth for the sardine-packing industry. After that, the small factories were absorbed by larger ones." With a further decline in availability of fish, the number of factories further diminished to the remaining few present.

An important event in the area is the North American Sardine Packing Championships. Held in Black's Harbour across the Bay, this has become one of the most popular events during the Black's Harbour Labor Day Fair at the end of August. Last year's winner filled 112 cans of sardines in the alloted 10 minutes time to receive first prize. Think about it. With a can holding an average of 6 sardines, that means that a sardine per second is accordingly plucked, prepared and placed. The winner actually packed 113 cans, but one was disallowed by the judges.

Near the Sardine Cannery plant is the John P. McCurdy Smoked Herring Plant (19). It is the last remaining facility of its kind in the U.S. Here, the adult herring are skewered in long rows on sticks and hung in the rafters of the smoke-house to be turned the color of deep, burnished gold by the hickory smoke. You won't need to inquire if any herring are being processed, for the enticing aroma of kippered herring will pervade the entire town. Go see how they do it!

**Wildlife and Whales.** The region abounds in all kinds of wildlife. Nearby Machias Seal Island is famous for its number of nesting small Atlantic puffins and Arctic terns. There are razorbill auks, bald eagles, osprey and great blue herons.

This is also one of the finest areas for whale watching. Within these waters are to be seen the northern right whale, minke whale, finbacks, humpbacks, seis and blue whales. These cetaceans arrive in late spring and early summer to mate and calf. They then depart in the late fall. It is possible to view them from land equally as well as from the water. Often they can be observed very close to shore from West Quoddy Head (4) and from East Quoddy Head at the entrance to Head Harbour Passage at the north end of Campobello Island.

The northern right whale, the rarest whale in the world, is the prime whale in the area. It has been proposed that the region be designated as a right whale refuge. The minke whales, a small, evasive species, are frequently seen in the Bay of Fundy. They often approach boats closely and swim into shallow coves, feeding on herring and other small schooling fish.

Many of these exciting animals present themselves to you as you sail in the area. There are tours and professional guides to help point them out to you and provide explicit information. One of these is Capt. E. "Butch" Huntly, and his Seafarers Expeditions, located in Lubec, he takes passengers out in his boat, the "Seafarer," on whale and bird sighting tours, or simply island-hopping. He may be reached at 207-255-8810, or 733-5584.

**West Quoddy Biological Research Station.** Another nearby attraction is the West Quoddy Biological Research Station (23), located in the former Coast Guard Station on West Quoddy Head. The buildings have been converted into laboratories and workshops. One of the buildings serves as a museum and display area of the work being done there. A staff member is usually present to give a tour and to answer questions.

Established in 1980 for the purpose of conducting marine research in the Bay of Fundy, the WQBRS work focused on the study of underwater acoustics and the behavior of the local whales and seals. In conjunction with this, a program of marine mammal stranding rehabilitation has been set up. Stranded or injured whales, purpoises and seals are rescued and helped to get back into deep water. Care and treatment of the injured is provided as needed. This forms an important link with the entire east coast stranding program. There have been massive whale strandings in Cape Cod Bay during the past few years.

If you sight an injured or stranded whale, dolphin or porpoise, call the West Quoddy Biological Research Station and they will provide immediate attention. Their telephone number is (207) 733-8895.

The following protocol for dealing with a stranded marine mammal has been provided by the WQBRS. Following these directions will assure the safety and well being of both the animal and the rescuer.

1. Upon discovery of a stranded animal or animals, there is one Golden Rule that takes precedence above all others: CALL FOR ASSISTANCE. It is extremely important to give detailed, exact directions to the location of any stranding. Precious time can be saved if these directions are compiled before calling.

2. If an animal is caught in pilings, rocks or other obstructions, remove the animal (if possible) into a stable position, BELLY DOWN. An animal lying on its side is likely to drown, or the uneven pressure of its weight causes blood to pool in one area and enhances shock.

3. Once the animal is in an upright position, make sure the pectoral flippers are not underneath the body or supporting all the weight. They are easily broken and this area, as well as the tail flukes, are instrumental in body heat regulation (thermo-regulation). Dig a hold around the animal, especially the flippers and fill the space with water. DO NOT TRY TO WARM THE ANIMAL. Their blubber layer is very thick and when they are out of the water they overheat very quickly. Cool the animal by applying wet towels to as much of the body as possible, keeping in mind those areas of thermo-regulation should be kept the coolest.

4. NEVER OBSTRUCT OR COVER THE BLOWHOLE, and make sure no water enters. Keep sand away from the blowhole and eyes.

5. Handle the animal as little as possible and keep noise to a minimum, since the animal is already undergoing a considerable amount of stress. No flashlights or bulbs should be shone directly into the eyes.

6. AT NO TIME SHOULD AN ANIMAL BE TOWED BY THE TAILSTOCK BACK TO THE WATER! Dislocation of the tail vertebrae can easily occur.

If you have been instructed by WQBRS to re-locate the animal by boat:

1. Load animal onto thick blankets, padding or sling; DO NOT pick it up by the tail or flippers. Flippers should be against the body, not under it.

2. Be as quiet as possible and keep the animal wet, but avoid getting water or sand into the blowhole or eyes.

If, for some reason, it is impossible to procur professional assistance:

1. Place the animal in water only AFTER it has taken a breath and the blowhole is CLOSED. IF POSSIBLE, support the animal behind flippers, rocking it gently side to side BEFORE letting it go.

2. Should the animal start to sink, support and rock it for a while before releasing again. If the animal cannot swim, bring it to WQBRS.

Nature walks, accompanied by one of the staff members, originate from the museum and are scheduled frequently. There are general nature walks, bird walks and bog walks. Some are in the morning, while others are in the evening along with slide shows. However, any small group of interested people may be taken on a non-scheduled tour if the museum staff are not otherwise occupied. Call 207-733-8895.

•

As you cruise farther downeast along Maine's coast, you're approaching the eastern edge of our Eastern Time Zone. There's a noticeable difference in daylight hours. The sun is up earlier and sets later than Boston, New York, Cleveland, Miami or anywhere else in the Eastern Time Zone. At Lubec, you're as far east as our country goes. Lubec and Eastport see the first sunrise in the U.S.A.

### Campobello Island

From Lubec it is only a short taxi ride to Campobello Island on the Canadian side of the bridge. Part of the Province of New Brunswick, Campobello is best known to Americans as the summer home of Franklin D. Roosevelt. From 1883 until 1921, when he was stricken by polio, most of his summers were spent here. He didn't return to Campobello until 1933, although Eleanor Roosevelt and the five children continued to visit the island.

Today, their home ("cottage") is part of a 2,600 acre park, jointly administered by the United States and Canada, known as the Roosevelt Campobello International Park (20). The house is open, with guided tours seven days a week during the summer from 9:00 a.m. to 5:00 p.m. (E.S.T.) and contains most of the original furnishing and interesting memorabilia. New Brunswick is on Atlantic Time, but Campobello stays on Eastern Standard Time.

A Reception Center near the cottage shows two films produced by the Park Commission; *"Beloved Island"* a portrait of the island with emphasis on how Franklin Roosevelt related to it, and *"Campobello—The Outer Island,"* a naturalist's view of the island and its shores.

Most of the Park is protected in its natural state, and includes lakes, beaches, bogs and the fog forests that are characteristic of this part of the country. Thus, the land, as well as the house still exists, and can be seen pretty much as it was during the time of the Roosevelts. Roads, hiking trails and picnic facilities make all these areas easily accessible. Maps of the trails and roads can be obtained at the Visitor's Center at the Roosevelt home, and at the Tourist Information Center (21) at the Canadian side of the bridge.

You'll enjoy a look at scenic Head Harbor, and clambering out to Head Harbour Light beyond East Quoddy Head, at the northeast end of Campobello. Be careful not to tarry too long. The tide comes up fast and can strand you at the lighthouse, only connected to land when the tide is out.

A less publicized resident of the region was the notorious traitor, Benedict Arnold. At the close of the American Revolution, he was engaged in the fishing business on Treat Island (22), north of Lubec. With his wife, Peggy Shippen from Philadelphia, he moved briefly to Snug Cove on Campobello. But to his wife, Snug Cove did not compare at all favorably to Philadelphia and in 1798 they moved to St. John, New Brunswick.

There are several good anchorages along both the eastern and western shores of Campobello Island where you can wait out fog or favorable tidal currents, or drop your hook late in the day, or just visit hospitable Canada. Herring Cove (28) offers better protection than it might appear from looking at the chart. Best anchorage is near the south end, where you must be careful of a fish weir. The entire length of Herring Cove has a beautiful shingle beach with a superb view of the Bay of Fundy and Grand Manan Island. The south end of the beach borders on the Roosevelt Campobello International Park where there are picnic facilities and public restrooms. At the north end is Herring Cove Provincial Park, with picnic and camping areas, restrooms, drinking water, and a telephone at the Park Information Office (29).

Protection and good anchorage is also found in Mill Cove (30) and Head Harbour (31). You can enter Head Harbour from either north or south of Head Harbour Island (32). The preferred channel is north. The west shore of Campobello Island could be followed and entry easily made into Curry Cove (33) or Otter Cove (34) of Harbour De Lute, both close to Eastport.

If you do make landfall at any of the harbors on Campobello and plan to go ashore, be sure to contact customs and immigration on your arrival. During the summer months, a temporary office is set up at Wilsons Beach (35) for the convenience of yachtsmen.

Though the navigation and buoyage sustem of Canada is practically identical to ours, there are some differences. Most notable are the small buoys, which may be spar buoys. There are slender poles, painted green, kept to port, or red, kept to starboard. At low tide they may be lying flat on the surface of the water, making them difficult to see. It may also be hard to determine their color when the light is behind them but the green buoys have a truncated, flat top, while the red ones have a pointed top.

In Head Harbour Passage (10), the flood tide sets southwest, and the ebb tide northeast. Here, in contrast to Friar Roads, the strongest currents are during the ebb tide, reaching 3.5 to 4.0 knots. You will find that due to the particular configuration of waterways, you may have currents within the passage in opposing directions occuring at the same time. There may also be cross-currents up to 1.5 knots. It can be quite an experience tacking your way in with a southerly breeze and a flood tide. Your mind tells you the currents are in your favor and you should be making progress but the boat reacts much differently. At times you will be uncertain whether you are sailing forward or backward!

**Lubec, International Bridge to Campobello**

# CHAPTER 18

# EASTPORT AND THE ST. CROIX RIVER

## EASTPORT—CHART NOS. 13328 AND 13328-INSET

***Where they pry the sun up out of the ocean***

Refer to chart no. 13328 in Chapter 17.

Eastport (24) was so named in 1798 as the most easterly port in the Massachusetts Bay Colony. The town immediately strikes you as having a different feel to it, different quality about the water, the surroundings, and even the light. This is the cold lavender-blue light of far north latutudes. Coming through Head Harbour Passage (10) and looking out over Passamaquoddy Bay toward the mountains of New Brunswick, the feeling is of sailing on the rim of the world. If any music could be determined to match the atmosphere of the region, it would be Sibelius's *Finlandia*.

### Approaches.

Approached from Lubec, through Friar Roads (25), the passage is straightforward and presents no problems. The strongest currents here are found on the flood tide, attaining 3.0 knots, while the ebb tide produces currents of 2.5 knots. Near Moose Island where Eastport is located, close inshore there will be a counter-current during the ebb tide. It sweeps around the south end of the island and into Cobscook Bay past Estes Head (26) and Shackford Head (27).

With a flood tide and the predominant southwest wind, there is little trouble making the run from Little River, Cutler to Eastport, a distance of 30+ nautical miles, in under 5 hours. Refer to the folded chart inside the rear cover of this book. If there is fog, following the 20 fathom curve all the way from the bell buoy off Little River to East Quoddy Head will keep you clear of all dangers. Should radio contact be necessary for assistance, the Canadian fishermen monitor Channel 68 on VHF. Distress calls should be transmitted to the Canadian Coast Guard on Channel 51 and the U.S. Coast Guard on Channel 16.

As you get closer to Eastport, the small lighthouse on Cherry Island (36) serves as a good landmark, with its fixed red light and alternating bands of red and white on the tower.

### Marine Facilities

The main pier (37), with its row of tall poles and lights, can then be easily spotted. If a freighter is tied alongside, you will certainly have no doubts about the location of the pier.

Refer to chart no. 13328-Inset.

The chart shows an "L"-shaped wharf with Margie Rock (38), near the south end. There have been some recent extensive changes in this harbor. The main wharf has been enlarged and expanded to accommodate large commercial vessels. A newly built, additional wharf extends from the shore and terminates at Margie Rock, so the rock is no longer present as a navigational hazard. This new wharf, called "Fish Pier" (39), is primarily used by fishing vessels to offload their catch. It is a poor wharf to tie up to because the vertical pilings are fairly widely spaced. Behind them are horizontal timbers which can catch and hold your boat under water on a rising tide. There have been some incidents where a boat was nearly sunk because of this. Furthermore, if the wind is from the north, you would end up being pounded against the pilings. For yachtsmen, it should be considered as a breakwater and not as a wharf to tie up to.

Extending from the float (40) within the basin is another dock, providing additional space for small boats and sailboats to tie-up. Space is allocated on the inner face, that part closest to the town, for small, open fishing boats—the "mosquito fleet" as they are called. Sailboats may lay along the outer face if room can be found. The harbor is small and space is at a premium. If your boat is 30 feet or over in length, a Township fee of $30 will be charged for use of the basin. This applies to both Canadian and U.S. citizens, and is in addition to the $25 fee for cruising permit for foreign-flag vessels. Coast Guard vessels (42) tie up at the foot of the dock. Neither water nor fuel are available at the float, but diesel fuel will be delivered by truck by Ramsdell Oil Co. (tel. 853-4321) or Eastern Oil (853-4202). Eastern Oil also has propane. For gasoline, carry your own container to Cummings Exxon Station (41), about 200 yards west on Washington St. (chart no. 13328 in Chapter 17).

Although there are two anchorage areas designated within the basin, it is inadvisable, if not altogether impractical, to actually anchor there. Fishing boats along the wharf take up much of the space and an anchored boat would leave no room for maneuvering.

For boats from Canada or other countries, first visiting American shores, Eastport is a port of entry where customs and immigration formalities may be taken care of. The offices are in the basement of the gray granite Post Office, marked on the chart as "Tower" (43). See Chapter 2, General Notes and Recommendations, for more specific information.

By far, the best place for visiting yachtsmen to land at Eastport is at the Northeast Marina (39a). It is only a short 10 minute walk to the center of town, you escape the Township users fee, and there is the added advantage of the many services provided by the marina. Their wharf is easily distinguished by the flags flown from the head of the dock and the two large fuel tanks at its foot. A float with ample space for tie-up has 9-12 foot depths at low tide. It is also easy in access, compared to entering the small, crowded basin behind the Eastport Breakwater. The only disadvantage is its exposure and the lack of protection in the event of a storm. In that case, it takes only a couple of minutes to move over to the Basin. Presently, there is no charge for short stays of a day or two to lie alongside the float. Eleven moorings are available—fee charged. Diesel fuel, gasoline, water and ice are available at the end of the wharf. Showers and laundry are in the shingled building at the foot of the dock. To facilitate provisioning, Northeast Marina will deliver groceries to your boat.

Many yachtsmen preferring a less commercial setting than at the main pier will take their boat to the Cannery Wharf Restaurants (48) (chart no. 13328, Chapter 17). This is sometimes locally referred to as Stinson's Wharf. Here, at the site of a former sardine cannery, dockage is available with power, water and ice (no fuel). There is a restaurant complex ranging from informal take-out service from the Clam Kibbin, to the more elegant dining room of the Cannery. Reservations are recommended for the Cannery. Views from the wharf can't be beat and an additional bonus is being able to watch the small ferry which plies the waters from here to Deer Isle.

Editor's Note. When I visited there in September, a whole fleet of sailboats had come down the length of Passamoquoddy Bay from St. Andrews Yacht Club, New Brunswick, and had their award dinner at the Cannery Wharf Restaurant. They stayed overnight rafted at the wharf. At low tide the wharf was even with their spreaders! Many of them knew your author, and a fun time was had by all.

Recently opened is the Flag Officers Mess Restaurant (48a) on Water St. in the center of town. In pleasant, comfortable surroundings they serve lunch and dinner, plus giving you superb views of the harbor and Friar Roads.

A short walk north out of town along Water St. brings you to Rolandos Restaurant (48b), featuring Italian fare, as well as steaks and seafoods. All menu items, including fresh dough made to order pizza are available for take-out.

As you proceed from Lubec to Eastport and on to Passamaquoddy Bay and the St. Croix River, tidal ranges **increase.**

Here are mean tide ranges:

Lubec 17.5 ft.
Eastport 18.4 ft.
Robbinston 19.2 ft.

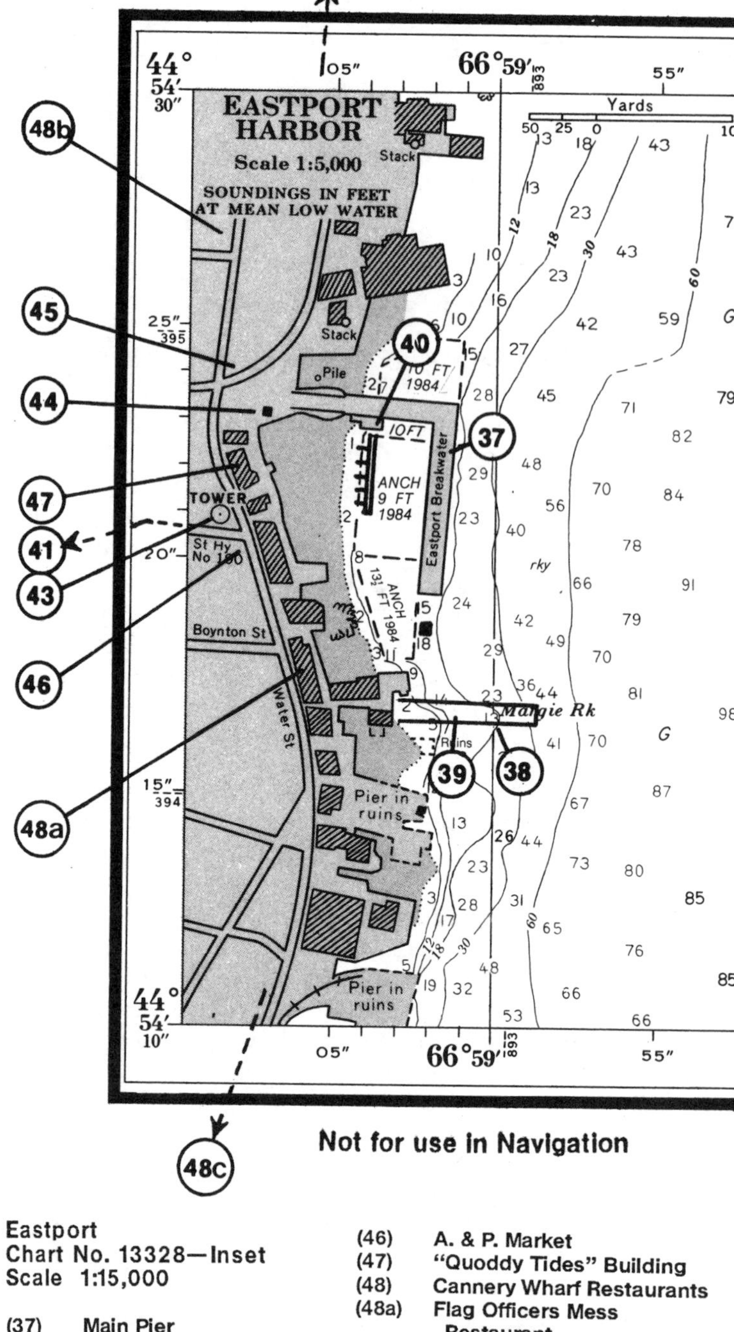


Eastport
Chart No. 13328—Inset
Scale 1:15,000

(37) Main Pier
(38) Margie Rock
(39) Fish Pier
(40) Float
(41) Cumming's Exxon Station
(43) Post Office and Customs Office
(44) Rosies Hot Dog Stand
(45) Moose Island Marine
(46) A. & P. Market
(47) "Quoddy Tides" Building
(48) Cannery Wharf Restaurants
(48a) Flag Officers Mess Restaurant
(48b) Rolando Restaurant
(48c) Downeast Lobster Shack

Calais 20 ft.

These are **mean** ranges. Two and one half feet more is not uncommon. Be sure you allow enough scope when you anchor, and stay away from non-floating docks.

## Supplies and Sightseeing

Most of the businesses of Eastport are located on Water St., the first street parallel to the waterfront. At the foot of the pier is a public telephone and Rosies

Hot Dog Stand (44). Across the road is Moose Island Marine (45) where marine supplies and charts are available. The nearest grocery is the A & P Market (46) on Water St. across the street from the Post Office (43). Several coffee shops and small restaurants are along Water St.

A pleasant time may be spent on a rainy afternoon in the Marine Library and Reading Room of the Quoddy Tides Newspaper building (47). Here, you may peruse their collection of books, periodicals and charts in comfortable chairs, overlooking the harbor and Bay. A thoughtfully placed pair of binoculars is at hand to help you watch boating and wildlife activity.

Nowhere will you find civic pride evidenced to a greater degree than the 4th of July celebration held at Eastport. It lasts the greater part of a week and culminates in a giant fireworks display. Activities that begin at 9:00 in the morning and last past midnight include many contests, e.g., the fastest knitter in the east contest, boat races and foot races, and street dances with live bands. A favorite is the relay race, Eastport style, done with a codfish! The motto is "exercise your bod, carry a slippery cod." Airplane rides are available over Passamaquoddy Bay and there are hourly boat cruises on the Bay.

### History

The city of Eastport, on Moose Island, is surrounded by frigid waters of the Bay of Fundy, which pour into the deep and navigable Passamaquoddy Bay. The sea has always been the basis of the existence and the history of Eastport. It provided an inexhaustible supply of fish, cod, haddock, and herring; and the means to transport these fish. As the fishing industry expanded, so did the construction of trading schooners and the development of a vigorous maritime trade in cargo and passengers to Europe, the West Indies and South Seas Islands. So thoroughly was the sea inextricably linked in the thoughts and activities of the residents that when the first horse was brought to the Island in 1804, it was greeted with "surprise, curiosity and even fear."

There had always been a brisk trade in foodstuffs, meat and munitions between the most easterly border towns of the U.S. and the Maritime Provinces of Canada, but this activity was markedly heightened after the famous embargo act of President Jefferson in 1807, wherein American ships wre forbidden to trade with England or France. With this new political climate, the complex shoreline, swift currents and the mask of fog and dark of night created an ideal arena for the development of contraband and smuggling.

When the U.S. declared war on Great Britain in 1812, effects were very little on both sides of the border in Passamaquoddy Bay. Both sides, by mutual consent, determined to carry on business as usual. But in 1814, when the British proclaimed a blockade of the Atlantic Coast, Eastport once again became a center for the smuggling trade.

Throughout the latter part of the 1800's, Eastport was a center of coastal trading, much of it in three, four and even five-masted schooners built there. It was also an important port in the North Atlantic Packet Trade. Barks and brigs from Eastport could make England in twenty-three days. When sailing ships gave way to steam, Eastport had four different steamship lines, making regular runs between Boston and St. John, New Brunswick. However, since the depression years, shipbuilding, shipping and the fishing industry have all gradually declined.

Eastport has perhaps been hardest hit of the eastern Maine towns, because of the demise of its industry and shipping. Many young people have moved away, and you'll see empty homes, factories, and commercial buildings. In recent years, some homes have been dismantled and moved to Deer Island, New Brunswick, just north of Eastport. Still, Eastport feels that the strength of her future lies in her past, and her waterfront has been modernized and piers enlarged to participate in a new era of international trade. There is now a steadily increasing number of vessels using this port and carrying the products of Maine, primarily wood-pulp, to the rest of the world.

## COBSCOOK BAY—CHART NOS. 13328, 13328A

Chart no. 13328 will be found in Chapter 17.

Cobscook Bay (49), a large and complex series of bays and waterways west of Moose Island, is mostly in a completely natural state, with no towns and few habitations along its shores. For all its beauty and abundance of wildlife, it is seldom used by visiting or even local yachtsmen. Navigational aids are few and the many channels with swift currents, the unmarked ledges and rocks require strict attention at all times. Notwithstanding, there are innumerable, beautiful coves where the adventuresome sailor may anchor with security and in solitude. There are bold headlands, steep forested hills, vast shallows, clear deep water, islands galore, and a maze of waterways. This is a great mini-cruising area, but you **must** keep track of where you are.

### Broad Cove—Chart No. 13328

Broad Cove (50), on the south side of Moose Island and west of Eastport, is easy to enter but there's little room to anchor. Favor the east shore to avoid the many unmarked rocks and ledges extending from Shackford Head (27). Two fish processing plants (52), each with a pier, are prominent on the east shore of the Cove. The northernmost has a float where you can land your dinghy. No fuel, water or ice are available at either pier. The plant processes fish scales into pearl essence, used in making iridescent jewelry.

Within Broad Cove are several moorings belonging to local fishermen, a fish weir, and several pens used for rearing salmon, a relatively new industry in the Quoddy area. Young salmon, brought from hatcheries on shore, are kept in the enclosures, fed, and allowed to grow to maturity. Each cage has a complex system of anchors extending outward to hold it in place. They are usually moored in at least 30 feet of water and do not necessarily display any lights at night, although there will always be a watchman.

Several hundred large, silver fish, flashing around inside a 40 foot square cage at feeding time makes an impressive sight. The value of these salmon is considerble, so any approach for inspection should be made with caution. Most of the watchmen have rifles or shotguns handy to deter marauding seals that have caused considerable losses to salmon farms at certains time of the year. Weapons could also be used to deter two-legged marauders. Do not approach the cages after dark unless you are expected, and under no circumstances do any diving in their vicinity. Many of the coves and inlets, in both American and Canadian waters are now utilizing this procedure which has considerable economic potential.

These pens are also present in the adjacent cove, Deep Cove (52a). The success of the program has prompted considerable expansion and starting last spring, 16 cages were placed in Broad Cove and 16 in Deep Cove. Successful as it is to the company owners and delightful as it may be to the lover of eating fresh salmon, the yachtsman cannot be quite as enthusiastic, for with all these cages and their surrounding system of support, little room for anchoring is left in either of these coves.

Contrary to the indication on the chart, the airport (53) bordering the cove is **not** disused. Clint Tuttle operates the Eastern Marine Aviation charter service from here. Available seven days a week, this makes access to any other commercial airport quite convenient and easy. Tel. 207-853-4410.

### Deep Cove—Chart No. 13328

As in Broad Cove, anchoring space has been fairly well pre-empted by the salmon pens. What room is left is in exposed and deep water. A well maintained pier (54) is on the east shore of the cove. 435 feet long, it has 12 feet depth at its outer face and a float for dinghy landing. Next to it is a boat ramp of flat, granite slabs, a former seaplane launching ramp. The pier is used by the adjacent Washington County Vocational Technical Institute (55). This is a marine vocational school, with courses in one and two year programs in boatbuilding, marine mechanics, marine painting and commercial fishing. Students have classroom instruction plus actual experience on the school's several fishing vessels.

On the north shore of Deep Cove are the remains of a pier, and at low tide, the barely discernible timbers of several abandoned coasting schooners. These relics of the four-masted schooners that once carried the cargo and fame of Eastport to the rest of the world, were brought here in 1932 as their final resting site.

### Federal Harbor—Chart No. 13328A

Excellent anchorage may be obtained on either side of Black Head in Federal Harbor (56), near the south end of Cobscook Bay. There are no docks or facilities on shore. Boats intending to make the passage through the reversing falls of Pembroke (Cobscook Falls-57) will frequently wait here until the most favorable state of tide is reached.

Cobscook Bay is one of the American eagle's four major wintering grounds in Maine. It has the densest nesting eagle population in Maine. Long Island, southeast of Federal Harbor (56) in South Bay, is a Preserve of The Nature Conservancy. No landing is permitted. Although no eagles nest there now, they have done so in the past, and Long Island is currently used as a roosting and feeding area.

Long Island was subjected to heavy logging during World War II. The Northern half was burned in 1958 by the Trescott fire which jumped across the narrow strait from the mainland. Harbor seals haul out on the northern ledges off Long Island, and you may see deer and smaller mammals that come and go between the mainland and the island.

### Cobscook Falls—Chart No. 13328A

As the tide rushes in to fill Dennys Bay (58) and Whiting Bay (59), it is compressed into the narrow channel between Mahar Point and Falls Island. In the middle, a huge boulder blocks the flow, creating the falls and a maelstrom of churning, boiling water. The 9-12 knot current trying to get past this obstruction will come straight up off the bottom creating high mounds of water which alternate with deep whirlpools. The process, with the same fearsome results, occurs on the ebb tide. At mid-tide there is a 12 foot drop between the two ends of the falls! A Maine State Park, with picnic facilities is on Mahar Point at the falls.

For some, the highlight of their cruise is taking their boat through the falls. It has been done without incident many times before, always with the presence with someone having "local knowledge." Those who want to run the falls, either in their own boat or in a charter boat should contact Bob Peacock in Lubec for specific information. The water is deep enough but the passage is narrow, and it snakes its way around the two boulders shown on the chart near the southwest end,. It's not passable safely when the current is at strength.

### Schooner Cove—Chart No. 13328A

Schooner Cove (57a) provides good anchorage, with mud bottom, amidst beautiful surroundings. Thirty to forty years ago, you could often see as many as 6 or 8 big four and five-masted schooners at anchor here. Plan to enter when the tide is in your favor for it runs quite swiftly past the constriction between Denbow Point and Leighton Point. You don't have to go through Cobscook Falls (57) to get to Schooner Cove from Eastport.

### Whiting Bay—Chart No. 13328A

I have not sailed Whiting Bay, having seen it only from the land side where I have admired its raw beauty. The main point of interest here is its large seal rookery.

COBSCOOK BAY
Chart No. 13328A
Scale 1:40,000 Reduced approx. 8%
(56) Federal Harbor
(57) Reversing Falls (Cobscook Falls)
(57a) Schooner Cove
(58) Dennys Bay
(59) Whiting Bay
Not for use in Navigation
Nautical Miles
Yards
Leach Pt
Sipp Bay
Hersey Cove
Hersey Pt
Herseys Upper Ledge
Pennamaquan River
Coggins Head
HERSEY NECK
Rogers Pt
EAST BAY
Pattangal Cove
Lincoln Cove
Nipps I
Redington I
Red Cove
Garnet Pt
Clement Pt
Pipeline
Middle Ground
Two Hour Rk
Gangway Ledge
Sheep Cove
Birch Pt
Kelly Pt
LEIGHTON NECK
Marsh
Red I
Birch Pt Ledge
Smith Rk
COBSCOOK BAY
Wilson Ledges
Gove Pt
Youngs Cove
Long Cove
Schooner Cove
Leighton Pt
Razor I
Denbow Pt
Leighton Rock
Youngs Pt
SOUTH BAY
Huckins Ledge
Little Dram I
Dram I
Mahar Pt
Cobscook Falls
Denbow I
Mink I
Fox I
Falls I
Ruth Pt
DENBOW NECK
Edgecomb Pt
Birch Is
Raft Cove
Race Pt
Huckins
Coffins Pt
Coffins Neck
Nutter Cove
Morrison Cove
Cobble Hill
Gooseberry I
Horan Head
Black Head
Long I
North Trescott
CROW NECK
WHITING BAY
Straight Bay
Parker I
Talbot Cove
Marong Cove
Federal Hbr
Carlos Cove
Dougherty Cove
Dougherty Pt
Bar I
Broad Cove
Bassett C
Scrub I
OVHD PWR CAB AUTH. CL. 45 FT

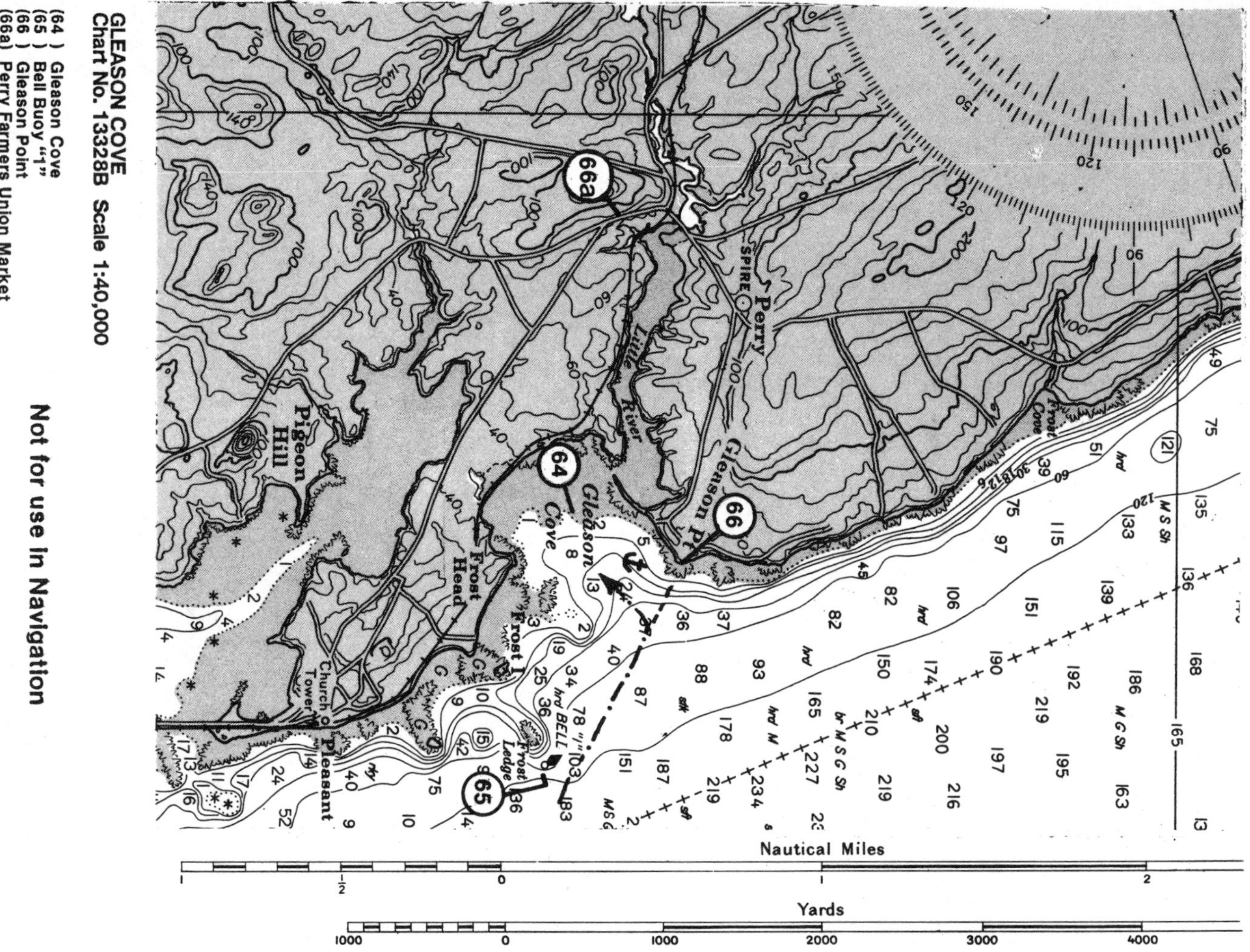


## WESTERN PASSAGE—CHART NO. 13328

Chart 13328 will be found in Chapter 17.

Western Passage (60), used as the principal entry to Passamaquoddy Bay, has as its most interesting feature what is affectionately called "the old sow." This is a whirlpool (61), which, when conditions are right, is the largest whirlpool in the world. It forms in the area between Dog Island (62) and Deer Island Point (63), slightly northeast of the center of the channel, that is, closer to the Canadian (Deer I.) side. To avoid it, keep closer to the American side of the channel near Dog Island.

This whirlpool is something to be treated with respect, for it can and has taken a 10,000 ton vessel out of control and spun it around a full 180 degrees. Small boats going into it come up in pieces. Its maximum strength is reached about 3 hours after low water, and passage through will usually be safe from one hour before to one hour after either high water or low water. Whenever going through this area, keep a firm hand on the tiller and a watch for numerous smaller whirlpools that can be seen in advance and circumvented.

On the flood tide in Western Passage, the strongest currents, about 5.0-6.0 knots, are closer to the Canadian east side, while on the American west side, they are about half that velocity. However, starting about 1.5 hours **before** full high water at Eastport, there will be a counter-current formed which will ebb at 0.5 to 1.0 knot. This current starts at Gleason Cove (64) at the north end of the passage, and continues down to Eastport, closely following the American shore. Thus, at this time, there is a flood current going up the Canadian side of Western Passage and an ebb current coming down on the American side.

## GLEASON COVE, PASSAMAQUODDY BAY CHART NO. 13328B

Refer to folded chart inside rear cover to show relationships between Western Passage, Gleason Cove, Passamaquoddy Bay and the St. Croix River.

Gleason Cove (64) is one of the few coves on the American side of Passamaquoddy Bay where you can take shelter. Be certain to give bell buoy "1" (65) at Frost Ledge ample clearance before turning to enter the cove. It appears to be farther out into the channel than it would seem from the chart and could be easily missed. After rounding the buoy, head over toward Gleason Point (66), traversing more than half-way across the Cove before heading in. By heading towards Gleason Point, you avoid the shallow 2 foot spot. Along the north shore of the cove, the land rises steeply as a bold cliff. Ledge extending into the cove from Gleason Point comes out much further than the chart shows and provides good protection from wind and seas from the north. Only in a strong and persistent norther will any appreciable swell coming down Passamaquoddy Bay be reflected into the cove.

Be prepared at all stages of the tide for a current which swirls within the cove. Anchor wherever there is space between the moored boats. The bottom is mud, but holding is only moderately good, for the mud is so soft a nature that your anchor will pull through it in any strong wind.

Along the entire north shore, about 150 feet out, is a row of poles that are difficult to see at high tide, for many have had their tops broken off during winter storms. Do not go between these poles and the shore lest you run the risk of fouling your propeller, because a closed loop of ⅜ inch polypropelene rope lies just below the surface and extends to shore where it is tied at a point on high ground. These are haul-ins, used to keep the fishermen's dories out in deep water until needed. Last fall your editor and author watched some Passamaquoddy Indian fishermen landing their catch, transferring it from a larger boat to a dory, then to a truck on the beach.

There are no docks, but dinghy landing may be made anywhere along the shore. Be sure to carry your dinghy above the high tide line, even if expect to be gone for only a short time. With a tide range of close to 21 feet, the water can rise with surprising rapidity. Some dinghies are tied to stakes above the high water mark.

The nearest grocery store is Perry Farmers Union Market (66a), approximately one mile west of Gleason Cove.

## ST. CROIX RIVER
## CHART NO. 13328C, AND INSET

A deep navigable channel leads all the way up the St. Croix River to a point where the river sharply turns west at Devils Head (67). This allows vessels of up to 6,000 to 8,000 gross tons to use the wharf (81a) 1.25 miles north of Sand Point, where a large tuna processing and canning plant is located. Vessels also come here for the transport of potatoes, pulpwood and to bring products to New Brunswick from other parts of the world. Even this far from the open sea, there's commercial traffic that must be watched out for.

Between the mouth of St. Croix River and Devils Head (67), current velocities are about 1.5-2.0 knots. From there west to the head of navigation at the towns of Calais (USA) and St. Stephen, New Brunswick, they attain a rate of 3.0 to 4.0 knots. The channel is well marked with a controlling depth of 7 feet beyond Whitlocks Mill (68). At strength of tide, buoys may be towed under at the Narrows (69).

At the bend of the channel past Knights Point (see Chart No. 13328-Inset) pay particular attention to your depths, for more often than not, buoy C "13" clearly shows where there is no water at low tide by lying on its side in the mud.

We have posted locations of three recently added large red buoys R "112c" (70), R "114C" (71), and R "114.6" (72) not shown on the chart. These were placed as an aid for vessels headed up river to the wharf and tuna plant (81a). They all show a flashing red light and have a radar reflector. There is no sound mechanism, although they look like bell or gong buoys. The southernmost, R "112C" (70) is near Joes Point by the 13 foot spot and replaces the red spar buoy there. The next, up river, R "114C" (71) is off the bluff of Lower Bayside in 35 feet depth. The third, R "114.6" (72), marks the edge of the reef north of Sand Point.

The few obstructions in St. Croix River are all marked. Little Dochet Island (73) always shows dry land above high water, while the shallow bank east of it is marked by black can C "1" (74). The southernmost ledge extending from St. Croix Island (76) is appropriately named Half-tide Ledge (75). Although not marked, it is seldom a problem.

Near the mouth of the St. Croix River, there's a free concrete Robbinston Launching Ramp at the public rest area off U.S. Route 1. The exact location is shown in the big folded chart inside the rear cover of this book. This is the best and most convenient ramp to use if you want to explore Passamaquoddy Bay and the St. Croix River in your trailerable boat.

St. Croix Island (76) was the site of the first attempted permanent settlement on the American Coast. It's now an International Park, jointly administered by Canada and the United States. Here, in 1604, Pierre du Gast, the Sieur de Monts with Captain Samuel Champlain and 70 colonists settled and stayed a winter before departing. To anchor here, go in as close as you feel you can north of the island. The holding ground is reasonably good, but make sure you have adequate scope, and come back before the tide turns in case it does anything

St. Croix Island at the mouth of the St. Croix River where the French established the first European settlement in New England, in 1604

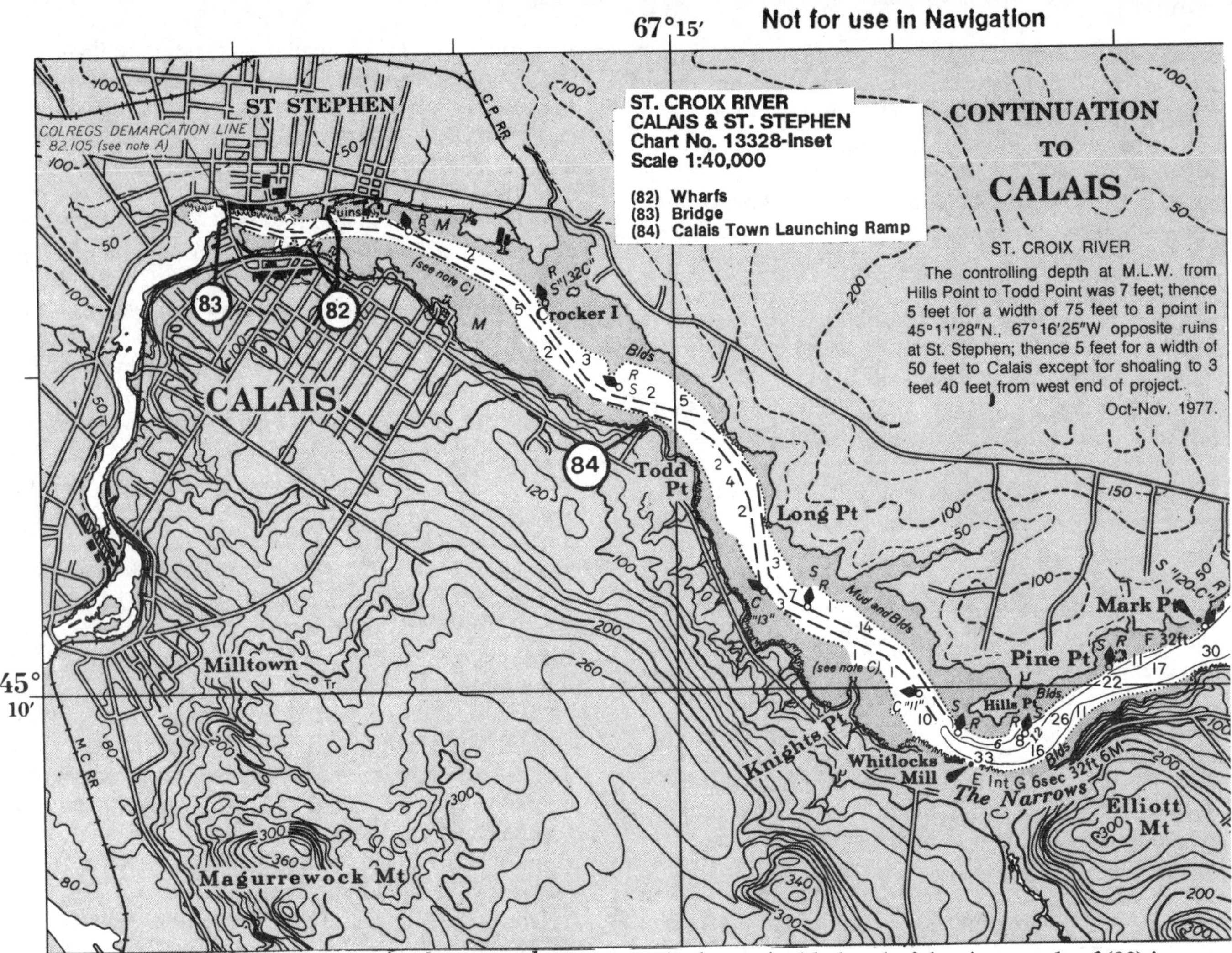


strange to the boat. You are permitted to go ashore. Like many of the Canadian lights, the intensity of the lighthouse beam is highly directional. In this case, the greatest intensity is towards Todds Point (77). There's a free, stone Red Beach Public Launching Ramp (81b) on the west shore southwest of St. Croix Island.

At Devils Head (67), where the river takes a sharp turn west, the ruins shown on the chart are no longer visible, and the pier no longer exists. Several small summer houses are present here.

Oak Bay (78) is all in Canada, and is a pleasant place. There is adequate water, with the bulk of the Bay having about 2 fathoms at low water. In the lower portion, the only spot that can be cause for concern is the spit of ledge (79), which extends west nearly 300 yards from the east shore. The rest of the Bay is navigable up to the latitude of Spoon Island (80), with only a few shallows.

Near Todds Point (77), close to the confluence of the St. Croix River, Oak Bay and the Waweig River, is the St. Croix International Yacht Club (81). Formed in 1981, their membership draws from both the American and Canadian sides of the border. Every summer they have a "St. Croix Weekend" with friendly rivalry races with neighboring St. Andrews Yacht Club. There are no moorings for visiting yachts, but a member's mooring might be available. If not, anchorage in mud bottom is quite satisfactory just outside the moorings.

Refer to chart no. 13328 Inset, Continuation to Calais. Local people pronounce Calais, Ca-liss.

At the navigable head of the river, a wharf (82) is present on each side for the towns of Calais, USA, and St. Stephen, Canada.

Both Town Wharfs (St. Stephen and Calais) have a float alongside with 4 feet of depth at low tide. The mooring between the two is a guest mooring, courtesy of the St. Croix Yacht Club. It is a good, heavy one (2,000 lbs.) with heavy chain and there is no fee for its use. The Calais Town Launching Ramp (84) is gravel and located off the street ending west of Todd Point. Both towns are ports of entry, with customs offices on each side of the bridge (83). You'll find all kinds of stores including groceries, in both towns.

•

Editor's Note. The scope of this book does not include New Brunswick although Don has covered Campobello Island and its anchorages in some detail and made reference to other Canadian land marks and passages. If you get up this far, do yourself a favor and take up to a week to enjoy Passamaquoddy Bay. This is a mini-cruising area of its own. There are many coves and rivers all around the bay. I particularly enjoyed the Magaguadavic River, and St. Andrews is one of the prettiest towns you'll ever see, with the kind of shopping opportunities your ladies will enjoy and one of the finest hotels anywhere. Deer Island is beautiful, with many anchorages, coves and harbors off both shores. These are all shown on the big folded chart inside the rear cover.

Chapter 2, U.S. Coast Pilot 1, or weekly Notice to Mariners which include new or

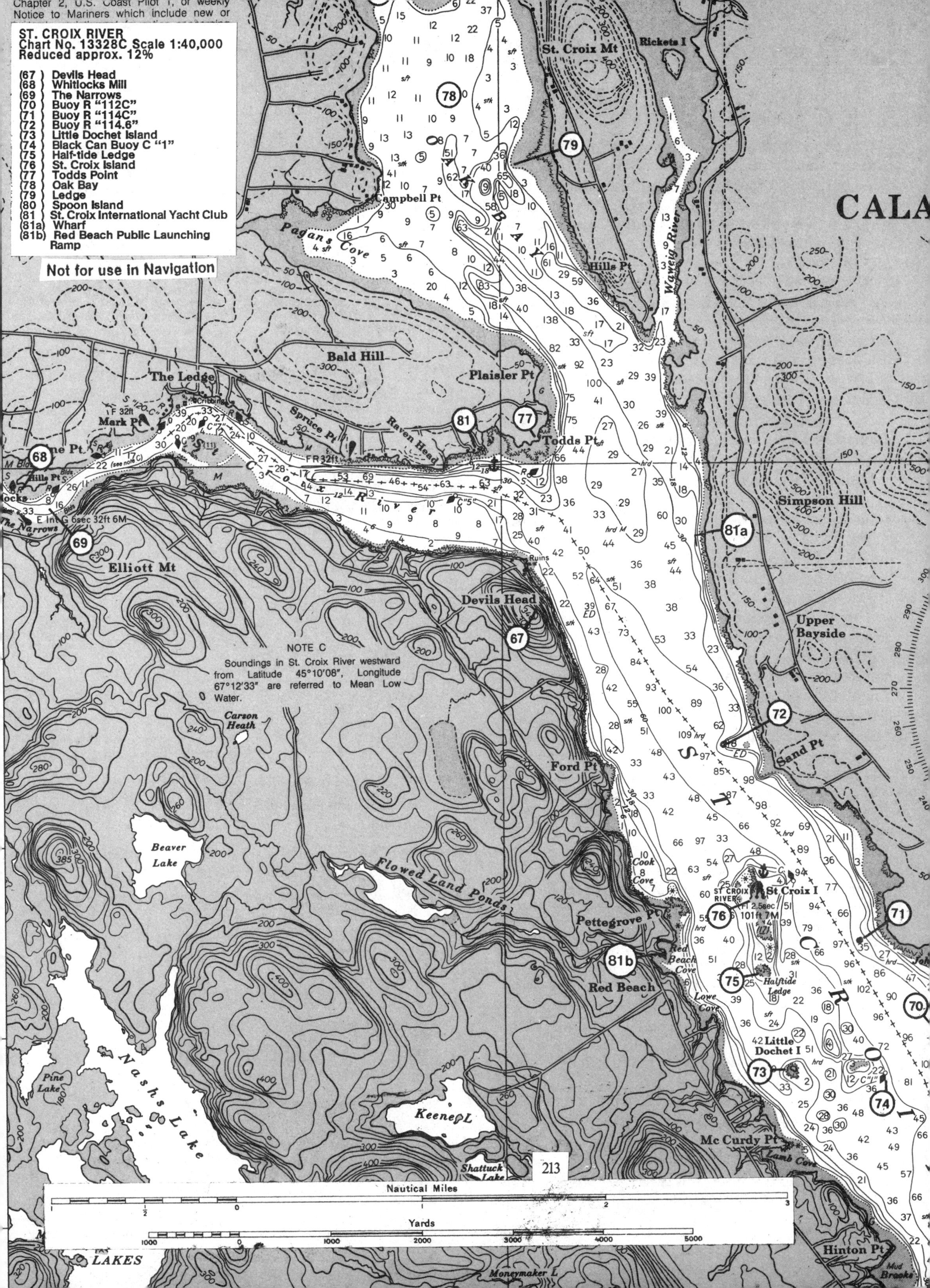

# APPENDIX I

## MAINE CHARTER LIST

Fortunately for those who live in other parts of the country, there's a thriving charter fleet in Maine, any kind of boat you could want. Some of the smaller ones are best suited to puttering around in bays (nothing wrong with Penobscot Bay or Mount Desert Island for a week or two!), and you can charter larger craft for coastal cruising.

The two lists that follow are separated into categories, bareboats and windjammers. If you're a landlubber or a neophyte sailor, the windjammers provide an economical and good introduction to the Maine coast. These boats are two-masted schooners, generally about 100 ft. long. Most of them were originally fishing schooners, working on the Grand Banks, or carrying fish or cargo along the coast. The "Isaac M. Evans" is a former Delaware Bay oyster dragger. A few were built specifically for the Maine Schooner passenger trade, e.g., the "Mary Day," "American Eagle," "Heritage," "Anglelique," and "Harvey Gamage." All are U.S. Coast Guard inspected and approved for safety. Nearly all are based in Penobscot Bay and most of them cruise for 5½ days. They will all send brochures and you can then make your choice. Maine is unique in the size of its windjammer fleet.

The bareboat fleets are useful not only to people from other parts of the country. If you're a working stiff and have only a limited time, you have to make a forced march from Long Island Sound or anywhere south of the Cape Cod Canal. You can get to Maine in a few days by sailing 24 hours, but you need a big crew to stand watches, and you'll get to Maine needing rest. If you ferry your boat most of the way up on weekends, you deprive yourself of the use of your boat evenings, and you lose time taking public transportation back home from where you left your boat. Why fight it? Take advantage of the excellent charter fleet. Charter the boat of your choice in Maine and enjoy a leisurely cruise for all the time you have.

Some of the bareboats listed can be optionally provided with a skipper aboard. For neophytes, this is advisable even with Don Johnson's excellent sailing directions. Maine cruising is not for beginners. In addition to these bareboats, there are a number of crewed boats in Maine. These fluctuate too much for us to make a useful list. Best advice is to work through charter agencies listed in the back pages of boating magazines. These agents know the boats and will match your desires to the best choices for you. Crewed boats are not cheap, but the crew will include a skipper, a cook, and sometimes a deckhand. You'll cruise in style, though for many reasons, your editor prefers bareboats.

We are not including prices because these fluctuate too rapidly. The Maine charter season is short, but prices are not out of line with prices charged in other popular east coast cruising areas.

Try to make arrangements well in advance. Most of the choice boats are booked for the season months ahead. Six months is not too much lead time for reserving a charter boat.

If you have time, sail your own boat up to Maine. This guide is designed to make Maine cruising easy for you, but it assumes basic cruising skills on your part, especially good navigation skills. You'll enjoy this lovely and dramatic shore, as thousands of skippers before you have done.

### Bareboat Charters

**Bar Harbor Boating Co.**
Sargent Drive, Mount Desert, ME 04660
(207) 276-5838
5 sailboats, 30′ to 38′

**Bay Island Yacht Charter Co.**
Camden, ME 04843
(207) 236-2776

**Beaman Yacht Charters**
Star Route 2
Robinhood, ME 04530
(207) 371-2827
Fred and Susan Beaman
Cape Dory 33 sloop

**Bristol Offshore Ltd.**
Gamage Shipyard, South Bristol, ME 04568
(207) 644-8181

**Bucks Harbor Marine Charters**
Box 296, Brooksville, ME 04617
(207) 326-8839

**Cape Dory Charters**
Robinhood Marine Center, Robinhood Cove, Robinhood, ME 04530
(207) 371-2525
12 Cape Dory sailboats, 25′ to 45′

**Classic Charters**
Box 206, Boothbay Harbor, ME 04538
(207) 633-2151
Located Boothbay Harbor, Southwest Harbor. 40 sailboats, 25′ to 41′, provisioning, skipper, sailing instruction available

**Coveside, Inc.**
Christmas Cove
South Bristol, ME 04568
(207) 644-8282
Mike Mitchell
Pacific Seacraft; daysailers

**Eastport Boat Yard and Supply**
P.O. Box 190
Deep Cove Road
Eastport, ME 04631
(207) 853-6049
Daniel MacNaughton
*Eric*, 32′ wooden Atkin double-ended gaff-rigged ketch (1925)

**Fitz-Patrick Sailboat Charters**
P.O. Box 825
Gardiner, ME 04345-0825
(800) 626-0769 or (207) 549-3196
Jim Fitz-Patrick
25′ and 30′; sail from Rockland

**Captain G.W. Full & Associates**
126 Beacon Street
Marblehead, MA 01945
(617) 631-4902
42′ and 44′ motor yachts only

**Getaway Charters**
Box 6084
Falmouth, ME 04105
(207) 744-2776
Mark Pentilescu
31′ Pearson and 322 O'Day

**Gull Haven**
Box 1282
Southwest Harbor, ME 04679
(207) 244-9233
John Bell
19′ to 40′ sail and motor

**Ed Hamilton & Co.**
Box 430
North Whitefield, ME 04353
(800) 621-7855 or (207) 549-7855
Ed Hamilton
40′ to 150′ sail and power

**Handy Boat Charters**
215 Foreside Road, Falmouth Foreside, ME 04105
(207) 781-5110
30 sailboats, 34′ to 42′, sailing instruction available

**Hinckley Yacht Charters**
Bass Harbor Marine, Bass Harbor, ME 04653
(207) 244-5066
Located Mt. Desert Island, ME. 40 sailboats, Sabres, Hinckleys, 30′ to 43′, provisioning, skipper available

**Holladay Marine**
Southport Bridge
West Boothbay Harbor, ME 04575
(207) 633-4767
Sally and Lou Holladay
30′ to 34′ Tartans; instruction

**$H_2$ Outfitters**
P.O. Box 72
Orr's Island, ME 04066
(207) 833-5257
Jeff Cooper; Whitney Smith
Sea kayak outfitter; tours and instruction

**Kimberly Yacht Charters**
Box 64, Boothbay Harbor, ME 04538
(207) 633-3717
Located West Southport, ME. 18 sailboats, 32′ to 40′, skipper, sailing instruction available

**Knight Marine Service**
525 Main St., Rockland, ME 04841
(207) 594-4068

**Long Reach Charters**
Rt. 1, Box 348
Orr's Island, ME 04066
(207) 833-6659
Gayle Ingersoll
27′ to 50′; power or sail

**Maine Sail**
P.O. Box 568
Kennebunkport, ME 04046
(207) 967-5043
George M. Kelley
24′ to 38′ sail and power

**Manset Yacht Service**
By Sea or By Shore Road
P.O. Box 681
Southwest Harbor, ME 04679
(207) 244-4040
Bob or Mia Brown
Sailboats 20′ to 30′

**Morris Yachts**
P.O. Box 58
Clark Point Road
Southwest Harbor, ME 04679
(207) 244-5509
Janet Vangeli
26′ to 36′ Chuck Paine-designed Morris sloop

**Newman Marine**
Main Street
Southwest Harbor, ME 04679
(207) 244-5560
Jarvis Newman
32′ Grand Banks

**Offshore Sail, Ltd.**
Box 769, Main St., North Conway, NH 03860
Fleet in Maine, 4 sailboats, 33′ & 38′, provisioning and skipper available

**Pierce Yacht Sales**
55 Atlantic Ave., Boothbay Harbor, ME 04538
(207) 633-2902

**Pleiàdes**
Isleboro Marine Enterprises
Box 19
Isleboro, ME 04848
(207) 734-6433
George H. Evans
35′ English wooden sloop

**Rockport Yacht Services**
Box 123, Rockport, ME 04856
(207) 236-4881

**Somes Sound Yachting**
Box 84
Mount Desert, ME 04660
(207) 244-3055
Keating Pepper
Hinckley 41; instruction

**Spindrift Cruises**
Box 399
Tenants Harbor, ME 04860
(207) 372-6245
Jim Brown

**Sun Yacht Charters**
Box 737, 36 Elm Street, Camden, Maine 04843
800-772-3500, (207) 236-9611
Located in Camden, 15 sailboats, 31′ to 45′ several different makes. Provisioning plan optional. Skipper, sailing instruction available.

**Michael Waters, Yacht Broker**
112 Beach Street
Rockland, ME 04841
(207) 594-4243
Michael Waters
28′ to 120′; Maine to Caribbean

**William Cannell Boatbuilding Co.**
Atlantic Ave., Camden, ME 04843
(207) 236-8500

**John M. Williams Co., Inc.**
Hall Quarry
P.O. Box 80
Mount Desert, ME 04660
John M. Williams
(207) 224-7854
33′ to 43′ power and sail

**Windward Mark**
Box 307, 60 Bayview St., Camden, ME 04843
800-633-7900, (207) 236-4300
50 sailboats, 30′ to 45′, provisioning, skipper, sailing instruction available

## Windjammers

**North End Shipyard**
Box 482
Rockland, ME 04841
(207) 594-8007
Schooners: *American Eagle, Heritage, Isaac H. Evans, Lewis R. French*

**J. & E. Riggin**
Box 571
Rockland, ME 04841
(207) 594-2923
89′ schooner *J. & E. Riggin*

**Timberwind**
Box 247
Rockport, ME 04846
(207) 596-0501 800-225-5800
Schooner *Timberwind*

**Yankee Schooner Cruises**
Box 696
Camden, ME 04843
(207) 236-4449 800 255-4449
112′ schooner *Roseway*

**Yankee Packet Company**
Box 736
Camden, ME 04843
(207) 236-8873
Steel ketch *Angelique*

**Maine Windjammer Cruises**
Box 617
Camden, ME 04843
(207) 236-2938
Schooners: *Mercantile, Mistress*

**Stephen Taber**
70 Elm Street
Camden, ME 04843
(207) 236-3520
Schooners: *Stephen Taber, M.V. Pauline*

**Coastal Cruises**
Box 798
Camden, ME 04843
(207) 236-2750
Schooner *Mary Day*

**Nathaniel Bowditch**
Harborside, ME 04642
(207) 326-4098
Schooner *Nathaniel Bowditch*

**Summertime Cruises**
Box 20R
North Brooklin, ME 04661
(207) 359-2067
53′ Pinky Schooner *Summertime*

**Downeast Windjammer Cruises**
Box 8
Cherryfield, ME 04606
(207) 546-2927
100′ schooner *Natalie Todd*, 65′ schooner *Janet May*

# APPENDIX II

## RADIO STATIONS, WEATHER BROADCASTS, RADIO TELEPHONE COMMUNICATIONS, RADIO DIRECTION FINDING BEACON LISTING

To receive weather forecasts in the area covered by this book, you need four different frequency bands. This might mean four differents sets, though many VHF sets have VHF-FM continuous weather frequencies, and many Radio Direction Finders have standard broadcast AM and FM bands.

1. A VHF-FM Receiver (Weather Radio) for continuous weather forecasts.
2. A standard AM broadcast band receiver. Although you can also receive weather on some FM stations, stations in the AM band broadcast weather more frequently.
3. Radio Direction finder to receive air navigation weather predictions.
4 Radiotelephone.

### WEATHER RADIO

If you have a VHF-FM receiver, you'll be able to hear 3-hour old (or less) weather reports any time you tune in.

Following are the continuous weather channels useful in Maine:

| | | | |
|---|---|---|---|
| Boston, MA | KHB35 | 162.475 mHz | WX-3 |
| Portland, ME | KD095 | 162.55 mHz | WX-1 |
| Dresden, ME | WXM60 | 162.475 mHz | WX-3 |
| Ellsworth, ME | KEC93 | 162.40 mHz | WX-2 |

The Boston Station can usually be heard at Isles of Shoals, Portsmouth, NH, and Kittery, ME. KD095 at Portland, has an antenna north of town at an elevation of 735 ft. It can be received almost to Kittery, at Cape Neddick, and up to Monhegan Island and into the western part of Muscongus Bay. WXM60 at Dresden is designed to improve coverage between Portland and Ellsworth. There is some overlap in range between Dresden and Portland. The overlap does no harm because the three Maine stations are all on different frequencies, and Boston is so far from Dresden that no overlap can occur on their frequency, which is the same as Dresden.

There's is a short gap in coverage on the west shore of Penobscot Bay. You lose WMX60, Dresden, just north of Camden, and you usually don't pick up Ellsworth until Lincolnville. Ellsworth usually can't be received in the southernmost parts of Penobscot Bay. It comes in good on all of Isleboro Island except the south tip, but doesn't cover North Haven Island or Vinalhaven Island. It can be received at Deer Isle, but not Isle au Haut. Coverage is good at Swans Island, all of Mt. Desert Island, and Great Duck Island. It can be received as far east as Dyer Neck, but reception is only marginal at Petit Manan Point, and non-existent farther east most of the time. See Canadian Weather Brodcasts below in this Appendix.

These VHF-FM radio stations are managed by the National Weather Service. Broadcasts include the following:

1. Description of the weather patterns affecting the eastern United States and coastal waters.
2. Regional and state forecasts with outlook for the third day.
3. Marine forecasts and warning for coastal waters. Fisherman's forecast for Georges Bank and Nantucket Shoals.
4. Weather observations from selected National Weather Service and Coast Guard stations.
5. Radar summaries and reports.
6. Local weather observation and forecast.
7. Special bulletins and summaries concerning severe weather.
8. Tide reports.

### STANDARD BROADCAST STATIONS IN THIS AREA THAT BROADCAST MARINE FORECASTS AND WARNINGS DIRECTLY FROM NATIONAL WEATHER SERVICES OFFICES

| Time | Call Letters | Location | AM Freq | FM Freq | Remarks |
|---|---|---|---|---|---|
| 7:10 a.m. | CJS | Yarmouth, Nova Scotia | 1340 | | Mon.-Sat. |
| 7:20 a.m. | WPOR | Portland, ME | 1490 | | Daily |
| 7:20 a.m. | WPOR-FM | Portland, ME | | 101.9 | Daily |
| 6:15 a.m. | WPOR | Portland, ME | 1490 | | Mon.-Sat. |
| 6:15 a.m. | WPOR-FM | Portland, ME | | 101.9 | Mon.-Sat. |

### STANDARD BROADCAST STATIONS WHICH BROADCAST WEATHER FOR THEIR AREAS, THAT CAN BE RECEIVED IN MAINE

| Call Letters | AM Freq. | FM Freq |
|---|---|---|
| | Boston, MA | |
| WHDH | 850 | |
| WBZ | | 1030 |
| WBZ-FM | 106.7 | |
| | Portsmouth, NH | |
| WHEB | 750 | |
| WHEB-FM | | 100.3 |
| | Portland, ME | |
| WPOR | 1490 | |
| WPOR-FM | | 101.9 |
| WGAN | 1560 | |
| | Augusta, ME | |
| WRDO | 1400 | |
| WFAU | 1340 | |
| WFAU-FM | | 101.3 |
| | Waterville, ME | |
| WTVL | | 1490 |
| WTVL-FM | | 98.3 |
| | Rockland, ME | |

| | | |
|---|---|---|
| WRKD | 1450 | |
| WRKD-FM | | 93.5 |
| | Bangor, ME | |
| WLBZ | | 620 |
| WABI | | 910 |
| | Ellsworth, ME | |
| WDEA | 1370 | |
| | Calais, ME | |
| WQDY | 1230 | |

## AIRCRAFT WEATHER REPORTS

Airways and pilot weather reports including aviation advice are transmitted continuously as issued by the following airport stations:

| Location | | Station | Freq. kHz |
|---|---|---|---|
| Boston (Lynnfield), MA | 42° 27′ 07″ N<br>70° 57′ 50″ W | LQ | 382 |
| Millinocket, ME | 45° 38′ 51″ N<br>68° 38′ 30″ W | LNT | 344 |

Within range, these reports are receivable on RDF sets.

## CANADIAN WEATHER BROADCASTS

The following stations broadcast forecasts by Canada's Atmospheric Environment Service covering areas of eastern Maine not receiving NOAA Weather Radio Broadcasts:.

| Call Letters | Location | Freq kHz | Times, Eastern Standard Time |
|---|---|---|---|
| CBH | Halifax, Nova Scotia | 860 | Mon-Fri, 5:06 am, 4:03 & 11:07 pm<br>Sat. 5:06 am, 6:07 & 11:07 pm<br>Sun. 6:03 am, 6:07 & 11:07 pm |
| CBD | St. John, New Brunswick | 1110 | Mon-Fri, 5:06 am, 4:03 & 11:07 pm<br>Sat. 5:06 am, 6:07 & 11:07 pm<br>Sun. 6:03 am, 6:07 & 11:07 pm |
| CBA | Sackville, New Brunswick | 1070 | Same time as CBD, St. John |
| CBI | Sydney, Nova Scotia | 1140 | Same time as CBD, St. John |

## NEW ENGLAND WATERS RADIOFAX BROADCAST SCHEDULES

| Time (Z) | Coverage |
|---|---|
| 0530,1730 | Surface Analysis |
| 0540 | 12 Hour Surface Prognosis |
| 0550 | 36 Hour Surface Prognosis |
| 0600 | Extended (Day 3 & 4) Surface Prognosis |
| 1740 | 24 Hour Surface Prognosis |
| 1750 | 48 Hour Surface Prognosis |
| 1800 | Oceanographic Analysis |

These Broadcasts are on the following frequencies:
3242(0530Z to 0615Z)
7530 (1730Z to 1815Z)

## VHF RADIOTELEPHONE CHANNELS IN COMMON USE IN THE AREA COVERED BY THIS BOOK

Channel 16—distress, monitored by Coast Guard
Channel 22 (also known as 22A, 22CG, or 22US)—Coast Guard working frequency (not distress), backup channel for Coast Guard, port operations
Channel 13—monitored by bridge operations
Channels 6, 9, 16, 68, & 78 are monitored by some marinas and waterfront restaurants. These are specified in text descriptions of marine facilities.
Channels 24, 25, 26, 27, 28, and 84 are used by marine radio telephone operators for public correspondence.

## COAST GUARD STATIONS THAT MONITOR CHANNEL 16

U.S.C.G. Group Boston, 427 Commercial St., Boston, MA 02109, (617) 223-6978
U.S.C.G. Station Portsmouth Harbor, New Castle, NH 03854, (603) 436-4414
U.S.C.G. Group Portland, 259 High St., South Portland, ME 04106, (207) 799-1680
U.S.C.G. Station Boothbay Harbor, Box 327, Boothbay Harbor, ME 04538, (207) 633-2643 and 2644
U.S.C.G. Rockland, ME 04841, (207) 596-6666 and 6667
U.S.C.G. Group Southwest Harbor, Southwest Harbor, ME 04679, (207) 244-5121
U.S.C.G. Station Jonesport, West Jonesport, ME 04649, (207) 497-2200
U. S. C.G. Station Eastport, Eastport, ME 04731, (207) 853-2845
The Canadian Coast Guard monitors VHF Channel 51. Many Canadian fishing boats monitor Channel 68.

## MAINE PUBLIC CORRESPONDENCE MARINE OPERATORS

| Call Sign | Location | VHF Channel | Licensee | Marine Operator Identification |
|---|---|---|---|---|
| KTD590 | Cape Elizabeth, ME | 24 & 28 | Portland Marine Radio | Portland Marine Operator |
| KQU620 | Camden, ME | 26 & 84 | Sea Jay Corp. | Camden Marine Operator |
| KVF856 | Southwest Harbor, ME | 28 | Sea Jay Corp. | KVF856 |

## RADIO DIRECTION FINDING STATIONS USEFUL IN MAINE

| Station | NOS Chart No. | Frequency | Sequence | Code | Range |
|---|---|---|---|---|---|
| Highland Light, MA (Cape Cod) | 13246 | 286 (marine) | I | HI .... .. | 100 miles |

| | | | | | |
|---|---|---|---|---|---|
| Lynnfield, MA | 13267 | 382 (aero) | continuous | LQ .—.. ——.— | 100 miles |
| Portsmouth, NH (New Castle on Fort Point) | 13278 | 322 (marine) | continuous | NCE —. —.—. . | 10 miles |
| Portland Light | 13288 | 301 (marine) | continuous | PH .——. .... | 30 miles |
| Halfway Rock Light | 13288 | 291 (marine) | continuous | HR .... .—. | 10 miles |
| Cuckolds Light | 13288 | 320 (marine) | continuous | CU —.—. ..— | 10 miles |
| Manana I. Signal Station | 13288 | 286 (marine) | VI | MI —— .. | 100 miles |
| Matinicus Rock Light | 13302 | 314 (marine) | continuous | MR —— .—. | 20 miles |
| Great Duck I. Light | 13312 | 286 (marine) | V | GD ——. —.. | 50 miles |
| West Quoddy Head Light | 13325 | 308 (marine) | IV | WQ .—— ——.— | 20 miles |

Some stations listed above have Roman numerals in the sequence column. Roman numeral I means that the beacon transmits during the first minute of each hour, and every 6 minutes thereafter. Stations marked II transmit during the second minute of each hour, and every 6 minutes thereafter. III transmits during the third minute, IV during the fourth minute, V during the fifth minue, VI during the sixth minute, and then the cycle repeats. You can't waste time tuning once you establish the signal. The last 10 seconds of each minute is a continuous dash to facilitate tuning.

# APPENDIX III

## PARKS

Refer to map on page 224

In order to fully avail yourself of all that Maine's coast has to offer, the superb sailing, the natural beauty and vast areas of undeveloped land supporting large populations of wildlife, you should take advantage of Maine's fine system of parks and other recreational facilities. They offer opportunities for camping, picnicking, cookouts, fishing and hiking. An abundance of wildlife; flowers; mammals, and birds can be observed in their undisturbed, natural habitat.

The following list of parks are those of immediate access to the cruising sailor all being sited on the coast. Some have already been described in the appropriate chapter of their region. For a complete list and description of all of Maine's State Parks, Public Lands and Historic Sites, write to: Maine Bureau of Parks and Recreation, State House Station #22, Augusta, Maine 04333.

### Camden Hills State Park

Camden Hills State Park is two miles north of Camden on U.S. Route 1. It has 112 campsites, flush toilets and hot showers. Without doubt, its greatest attraction is the 25 miles of marked trails which take you to the summit of Mt. Battie and Mt. Megunticook. From the tops of these mountains, all of Penobscot Bay is laid out before you. Refer to Chart No. 13307—Camden Harbor.

### Warren Island

Warren Island, north of 700 Acre Island, is one of the few places where camping is permitted on this chain of islands in the middle of Penobscot Bay. Facilities include 10 campsites, 2 Adirondack shelters, a group campsite and fresh drinking water. Both docking and moorings are available on the lee side of the island. Refer to Chart No. 13305-13309—Islesboro Island.

### Moose Point

Moose Point, at the head of Penobscot Bay, offers open fields, spruce groves and the opportunity for a picnic or cook-out with a panoramic view of the Bay. Refer to Chart No. 13302—Penobscot Bay-Upper Reaches.

### Fort Point (Fort Pownall)

Not much remains of Fort Pownall now, only a few earthworks. Built in 1759 by the newly-appointed Royal Governor of Massachusetts, its purpose was to prevent French invasion from the north, of English controlled coastal regions of New England, by way of the Penobscot River. Additionally, it would keep the Indians well inland. Fort Pownall never saw action, for shortly after its construction, the French empire in North America began to dissolve. It did, however, encourage Anglo-American settlement in the Penobscot region. The Fort is part of Fort Point State Park. Refer to Chart No. 13309—Searsport.

### Halbrook Island Sanctuary

Halbrook Island Sanctuary in Brooksville, across the Bagaduce River from Castine, contains 1345 acres of prime wildland and great scenic beauty. Although it has no developed facilities, it does provide a wonderful opportunity for hiking and the appreciation of nature in undisturbed surroundings. Refer to Chart No. 13309—Castine and Nearby Anchorages.

### Acadia National Park

Acadia National Park, which covers much of Mt. Desert Island, Isle au Haut Island and nearby Schoodic Peninsula, is extensively described in Chapters 8 and 12. Editor's Note. This is our nation's second most popular national park, and should not be missed if you're cruising this coast. A complete list of activities, facilities, descriptive literature and maps may be obtained by writing to: Superintendent, Acadia National Park, Bar Harbor, Maine 04609. Refer to our fold-out chart inside the front cover.

### Roque Bluffs

Roque Bluffs, just north of Roque Island, offers the unique opportunity to choose between freshwater and saltwater swimming. A narrow strip of beach separates the sea from a freshwater pond. Facilities include tables, grills, toilets and a children's playground. Refer to Chart No. 13326B—Roque Bluffs.

### West Quoddy Head

West Quoddy Head—the most easterly of all the State Parks, provides spectacular views of the Bay of Fundy and Grand Manan Island. Its lighthouse, trails and scenic beauty is bound to please photographers. While there, you might want to make a short side trip to nearby West Quoddy Biological Research Station, where there is a small museum and display area describing their work on local whales and seals. There are frequently scheduled nature walks, bird walks and bog walks, accompanied by one of the museum staff. Refer to Chart No. 13328—Lubec.

### Campobello

Jointly administered by the United States and Canada, under the title of Roosevelt Campobello International Park, it is best known as the summer home of President Franklin D. Roosevelt. Most people who visit the park do so to view his "cottage," but not to be overlooked are other extensive parts of the park which includes lakes, beaches, bogs and fog forests. For a more complete description, see Chapter 17. Refer to Chart No. 13328—Eastport, Western Passage.

### Cobscook Bay State Park

Cobscook Bay State Park, although the least accessible, is nonetheless, the loveliest of all—well worth the trouble it may take to reach it. There are many campsites and shelters, but they are so carefully situated in this 888 acre park that you would believe you are the only person present for many miles around. All have wonderful views of Cobscook Bay and there is the real bonus for the cruising sailor of having hot showers. Here is your best chance to observe the Bald Eagle, not to mention the possibility of sighting many of the 200 different species of birds that have been identified in the Park. Try digging for your own soft-shell clams. You are allowed, one peck of claims per person, without having to get a license. Rangers will direct you to the nearby, fascinating reversing falls of Pembroke. Refer to Chart No. 13328—Cobscook Bay.

### St. Croix National Monument

St. Croix National Monument, like Campobello National Park, is jointly administered by Canada and the U.S. In 1603, Pierre du Gast, the Sieur de Monts, was granted land in Acadia by Henry IV of France. Sailing with Samuel Champlain, much of this coast was charted and settlement was made on St. Croix Island in 1604. This was the first attempted permanent settlement by the French in New England. Refer to Chart No. 13328C—St. Croix River.

## PLACE NAME INDEX

Criehaven I. Harbor (Ragged I.), Chapter4

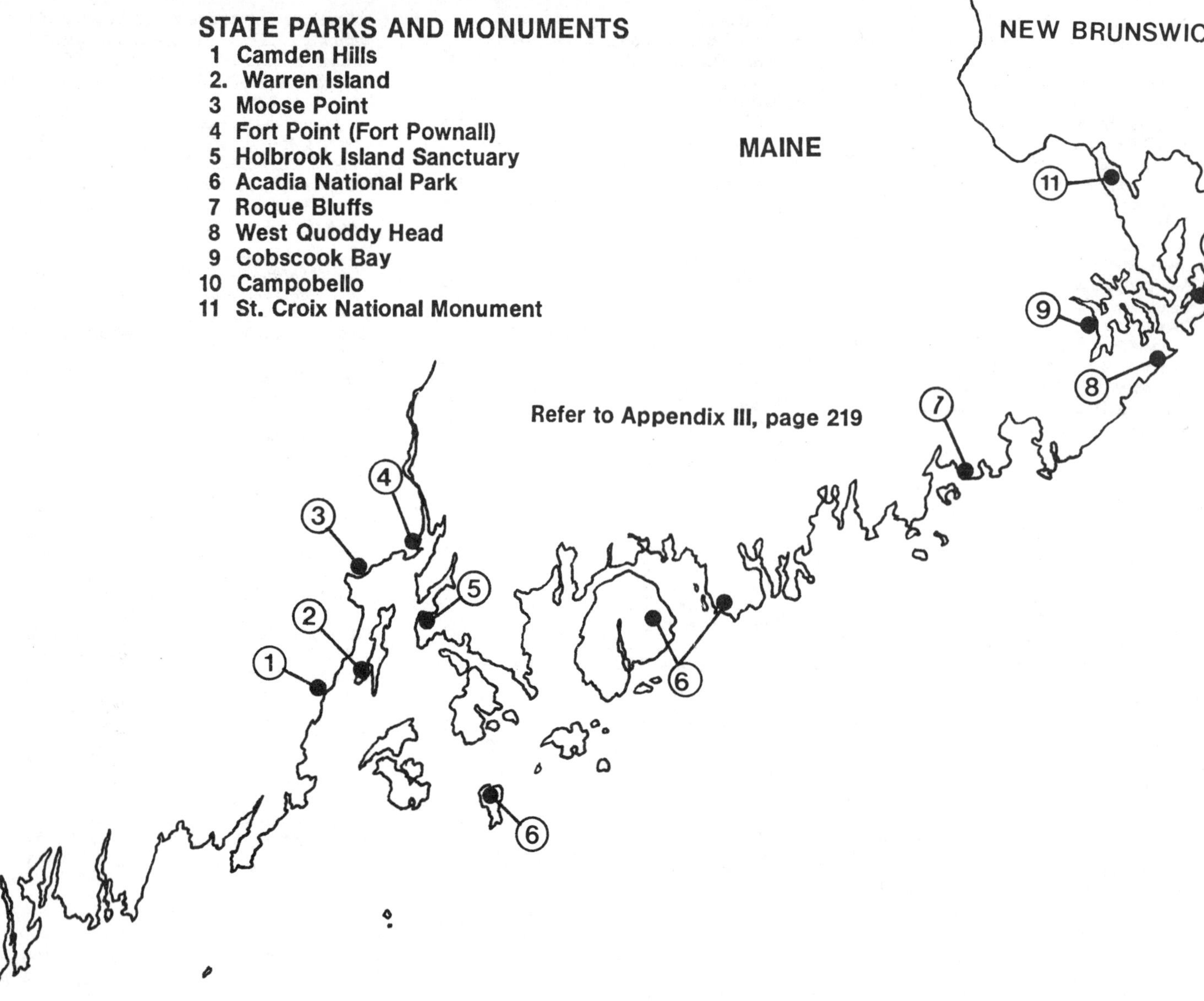


Other cruising guides and nautical books published by
Wescott Cove Publishing Co., Box 130, Stamford, CT 06904

Cruising Guide to Belize and Mexico's Caribbean Coast including
Guatemala's Rio Dulce by Freya Rauscher
Pacific Wanderer by Earl R. Hinz
Irma Quarterdeck Reports by Harley L. Sachs with cartoons by Peter Wells
Cruising Guide to the Turquoise Coasts of Turkey by Marcia Davock
Cruising Guide to Maine—Volume I, Kittery to Rockland by Don Johnson, 2nd Ed.
Cruising Guide to the Abacos and Northern Bahamas by Dr. Darrel Wyatt
Yachtsman's Guide to the Windward Islands by Julius M. Wilensky
I Don't Do Portholes, a compendium of useful boating tips
by Gladys H. Walker and Iris Lorimer with cartoons by Peter Wells
Lights and Legends—An historical guide to the lighthouses of Long Island
Sound, Fishers Island Sound, and Block Island Sound by Harlan Hamilton
Beachcombing and Beachcrafting by Anne Wescott Dodd
Inside American Paradise by June Wilcoxon Brown
Beachcruising and Coastal Camping by Ida Little and Michael Walsh
Circumnavigation: Sail the Trade Winds—2 volumes
Volume I—Fort Lauderdale to Fiji
Volume II—Vanuatu to Fort Lauderdale